THE HISTORY OF CLAY COUNTY, TENNESSEE

1986

Clay County Courthouse in the Early 1950's

Publishers of America's History
TURNER PUBLISHING COMPANY

Copyright © 1986 by
Clay County Homecoming '86
Historical Book Committee
Celina, TN 38551

Library of Congress Catalog
Card Number 86-51319

ISBN 978-1-68162-034-3

First Printing 1986 - 1000 Copies
Second Printing 1995 - 300 Copies
Third Printing 2001 - 300 Copies

CLAY COUNTY
TENNESSEE

1986

Building first bridge over Little Trace Creek on Highway 52 in the early 1900's

TABLE OF CONTENTS

ACKNOWLEDGEMENTS

Frances Donaldson — Co-Chairman

Margaret Reneau — Co-Chairman

Dayton Birdwell — Chairman
History Book Committee

The "Homecoming '86" Committee co-chairmen, Frances Donaldson and Margaret Reneau, selected as one of the major projects of the "Homecoming '86" Committee the publication of a Clay County History, as Clay County has had no major historical publication since Isaiah Fitzgerald's "History of Clay County" was published in the early 1900's. Dayton Birdwell was chosen to serve as Chairman of the History Book Committee and Publication Staff. This book was written by Clay Countians to preserve the heritage of the past and to be a treasure for those who own a copy.

History Book Committee and Staff: Dayton Birdwell, Chairman; Laquanah Crowder, Technical Editor; Brenda Kirby and Laura McLerran, typists; Mel Lee Head, Donnie Pealer, and Allen C. Birdwell, photographers; and committee members, Peggy Davis, Hilda Brown, Phyliss Boyce, Joy Key, Don Sherrell, Mary Etta Sherrell, Joyce Witham. The following people assisted with research and the collecting of pictures: Layne Boyce, Hilda Brown, Jeff Brown, Lona Capshaw, Blanche Carver, Lex Cherry, "Tootsie" Clark, Ray Clements, Jo Frances Craighead, Ralph Craighead, Annis Crawford, Carl Davis, Geneva Fowler, Bonnie Grace, Elaine Groce, Elsa Hampton, Doris Jackson, Ina Kemp, Mattie Kyle, Rachel Langford, Rebecca Leonard, Belva Pennington, Gwen Sadler, Lucy Sherrell, Paula Sidwell, Gerry Smalling, Martha Smith, Randall Smith, Betty Teeples, John Teeples, Billie Fay Thurman, Pearl Brown, Billie Stone, Lavelle Buford, Norma Jean Hawkins, Judy Groce, Don Napier, Robert Daniels, Mattie Kyle, Kevin Donaldson, Tammy Dulworth, Edwina Upton, W.B. Upton, and W.H. Reneau.

"Homecoming '86" Committee Members: Frances Donaldson and Margaret Reneau, Co-chairmen; Geneva Spear, Wilma Jean Hayes, Joy Key, Beth Windle, Betty Jo White, Bobby Meadows, Jackie Lynn, Donna Burnette, Sandra Eads, Beth Gentry, Mike Gentry, Debbie Nevins, Phyliss Boyce, Sue Stone, John H. Stone, Al McLerran, Joe McLerran, Corinne McLerran, Mary Loyd Reneau, Jerry Burnette, Mary Emma Reneau, Jean Hill, Gale Thompson, Mary Ann Hamilton, Alan West, Margaret Birdwell, Anna Ruth Locke, Ann Dalton, Butch Burnette, Joan Burnette, Mayfield Brown, Thomas Watson, Doye Windle, J.H. Reneau, III, Randall Kimes, John Sparkman, Dale Birdwell, Shirley Meadows, Mike Richardson, Nell Stone, Russell Cherry, Rachel Langford, Debbie West, Anna Mae Coe, Bill Coe, Donna Smith, Linda Green, Virginia Dale, Paul Boyce, Sadie Napier, Junior Napier, Buddy Thompson, J.D. Donaldson, Bobby Bartlett, "Butch" Young, and "Cobby" Smith.

CLAY COUNTY — FACTS AND LEGENDS

1929 — Gigantic snowfall with Haskell Neely — Homer Gates

Digging a water well on the courthouse square in the 1920's.

EARLY INHABITANTS

Probably the cave dwellers, who settled along the water courses where fish and game were plentiful and overhanging cliffs afforded natural dwellings, were the first inhabitants of what is now Clay County. Caves showing signs of occupancy are especially numerous at the headwaters of the Cumberland River and its tributaries. In 1917, when the Cumberland River was at a very high stage, the river bank gave away just below the mouth of the Obey River and slipped into the river, causing a depression some ten or twelve feet deep and exposing various pieces of pottery and other relics of Indian habitation. On the east bank of the Cumberland River three miles above Celina is located an old campsite where pieces of pottery and Indian arrowheads can be found on the surface of the earth following heavy rains. Three miles north of the Willow Grove area and on the north side of the Obey River is located a river bluff called "skull bluff" because of the many human skeletons found there which clearly indicates that these caves were used for burial purposes. Along the Obey River, many rock shelters have been found which are very similar to the Pueblo Communal ruins in the Southwest. Many Indian relics and remains have been found in a cave located approximately three miles from Hermitage Springs. Two Indian mounds are located in the "Old Town" section of Celina.

The Mississippian Statues

In 1983, James Capps and Edward Arms discovered two Mississippian Indian statues. James Capps first discovered the female; and about one week later, Edward Arms discovered the male near the Cumberland River at the same site where the female was discovered. An archeologist guessed that they were carved between 1000 and 1400 A.D. by the Mississippian Indians who were forerunners of the Cherokees. These statues were used in religious ceremonies by the Mississippians who usually spent most of their lives in one general area near a river where they could hunt and fish. (Excerpts from the *Clay Citizen,* March 9, 1983.) Other Indian tribes who lived in the Clay County area were the Shawnee, the Cherokee, the Chickasaw, and the Iroquois.

A Frenchman, Martin Chartier, was believed to have been in this area as early as 1691. He was a Canadian who came South probably with a Shawnee wife. Chartier spent about two years on the Cumberland with the Shawnee, hunting and fishing. They may have stayed in one place long enough to raise a corn crop, as game was plentiful here; and even in the late 1700's, the area had plenty of buffalo. (Mary U. Rothrock, *Discovering Tennessee*)

About the end of June 1766, Colonel James Smith, Uriah Stone, William Baker, Joshua Horton, and a slave, eighteen years of age belonging to Horton, came down the Cumberland River and explored the country south of Kentucky, and no white man could be found. On the second of June 1769, a company of adventurers was formed for the purpose of hunting and exploring in what is now Middle Tennessee. There were more than twenty men in this party. Some of them were John Raines, Kaspar Mansker, Abraham Bledsoe, John Baker, Joseph Drake, Obediah Terrill, Uriah Stone, Humphrey Hogam, Henry Smith, Ned Cowan and Robert Crockett. They camped for the summer at the mouth of Obed's River which was named for Obediah Terrill. Down through the years, the spelling and pronunciation of Obed's River has been changed, and at the present time, it is called Obey River. At the end of the year, most of these men returned home taking with them the peltry, dogs, and horses. However, Kaspar Mansker, John Raines, Isaac Bledsoe, Uriah Stone, Humphrey Hogam and others, ten in all, stayed several months longer and went into the meat packing business. (*Early Times in Middle Tennessee* by John Carr)

Obediah Terrill stayed on for several years as a farmer-hunter before permanent settlement was made in Tennessee. A lonely creature, he "had not children, perhaps no wife" was the statement Daniel Smith made in his "Journal" after spending a night in Terrill's camp near the mouth of the Obed's River while on a buffalo hunt. The date of this journal entry was January 4, 1780. (*Seedtime on the Cumberland,* by Harriette Simpson Arnow)

In the notes kept by Daniel Boone on his second trip from the earlier settled colonies into Kentucky is found an account of his having crossed the Cumberland River at a place he called "Twin Creeks." This point is located seven miles south of Celina on State Highway Number 53, where the two Mill Creeks flow into the Cumberland River at the same point. (*History of Clay County,* by Isaiah Fitzgerald)

Some of the first settlers within the present boundaries of Clay County were Quakers from Pennsylvania and Maryland. Hugh Roberts was supposedly the first white settler in the present town of Celina. His home stood on a knob elevated

The Hugh Roberts Home built in 1780

some 50 feet above the surrounding area. This building has been located in three states — North Carolina, Franklin, and Tennessee, and in seven different counties — Washington, Davidson, Sumner, Smith, Jackson, Overton, and Clay.

John Plymley (Plumlee) is said to have been the first white settler west of the Cumberland River in the present Clay County. He came here from Pennsylvania while George Washington was President. Being a Quaker, he left the State of Pennsylvania because of religious persecution.

Another one of the early settlers of this section was Isaac Johnson, who came to the mouth of Obed's River from Virginia in 1797. He died in 1869 and selected the following epitaph for his grave marker: "Remember, friends, as you pass by, as you are now, so once was I; as I am now, you are sure to be; prepare for death and follow me."

The Gearheart family settled near the mouth of Obed's River in 1795. They came from Pennsylvania and were of Dutch descent. Valentine Gearheart was born in 1775 and died in 1835. He was buried near Celina.

William Donaldson, who was born near Mt. Juliet in Wilson County, Tennessee, traveled partly by trail on horseback to a new settlement on Obed's River. This was a distance of about one hundred miles. He was a well-educated man of Scotch-Irish descent and a descendant of John Donelson who took an active part in the early settlement of Middle Tennessee. Donaldson married Nancy Hoard, the daughter of a family who had come to the new settlement from Virginia. Her family owned a large tract of land in what was known as Modoc Bottom on Obed's River. This land was purchased for the price of one pony. Donaldson acquired quite a large tract of land, and in the Southeast corner of his land was located a large spring near which a man named Fox, a shoemaker, had settled in 1800. This place was named for Fox and called "Fox Springs."

Perhaps the earliest settlement in the County of a family of any historical prominence was located in the Fairview Community in the extreme eastern section of the County. This settlement was made by the wife of Governor John Sevier, Catherine, better known as "Bonnie Kate," in 1815. This settlement was made on a grant of 57,000 acres of land acquired by the Governor for his service to the United States during the Revolutionary War. This area was called "The Dale" and was near a large cave spring.

"The Dale" — Home of Bonnie Kate Sevier

The surnames of other early families who settled in what is now Clay County were Willis, Peterman, Brown, Hughes, Davis, Roberts, Boles, Rich, Stone, Fitzgerald, Arms, Arterbury, Bean, Biggerstaff, Armstrong, Birdwell, Butler, Cherry, Clancy, Comer, Copas, Cross, Dale, Denton, Fowler, Gass, Gates, Gettings, Goodpasture, Hamilton, Hampton, Hinson, Holman, Kyle, Kendall, Kirkpatrick, Langford, Mayfield, McColgan, Moore, Monroe, Poindexter, Newman, Nevins, Rose, Tinsley, Waddell, Whitson, York, Williamson, Young, Strong, Southworth, Plumlee, Stone, Miles, and Osgathorpe. These people were mostly of German, English, and Welch ancestry as well as Scotch-Irish and French. Many of these people married Indians.

Home of the Kerrs on Pea Ridge

These early settlers were very industrious and self-supporting. Their houses were built of hewn logs, and the cracks between the logs were filled with a plaster made of mud. The roofs were usually made of chestnut boards which were rived from logs which had been cut into two-foot lengths. The windows were covered with shutters which were left open during the summer with no covering to protect from various insects. Sometimes the houses had no floor as the earth was just evened off and packed down. Others had a puncheon floor which was made by splitting logs in half and placing the flat side up to make the floor as level as possible. Large rock chimneys were usually built at each end of the house, and these were used not only for heating but also for cooking. Many of these houses had two large rooms connected by a wide open hallway called a "dog trot." Many times the kitchen was built separately at the back of the house or was connected to the house at the back by another open hallway. The furniture was constructed from rough lumber usually put together with wooden pegs. The chair backs and seats were made of woven cane or hickory bark. The first homes were lighted with candles made from tallow saved from slaughtered meat. Many used grease lamps which were made by twisting strings together and placing them in containers of grease leaving one end of the string out of the container. Later, lamps were used for lighting purposes. Each family usually raised its own fruits and vegetables. The fruits were either smoked with sulphur or dried in the sun to preserve them for the winter. In the early winter when it was cold enough to insure the farmers that if livestock were slaughtered it would not spoil, "hog killings" were held. Many times all the people in one community would meet at a given location to butcher the hogs. The meat was salted and allowed to stay in the salt for a few weeks, and it was then taken up and smoked until it was cured. Hickory was the wood preferred for smoking the meat for preservation. The women made their soap from grease drippings and lye water. Clothing was made from wool sheared from their own sheep, or from cotton grown on the farm. Wild berries, walnuts, walnut bark, etc. were used to make dyes.

The pioneers had many home remedies used for medicines. Much of the medicine was made from hickory bark, slippery elm, mullen, Jerusalem oak, snake root, honey and whiskey, turpentine and sugar, and beet poultices.

EARLY INDUSTRY

The earliest industry was the tanning of the hides of cattle, deer, bear, raccoons, and hogs. Next came the manufacturing of whiskey, the making of gunpowder, and the installation of water mills for grinding cornmeal. In 1820, whiskey was 50 cents per gallon and cornmeal was 40 cents per hundred pounds.

Vanus Eads, Cancil and Geirrus Moore preparing pelts for sale (Esco Moore on the porch)

Flatboats were constructed by James Stone and others about 1804 or 1805. These boats were used for shipping cured meats, hides, hemp, cotton, tallow, beeswax, and other produce down the rivers to New Orleans for sale.

Sunday outing on a flat bottom boat.

Each community usually had a tanning yard; a saddle shop which made saddles, harnesses, boots, shoes, etc.; and a blacksmith shop. One of the earliest known blacksmiths was Riley Rich, and one of the first harness and saddle makers was Blue Gist.

The first postal riders received so little pay that they carried whiskey with them to sell for ten cents a pint.

"Henry Harley" docking in "Old Town"

A new era dawned for the Upper Cumberland area in the early 1800's when the first steamboats came up the Cumberland River opening the region for industrial development. For the next 100 years, they were the principle means of transportation for both people and salable goods. Some of these boats were: "The Rambler," "Tom Yeatman," "B.S. Rhea," "J.H. Hillman," "Benton McMillan," "L.T. Plumlee," "Albany," "R. Dunbar," "Henry Harley," "The Celina," "The Nashville," "Rowena" and the "Jo Horton Falls."

RELIGION

The majority of the people were Quakers (Friends), Presbyterians, and Baptists in the late 1700's. Barton Warren Stone came into this area to preach in 1796. He had been reared as a Presbyterian, but was now in disagreement with some of their precepts. He thought that the Presbyterians and other religious groups had gotten away from the strict teachings of the Bible, and he proposed to teach only what was (in his opinion) found in the Bible. He had a group of followers called "Stoneites" or "New Lights."

In 1823, Alexander Campbell, a native of Scotland, came to this area, and he, like Stone, did not fully agree with the prevailing Church doctrines. He organized a following of those that believed in only teaching from the Bible, and they were called "Christian Baptists" or "Campbellites." These two groups later became known as the "Church of Christ."

Other early religious leaders were McDonald Moore, Hugh Gearhart, Marion Harris, Martin Luther Moore, F.B. Srygley, W.C. Hamilton, W.L. Brown, Doc Hall, John Arms, Sam Spears, Milt Burnette, Eli Bronstetter, Earl Cunningham, Tollie Phemister, Sam Strode, Willie Hunter, John Savage, Jesse Savage, Elijah Keeling, Isaac Denton, Cornelius Clancy, and John L. Roby.

9

EDUCATION

One of the earliest schools in what is now Clay County was Philomath which is the Greek word for "lover of learning." It was located in Tinsley's Bottom. It was the first school in this area to have manufactured desks. Many of the leading citizens of what was to become Clay County attended this school: the McMillans, the Mitchells, the Kirkpatricks, and the Johnsons. Joseph McMillan, after attending Philomath and Buritt College, later became head of Montvale Academy. Montvale Academy had many prominent students including Cordell Hull and Benton McMillan, a governor of Tennessee. Montvale Academy, located in Celina, later became Montvale College.

Prior to the Civil War, most communities had at least one school called a subscription school where tuition was paid for attendance. These schools usually had a term which lasted for only three to four months per year. Some of the early teachers at these subscription schools were Mack Moore, Garland Kuykendall, William Kuykendall, George Stephens, J.A. McMillan, J.B. Lea, J.L. Algood, S.D. Bilyew, W.B. Boyd, R.L. Fitzgerald, Luther Moore, Douglass Woods, Hill Edwards, O.B. Maxey, and Scott Smith.

At this time, there were no more than three comfortable school buildings in the area. The others were crude log houses with rough floors and seats made from logs which had been split in the center and hewn smooth on one side with a broad axe with legs attached at each end. These benches were about ten inches wide, with no backs, and were so high that the smaller children's feet would not touch the floor. In many of the buildings, a log cut out of the wall answered for a window.

Highland School — 1910

The teachers received a salary of about $20 per month for a term of three or four months. Twenty-five dollars per month was the highest salary received by any teacher.

THE CIVIL WAR

Just prior to the Civil War, the majority of the citizens who lived in what was to become Clay County were prosperous, owned nice homes, and had fine livestock. They had beautiful orchards, rows of bee stands in the yards, gardens, and excellent corn and wheat crops. Many of the farm owners along the Cumberland and Obey Rivers also owned slaves. There were at least 25 slaves in the Arcot Community, and other communities had even more.

Kibbie Tinsley Williams Gardenhire was a young girl of only

The Keisling Home

seven when the War broke out. She lived in Tinsley's Bottom, and she gave the following account of how the War affected her community. "I stood on the porch and watched the first steamboat load of Confederate Volunteers go down the Cumberland River. The flags were waving in the breeze; and the women were in tears. My brother, Penbroke, was but sixteen when he volunteered, and they made him a lieutenant. I remember being with my father and mother when the Yankees came and drove out fifteen head of fine mules and horses. One time a regiment of Yankees crossed the Cumberland River at the mouth of Brimstone Creek, and they formed a line of battle and came marching across those broad fields with their guns glittering in the sun. The Yankees marched on. Part of the line passed through our yard. One soldier shouted that someone had shot at them from our house and threatened to burn it, but the Captain said they would not do that. They questioned my father and released him when they got to the big road. Yankees later came and plundered the house. They even went into the negro houses and took some of their clothes. Emarine, our head cook, fixed something for them to eat, and they went on down the bluff road. A Texas Ranger was on top of the bluff, and he fired into the Yankee troops killing two men and seven horses. We did not suffer for things like the people farther South, but we knew that we had to feed the soldiers on both sides. When someone would say that the Yankees were coming, we did not know what to expect, whether someone would be killed, the house burned or plundered; but one thing was sure, they had to be fed."

Since Clay County had not yet been formed, men from this area enlisted to serve in both the Confederate and Union Armies in Jackson County, Overton County, and in various towns in Kentucky. People in the eastern and Cumberland River sections of what is now Clay County were usually Confederate sympathizers while residents of the western section were usually Union sympathizers. One of the first Confederate Regiments to be organized was Hamilton's Tennessee Cavalry Battalion, also called the Fourth Tennessee Cavalry Battalion, the Fourth Tennessee Cavalry Regiment, and later called Shaw's Tennessee Cavalry Battalion. It was organized in Jackson County in December of 1862, was in Confederate service on April 11, 1863, and was consolidated with Allison's Squadron in July of 1864. The Adjutant General's Office, State of Tennessee, advised Adjutant General S. Cooper, Richmond, Virginia on April 18, 1863: "Hamilton's Company was mustered into service for the local defense of the border counties lying up the line of Tennessee where the counties and mountains strike the Kentucky line pursuant to an order from General Johnston authorizing the muster of companies for that purpose. This company has done good service, and is now organized, and has been, and is now, in general service." Hamilton was first elected Major of the Battalion and then promoted to Lieutenant Colonel on July 1, 1863. Major O.P. Hamilton was captured at Celina on March 4, 1864. He was charged by the Federal officials with being a guerrilla, and was being forwarded to Lexington, Kentucky for trial, when he was killed by his guard — circumstances unknown. There are several Federal communications concerning Hamilton's exploits. A communication from Lieutenant Colonel Hamilton, dated July 25, 1863, reported that the battalion, with six companies, was mustered into Confederate Service April 11, 1863; and on April 20, 1863, Federal General E.H. Hobson reported that troops of his command had attacked Hamilton's command at Celina, destroying his camp and killing seven of his men. On the next day, they took possession of the town, killing 30, and reported the rebels to be in full retreat and in total disorder. On June 9, another Federal report described the total rout of Hamilton's command at Kettle Creek, with 40 killed, 36 captured, and the capture of two howitzers and the entire wagon train and equipment. At this time, Hamilton's command was a part of Brigadier General John H. Morgan's forces, who in reporting the disaster stated that Major Hamilton was ordered to report to Colonel R.C. Morgan, but Hamilton refused. A Federal Report told of a skirmish with "Hamilton's Marauders" at Flynn's Lick on January 31, 1864. After Hamilton's capture and death, the battalion was under the command of Major Jo Shaw.

Re-enactment of Civil War Battle

Men from this area also served in the Fourth (Murray's) Tennessee Cavalry Regiment, the Thirteenth (Dibrell's) Tennessee Cavalry Regiment, Eighth Tennessee Infantry Regiment, Seventeenth Tennessee Infantry Regiment, Twenty-Fifth Tennessee Infantry Regiment, Twenty-Eighth Tennessee Infantry Regiment (also called the Second Tennessee Mountain Volunteers), Thirty-Fourth Tennessee Infantry Regiment, and the Eighty-Fourth Tennessee Infantry Regiment. Federal regiments with men serving in them from this area were the Fourth Tennessee Mounted Infantry Regiment, U.S.A. and the Eighth Tennessee Mounted Infantry Regiment. (Data taken from: *Tennesseans in the Civil War.*)

The War of the Rebellion, Ser. I, V. 10 gives the following reports of battles in Celina and what is now the Clay County area. A report of Colonel Edward C. Williams, Ninth Pennsylvania Cavalry, June 13, 1862, stated that Captain McCullough, with 60 men, had been attacked on this side of Celina by 180 mounted men, under Hamilton. Captain McCullough was killed and four men seriously wounded; two horses killed. One of the men will probably die. It further stated that Lieutenant Longsdorf, who succeeded Captain McCullough in command, routed the rebel force. This same communication stated that upon hearing that this marauding band (Hamilton's and Ferguson's men) had taken refuge in Celina, Colonel Williams directed Major Jordan to join him at McMillin's Ferry at Turkey Neck Bend where it took them until after dark to cross the river as only six horses could be ferried at one time. The next morning they marched on Celina with nine companies of soldiers. Hamilton heard of their coming and scattered into the hills where the mounted troops could not go. However, it stated that four of his men were captured — Samuel Granville, Smith Butler, Tipton T.C. Settle, and William Henry Harrison Peterman. Major Jordan was ordered to Butler's Landing where he discovered the property captured by Morgan from the steamer, John A. Fisher, as well as some Confederate stores, and, having no means of transportation, he destroyed them by throwing them in the river. He also captured Hamilton's celebrated racehorse.

Major Thomas J. Jordan of the Ninth Pennsylvania Cavalry gave the following report on June 6, 1862 at Glasgow, Kentucky. " On the morning of the 10th, by command of Colonel Williams, I took the two companies and proceeded from Celina to Bennett's Ferry. While at the ferry, I captured and destroyed 20 boxes of army bread, 10 barrels of the same, two barrels of sugar, 100 bags of wheat, and 23 hogsheads of tobacco, which I destroyed by throwing them in the river. They are the remainder of the property captured some two months ago by the rebels from the steamboat, John A. Fisher, while passing that point on her way to Nashville."

Major Thomas J. Jordan made the following report at Louisville, Kentucky on December 29, 1862. " With this force (230 men) I determined to attack Salina (Celina), and, if possible, capture or disperse the forces of the enemy at that point. I succeeded in crossing the Cumberland at a point 12 miles north of Salina (Celina), and at daylight on the morning of the 8th entered the place, but I was disappointed in not finding the enemy. I made every inquiry possible from the inhabitants, but all denied any knowledge of forces being either there or in the neighborhood. I marched back to my camp. As day broke on the morning of the 9th, revelle was sounded. . . . A faint discharge of firearms was heard far out on the Salina (Celina) road. . . . My pickets reported the enemy approaching in a large force. . . . Colonel Morgan's command began to deploy from the woods. . . . I soon found that his force outnumbered mine by six to one. . . . The Burkesville road being gained, my retreat was conducted in a most orderly manner. The forces of Colonel Morgan consisted of his own brigade, Colonel Hunt's cavalry, two squadrons of Texas Rangers, and the independent companies of Captains Bledsoe, Hamilton, McMillin, and Ferguson, numbering in all some 2,000 men, with two pieces of artillery. Colonel Hunt was mortally wounded and died at Tompkinsville."

The War of the Rebellion, Ser I, V. 23 gives the following reports of battles at Celina and Bennett's Ferry. The report of Major General Horatio G. Wright, U.S. Army, made on April 23, 1863 stated: "The expedition to Celina was entirely successful. Colonel Graham reports, through General Hobson, that they destroyed the town, 100,000 pounds of bacon, 10,000 bushels of wheat, 10,000 bushels of corn, 100 barrels of whiskey, 100 barrels of flour, considerable quantity of sugar, coffee, tea, meat, and other stores, and 40 boats, which had been used in transporting supplies from Burkesville and other points on the Cumberland."

On April 29, 1863, General Hobson reported that Colonel Graham in his expedition had captured 30 rebels, shelled the enemy at Celina and drove them from that place. They attacked 600 at Bennett's Ferry by shelling from long range. One was killed. He reported that no rebels could be found at Celina or Bennett's Ferry.

Garret Home struck by a cannon ball during the Civil War

Brigadier General John H. Morgan of the Confederate Army gave the following report on the burning of Celina to Colonel George William Brent on April 26, 1863 at Sparta, Tennessee. "... I have received information from Celina, stating that the enemy, between 1,200 and 1,500 strong, crossed the river at that point on the 19th instant, shelled and burned the town, together with the churches, not even giving the citizens any warning of their intention. Major Hamilton had to fall back some four or five miles, but being reenforced by Colonel Johnson's regiment, attacked and drove the enemy back across the river. (Rebel troops from Celina marched to Tompkinsville, Kentucky where they burned the courthouse in retaliation for the burning of Celina.)

Since Clay County had not been formed at the time of the Civil War, exact records of the men who fought in the War from this area are not available. Robert Daniels has done extensive research in this field and provided the following list of men who served in the Confederate Army and the Union Army from this area. (Mr. Daniel's list came from census records, service records, cemetery records, and pension lists.) Men who fought for the Confederacy were: Thomas Manion Rabon, Allen G. Parker, Robert B. Parker, William Sidwell, John A. Fletcher, Andrew J.W. Maxfield, J.C. Garrett, J.C. Bennett, J.K.P. Davis, Pleasant A. Huffer, Thomas Henry Huffer, P.H. Wilborn, O.P. Hamilton, Allen Davis, James T. McColgan, Lipscomb Pettett Abeston, Alvin Cullom Arms, Henry Martin Arms, John Hudspeth Black, John Burchett, John Carson, Jessie L. Davis, James Dulworth, Francis Marion Evans, Pearce Evans, Milton A. Fletcher, Thomas Harrison Haile, William C. Hamilton, E.D. Hestand, James M. McDonald, Lewis Mainard, Thomas Carrol Masters, Milton P. Nevins, Joe Rich, J.W. Sells, Joseph Smith, Mordica Smith, William R. Stone, James Terry, Marcus Aurelias Turner, James Francis Watson, Eli E. White, Andrew J. Whitson, Samuel Brown, N.M. Amis, T.R. Armes, A.C. Arms, S.W. Atkinson, Esibins Bemon, J.H. Black, Eusibius Bowman, O.B. Brady, Joseph Brewington, Enoch Brown, John P. Brown, Henry C. Butler, John L. Carson, Z.B. Carter, J.D. Changler, John D. Chandler, James B. Cherry, A.L. Chilton, John F. Clinton, P.P.

Cooper, W.M. Copeland, G.W. Dailey, A.L. Dale, C.E. Dale, J.F. Dale, J.L. Davis, T.V. Davis, W.S. Davis, Davis Delk, John R. Donaldson, J.M. Dubree, James L. Hogan, B.F. Hall, Benjamin Harris, Arthur L. Hill, J.M. Hummell, William Jones, William H. Jones, Andrew Lynn, David Lynn, S.R. Martin, L.B. Mayfield, David H. Nelson, E.G. Osgathorp, G.B. Osgathorp, Samuel K. Plumlee, J.J. Poindexter, J.H. Prichard, John Rains, George Washington Reels, John Roberts, David Richardson, James K. Scurlock, J.A. Sherrell, Thomas J. Sims, M.M. Smith, J.P. Smith, William F. Smith, F.M. Stanton, Jerre B. Stephens, J.R. Stone, William R. Stone, William A. Stuart, W.C. Terry, John B. Waddle, J.A. Watson, John Williams, and D.D. Worley. (This does not purport to be a complete list of men who served from what is now Clay County.)

Men from this area who served in the Union Army were: Josiah Daniel, G.W. Hoots, R.N. Davis, Joel Moore, James Crawford, J.A. Birdwell, R.S. Browning, Daniel Rhoton, J.W. Rhoton, Alpheus Kendall, William W. Chitwood, Philip Emmert, Elisha Rich, John Johnson, Samuel N. Plumlee, William Rich, Caleb Head, Joshua McAlpin, Joel White, James L. Goolsby, John Smires, Russell D. Frazier, David J. McAlpin, John Sims, Benagy McLerran, Thomas P. Dickens, George W. Carter, Jeremiah Stone, Marquis Ross, John H. Dearning, Walker Grace, James M. Tolman, Samuel Tinsley, Samuel Grisham, Harrison Perdue, James Adams, Abram Keen, David W. Pennington, Sam Likins, Joe Stewart, James R. Ray, George W. King, Andrew Watkins, Logan Huffines, Keith Henry, William B. Decker, John C. Davis, John W. Gentry, William F. Birdwell, John Grider, Hiram Grist, Henry Eakle, Shelton Craighead, Pennington (first name unknown), George W. Clements, John Right, Joseph Gulley, Isaac M. Crawford, Argarts A. Wilkerson, Johnathan B. Crawford, John T. Billingsley, James Trisdell, Isaac Cross, James Cross, William H. Grider, Arthur B. Jackson, Andrew J. Moss, Samuel A. Moore, Robert A. Welch, George Murray, Perry Morgan, Obedia Leonard, Lemuel Leonard, Meridith Davis, James Bean, Anthony C. Moss, Robert Morris, Robert Thurman, Lafayette Smith, James Bowman, Louis Massingale, William Overstreet, William Spivey, William Day, George Garrett, John L. Carson, Daniel W. Cullom, Harrison White, John Kerr, Curtis Dowel, James Sullivan, John Cash, Benjamin Waddell, John Billings, William Pryor, Jessie K. Thompson, Joshua Johnson, John Harvey, Zachariah Vaughn, Fountain R. Riddle, Granvil Hogan, James L. Hogan, M.T. "Tice" Dulworth, Hardy Thrasher, Milton K. Colson, Meredith York, Isaac Rush, William C. Brown, George Davis, Jesse A. Pedigo, Franklin Reeves, Luke M. Reeves, Zachariah Pedigo, Calvin Baker, Robert Hudson, Hawood Wilson, Stewart Vinson, William Strong, Henry Asberry, James Green, John A. Murray, David Mortin, John J. Miles, James McCarter, Claborn Kirby, Andrew Davis, Thomas Bean, Wilson Cherry, William Carnahan, James H. Gaines, Allen Davis, Gideon B. Long. (Lists copied from National Archives Microfilm by Robert Daniel. Some names were illegible. This does not purport to be a complete list of men who served from what is now Clay County.)

Civil War Veterans

CLAY COUNTY ESTABLISHED

Clay County was authorized by an Act of the Legislature passed on June 16, 1870. It was taken from the northern sections of Overton and Jackson Counties. Five commissioners were named and given the power and authority to hire a surveyor to run the proposed boundary lines to meet the requirements of the Constitution. A map was to be made and submitted to the Secretary of State; and then an election was to be held to see if two-thirds of the people in the area wanted this new county. The five men in charge of these preliminary activities to the formation of this new county were R.P. Brooks, James G. Cunningham, and J.M. Morgan of Jackson County and W.H. Turner and Thomas Armstrong of Overton County. The survey, ordered by the five commissioners, was made by William (Bill) Gore with the assistance of B.M. Smith, "Yankee John" Stafford, M. Boles, R. Greenwood, J.H. Jones, Milton Meadows, and W.H. Davis. These assistants acted as chain carriers and ax men. The five commissioners ordered the election held, and two-thirds of the people within the boundary voted to establish a new county. The new county was named Clay County in honor of the Kentucky Statesman, Henry Clay.

In an election held in February of 1871, the following county officials were selected: John J. Brown, County Court Clerk; John L. Maxey, Chairman of the County Court; H.G. Tinsley, Tax Collector; Adam Thrasher, Sheriff; Richmond Darvin, Chief Deputy by Appointment; Isaac Miller, Register; and A.P. Green, Trustee.

The following members of the County Court were appointed on the first Monday in March of 1871: John L. Maxey, E.C. Smith, Scott Moore, S.N. Plumlee, Hiram Crabtree, W.B. Harris, Robert Pedigo, Robert B. Overstreet, J.A. Smith, L.L.

Brown, John Arms, A.W. Colson, William Dale, Eli Pentecost, John J. Miles and Samuel Ellis. These men became the Justices of the Peace as commissioned by Governor D.W.D. Senter. On motion, Samuel Ellis was called to the chair to serve as temporary chairman. The court then proceeded to organize, and John L. Maxey was elected chairman. W.H. Denton was elected coroner, and S.H. Calloway was elected co-surveyor.

The first session of the County Court was held in a store in Butler's Landing belonging to Mary S. Roberts. Celina was chosen to be the county seat by a narrow margin over Bennett's Ferry; and the commissioners ordered the Court sessions moved to Celina.

COUNTY DEVELOPMENT

The first superintendent of education was Sylvanus Kirkpatrick who apparently received no salary. His successor, George W. Stephens, received the sum of $125 per year from 1874 and 1878. In 1874, there were 1644 white and 119 black students in Clay County. The average teacher's salary was $31.45 per month. In 1876, the average teacher's salary was $26.15 per month, and the average tuition was 53 cents per month per pupil. In 1878, there were 19 male and five female teachers with a total of 2417 pupils between the ages of six and 21. B.F. Bray was the superintendent in 1878 and reported a total school revenue of $3440.

When Clay County was created there were no roads. There were a few trails which were called roads. These were hard to travel over with anything other than horses and in many places the going was hard on horseback. The best road into the county was the road leading from Butler's Landing through Hilham to Livingston. So many freight wagons passed over this road hauling goods from the steamboat landing at Butler's Landing that some attention had to be given to it. An old stage road came from Georgia and Alabama to Cookeville, and from Cookeville one fork came through Hilham and crossed the Obey River about the present site of Dale Hollow Dam continuing on to Burkesville, Kentucky. Some called this the "Old Kentucky Road," and others called it "The Great Road."

Mules and horses — Main method of transportation

When Clay County was formed, it had a dense virgin timber crop. During the last ten years of the 19th century and first ten years of the 20th century, the harvesting of this timber was at its peak. There were over 20 large sawmills in the county and many smaller mills whose combined cut of timber ran well over a million feet per day. In addition to these mills there were handle mills, heading mills, stave mills, shingle mills, shuttle-block mills and mills for using every type of timber. In addition to the mills, there were millions of feet of timber that were cut,

Cordell Carter's Saw Mill — Dry Creek — Arcot Community

Cordell Carter's Mill crew

rafted, and floated down the Cumberland and Obey Rivers to Nashville. The leaders in this logging industry were Hugh H. Kyle, Captain A.C. Dale, J.D. Hatcher, Captain Jim Davis, W.C. Keen, Benton McMillan, Arch P. Green, Ed Myer, M.C. Gore, David Hughes, John Fite, Pleas and Hob Harrison, Jim Gamble, Buck Baker, Cabe Beatey, "Uncle Billy" Hull, Bob

William "Uncle Billy" Hull — A leader
in the logging industry

Riley, and M.M. Smith. As early as 1874, Killebrew wrote in "Resources of Tennessee" that an estimated 22,500,000 feet of saw logs came down the river to Nashville in one year. Most of the Cumberland rafts were put together according to the number of feet of lumber desired. They ranged in size from those containing 40,000 feet to those with as many as 90,000 feet. No logs were cut less than ten feet in length and the longest were sixteen feet. The average raft was manned by a crew of six men, one of whom was the pilot. It usually required about five days to run a raft on a good tide from Celina to Nashville.

During this period, the county's assessed valuation reached nearly four million dollars on a basis of thirty cents to the dollar or an actual property value of more than $11,000,000, and the county had a population of better than 9,000.

In the early years of this century, telephone service became available to the people of Clay County. In 1910, there were switchboards at Celina, Butler's Landing, Moss, Boles, Spivey (now Hermitage Springs), Fox Springs, Willow Grove, and Lillydale.

WORLD WAR I, WORLD WAR II, THE KOREAN AND VIETNAM CONFLICTS

In 1918, World War I began. A conscription law was passed that called all men to enlist between the ages of 21 and 35. During the years of the war, this law was changed to call men between the ages of 18 and 35. When the men were called to duty from Clay County, they would gather on the square at Celina and wait for cars to come and pick them up. The people of the town and the men's families would come to see them off. As the cars left to take the men to Nashville, the drivers would drive around the square so that the men could wave goodbye to their families and friends. Some of the local people went to Old Hickory to work at the powder plant that helped supply the soldiers with needed war materials. Many of the men from Celina rode down to Old Hickory on steamboats to work at this plant. An influenza epidemic hit the entire country during the early months of the war. Many local citizens, including Dr. Herman Sidwell, and soldiers died during this epidemic. The communities worked together and had meatless days and wheatless days in order that there would be enough food for all the people. The women of Clay County had sewing circles that made items to be sent to the soldiers through the efforts of the Red Cross. In 1920, news came by telephone that the war was over. A celebration took place at the Meadows Hotel with fireworks and a dance.

Between the two world wars, a bridge named for Henry Horton was built across the Cumberland River at Celina; and a great depression struck the country. The people of Clay County worked any way they could to supply their families with food and clothing. People here did not fare as badly as people in other areas as they had gardens for a food supply and livestock to provide their meat. While most of the banks were being closed, the Bank of Celina stayed open to help the community in any way it could. Near the end of the depression, the Henry Horton Bridge was completed, and Governor Henry Horton came to Celina to dedicate the bridge.

By the middle 1930's, Clay County was beginning to prosper. Farm production was increased, and new businesses began to move into the county.

In December of 1941, news came over the radio that the Japanese had attacked Pearl Harbor, and World War II was declared. All the young men of the County were called into service; and the women of the community took their place in the work force to supply the needs of the families. People gathered nightly at the homes with radios to hear reports of how the war was progressing. Ration books were issued to each household which were needed to purchase sugar, gasoline and other items. Victory committeemen were selected, and they, along with local leaders, encouraged people to buy war bonds and stamps. They collected over six hundred tons

Scrap Iron piled at the Court House in 1943 — 600 tons collected

of scrap iron to make needed war equipment. They volunteered their service in the vaccination of thousands of hogs in the worst outbreak of hog cholera in the county. They financed a 10,000 baby chick project for 200 4-H Club boys and girls. They asked that the people produce more of everything, sell more, use less, buy less and pay more debts. Their motto was drive! drive! drive! fight! fight! fight! for more of everything that would contribute to the winning of the war.

There was a 20% increase in farm production; a 10% increase in cattle production; a 30% increase in poultry production; and a 20% increase in food for home use. In August of 1945, the war was over. Ration books were burned as part of the celebration. Prices soared after the war; but jobs were plentiful, and the people prospered.

Two other conflicts — the Korean Conflict and the Vietnam Conflict — took young men from Clay County to serve their country on foreign soil.

In these wars and conflicts, people waited for news of the young men of Clay County. Telegrams often brought the devastating news that young men had lost their lives. During World War I, the following young men gave their lives for their country: Bedford W. Bean, Ezra Adam Brown, John Cherry, Stone F. Cherry, Elmer C. Colson, Comer Cross, Clyde F. Hestand, Willie Kendall, James A. Waddle, Reubin J. Watson, Amos Spear, and Ben Cunningham.

During World War II, the following young men lost their lives: Luke S. Anderson, John Thomas Barlow, R.J. Bean, Willis L.R. Brown, Cecil Bullock, Willis Collins, Will H. Collins, J.B. Dennis, James R. Fitzgerald, Fred T. Garrett, George S. King, James C. Lancaster, Isaac A. Mansfield, Vernon Page, Noel G. Pitcock, Edwin L. Short, Fred Short, John Smith, Willis D. Smith, Sherman C. Teeples, Edward C. Walker, Marshall C. Webb, Riley Rich, Loy C. Hogan, Oscar Welch, Coell Wood, William Fowler Pennington, Noel Ralph McLerran, Huey E. Browning, and Fred King.

Noble Larry Crawford and Willard Welch lost their lives during the Korean Conflict.

Three young men died during the Vietnam Conflict — Jerry L. Cherry, Larry Strong, and William Bethel Watson.

Requests were made in the local newspaper and over the local radio station for bibliographies of the young men who died in these wars and conflicts. The following were submitted by families and friends.

WORLD WAR I

Adam Brown — died in WW I

Ezra Adam Brown, the son of Martha Jane and James McHenry Brown of the Arcot Community, died on a ship enroute overseas as a result of influenza during World War I. So many of the soldiers on the ship became ill that the ship returned to the United States. Adam's body was returned to Glasgow, Kentucky where family members traveled by horse and wagon from Arcot to receive the body. The people were so terrified of the influenza that his coffin was never opened. He was married to Fannie Sallee, and they had one daughter, Ada Dean, whom Adam never saw. He is buried in the McColgin Cemetery at Arcot.

Luke Shields Anderson, the son of Luke Baylos and Cora James Anderson. He lost his life in the battle of Bastogne in Germany on December 22, 1944.

Private Loy Cecil Hogan was born on May 22, 1921. He was the son of Tommie and Vela Davidson Hogan of Willow Grove, Tennessee. He was drafted into the Army of World War II in July of 1942. After only six months of training here in the United States, he was shipped overseas.

Loy Cecil was a passenger on a ship which was attacked shortly after midnight in the North Atlantic by an enemy submarine which struck without warning; and Loy Cecil was killed. This occured on February 3, 1943.

Willis LaRue "Biggon" Brown, the son of Cora and Luke Brown of the Pine Hill Community, was killed in action on Luzon Island on June 2, 1945 during World War II. His parents decided that he should be buried in Arlington National Cemetery in Washington, D.C. He was awarded the Purple Heart posthumously.

Fred King, the son of Benton and Sally King, died in World War II.

Huey E. Browning, born April 11, 1912 was the son of Benton and Carrie (Long) Browning. He was a P.F.C. in 306 Infantry, 77 Division, World War II. He was killed May 20, 1945 on Okinawa.

George S. King, the son of Hiram and Floy (Reneau) King, was born May 20, 1920. He was the stepson of Lillie (Ritter) King. He was killed in World War II in July of 1945.

Noel Ralph McLerran was born June 2, 1922, the only son of Albert Harrison and Zona Caruthers McLerran. He graduated from Hermitage Springs High School; and soon after in 1942, he went off to serve in World War II. He was a member of the 77th Division and served in the South Pacific. He fought in three major battles before being killed in action on Leyte, Philippine Island, on December 16, 1944. His body was returned home for burial in 1949. He is buried in the Pitcock Cemetery in Oak Grove near where he played as a child. We hope your sacrifice was not in vain, Noel. June 29, 1986 — B.M.C.

Short Brothers — Fred and Edwin Leon Short were the sons of David Franklin and Sarah (Moore) Short. Fred was born January 20, 1924. He was killed in action in the Pacific Theater in World War II. Edwin Leon was born November 3, 1917. He was killed in action in the European Theater in World War II.

PFC Edward C. Walker, the son of Benton T. and Dovie (Reecer) Walker, was born January 4, 1924. Just after he graduated from Celina High School, he was called into the Army. He died in World War II on August 6, 1944. The following is inscribed on his tombstone: "Died in France. Nobly he fell while fighting for liberty."

Coell Wood, the son of Herman and Dora Wood, was killed in the South Pacific during World War II when the tank in which he was riding ran over a land mine and exploded.

KOREA

Noble Larry Crawford was born June 6, 1937, the son of Irvin and Florida Coons Crawford. He died in Korea at Heartbreak Ridge on April 5, 1953.

VIETNAM

Jerry L. Cherry, the son of Estes "Larkin" and Estelle Cherry of the Union Hill Community of Clay County, was born July 7, 1947. He was killed in Vietnam on May 8, 1968.

VIETNAM ★★★★★

PFC Larry Strong, the son of Mr. and Mrs. Joe J. Strong of Celina, was killed in Vietnam on September 17, 1970. He was married to the former Connie June Kendall. He was killed while on patrol near Da Nang when the patrol encountered enemy fire. Larry Strong was a quiet young man and a good citizen.

William Bethel Watson, the son of Ersie and Johnie Watson of Route Two, Celina, died in Vietnam on April 18, 1969.

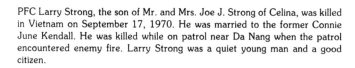

PROFESSIONAL SERVICES

Medical and legal services have been available to the people of this area since the mid 1800's. The very earliest doctors and lawyers usually had additional occupations as they did not have enough medical and legal practice to keep them busy.

Dr. William F. Plumlee, who was in the medical section of the army during the Mexican War in 1847, attended the University of Louisville for one year before starting his medical practice. One account stated that Dr. Wilson McColgin and his son, James Talleyrand, were graduates of Harvard University. The McColgins practiced medicine at Arcot. Dr. Wilson McColgin was practicing there before the Civil War. Dr. Talleyrand McColgin served in the Civil War, and entered the field of medicine just after the War.

Dr. Talleyrand McColgin

Other doctors who have served the people of Clay County are Dr. Jonathan Davis, Dr. Robert Chowning, Dr. Barton Stone Plumlee, Dr. John T. Chowning, Dr. T.H. Haile (also an ordained minister), Dr. W.N. Gray, Dr. Cullum Sidwell, Dr. Herman Sidwell, Dr. Edward Clark, Dr. John Bethel Lansden, Dr. Stuart F. Grace, Dr. Lindsey, Dr. Miller, Dr. J.R. Murray, Dr. D.D. Howser, D. W.L. Davis, Dr. James Barlow Boles, Dr. Thomas L. Willis, Dr. J.R. Webb, Dr. William P. Bean, Dr. O.S. Deathridge, Dr. J.W. White, Dr. Charles L. Kyle, Dr. John Orville Ewert, Dr. Arthur L. Buell, Dr. Emmett Root Johnson, Dr. Champ Edward Clark, Dr. A.E. Draper, Dr.

Dr. Champ E. Clark

Roscoe C. Gaw, (names from the *Physicians* Certificates Book I, Celina Courthouse), Dr. Art. Cardona, Dr. Billy C. Nesbitt, Dr. R.G. Kloss, D. Renaldo Olechea, Dr. Manuel Crespo, Dr. Terry Rounsavall, Dr. Arun Bajaj, Dr. Renu Bajaj, Dr. Nora

Carl Davis — Administrator, Margie Boone — Medical Records, Dr. Arturo Ruanto, Dr. R.V. Tiongson, Dr. Nora Bolonas (Tiongson) and Dr. Roberto Mauricio

Bolanas (Tiongson), Dr. Rod Tiongson, Dr. Roberto Mauricio, Dr. Arturo Ruanto, and Dr. Michael D. Littell.

Clay County did not have a hospital until 1965, when a modern facility was constructed. In February of 1976, a new clinic was completed at a cost of $100,000. The hospital and clinic are constantly upgrading their facilities and services. Mr. Lloyd Black was the first hospital administrator; and in 1986, Carl Davis serves as administrator. Eva Craig was the first Director of Nursing. In 1986, Mrs. Finley is the Director of Nursing.

In the early 1900's, a Dr. Green practiced dentistry on the back porch of Roxie Lynch's boarding house in Butler's Landing. In January of 1973, Dr. John H. Stone, a graduate of the University of Tennessee College of Dentistry at Memphis, Tennessee and a native of Clay County, began his practice of dentistry in Clay County.

Dr. John H. Stone — Dentist

In 1967, Dr. John Clark Donaldson, a native of Clay County, became the first veterinarian to establish a practice in veterinary medicine in Clay County.

Dr. John C. Donaldson — Veterinarian

In 1972, an ambulance service was established. Three ambulances now serve Clay County. They are manned by six emergency medical technicians and one paramedic.

Clay County has a modern Health Department housed in an excellent facility. The department provides numerous medical and environmental services to the residents of the County.

Clay County Health Dept.

Clay County Nursing Home (Clay County Manor)

The Clay County Nursing Home was opened in 1976. The Nursing Home was established by Francis (Brownie) Brown and his father, Sam T. Brown, who sold stock to anyone wanting to buy shares in the nursing home. The nursing home has sixty beds and is always fully occupied. In 1985, the stockholders of the nursing home agreed to sell the nursing home. It then became Clay County Manor.

The forerunner of the present-day Department of Human Services was the relief program started during the depression which was directed by Mrs. Della Reneau. Next came the Welfare Department; and one of its directors was Ms. Lou Hamilton. The present-day Department of Human Services provides many programs for the people of Clay County: aid to dependent children, supervision of foster care, investigation child abuse cases, assistance with medical care, and the food stamp program, etc. Two of the past directors of this Department were Ralph Craighead and Cordell Masters. Willodean Webb is now the Director of the Department of Human Services.

Otis and Willodean Webb — Willodean is Director of the Department of Human Services

Many of the early lawyers did not attend a formal law school but read law with an experienced attorney or judge. Clay County has had many prominent attorneys. Benton McMillan attended Philomath Academy and the University of Kentucky. He was admitted to the bar and began practice in Celina in 1871. He became a member of the State House of Representatives in 1874; was commissioned as a special judge of the Circuit Court in 1877; became a member of Congress in 1879; and became Governor of Tennessee in 1899. Cordell Hull attended Montvale Academy and graduated from Cumberland University in 1891. He was admitted to the bar the same year and began his law practice in Celina. He was a member of the State House of Representatives. He served as a Captain in the Spanish-American War. He was judge of the fifth Judicial Circuit. He was a member of Congress. He was chairman of the Democratic National Committee, and he was a United States Senator. He was appointed Secretary of State by President Franklin D. Roosevelt on March 4, 1933. He was awarded the Nobel Peace Prize in 1945. He retired as Secretary of State on December 1, 1944. John McMillan, a younger brother of Governor Benton McMillan, was considered one of the best criminal lawyers in Tennessee. Dr. Barton Stone Plumlee, in addition to being a medical doctor, was also a well-known attorney in the late 1800's. O.B. Maxey came here in 1878; and Milton Graven Sidwell practiced law in the early 1900's.

J.H. Reneau, III, J.H. Reneau, II and J.H. Reneau, Attorneys at Law

James H. Reneau was educated at Montvale College. He was a teacher in the Clay County School System before entering the legal profession. Mr. Reneau held the following elected offices in Clay County: tax assessor and county court clerk. His son, J.H. Reneau, Jr. and his grandson, J.H. Reneau, III, also became attorneys. The three Reneaus were considered to be the most outstanding criminal lawyers in the area. J.H. Reneau, III still carries on this tradition.

W. Grady Sidwell, Attorney

Watterson Grady Sidwell received his education in the public schools of Clay County, Burritt College and Vanderbilt University, where he received his law degree in 1919. In addition to his legal duties, Mr. Sidwell served as trustee of Clay County and as Floterial Representative in the Tennessee General Assembly.

Charles L. Haile   Judge Thomas H. Haile

Charles Laishley Haile was educated in the public schools of Clay County, David Lipscomb College, and he received his law

degree from Cumberland Law School in 1923. He also served as County Judge of Clay County and as mayor of Celina. He was known for his writing and was a national winner of the Freedoms Foundation Award at Valley Forge, Pennsylvania.

His son, Thomas H. Haile, received his law degree from the YMCA Law School in 1948. He was elected county attorney in 1957 in Cookeville where he practiced law. He was later appointed Judge of the Fifth Judicial Circuit.

Other attorneys who have practiced in the county were William Davidson, Jim Crabtree, Tony B. Maxey, L.A. Webb, Thomas Crawford, Samuel Turner, Marcus Turner, A.P. Green, Lewis Dodson, John H. Daniels, Joe S. McMillan, Samuel M. Plumlee, W.R. Officer, Turner Roberts, E.C. Sidwell, Jacob Jenkins, W.D. Fiske, F.W. Fitzgerald, J.T. Ford, B.R. Grace, James Spicer, M.C. Sidwell, W.D. Davidson, J.J. Gore, J.M. Crabtree, Karl E. Monroe, who also served as General Sessions Judge, Isiah W. Mitchell, and Willis E. Spears, who also served as General Sessions Judge.

In 1986, Clay County has three attorneys — J.H. Reneau, III, James Dale White, Jr., and John Heath. J.H. Reneau, III also serves as General Sessions Judge.

AGRICULTURAL SERVICES

Clay County's first agricultural agent was Joe Eastes who served from 1918-1920. E.B. Wright was the second county agent and he served in 1929-1930. Charles Vaughn became county agent in 1934, and he served longer than any other person in this position, retiring in 1969. The last two county agents have been John C. Beaty, who retired in 1985, and John W. Sparkman, who came in 1985.

John Beaty — County Agent Bicentennial Year

Phyliss Boyce — Home Demonstration Agent — Bicentennial Year

The years between 1919 and 1934 are sketchy as to how much extension work was actually done in Clay County. Farm enterprises for 1934 included: 1400 bushels of Irish potatoes; improved methods of breeding, feeding and management practiced in 24 leading communities; 15 farmers built poultry houses, eight brooders were constructed; 3500 acres sown to pasture; 5500-6000 acres sown in lespedeze; and 78 farm meetings held with 1875 people in attendance.

In 1938, Rural Electrification Administration began building electric lines to the rural homes of Clay County. Charles Vaughn stated: "There is no project that rural people appreciate as much as they appreciate having electricity in their homes. I have heard farmer after farmer say that he would rather have his electricity in his home than to have all the aid that has been received from State, Federal and Local Agencies. Extension Service has done everything possible to make

Strawberry Processing Plant

this convenience available for the farmers. (1941)"

The 1950's found Clay County people actively involved in strawberry production for Breyer Ice Cream, which established the first plant of any kind in Clay County. It was an ideal spring enterprise, for the entire family could work to make the crop and increase the family's income. Strawberries were in the limelight for a cash crop for Clay County families until the early 1960's when labor became a problem.

The 1980's have been trying times for Clay County farmers. Prices for hogs and beef cattle fluctuate. Tobacco support prices have been reduced. New enterprises of orchards, vegetables, and small fruits are being tried on a trial basis to keep the small farm in the hands of the small farmer. In 1986 only 55 people are engaged in full-time farming, while an estimated 583 are part-time farmers with incomes being supplemented by off-the-farm work.

The first county Home Economist (Home Agent) was Mattie Dowling, who served Clay County from 1917 until 1919. Other home agents have been Lillian Robinson, Mary Ruth Patton, Amanda A. Deweese, Lois Lee White, Thelma Leeth, Agness M. Jackson, Maurene Cassetty, Elna Gaw, Patsy Anne Reynolds, Carolyn Hamilton, and Phyliss Robinson Boyce. There have been two expanded foods nutrition workers — Linda Diane Ballard and L. Rene Loggins.

In the 1940's, four hundred women were enrolled in Home Demonstration Clubs. In 1940, one hundred and thirty bales of cotton and eleven bales of mattress ticking were obtained from the Federal Surplus Commodity Corporation. Thirteen hundred mattresses were made from October 8th to November 30, 1940. More than 200 old mattresses were reworked in the 30 mattress centers which were set up in various communities.

Special interest groups were organized in the 1970's and 1980's with an average of 15 sessions being held each year dealing with interior design, foods and nutrition, and family living.

George F. Luck became Clay County's first County Agricultural 4-H Agent in 1946. Other 4-H Agents have been Frank C. Pharris, Henry J. Stamps, J. Newt Odom, J.D. Beaty, John C. Beaty, Earl W. Law, Hugh Davenport, James Bell, Ronald Rogers, and Randall Kimes.

In 1919, the County had a Corn Club with 160 boys participating in the Club. In 1934, Charles Vaughn had 112 members enrolled in 4-H projects: poultry, Irish potatoes, corn, pigs, tomatoes, tobacco, sweet potatoes, peanuts, farm accounting, baby beef, bees, and soybeans. In 1940, girls began to be organized into 4-H Club work, and over 300 girls enrolled in

fourteen clubs. Projects of the 4-H Club down the years have been clothing, canning, poultry, gardening, wildlife, horse, veterinary sciences, public speaking, livestock judging, interior design, marketing lambs, breadbaking, arts and crafts, and camping.

During the 1970's, Clay County 4-H Club members received trips to Chicago to National 4-H Congress. Jimmy White went in 1975, Ricky Buford in 1976, Ronnie Buford in 1977; and in 1983, Johnny Donaldson became the first national winner from Clay County in the project in Agricultural Careers. Janice Strong and Freeda Smith also competed in projects in Chicago. Clay County 4-H members who have attended the Commodity Marketing Symposium in Chicago have been Jimmy White, Teresa Cherry and Janice Strong. (Extension data provided by Phyliss Boyce.)

The Clay County Soil Conservation District was organized under the provisions of the Tennessee Soil Conservation District Enabling Act of 1939 to protect and promote the wise use of Clay County's soil, water, and related natural resources. County Agent Charles Vaughn was instrumental in organizing the Soil Conservation District. Mr. Vaughn, along with Frank Thurman, W.H. Langford, Grady Sidwell, W.D. Terry, Bill Fiske, and a Mr. Arnis helped organize a soil conservation district for Clay County. Their objective was to fight the soil erosion that was devastating farms in the county. The first farm conservation plan accepted was the one for the Amos T. Stone farm on July 8, 1945.

The following Clay Countians have served as Soil Conservation District Supervisors: Amos Stone, W.D. Terry, J.H. Overstreet, Frank Thurman, Amo Osgathorpe, Elmo Henson, A.E. Craighead, Phillip Cherry, C.W. Clements, Jr., W.L. Russell, Harold Stone, Wayne Head, Bruce Turner, David Browning, Henry Boyd Stone, Joe Melton, Robert H. Jackson, Corinne McLerran, Ricky Melton, and John M. Hayes.

Soil Conservation service personnel who have worked in Clay County have been Frank Pharris, Wayne Thomas, Jack Enoch, Alfred Smith, Marion Simpson, and Michael Richardson. Local people who have served as part-time employees for Soil Conservation Service include Nelson E. "Jigs" Craighead and Willie George Roberts. (Soil Conservation District data submitted by Mike Richardson.)

The Agricultural Stabilization Conservation Service has provided valuable services to the farmers in the allotting of tobacco poundage, overseeing corn and hay production (acreages) and in developing conservation plans, etc. Amo Osgathorpe is the director of this service. Jewel Dean Arms and Shirley

Stone Sharp also work for this service.

The Clay County Farm Bureau, an organization strictly for farmers, has been instrumental in working to secure better lives for all its members by making the membership aware of many services available to farmers. One of its strongest programs has been health insurance. Its property insurance is also vital to farmers.

The Farmers Home Administration was organized after the great depression in the early 1930's. In the early years, it was called the "Feed and Seed." The "Feed and Seed" provided loans to the farmers to purchase seed for crops and feed for the mules and other livestock. Hugh Kyle was the manager of the first "Feed and Seed" Store. In later years when it was changed to Farmers Home Administration, Mr. Kyle remained as the manager. He retired in 1965. Most of the loans from this organization go for industrial use, farm loans, and for low income housing. Other managers have been William G. Gravette, Ray Smith, and Don Haston. Clerks have been Cleo Donaldson, Greta Witcher, Rita Reed and Janith Reecer.

INDUSTRIAL AND COMMUNITY GROWTH

The first "plant" to come to Clay County was the Breyer Ice Cream Company plant built around 1950 by Dr. Champ Clark and Bill Moulton in conjunction with Breyer Ice Cream Company. Through the combined efforts of the County Agent, Charlie Vaughn, and the farmers of the area, strawberries were grown and sold to the plant to be processed into ice cream. During the peak of production farmers raised several hundred acres of strawberries. Due to a decrease in man power, primarily people to pick the berries, the plant closed after being in operation for several years.

The first major corporation to establish a factory in Clay County was OshKosh B' Gosh, Incorporated which was originally founded by Frank E. Grover in Oshkosh, Wisconsin in 1895. It was then called Grover Manufacturing Company. When the business was sold to Messrs. Jenkins and Clark in 1896, the name was changed to OshKosh Clothing Company. In 1953, OshKosh opened a plant in Celina employing 86 persons. T.H. Holland was the plant manager and served in this position until his retirement in 1974. He was succeeded by Kenneth Masters. The factory was expanded in 1979 when a branch factory was opened in Hermitage Springs. This plant is managed by Mickey Clements. The Celina factory is now managed by Eddie White. These two plants employ approximately 1,000 people in the production of shirts, pants, and overalls. Crotty began operation in Clay County in 1971, with Bill White as its supervisor.

OshKosh B'Gosh, Inc.

Crotty makes sun visor's for Ford, GM, and AMC cars and trucks.

In July of 1974, Hevi-Duty started the manufacture of transformers at its Celina plant. In September of 1975 a night shift was added. The company presently manufactures a line of transformers from 15KVA to 330KVA, which weigh as much as 2000 pounds. Gerald Block is the plant manager.

Green Forrest, owned by Douglas Smith, is located near Moss, Tennessee. It is a very diversified organization with the manufacture of log homes being its prime industry. These homes are sold throughout the United States under the trade name of "Honest Abe" Log Homes.

Two other factories in the county manufacture clothing — Celina Apparel located in Celina and Clay Sportswear in Moss, Tennessee.

Tennessee Mills, located at Hermitage Springs, manufactures pallets. This business is owned by W.C. White.

The project that first brought "outsiders" into Clay County on a large scale was the building of Dale Hollow Dam. It was authorized by the Flood Control Act of 1938. Dale Hollow Dam was built to harness the wild Obey River, the second largest tributary to the Cumberland River. The dam was named for its location near Dale Hollow, which was settled in 1808 by William Dale, a pioneer who had come to the area earlier to help establish the state boundaries between Kentucky and Tennessee.

Dale Hollow Dam

The construction of Dale Hollow Dam was to be done concurrently with the Wolf Creek and Center Hill Dams, but, with the advent of World War II, construction was halted at Wolf Creek and Center Hill due to shortages in labor and materials. These resources were pooled, and construction was continued on Dale Hollow due to the decision to complete one dam and to get one power plant on-line, which would aid the development of the then secret Manhattan Project. The decision was made later to house the Manhattan Project at Oak Ridge, but construction continued on Dale Hollow Dam which was completed in 1943. Power-generating units were added between 1948 and 1953 to give a combined generating capability of 54,000 kilowatts. (Data given by Jim Hunter)

Dale Hollow is the oldest lake in the Nashville District. It has 620 miles of virtually unspoiled shoreline and crystalline waters reaching to depths of 150 feet. The construction of the project displaced about 1,500 people located in two major communities. This removal of people could be called Clay County's "Trail of Tears." The county and area has been greatly benefited by the flood control of Dale Hollow Dam. Recreation is another important asset provided by Dale Hollow Lake. In 1985, 3.2 million people visited Dale Hollow. With its 27,700 acres of water and 25,000 acres of land, Dale Hollow never seems crowded.

Many volunteers work with the Corps of Engineers to develop a variety of programs such as the annual Ecology Dive usually held in July. Scuba divers retrieve trash off the bottom of the lake and compete for the largest amount. Several diving clubs and some individuals take part in this Ecology Dive each summer. An Eagle program has been organized to stimulate greater public awareness and to present factual information about the eagle. One of the major activities of this program is the eagle watch which is held at Dale Hollow each winter. An environmental education camp which teaches students about natural resources is held the first week in May, and it includes such topics as endangered species management, fisheries management, forestry management, plant identification, et cetera (Data furnished by Jim Hunter, Jack Donaldson, Keith Crowe)

Forrest Rich — Fishing in the 40's was excellent

Fishing has always been a major recreational activity on Dale Hollow Lake. Dale Hollow is known for a variety of fish: trout, bass, muskellunge, et cetera. Many of the Tennessee and Kentucky fishing records have been set at Dale Hollow. In 1955, the world record small mouth bass, 11 pounds 13 ounces, was caught on Dale Hollow by David L. Hayes.

Many resorts are located on the shores of Dale Hollow Lake. Some of the better known Clay County resorts are Cedar Hill, Holly Creek, Horse Creek, Willow Grove, and Dale Hollow.

Dick and Betty Roberts and their two small children, Dicky and Ray, came to Celina in January of 1946 after Mr. Roberts was discharged from the Air Force at the end of World War II. The first summer, they used their own home or "shack" for an office and restaurant. They purchased and tore down old buildings at Smyrna Air Force Base to build cabins. Betty cooked and waited tables in the restaurant which they built the second year. The Roberts' twins, Roger and Ronnie, were born this second year also. Outhouses were used for bathrooms. Rainwater was used for drinking and cooking. As the years passed, the cabins were updated as money permitted. The resort is now run by the four sons, with Dick and Betty still active in the bookwork and planning. The resort now employs about 40 people during the peak season. (Data provided by Roger Roberts.)

The Holly Creek Fishing Camp and Boat Dock was established by Alvin C. Yates while he was living in the Pea Ridge area operating his sawmill. Mr. Yates built most of the cabins for the fishing camp. Before the actual floating dock was built, the boats were tied to a large cable along the edge of the bank. Mr. Yates purchased several military surplus boats to be used as rental boats for the public. He created several jobs for people in the Pea Ridge area. He purchased red worms for resale for fish bait, et cetera. J.H. Reneau, a prominent Celina attorney, purchased the Holly Creek Fishing Camp and Boat

Dock from Mr. Yates and moved to the Pea Ridge area. They made many improvements on the property, and they made many jobs available to the people of Pea Ridge. In later years, Mrs. Reneau took over the management of the camp and dock. In the early 1980's, she sold the dock but kept the cabins, some of which she later sold for private ownership. David Sharp, John Officer, and Kenneth Winninghan are now the owners and operators of the Holly Creek Boat Dock. (Data provided by Don and Mary Etta Sherrell)

Holly Creek Dock — 1951

A new occupation for Clay Countians became available with the advent of Dale Hollow Lake — fishing guide. There have been many fishing guides on Dale Hollow; but perhaps the most famous is Billy Westmoreland who is also a championship fisherman and a lure manufacturer. Billy has a TV program which is shown on cable television in 135 cities called "Fishing Diary." Billy's father, Lester Westmoreland, was noted for the houseboats that he built, many of which went to Dale Hollow Lake. This was another business that was opened to area residents because of the Lake. Over 400 houseboats were used this past year during the recreation season.

An annual fish fry is held on Corps property each year at Donaldson Park. The fish fry is sponsored by local residents

Annual Fish Fry — Jerry Brown and Jimmy Dale

and is open to the public. Between 4,000 and 6,000 people attend this event annually. Other events are now held in conjunction with the fish fry: simulated Civil War battles, arts and crafts shows, displays by the National Guard, et cetera.

The Dale Hollow National Fish Hatchery, located about 1,000 yards downstream from Dale Hollow Dam, went into operation in 1966. The hatchery has produced millions of pounds of rainbow, lake, and brown trout. The current annual trout production is close to 200,000 pounds. These trout are

23

distributed to the Tennessee Valley Authority's and to other Corps of Engineers' lakes, located mainly in Tennessee. Lakes in Alabama receive approximately 35,000 pounds of trout a year. The main bulk of these fish are stocked at nine-inch lengths because smaller sizes have proven to have poor survival rates. The hatchery is open to visitors. It has an indoor aquarium, starting tanks and an outdoor rearing raceway. It is operated by the United States fish and Wildlife Service, United States Department of the Interior. (Data furnished by Jack Donaldson)

In 1976, the Clay County Community Center was built. It is used for a variety of community activities. One of the major programs at the center is the nutrition program which provides meals for those 65 and over. Governmental offices are also housed at the center. The large recreation room is used for benefits and other community activities.

Clay County Library

Clay County has a modern public library which is part of Tennessee's Regional Library System. The library houses over 12,000 volumes which may be checked out free of any charge. Louise Hayes is the librarian.

The people of Clay County are followers of the old-fashioned work ethic but they are also fun loving and community conscious. Some of the events that may take place at any time during the year, but particularly in the summer and fall are fish frys, barbeques, "outhouse" races, quilt shows, antique shows, horse shows, marble championships, bible schools, and protracted meetings. In the winter, hunting is a favorite sport.

Clay Countians demonstrating the game of Marbles in D.C.

The game of "Rolley Hole" marbles is only played in two locations in the United States — Clay County, Tennessee and Monroe County, Kentucky — according to an article in the *Nashville Banner*. The National Rolley Hole Championship Tournament is held each year at Standing Stone State Park, which is located in adjacent Overton County. For three years in a row, the champions of this tournament have come from Clay County. They are Wayne Rhoton and Ralph Roberts. In

the summer of 1986, four Clay Countians were invited to the Smithsonian Institute's twentieth annual Festival of American Folklife to demonstrate the game of Marbles. They were Ralph Roberts, Wayne Rhoton, Doyle Rhoton, and Russell Collins. One master marble maker, Bud Garrett, lives in Clay County, Tennessee. He and his wife, Edith, an expert quilt maker, also were invited to attend this annual Festival of American Folklife.

COUNTY OFFICIALS

Early chairmen of the Clay County Court were John L. Maxey, 1871-1879; Milton Meadows, 1882; Robert Pedigo, 1882; M.F. Green, 1884; Samuel L. Plumlee, 1887; A.P. Williams, 1888; O.B. Maxey, 1889; J.R. Donaldson, 1890; John R. Leslie, 1892; H.L. Gist, 1893; O.B. Maxey, 1894; D.W. Cullam, 1895; T.J. Mabry, 1899; John Willis, 1900; T.J. Mabry, 1901. County judges then replaced chairmen of the County Court. County judges have been O.B. Maxey, 1904; T.J. Mabry, 1904; H.B. Plumlee, 1916; L.A. Webb, 1926; W.F. Brown, 1935; Charles Haile, 1936; J.B. Bailey, 1937; Willie Hunter, 1938; J.B. Bailey, 1942; W. Grady Sidwell, 1955; C.J. Mabry 1955; and Frank B. Halsell, 1966-1982. In 1982, the title was changed from County Judge to County Executive. Cecil Langford was elected the first county execu-

| Cecil Langford | Frank B. Halsell — Trustee |
| Former County Executive | County Judge, County Executive |

tive in 1982. In 1986, Frank B. Halsell was elected as county executive.

General Sessions Judges have been O.B. Maxey, 1900; H.B. Plumlee, 1912; J.B. Bailey, 1937; Willie Hunter, 1938; W. Grady Sidwell, 1949; Willis E. Spear, 1950; Guy B. Johnson, 1958; Willis E. Spear, 1966; Karl E. Monroe, 1978; and

J.H. Reneau, III General Sessions Judge

J.H. Reneau, III, 1984. These judges were appointed by the Court until 1970 when they were elected by the people.

The trustees of Clay County have been A.P. Green, 1871; John R. Hampton, 1876; William C. Purcell, 1882; E.C. Fowler, 1886; M.F. Green, 1890 (died in office); P.M. Moore, 1897; Joe Chatt Chowning, 1898; M.M. Smith, 1902; P.M. Moore, 1904; J.B. Denton, 1906; W.L. Stone, 1910; D.W. Mabry, 1916; J. Cleve Scott, 1918; W. Grady Sidwell, 1928; J. Cleve Scott, 1932; W. Andrew Cook, 1936 (died in office); Guy B. Johnson, 1941; Frank B. Halsell, 1950; Paul White, 1966; and James R. Bailey, 1974 and re-elected 1986 for fourth term.

James Reed Bailey — Trustee

The following have served as County Court Clerks for Clay County: John J. Brown, 1871; M.F. Green, 1886; John J. Brown, 1890; L.S. Brown, 1892; J.T. Donaldson, 1894; O.B. Maxey, 1906; W.F. Sevier, elected in 1914 but died before taking office; T.L. Gist, 1914 (resigned); O.B. Maxey, 1915; J.H. Reneau, 1918; Baby Reneau, 1934; J.H. Reneau, Jr., 1938; Mary Emma Reneau (served while her husband was in service); Oopie Reneau, 1946; J.D. King, 1960; Harold Car-

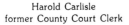

Harold Carlisle
former County Court Clerk

Pat Hix
County Court Clerk

lisle, 1960; and Pat Hix, 1986. Baby Reneau served as J.H. Reneau's deputy while she was still in high school. Senate Bill No. 80, introduced by Senator W.F. Officer, allowed Baby Reneau to serve. She was the youngest and first woman to hold this office in the State of Tennessee. Five members of the Reneau family have held this office: J.H. Reneau, Baby Reneau, J.H. Reneau, Jr., Mary Emma Reneau, and Oopie Reneau.

Circuit Court Clerks for Clay County have been William H. Hawkins, 1871; W.B. Chowning, 1875; Joe P. Thompson, 1878; A.B. Jackson, 1891; C.S. Laishley, 1894; E.F. Plumlee, 1898; John Monroe, 1902; James M. Gray, 1910; W.G. Masters, 1924; W.F. Waddell, 1930; Henry E. Neely, 1942 (re-

Oopie Reneau
Former County Court Clerk

signed); W.F. Waddell, 1942 (appointed to serve Neely's term); David Hunter, 1946 (resigned); Clara Hunter Bryant, 1949 (appointed to serve out Hunter's term); John T. Stone, 1954; Fannie Ruth Atchley Gribble, 1978; and Bobby Meadows, 1982. William H. Hawkins, the first Circuit Court Clerk, was born in 1807 and died in 1876. He was married to Elizabeth Hamilton. One of his sons, Harvey H., was killed in the Battle of Murfreesboro during the Civil War. He is buried in the Butler Cemetery near Butler's Landing. He is the great grandfather of Willie Butler Upton.

William H. Hawkins
First Circuit Court Clerk

Bobby Meadows
Circuit Court Clerk

The following people have served as Register of Deeds: Isaac H. Miller, 1871; Daniel W. Cullum, 1881; John Monroe, 1890; J.R. West, 1894; W.B. Dale, 1898; Fannie Overstreet Clark, 1930; Mary Dale, 1934; George Butler, 1938; Lockie Butler (Mrs. George Butler), 1962; Joe Ridge, 1966; and Ray Frogge, 1978. The first deed was recorded on April 6, 1871 at 3 p.m. transferring ⅛ of an acre from L.B. Butler to S.H. Jones and Brother.

Ray Frogge — Register of Deeds

The following have served as tax assessor: H.S. Tinsley, 1871; E.S. Dale, 1900; O.B. Maxey, 1900; J.J. Plumlee, 1900; D.A. Sprat, 1900; J.M. Tuttle, 1900; A. Crabtree, 1901; J.D. Chandler, 1901; W.L. Colson, 1903; F.P. Waddle, 1904; J.P. Condra, 1905; W.L. Reecer, 1911; J.H. Reneau, 1913; E.C. Edens, 1916 (resigned); J. Will Mayfield, 1921; John B. Overstreet, 1924; H.O. Pennington, 1928; Paul Stone, 1946; Bobby Stone, 1964; and Joe Melton, 1984. No explanation is given for having five tax assessors listed for 1900 and two listed for 1901.

Joe Melton — Tax Assessor

The following have served as sheriff of Clay County: Adam Thrasher, 1871; J.C. Bennett, 1872; W.C. Mayfield, 1874; William C. Percell, 1878; William C. Mayfield, 1880; Samuel Comer, 1886; Joseph A. Parker, 1888; S.H. Hance, 1894; Joseph A. Parker, 1896; Champ Williams, 1902; W.C. Waddell, 1904; Champ Williams, 1906; M.E. Sanders, 1910; J.M. Gray, 1916; T.M. Hampton, 1918; Champ Williams, 1922-23 (died in office); T.L. Meadows, 1923; Vanus B. Spear, acting sheriff, 1924 (killed at the Butler's Landing Schoolhouse while performing his duty as acting sheriff); J.M. Gray, 1924; Alex Spears, 1928; J.C. Eads, 1932; B.B. Masters, 1938; George Abney, 1940; Bryan Davis, 1942; Hershel Dowell, 1946; Everett Spear, 1948; Roy Boles, 1950; Raymond Strong, 1952; Jesse Copeland, 1958; Lester R. Boles, 1964; Jesse Copeland, 1968; Hugh Davis, 1972; Austin Thompson, 1982; and Jerry Rhoton, 1986.

Austin Thompson — former Sheriff   Jerry Rhoton — Sheriff

The following have served as road commissioners of Clay County: James J. Amonett, George W. Stephens, and W.M. Rich, 1880; M.F. Green, H.H. Spivey, John L. Maxey, Newton Plumlee, 1881; J.A. Stephens, R.T. Thurman, H.H. Spivey, J.G. Glasson, J.K. Gilland, E.C. Fowler, 1882; W.S. Davis, John R. Hampton, S.B. Langford, Hamilton Brown,

F.P. Pedigo, George M. Kirk, J.T. Coffee, 1886; Milton Thurman, Thomas Butler, Amos Kirkpatrick, T.B. Mayfield, S.T. Tinsley, 1871; W.C. Johnson, Milton Burnett, Sam Keisling, 1890; E.S. Dalton, 1900; George Abney, Andrew Johnson, Frank Halsell, 1946; Frank Brown, 1954; D.A. Eads, 1958; Roy Boles, 1970; and Press Browning, Jr., 1978. Up until the 1940's, each district had a road commissioner.

Press Browning — Road Commissioner

The following have served as superintendent of schools: G.W. Stephens, 1873; James L. Brown, 1878; B.F. Bray, 1880; William L. Brown, 1883; B.F. Bray, 1887; L.S. Smith, 1889; W.C. Sidwell, 1892; M.L. Moore, 1895; W.J. Cherry, 1898; J.T. Ford, 1903; W.B. Boyd, 1907; J.T. Ford, 1909; B.C. Ledbetter, 1913; H.G. Maxey, 1921; B.C. Ledbetter, 1923; Edward Mayfield, 1932; Willie T. Cherry, 1936; Clarence Holman, 1947; Melvin Brown, 1948; Elsie Jo Vaughn,

Elsie Jo Vaughn
Superintendent of Schools

Carmon C. Brown   Frankie M. Brown
Superintendent of Schools   Superintendent of Schools

1958; Carmon C. Brown, 1964 (died in office); Frankie M. Brown, 1967 (completed her husband's term — Carmon C. Brown); Joe E. "Dickie" Masters, 1968; James L. "Jimmy" Watson, 1976; and L. Mayfield Brown, 1980. Four members of the Brown family have served as superintendent of schools: Melvin Brown; his brother, Carmon C. Brown; Carmon's wife, Frankie; and Carmon and Frankie's son, Mayfield. Melvin and Carmon are the nephews of another superintendent, W.T. Cherry.

L. Mayfield Brown
Superintendent of Schools

The following have served as school board members: 1881, trustees of the Oak Grove District — Augusta Pitcock, Shelton Craighead, and John S. Harlin; 1882, Montvale Trustees — A.J. Maxey, Isaiah Fitzgerald, J.J. Stephens, A.P. Green, J.J. Brown, John J. McMillan, Rial Rich, M.A. Turner; 1893, School Directors of District One — Phillip Dalton, J.B. Stephens, and T.J. Mabry; 1894, School Directors of District Two — S.J. Spear, Jeff Nevins, L.S. Smith; 1894, School Directors of District Three — J.T. Clancy, J.B. Denton, and J.B. Kendall; 1902, School Directors of District Five — Add Green, James Davis, and Cyrus Rush; 1908, W.P. Windle, J.G.H. Windle, J.A. Rich, Bug Griffith, Thomas Hogan; 1909, M.C. Sidwell, J.T. Ford, W.P. Windle, J.G.H. Windle, A.W. Raines, J.A. Rich, H.T. Gettings; 1912, W.B. Clark, Bedford Arnold, William Rich, G.B. Gates, James A. Pedigo; 1913, E.C. Edens, W.B. Clark, W.A. Marcom, Andrew Mullinix, Scott Reneau; 1915, W.B. Clark, B.C. Ledbetter, W.A. Marcom, Caleb Ledford, B.R. Grace, Sam Leonard; 1916, W.A. Marcom, B.R. Grace, A. Bean, C.R. Stockton, W.B. Clark; 1918, W.B. Clark, T.B. Huffines, W.A. Marcom, A.T. Sallee; 1919, A.T. Sallee, W.A. Marcom, W.B. Clark; 1920, W.B. Clark, W.A. Marcom, B.R. Grace, W.W. Grace, T.B. Huffer; 1921, B.R. Grace, W.W. Grace, W.A. Marcom, T.B. Huffer, F.B. Mayfield; 1923, B.R. Grace, W.W. Grace, G.L. Bilbrey, Frank Kyle, F.B. Mayfield, J.T. Ford, Forrest Arney; 1924, F.B. Mayfield, Frank Kyle, W.W. Grace, J.A. McLerran, J.T. Ford, B.C. Ledbetter; 1925, W.A. Marcom, Frank Kyle, W.W. Grace, G.L. Bilbrey, J.A. McLerran, J.T. Ford; 1926, W.W. Grace, W.A. Marcom, Frank Kyle, J.T. Ford; 1927, J.A. McLerran, W.W. Grace, W.P. York, W.A. Marcom, Frank Kyle, C.E. Clark, J.T. Ford; 1928, J.T. Ford, C.E. Clark, W.A. Marcom, J.A. McLerran, W.P. York, W.W. Grace, Gordon Smith, Frank Kyle; 1929, W.A. Marcom, Frank Kyle, C.E. Clark, Gordon Smith, J.A. McLerran, W.W. Grace, W.P. York; 1930, W.A. Marcom, W.C. Monroe, C.E. Clark, Gordon Smith, J.A. McLerran, W.W. Grace, W.P. York; 1933, W.C. Marcom, W.C. Monroe, J.A. McLerran, C.E. Clark, Gordon Smith, Wilson Grace, Smith Roberts; 1934, J.M. Hamilton, Bert Hestand, Smith Roberts, W.W. Grace, Gordon Smith; 1937, W.B. Bean, Bert Hestand, Roy Maynord, J.M. Hamil-

ton, H.B. King, H.E. Neely, J.R. Colson; 1940, J.M. Hamilton, Roy Maynord, W.B. Bean, B.E. Hestand, H.B. King; 1941, J.B. Hamilton, B.E. Hestand, W.F. Brown, Gordon Smith, S.R. Roberts, Joe Moredock; 1942, W.F. Brown, J.B. Hamilton, Bert Hestand, S.R. Roberts, Willis Hay, Joe Moredock, V.M. Birdwell; 1943, W.F. Brown, B.E. Hestand, S.R. Roberts, V.M. Birdwell, J.B. Hamilton, Joe Moredock; 1945, Jewell Terry, H.B. King, J.B. Hamilton, Bert Hestand, S.R. Roberts, Joe Moredock, J.H. Overstreet; 1946, B.E. Hestand, Joe Moredock, J.H. Overstreet, S.R. Roberts, H.B. King, Jewell Terry, Joe Moredock; 1947, J.B. Hamilton, J.H. Overstreet, Jewell Terry, S.R. Roberts, H.B. King, and Henry Moredock; 1948, Harmon Overstreet, J.B. Hamilton, Bert Hestand, Smith Roberts, Bedford King, Jewell Terry, H.F. Moredock; 1949, J.H. Overstreet, Thomas Langford, Fred Smith, Montie Savage, Lemuel Smith; 1953, Jimmy Smith, Grady Savage, R.L. Goodpasture, Fred Marshall, Katherine Spivey; 1957, W.G. Roberts, Herman Roberts, Minor Buford, Floyd Collins, Fred Marshall; 1961, W.G. Roberts, Ray Emerton, Raleigh Melton, Johnny Crowder, Cecil Langford, Herman Roberts; 1965, Alfred Young, Louis McLerran, Ben Melton, Melvin Grace, Cecil Langford, (Selma Young served out her husband's, Alfred Young, term); 1968, Selma Young, Joe Melton, Ernest Hummel, Cecil Langford, Melvin Grace; 1969, Curtis Taylor, Selma Young, Ernest Browning, Cecil Langford, Joe Melton; 1970, Joe Melton, Lester Westmoreland, Randall Scott, Curtis Taylor, Ernest Browning; 1973, Bert Hestand, Jr., Harvey Webb, Ernest Browning, Kerry Eads, Cecil Langford; 1976, Bert Hestand, Jr., Cecil Langford, Harvey Webb, Huel Boles, Ernest Browning; 1977, Bert Hestand, Jr., Cecil Langford, Harvey Webb, John C. Donaldson, Ernest Browning; 1979, Cecil Langford, Louis McLerran, Wayne Strong, Connie Mac Clements, John Clark Donaldson; 1982, John Clark Donaldson, Harold Wix, Louis McLerran, Billy Grace, Dicky Roberts; 1986, John Clark Donaldson, Harold Wix, Leslie Meadows, Russell Cherry, Dicky Roberts.

In 1919, a high school board of education was composed of Luke M. Brown, J.B. Walker, H.B. King, O.L. Carnahan, A.C. Willis and P.T. Biles. In 1920, Luke M. Brown, B.C. Ledbetter, Bedford King, Joe Walker, Mattie Capshaw, and O.L. Carnahan served on this high school board.

(Data for this section was compiled by Laquanah Crowder. Contributors were Edwina Langford; unpublished writings by W.L. Brown, William Curtis Stone, Landon Anderson, Kibbie Tinsley Williams Gardenhire; Robert Daniels; the *Citizen-Statesman;* the *Nashville Banner;* "Tootsie" Clark; Debbie Roberts; Kathy Poindexter; Sharon Thompson; Helen Walker; Billie Fay Thurman; J.H. Reneau, III; Margaret Reneau; Paula Sidwell; Mary Loyd Reneau; Blanche Carver; Ralph Craighead; Louise Hayes; Carl Davis; Jimmy Burchett; Jim Hunter; Jack Donaldson; Keith Crowe; Jerry Eads; Mayfield Brown; Frances Donaldson; Phyliss Boyce; Louise Melton; Laura McLerran; Tammy Dulworth; Don Napier; Kevin Donaldson; and Dayton Birdwell)

Mell Lee Head — Photographer

The Steamer Helen Fitzgerald — 1938

"Gathering at the River" in the early 1900's

CELINA —
THE COUNTY SEAT

Hotel Celina — "Old Town"

Gathering at courthouse for a public speaking by Governor A.H. Roberts about 1918 or 1919.

CELINA — THE COUNTY SEAT

According to at least two historical records, Colonel James McColgan and Hugh Roberts purchased 113 acres of land from Spilby C. Winston of Sumner County, Tennessee on September 22, 1932 for $250, and they laid off lots and streets for a town site just south of the Obey River and just west of the Cumberland River. This became the village of Celina which was named for Celina Fiske Christian, the daughter of Moses Fiske, an early educator in the area. The town was incorporated on February 2, 1848. One-half of the original 113 acres purchased was sold to Charles Moore for a ferry. This ferry was later sold to B. Peterman, and later to Kyle Brothers. Celina was burned by the Yankees in April of 1863; and it ceased to function as an incorporated town until after Clay County was formed.

A post office was established near the town of Celina (One record has it listed as being approximately four miles from Celina on the Livingston road) May 27, 1828. James O. Barnard was listed as the postmaster. Other postmasters have been: Robert Nivins, October 10, 1828; John F. Vass, March 18, 1832; Micajah L. Armstrong, September 14, 1836; Robert Hemphill, April 10, 1838; Washington L. Vawter, November 2, 1842; Robert Hemphill, September 29, 1843; S.B.M. Fowler, February 10, 1846; Loudon C. Armstrong, August 23, 1847; Zachariah Van Hooser, November 5, 1849; Landon W. Oglesby, December 13, 1854; L.B. Peterman, December 5, 1860; Robert P. Brown, September 18, 1866; (Post office changed from Jackson County to Clay County) James L.F. Brown, July 15, 1878; John J. Brown, March 30, 1880; Daniel W. Cullom, June 24, 1884; John Monroe, December 13, 1889; Zerilda W. Monroe, August 22, 1890; Alfred J. Maxey, June 1, 1893; Mrs. Ann Maxey, September 8, 1894; William T. Moore, July 8, 1897; Hampton G. Maxey, May 6, 1914; Woodford C. Monroe, April 12, 1921 (acting postmaster); Woodford C. Monroe, May 15, 1922; Mrs. Dora W. Williams, July 1, 1934 (acting postmaster); Albert Jackson Dale, October 24, 1936 (acting postmaster); Albert Jackson Dale, February 2, 1937; John B. Overstreet, August 26, 1944 (acting postmaster); John B. Overstreet, June 16, 1948; Kenneth W. Overstreet, December 29, 1965 (acting postmaster); Kenneth W. Overstreet, November 7, 1967; and Burton E. Carter, March 29, 1986. (Researched by Edwina Napier, who has served as postal clerk under the last four postmasters at the Celina Post Office.)

After 1863, the first Celina became known as "Old Town." It was a thriving center of commerce. It had one main street,

Union Street — "Old Town"

Union, which began at the riverbank and ran southeast for approximately 340 yards. Three other streets, Water, Walnut, and Spring, ran westwardly and ended at Union Street which terminated at the public road going over the Low Gap to Livingston and Gainesboro. "Old Town" had many businesses over the years. Some of them were: a general merchandise store built by Hibbit and Maxey, which was later purchased by A.P. Green and then by W.L. Brown in 1883; a general

W.L. Brown Store "Old Town" — Celina

merchandise store operated by L.T. Armstrong; A.A. Moore's Mercantile; a general store and drugstore owned by Stone and Oglesby; a saddle shop owned by Joe Gist; Alex Spear's blacksmith shop; a livery owned by Champ Williams; a millinery shop owned by Pearl Farrell; an icehouse; a casket house

"Old Town" Icehouse

owned by John Buchanan; a warehouse owned by the Cumberland Grocery Company; and the Kyle Ferry owned by Millard Kyle. Occupational licenses issued in 1892 on record in the Clay County Courthouse were: Willis and Bradley, retail liquor dealer; Mills and Haile, auctioneers; Nop Harrison, log merchant; A.J. Whitson; Willis and Hull; Gilliland and Brother; W.C. Willis; Hull and Willis, log merchants; McDonald Moore;

Kyle and Hatcher, log merchants; Stephen Mills, peddler; R.B. Sullivan, peddler; Green and Comer; J.L. Wood; J.R. Gist; J.C. Chowning; and Ellis Kirkpatrick. In 1893, the following occupational licenses were issued: W.G. Parker; W.C. Willis; J.N. Nixon; Hull and Arnold; M.D. Moore; J.C. Chowning; John L. Wood; Green and Corner; Ellis Kirkpatrick; A.J. Maxey, hotel; D.W. Cullom, hotel; John Monroe, hotel; and Chapman and Steel, photographers. In 1895, the following occupational licenses were issued: merchants—L.S. Brown; I.J. Gregory; and Moore Brothers; hotels—D.W. Cullom and William L.A. Maxey; peddlers—Bernie Davis; J.C. Thompson; I.C. Hale and Brothers; and Ike Selinskey; distilleries—R.L. Sherrell; B.S. Johnson; L.A. Williams; J.L. Wood; Hargrove and Willis; E. Kirkpatrick; J.W. Reeder; J.C. Chowning; I.H. Hale; E.D. Maynord; Willis and Hull; logging—Kyle and Hatcher; W.H. McCormack; M.M. Smith. Occupational licenses issued in 1896 were: William Spivey; W.J. Moore; W.L. Brown; M.F. Green; P.D. Staggs; D.W. Cullom; A.J. Whitson; I.J. Gregory; M.M. Smith; W.C. Sillis; W.G. Parker; J.R. and M.S. Baker; J.H. Nixon; Arnold and Johnson Hull; Moore Brothers; Willis and Bradley; E. Maynord; D.W. Biles; Hargrove Willis Company; E. Kirkpatrick; Willis and Hull; and distillery licenses were issued to I.A. Williams and Willis and Bradley. Occupational licenses issued in 1898 were: merchants—W.H. McCormack; Kyle and Sons; Green and Windle; L.S. Brown; M.C. Green; Green and Jenkins; J.H. Nixon; A.J. Whitson; H.H. Kyle; I.J. Gregory; S.D. Denton; Hull, Willis and Johnson; Cecilia Parker; J.H. and M.A. Baker; Biles and York; A.W. Crabtree; Allen Rich and Company; Moore Brothers; logging—W.H. McCormack; Hull and Willis; M.M. Smith and Company; livery—I.A. Maxey and W.C. Lowery; Innkeepers—W.C. Lowery; D.W. Cullom; lunch stand—W.C. Lowery; other merchants—Copas and Ross; D.W. Biles; Chowning and Hunter; Laishley and Rich; E. Maynord. The following purchased licenses in 1899: log merchants—Hull and Riley; Green Brothers; Weaver and Kirkpatrick; Green and Weaver; W.H. McCormick; U.J. Moore; W.L. Brown; merchants—A.W. Crabtree; H.L. Harlan and Company; Allen Rich and Company; Chowning and Hunter; Kirkpatrick and Harlan; Copass and Ross; J.W. Reeder; L.S. Brown; G.J. Jenkins; Green and Jenkins; Al J. Whitson; and J.H. Nixon; hotels—W.C. Lowery; and Mrs. E. Cullom; feather renovators—Beard and Kemp; livery stable—W.C. Lowery; and auctioneers—J.F. Haile and Company. Licenses purchased in 1900 were: merchants—J.H. Stephens; J.W. Green; E. Maynard; J.H. Baker; J.W. Reeder; Willis and Johnson; Chowning and Hunter. Licenses purchased in 1901 were: merchants—Staggs and Arnold; J.M. Staggs and Company; J.M. Robinson and Company; Butler and Deceter; Hogan and Deices; A.J. Whitson; Baker Brothers; J. Luck Brothers; J.J. Harlan; hotels—W.C. Lowery; Mary Peterman; Ella Cullum; feed stables—W.C. Lowery; Mary Peterman; and Ella Cullum; distillers—N.W. Riltes; T.A. Williams; peddler—J. Luck Brothers; other merchants—E. Kirkpatrick; G.J. Jenkins; Hill and Hogan; Willis Hull Johnson; C.R. Willis; Hawks and Company; P.T. Biles; John Bean; A.L. Harlan; A. Rich and Company; Moore Brothers; R.C. Russ; Chowning and Hunter; J.H. Baker; Allen and Cannon. Merchants listed in 1905 were: E. Kirkpatrick; R. Heard and Company; R.L. Ross; Saddler, Griffith and Clark; Hawkins and Carmack; Whitson and Dale; E.S. Dale; J.C. Chowning; Baker and Company; Davidson and Willis; Plumlee Brothers; Saddle and Hudson; J.A. Pedigo; and George W. Davidson.

Riverboats brought merchandise into Celina for distribution not only in Celina but throughout the Upper Cumberland area. In 1833, at least three riverboats came to the upper reaches of

Riverboat nearing "Old Town" Landing.

the Cumberland River—the Mayflower, the Tom Yeatman, and the Rambler. Other riverboats that plied the Cumberland during the years of the riverboat traffic were: the Celina, the Burnside, the L.T. Armstrong, the L.T. Plumlee, the Quick Step, the J.J. Gore, the Dunbar, the Will J. Cummins, the B.S. Rhea, the J.H. Hillman, the Benton McMillan, the Henry Harley, the Albany, the Rowena, the Bob Dudley, and the Joe Horton Falls. The Joe Horton Falls was constructed in 1913, and it operated for many years. When she was a young girl, Billie Faye Brown Thurman made several trips to Nashville on the Joe Horton Falls. She described it as being a very luxurious riverboat with three levels. The first level held livestock that was being shipped to market; and the second level had berths for sleeping on the sides. This second level also had the cooking area, and at mealtimes, long rows of tables covered with white tablecloths were set up for dining. Mai and Madden Davis of the Free Hills Community were the cooks on this riverboat. A piano was located on this second level, and if someone on board could play the piano they had music and dancing for entertainment. On the third level was located the pilothouse. Mrs. Thurman remembered being invited up to the pilothouse where the pilot kept a stalk of bananas, and he would allow his visitors to pick a banana from the stalk. Mrs. Thurman remembered that this was the first stalk of bananas that she had ever seen. It took about one week to make the trip from Celina to Nashville. The riverboats brought many visitors to Celina, thus causing many hotels to prosper such as: The Riverside Hotel owned by Champ Williams; the Dale

Red Letter Hotel in "Old Town"

Hotel owned by W.T. Dale—later called the Red Letter Hotel;

L.B. Peterman's Hotel; and the Meadows Hotel owned by Tom Meadows. The Meadows Hotel had several full-time boarders. When the community fair was held, people came from miles around and stayed at the the hotels to attend the fair.

Celina had an outstanding fairgrounds with excellent facilities. It had a reviewing stand, a bandstand, grandstand with promenade, excellent areas for horse shows, livestock shows, and entertainment. Skagg's Circus also performed at the fair grounds.

Prominent families living in or near "Old Town" were: W.C. Willis, L.B. Peterman, R.P. Brown, Captain Hughes, Dr. Johnthan Davis, John J. Brown, Joseph Roberts, James Roberts, Landon Oglesby, Nancy Rich, Albert Rich, Rial Rich, Joseph Rich, John H. Stone, Sallie Gearheart, Hugh Gearheart, Ben Gearheart, Abe Gearheart, Dr. William Shields, Richard Stone, Isaiah Fitzgerald, Dr. B.S. Plumlee, Varney Andrews, William Hamilton, Evan Arms, Vanus Fowler, the Biggerstaffs, Walt Comer, H.G. Tinsley, Palo Conkin, M.G. Hayes, J.J. Amonette, Newton Plumlee, William Walker, Hugh Plumlee, W.C. Lowery, Mike Kirkpatrick, Thomas Stone, W.S. Waddle, Hall Holman, P.A. Dalton, Thomas Minor, L.S. Dalton, Randolph Langford, T.J. Mabry, Wilson and J.T. McColgan, Irvin Langford, Lafayette Harlow, Millard Kyle, G.W. Stone, Allen Skipworth, John L. Maxey, E. Kirkpatrick, M.F. Green, A.P. Green, W.G. Parker, and the Poindexters.

In 1870, the new town of Celina was formed. Most accounts state that ten acres were purchased from A.P. Green, and then surveyed and divided into lots by Bill Gore. The lots were then sold at public auction by Richard Brooks, auctioneer. However, one account states that Arch P. Green, Blew Gist, and W.M. Savage, as a committee, purchased the town site from Mrs. Susan Hannah Davis, the widow of Isaac Davis, for $40 a year for the remainder of her life. It further states that on June 22, 1872, town lots were sold at public auction with Richard (Dick) Brooks serving as auctioneer. As the lots were sold, Mrs. Davis made a deed to the above named committee, who in turn made a deed to the commissioners. The commissioners then made deeds to the purchasers. As Mrs. Davis only had a lifetime dowry in the lots, the town was sold through Chancery Court in Gainesboro to clear the titles after Mrs. Davis' death.

All accounts agree that on April 27, 1872, contracts were awarded for the public buildings to be erected in the new county seat, Celina. D.L. Dow of Cookeville, Tennessee was awarded the contract for construction of the courthouse. The contract price was $9,999.00, with a completion date set for October 1, 1873. The brick for the courthouse was made from clay dirt taken from the public square, and the lumber was

dressed by hand. Carpenters who assisted Mr. Dow were David Buchanan, F.M. Buchanan, and W.C. Garrett. The first court session was held in the courthouse in June of 1874. This

John Buchanon, Contractor for Clay County Courthouse.

building has been in constant use from 1874-1986. The contract for the jail was awarded to W.H. Watts of Oak Grove for the construction of a log jail with a contract price of $2,200 and a completion date of January 1, 1873. Celina has had three jails — the latest built in the mid 1960's.

The first business started in the new town of Celina was a hotel owned by Coe and Martin. It was later owned by A.J. Maxey; and it was next sold to E.S. Dalton, who owned it when it was destroyed by fire in 1924. Benton and John McMillan built a general store and law office, which was later sold to Mrs. Hattie Brown and W.F. Brown who operated it until it burned on Christmas night in 1902. Captain J.K.P. Davis ran a saloon on the southwest corner of Dow and Martin Streets for several years. Some of the later businesses were J.A. Howard Hardware, Buford and Cherry Dry Goods, Bob Parsons Gro-

Kirkpatricks General Store and Miss Aries Cafe around 1900

cery and Icehouse, Ford Garage, W.L. Brown and Sons' Dry Goods, Mrs. Lovie Napier's Restaurant, Bob Ray's Restaurant, Kirkpatrick's, Maxey's Drug Store, Dale's Theater, Burnette's Dry Goods and Furniture Store, Ell Dale's Grocery, Lawson's Department Store, the Dollar Store, Eads Department Store, Napier's Grocery, Napier's Drive-In, "Blooney" Napier's Restaurant, "Blooney" Napier's Market on East Lake Avenue, Boone's Grocery, Dennings 5 and 10, Clay County Co-op, W.T. Marshall Feed Supply, Goodpasture's Grocery, and Lay-Simpson. At least two gristmills have been located in Celina. W.L. Brown tore down the old Hibbitt and Maxey Store, and the lumber was used to build the Bank of Celina. This bank was located on the northwest side of the

Fairgrounds in early 1900's.

Osco Pennington, Bill Dale, Vanus Spear, Paul Hamilton at the "Old Town" Barber Shop and Cafe — 1915.

public square. The Bank of Celina has been in three different locations in Celina. In 1970, the Bank of Celina constructed a new building on East Lake Avenue. The Bank of Celina was organized in 1895 by M.F. Green, A.P. Green, H.H. Kyle, J.T. Anderson, A.G. Maxwell, and George W. Stephens and is the oldest existing business in Clay County. Another bank was located in Celina at this time, the Farmers and Merchant Bank, which merged with the Bank of Celina in 1928. The president of this bank was Dr. Bilyeu, and the cashier was R.L. Donaldson. When the merger of both banks took place, the Bank of Celina moved to a new building where Terry's Drug Store is now located. In 1918, the president of the Bank of Celina was W.L. Brown who served in this capacity until 1944 when Ed Fowler replaced him. Other presidents of the Bank of Celina have been J.A. Howard, M.D. Cherry, Grady Sidwell, H.R. Gates, Clyde King, and Kerry Eads.

In 1909, Celina was incorporated by an act of the Legislature. Hugh H. Kyle was the Mayor, and W.C. Davidson was City Recorder. Other mayors of Celina have been: W.F. Brown, 1917-1932; Charles L. Haile, 1932-1937; J.B. Hamilton, 1937-1941; E.P. Fowler, 1941-1947; Edward Mayfield, 1947-1955; Cecil Buford, 1955-1957; Clyde King, 1957-1959; Joe A. Clark, 1959-1960; W.H. Mayfield, 1960-1961; Willis Spear, 1961-1963; J.H. Overstreet, 1963-1969; Durell Brown, 1969-1970; J.B. Dale, 1970-71; Ralph Hamilton, 1971-1981; Wayne Rich, 1981-1985; and W.H. Reneau, 1985.

Bank of Celina — Cordell Donaldson, Edd Fowler and W.L. Brown.

Mayor W.H. Reneau

The Connecting Link — The Henry Horton Bridge

The Henry Horton Bridge spanning the Cumberland River at Celina was begun in 1928 and completed in 1930. For approximately four years, it was a toll bridge. Toll collectors

Forrest Rich *(standing in doorway)* — toll booth operator.

were Walter Roberts, Forrest Rich and Cordell Donaldson. Completion of the bridge brought an end to "Old Town" as a business district, and the people moved to the new sections around the square. The first switchboard was installed in

South Side of the Town Square in 1940's.

Celina in 1910. In 1914, Charlie Kyle became the first person to own and drive a Model "T" Ford; and in 1926, Jim Guffey was the first person to have electricity installed in his home.

The very first home built within the present city limits of Celina was the Hugh Roberts' home which was built in 1780. He was of Quaker origin and his home was probably used for a meetinghouse. This house stood within the boarders of three states — North Carolina, the State of Franklin, and Tennessee. It has been a part of a territory and seven counties. Legend has it that Mr. Roberts migrated here to avoid military service. He was the first settler in the Celina area. The first brick home

First Brick home in Celina built by Albert Jackson Dale.

in Celina was built by Albert Jackson Dale. This home is now owned by Mode Denning. This home was the first in Celina to have indoor plumbing.

The first school in Celina after the Civil War was taught by George W. Stephens in 1868. Later schools were taught by Mrs. Emma Colson, Miss Martha Maxey, and J. Fay Brown. The first outstanding school was Montvale Academy, which was organized on April 13, 1882 by Isaiah Fitzgerald, A.P. Green, John H. McMillan, J.H. Stephens, V.P. Smith, and William Love. J.S. McMillan, the brother of Benton and John H. McMillan and a graduate of Burritt College, was elected to head the school. He served as administrator for approximately ten years. Some of the Montvale students became lawyers, doctors, judges, and teachers. Two of the most famous graduates were Congressman, and later Secretary of State, Cordell Hull and Benton McMillan, Governor of Tennessee. Teachers at Montvale were R.L. Fitzgerald, Luther Moore, Douglas Woods, Hill Edwards, O.B. Maxey, and Scott Smith. Interest

Montvale Academy and College

in the school abated, but it was rejuvenated in the early 1900's, when a new board of trustees was elected. The members of the new board were M.M. Smith, W.C. Lowry, S.B. Anderson, and L.S. Brown. They employed W.B. Boyd, who was so well-liked that the school had to be enlarged at the beginning of his second year. About $3,000 was raised by private subscriptions to enlarge and remodel the school which became Montvale College. The daily attendance at the college was approximately 200 students. Montvale was in existence for 37 years, and students came from far and near to attend this outstanding institution. Students attending Montvale in 1904 were Frank Brown, Herman Brown, J.D. Brown, C.J. Mabry, Herman Plumlee, O.L. Carnahan, Milton Boles, Ellis Boles, A.J. Dale, J.B. Hamilton, Shields Plumlee, Samuel Weaver, G.O. Arms, G.B. Arms, A.T. Arms, T.C. Crabtree, Fred Clark, Perry Dale, Breck Dickens, Hubert Donaldson, B.G. Edens, A.B. Edens, M.L. Fowler, H.H. Grider, Bennett Gates, C.B. Hamilton, Paul Hamilton, B.J. Hampton, Charlie Hampton, R.L. Irwin, Terry Irwin, Knox Inness, Walker Inness, M.F. Lynch, Mark Lowery, H.H. Maxey, Tony Maxey, J.F. Monroe, Eddie Monroe, W.B. Nevins, A.E. Plumlee, Charlie Poindexter, W.M. Poindexter, Fred Rich, Porter Rich, Ellis Spear, Amos Spear, Guy Stephens, G.P. Stone, A.T. Stone, Wade Stone, Waterston Stone, N.F. Stone, B.C. Stone, Oscar Simmons, Arthur Terry, Austin Terry, B.C. Waddle, B.S. Waddle, James Waddle, H.W. Waddle, Willie Waddle, Fowler Webb, David Williams, J.M. Crawford, Charlie Hatcher, Antne Netherton, Herod Birdwell, Sr., W.L. Murphy, E.G. Murphy, J.W. Smith, Herman Estes, W.A. Hensley, D.A. Clark, Clyde Martin, W.M. Bibee, L.M. Botts, W.C. Hill, Guy Johnson, Hollis Carroll, Frank Norman, Evert Spear, Edward Spear, Fred Spear, Mac Scott, Mildred Mabry, Alice Carnahan, Nannie Smith, Willie Mayfield, Stella Windle, Golda Walker, Ada Arms, Ethel Brown, Nina Brown, Lula Brown, Bertha Brown, Zora Dickens, Ora Dickens, Martha Dale, Lillie Dale, Pauline Dale, Ruby Donaldson, Emma Donaldson, Mattie Edens, Dayse Fowler, Maude Fitzgerald, Pauline Gray, Lucy Price Gray, Hettie Grider, Ella Hamilton, Rose Hampton, Pearl Hampton, Minnie Irwin, Dayse Johnson, Annie Lowery, Nardie Lowery, Carrie Maxey, Dixie Maxey, Bettie Monroe, Bonnie Poindexter, Bessie Rich, Gracie Rich, Clara Roberts, Beulah Roberts, Dora Spear, Lean Terry, Emma Terry, Dee Terry, Ruby Tinsley, Sophia Williams, Myrtie Williams, Pearl Kuykendall, Letha Netherton, Duleenia Smith, Etta Neely, Clyde Harris, Bettie Sewell, Verda McGlasson, Minnie McGlasson, Flora Smith, Verna Spear, Ova Spear, and Dora Scott.

In 1905, the Board of Trustees had the following members: W.C. Lowery, President; W.B. Boyd, Secretary; W.L. Brown; S.B. Anderson; W.N. Gray; E. Kirkpatrick; and C. Hull. Other teachers at Montvale were R.L. Fitzgerald, Luther Moore, Douglas Woods, Hill Edwards, O.B. Maxey, Scott Smithland, Joseph McMillan, Daisy Dale, Walter Boyd, Billy Boyd, Della Boyd, Ida Johnson, Ollie Hughes, and Virginia Myers.

The Montvale College Trustees' Circular published in 1905 stated, "The scholastic year, beginning in September, will continue for a period of nine months, and will be divided into two sessions. The rules are few and reasonable, but are never relaxed, and a strict observance of them is required of all alike. This is not a school of favorites and pets, but a place where the sluggard finds no rest and the meritorious get their reward. Students are not permitted to loiter about town, and are required to remain at their homes or study rooms at night."

35

The following rules and regulations were stressed as it was believed that the importance of discipline could not be overestimated.

1. No fighting, quarreling or riotous conduct of any kind will be allowed.

2. All students are required to obstain from rough boxing, wrestling and scuffling.

3. No student shall bring any pistol, dirk, fireworks or explosive of any kind about the school premises.

4. No student shall bring any obscene book, obscene pictures or gaming cards of any kind upon the school campus.

5. All cursing, swearing or indecent language is strictly forbidden.

6. No student is permitted to interfere with the property of another, whether student or citizen.

7. No student shall mark, cut, or in any way deface the school property and should this regulation be violated, the offender shall pay all damages and be subject to such punishment as the Principal may see proper.

8. Every student must abstain from smoking and chewing tobacco while on the school campus.

9. Every student must occupy the desk assigned, or his room, and must refrain from all visiting, sport, communication, or unnecessary noise.

10. No student shall at any time leave the premises without permission.

11. Every student is expected to obey promptly every summons of the school bell.

12. No student, save the regular bellman, shall interfere with the school bell.

13. On the ringing of the evening bell, every student must retire to his/her room and use the time as designated by the faculty.

14. Except at times designated by the faculty, there shall be no communications of any kind between boys and girls.

15. Every student must obstain wholly from intoxicating liquors and association with characters of ill repute.

The school had a series of dormitories for use by the young men. Students occupied these rooms both day and night.

R.C. Spear at Montvale Barracks for men.

During the day, they were removed from the noise and general "bustle" of the study hall; during the night they were under the immediate supervision of the Principal. This enabled the faculty to keep students at their places and work, and allowed them to keep them away from all pernicious associations and influences.

Students wishing to enter the school had to present evidence of moral character and had to pay in advance for all room rent and contingent fees. The itemized expenses were as follows: board, $6-8 per month; tuition, primary $1.25 per month, intermediate $2 a month, preparatory $2.50 a month,

academic $3 a month, teachers course $3 a month, elocution, $2 per month, instrumental music, $3.50 a month, and a contingent fee of 50¢ a month. Young men who occupied a dormitory room had the following expenses: board for 5 months, $30; tuition for five months, $10-12; room rent, $2; fuel and incidentals, $2.50-5.00. The total bill was from $44.50 to $49.00. The cost for young ladies and/or young men who lived in town per session was from $50-$55. Any student who was expelled or stopped before the end of a term, without reasonable cause, forfeited the tuition for the entire term.

The following course of study was offered in 1905: Primary Department — primer, reading, writing, speller, numbers work, and home geography; Intermediate Department — reading, spelling, United States history, Tennessee history, geography, practical arithmetic, English grammar, and intermediate physiology; Preparatory Department — intellectual arithmetic, higher arithmetic, algebra, geography, and higher English; Academic Department — first year: higher arithmetic, rhetoric, geometry, higher algebra, latin, and civil government; second year: geometry, physics, English literature, Latin, ethics, and geology of Tennessee; third year: trigonometry, astronomy, botany, chemistry, logic, and zoology; Special Courses — psychology, art of study, pedagogy, and school management. Montvale had two special departments — the Department of Elocution, a four year course of study, which included simple breathing exercises, articulation, delarte exercises, short recitations, vocal training, study of gesture, gymnastics, harmonic pose, pantomime expression, dramatic readings, et cetera; and the Department of Instrumental Music, a five year course of study which included Lebert and Stark's Piano School, pieces by Shumann, Gurlitt, Hullah, Reinecke, Vokmon, Clementi's Sonatinas, and selections from Beethoven, Mozart, Chopin, and Mendelssohn. Some of the students enrolled in these special programs in 1906 were Ethel Brown, O.L. Carnahan, G.P. Stone, G.O. Arms, L.M. Botts, J.H. Reneau, Lockie Webb, Lee Anderson, Belew Edens, Maude Fitzgerald, W.T. Sewell, F.C. Maynard, C.J. Mabry, W.L. Roberts, H.L. Long, Myrtie Dowell, O.R. York, Beryl Haile, Fred Maxey, Paul Hamilton, Fowler Webb, Charlie Haile, Nina Brown and Della Elam. The *Montvale Bulletin* described the town of Celina as: "a small town, on the east bank of the Cumberland River. ... blessed with a solid, sober-minded, conservative citizenship. Its order and morality are unequaled by any town in this part of the country, free from 'quacks, frauds, sideshows,' and it is also free from the light and fastidious characteristics in manner and dress. Celina has a refined country society, from which at all times the great and good have come."

Montvale Class of 1914

In 1907, Clay County had three school systems governed by three separate boards of education, one of which was the Celina Board of Education. In 1919, Celina came under the Clay County School Board and a public high school, Clay County High School, was established. Professor J.J. Hendrickson was principal of Clay County High School. Clay County

C.H.S. Faculty 1930's

High School became Celina High School in 1933.

According to Charles P. Gray, editor of the *Celina Messenger,* basketball was inaugurated at Montvale College in 1908-1909. He wrote: "Under the supervision of the Editor, they have been playing in the open air for a week. There is no house in the city in which the game can be played; therefore, it must be played in the open air. The boys have been practicing under many difficulties, and yet they have done well. The

L. to R. Lizzie Rich, Bennie Stone, Peggy Williamson, Lockie Masters, Brownie Anderson, Katherine Rich, Mary Fitzgerald, Docia Masters, Rachel Riley, Hallie Ruth Fiske.

Celina's Girls Basketball Team wearing first manufactured uniforms — 1922.

Clay County High Football Team — 1923

Celina High School

Class of 1925 — Celina High School

game will be played solely for practice and exercise. It is devoid of rough features when properly played. It is a splendid cultivator of the muscles and the wind. It is hoped that the boys will be successful and that hereafter this place will be represented by a good team." Mr. Gray's wish for good teams in the future certainly came true. In 1984, '85, and '86, the Celina High boys' basketball team played in the Tennessee State Tournament. In 1986, they advanced to the semi-finals

Joey Coe — Celina High's first "All American" basketball player.

selected to McDonald's High School All-American Team. Coe scored 2,966 career points and broke all Celina records but the one held by David Short for most points per game — 51 scored in 1951. Celina High School's football team, the Bulldogs, went to the state semi-finals in 1986.

Celina High boys basketball team — 1986 — State Semi-Finals.

of the Tennessee State Basketball Tournament. Coach Thomas Watson's team was made up of the following players in 1986: John Carlisle, Greg Brannon, Jeff Arms, Jeff Rich, Tracy Strong, Kevin Watson, Scotty Likens, Chris Smiley, Donnie Copeland, Jerry Arms, Jody Reecer, Billy Cherry, Rob Weir and Michael Fox, Manager. In 1985, Joey Coe was

Billie Faye Brown Thurman, "Mrs. Billie" School Librarian for over 20 years.

New Celina High School in 1955.

Some of the teachers at Celina High School have been: Herman W. Taylor, Brownie Anderson, Karl E. Monroe, Bennie Stone, E.W. Fox, Helen Hancock, Charles P. Jennings, Alyne Young, Ruth Plumlee, Karl Monroe, Lucille Mayfield, R.B. Smith, Elsie Jo Vaughn, Edward Mayfield, Dan Masters, Frank Sidwell, Billie Faye Brown Thurman, Eddie H. Watson, Martha Belle Kyle, Jack Clark, Cleo McGlassion, Hanson Carr, Lona Walker Capshaw, Edna (Mrs. M.D.) Cherry, Ruth Patton, Carmon C. Brown, Sue Sidwell, Hugh Dowell, Patsy Sidwell, Jewell Dean Arms, I.W. Finley, Katherine Clark, Kathleen Brown, Jessie (Boles) Hord, Mrs. Russell Hinson, Clarice Qualls, Charles Hord, Robert Teeples, Leonidas Holland, Mary Lou Gates, Alvirtta Copas, Lillian Chitwood White, Clifton Carter, John W. Brown, Eddie Mae Langford, Betty Hale Webb, Willodean Webb, Laquanah Crowder, Lecta Grace, Helen Brown, Mary E. Cherry, Mary Fitzgerald, Christeen West, Olyne Gates, Marvena Maynord Lynch, Betty Teeples, Lincoln Wilkerson, Imogene Spear, Joe E. Masters, Sara Lynn, Marshall Donaldson, Dayton McLerran, Larma Holt, Hance Wilkerson, Henderson Grace, Byron Gray, Ann Bryant, Odell Swann, Douglas Young, Mayfield Brown, Bobby Westmoreland, Joe Lynn, Eva Nell Plumlee, Jerry Eads, Johnny Dowell, Christine Poindexter, Ann Townes, Jane Smith, Ed Tinch, Brenda Mabry Kirby, Joe Neil Eads, Russell Richardson, David Browning, Judy Bailey, Tim Reecer, Carolyn Melton, Donna Capps, Jean Stephens, Thomas Watson, Dennis Smith, Emily Hayes, Lucy Head, John Cullen, Joe Dan Fox, Jerry Fox, Jimmy Watson, Harold Watson, Harry T. Matthews, Geneva Bartlett, Jane Clark, Stuart Eiland, Champ Langford, Joyce Scott, Junior Buford, Martha Cropper, Eldon Scott, Jerry Coates, Mary Loyd Reneau, Peggy Davis, Kathy Graves, Alan West, Diana Monroe, Elizabeth Holtam, Brent Wells, Diana Sullivan, Corryne Clements, Beth Gentry, Dona Tade, Elizabeth Reneau Burch, Hilda Brown, Phyliss Buford, Gary J. Strong, Johnny McLerran, Randy Birdwell, Janet Swan Craighead, Bobby Bartlett, Linda Green, Sharon Hayes, and Janice Graves. Many of these same teachers also worked at Celina Elementary School. Celina Elementary School was changed to Celina K-8 School when the new school was constructed in the early 1970's. Principals of Celina Elementary and/or Celina K-8 have been: Elmo Burris, Glin Emerton, Larma Holt, Carmon Brown, Elsie Jo Vaughn, John Teeples, Peggy Davis, Charles Hampton, Homer Gates, Finis Maynard, Herman Waddell, W.H. "Bill" Smith, and Geneva Clark Fowler. Some of the teachers at Celina Elementary School and Celina K-8 School have been: Erma York, Vera York, Daisy Dale, Mrs. John J. Hendrickson, Lillie Ashburn, Cassie Smith York, Mae Swan Gilpatrick, Winnie Brown, Pearl Brown, Jewel Qualls, Amos Arms, Patsy Sidwell, Frankie Brown, Odell Swann, Janet Swann Craighead, Hilda Brown, Mary E. Cherry, Lizzie Langford, Lucille Melton, Alice Sanford, Karen Bowman, Eddie Rose Cherry, Christine Poindexter, Geraldine Clark, Jane Clark Robbins, Billie E. Marcom, Geneva Clark Fowler, Clyde Atchley, Homer Gates, Olyne Gates, Diane Browning, Mary Fitzgerald, Mrs. I.W. Finley, Mrs. John W. Brown, Marvena Maynard Lynch, Sara Lynn, Maude Fitzgerald, Billie Brown Thurman, Helen Wells, Carolyn Hindman, Martha Thurman, Katherine Roberts, Martha Poston, Betty Teeples, Linda Hamilton, Johnny Dowell, Jerry Eads, Ann Watson Rich, Connie Lynn, Judy Fox, Lura Parsons, Debbie Seber, Donna Burnette, Debbie West, Margaret Taylor, Barbara Butler, Margie Garrett, Bobbie McClain, Mary Addie Hinson, Margaret Birdwell, Jayne Donaldson, Linda Strong, Champ Langford, Margaret Arms, David Threet, Carlotta Grimsley, Leslee Korth, Brenda Kirby, Dennis Smith, Randall Walker, Anna R. Locke, Faye Watson, Randall Smith, Bobby Bartlett, Geneva Bartlett, Stephen Chitwood, Lana Chitwood, Sue Stone, Betsy Holtam, Debbie Craighead, Christeen West, Mary L. Reneau, Johnny McLerran, Joe Simms, and Donna Capps.

Dorothy Dale Rich
Music Teacher and volunteer for all events requiring music.

CELINA CHURCH OF CHRIST

The oldest church in Celina is the Celina Church of Christ, first called the Christian Church, which was established in either 1833 or 1834. The first building was located in "Old Town" facing the Cumberland River. It was later turned to face the Montvale Academy. This same building was used for the county court meetings when the site of the court meetings was changed from Butler's Ferry to Celina, according to one report.

In the early years, the Church had no regular preacher. W.L. Brown, who was a leader of this Church, usually held the regular Sunday morning service. When week-long meetings were held, a visiting preacher would come and stay for the entire week of the meeting. W.L. Brown (affectionately called "Billy Pa") was in charge of inviting the speaker for the meeting. These visiting preachers would lodge at Mr. Brown's home until the close of the meeting. There were approximately 100 members of the congregation in the earlier years of the Church.

The new Celina Church of Christ was built around 1954.

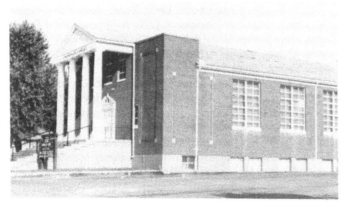

Celina Church of Christ

The land for the Church was purchased from Mrs. Mattie Smith for $250. Some of the preachers for this Church have been: Bill Dossett, Lovell Clark, Ralph Kidd, Herbert Ledford, William B. Yates, Monroe Lawson, George F. Raines (first preacher to live in the new parsonage), Charles E. Cheatham, James C. Allen, John Hollaway, Harry L. Hastey, Nat Evins, Kenneth McClain and Robert Crabtree.

LAKE AVENUE CHURCH OF CHRIST

The Lake Avenue Church of Christ was established in 1976. Its first meeting place was above Charlie's Restaurant. Chester Thompson and Joe Finch from Nashville helped this congregation with the assistance of Paul Bates of Bayfield, Colorado. In May of 1976, Donald Bryant came to Celina from Booneville, Arkansas to work full-time with the congregation. At this time, land was purchased from Jack Roach and his wife, Betty, for the sum of $4,000 for property to erect the church building. At this time, there were six lady members and an attendance of about twenty. By December, the membership had reached thirty and the attendance at worship services averaged 50 to 60.

The actual construction of the new building was started in March of 1977, and it was completed in July of 1977. The members of the Congregation helped with the construction along with Everett Holloman of Booneville, Arkansas. The first meeting was held in July of 1977, with Paul Bates as the pastor. Donald Bryant served as pastor of the Church for a number of years.

RIVERSIDE CHURCH OF CHRIST

This Congregation first met in the old processing plant with Paul Hamilton as the first preacher. The congregation later moved upstairs at the Buford Bait Shop.

In 1973, land was purchased for a building in the Riverside Subdivision. The land was purchased from Jessie Lee and Jewell Copeland, Ronald and Judy Bailey, and Clyde and Ruth King. The trustees were W.B. Napier, Jr., Carlos Spurlock and Robert Hix.

Riverside Church of Christ

The Congregation erected a brick building with an auditorium and two classrooms. The Congregation has approximately 50 in attendance for the Sunday morning worship service. Brother Paul Hamilton served as preacher for this Congregation up until his untimely death.

CELINA FIRST BAPTIST CHURCH

On the first Sunday in November of 1933, the First Baptist Church was organized by six charter members: Mrs. Mary B. Spear, E.W. Fox, Mr. and Mrs. James S. Ray, and two children. Reverend James S. Ray was called as the first pastor of the Church.

Reverend G.L. Winstead (pastor at Gainesboro) served the Church for a few months. The Church was using the Methodist Church building at this time. In January of 1935, Brother C.B. Pennington came to live here and served as pastor. Next, the Church began having services at the Courthouse. Brother Pennington organized a Sunday school with meeting days being the second and fourth Sundays. In the early years of the Church, Mrs. Mary B. Spear has been known to be the only person at the services, bringing wood for the fire, making the fire, saying a prayer and then leaving. In March of 1935, Mrs. Mary B. Spear and E.W. Fox began working toward the building of their first Church building. A total of $77 was collected for the building fund. This money assisted in the building of a small box building. The land for the building was acquired from Fred and Ollie Maxey on April 24, 1935, for the consideration of $200. The trustees were Mary B. Spear and E.W. Fox.

Celina First Baptist Church

Brother C.B. Pennington started to build the Church building with the assistance of the Church members and members of other Baptist Churches. The house was ready for use in the winter of 1936.

W.T. Parrott held the first revival in the new Church building in January of 1936. Three members were added to the Church: Mrs. Frank Ledbetter, Miss Marie Ledbetter and Mrs. Betty Brummett. In October of 1943, additional land was acquired from P.M. and Ida Mary Cherry for the consideration of $500. Additional renovations have been made to the original building over the years. In the early 1980's, a new building was completed.

CELINA METHODIST CHURCH

The Celina Methodist Church was established around 1899 on land purchased from William and Elizabeth Hull. The Methodist trustees were M.M. Smith, Mrs. Alva Sidwell, H.H. Kyle, and M.C. Sidwell. A two-story frame weatherboard building was erected on the land with a steeple that was visible all over town. The first floor was used by the Church, and the second floor was used by the Celina Masonic Lodge and Eastern Star. It has been said that H.H. Kyle donated most of the lumber for this building. The building had a gas light outside the main door, which was a novelty at that time. Pastors who served the early Church were Brothers Rochelle, Taylor and Kirby.

In 1911, E. Kirkpatrick and his wife, Mollie, sold the Church a lot for a parsonage. Trustees at this time were W.J. Maynord, W.E. Sullivan, J.H. Myers, Mayhew Neely, John Patterson, A.P. Chilton and S.B. Anderson.

The Church sold this building to the Celina Masonic Lodge for $200 in 1954; and they sold the land on which it stood to Karl Napier for $7,000. The trustees were Rachel Langford, W.H. Hay, Roy Maynard and Sue Sidwell. On March 12, 1954, land was purchased from Hattie Coffee for $2,250. A modern brick sanctuary was built with stained glass windows and double front doors on the new property on South Brown Street. Members of the Church purchased walnut pews for the new building. These members were Mr. and Mrs. Grady Sidwell, Betty and John Teeples, Paula Sidwell, Mr. and Mrs. Thomas Langford, Dillard and Zettie Sparks, Roy Maynord, Dick and Betty Roberts, Karl and Reba Napier, the Flora Collins Family, Mr. and Mrs. Edward Swann, Lee Ann and Lisa. The Church has received many gifts from the members of the Congregation, including a baptismal font donated by Mr. and Mrs. David Stooksbury in memory of Bob and Trudy Riley; and a steeple was placed on the Church by Sue Sidwell

Celina Methodist Church

in memory of her husband, W. Grady Sidwell. The organ in the Church was purchased with money given by the Haskel Howard estate.

SEVENTH DAY ADVENTISTS CHURCH

The Celina Seventh Day Adventists Church was organized in 1940 through the Georgia Cumberland Conference Association. In the entire county, there was not a representative of the Seventh Day Adventists Church. Plans were made to awaken an interest in this Church. The city fathers offered the facilities of the courtroom for Church services. The Baptist Church offered the use of a pedal organ. A series of meetings were held, and the first family to join the faith was the Amos Keisling Family. Soon a company of twenty was organized. The land for a church building was obtained from J.C. and Nannie Eads for the sum of $150. A rock veneered building was erected on this property in 1941, through the diligent efforts of Dr. Ewert and his wife, a Mr. Rush and the Keislings. This building also had provisions for a private school which could accommodate about one dozen children.

Celina Seventh Day Adventist Church

This Church was associated with the Georgia Conference until February 27, 1951, when it was conveyed unto the Kentucky-Tennessee Conference Association. This Church served other communities' spiritual needs that did not have a place of worship. Jim McCormick served this congregation for several years.

Celina only has one civic organization that has met continuously for a number of years, and this is the Celina Lions Club, which was organized on October 28, 1952 at Napier's Restaurant on the square (now Mr. B's). The Lions Club meets on the second and fourth Monday nights of each month. The regular meeting place has been Napier's Restaurant, which is now Wilma's Restaurant.

Mops, brooms, fruit cakes, light bulbs, and anything else that would sell have been sold to raise money for club projects. For the past 23 years, the main fund-raising project has been the annual Lions Club Horse Show. Sight conservation is one of the main projects of the Lions Club. They have pur-

Don Sherrell with sight conservation recipients Velma Threet and Nan Stacy.

chased eye glasses for numerous people in Celina and Clay County They also contribute to charities and other benevolent campaigns. Other projects of the Lions Club are the annual Easter Egg Hunt, aid to school children, help for the elderly, et cetera. They also assist in the promotion of community and school progress, including enrichment activities and industrial development. They provide assistance with the annual Fish Fry, which is free to the public and attracts hundreds of visitors each year in the month of August.

For the past three years, beginning in 1983, the Lions Club has given a "Citizen of the Year" Award to the person who deserves special recognition for outstanding service to the Community. This award has been presented to Kenneth Masters, Doug Smith and Frances Donaldson.

The first officers of the Lions Club were: Jesse Goodpasture, president, and Leslie Upton, secretary-treasurer. Other members who have served as officers have been Luke Martin, William G. Redmon, Carmon Brown, E.L. Monroe, William B. Yates, W. Grady Sidwell, W.B. Upton, John Teeples, Herbert Higdon, Frank B. Halsell, Joe E. Burnette, Leslie Upton, Earl Napier, James K. Sparkman, John D. King, Dr. James E. Brown, Ezell Nevans, Joe F. White, Bobby Westmoreland, Douglas Young, Clyde Dowell, Jr., John Donaldson, Joe Lynn, Ronald Bailey, Kerry Eads, Roy Burnette, Earl Law, Donald Haston, Don Napier, Jerry Eads, John Bell, Gerald Block, William Burnette, Robert Weaver, Mike Bailey, James H. Reneau, III, John Heath, Donald Sherrell, and James D. White, Jr.

One of the primary social events in Celina for over 20 years has been Earl Napier's "Chitlin' Supper," held each winter through 1985. Earl started this event as a small "get-together" for his friends at his Drive-In on East Last Avenue. Each year the event grew larger until it had to be moved to the cafeteria at Celina K-8 School where hundreds attended the event from all over the State of Tennessee and neighboring states. State and local politicians and TV personalities came to enter the "Chitlin' Eating Contest," and many of them, as well as local citizens, did win the yearly contest. Mr. Napier died in 1985;

Earl Napier — "Chitlin' Supper" host.

and plans have been made to continue this event in his memory.

One of the favorite pastimes for the men of Celina has been playing cards, rook and "pitch." These games were often held in local stores, particularly W.A. Marcom's and Johnny

Card Game at W.A. Marcom's Store.

White's. Another favorite pastime is gathering on the public square to whittle. The men use cedar sticks for their whittling; and by the end of the day, large piles of cedar shavings have accumulated on the square.

Celina is proud of its heritage, which was evidenced by the many events held during "Homecoming '86," a celebration held throughout the State of Tennessee. "Gathering on the Cumberland" was the theme for Celina and Clay County. The following events were held in downtown Celina: quilt show, square dancing, pie auctions, parade, farmers' market, civil war exhibit, art show, antiques display, and the reopening of the Cordell Hull Law Offices.

The Cordell Hull Law Office

COMMUNITIES

Pine Branch Church of Christ

Vacationers at the Long Hotel — Hermitage Springs, TN.

Eastern Clay County

"I can still imagine that I am a barefoot boy roving the banks of Iron's Creek from Obey River to the head of Wiley's Fork. . . . I know that you, too, have the same longings and have similar imaginative scenes," wrote Dr. Champ E. Clark in his "Reflections," published in the Homecoming Edition of Willow Grove in 1968. "Longings and imaginative scenes" are all that is left of a beautiful valley surrounded by towering hills with a peaceful river fed by smaller creeks coming down from the hollows into this valley; as this large, fertile section of Clay County, consisting of several small communities and the village of Willow Grove, was covered by Dale Hollow Lake in the 1940's."

Willow Grove

Willow Grove, as a village proper, was small and nestled in the valley of the Obey River on the banks of Iron's Creek. The

Willow Grove

Willow Grove Community extended over a vast area from hill to hill. There was no approach to the community, except by river, without going down a hill into the valley. According to tradition, it derived its name from a grove of willow trees which, at one time, surrounded a spring that flowed out of the village into Iron's Creek. The creek received its name from a man by the name of Iron who was one of the early settlers of the area and whose son was killed in a horse race and interned on a knoll in the village over which the schoolhouse was erected during the 1800's. When the old building was moved from the knoll for a new school building to be erected about 1933, John Brewington, an elderly resident of the community, pointed to a spot from which the old building was removed and said, "The Iron boy's grave should be near here." As the excavation proceeded, a walnut casket was found that was put together with wooden pegs. The casket was placed under the new building, and insofar as is known, it is under the lake to this date. Another story that is told is that on a farm last owned by Haskell Buford there was a hill covered with cedars, and at a certain time each year, wild pigeons would come to this cedar grove in such flocks that the skies would become darkened. The people would come from miles around to catch the pigeons for food by using torches to blind the pigeons.

The people who inhabited this valley were of modest means, yet they were self-reliant and honorable. It was a close-knit community with common ties. Members of the community consisted of pioneer settlers such as the Sidwells, Marcoms,

Colsons, Clarks, Smiths, Watsons, Stovers, Hawkins, Hargroves, McCluskeys, Holmans, Maynards, Ledbetters, Sewells, Hatchers, Seviers, Davidsons, and Fords.

The most famous of the pioneer settlers who came to this section of the County was Bonnie Kate Sevier, the widow of Governor John Sevier, who owned 57,000 acres of land in this area. Bonnie Kate moved to "The Dale," later known as the "Clark Place" in 1815. "The Dale" was located near Fairview and Willow Grove near a large cave spring. She later moved to Alabama. Some of Governor John Sevier's family who lived here and who have descendants still living here are Dr. Sam Sevier, a son, who lived near the mouth of Wolf Creek; George W. Sevier, who lived on Sulphur Creek; Joanna Windle, a daughter; Valentine, a son, who lived on Iron's Creek; Mary Overstreet, a daughter, lived on the Obey River; another daughter, Sarah Brown, who lived at the "Old James McMillen Place;" another daughter, Ann Corlin, who lived on Ashburn's Creek; and another brother of the Governor's who lived near the mouth of Ashburn's Creek, whose name was Joseph. John Sherrill, a brother of Bonnie Kate, lived near the mouth of the Wolf River.

Families who have owned and operated stores in Willow Grove were John Craft General Merchandise, Grimsley's Drug Store, Hay and Martin General Merchandise, Martha Marcom Millinery Shop, Ed Hargrove General Merchandise Store, Y Store, Jim Watkins Blacksmith Shop, Hay and Watson Truck Line, Bob and Christine's Garage, and Bill Smith's Garage.

The following people had gristmills at Willow Grove: Lewis Daniels, Hoy Ford, Willie Colson, and Jim Watkins. Bill Boykin and Bill Estep operated a water mill and cotton gin on the head of Iron's Creek which ceased operation in 1926.

The first doctor to practice in the Willow Grove Community was Dr. J.M. Turner. In the early 1900's, Dr. Walter Frank

Dr. Walter Sidwell   Dr. Edward Clark

Sidwell and Dr. Edward Clark administered to this and other outlying communities riding on horseback in all kinds of weather to attend the sick. Records on file in the Clay County Courthouse in Celina show that John Bethel Lansden (1901) and Thomas L. Willis (1908) were doctors who listed their residences as Willow Grove.

William Stovall was the first postmaster at Willow Grove. He was serving in this position in 1837. The post office was discontinued in 1858; but it was reopened on December 6, 1976 with Thomas H. Johnson as the postmaster. Other postmasters were Joseph Smith, P. Virgil Hawkins, George V. Grimsley, Jesse L. Smith, William S. Smith, and Sernadus G. Sewell. The post office was closed December 30, 1942, because of Dale Hollow Lake.

All of the people in the Willow Grove Community had a common interest — the school. There seems to be no record of the first school, but it was possibly located in the area known as Watsons' Bend of the Obey River. The Honorable Cordell Hull attended school there before moving further down the river to Celina. Willow Grove Academy began November 13, 1899. (This was known as a subscription school.) The tuition varied from $1 to $3. Students could "board" in private homes for $1.25 a week. Public schools were established in the early 1900's. At this time a two-story weatherboard building was erected. In 1919, the county established a two year high school at Willow Grove, with Lindsey Hunter as principal. In 1927, the school became a three year high school. Principals and teachers serving during this period were Raymond Hamilton, a Miss Bilbrey, John Bell, Elmos Gentry and Jesse P. Price. It became a three year high school in 1927-28, with Ben E. Groce as principal. It became a four year high school in 1928-29, with Frank Spear as principal. Other principals of the high school were J.B. Lea, J.L. Algood, S.D. (Doc) Bilyeu, W.T. Cherry, F.L. Sidwell, Eddie Watson, Earl Watkins, Winfred Kirby, Maurice Anderson, and Kermit Smith. In 1938, with the help of the Works Progress Administration, a modern high school was built on the same site. This was a two-story, brick building with the grammar school on the ground floor and the high school occupying the second floor. (The Masonic Lodge had access to the second floor until they disbanded.) A gymnasium was built through the efforts of the people in the community. The gymnasium was built at the back of the high school, and gas-powered generators were used to supply lights

Willow Grove Class Of 1940

for the games. The school was disbanded in 1942-43 due to the construction of Dale Hollow Dam.

The Willow Grove Baptist Church was built on the banks of Iron's Creek. The land on which the church was built was given by Eugene and Martha Marcom in the early 1800's. Some years later, a second church was built near the site of the first. The Marcoms provided a parsonage for the Baptist Church. In 1929, when a new road was built, the Church was moved across the road to a new site deeded to the Church by B.C. Marcom and his wife. The Willow Grove Baptist Church continued to function with the following member families: Marcoms, Andersons, Crafts, Hays, Martins, Grimsleys, Hogans, and Burroughs, until the Church closed its doors with the construction of Dale Hollow Dam in the 1940's. The elders at this time were C.V. Grimsley, J.L. Conner, and R.R. Little. The Church was paid $1,550 for its building and 1.19 acres of land.

The Willow Grove Church of Christ was established by Dr. J.M. Turner, who came from Virginia to Tennessee in the early 1800's. Having no meeting house, the little congregation met in the groves in the summer and in the home of Squire John "Jack" Sevier in the winter. This John Sevier was the father-in-law of Dr. Turner, and a nephew of the first governor of Tennessee, Colonel John Sevier, whose wife, Bonnie Kate, had a large land holding in this section. Squire Sevier was an

Willow Grove Church of Christ

elder in the congregation and gave the land for the meeting house. Another early leader in the Church was William B. Sewell. He served as an elder for 40 years. Some of the early preachers here were Newton Mulkey, Andrew P. Davis, Isaac T. Reneau, the Sewells (Jessie, Isaac, Caleb, Elisha), J.M. Kidwell, and James Ownsby. In later times, the Kirbys and F.B. Srygley, along with Marion Harris and Willie Hunter, served this church as preachers. In 1910, the membership outgrew the first building and a new building was erected on land conveyed to the elders by G.W. Sevier and his wife. The elders were J.M. Copeland, G.W. Davidson, and James M. Smith. Marion Harris delivered the sermon when the new building was dedicated. When the construction of Dale Hollow Dam began, the Church was paid $2,240 for the building and 1.65 acres of land. The elders were R.A. Sewell, R.R. Clark and Edward Clark.

The Willow Grove Methodist Congregation met jointly with the Baptist Congregation for many years since they had no building of their own. In 1939, a new road was built, causing the Baptist Congregation to move from this location. The trustees of the Willow Grove Methodist Church — J.W. Gentle and C.T. Hogan — decided to build their own church building. They obtained land for the building from J.W. and Cynthia Gentle. The deed stated that the two-story building was to be used for Church and Lodge purposes. The Methodist Church was to have the first floor and Mount Pisgah Lodge F.&A.M. 481 was to have free access at all times to the second floor of the building. Trustees of the Lodge up until the 1940's were J.W. Gentle, O.F. Meadow, and Ray Dulworth. Early preachers who led this congregation were Everett Edens and Alf Jenkins. The Willow Grove Methodist Church was closed with the construction of Dale Hollow Dam. The Church and the Lodge each received $899.00 for their share of the building and the property. — *Contributors to this article: Clarence M. Holman, Champ E. Clark, Geneva Clark, Paula Sidwell.*

Willow Grove residents in Nashville lobbying for a road into this section of Clay County and on into Pickett County

Fox Springs

In 1834, William Donaldson operated a post office at Fox Springs. In 1835, it was operated by D.W. Cullon until it was discontinued in 1847. Henry D. Johnson was the postmaster when the post office was reestablished. Other postmasters have been L. Daughter, Charles Smith, Thomas C. Webb, Jonathan C. Sewell, Josh C. Chowning, William C. Brown, Joseph C. Chowning, and John E. Sidwell. The post office was discontinued February 15, 1911.

Joe Chatt Chowning operated a store in Fox Springs in the 1890's. John F. Sidwell later ran this store and added a drugstore. Fred Clark purchased this business and operated it for three years. The next owner was Cattie Clark. Bub Maynard obtained the store in 1935 and operated it until 1946. The Fox Springs Store was a general merchandise store with dry goods, flour and sugar being kept in one store and salt, lamp oil, et cetera, being kept in a separate building.

The Fox Springs Congregation erected their first meeting house in the late 1800's. This was an all denominational church. However, only the Christian Order, now called the Church of Christ, used this building for services. John Chilton, Bob Riley, and Bob Fletcher donated the lumber for the initial building. Jennie Chilton, the mother of John Chilton, donated the land for the building. Early preachers here were Brother Tracy, Brother Kennedy, Brother Taylor, and Doc Hall. With the construction of Dale Hollow Dam, the building was dismantled; and Ebb Chilton purchased the lumber to construct a dwelling house.

G.L. Maynord had a gasoline gristmill in conjunction with a store at Fox Springs. It was operated by Ruffin Smith and later by Jim Jackson. It operated only on Saturday as this was the day the farmers brought their corn in to be ground into meal. Vannie Neely operated a mill at his home about one mile from Fox Springs in the early 1930's.

In the early 1870's, The New Salem Methodist Espicopal Church was built on the banks of Mitchell's Creek just south of Fox Springs. The deeds for this land were conveyed to the Church by William and Sarah T. Davis and John and Della Chilton. The land was donated to John Riley, Webster Cullom, and Thomas B. Davis by William and Sarah T. Davis in their deed made in 1871. The second deed by John and Della Chilton was recorded in 1904. Joe Chatt Chowning and other families raised the funds for the Church. Walter Smith erected the building with the help of Bob Riley, who sawed the lumber for the construction of the building. The Church was in existence for more than 75 years. It closed its doors when Dale Hollow Dam was built.

Lillydale

Lillydale was located in the extreme northeast corner of Clay County in a valley formed by the Wolf and the Obey Rivers. It was there that the Wolf joined the Obey, and the community was called Mouth of Wolf until 1892. A special school was held that summer with three visiting teachers in charge. One of the teachers much admired the charms of two of the local girls, Lily Gilliam and Sally Dale. He contended that the valley was too beautiful and the people too nice for the name "Mouth of Wolf", so he renamed it for the two girls. The folks who lived there liked the name, so the name of the Post Office was changed to Lillydale.

For most Clay Countians, Lillydale was, at that time, the "Land Beyond the River". Actually, Lillydale might have more appropriately been claimed by Pickett County or even one of the Kentucky counties of Clinton or Cumberland. A small section of those two counties separated Lillydale and the Pickett County community of Vans Branch. During a "High Tide" in those early days, Lillydale was completely cut off from their Willow Grove neighbors and their county seat town of Celina.

Two fords on the Obey River connected Lillydale with the rest of the county. One led to the Gamewell Hill and Willow Grove while the other, the Holman Ford, connected Lillydale with the Ashburn Creek area. Two fords across the Wolf, the Rocky Ford and the Bryson Ford, led to Albany, Kentucky.

In later years a bridge, located between the two fords, was built across the Obey, making Willow Grove and Celina easily accessible to the residents of Lillydale.

The people who lived there were of hearty pioneer stock, their lives closely interwoven with each other. They enjoyed music and the old songs and dances that had been brought across the mountains by their old world ancestors.

Prior to 1800, Colonel James Armstrong had a boat work at the mouth of the Wolf River. One of the first oil wells in this section of the state was discovered about a mile from the mouth of the Wolf by two boys also named Armstrong. They were drilling for salt water. According to legend, the oil flowed out over the ground and down into the river where it caught fire. The residents of the area thought the world was coming to an end, and indeed, for awhile, it must have appeared to be the actual Day of Judgment.

Because of the steamboating and rafting, most of the early growth of the settlement was clustered near the rivers. Even after the name Lillydale had been adopted, the more common usage was Lillydale Landing, thus showing the importance of the two rivers in the development of the settlement.

After 1900, Lillydale village began to spread out more and draw back from the river. One building doubled as the school (grades primer through eight) and the Church of Christ meeting house. In the very early years, the Methodist Church also used the building for their meetings.

Lilly Dale School — 1936 Esther Clark — teacher.

Some of the Lillydale teachers were Ida and Esther Clark, Waymon Hogan, Earl Watkins, Riley Stockton, Forest Long and Jack Clark (now a medical doctor in Cookeville, Tennessee).

One of the 8th grade graduates of Lillydale School, Keith Arney, later became a Doctor of Medicine and was personal physician to President Lyndon Johnson for a time. Before his untimely death, he taught medicine at the University of Texas Medical School.

Some of the Postmasters were Jim Speck, Jang Scott,

Milton Pryor, George D. (Cap) Arney, Mrs. Ola Sevier (her husband Frank was a direct descendant of Governor John Sevier), and Gwendolyn Phillips (Sadler) who was Acting Postmaster during the interim between Mrs. Sevier's resignation and the floodwaters of Dale Hollow Dam.

The most popular location for the post office was the side

Lillydale Post Office — Gwendolyn Phillips — Postmaster

room of the general store. However, Mr. Arney and Mr. Scott provided nice (post office only) buildings during their tenure. One rural route out of the post office served the people of the area in parts of both Clay and Pickett Counties, as well as the small K section.

Gratton D. Phillips was the Rural Carrier from 1919 until his untimely death in 1941. His brother, Haskell Phillips, served as substitute carrier. Geraldine Phillips (Smalling) was appointed Rural Carrier in September 1941. Geraldine and Gwendolyn (Acting Postmaster) Phillips were daughters of Gratton D. and Lorene Pickens Phillips.

Some of the Lillydale doctors were Dr. Dalton, Dr. Strange, Dr. Sidwell and Dr. Bill Tom Pickens.

Some of the merchants were Jim Speck, the Daltons, Luther Stanford, Clark Arney, John B. Jennings and Frank Sevier.

The first mill at Lillydale was owned by Ransom Mercer and the first blacksmith shop by Morgan Copeland. In later years, Gillis Smith operated the Lillydale mill. Ina Murry was the telephone operator.

Some of the family names were Dalton, Dale, Clark, Smith, Phillips, Hatcher, King, Boles, Upchurch, Mullins, Shipley, Short, Coop, Mercer, Officer, Gilliam, Sells, Scott, Hurd, Stanford, Arney, Wright, Sherfield, Gamewell, Stamps, Melton, Norris, Pryor, Ellis, Groce, Murry, Holman, Hardin, Jennings, and Speck.

POST OFFICES

Other post offices in Eastern Clay County were located at Speck and Mouth of Wolf. The postmasters at Mouth of Wolf were Spencer M. Henry, July 31, 1856; Allen T. Gilliand, 1874; James C. Gilliand, 1887; and Allen T. Gilliand, 1891. This post office was later called Lillydale. The postmasters at Speck were Landon L. Maxfield, 1880; John M. Sidwell, 1884; Elizabeth J. Sidwell, 1901; Abram McKines, 1904; and Mary E. Maxfield, 1910. This post office was discontinued in 1911.

CHURCHES AND SCHOOLS

Other churches and schools located in Eastern Clay County were Mount Pisgah; Gum Grove Church of Christ, Ashburn's Creek Church of Christ, Poor Branch Church of Christ, Ashburn's Creek School, Pleasant Hill School, Pleasant Hill Methodist Church, St. John's School and Church, Fairview Methodist Church, Buzzard's Roost School, Hong Kong School, Fairview School, Meadows Chapel School and Church, and Cross-Plains Church.

Mount Pisgah was organized prior to 1884. The building was jointly owned by the Church and Mount Pisgah Lodge No. 481. A deed given to the church and the lodge by T.H. Johnson was never put on record. Another deed conveying property to the Church and Lodge was made by Amy Bennett, Mayford Maxfield, Kate Maxfield, Parrs Maxfield and Bertie Maxfield. This building was also used as a school. In the 1940's, attendance at the Church began to drop off. Members living on the main road decided to build another Church that was closer to their homes. The Fairview Methodist Church was built, and the members of Mt. Pisgah brought with them the benches from this church. The Mt. Pisgah Building was torn down in the 1960's.

Ashburn's Creek Church and School were organized prior to 1922. C.A. and Mary B. Wilborn deeded the land to the Clay County Board of Education for $80. Teachers at Ashburn's Creek have been Ida Clark and Mary Lou Melton. The Ashburn's Creek Christian Church was paid $100 for the building when Dale Hollow Dam was built.

Pleasant Hill School was a one-room log building. It was built on land deeded by J.R. and Rettie Nelson. In 1925, a second school was built. The daily attendance at this school was approximately 100 students. Teachers who taught there were Lillian Sevier, Lillie Marcom, Dudley Hogan, Tula Ledbetter Clark, Willie Arms, Joe Arms, Laura Melton and Pearl Smith. In the early 1940's, a third building was constructed here. In 1945, the school was presumably sold, and the building was deeded to the Pleasant Hill Methodist Church. This Church had been in existence prior to the 1900's with a large membership recorded. Early members and leaders in the Church were Hogans, Daniels, Pattersons, Chiltons, Collins, Chowning, and Stocktons. Appointments to this Church were made by the Bishop; and the first pastor according to the Church Register was John L. Roby, who was appointed on October 29, 1900. The Church continued to function until the late 1970's, when it merged with Fairview and Taylor's Cross Roads to build Martin's Chapel in Overton County.

The St. John's School and Church of Christ used the same building for about 49 years. The land for the building was given by I.E. Sewell and his wife. Early teachers here were Elmer Colson, Willie Colson, Mae Edens, Cleston Grimsley, Myrtle Marcom, Forrest Long, and Chester Ledbetter. The Church and School closed in 1953.

The Fairview Methodist Church was built on land purchased from S.C. Heard in 1945. In the late 1970's, the once large attendance began to dwindle, and the Church closed. The leaders of the Church sold the building to E.C. Reagan who converted the building into a grocery.

Buzzard's Roost School was established in the late 1800's near the present site of Dale Hollow Boat Dock. Classes were held in a small building accommodating twenty students. Teachers were B. Wright, Henry Neely and Cecil Dowell. In 1915, the Hong Kong School was built about 50 yards from where the Buzzard's Roost School stood. The residents wished for a new name other than Buzzard's Roost, and they called it

Hong Kong. This school consolidated with the Pleasant Grove School approximately 22 years after its opening.

The Fairview School was built on land conveyed by M.F. Clark in 1899. Around 1913, a second building was erected on land obtained from Margaret and James Boyakin. Teachers at this school were Cullum Sidwell, Betty Sewell, C. Willis, Lillian Sevier, Ula Sevier, L. Maxwell, Clyde Ford, Vinas Maynord, Forrest Long, Ester Clark, Joe Arms, and Sallie Spicer. This school was later consolidated with Maple Grove.

The Meadows Chapel School was established in the 1880's. This was a small school for grades one through eight. Early teachers were Lil Maxey, Dave Kyle, and Lizzie Dillion. The Christian Order Church did not meet regularly, but they did hold meetings in this building. John Arms was the minister that conducted the services in the early 1900's. The building of Dale Hollow Dam brought about the removal of this building.

The exact location of the Cross-Plains Church is not known, and the specific religious persuasion and teachings of this Church is also a mystery. The official County Court Minutes dated April 5, 1871 states: "On motion it is ordered by the Court that Saddler Holman be appointed overseer of a road leading from the Cross-Plains Meeting House to Celina by the way of J.W. Gates and that he have all the hands living on the farm of John Webb, W.P. Overstreet, A.B. Holman, T.J. Meelys, Martha Nevins, M.W. Davis, W.L. Hall, J.A. Gates, R. Peterman, M.M. Williams, James R. Stone, Sarah Gearhart, Isaiah Fitzgerald, Henson Smith, and Hiram Tinsley's farms which road is to be worked as a second class road." This is the only record of this Church.

The Maple Grove School was erected in 1936 on land donated by John Martin. The second Maple Grove School was erected on land purchased from J.B. and Ella Martin. This school is still in existence and is the only school located in the Eastern section of the County. Some of the teachers here have been Cornelia Huffer, Forrest Long, Lizzie Langford, Isabell Garrett, Randall Walker, Mildred Daniels, Roger Watson, Champ Langford, Lura Parsons, Jayne Donaldson, and Joy Langford.

On July 18, 1942, Dr. Edward Clark made the following address to the people of this section just prior to their having to leave.

"I have been asked, urged to try to talk to you a little. I am a sick man, both in mind and body. Those of us in this area which is soon to be inundated with water have a double problem to the rest of you. I do not know what to say to you, or what I ought to say to you. I do not know how to say it.

" . . . We, people in this Valley, are soon to have to seek new homes somewhere. All that has been dear to us, we are going to have to turn our backs upon and leave. Many of us have sons in that awful conflict that is raging now and will have for the balance of this war. Many of you have other sons who will be inducted into the service; and I am telling you now many of them will be sacrificed in this conflict and before it is over, their blood will be spilled on foreign soil. All of the sad things I know anything about and all the horrible things I know anything about is war and hell. Sherman said, 'War was hell,' and I believe he is right."

"In addition to this problem, we are having to give up the dearest thing that any human has ever had from a human standpoint, and that is our little castle called home. There are three words that stand out in the English language. Those words are Home, Mother and Heaven. I realize that in this great crowd of people here today who have gathered to make contact for new homes, the majority of you will never see each other again. Some will go one way, some another. But I want to tell you that with that kind of dark picture before you, you

should be thankful because we are living in a country and under a flag that so far has guaranteed to you the right of 'Liberty, Justice and the Pursuit of Happiness.' You can and will find homes in other communities. We hope and trust that after this is over, and we settle back to normal, you will be useful citizens and happy the rest of your lives. I am thankful that we have had this get-together meeting here today. I hope that much good in the way of directing the tenant farmer to the people who can furnish them homes will be accomplished; and I believe that if we will just use our judgment along with the help the Extension Service of the University of Tennessee is giving us, and will continue to give us, we can and will all find homes.

"I want to say this to you — be careful! The price of land is 40 to 50 percent higher than it was a few years ago. The man who has land to sell wants to get all he can for it, and the man who has to buy feels he has to buy regardless. Remember that after the other war, there was an awful letdown. It is coming to all of us again to some degree. To those of you who are going to buy land, let me admonish you to be careful. Buy your home in a community where you think you would like to live — where there are churches, schools, and in an enterprising community that will help you to be better citizens. So far as knowing what you ought to do, I do not. I do not know myself. I do not know what I can do, but by the help and direction of the almighty God I am going to live somewhere and try to make an upright, useful citizen the remainder of my active life, which is not long, and I trust that you will do the same."

Most of the Eastern Section of Clay County is history. The building of Dale Hollow Dam forced the citizens to go in all directions at the close of 1942. The timber was cut, the homes torn down, the schools, churches and stores demolished. This area was taken from the maps, but not from the hearts of its people.

Contributors for this section were: Paula Sidwell, Rachel Langford, Lavelle Buford, Geraldine Smalling, and Edwina Upton. Compiled by Laquanah Crowder.

The Dale Hollow Dam

ARCOT COMMUNITY

Colonel James McColgan settled what is now the Arcot Community in approximately 1810. He was granted this large tract of land for his services during the Revolutionary War. In the early 1800's, the community was called Hix. It was next called Bennett's Ferry, but this name applied to the lands on both the eastern and western banks of the Cumberland River. In the late 1880's, it was named Arcot by the McColgan's, who according to legend named it for a community in their native Ireland.

Colonel James McColgan's son, Wilson, T., was a physician and was practicing medicine in this community as early as

The home of Dr. Wilson McColgan. (present owner — Melvin Brown)

Cumberland River — site of Bennett's Ferry.

1845. In this remote section of Tennessee, the practice of medicine was not a full-time occupation, so he became interested in woodworking and furniture making. He and his friends also made a printing press, and in later years, he and his son, James Talleyrand, (called Dr. "Tallow Ann" by local residents) used this press to publish a medical journal called "The Country Doctor," which was postmarked from Arcot, Tennessee.

The McColgans were slave owners, and these slaves made

The home of Colonel James McColgan. (renovated by O.N. Cherry)

the brick to construct an imposing 14 room brick home which was completed by 1858.

The total Arcot Community can be divided into smaller segments — Knob Creek, Dry Creek, the Upper (or Stone's) Bottom, and the center section (Gnatty Branch). Knob Creek was the home of the Daltons, Harpes, Browns, and Atchleys. Dry Creek was the home of the Langfords, Plumlees, Browns, Crowders, and Adkins. The Upper Bottom was the home of the Chapmans, Stones, Kirkpatricks, Roberts, and Smiths. In the middle section lived the McColgans, Cherrys, Delks, Garretts, Dales, Farris, Mabrys, Frogges, Cunninghams, and Walkers. The 1880 Census listed 53 households for the Arcot Community. Most of the people were farmers. However, there were two doctors, a teacher, and 25 blacks (former slaves), who worked for the other families in the Community.

A post office was located in the home of Dr. McColgan who served as postmaster from 1888 until 1905. Other businesses in the community were a sugar mill, a sawmill, and three stores. Farming was the prime occupation of the community. Many of the men worked at logging and rafting — building rafts and floating them down to Nashville.

Bennett's Ferry was a major center of trade. It was one of three sites voted on as a possible county seat for Clay County. It lost by two votes to Celina. Riverboats stopped regularly to leave merchandise and to buy produce from the farmers. During the Civil War, a riverboat was sunk here in an effort to

block the Cumberland River. However, it was soon raised and put back into service. Several other skirmishes between the Yankees and the Rebels took place at Bennett's Ferry. At one time, a gunboat shelled the community hitting the home of one of the McColgans. Smith "Son" Crowder operated the Ferry for many years. This ferry connected the eastern and western sections of the County until the Henry Horton Bridge was built at Celina.

Arcot School

There have been at least three schools in the Arcot Community: Knob Creek, Arcot, and Plumlee's on Dry Creek. T.J. Mabry deeded the land to the County for the Knob Creek School for the monetary sum of one cent in 1914. The school was actually built in 1899 at the foot of the Knob Creek Bluff facing the Cumberland River. The teachers dismissed classes when the riverboats passed in order for the children to go out and wave to the boatmen who in turn sounded the boat whistle. The children attending Knob Creek School ranged in age from five to twenty-five. Some of the teachers were Belvia Plumlee, Maude Fitzgerald, Mattie Meadows, Belle Mabry Kyle, Bonnie Poindexter, Ollie Hamilton, and Hampton Maxey. Some of the students were Paul (Bowser) Stone; Bonnie Waddell; Alice, Helen, and Amos Arms; Kate and Ernest Harpe; Bed and Belle Day; Fred Mabry; Luke Smith; Edward (Matt); and Charlie Mabry. This school closed in 1922.

The Arcot School was built on land donated by the McColgan Family in the late 1800's. The first building was made of logs. The next building, built on the same land, was constructed of weatherboarding and painted white. It had two classrooms, two cloakrooms, and a large front room used for a kitchen and dining area. At the beginning of the school term each student would bring his eating "utinsels" — plate, bowl, glass, fork, and spoon — to use for the year. Lunches were paid for by bringing potatoes, greens, home-canned vegetables, meat, et cetera. Some of the teachers were Rose McColgan Hall, Charlie Hampton, Asia Plumlee, Beulah Spicer, Vera

York, Dona Harpe, Harold Sain, Dorothy Sain, Captola Brown, Alvirtta Copas, Gertrude Arms, Adele Birdwell, Larma Holt, and Christeen West. Children from the following families attended Arcot School: Cherry, Atchley, Brown, Delk, Walker, Harpe, Mabry, Goolsby, Morris, Spears, Stone, Dale, Eads, Moss, Cunningham, Adkins, Crowder, Baxter, Jones, Harris, Farris, Strong, Frogge, Arms. The Arcot School closed in the early 1950's.

Plumlee's School was located on Dry Creek and was built by Samuel Plumlee to educate his children and the children of others who lived on the "Creek." This school closed in the late 1800's. Mrs. Bertha Pedigo Brown taught school in her home on Dry Creek for one winter term.

The Arcot Church of Christ first met in the Arcot School building. William Jackson Cherry was instrumental in the organization of this church. In the 1940's, the Church built its own

Arcot Church of Christ renovated 1970's.

building on land donated by O.N. Cherry, the son of William Jackson Cherry. Families who have attended this Church down through the years are: Cherrys, Browns, Crowders, Stones, Harpes, Atchleys, Dales, Walkers, Delks, Cunninghams, Roberts, Williams, Jones, Strongs, Eads, Mabrys, Donaldsons, Masters, Roaches, Kyles, Kirbys, Rhotons, Robinsons, Holts, Smiths, Farrises, Goolsbys, Meltons, Copas, Moss, Frogges, and Sharps. Some of the preachers have been John Arms, Marion Harris, Tolley Phemister, Willie Hunter, Harold Sain, Freeman Crowder, Leslie Spear, J.B. Gaither, Edward Anderson, Jerry Coates, Donald Short, Horace Burks, and Levi Stephens. The Arcot Church of Christ has had two regular preachers: Arkley Billingsley and Jack Gaw.

Arcot in the 1980's is still primarily an agricultural community although many of its residents work in Celina. The majority of the residents are descendants of the early settlers of the community. They are proud of their heritage and take pride in their community. *Researched and compiled by: Jeff Brown, Layne Boyce, and Laquanah Crowder. Contributors: O.N. Cherry, Ethel Cherry, Ethel Crowder, Ezra Brown, Vanus Eads, Paul Stone, Berah Stone.*

BAKERTON COMMUNITY

In 1900, Melanthon Kirby established the first post office in the Bakerton Community. In 1904, John Baker was the postmaster. The mail was delivered to the Bakerton Post Office by Babe Smith. Mr. Smith would ride a horse from Nashville with the mail. The mail was kept in locked saddlebags. The postmaster kept the key that unlocked the mailbags. People of the

community would then go to John Baker's Post Office to pick up their mail. By having the post office in his store, John Baker was bringing in more customers on a regular basis. Tradition has it that the community was named for this same John Baker. Mr. Baker retired from his business in 1906. Farmers in this area took eggs, feathers, sometimes wool, and coups of chickens to Lee's Landing near Gainesboro. As they were in route during the rainy seasons, farmers would sometimes have to wait for floodwaters to go down in the North Springs area. After the waters abated, they would proceed to their destinations. While the farmers were at the Landing, they would pick up goods for John Baker's Store. He paid these people for delivering his goods.

In 1906, Mr. Baker sold his general store to Bud Hudson. He operated the store and also the post office until it was discontinued in 1907. The next owner of the store was Joe Griffith. The last owner was Avery Clark. Another store was erected by LeRoy Whitley who sold the store to Wesley Clark.

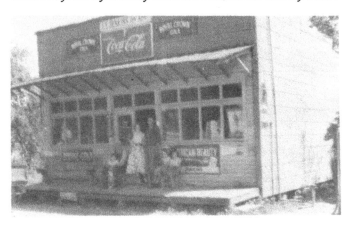

J.S. Jenkins Store

Jake Jenkins and his family next purchased the store and operated it until his retirement several years later.

The first Church built in the Bakerton Community was called the Rose Hill Church of Christ. This Church is believed to have been established over one hundred years ago. Mr. Lonnie McMillan donated the land for the church, which was located near the Vinson Cemetery. Several years later, the members decided to move the building up on a hill from the original site. After the building was moved, extensive remodel-

Bakerton Community Church of Christ

ing was done. A new, more accessible building was erected near where the Bakerton Store once stood in 1970.

BAPTIST RIDGE COMMUNITY

The Baptist Ridge Community is between Butler's Landing and Overton County. The following families established, and many still live in, the Baptist Ridge Community: Bronstetter, Holt, Gilpatrick, McBride, Spear, Abney, Waddell, Moore, Rich, Hall, Kellow, Boles, Langford, Spivey, Cunningham, and McClain.

There have been at least two general merchandise stores on Baptist Ridge — Holt's General Store and B.C. Waddell General Store. A "rolling store" was operated by Leon Holt from Holt's General Store. This "rolling store," which was a large truck fitted with shelves, carried all types of merchandise into the many rural communities that did not have a store.

The first school on Baptist Ridge was a log building. It was called Oak Grove. A Mrs. Williams taught here for many years. In 1905, a new school and church building was erected. The property was donated by Allen Rich. The County paid for the materials, and the people in the community supplied the labor. Some of the early teachers were Miss Ova Dale, Stella Windle, Hettie Windle, Turnie Clark, Leslie Davis, Walter Roberts, Laura Melton, B.C. Waddell, Lena Sevier, Charles Poindexter, Susie Maynard, and Roy Maynard. In 1913, approximately 100 students were enrolled in this school. In 1929, a new school was built on property bought from Walter and Pearlie Boles. This school was consolidated with Celina in the 1960's. The building was used as a community center until it burned around 1971.

The Baptist Ridge Baptist Church was organized in an old store building belonging to Della Bronstetter. She deeded to the Tennessee Baptist Convention a lot for a church on October 25, 1941. This Church disbanded in the 1950's.

The Oak Grove Church of Christ on Baptist Ridge was established in 1956 on land deeded by Charlie Burris. The trustees of the Church were Fred Abney, B.C. Waddell and Granville Gilpatrick. Kenneth Poindexter and Palmer White did the initial building of the Church. Lester Coates delivered the first sermon in the new building.

BEECH BETHANY

Beech Bethany is located on the Western banks of the Cumberland River and extends to the foot of the Walker Hill. It has two major creeks — Big Proctor and Little Proctor. This community was settled by the following families: Hayes, Arms, Stones, Riches, Nevins, Walkers, Plumlees, and Tinsleys. The following families still reside in this community: Hayes, Plumlees, Stones, Scotts, McLerrans, Walkers, Watsons, Reecers, Beasons, Dulworths, and Butlers.

Beech Bethany School from the 1840's.

One of the first schools in this Community was built on the farm now owned by the Hayes Family in 1845. Abram Sallee was one of the teachers here. Classes were held in this school until the late 1800's. In 1895, a new school and Church building was erected. The land for the school and Church was obtained from Joe and Kathryn Rich. Among the early teachers were Lizzie Kyle Boles, Herman Waddle, Margaret Plumlee, Bill Dale, Lillian Stone Dale, Frank Poindexter, and Ora Crabtree. This school closed in the late 1940's or early 1950's.

When the community began construction of the Church building, the building materials were sent up from Nashville by steamboat. The Church was a weatherboarded building. People from the community made the pews. Some of the early leaders of this Church were J.H. Arms, Ben Stone (song leader), Newt Plumlee, Hy Tinsley, and Amos Tinsley Stone. Among the first preachers were Luther Moore and John H. Arms. In later years, a new church was constructed; and

Beech Bethany Church of Christ

services are still held there with many of the same families in attendance.

Farming is still the number one occupation of the residents of this community. In addition to farming, several of the people work in Celina.

BEECH SPRINGS COMMUNITY

The Beech Springs Community was located near the Overton County line. In 1916, Tom and Parmeliah Dailey and Frank and Eller Roberts deeded the land to the Board of Education for a school. The building was a weatherboarded building and was said to have been built by Thomas Gentry. This school, like so many others, was heated by a potbelly stove and students walked to school bringing their lunches. Early teachers of this school were Mae Swan Gilpatrick, Jessie Boles, Christine Hull, Larma Holt, Roy Maynord, and Lizzie Holt Langford.

The Church of God held services in this building for some years. Hubert Hammock and Quarles Smith were two of the early preachers. This building was destroyed by fire in the late 1950's.

In 1911, Lonnie McClain started operating a general store in an old building on his farm. In 1917, a new store building was constructed. Among the many items in this store were groceries, clothing, yard goods, shoes, hardware, oil cloth, wallpaper, feed, kerosene, and motor oil. Farmers brought their produce to this store for Mr. McClain to sell to other markets. This store served the community until Mr. McClain's retirement in 1958.

BRIMSTONE COMMUNITY

The first known school in the Brimstone community was located at the head of what is known as Little Creek. This school was a one-room log building. The first known teacher was Lee McGlasson. This building was later torn down because of backwater and a second building was erected around 1910.

Teachers — Noel Pitcock and George Newton Plumlee

This was a weatherboard building. Early teachers were Willette Marshall, Edna Crabtree, Frank Spears and Lassie Hinson.

In 1957 a new block building was erected on four acres of

Brimstone School — 1958 — Eulice and Irene Anderson had eight children in the group, one in each of the eight grades. First row — Oma Crawford, Dennis Jenkins, Gay Jenkins, Harold Anderson, Faye Anderson, Coell Smith, Kay Strong Second row — Peggy Asberry, David Lancaster, Thomas Anderson Third row — Wilma Crawford, Roger Dale Crowder, Winston Anderson, Thurman Crawford, Robert Strong, Illona Anderson, Pathrisa Crowder Fourth row — Joann Roberts (teacher), Ardell Anderson, Buddy Hammons, Danny Jenkins, Glynn Anderson, Edgar Lancaster, John Anderson, Richard Hammons, Willodean Crawford, Nyoka Smith, Wonnie Smith, Willodean Crowder, Francis Jenkins, Harold Carlisle (teacher).

land bought from Lester Brown for $400.00. This building was only used for 10 years, and then the school was consolidated with Moss.

In 1960, the Brimstone Church of Christ bought the second building and remodeled, adding two classrooms on the back.

There were three known postmasters at Brimstone, Montgomery Huffines, September 19, 1902; Chalmers Holder, July 22, 1904; and Wheeler M. Cherry, October 18, 1905. The post office was transferred to Moss on October 15, 1906.

The only families left living on Brimstone are Crowders, Lancasters, Moores and Smiths. *Compiled by Peggy Davis.*

BUTLER'S LANDING COMMUNITY

Daniel Boone, in his second trip to the Western Territory,

followed the old game and Indian trail to where two creeks flowed into the Cumberland River. He refers to them as the Twin or Double Creeks in his Journal. On this trip, he spent the winter on the bluff down the river below what is now Butler's Landing and the mouth of the Twin Creeks — Dry Creek and Mill Creek. Butler's Ferry was established between these two creeks before it became Butler's Landing. It was here that five Butler boys secured land. Thomas J. and Bailey C. Butler later acquired extensive acreage on both sides of the river and established the ferry. This became the main road into Kentucky, and it was the fourth post road established by an Act of Congress on March 3, 1820. The road ran from Sparta, to Cookeville, to Gainesboro, to Meigsville, and crossed the river at Butler's Ferry and on to Tompkinsville, Kentucky. The Butler brothers built a large log store and started a thriving town. The town consisted of a large distillery, a race track, a blacksmith shop, a saddle and leather shop, and some large warehouses. At one time, Wilburn Hamilton Dale had a blacksmith shop at Butler's Landing.

Butler's Ferry had its first post office in 1831, with Bailey Butler acting as postmaster. In 1838, Butler's Ferry changed to Butler's Landing, with Thomas Poteet listed as postmaster. Postmasters who came after Mr. Poteet were William Hawkins, Franklin W. Butler, John R. Hampton, Stephen S. Kirk, Stephen H. Jones (1870 — first postmaster to serve Clay County rather than Jackson), C. Terry, Vanus M. Fowler, William H. Dale, M. Masters, Vanus M. Fowler (second term), Ellis Kirkpatrick, John J. Harlan, Robert E. Cullon, and Javannah Smith. The post office was discontinued on November 30, 1910.

In 1871, Albert Kirkpatrick and A.F. Kirkpatrick made a $2,000 bond for the furnishing of all vessels needed for a public ferry. In 1872, Rickman Darwin, John Dale, W.B. Butler, J.J. Amonett, and W.N. Dale made bond to operate the ferry. Frank Brown was the last person to operate a ferry at Butler's Landing. Freight and merchandise coming up the river from Nashville were stored in warehouses, as Butler's Landing was the pickup point for stores in the Hilham and Livingston areas. The last known warehouse in this area was operated by Porter Windle and was destroyed by floodwater from the Cumberland River in the 1920's.

The first county court of Clay County was held in a storehouse at Butler's Landing belonging to Mary S. Roberts. It met there from March 1, 1871 until March 1, 1872, when it was ordered by the county commissioners to the old town of Celina, which was chosen as the county seat over Butler's Landing and Arcot (Bennett's Ferry).

In 1876, a blacksmith shop was operated by Mr. Terry, and later a blacksmith shop was operated by Lindsey West. At one time, three gristmills were in operation in and/or near Butler's Landing. The earliest known water mill was located on Mill Creek about two miles from Butler's Landing. This mill was owned and operated by John Chism Hamilton until his death in 1909. His son, John Bed Hamilton, operated it until 1914. Gasoline gristmills came into the community in the early 1900's. One such mill was operated by Frank Brown, grinding 50-75 bushels of meal a day, with grinding days on Wednesdays and Saturdays. Another gasoline mill was operated by Hub Young until his death. It was then operated by Andrew Carmack and Howard Young. A sawmill was operated by John White.

The community's first telephone service was established in the early 1900's. At this time, switchboards were located in dwelling houses. Homes that housed the switchboard at Butler's Landing were the Ell Dale home, the home of Walter and Beulah Lynn, and the home of Lindsey West. The average cost for telephone service was three dollars for six months.

In the early 1900's, a boardinghouse was run by Mrs. Roxie Lynch; and a Dr. Green practiced Dentistry on the back porch of the rooming house.

Perry Baxter and Jesse Brown in Butler's Landing — 1920's.

E.L. Young operated a general store until 1936 when it was destroyed by fire. I.W. Mitchell had a general store and pharmacy. He sold the business to Ell Dale in the 1930's, and he, in turn, sold it to Bob Ray in the 1940's. The store closed in the early 1950's. Flora Young operated a store in Butler's Landing until 1953 when her son, Howard, took it over. In 1958, it was sold to Jim Tom and Polly Weaver, who operated it for two years.

S.C. Fowler and A.F. Kirkpatrick conveyed the land for a school and church at Butler's Landing on the 16th day of December, 1894. This building was located on the edge of the Cumberland River. The school term was for three and four months each term, and the attendance was large. The Butler's Landing Church of Christ met here with an attendance between 50 and 100. In the 1920's, floodwaters from the Cumberland River washed this building away. The second school and church was built above the first site and across the road. This sight was deeded by Ben Lynch. The building was constructed in the early 1920's. Some of the teachers at Butler's

Students at Butler's Landing School — 1939 — Teacher Charlie Hampton.

Landing were Charlie Hampton, Doc Thurman, Elizabeth Dale, Olyne Gates, Anna Bell Denton, Lexie Overstreet, Olyne Boles, Nell Lynch Stone, Lois Marshall, Ellen Moore, and Clyde Atchley. This school was consolidated with Celina in the 1960's.

The Butler's Landing Church of Christ renovated the Butler's Landing School building; and services are held there each Sunday. Families who have attended and still attend Church

Butler's Landing Church of Christ

services there are: Mitchells, Loftis, Roberts, Baileys, Cooks, Smiths, Atchleys, Phillips, Dales, Marshalls, Eads, Weavers, Boles, Youngs, Browns, and Lynch. Some of the preachers have been J.B. Gaither, Lester Coats, Logan Fox, Jerry Coats, Crowder Wayne Coats, Walter Neal, and James Cramer. Some of the men who have served as treasurer of the Church have been I.W. Mitchell, Jerry Roberts, Lee Bailey, D.A. Eads, Wheeler T. Marshall, and Edgar Phillips.

CAMPGROUND UNITED METHODIST CHURCH

Campground United Methodist Church is located about one mile north of the Oak Grove Community. This white frame church building houses one of the oldest, continually active churches in this area. The name "Campground" came from the early use of this site for a "protracted" camp meeting which would last for several days with people gathering from near and far. The people came on foot, on horseback and in buggies and/or wagons to attend these meetings. A local evangelist or a circuit rider would hold these services in the shade of a brush arbor.

The present building was erected in 1885 and has been renovated and repaired to continue to serve its rural congregation. The old wood heating stoves have been replaced by gas heaters, and new roofing and storm windows help keep out the cold winter winds. However, the old poplar benches, made from planks wider than trees now grow, and the cool, high-ceilinged sanctuary still remain as mute witnesses to the foresight of the early builders. Prior to the present structure, a log building stood at the same location.

Campground — United Methodist Church

Campground is on the Red Boiling Springs Charge of the Cumberland District of the United Methodist Church. Earl Davis is the current minister. Other ministers who have served this church are Draper Murphy, Wes Robbins, Mark Forester, James Lauderdale, Sam Hughes, Arnett Creasy, Donald Draper, Sam Cherry, Lemuel Davis, Goldman Marion, and John Elisha Hale.

Surnames of families attending this Church are: Hanks, Odle, Crowe, Davis, Clements, McLerran, King, Cherry, Eakle, Hale, Watson, and Grace.

CAVE SPRINGS COMMUNITY

The Cave Springs Community is located between Celina and Pine Branch — just off the main highway to Dale Hollow Dam. Some of the families who have lived in this area are: Tinsleys, Poindexters, Longs, Holmans, Keislings, Ashlocks, Arms, Taylors, Uptons, Johnsons, Adams, Napiers, Keys, Williams, Jones, Scotts, and Wixes.

The first known school at Cave Springs was established in 1897. This land was deeded to the citizens of the neighborhood for the consideration of five dollars by George W. and Eliza Tinsley and Sadler and Sallie Holman for school purposes and religious worship to be used for free and subscription schools and to be used freely by any and all religious denominations. When classes first began in the building, students met for about three months a year. This school was consolidated with the Celina School in 1954. Some of the teachers at this school were Mai Swann, Katherine Roberts, Will Allen Donaldson, Miss Dale, and Marshall Donaldson.

The first Cave Springs Church building was thought to have been erected in 1879. Among the congregations to use this Church building were the Methodists and the Christians (Church of Christ). The morning services were conducted by the Christian Church, and the afternoon services were conducted by the Methodists. A second building was erected in 1897. This building sat next to Neely's Creek. The building remained there until 1929, when the backwater from the flooded Obey River moved the church from its foundation. Members of the community took ropes and pulled the church building back up the creek. It was probably at this time that the people decided to move the building from this low area up above the road to a slight hill. In later years, the building was moved again to make room for the widening of the Celina-Kettle Creek Road. In the 1920's, Walter Keisling, who was a leader of the Methodists, disbanded the Methodist Church. The Christian (Church of Christ) maintained the building. For the last several years, the Church of Christ has been the only congregation meeting in this building. Early leaders in the Methodist Church were N.B. Taylor and Walter Keisling. Early leaders of the Church of Christ were Jim Arms, Lum Ashlock, and Dave Knight.

CLEMENTSVILLE COMMUNITY

The Clementsville Community was first called McLeansville. It was not called Clementsville until 1857. The first settlers in this area were members of the Peter White family who came here in 1812. Mr. White gave the land for the first church and school building in this community. The second church and school building was erected around 1903. George W. Clements furnished the materials for the building.

Clementsville Water Mill

Several doctors practiced medicine at Clementsville. Some of them were John Murray, James C. Wier, R.F. Crabtree, and Andrew Jackson Clements.

The first post office was established on June 28, 1831, by Alexander Keith, and it was called McLeansville. The following people served as postmasters: Benjamin Gist, 1842; Christopher Clements, 1842-1854; Hiram Crabtree, 1854; James P. Keen, 1854-1856; William C. Brockette, 1856-1857; Henderson M. Clements, 1857-1858; Andrew Jackson Clements, 1858; Abram J. Martin, 1858-1861; V.B. Keen, 1861-1867. The post office closed in 1867 and was reestablished in 1870 by Hiram Crabtree who served as postmaster until 1884. Other postmasters were: John L. Wood, 1884; W.B. Green, 1884-1885; Burl W. Green, 1885-1888; Alexander Crabtree, 1888; James H. Nixon, 1888-1904; Bethel Harlan, 1904-1905; and Mary S. Harlan, 1905. The last postmaster was George C. Brown. The post office closed in 1907. Another post office located near Clementsville was called Tilford. It was established in 1883. The postmaster was Robert Tilford Miles, a brother of John J. Miles of Miles Cross Roads. This post office closed in 1883.

Some of the merchants in the Clementsville Community were James H. Nixon, Jessie Crawford, Tandy Head, Clar-

C.W. Clements Mill

ence Clements, Press Butler, and Kit Clements.

Laurel Bluff School was located near Clementsville. The first school was built in 1877, when a one-room building was erected. A new building made of blocks was built in 1948. This school closed in the early 1950's. The building is now used as a dwelling house.

The Campground Methodist Church and the Clementsville Church of Christ are both located on the Oak Grove and Clementsville Roads.

DRY MILL CREEK COMMUNITY

Dry Mill Creek Community is located just below Butler's Landing. In the early 1900's, there were approximately fifty families living there. Poley Brown owned and operated a gristmill in the community around 1932. A family named Puckett came to the community around 1910 and ran a sawmill. While they were there, they lived in a tent. "Aunt Add" Stafford lived in this community and is perhaps its best known resident. Her Easter dinners and Christmas dances were famous far and wide. Guests came by the hundreds to these affairs. Other families who lived in the area were: Williams, Boles, Burks, Youngs, and Penningtons.

The first school on Dry Creek was called Forks Creek School. It was a large log house. In 1908-1910, it was filled with students. Later, the name was changed to Dry Creek School. Only 40 to 50 students were enrolled in the new school. Some of the teachers were Amos Arms, Jewell Parsons, Leland Kirkpatrick, Roy Maynard, Frank Thurman, and Martha Thurman.

At the top of the hill going up Dry Mill Creek is located the large Turkeytown Cemetery and Turkeytown Community. Many of the people who had lived in Butler's Landing, Weaver Bottom, Turkey Creek, and Dry Mill Creek are buried in this Cemetery — Williams, Staffords, Roberts, Boles, and many others. A large decoration is still held each year at the Turkeytown Cemetery.

FREE HILLS COMMUNITY

The Black population of Clay County is made up completely of one family which was placed here by a white woman, a slaveholder from North Carolina, by the name of Virginia Hill. This was before the days of the War Between the States, and the Negroes were still in bondage.

Mrs. Hill liked the Clay County area so well that she purchased a tract of land, approximately 2,000 acres, from Samson William and moved all the Blacks over in this area. This tract of land was composed of hills and hollows, and at the time of purchase, it was covered with virgin timber. It was located northeast of Celina and separated from the town by the Obey and Cumberland Rivers.

The oldest Black woman who came from North Carolina with Mrs. Hill was Betsy Manny. Betsy was not a slave, but she had a son by the name of Rubin who was a slave. Rubin would labor daily as a blacksmith, making tools, and as a handyman cutting logs, clearing land and doing other jobs that needed to be done. Rubin did not live with his mother, but he was allowed to visit her very often.

At the age of 31, Rubin became infatuated with a girl named Sarah. She was a housekeeper for Betty and Bye Stone. She was just 15 years old. He married her, and they had two sons, Tom and Joshua Polk Hill. The tract of land Mrs. Hill owned was divided between Rubin and the other slaves who came over with her. Rubin was given 400 acres of land. Rubin and the other slaves were given their freedom by Mrs. Hill and were referred to as "the free Hills". It was a coincidence because of the name, Hill, and of the fact that the tract was very hilly and rough. It was always referred to as "The Free Hills". Some of the direct descendants of that family still own portions of the 400-acre tract today.

After the people received their freedom, they needed training in various fields in order to obtain jobs. Since education was a necessity for her sons and grandsons, Betsy Manny gave

the first logs for the construction of a schoolhouse. A one-room log cabin was built with the logs and was used for school, church, and other events because it was the only public place in the community. The foundation is still visible today.

The economy was geared to rafting on the Cumberland River. The greatest resource of the county was the supply of timber, which was floated to market on the waters of the Cumberland River by flatboats and rafts. Taking a big raft down the Cumberland on a high tide was no easy matter. It took great physical strength to manipulate the sweeping oars and courage to hold onto them in wind and storms. It took from five to seven days to run a raft on a good tide from Celina to Nashville. However, with Joshua Hill as the main pilot and Bailey and Verney Andrews, Uncle Cal Hamilton, High Hamp, and Porter and Hardy Page as assistant raftsmen, the task was not one to worry about. These men had worked at the job for many years. Joshua Polk Hill was a skilled worker. He took the tools that his father, Rubin Hill, and some other slaves had made and hewed the logs to build the cabins for the rafts and flatboats. Life on the raft was a world unto itself. The raft cabin was the center of social life on the trip. The men slept on straw but had plenty of quilts to pull over them. Their meals were well prepared even though they were cooked on a small rock grate above a hearth of mud and clay. Oscar Page was the cook. Mai and Madden Davis were cooks on the riverboat, Joe Horton Falls.

The first Church of Christ and school for the Free Hills area was established in 1816. The building was constructed of logs and was located on the Brady Plumlee farm. Some of the early song leaders of the church were Josh Hill, Porter Burris, Clifton Hamilton and John Hickman. The early members were Rachel Page, Susie and Harvie Langford, Bessie Hamilton, Mint Hamilton, and Eda Webb. Some of the early preachers were Brother Johnson from Cookeville, Brother T.H. Busby from Little Rock, Arkansas, Brother Major Boyd and Brother Winston, both from Nashville, Perry Smith, and G.H. Bowser.

Because the building became inadequate, a new church was

Free Hills Church of Christ

erected in 1938. This church was built from some of the logs from the old church, with the members of the community providing the labor for the construction of the building. The land for this building was donated by Joe Walker. The earliest preacher was Gilbert Johnson, with Brother D.P. Phillips next.

The African Methodist Church was established shortly after the close of the Civil War by a group of recently freed slaves and was situated in the Free Hills Community. The church was located where Mrs. Bertie Plumlee now lives. Their church building was completed and in use sometime prior to 1903. This church had a small membership from its existence. There was said to be only a few families who attended this church regularly, with the Page and Hickman families being the leaders of this church. After some time, these families moved to Nashville, thus bringing about the eventual closing of this church. Some of the early preachers of the church were Brother Tucker and Brother Clay.

The first school of the Free Hill Community was held in the old church building and continued until the late 1920's, when a new school was constructed. In 1928, Martin Bailey and his wife, Enner, and Mary Davis and her heirs sold approximately three acres of land to the Clay County Board of Education for the construction of a new school. The building was a weatherboard structure, containing two classrooms, a cafeteria, and

The Free Hills School (now the Community Center).

indoor restrooms, with grades one through eight attending. Major Boyd was instrumental in getting the hot lunch program for the thirty or more students under the supervision of Mary Alice Lewis. Students attending high school were taken daily by bus to Darwin High School in Cookeville until 1964 when Darwin burned. At that time all the Free Hills students began attending school in Celina.

Some of the teachers of the Free Hills School were Daniel Johnson, Edexine Page, Estelle Chaffin, Cordella Bohanon, Mr. Rickman, Jacob Gay, Porter Burris, Major Boyd, Mary Alice Lewis, and Geneva Andrews (Bartlett).

Some of the families residing in this community in 1986 are: Hills, Bartletts, Andrews, Hamiltons, Garretts, Philpotts, Paiges, Burrises, Williams, Baileys, and Williamsons.

Two of the better known businesses in the area are the Hilltop Cafe, owned by Clorina and George Andrews, and the catering service operated by Jean and Ann Hill. After Ann's marriage and subsequent leaving the Community, Jean has continued the business with the help of others — Jessie Lee Bartlett, et cetera. — Compiled by Brenda Kirby.

HAMILTON'S BRANCH

Hamilton's Branch was located between Celina and Butler's Landing. Some of the people who lived in this area were Arms, Hamiltons, Baileys, Hamptons, and Eads. There was a school located in this community, but it did not last for too many years before it consolidated with other schools.

The Hamilton Christian Church was organized by William Carol Hamilton in the late 1800's. Early congregations held Sunday afternoon services under a shade tree. Seats for this Sunday afternoon congregation were taken from a nearby rail fence. W.C. and Maggie Hamilton gave the land for the school and the church to revert back to the Hamiltons if the school or church abandoned the building for five consecutive years. This building was used by the Christians (Church of Christ), the Methodists, and the Baptists. Many times the congregation

would number as many as 75 to 100. During a protracted meeting, the building would not begin to hold the people, and they would sit in the windows and outside to listen to the sermons. Mr. Hamilton, who was the leader of the church, attended each time a congregation met regardless of the denomination. After services, the preacher always knew he had the invitation of Sunday dinner at the Hamilton home. This church prospered until the death of Mr. Hamilton in 1919, thus bringing about the eventual closing of the Church. Early Christian preachers were Doc Hall, Marion Harris, John Arms, Sam Spears, and Milt Burnette. Other denominational preachers were Earl Cunningham and Eli Bronstetter.

With the advent of better roads, the people aligned themselves with other communities, and Hamilton's Branch ceased to be.

HERMITAGE SPRINGS COMMUNITY

This Community was settled in the early 1800's; and the name has been changed several times. It was first called Trace Creek. Around 1885, it was known as Sugar Orchard because the valley was covered with sugar maple trees. A sugar camp was located in the valley. This camp was onced owned and operated by Carrol Purcell. The camp consisted of a shed with wood fire furnaces and large kettles. The sugar maple trees were tapped for sap which was caught in buckets and boiled down into syrup or sugar for the local residents, or it was sold to peddlers who hauled it into Nashville by covered wagons. These sugar maple trees were killed by insects which got into the sawdust from the Turner Axe Handle Factory.

The first post office in this area, Trace Creek, was established on August 30, 1833. Postmasters here were Claiborn D. Witcher, John Vinson, and Curtis Wood. The post office closed on April 3, 1860. It was reopened January 8, 1861 with James Tinsley and Lewis C. Merritt serving as postmasters. The post office was again discontinued on September 22, 1866, probably due to the Civil War; 1870 brought about the re-opening of the post office. George Waddell, William C. Purcell and Robert Pedigo served as postmasters. The post office closed again in 1875. Around 1883, Ham H. Spivey opened a general merchandise store, which also housed the reestablished post office. In 1883, the name of the post office and the community was changed from Trace Creek to Spivey. Postmasters in Spivey were George W. Purcell, 1885; John L. Wood, 1887; John H. Baker, 1897; John W. Green, 1899; and Bernetta Green, 1909. In 1912, John (Squire) Bean operated the post office in the store which he had purchased from Ham Spivey. Bernetta Tinsley took charge of the post office while it was still located in the John Bean Store. In 1919, the post office and community name was changed to Hermitage Springs. Bernetta Tinsley Christian served as postmaster until 1935. Miss Gladys York and Mrs. Dona Sims served as postmasters until the post office was again closed in June of 1936.

Hermitage Springs was a farming community; however, around 1900, efforts were made to change this to a resort area similar to nearby Red Boiling Springs. Hermitage Springs had the mineral waters as did Red Boiling Springs. Sulphur wells were put in operation in the early 1900's. Shortly thereafter, hotels began to be constructed.

The Long Hotel was a two-story building owned and operated by Tom Long. He later added an annex on the side of the hotel. This hotel was located near the present Hermitage Springs Church of Christ. Later a physician, Dr. Flippin, assumed operation of the hotel. It was a popular summer resort.

James and Floretta Biles owned and operated the Biles Hotel, which contained thirty or more rooms. This hotel was destroyed by fire. P.T. Biles owned and operated the Central Hotel which was located near the present Bert Davis residence. This was a two-story structure with twelve large rooms. This hotel also burned.

The main attraction of this resort area was the mineral waters which were recommended for various ailments. "Boarders" in these hotels would come to enjoy the peaceful atmosphere, delicious meals, and the social activities — piano playing in the parlor and group singings.

Over the years many stores were established in this community. A few of the store owners were Hamilton H. Spivey, John (Squire) Bean, J.C. Pedigo, S.S. Jackson, James H. Yeamon, John William Green, Granville Green, Bob Ross and

The Will Green Store

other merchants. Other businesses of this area were an axe handle factory owned by Captain Ford located near the Emmert Store; a blacksmith shop operated by Anderson Browning, the father of Bob Browning and Ava Green; and a blacksmith shop operated by Bertie Copas. The Spivey Manufacturing Company was active in the area in the 1920's. This company, which dealt mainly in lumber, was owned by G.G. Griffith, Lans Bilbrey, Pleas Biles, and Sylvanus Carter. Green Brothers Planing and Sawmill was also in operation for many years.

The first school in the Hermitage Springs area met in a log building situated near the present residence of Misses Vina and Gladys York. The log building, which was used for both school and church, was here as early as August 15, 1840, according to the Hermitage Springs Church book. Jim Wood was the only known teacher of the first school with classes only being held a few weeks each year. The next school was relocated a short distance from the first building, and it was also of log construction. It was called the York School. The exact date it opened is unknown, but it is believed that it opened in the mid 1850's. Some of the early teachers of the York School were Jessie Wood, Camelia Griffity, Ephriam Dalton, and M.O. Goodpasture. The York School was destroyed by fire. Jesse Woods, the teacher, began having classes in the John Woods home, which was located closer to the Hermitage Springs area. Classes were assumed to have been held in his home until a more suitable location was found. They next met in the Log Church at Trace Creek, now Hermitage Springs. This church probably was used from the 1870's until the 1880's, when a one-room frame building was constructed across from the Lynn Spivey residence. There were two teachers who taught in this one-room school at the same time due to the large enrollment. The first library was added in 1909. Some of the teachers at this first Hermitage Springs School were Jesse Woods, Hampton Maxey, Harley Long, Stella Birdwell, Thomas Bean, Jesse Copas, and Oscar Carnahan. In 1912, a two-story building was constructed and placed farther back from the road to insure a larger playground for the students. The

older one-room school was moved up to the new building to provide even more classrooms. In 1912, there were approximately 130 students attending the Hermitage Springs School.

In 1916, the first basketball court came into existence. The coach was Mrs. Emma Capshaw Wilson; and her team members were Rad Bean, Pleas Capshaw, Jim Long, Thomas Long, and Earl Biles. Mrs. Wilson also coached the girls' team consisting of: Lois Reeves, Beulah Wood, Ethel Pedigo, Rosa Mae Green, Blanche Ford and Clements Ford. In 1919, a two-year high school curriculum was added to the school. In 1926, this building was destroyed by fire.

In 1927, a new brick school was erected. Additional land was acquired for the school grounds in order for the school to be placed a greater distance from the road, thereby enabling the school to have a baseball field and playground. In January of 1928, a little over four acres were acquired from Sarah, Zula, Esther and Sam Pedigo for school property. In the same year, four acres were acquired from John (Squire) Bean. This building was a one-story structure with several classrooms and an auditorium. It was not equipped with a cafeteria. One was added in 1930 adjacent to the school. It was equipped with indoor plumbing.

A four-year high school was established in 1927 primarily due to the diligent efforts of Mattie Capshaw, a teacher at the school. Students could now finish school at Hermitage Springs rather than having to go to Celina or Red Boiling Springs or

The Hermitage Springs School destroyed by fire in 1951.

possibly dropping out of school. The first high school class to graduate had six members: Amo Osgathorpe, Verna Cherry, Guy Roberts, Will Bean, Mildred Wilson, and Ora Cherry. The

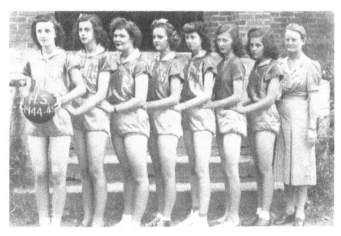

Hermitage Springs Girls Basketball Team — 1944-45: Mable Reeves Clark, Ruth Ritter, Dorothy Smith, Catherine Dyer, Lavelle Rich, Lucille Jenkins, Emma Lou Cherry and Teacher, Cassie York.

graduation exercises were held by the light of an oil lamp. Of the six graduating in 1930, four entered the teaching profession. This building was destroyed by fire in 1951. After the fire, classes were held in the gymnasium, the Hermitage Springs Church of Christ, and the Laurel Bluff School. The new building contained ten classrooms, an auditorium, and offices. In 1960, a new gymnasium, four elementary classrooms, and a cafeteria were added.

The Popular Bluff School (just outside Hermitage Springs) was established on or before 1889. Granville Turner conveyed the land for the school on the waters of Line and Trace Creeks. This school was located near the W.J. Capshaw and Pleasant Biles farms. Classes were held here until around 1906.

The Capshaw Watermill was located on Trace Creek about one-half mile north of Hermitage Springs, near the road leading to Gamaliel, Kentucky. It was built by a family named Parslay prior to the Civil War. The power was furnished by water flowing through a wooden tub wheel. Later it was run by a metal tub wheel. The Parlays sold this mill to Dave D.

Capshaw Mill Pond — Hattie Capshaw, Loma Jackson and Silva Capshaw.

Capshaw who rebuilt it around 1910 adding a bolter to make flour. Two brothers, Bob and Fuller Capshaw, bought this mill from the heirs when their parents, Mr. and Mrs. Dave D. Capshaw, died around 1935. Again, it was rebuilt adding a Simpson turbine waterwheel. The mill was washed away in a flash flood in June of 1969. This mill also ran a saw for sawing lumber. The mill served the people in the area for more than 150 years.

The first church in the Hermitage Springs Community was located near the present residence of Miss Vina York. The following was taken from the original handwritten church book that was kept by the congregation at Hermitage Springs (then called Trace Creek) which began meeting for worship on August 15, 1840. The first elders of the Church were Meredith York, Jesse Vinson, and Robert Pedigo. This log building was used for an unknown number of years. The Church was then relocated closer to Hermitage Springs by about one-fourth mile. This meeting house was also in the log building used by the York School. In 1879, the meeting place was changed to a log church building in the Hermitage Springs area near where the present church is located. The present church was renovated in the late 1960's. It was bricked, and classrooms and a baptistry were added.

Some of the businesses now located in the Hermitage Springs Community are: E.H. Biles Garage; Carlon Carnahan Beauty Shop; Darlene Comer's Beauty Shop; Kenneth Birdwell's Garage; Harold Dillehay's Garage; Melvin Grace's Laundry; Hermitage Springs Grocery, run by Dale and Dorothy

Collier; Country Grocery, owned by Melvin Grace; Tennessee Mills, owned by W.C. White; Hermitage Springs Bank; Western Auto, operated by Melvin Grace; Dairy Burger; OshKosh B' Gosh; Variety Shop, operated by Brenda Smith; Car Wash, owned by Glyn Birdwell; Hermitage Springs Feed Mill, operated by Coel Hickman; Hermitage Hill Restaurant, operated by Ollie Ethridge; and Birdwell's Electric Company, operated by Earnest Birdwell.

The first bridge built in Hermitage Springs — man on bridge is Granvil Green.

LEONARD COMMUNITY

The Leonard Community is located in the west end of Clay County, bounded on the South by Jackson County, and on the West by Macon County. The land area was at one time a part of Monroe County, Kentucky until Kentucky and Tennessee realigned their boundaries.

A large cave, known by archaeological evidence to have been inhabited by Indians, is almost in the center of the present Leonard Community. The cave (and the Community) were called Leonard because it was on the farm owned by

Sarah (Sal) Coons Leonard — Widow of Lemuel Leonard.

Lemuel Leonard, whose widow, Sally, donated the land for the community cemetery. The cave is still, for the most part, unexplored. The opening of the cave is larger than the Mammoth Cave in Kentucky. A large stream runs within the cave at all times. The "spring" in front of the cave is actually the headwaters of Trace Creek. The cave is unique in that it has a very large room at the entrance. The main passageway to the right of this large room leads to another room. A stairway from this room leads to an upstairs room. The large room at the entrance was made into a combination dance and beer hall in the late 1930's. It had a large volume of business for a year or so. The cave came to the attention of the Tennessee

Government in the early 1900's when the State Geology Department unearthed four skeletons in the large room of the cave in the early 1920's, thought to be the remains of two men, one woman, and one child. Artifacts found in the graves established that the Leonard Cave had served as a burial ground for the Indians. Two of these skeletons were placed in the State Museum in the War Memorial Building in Nashville, Tennessee.

The original mailing address of the community was Bakerton, Tennessee. The Bakerton Post Office provided no rural delivery. All the people had to transact their mail business personally, or send someone for their mail. James W. (Bill) Bean, Sr., canvassed a large area in Eastern Macon and Western Clay Counties to acquire signatures on a petition to present to the United States Post Office Department asking for Rural Free Mail Delivery. The attempt was successful and Rural Route Four was established out of Red Boiling Springs, Tennessee. Mail delivery began in 1925, with James W. Bean, Sr. serving as the first Rural Mail Carrier. The new rural route gave people not only free mail delivery, but put them in direct contact with the big mail order companies — Sears Roebuck, Montgomery Ward, Aldens, and all the seed catalog companies. Parcel post rates were cheap, and people could buy anything by mail with a delivery time of from seven to ten days. Even baby chicks were delivered by parcel post.

Common family names in the "original" Leonard Community were Leonard, Baker, Bean, Browning, Cherry, Clark, Coons, Davis, Griffith, Franklin, Kirby, McCarter, Pedigo, Purcell, Rush, and Wilson.

The Leonard Community has made many cultural, economic, and patriotic contributions to the well-being of Clay County, Tennessee and the United States. Fifteen or more of Leonard's young men served in World War I, and many more served in World War II. Others served in the Korean War and the Vietnam conflict.

Time has drastically changed the "Leonard" that once existed. The Christian Church, which started in the early 1850's, became the Church of Christ, and it is still active. The elemen-

Leonard Church of Christ — 1961

tary school was consolidated with the Hermitage Springs School. The cemetery is maintained better than most, and most native residents still expect to be buried there.

Probably the oldest home that has continuously been occupied is the ancestral home of the James W. (Bill) Bean family. Most of the older people left believe the home to be approximately 130 years old. It has been occupied by some members of the Bill Bean family since 1907. The home was completely renovated and landscaped in 1984. It is presently the home of the youngest son of James W. (Bill) Bean, Sr.

Around 1900, a gristmill was operated by Rice Browning. He kept this mill in operation for approximately 40 years. He also had a General Store near the gristmill where he sold dry goods, hardware, and food products. The store was later operated by Woodard Jackson. Mr. Jackson later built a new store and sold not only goods, but gasoline. This store was in operation for several years until Mr. Jackson's retirement.

After the death of Rice Browning, his son, Silas Browning, purchased and operated the mill. This mill not only ground corn meal but also whole wheat flour. It was also used to grind feed for the farmer's livestock. During the winter of 1914, the mill was needed to grind most of the meal for residents of Macon, Jackson, and Clay Counties, as well as neighboring Kentucky, because of the severe weather which froze the water mills and they were unable to operate.

The first school built in the Leonard Community was constructed in the 1870's or 1880's. The land was conveyed to the school by William Leonard. This was a one-room log building that was later weatherboarded. The school was for grades one through eight. The school term lasted for approximately three months each year, and it was usually dismissed when it came time to pick fodder. The first teacher of the school was Aesop Wilson. Some of the later teachers were George Hix, Pate Bean, Bish Bean, and Thomas Bean. The second Leonard School was erected around 1910. Bill Grissom was hired to construct the main building. Additional classrooms were added later. Handy Wright and Silas Browning were employed to add the additional rooms. The school also contained a library for the use of the students. Some of the teachers were Bill Bean, Sam Birdwell, Herod Birdwell, Sr., Rad Bean, Mr. Reecer, and Benton Wright.

The Leonard Church of Christ was established around 1895. The first congregation met at the log schoolhouse at Leonard. As the congregation grew, it felt a need to erect a church building. Elizabeth (Betz) Leonard said that she would donate the land for the church if they would build the church on her farm in order that she might be able to attend church regularly. The church was constructed on her farm and the same building is still being used today. Some of the members who helped establish the church were Bill Smith, Arie Davis, Navie Smith, Bill Smith, Charlie Slate, Tom Bean, John (Squire) Bean and Marg Bean.

Some of the families living in the Leonard Community in 1986 are Beans, Brownings, Coonses, Jacksons, Davis', McCarters, Pedigos, Brays, Leonards, Hixs, and Gentrys.

LIBERTY HILL COMMUNITY

Liberty Hill was located on Proctor's Creek about three miles west of Celina at the bottom of Liberty Hill near the road leading from Proctor's Creek to New Hope. There was an old Baptist Church in the Community prior to the Civil War, but the membership dwindled to three or four. Elder W.H. Smith, Missionary for the Enon Baptist Association, visited with them and gathered a number of members which were supplemented by a number from the Oak Grove Baptist Church. These were organized into a Church in 1885 by Elders W.H. Smith, T.W. Matthews, and M.B. Ramsey. The Church prospered for a while. It cannot be stated accurately just when this church ceased to exist, but it is certain it was active as late as 1902. (Willis Spears' mother, Mary Belle Savage Spear, and his grandmother, Rachel Odle Savage, were members of this church.)

It is the opinion of former residents of this community that the Liberty Hill School was erected in the 1890's. The land for the Liberty Hill School was purchased from George W. Stephens for $32.50. There were no bookshelves in this school to provide a small library for the children, so George Walker provided a place in his home for the library books and school books to be stored. Classes were held for three months each year for grades one through eight. It had an enrollment of about thirty during most of the years it was in operation. On days when the different classes had long lessons, classes began at 7 a.m. and lasted until 5 p.m. This school was destroyed by fire in the summer of 1936. Some of the early teachers were Adder Hayes, Ollie Hamilton Plumlee, Jake Jenkins, Vesha Plumlee, Dona Harpe, Belva Plumlee, Asia Plumlee, Deshie Coglen, Sam Birdwell, and Doshie Plumlee. *Compiled by Willis Spear (deceased).*

MACEDONIA

Macedonia is located adjacent to Midway, and many consider it part of the Midway Community. The first Macedonia Baptist Church was established prior to the Civil War. According to legend, church members guarded the church day and night for fear the Yankees would burn it. Around 1925, the congregation saw the need for a new building. They purchased the land from James and Mary Ann Rich for the sum of $10. Around 1970, the building was remodeled. The membership has fluctuated through the years, but it stays at around 100.

The Macedonia Cemetery is located close by the church. Many people who settled this area are buried there along with their descendants. Some of the families are Rich, Spear, Brown, Strong, Reecer, Kendall, Strode, Trobaugh, Perrin, Plumlee, Rhoton, and Cunningham.

MIDWAY COMMUNITY

One of the first churches and schools in the Midway Community was held in the late 1800's about two miles from the present site of the church. The name of the building was Mars Hill, and it was located near Charlie Rhoton's farm. From Mars Hill, the church and school was moved about half a mile to a spot on a farm owned by "Elick" Spears. At this location, the school and church were named Midway. The seats were made out of split logs with legs made by using pegs. The logs that were used in this building are still in use today in a barn on the farm of Reed Brown.

In 1906, John Rich gave land for a church and school near the present church site. A frame building was constructed by John and Hans Burks for the dual purpose of a church and school. In the late 1940's, a new school was constructed by Charlie Moore and sons on property purchased from Mose Strong, and it is still standing today. School was held at this site for about four years until students were placed in the Moss Consolidated School.

The schools in the Midway area had several teachers. The following is a partial listing: Verta Dalton, George Newton Plumlee, Raymon Spears, Euna Denton, Ethel Hogan, Ray Cherry, E.D. Cherry, John Tom Stone, Nell Stone, Edna Melton, Hance Wilkerson, Pearl Brown, Evelyn Cherry Birdwell, Bill Stone Denton, Carl Walker, Tim Reecer, and Larma Holt.

After the school was moved in the late 40's, the Church of Christ continued to meet in the old building until a new build-

Midway Church of Christ

ing, which is still in use today, was constructed in 1960.

Several stores were once located in the Midway area. The first store was said to have been operated by Rosco and Tandy Head at the present location of Clarence Reecer's house. Later Gilbert and Norman Clancey owned a general store in the same location. Other owners of this store were Elisha Rich, Tom Perrin, Mr. Todd, and Joe Burnette. Other stores were operated in the Midway area by Mose and Docie Strong, Buford and Dorie Rich, and Will Herman (Bouse) Strong. The last store in the Midway area closed in the 60's.

Around 1908, the Midway area was noted for making hoops for barrels. A shed was located near the entrance to the present farm of Reed Brown where hoops were shaved out for barrels that were used to hold merchandise, such as sugar, salt, et cetera. These hoops were shipped out to other areas by boat to barrel factories.

Another noted sight in this area was sawmills. Brian Crabtree moved a mill on the Midway Road in 1946 that employed around twelve people from the local area. The lumber from the mill was transported to other areas for use. This mill closed in 1953. Another mill was run by Will and Patton Cassetty on the Bennett's Ferry Road.

The Midway area was also noted for molasses mills. Calley Strong, Lem Rhoton, and Will Dodson all operated mills in the 30's. Sid Rich started making molasses in the early 40's and made molasses until the early 60's. In one fall during World War II, Sid made 1450 gallons of molasses.

Like other areas of the county, Midway had workers in the

WPA Workers constructing Dry Creek Hill — Midway.

late 1930's that did construction work with the Works Progress Administration. These workers constructed the Dry Creek Hill.

An event that was certainly unusual for the time was the emergency landing of a plane in the Midway area in 1946. An Illinois man, Melvin May, his wife, and niece were on their way to Florida when they ran out of gas over the Brimstone Hills, came back, and landed in a wheat field they had seen on the Sid Rich farm. He tried to take off from this spot several times in a three day span but was unable to gain enough speed on

Emergency landing — 1946.

this short area. After much timber cutting along the road going to Moss, Cordell Carter hauled the plane to a straight stretch of road close to Moss and here it became airborne again.

In 1985, the following families reside at Midway: Browns, Riches, Kendalls, Strongs, Cunninghams, Copelands, Reecers, Strodes, Rhotons, Nethertons, Renodins, Bonnors, Scotts, and Heads. Many of these residents are descendants of the early settlers. — *Compiled by Hilda Brown.*

MILES CROSS ROADS (MOUNT VERNON)

Miles Cross Roads (Mount Vernon) is located in the west end of Clay County on the headwaters of Jennings, Little Trace and Big Trace Creeks. The first settlers in this community came around the 1820's. At this time, the territory was claimed by both Kentucky and Tennessee. Kentucky was given the right to grant the land, but the territory belonged to Tennessee. These grants were called Grants South of Walker's Line, and many of them were recorded in Monroe County, Kentucky. The earliest grants that can be found for this area were granted to the following: Robert Davis, 1829; Wilson Cherry, 1829; Edward Purcell, 1830; George Miles, 1835; and Hawkins Browning, 1838. Many of their descendants live in this community today. When Miles Cross Roads was settled, it was located in Jackson County. By 1850, it was a large settlement. Some of the families listed in the 1850 Census as living in this area were Cherrys, Davises, Brownings, Miles, Woods, Yorks, Armers, Prewitts, Pedigos, and Propes. Most of them were farmers. Although there were no known slave owners in this area, it was still interrupted by the Civil War with the majority of the people supporting the Union cause. Many of them joined the Union Army. Some of the men who fought in the Union Army from this community were John Jackson Miles, William Calvin Miles, Wilson Cherry, Jr., Robert Browning, and John Alexander Murray. Issac C. Rush fought in the Union Army, however, he was not living in this Community at this time but at Monroe County, Kentucky. Two of these men lost their lives in the War. They were William Calvin Miles and Wilson Cherry, Jr., who were brothers-in-law. General Bragg marched his entire army through this community on his way to invade Kentucky.

In the 1870's, John Jackson Miles established the first store in the community. This store also served as a post office with John J. Miles being the postmaster. The post office was established May 4, 1877 and continued until July 17, 1907. The mail was brought from Boles, Kentucky by Elic Murray to Miles Cross Roads in locked saddle bags, and only the postmaster had the key to unlock them. After John J. Miles retired, Bird Monday operated this store.

Other merchants in the Community were Drew Allen and Tip Cannon, who operated a store across the road from the

Miles Store; Andy Stafford and Benton Reeves; and John Hopkins, who operated the Benton Reeves store until he returned from Illinois to this area when Mr. Reeves again assumed the operation of the store.

John (Squire) Bean acquired the Drew Allen and Tip Cannon Store from R.S. Miles who had purchased it in 1911. Squire Bean operated this store until he purchased the store located near the cemetery as it was a newer and better building. Sam Saddler and Stant Capshaw next operated this store. The store was next operated by Benton Reeves until he decided to reestablish the old Allen and Cannon Store. He remained in business at this location until 1948. Herman and Cancel Roberts purchased the store in 1948 and made extensive renovations. They operated the store until they retired in 1977. They sold their inventory and leased the building to Bobby and Sue Meadows, who operated it for several years.

William and Viola Hatcher owned and operated a store here for 25 years. Other merchants have been Girvous Birdwell, Mamie Birdwell, Clure and Nellie Birdwell, Carlos Birdwell, Herod Birdwell, Perry Copas, Andrew and Susan Davis.

In 1912, a steam gristmill, owned by John J. Miles, was operated by Hove and Press Browning. Andrew Davis also operated a gristmill in this community. Pleas Browning and Sam Rush owned well rigs and drilled water wells. Edd Copas operated a blacksmith shop for over 30 years. His son, Pleas Copas, Sr., has owned and operated a garage in this community for over 30 years.

There were several sawmills in this community. One was located on the Union Hill and Mt. Vernon Roads on the Jim Cherry farm. John J. Miles ran a sawmill located on the Dean Roberts' Farm. Another mill was set up in the Happy Hollow section of the community by a Mr. Strong. In the late 1920's, Tom McClard established a sawmill here. The mill was set up in the area where the John J. Miles mill had been located. This mill was in operation for approximately ten years. Railroad ties were sawed at this mill as well as first-class lumber. This mill employed as many as 25 people at one time.

Around 1936, Mrs. Ova (York) Reeves built a movie theater in this community. It was constructed out of rough lumber. Her uncle, William (Billy) Birdwell, built this structure. There was no electricity in this part of the country in 1936, but Ova did not let a little thing like that stop her. She had a small gasoline driven generator installed to produce the needed electricity. This building is still standing, but it has been moved across the road from the Roberts' Store.

The first known school in this Community was the Rush School. It was established in the 1880's and was located on the Hermitage Springs and Mt. Vernon Roads where Dumas Grace now lives. This school was named in honor of Isaac C. and John Rush who conveyed the land for the school. The building was constructed of logs and had only one room. This building was also used by the Christian Church, now known as the Church of Christ. The first teacher at this school was Sercie Smith. Isaac Denton was also an early teacher. The next school was located in front of the Rush School. It was called Pout Hill and was built around 1903. Elic Birdwell built this building. As legend goes, the workers were constantly disagreeing on the way the building should be constructed. A man came by one day and overheard them arguing over some aspect of the building, and he suggested that they should call the school Pout Hill because they were always disagreeing. This name stayed with the school as long as it was in existence. It closed around 1922. Another school located on the North Springs and Mt. Vernon Roads on the Sam Clark farm was called Highland. It was built around 1902. The school directors were Cyrus Rush, Sr., Add Green, and James Davis. Sam

Clark and James Davis built this school which contained only one large room. Lula Woods is thought to have been the first teacher. Other teachers have been Bill Bean, Gilbert Watson, Jim Davis, and Rad Bean. This school closed in 1922 when it was sold for a dwelling house, which burned in 1925. By 1923, the community had grown and Pout Hill and Highland Schools were not large enough to accomodate the number of students in the area. A much larger building was erected near the Miles Store, because of this being a central location. This school brought about the changing of the community name from Miles Cross Roads to Mount Vernon. The Mount Vernon School had four classrooms, a library, and a kitchen. The first teachers were Phocian York, Vina York, Mattie York, and Sam Birdwell. This school served the Community from 1923 until 1968, when it was consolidated with the Hermitage Springs School. The building was destroyed by fire in 1974.

The first known church in the community was the Christian Order Church, now known as the Mount Vernon Church of Christ. This congregation began meeting in the old Rush School building in the 1880's or 1890's. Services were held in this building until 1903, when they changed the meeting place to Pout Hill School. This congregation also met in the Con-

The Mt. Vernon Church of Christ

gress Hall building located near the Mount Vernon Cemetery which was owned by John T. Miles. In 1923, the congregation began meeting in the Mount Vernon School building. At this time, the congregation became the Mount Vernon Church of Christ. Worship services were conducted here until the 1940's. Jahue Smith (Coone) Browning donated the land to build a church building. Members of this congregation and the men of the community donated their time to build the building. The original building had only one large room. Later classrooms and a baptistry were added, and the entire structure was bricked.

The Milestown Church of Christ was organized on Sunday, April 13, 1969, with around 55 to 60 members. They met in

Milestown Church of Christ

the Mount Vernon School building until it was destroyed by fire on August 23, 1974. The next Sunday, the congregation held their services outside. The following week, they began meeting in a vacant store building that belonged to William and Viola Hatcher. The Church purchased one-half acre of land from Ocia Birdwell upon which they built a new building. They moved into this building on Sunday, June 22, 1975. They now have between 65 and 70 members. Elders at this congregation are Harris Johnson and Claude Browning. The present minister is J.T. West of Lafayette, Tennessee.

The Mount Vernon Charity Tabernacle Church was dedicated on May 30, 1976. Mrs. Elma Jenkins was instrumental in

Mount Vernon Charity Tabernacle Church — 1986

securing the land for the church and in acquiring funds to begin the initial construction. The building was built by the men of the community who donated their time. Some of the workers were Orville Hatcher, Rickey Hatcher, Phocian Wilkerson, and Eddie Trobaugh. This church was not sponsored financially by other churches but mostly through the work of Mrs. Jenkins and her sisters, Isabelle Hatcher and Bessie Davis. Raymond Denton served as the Church's first pastor.

The names of families living in this community in 1986 are Birdwell, Browning, Grace, Rush, Profitt, Copas, Roberts, Bean, Davis, Jenkins, Hatcher, Delk, Coons, Buford, Wheat, Cherry, Cross, Carlisle, Reecer, Long, Purcell, Dodson, Lee, Goolsby, Rich, Likens, Meadows, Ritter, Smith, McDonald, Gentry, Johnson, and Wilburn. — *Compiled by Dayton Birdwell*

MOSS COMMUNITY

The Moss Community was first called Lodi. In 1833, John Whitson was postmaster at Lodi. Other postmasters who served Lodi were Garrett Moore and then Richard B. Gass. A mail rider, Mr. Patterson, brought the mail from Lafayette, Tennessee to Lodi once a week. The Lodi Post Office was discontinued in 1866. It was reestablished in 1870. The postmasters were Richard Gass, Columbus T. Neely, Albert G. Plumlee, and James Goad. It was discontinued in 1871 and reopened in 1878 with Charles F. Green, Albert G. Plumley and Henry Hughes serving as postmasters. The exact dates this community was called Shattersburg are unknown. In January of 1883, the post office was named Moss. The postmasters of Moss have been as follows: Francis M. Gass, William H. Rush, Andrew J. Whitson, Melanthon Moore, Ulysses J. Moore, Phillip M. Moore, Etta Comer, Claude W. Head, Dick A. Clark, Fred Osgathorpe, and Avos B. Halsell. In the late 1800's, there were two other post offices in the vicinity of Moss — Snakepoint and Exeda. The postmasters of Snakepoint were Thomas A. Williams and James M. Bradley. This post office was moved to Moss in 1908. The postmasters at Exeda were Harrison M. Osgathorpe, Arthur Jackson, James A. Brown, and Erasmum G. Osgathorpe. This post office was discontinued in 1894 and the mail sent to Moss.

One of the first businesses located in Moss was a water mill which ground cornmeal. This mill was built before the Civil War by Jim Condra. The large wheel full of buckets was turned by water power. Later the mill house was moved to the top of the Big Creek hill and was run by a long wire cable. If this cable happened to break the only one who could tie this wire rope back together was Alex Birdwell, Sr., who was a carpenter. This mill was operated by Lisha Rich.

There were two blacksmith shops in Moss during the early 1900's. Ross Burnette ran one of the shops which was located in a building later used as the Hestand Garage. Mr. Burnette built wagon wheels, shoed horses and sharpened plow points for the farmers. Mack Burnette worked for Ross Burnette and did the shoeing of the horses. The other blacksmith shop was operated by Spergen Savage in a shop located near the old Moss School.

In 1922, D.A. Clark had a general merchandise store combined with a post office in Moss. G.D. Clancy, B.R. Grace, W.D. McAlpin, O.D. McLerran, Gene and Fred Osgathorpe, Langton Moore, Jim and Zona Rich, and Ada Rich have operated general stores in the Moss Community. Boss and Laura Stone operated a restaurant in Moss for approximately 20 years. In the 1930's, Bert Hestand established a garage in the building where Ross Burnette had had his blacksmith shop. Dave and Dorothy Hestand operated a general store in Moss.

One of the first schools to be located near Moss was called Concord Academy which was operated by McDonald Moore, a preacher and a teacher. He taught only in subscription schools. McDonald Moore's son, Luther Moore, established Excelsior Academy in the late 1800's. The following was taken from the second annual announcement of the Excelsior Academy printed in 1898. "In making our Second Annual Announcement of the Excelsior Academy, we feel it our duty to make therewith a brief report of the work accomplished: last years enrollment reached 90, with an average daily attendance of 65. Excelsior Academy is located nearly equal in distance from Celina and Tompkinsville. The people of this place are very kind and hospitable. Two of the leading churches of our country are represented here. Good board, including fuel and lights and comfortable rooms, can be obtained for the very low rate of $1.50 per week. The tuition per month is as follows: Primary Department, $1.50; Intermediate, $2.50; and Academic $3.00." Family names of students enrolled there were: Dalton, Plumlee, Scarlet, Neely, Smith, Wright, Birdwell, Grace, Dix, Gas, Moore, Spear, Odle, Fowler, Arterberry, Cherry, Savage, Richardson, Sims, Pennington, McLerran, Copeland, Davis, Bean, Terry, McGlasson, Hix, Grissom, Looper, Crabtree, Holman, Hamilton, Comer, Fitzgerald, Gettings, Sanders, Hinson, Hestand, Reneau, and Harlin.

Excelsior Academy also offered a preparatory course for teachers. The entire cost for one term was guaranteed not to exceed $8-$9. The school urged teachers to "prepare yourselves to do more efficient work, and you will receive better wages, and be of greater worth in your profession."

Shiloah was another school located near Moss. The first school to be established in Moss was located near where Bert Hestand's home now stands. Some of the teachers at this school were Oscar Carnahan, Dorie Carnahan, and Phillip Dalton. Louis Franklin Salee was another pioneer teacher in the Moss area, and so was Nathan Scott Reneau. After this school became inadequate, a new building was constructed. It was a two-story framed building. This building was destroyed by fire in 1945. The last school building to be constructed at Moss was a brick structure, which contained classrooms, a

Moss School — 1930's

cafeteria, auditorium, and gymnasium. Some of the teachers at this school were Carl Walker, Larma Holt, Horace Bean, Captola Brown, Stella Wilkerson, Mary A. Hinson, Loucille Melton, Loretta Masters, Jimmy Watson, Roy Hinson, Joy Hinson, Linda Hamilton, Tommy Denton, and Eva Nell Plumlee. This school was consolidated with Celina K-8 School in the 1970's.

One of the first churches in the Moss area was located on the Pine Hill Road. In the late 1800's, the church (Church of Christ) was moved to Moss. In 1916, land was purchased from G.D. and Marselous Osgathorpe to construct a new building. Other property was also purchased from R.V. McLerran. In 1961, additional land was donated by C.H. and Lorene Carter when a new brick structure was erected.

Some of the pioneer families in the Moss area were Southworth, White, Sallee, Henson, Moore, Hestand, McLerran, Waddell, Moss, Plumlee, Condra, Gass, Osgathorpe, Green, Pennington, Neely, Whitson, Head, Strong, Spear, Kendall, and McAlpin.

The Eminence School was located on the Boles Road, one-half mile off Highway 52. The one room structure was on land fomerly owned by Scott Reneau. The building burned in 1938, and the students were transfered to Moss. There were one or two teachers and sometimes as many as 60 students. — *Information contributed by Tippy Hinson Condra and Belva Pennington. Compiled by Joy Key.*

NEELY'S CROSS ROADS

Neely's Cross Roads is believed to have been named for Albert B. Neely who operated a corn gristmill in conjunction with a general store from 1925 to 1944. After his death in 1944, the Neely descendants moved the gristmill to Florida. The demand for meal at Neely's Cross Roads enabled another mill to be set up. In 1927, Cecil Hunter Buford ordered a complete outfit for grinding cornmeal from Sears, Roebuck or Montgomery Ward. It was first operated by William Daniel Webb and later by John Robert Key. The mill was located at Buford's General Merchandise Store at the junction of the old Hilham-Burkesville-Celina-Fox Springs Road, at the point that went over the big hill to the Obey River.

In the 1920's, the citizens decided there was a need for a public school. The land for the school was purchased from Walter and Arie Davis in July of 1928. Approximately fifty students attended this school. Some of the teachers were Suzie and Wid Maynord, Elmo Burris, and Katherine Roberts.

In this same building, the Church of Christ began meeting.

Some of the early members were Mrs. Ella Langford, Zou and Fred Rich, Johnny Burchett, Goldie Keen, Dee Gentry, Domer and Irene Killman, Jim Keen, Lewis Langford, Sam Keen, and Homer Marshall. In 1955, land was purchased from Vernon Hall Deck for a new building. Some of the families who presently attend church here are Killmans, Atchleys, Daniels, Hardens, Whites, Smiths, and Kyles.

The Indian Graves Baptist Church was also located near Neely's Cross Roads. This congregation first met on the John B. Brown farm in the early 1900's. In 1944, Thomas and Mamie Hayes sold the congregation a tract of land for $50 for a building. It was a block structure with long wooden benches. George Hayes and John B. Brown did most of the construction on this building. Some of the early preachers were Brother Woods and Brother Nevils. Some of the early members were Hamilton and Mary Daniels, J.B. Brown, Jim Polk Morris, Haskell and Ethel Brown, Ada Ledbetter and Orval Daniels. The congregation closed in 1962, and the membership was transferred to the Celina Baptist Church.

NEW HOPE COMMUNITY

The New Hope Community is located between Celina and Moss. Some of the early residents of this area were Spears, McLerrans, Walkers, Smiths, and Morris.

The first school building was thought to have been built in the 1880's on property deeded by Benajy and Amanda McLerran. This was a log building; and classes were held here until 1904 when a new building was erected. Some of the early teachers here were Garrett Smith, Delia Arms, Vesia Plumlee, Gertrude Arms, Bertha Pedigo, Ermon Henson, and Sam Birdwell.

Benajy and Amanda McLerran included in their deed for the school the provision that it would also be used as a church. It was to be used for no other purpose other than a school and a meetinghouse (church). Among the early leaders in the Church of Christ were B. Tom Morris, Elza Walker, Harlan McLerran, Calvin Smith, and Sam Spears. Some of the early preachers were John Arms, Milt Burnett, Sam Spears, and Sam Leonard.

OAK GROVE COMMUNITY

The Oak Grove Community was first called Memorial, when a post office was established there in 1930. The following people served as postmasters at Memorial: Allie Chitwood,

Oak Grove School — 1910

1930-1932; Edd Jones, 1932-1934; Leslie L. Spears, 1934-1935; Eula Copas 1935-1937; and Lex Cherry from 1937-1954. This post office closed in 1954.

The first school was established in approximately 1881. John Wright conveyed the land for a school and church to Augusta Pitcock, Shelton Craighead, and John S. Harlan, Trustees of the Oak Grove Schoolhouse. A second school was built very near to the site of the first school and was situated on approximately a one acre lot with a well on the grounds to provide water for the school. A cafeteria or kitchen was not included in this building. A kitchen was located across the road from the school, but eventually a kitchen was added to the original building. In 1923, as many as 75 students attended this school. The school was consolidated with Hermitage Springs in the late 1950's. The school building was sold and is now a dwelling house.

The Oak Grove Church of Christ first began meeting in the school building in the early 1900's. The congregation continued to meet here until 1948 when a brick building was constructed on land donated for a church by Guy and Mae White.

The Oak Grove Baptist Church was located about two miles southeast of the Centerville area near Line Creek on land that is now known as the Buford Pitcock farm. It was established on April 14, 1883 due to efforts of Elder W.H. Smith while he was acting as a missionary of the Enon Association. The presbytery that constituted this Church was composed of Elders W.H. Smith, J.L. Talmon, and Deacon George W. Glover, with six members present. So far as can be ascertained from all available sources, Brother S.A. Pitcock served as Clerk throughout the life of this church. S.A. Pitcock, E.C. Grisham, J.A. Parker and C.W. Copas were the Deacons in 1902. This church was active as late as 1902, but the exact date it was disbanded is not known.

Some of the merchants of this community have been Harrison Cherry, Weaver Hinson, Guy White, Lex and Edith Cherry, Nevil and Cena Chitwood, Billy and Shelba Stone, Robert Jackson, Billy Grace, Bobby Grace, Buford Pitcock, Virgil Browning, Whiley Thompson, Jim Billingsley, Rad Billingsley, John Billingsley, Dumas and Allie Chitwood, Herbert Clancy, Ed Jones, and Cryal Dodson.

PEA RIDGE COMMUNITY

In the early 1800's, there were approximately fifteen families living in the Pea Ridge Community. They lived in log homes with paths running from one home to another. Folklore has it that the ground in this area was so poor that it would not sprout a pea, thus producing the name Pea Ridge.

Some early family names of those living in the Pea Ridge Community include Stephens, Sherrell, Williams, Watson, Webb, Ashlock, Colson, Poindexter, Kerr, Thompson, Key, Scott, Gray, Donaldson, Johnson, Taylor, Kilmon, Rich, Davis, Bowe, and Adams.

Most of the families raised large gardens and cotton. The men farmed, raised livestock and logged. The women gardened, made clothes from homespun wool, and stored food away for the winter.

The children from these families attended school at Plainview or Ashlock. The Asklock School was located in Cumberland County, Kentucky. The school term was from three to six months. Spelling matches were held every Friday morning at the Plainview School. This was considered a social event and all the community would attend.

In the early 1900's, the population had grown considerably

Plainview School — 1950's.

due to the fact that timber became a sellable item. Sawmills moved into the community along with gristmills for grinding corn into meal. There were approximately fifteen mills in operation from 1900-1935. The families would sell their timber to a mobile mill operated by the Swann Brothers, who would then set up the mill on the family's property. Other people operating mills in the area were the Kyles and the Hulls.

In the 1920's, there were approximately six stores that supplied the community with such items as coffee, sugar, and flour. Lawrence Coffee began making soft drinks in the early 1920's and sold them to the store owners. The "cokes" were in bottles and sold for five cents. The stores also had shoes and calico for sale. In the fall, the children would gather chestnuts and sell them to the store owners to buy themselves a pair of shoes for the winter.

Radio came to Pea Ridge in 1930. Among the first to own a radio were Jimmy Colson, Orville Scott, Bob Daniels, Tee Thompson, D. Martin, Ben Sherrell and Bob Thompson. Families would gather at these homes to listen to the Grand Ole Opry and other country singers.

Among the first owners of cars were Sylvanus Watson, Lum Ashlock, Virgil Ashlock, George Webb, Radford Blythe, and Dillard Webb. In 1944, with the completion of the Dale Hollow Dam, the people of Pea Ridge had an easily accessible road to Celina which helped the growth of the community.

Descendants of the early inhabitants continue to live in this area. Family names in the Pea Ridge Community in 1986 include Watson, Stephens, Sherrell, Williams, Ashlock, Colson, Daniels, Raines, Webb, Thompson, Poindexter, Key, Gray, Groce, Kilmon, Reneau, Scott, Melton, Anderson, Emerton, Jenkins, Davis, Grogan, and Hogan.

There have been at least five schools in the Pea Ridge Community. In the late 1800's, an elementary school called Sweet Gum Plains was established near Crossroads (road to Holly Creek). Lela Sherrell Waddell attended this school when she was four, and her teacher was Mr. Wright. Another known teacher was Sidney Sherrell.

The Plainview School was located on the Bert Kerr farm in 1905. Enrollment at this time was around a hundred, with two teachers. Around 1922, the road was changed and a new location was obtained from R.C. and Myrtie Williams for the

second Plainview School building. During the 1930's, Works Progress Administration workers hand dug a basement underneath part of the building for a recreational area and later for a cafeteria. A distinguished feature of the building was a bell tower and its large bell which was rung six times a day — to signal the beginning of the day, "to take up books," morning recess, lunch, afternoon recess, and the end of the school day. (This bell is now located at Celina K-8 School) The students enjoyed many games including marbles, "stink" base, tag, "skip to my Lou," volleyball, softball, "fox and hounds," "drunkards and sheriff," and basketball. Known teachers for this school were Ethel Hogan, Dud Thompson, Jack Clark, Riley Stockton, Agnes Terry, Josephine (Hunter) Stephens, Elmer Thompson, Lena Martin, Andrew Phillips, Waymon Stone, Forrest Long, Roy Maynard, Susie Maynard, Amos Arms, Alfred Keisling, Winnie Brown, Geneva Clark, Lockie Burnette, Odell (Looper) Swan, Christine Poindexter, Katherine (Terry) Clark, Enoa (Terry) Harper, Carmon Brown, Clint Johnson, Willodean Webb, Helen Wells, Anna B. Denton, Carl Walker, John Teeples, Clyde Atchely, Larma Holt, Elmo Burris, Frankie Brown, Homer Gates, Martha Thurman, Evelyn Martin, Polly Barlow, Ruby Barlow, Cordell Masters, and Marvena Maynard.

The Holly Creek School was established around 1890 on the property of Bud Arms. This school closed in the mid-1920's. However, in the early 1930's, the school was reestablished and a second building was located near the present Holly Creek Boat Dock. The lumber was hauled from D. Martin's sawmill by Cordell Sherrell and transported by mule and wagon over the old Grogan Hill, for which Mr. Sherrell received about fifty cents a load. The building was erected by Shell Nolan. Teachers at this school were Josephine Hunter, Hettie Clark Buford, Ida Clark, Gordon Smith, Lillie Marcom, Mrs. Chester Ledbetter, Clarence Waddle, Delia Sewell, Waymon Stone, and Lena Martin.

The Ashlock School was under the control of the Cumberland County, Kentucky School District, but it is part of the Pea Ridge Community. There have been two schools located in this area. After the school closed, some of the students came to Celina and others went to Cumberland County. Some of the teachers have been Ada Spears, Mauzie Gibson, Ruby Rainey, Dora Lawrence, Nellie Glidwell, Grady Key, Lora (Arms) Goodpasture, Lee Williams, Robbie Logan, William Wells, Lyda Scott, Helen Wells, Winnie Brown, and Lovie McCoy.

The first Pleasant Grove School was located near Cedar Hill Boat Dock. The land for this combination school and church was obtained from J.P. Nevins. About 1927, the Clay County Board of Education built a new schoolhouse on the top of the Gray John Hill.

One of the oldest landmarks in Clay County, having been in

Rock Springs Church of Christ

existence for 181 years, is the Rock Springs Church of Christ. It is the oldest body of the Church of Christ to meet continuously, not only in Clay County but in the United States. This church was established in 1805 on the hills and rocks of the Pea Ridge Community. It was named Rock Springs because of the stream of water that ran over the hills behind the building into the Obey River, which is now Dale Hollow Lake. The membership has maintained a number from 150 to 300 from 1805 until 1986. There have been three buildings all located on the same grounds but not the same site as the present building. The first log building was used until around 1820. The second log building was much larger, and it was used until about 1903. In 1903, more land was purchased from Henry Raines, with Jim Arms as contractor to build the present building. This building was renovated in about 1965. A few of the earlier preachers at Rock Springs were Alexander Campbell, John (Racoon) Smith, Isaac T. Reneau, John N. Mulkey, John Arms, Dave and John Knight. Some of the Elders have been John Watson, George H. Watson, Lum Ashlock, Cleve Scott, Johnny Watson, Andrew Johnson, Jewell Terry, Frank Stephens, Guy Watson, Marvin Ashlock, and Willard Webb. Some of the Deacons have been J.T. Colson, Dan Webb, Curb Watson, Edgar Stephens, Raymond Rich, Cordell Sherrell, Harlon Sherrell, L.B. Williams, Cecil Webb, Domer Webb, and Vernon Groce. The church records have been kept by Andrew Johnson and Guy Watson, presently. Otis Webb is church treasurer. In 1975, the church employed its first full-time minister, Jerry Coats. The present minister is Edward Anderson. Rock Springs is noted for its fellowship, hospitality, and singing. A Memorial Day Service, better known as "dinner on the ground," is held the last Sunday in May of each year. This is the time when relatives return to visit with family and friends and to pay respect to family members who are deceased. The Rock Springs Cemetery is located adjacent to the building, and it has graves dating back to the 1800's.

The Ashlock Church of Christ was established in 1936 by Stanford and Sylvanus Watson. Some of the early preachers were Willie Hunter, Leslie Spears, Lum Ashlock, Robert Grider, Dave and John Knight. A new building was erected in the 1940's on land donated by Vanus and Ova Watson.

The Pleasant Grove Church of Christ was probably established about 1900. It met in the Pleasant Grove School building. C.H. and Bonnie Buford donated land for a new church to be built on top of Gray John Hill. The church disbanded in 1945 or 46 due to so many members having to leave the area because of the impoundment of Dale Hollow Lake.

Between 1870 and 1930, a telephone system was in operation which served the communities of Pea Ridge and Kettle Creek. It was in the home of Jim and Sara Short and was operated by Mr. Short's stepdaughter, Susie Moore.

In addition to sawmills and gristmills, several small grocery and general merchandise stores have served the area. Edgar Stonewall Jackson Stephens sold goods in a small room in his home in 1936. He built a building for his store in the 1940's. Jewell and Agnes Terry began a general merchandise store in the Pea Ridge area in 1934. Domer Ashlock and his wife, Minnie, rented the Terry Store in 1944. In 1946, they sold their remaining goods to Clyde Bowe. Ray Williams then operated the store for a short time before it was closed in 1948. In the 1920's, Pete Daniels built a store near the Rock Springs Church. In the 1930's, it was rented to Iva and Murlene Watson, and they operated it until it was destroyed by fire. In 1902, Ed Scott built the first store in Ashlock. He sold it to Lum Ashlock after operating it for approximately twelve years. This store was next operated by Lewis Fletcher. In the 1930's F.P. Ashlock purchased this store, which was later

purchased by Brance and Mattie Capps, and they sold goods here for 34 years. Mr. and Mrs. Claude Scott presently run the store.

Charlie Key operated a store in the 1930's and 1940's. The Crossroads Store was operated by several different merchants: Wofford Gray, Bob Thompson, Dan and Winfield Webb, and Savage Webb and his wife, Stella. Dan Webb separated his business interest from his brother, Winfred, and built a new store near the Crossroads Store which he operated for about 20 years. In the 1960's, he returned to operate the Crossroads Store. Jimmy Colson operated a store near his home close to Pilot Knob for several years. Cordell and Lucy Sherrell operated a store near their home on the Holly Creek Road for about seven years. This store had the first ice cream and the first delivery service from R.C. Cola and a bread company. Later Edward Davis, then Fowler Thompson, and

Thompson Grocery in Pea Ridge.

then Jay Thompson operated this store. Domer Davis operated a store in the Ashlock area for a number of years. Archie Poindexter later operated this store. J.B. Webb and Allie Webb went into the grocery and restaurant business. The restaurant operated for about ten years. They now sell groceries only.

Otis Webb has operated a grocery store for several years. The first store was built by Otis and his father, W.T. Webb, at the foot of the Webb hill. In 1968, Otis built a new store at the top of the hill where he has sold groceries for 18 years. In 1969, he constructed a greenhouse next to the store. Cal Burton and his wife, Norma, own and operate a grocery store on the Holly Creek Road. They also have a storage area for boats.

According to records, two post offices operated in and/or near the Pea Ridge Community. Sweet Gum Plains Post Office operated from June 2, 1873 until December 1874. The postmasters were James R. Terry and Jerry W. Stephens. Reeder Post Office (thought to be near Willis Bottom) operated from 1900 until 1907. The postmasters were James W. Reeder, John Willis, and Andy M. Davidson. — *Researched and compiled by Don and Mary Etta Sherrell.*

PINE BRANCH-KETTLE CREEK COMMUNITY

The "Pine Branch" Community gets its name from the Poindexters who helped to settle the area in the early 1800's during the religious revival that took place as people began to move into Tennessee and Kentucky. It extends beyond the

Kentucky state line to the Kettle Creek Church. In the early days, churches and schools were the link that helped to bring communities together. With no modern conveniences, telephones, et cetera, the latest news was gotten at church and school. It was not unusual on a Sunday morning to see more people outside the church building than had gone inside for the service.

When the "Big Meeting" took place (when a preacher came from someplace way off to preach), people would visit from one church service to the next. They usually had a service at around 11:30 a.m. and then go back for another service at 7:00 p.m. Most work was put on hold, except for the essentials, like feeding the animals and milking. Families would take turns feeding and putting the preacher up for the night. It was almost like a vacation for the young people. Each family would cook and share with anyone who wanted to take dinner with them after the church service. When school was in progress during the "Big Meeting", all studies would stop as parents began arriving for the services. Students would help to prepare the building and make sure everything was clean and in order. The teacher always expected the best behavior during the church service. After the church service was over, it was back to the studies until time to go home. Most people traveled in wagons or horseback, as automobiles were few. It was not unusual to see a wagon with two or three families in it on their way to church. In some places there was no road (as we know them now), and travel was done in the creek bed.

In the early 1900's, Bob Parsons owned and operated a general merchandise store near the Mary Keen Hill. When Mr. Parsons moved to Celina, he sold the store to Johnny Williams who operated the store for almost forty years until his death on February 8, 1960.

The "Box Suppers" were always a big event at the school. Girls would decorate a box with crepe paper and put delicious food inside and hope that her favorite boy would be able to bid high enough to buy it. Whoever got the box, the girl had to eat with them. School during this time was a family affair. Parents planned and worked during the Box Suppers and Cakewalks. There were no school buses, and children walked three and four miles to school carrying their lunch in a "lard bucket", usually consisting of biscuits, fried pies, et cetera. Teachers at Pine Branch were W.L. Brown, Jim Reneau, Della Reneau, Maude Fitzgerald, Frank Thurman, Isaish Fitzgerald, Gladys Windle, Alice (Arms) Overstreet, Helen (Arms) Overstreet, Edith (Arms) Bilbrey, Laura Lee (Arms) Mayo, Una Denton, Pearl Brown, Sammie Parsons, Katherine Roberts, Olyne Gates, Josephine Hunter, Lavell Buford, and Clyde Atchley

Families who lived in this community from about 1840 through 1948 were: Edens, Parsons, Holmans, Roberts, Cooks, Scotts, Arms, Tinsleys, Perdues, Poindexters, Roachs, Browns, Stones, Hulls (Cordell Hull's brother), Waddells, Nevins, Williams, Conners, Dunhams, Richs, Halls, Ashlocks, Hills, Overstreets, Murleys, Butlers, Davis, Shootmans, Shields, Kings, Spears, Keys, Coffees, Wells, Logans, Dowells, Crawfords, Kerrs, Shorts, Coes, Kilmons, Pruitts, Hamiltons, Blythes, Watsons, Grays, Grogans, Stephens, Webbs.

Church services are still held at Pine Branch and Kettle Creek churches. It is still a farming community, but most people who live here today also work at public work.

Most of the people who live here today had ancestors who lived and farmed in this community. Some of them moved away for awhile but something about this part of the country brought them back. The Pine Branch-Kettle Creek Community holds many good memories for those of us who were fortunate enough to be able to return here to raise our families. *Compiled by Joyce Scott Witham*

PINE HILL

The first school in the Pine Hill Community was called the Chestnut Mound School located near where Dean Short now lives. The land was conveyed by William A. Right and his wife, Alvira, for $10.00 for one acre. This was in the 1880's. The building was of logs with split log seats. School was held for approximately three months each year with about thirty students attending. Sarah Denton and John A. McLerran were early teachers.

In 1907, a new building was erected. The location was changed and the name of the school was changed to Pine Hill, because the new building was situated on a hill that was covered with pine trees. The land for the school was obtained from M.W. Denton and conveyed to Fay Head, John Kendall, and G.W. Lee, trustees of the Pine Hill School property, for $15.00. This tract contained about one and a half acres and was to have free access to and from a spring located seventy-five yards from the tract of land. This was a weatherboard building. Mr. Abraham Salee, Hance Wilkerson, Alvirta Copas and Lona Capshaw were some of the teachers.

At the time this picture was taken, George C. Scott lived on the last farm in Tennessee. His farm joined the Kentucky State line. This is Mr. Scott, his son Jack and his team of horses that were so familiar in the community at this time. The horses names were Dan and Frankie. This picture was taken around 1943. Mr. Scott used this mowing maching to mow the county road from Pine Branch to Cave Springs Road. He also mowed the church and school grounds.

E.H. Wilkerson at Esco Moore's.

In 1946, a new Pine Hill School building was erected near where the old building was located. It was built of blocks. The land for this building was obtained from the Miles W. Denton heirs and was bought for $25.00. Classes were held here until the school was consolidated with Moss and Celina. Some of the teachers of this third school were Hance and Stella Wilkerson, Dorothy Hestand, Helen Turner, Frank Wilson, Bell Wilmouth, Bernell Head Smith, John Teeples, and Loucille Melton.

The only church in Pine Hill is the Church of Christ. It first met in the school buildings already described. Denton Moore,

Pine Hill Church of Christ

who was one of the leaders of the church when it was located in the log building, Tilda Francis Kendall, and many others were instrumental in helping to establish the church. In 1949, the Pine Hill Church building was erected. It was built by people in the community donating standing trees. A sawmill was brought in and the trees were cut and sawed into lumber. The dedication of the church was held November 1950 by Mr. Harold Sain. Leslie Spears was one of the first preachers.

Early preachers of the church were Phelix Rose at the Chestnut Mound building, Mac Moore, Marion Harris, John Pendergrass, and later Willie Hunter.

Some of the family names prominent in Pine Hill are Denton, Collins, Kendall, Moore, Brown, Wilkerson, Head, Copas, Moss, and Smith. *Researched by: Peggy Davis.*

PLEASANT RUN

The minutes of the Pleasant Run Baptist Church disclose that it was constituted and established the 15th day of July, 1815 on McFarland Creek by Elders James Fears and John B. Longden. It is difficult to say exactly where Pleasant Run was located. It was either just inside the Tennessee state line or just across in Kentucky, or it could have straddled the line. The old church cemetery, though overgrown and ill kept because of years of nonuse, is still very identifiable and shows signs of perhaps a hundred graves. Brother John Savage was granted a license to preach by this church in 1838, and the following month, August, a license to preach was issued to Brother Jesse Savage. They were ordained in May of 1839 with Brethren Elijah Keeling and Isaac Denton attending as a presbytery. The final entry into the minutes of this church read: "Church met and after worship proceeded to business; 1st, the church doors were opened for the reception of members; 2ndly, the church with the committee appointed by the Association to attend this church to consult and give council is of the opinion that this church will dissolve and letter out and join other churches. These minutes were recorded on the second Saturday in October of 1844. *Compiled by Willis Spears (deceased).*

SHANKY BRANCH

Shanky Branch is located just outside Celina on the road to Livingston. Families who have lived in this area are Masters, Brown, Collins, Webb, Boles, Johnson, Cunningham, Bailey, Teeples, and White.

Shanky Branch has a grocery store, a beer tavern, and at one time it had a garage.

The Shanky Branch Church of God is a large congregation that meets regularly. This congregation was established in 1939. The contributors for purchasing the building for the Church were Sam and Clarence Cunningham, Fowler Dulworth, and Ress and Allen White. The first pastor was James T. Hooten. In 1943, a larger building was erected on land conveyed by J.R. and Linnie May Carmack for the consideration of $1. Mrs. Allen (Rosa) White, a pioneer member, taught class, led singing, was church secretary and treasurer, Sunday School Superintendent, and janitor for many years. In 1948, the church purchased its first piano. The land for the next church building was purchased from Paul and Versa White. The first pastor to serve in this building was Lloyd Kidger and his wife, Mae. Others who have served the church are Fred Hawkins and his wife, Sonja; Bradie Reed and his wife, Selma; and Leslie Wright and his wife, Mae. Some of the trustees of the church have been Will Hull, Jesse Copeland, Clyde Cunningham, Rosa Rich, and Max Hoese.

TINSLEY'S BOTTOM

In the early 1800's, there was a fine citizenship in Tinsley's Bottom. They were all in prosperous circumstances — owned good homes, had slaves, and much fine stock. They had fine orchards, rows of bee stands in their yards, and fowls of different sorts. They raised fine gardens and fine crops of corn and wheat. They had a Christian Church and all attended church on Sunday; but the war came, freed the slaves, and took their stock and most everything except the land and the children.

Tinsley's Bottom School — the first known school to have been in Tinsley's Bottom was the Philomath Academy. It was established in the early 1800's by John Tinsley and wife, Alice Mulkey, the daughter of Reverend Phillip Mulkey. Thaddeus Tinsley became president of this school, and the academy

The Tinsley home

prospered and became widely known for some of its famous pupils, including the McMillan brothers. At this time, the school was only a three months school. For these three months, a teacher would come in and have subscription school. Ida Hamilton taught here in 1902. The school burned in 1903. A one-room school was built. Two of the early teachers were Edgar Fowler and Pauline Gray. This building was destroyed by fire, and another building was erected. There were about thirty to forty students in attendance at this time. Not long after this building was completed, it was also destroyed by fire. The fourth building was built around 1929. Approximately fifty students attended this school.

Philomath was located on the Gearhart farm, an early settler in the Tinsley's Bottom area. This property is now owned by the descendants of Asa Lynn, also one of the early settlers in the Tinsley's Bottom area. It has been told that Reverend Phillip Mulkey, Alice Mulkey Tinsley's father, would come from Kentucky and hold meetings in this building.

Tinsley's Bottom Church of Christ, earlier known as the Christian Church, came into existance through the financial assistance of two men, Edgar Williams and Hamp Lynn. Each of these men gave $500.00 for the erection of the church in the year 1916. The renters from Tinsley's Bottom furnished the labor, building the church on the land of Edgar Williams.

The building was a weatherboard building with a bell tower on top. The congregation bought a bell, which was shipped by riverboat from Pennsylvania. The building was one of the few in this section to have factory made benches, a gift from a church in Nashville. A congregation in Kentucky gave the church stained glass windows. The church also had an organ which became the center of controversy, due to the teachings of Marion Harris. Half of the congregation began meeting in the school, but the congregations were soon reunited when the organ was removed from the church. At this time the church became known as the Tinsley's Bottom Church of Christ. This church had a large congregation during the early years but declined in attendance with the moving out of the renters in the late 1940's. Services are no longer held at this church.

Tinsley's Bottom Post Office — The following people served as postmasters for the Tinsley's Bottom Post Office: Perry Terry (January 27, 1910); Sib Rich (October 4, 1911); Maggie S. Kirkpatrick (September 22, 1913); Labron Mabry (October 11, 1916); James R. Meadows (January 12, 1918); Vester Cook (December 27, 1918); Edgar Williams (July 11, 1919); and Georgia Mai Lynn (January 13, 1922). Mail service was discontinued at the Tinsley's Bottom Post Office on January 14, 1925; effective January 31, 1925 mail was sent from Gainesboro. *Compiled by Brenda Kirby.*

TURKEY CREEK

In the early 1800's, Turkey Creek could have been considered a surburb of Butler's Landing and Tinsley's Bottom. Although the Cumberland River separated Turkey Creek from the other two communities, contact between these communities flourished because the river was the main artery of transportation in the area. Bailey Butler and his brothers were among the first settlers in Butler's Landing, yet the Bailey Butler Cemetery is located on Turkey Creek. Early records indicate that Dr. David B. Plumlee and Dr. William F. Plumlee were residents of Butler's Landing, but they are also buried on Turkey Creek. Relatives of the Tinsleys and Mulkeys of Tinsley's Bottom lived on Turkey Creek. Other families living on Turkey Creek in the 1800's were Pyrons, Condras, Ander-

sons, Loftises, Armstrongs, Dales, Browns, Kirks, and Harpes.

It is estimated that at least seventy-five slaves lived in this area just prior to the Civil War. Farming was the number one industry in this area. The people of this area were very interested in education and the Christian religion as preached by the Mulkeys; therefore, they built a log building which served as both school and Church. As many as forty to fifty children attended this school. Some of the teachers on Turkey Creek were Mary Plumlee, Hettie Windle, Willie Colson, Bransford Kerr, Charlie Davis, Docia Masters, Ben Brown, Bob Abney, Ray Dale, Hallie Ruth Fiske, Will Allen Donaldson, Pearl Brown, Cordell Masters, Clyde Atchley, Guy Rob-

Turkey Creek school — 1943-44 — Teacher — Pearl Brown

erts and Katherine Waddell. This school was destroyed by fire in 1952. The names of some of the last families to send children to school on Turkey Creek were Williams, Eads, Jones, Strong, Phillips, Roberts, and Long.

After the demise of river transportation, many families left this area; and in the 1980's fewer than eight families live here.

UNION HILL COMMUNITY

The Union Hill Community was first called Cherry Hill. The Lemuel Cherry Family was the first known settler in this area, and he is listed on the Jackson County, Tennessee tax list in the early 1800's. Other early settlers were Dentons, Crosses, Asberrys, Crawfords, Johnsons, Prices, Riches, Shorts, Smiths, Condras, Hestands, Newmans, Jones, Likens, Vaughns, and Butlers.

Virgil Cherry Store in 1946.

When a post office was established by Thomas J. Gregory in 1895, the name of the community was changed to Gregoryville. Other men to serve as postmasters were James Short, John B. Denton, Cary Press Butler, and Richard A. Clark. The post office was closed April 9, 1906. After the post office closed, the community was called Union Hill.

The following people have owned or operated stores in this community: Thomas J. Gregory, John B. Denton, Cary Press Butler, Ensley Hestand, Bransford Hestand, Willis Hinson, Virgil Cherry, Dona Smith, Jack and Laura Smith, Douglas and Brenda Browning, and Eulas Cross.

Sid Jackson operated an ax handle factory. George Newman and Parkes and Russell operated sawmills in the community. Clarence Franklin had a sawmill as well as a gristmill.

Clarence Franklin Sawmill

Ensley Hestand and his son, Bransford, had a sawmill. Wilson Coffelt was a blacksmith, as was Pony Asberry.

Several cemeteries are located in this community: Union Hill, Cherry-Denton, Pricetown, Jonestown, Hinson, Vaughn, Cherry-Price, Joe Cherry, Newton Cherry, Painter, Newman, and Henry Asberry.

Two doctors have practiced medicine in the community, Dr. Miller and Dr. Stuart F. Grace.

The first Union Hill School was probably established as

Union Hill Girls Basketball — 1926 — Novella Green, Neta Beeford, Zora Asberry, Lucil Cherry, America Murray, Lou Ann Cherry and Gracie Smith.

early as 1878. The second school was located near the present Community Center. This building was erected in 1927 and was a frame structure with three classrooms. In 1948, a third schoolhouse was constructed of blocks and contained three classrooms, an auditorium, and a kitchen. This building served the community until 1970, when this school was consolidated with Hermitage Springs School. The cafeteria is all

that is left of this school; and it is now a Community Center.

Another school located in this community was the Fairview School, which was on the property of Dr. Stuart F. Grace near the present Harold Carlisle farm. This log building was constructed in the early 1880's. There were usually thirty or more students in attendance each year for a term of three months. Ruby Grissom was the first teacher at this school. The school was closed in either 1912 or 1915; and it was sold for a dwelling house.

The Union Hill Church of Christ was the first church in this community. It is believed to have been established in the early 1900's. Services were conducted in the school building until 1943, when the first church building was constructed. The men of the community donated their time to build this church. The materials were donated by George B. Hinson, Bransford Hestand, and Lemuel Smith. Clarence Franklin sawed the lumber for the building, with Henry Swann making the flooring. The original building included only one main room for worship. In 1960, classrooms and a baptistry were added. In 1969, the structure was renovated with two more classrooms being added, and the entire structure was bricked on the outside.

There is another church in this community, the Wesleyan Church, located on McCormick Ridge.

Raymond Spear — 1923 — one of the first cars in Clay County

Do I have to wear my hat?

FAMILIES OF CLAY COUNTY

Pedigo Family

W.L. Brown Family — 1905

COLONEL JOHN B. ANDERSON

Colonel John B. Anderson was born March 1, 1832 – died April 28, 1890. He was the son of Lawrence Manning Anderson, born 1788 – died 1848, and Edna Cason, the daughter of Edward M. Cason who was a Revolutionary War Pensioner. Lawrence Manning was a Justice of the Peace in Jackson County. He owned and operated a Saddle Shop. His second wife was Mary Polly Butler.

Colonel John B. Anderson married Mariam Butler, the daughter of Colonel Bailey Butler and "Polly" Mary Stafford Butler. Colonel Anderson was a dashing young Calvary Officer who was attached to Forrest Calvary – the 28th Tennessee, Army of the Confederacy. He was in the invasion into Ohio, the Battle of Nashville, the battle at Vicksburg and the campaign in Mississippi. He was paroled from the Civil War in Columbus, Mississippi. He, with a trusty negro ex-slave, walked from Columbus, Mississippi back to Butler's Landing, where, with his family, he built a steamboat and started back in steamboating. In 1878, he purchased the steamboat, "Arch P. Green," from Arch P. Green of Celina.

Captain John Anderson w/three daughters: Lou M., Marjorie and Ada Belle

Colonel Anderson was a farmer, a riverboat pilot, and a lawyer. He and Mariam had nine children as follows:

Lafayette Shields, born February 4, 1855 – died July 29, 1897, was a pharmacist and a farmer. He married Mary D. Lowe.

Martha Susan Anderson was born March 10, 1858 and died in 1941. She married James Bedford Cunningham, one of the first settlers in Celina, Texas.

Ada Belle Anderson, born December 15, 1850 – died July 8, 1948, married William "Bill" Kirkpatrick Tinsley. They owned and operated a farm in Tinsley's Bottom.

Majorie Anderson was born June 27, 1852 and died September 10, 1858. George Anderson was born and died February 4, 1854.

Lou M. Anderson, born July 24, 1866 – died July 24, 1890, married Jim Loftis.

Dr. Landon B. Anderson was born June 24, 1869. He died December 16, 1893. He was a Mason.

Nannie Butler Anderson, born April 4, 1872 – died December 30, 1955, married Byrd Lee Quarles, Sr.

Luke Bayles Anderson, born August 14, 1874 – died April 1, 1938, married Cora Lee James. He was a planter, a pharmacist, and a Master Mason.

LUKE BAYLESS ANDERSON

Luke Bayless Anderson, born August 14, 1874, in Meagesville, Tennessee, married Cora Lee James of Forrest City, Arkansas on April 22, 1900. The wedding took place in Gainesboro, Tennessee. Luke's father was Captain John Bayless Anderson, born March 1, 1832 – died April 28, 1890. His grandfather was Lawrence Manning Anderson. His mother was Martha Miriam Butler, born October 1, 1832 – died February 6, 1876, the daughter of Colonel Bailey Butler.

Luke Bayless was a druggist, a Master Mason, and a planter. Cora Lee was a painter, a Methodist, a member of the Eastern Star, and a member of the United Daughters of the Confederacy. She was born January 18, 1880 and died August 28, 1966. She was the daughter of Lafayette "Lum" Pleasant James and Martha Thompson James.

Luke and Cora purchased the Dalton farms in Clay County in 1932, which were located on Knob Creek and the Cumberland River. They had five children. Landon Butler Anderson, born December 28, 1901, married Dora W. Dale on April 10, 1937. They have one son, Dr. Landon B. Anderson, who received his M.D. from Vanderbilt University Medical School. He married Connie Heflin who received her B.S. Degree from David Lipscomb and her M.S. Degree from Middle Tennessee State University. They have three children: Landon B. Anderson, IV, Tinsley Anderson, and Luke Bayless Anderson. Landon Anderson is a retired Supervisor of the Celina Water System and Clay County Historian. He and Dora Willette live in Celina.

James Ben (Bayless) Anderson was born August 13, 1904 in Gainesboro, Tennessee. He graduated from Aberdeen High School in Mississippi and attended the University of Mississippi. He married Katherine Lashley of West Point, Mississippi on January 19, 1945. They had one daughter, Catherine Lee Anderson. She attended Middle Tennessee State University. On April 15, 1971, she married Steven Joseph Hilton. They were divorced on August 15, 1976. On August 16, 1980, she married Ralph Staffins, Jr. of Atlanta, Georgia. They have one son, Ralph Calvin Staffins, III. James "Pup" Anderson was an outstanding athlete. He was a member of Company G, 155 Infantry, Mississippi National Guard, and served in World War II. He died December 24,

1969 and is buried in the Draper Cemetery near Gainesboro, Tennessee.

Luke Shields Anderson was born March 23, 1906 in Gainesboro, Tennessee. He attended Hamilton High School in Hamilton, Mississippi. He never married. He was a farmer. He was killed in action in the Battle of Bastogne, Belgium on December 20, 1944. He was a member of Company B, 327th Glider Infantry. He is buried in the Draper Cemetery near Gainesboro, Tennessee.

Donald McGuffee Anderson was born January 30, 1911 at Gainesboro, Tennessee. He graduated from Hamilton High School, Hamilton, Mississippi and attended Middle Tennessee State University. He was a conservationist and worked with the Soil Conservation Service of the U.S. Department of Agriculture. He married Evelyn Fite on April 23, 1944, who was a graduate of Tennessee College. Donald served in the CBI Theater of World War II attaining the rank of Captain, Quarter Masters Corps. He was a member of Company G, 155th Infantry and the Mississippi National Guard. He had no children. He died April 23, 1968.

Martha Miriam Anderson was born May 16, 1913 in Gainesboro, Tennessee. She graduated from Hamilton High School in 1931. She was an outstanding 4-H Clubber, won National Dress Contest, attended Mississippi State College for Women in 1932 and graduated from Middle Tennessee State University in 1935 with a B.S. Degree in Education. She received her Masters Degree from Peabody College in Nashville. She taught in the public schools of Rutherford County, Davidson County, and Metro Nashville. She served as principal of a secondary school in Nashville. She married Sam Clemons Upchurch in November of 1936. She had one son, Dr. Sam Bylis Upchurch, geologist, B.S. Degree from Vanderbilt, M.S. and Ph.D. from Northwestern. He was a First Lieutenant with the Corps of Engineers and worked with the Department of Geology at the University of Southern Florida in Tampa, Florida. He married Mary Ann Comer, B.S. and M.S. Degrees in Library Science from Vanderbilt University. They have two children: Samantha and Sam Joseph Upchurch.

Maurice Manning Anderson, Colonel, U.S. Air Force, Retired, was born May 16, 1913 in Gainesboro, Tennessee. He is a Master Mason, a

The Anderson Family — 1986

Shriner, and a member of the Scottish Rite, and the Kiwanis Club. He married Ethleen Wilson, the daughter of R.H. and Emma Capshaw Wilson, of Red Boiling Springs, Tennessee. Ethleen graduated from Middle Tennessee State University. She taught school in Clay, Hickman, and Maury Counties of Tennessee. They were married November 10, 1937 at Albany, Kentucky. Maurice graduated from Hamilton High School in Hamilton, Mississippi. He graduated from Middle Tennessee State University in 1936 and did postgraduate work at the University of Georgia and the University of Tennessee. He was a teacher and served as principal of Hermitage Springs High School and Willow Grove High School in Clay County from 1936-1942. He served in World War II from August 1942 until December 1948. He retired from the United States Department of Agriculture on June 30, 1973. Maurice and Ethleen Anderson had three children. Dr. Maurice M. Anderson, Jr. was born September 15, 1945. He married Evalia Jean Rogers, born June 9, 1947. They have two children: Maurice M. Anderson, III, "Trey", born November 26, 1968, and Elizabeth Rae, born May 12, 1971. Dr. Anderson is a nuclear engineer. Haywood Shields Anderson was born August 3, 1947 in Oak Ridge, Tennessee. He graduated from Columbia Military Academy in 1965 and received a Bachelor of Science Degree from the University of Tennessee and an Master of Science in Business Administration in 1971 from the University of South Carolina. He is married to Harriett Ivey. They married February 26, 1971, and they have two children: Heath Shawn, born March 26, 1976, and Hal Stephen, born February 25, 1980. Haywood was Chief Design Engineer with Georgia Power Company and Nuclear Consultant with Impell Company. Donald Bayless Anderson was born December 1, 1955. He graduated from Columbia Military Academy and the School of Business Administration at the University of Tennessee.

JAMES RUSSELL ANDREWS

James Russell Andrews was the son of Bailey and Nannie Mae Andrews of the Free Hills Community of Clay County. He was one of ten children in this family.

James married Minnie Brown Plumlee, the daughter of Walter and Bertie Plumlee. There were seven children in this family. Minnie was born and raised in the Free Hills Community.

James was a farmer for several years. He worked on the construction of Dale Hollow Dam. He worked for several construction companies. He worked on the construction of a new wing on the Monroe County Hospital in Tompkinsville, Kentucky. Minnie worked for several families in their homes and worked at the Breyer Strawberry Plant in Celina.

James and Minnie had five children, one son and four daughters, among whom were Russell, Dorothy, Mary Ann and Jo Ann (twins).

James was injured while working in Tompkinsville when he tried to catch a falling window. He never fully recovered. He died several years ago and is buried in the Free Hills Cemetery.

WILLIE M. ARMER

Willie M. Armer, born October 6, 1882 in Clay County, Tennessee, was the son of Samuel Thomas Armer, born in March of 1856 and died July 21, 1907. Samuel had four children: Willie, Benton, Vada, and Amanda. Willie married Flora G. Denton on June 7, 1914. Flora was born on November 3, 1895. Willie was a farmer and sawyer, and Flora was a housewife. They had ten children: Essie, Mertie, Lassie, Ruby, Sam Thomas, Elise, Wealtha, Lovie Pauline, Jewel Marie, and Delbert. Willie died May 4, 1962. Flora resides near Moss.

Samuel Thomas Armer, born 1856 — died 1907

Essie Armer, born November 28, 1914, married Norman Smith on July 27, 1940. Norman was born September 8, 1916. They had two children: Jerlene, born May 5, 1941, married David Lynn, born October 12, 1951, August 9, 1972; and they have one son, David, born December 25, 1982. Troy Smith, born August 17, 1956, married Betty Sue Connun, born May 15, 1960, on February 28, 1977; and they have one child, Lania Sue, born February 19, 1977.

Mertie Armer, born April 15, 1917, married Earnest Smith, born October 12, 1911, on July 18, 1934. They have four children, Richard, born July 4, 1935, died December 24, 1955; Willis, born March 22, 1937; Weldon, born February 27, 1939, married Nina Trobaugh, born July 12, 1939, on December 21, 1957; and Frances, born September 11, 1941, married Daniel Dumas Crawford, born May 4, 1940, on May 20, 1957. They were divorced in 1963. They had one child Rickey Gene, born February 6, 1958. He married Gale Denise Shockly, born October 25, 1957, on August 1, 1981. They have one child, McKeshia Leat, born April 21, 1983.

Lassie Armer, born February 6, 1919, married Charlie Short, born December 8, 1912, on April 17, 1938. He passed away August 13, 1967. They had five children. Charlie Junior Short, born February 17, 1939, died July 10, 1981. Anna Lee, born December 31, 1940, married R.V. Cherry, born September 18, 1937, on April

Willie M. Armer and Family

16, 1960. They have two children: Tammy Evon, born October 26, 1965 and Melinda Gayle, born May 10, 1970. Nina Dean Short, born July 17, 1942, married J.C. Price, born October 2, 1941, on December 26, 1959. They have two children. Sheena Ann, born May 17, 1963, married Robbie Pero, born March 3, 1962, on June 18, 1983. They have one child, Robert Paul, Jr., born June 11, 1986. Tina Price was born September 12, 1966. J.C. Short, born September 28, 1947, married Patricia Ann Tice, born July 1, 1956, on October 12, 1985. Rita Joan Short, born May 13, 1950, married James Kenneth Adcock, born August 3, 1942, on November 29, 1975. They have two children. Curtis Allon Adcock was born July 9, 1970. (Father was Willie Alton Davis, born April 8, 1949.) Gidget Nicole Adcock was born March 23, 1980.

Sam Thomas Armer, born June 13, 1923, passed away on June 17, 1925.

Delbert Armer was born May 27, 1936. He and Zora Armer were divorced in 1970.

RUBY ARMER ODLE

Ruby Armer Odle was born February 14, 1921. She married James Odle on May 13, 1942. James was born on May 7, 1925. He passed away on February 17, 1980. They had three children. Sue was born May 22, 1943. She married Willie Tallent on December 5, 1959. Willie was born June 11, 1935. They had two children. Tammy was born October 12, 1960; and she married Tom Armstrong on February 1, 1986. Tom was born March 31, 1959. Terri was born April 25, 1962. She married Kenneth Kerkes on November 30, 1985. He was born December 3, 1960. Jimmy Odle was born on December 4, 1946. He married Cindy Pryor on November 12, 1965. She was born May 13, 1947. They had three children. Melissa Gayle, born July 14, 1966, married Mark Barton July 19, 1984. They had one child, Ashton Odle, born February 28, 1983. Dale Odle was born June 23, 1968; and James Ray Odle was born September 1, 1970. Tammy Odle was born July 8, 1949. Bonnie Odle was born January 8, 1948.

Lovie and Ruby Armer Odle

ELISE ARMER MOORE

Elise Armer was born November 4, 1925. She married L.D. Moore, born July 14, 1919. He passed away September 29, 1979. They were married April 28, 1945. They had six children.

Lacy Thomas was born April 27, 1948. He married Debbie Schell on December 24, 1970. They have three children: Lisa Ann, born August 22, 1975; Seth Thomas, born September 15, 1978; and Crystal Lynn, born December 16, 1982.

Debra Elise Moore married Jackie Dyer on May 26, 1967. They have two children: Thomas Wayne, born July 15, 1968, and Sidney Mitchell, born June 12, 1969.

Patricia Anna Moore was born November 26, 1950. She married Gary Wix on December 20, 1967. They have two children: Gary Michael, born January 23, 1971, and Cynthia Casay, born July 21, 1975.

Mary Ellen Moore was born December 25, 1958. She married Michael David Woods on June 27, 1975. They have one child, Dan Dusty, born November 11, 1985.

WEALTHA O. ARMER STRONG

Wealtha Olyne Armer was born on October 16, 1927. She married Carlos Caye Strong, born August 20, 1922, on August 8, 1947. She has nine children.

Faye was born February 15, 1947. She married Thomas Ray Watson on January 1, 1967. Thomas was born in 1944. They attended school in Clay County, both graduating from Celina High School. They are now teachers with the Clay County School System. They are both also coaches. Faye coaches girls' softball at Celina High School; and Thomas coaches boys' basketball at Celina High School.

Gaye Strong was born September 8, 1948. Randy was born May 8, 1950. He married Susy Beaty, born January 14, 1951, on December 9, 1970; and they have one child, Candy, born March 20, 1970.

Landy Strong was born March 22, 1952. Sherry Strong was born October 5, 1951. She married Michael Barlow on May 5, 1972. They have two children: Cristy Michell, born April 14, 1976, and Matthew Kyle, born September 4, 1981.

Gary Strong, born January 9, 1957, married Cynthia Brewington on September 3, 1984. Cynthia was born on June 11, 1964. Gary was a teacher with the Clay County School System. He now coaches in Cookeville, Tennessee.

Mark was born March 10, 1961. He married Mickie Michelle Johnson on November 3, 1983. They have one child, Amber, born December 19, 1985.

Michael Trent Strong was born September 23, 1963. Tracy Lee Strong was born in May of 1967. He was an outstanding basketball player at Celina High School and has been awarded a full scholarship to Cumberland College in Lebanon.

LOVIE P. ARMER McLERRAN

Lovie Pauline Armer was born on May 20, 1930. She married Louis McLerran on September 10, 1951. Louis was born on October 18, 1920. They reside in the Moss Community. Lovie is a housewife. Louis works for the Tennessee State Highway Department; and he is a farmer. He is a past president of the Clay County Republican Party; and he served on the Clay County Board of Education for a number of years.

Lovie and Louis have three children: Louis Lynn, Joan Marie, and Joy Frances.

Louis Lynn was born January 20, 1951. He married Brenda Carol Bishop on December 22, 1970. Brenda was born April 23, 1952. They have three children: Louis Issac, born March 29, 1974; Waylon Elliot, born November 2, 1976; and Cameron Lynn, born January 15, 1982. Waylon and Issac attend school at Celina K-8. The family resides near Moss.

Lovie, Joy, Lynn, Lois and Joan McLerran

Joan Marie was born April 2, 1956. She married W. Roy "Butch" Burnette on February 16, 1975. Butch was born on December 26, 1949. Butch and Joan are graduates of Celina High School. They both work at B & B Distributing Company in Celina and are active in civic affairs. They have two children: William Joseph, born June 12, 1978, and Amanda Joy, born October 11, 1978. The children are students at Celina K-8 School. The family resides in Celina.

Joy Frances was born April 14, 1958. She married James Ronald Key on June 30, 1978. James was born March 16, 1957. Joy and James are both graduates of Celina High School. Joy is a bookkeeper in the Central Office of the Clay County School System. James works for Tri-County Electric Membership Corporation. Joy and James have two children: James Derick, born August 21 1981, and Christopher Louis Edward, born January 19, 1985. The family attends Church at the Cave Springs Church of Chirst; and they reside on Neely's Creek near Celina.

JEWEL M. ARMER McBRIDE

Jewel Marie Armer was born August 4, 1932. She married Landon McBride on September 5, 1953. Landon was born December 14, 1930. They have three children.

Ronald L. was born December 21, 1954. He married Angie McJhoregy on March 25, 1977. She was born September 9, 1955. They have one child, Nicole McBride, born November 13, 1978.

Johnny McBride was born February 6, 1957; and Landon Jr. was born October 15, 1961.

ARCHIE THOMAS ARMS

Archie Thomas (Tommy) Arms was born February 22, 1886 and died January 11, 1968. He was the son of Robert Arms, Jr. and Helen Moses (Poindexter) Arms. Tommy's parents died young, leaving three children, Lovie, Laura and Tommy. Matthew Smith was appointed their guardian.

Tommy and Dayse Lucretia Stone were married March 3, 1906 by Professor W.B. Boyd,

Tommy and Dayse Arms

President of Montvale Academy. They were the first couple that he married where both persons had been his students. They had six children, Alice (Arms) Overstreet, Nancy Helen (Arms) Wells, Billy Amos, Laura Lee (Arms) Mayo and Walter Arms.

During the Great Depression, Tommy owed for part of his farm and had six children to rear. His wife, Dayse, wrote to President Franklin D. Roosevelt for help. The President referred her to the Federal Land Loan Association in Louisville, Kentucky. Tommy and his brother-in-law, Amos Stone, became two of the original directors of the Federal Land Loan Association in Clay County. This association helped the farmers of Clay County during the depression.

Helen Poindexter Arms' ancestry came from the Isle of Jersey, moving to Normandy, France. The family was prominent in religion and politics. Some of the American ancestors were John Poindexter, Edward Poindexter and Thomas Poindexter. Thomas was a captain in the Revolutionary War. It is recorded by the *Daughters of the American Revolution* that Thomas had a little daughter who passed messages to the army by sewing them between her petticoats. The enemy never harmed her.

Tommy and Dayse's children married and had families. Alice married Harmon Overstreet. Their children are: John Thomas, Mitchell, and Dayse. Helen married Dewey Wells. They had no children, but reared Lura Arms Parsons and Walter Lee Arms. Edith married Charlie Bilbrey, and they had two daughters, Brenda Bilbrey Stubblefield and Charlene Bilbrey Groves. Billy Amos married Lorene Neely, and they had two children, Billie June Arms Watson and Thomas Edward Arms. Laura Lee married Ronald Mayo, II, and they had three children, Ronald, III, Sharon Mayo Mathias, and Thomas Mayo. Walter married Claudine White (deceased), and they had two children, Lura Arms Parsons and Walter Lee Arms. Walter's second wife is Josephine Davis, and they have four children, Bobby, Lester Earl, Warren and Rama Arms.

Tommy died on January 11, 1968. He was buried beside his beloved Dayse in the Stone Cemetery in the Beech Bethany Community of Clay County. — *Submitted by Helen Arms Wells*

HENRY ASBERRY FAMILY

Henry Asberry and his wife, Polly Prock Asberry, came to Clay County about 1880. Polly was born and grew up in Monroe County Kentucky. She lived in Clay County for nearly 40 years.

Polly Asberry

Henry and Polly had six children: Newton, born in 1866; Hewett, born in 1867; Loucinda Jeanetta, born in 1875; Mary Sara, born in 1877; Susan B., born in 1882; and Luana, born in 1885. Mary Sara, Susan B., and Luana were all born in Clay County

Loucinda Jeanetta (Nettie) married Samuel Hice Turner on October 28, 1900. They had seven children: Otis, Estle, Edward, Buford, Woodrow, Ruby and Bessie. After Nettie's death, the children moved to southeastern Indiana. — *Submitted by Delma Williams McLeod*

HEWEL "PONY" ASBERRY

Hewel "Pony" Asberry, born on September 20, 1870, was the son of Henry and Polly Asberry. It is said that Henry first came into Jackson County (now Clay County) shortly after the Civil War, and at this time, he had the surname of Hammond, but he changed it to Asberry. The now called Hewel Asberry married Polly Turner, and they had five children — two boys and three girls. The children were Hewel, Newt, Sude, Nette, and Bell. Henry was born in 1822 and died in 1921. Polly was born in 1835 and died in 1925.

Hewel and Louisa Asberry

Hewel was called "Pony" all his adult life. It seemed that Hewel's older brother, Newt, was called "Horse," and so the younger Hewel was called "Pony." This did not bother "Pony" at all, but Newt would become fighting mad at the mere suggestion of the hated nickname, "Horse." "Pony" was a multi-talented man with many vocations to his credit. He was a farmer. He dabbled in illegal whiskey operations earning the name "Sly Red Fox," because he was redheaded and was never caught selling or making moonshine. He also did photography, blacksmithing, and operated a gristmill for Clarence Franklin by the old graveyard at Union Hill. "Pony" was a deputy sheriff. He served as singing master at the Union Hill Church of Christ in Clay County

As a young man, "Pony" courted and married Louisa Jones, who was born on April 5, 1875. Louisa kept one of the two local switchboards for the telephone service. This switchboard was destroyed in a tragic fire which consumed the home of Louisa and "Pony."

"Pony" and Louisa had eleven children — four boys and seven girls — Bedford, Tressa, Roxie, Dewey, Rosco, Zora, Donna, Esco, Edna, and twins, Nora Bell and Laura Mae, who died after one year of life.

"Pony" was born on September 10, 1870, and he died on December 2, 1940. Louisa was born on April 5, 1875, and she died January 20, 1955.

They are buried side-by-side in the Jonestown graveyard.

BOB AND OLLIE ATCHLEY

Vernon Miles Atchley lived in the Arcot Community in the late 1800's. He married Catherine Reecer, the daughter of Frederick Hison and Mary Jane Reecer. They had five sons, Bedford, Benton, Luke, Bob, and Hubert; and they had three daughters, Mary, Maudie, and Mattie.

Ollie and Bob Atchley

Bob Atchley was born April 19, 1906 in the Arcot Community of Clay County. He married Ollie Collins, the daughter of Lee Ann Collins of the Pine Hill Community. Bob was a farmer, and Ollie was a housewife. They had seven children. Clyde and Claude, twins, were born December 27, 1925. Claude died in infancy. Clyde attended Clay County School and Tennessee Tech. Clyde taught in the Clay County School System for 37½ years. He retired from teaching in 1983. Clyde has owned a flower shop, and he currently works as a florist at Clark Drugs in Celina. Clyde attends Butler's Landing Church of Christ.

Lee Kathryn married Alva Sherrel of White County, Tennessee. They have one daughter, Vickie. Lee Kathryn works at a factory near Sparta, Tennessee

Billy Ray married Joy Allen. They have one daughter, Lori. Billy works for the Corps of Engineers. Joy is a beautician. They attend the Celina Baptist Church. Billy Ray, Joy, and Lori live on Route 3, Celina.

Fannie Ruth married Horace Gribble of White County. Fannie has one son, Robert. Robert is a funeral director and co-owner of Anderson's Funeral Home in Gainesboro. He is married to Glenda Poindexter. Glenda works for J.H. Reneau, III, an attorney in Celina. Robert and Glenda have two children, Emily and Curtis. Fannie served one term as Circuit Court Clerk of Clay County. She is now employed at OshKosh B'Gosh in Celina.

Paul Edward married Faye Davis. They have three children, Greg, Kent, and Rhonda. Paul Edward works at Scott's Bestway in Celina. Faye works in Medical Records at the hospital in Livingston, Tennessee. They attend Neely's Cross Roads Church of Christ near Celina. They live at Timothy, Tennessee.

Rosa Nell married Frank Marsh of White County. Rosa Nell is an office employee in Sparta, Tennessee. They live in Sparta.

Bob died December 6, 1967. He is buried in the Fitzgerald Cemetery in Celina. Ollie lives in Celina. She attends Butler's Landing Church of Christ.

HUGH BARTON BAILEY

Hugh Barton was born in the Shanky Branch Community of Clay County on June 27, 1906. He is the fourth of six sons born to John Bennett Bailey, who served for sixteen years as Clay County Judge, and Sally Frances Clinton. Bart is the grandson of Calvin Bailey (wife's name not known) and Frank Clinton and Marjie Masters. Bart attended school at Baptist Ridge, Butler's Landing, Hamilton's Lane and Montvale Academy.

Bart grew up on a farm and was a farmer until the 1950's. He was Clay County Road Commissioner from 1944-48. He worked as an employee of the State of Tennessee from 1951-55 and an employee of the county from 1962-68. He was a member of the County Court from 1960-82, thus serving as a justice of the peace for 22 years.

He married Mary Daffo Weaver on July 6, 1924. Daffo was born in Weaver's Bottom on March 18, 1911. She is the daughter of William Radford Weaver and Rosa P. Jones. She is the granddaughter of Tom Jones and Sally Brown, and Martha Elizabeth Arterberry and James Bailey Weaver. Daffo has been a housewife and mother for most of her life. She has served as a member of the Clay County Library Board. She enjoys quilting, sewing, gardening, and needlework.

Barton and Daffo Bailey

Bart and Daffo are the parents of nine children — five sons and four daughters. Hugh Odell Bailey was born on December 31, 1925 in Butler's Landing. He married Evelyn Gail Hay. They had five children. Bill married Ann Burnette, and they have three children. Charles married Judy Fisher, and they have one son. Steve married Rhonda Smith; and they have three children. Deborah married Michael Brown, and they have two children. Tamara married Larry Ford, and they have two children. Hugh was married a second time to Donna, who has three children.

Wilma Jean was born on September 15, 1928. She married Clint Boles. She has two daughters. Freada married Jeffery Hinson, and they have three children. Joyce first married Champ Langford, and they had one son. She then married Perry Scott, and they have two children.

Edith Christine was born on April 25, 1931 in Butler's Landing. She married Willie Virgil Savage. They have four children. Carolyn married Keith Plumlee, and they have one daughter. Charles married Leah Craighead, and they have two daughters. Vickie married David Harrell, and they have two sons. Rita Ann married Robert Deal, and they have two sons.

Betty Joyce was born on November 4, 1934 in Butler's Landing. She married Bertie Walker. They have one daughter, Patricia Ann, who married William Fouch. They have one son.

Elsie Rose was born on February 3, 1938 in Butler's Landing. She married John Martin Rich. They have three daughters. Deborah married Chris Stoner, and they have two daughters. Diana married Gregg Kincaid. Donna Jean is single.

Ronald Douglas was born on January 22, 1943 in Butler's Landing. He married Judy Boone, and they have one son.

Kenneth David was born on March 11, 1946 in Butler's Landing. He is single.

Michael Keith was born on May 11, 1954. He married Marilyn Beard; they have one daughter and one son. Michael is the only child of the nine who was born in a hospital.

Bart and Daffo have lived in the same house since 1937. The house is located on Highway 53 near Butler's Landing. Bart's farm is located on the Cumberland River.

BOBBY LEE BARTLETT

Bobby Lee Bartlett was born February 1, 1939 in the Free Hills Community of Clay County. He is the son of Jessie Hill Bartlett and the late John Lee (Pete) Bartlett of Celina, Tennessee. Bobby is the grandson of Joshua Bill and Fannie Philpotts Hill. Josh and Fannie are deceased.

Bobby attended grades 1-8 at Free Hills Elementary School and graduated from Darwin High School in Cookeville, Tennessee. He received a Bachelor of Science Degree in Health, Physical Education and Recreation from Tennessee State University in 1974 and a Master of Science Degree from Tennessee Technological University in 1980 in Administration, Supervision, and Principalship.

For the past 14 years, Bobby has taught at Celina K-8 School and Celina High School. Along with teaching, Bobby has coached basketball for many years. He was junior high boys basketball coach at Celina K-8 School for ten years. During this time, he won the State Championship game and many trophies. His team won 200 games and lost 12.

Bobby Lee Bartlett

Bobby is active in civic affairs. He works with various clubs and the Free Hills Utility District. He is a member of the Masonic Lodge in Algood, Tennessee and the Hella Temple Shrine in Nashville. He is a 32nd Degree Mason and Shriner.

Bobby was married December 25, 1961 to Geneva Andrews, the daughter of Olli Mai Hamilton and Robert (Bud) Garrett of the Free Hills Community.

Bobby and Geneva have two daughters — Angela Janeene, born March 20, 1967, and Anita Juliette, born October 7, 1974.

Bobby is a member of the Free Hills Church of Christ. He is a part-time pastor at the church and at the Kingdom Hill Church of Christ in Tompkinsville, Kentucky.

During the summer, Bobby works as a park technician for the United States Corps of Engineers. He has done this since 1972.

GENEVA BARTLETT

Geneva Andrews Bartlett is the daughter of Mrs. Ollie Mai Andrews Hamilton and Robert (Bud) Garrett of the Free Hills Community of Clay County. Bud is well-known for marble making in the Celina area.

Geneva Bartlett

Geneva attended grades 1-8 at Free Hills Elementary School and graduated from Darwin High School in Cookeville, Tennessee in 1956. She received a Bachelor of Science Degree in Business Education from Tennessee State University in 1960. She has attended Tennessee Tech, The University of Tennessee, and Middle Tennessee State University for workshops, and has worked to earn credit toward a Masters Degree in library certification.

For the past 26 years, Geneva has taught in the Clay County School System. She was librarian at Celina High School for nine years before going to Celina K-8 School where she is now teaching.

Geneva was married on December 25, 1961 to Bobby Lee Bartlett of Celina, Tennessee. Bobby is the son of Jessie Lee Hill Bartlett of Celina and the late John Lee Bartlett. Geneva and Bobby have two daughters, Angela Janeene and Anita Juliette. Angela was born March 20, 1967, and Anita was born October 7, 1967.

Geneva is a member of the Free Hills Church of Christ. She belongs to the Free Hills Home Demonstration Club and works with many other clubs and organizations.

THOMAS BEAN

Thomas Bean was born November 25, 1814 in Tennessee. He married Mahala Moore, born in 1817 in Kentucky. They were living in the Fifth District of Jackson County, Tennessee in 1850. In the 1880 Census of Clay County Tennessee, Mahala Bean was living in the Leonard Community of Clay County. They had the following children: Jeremiah, born 1834; Ragena H., born 1836; Peter, born 1839; Frances, born 1841; Rebecca, born 1843; Thomas Marion, born January 1846; Walter, born 1849; John, born 1851; and James, born September 16, 1854.

Mahala (Moore) Bean

Thomas Marion Bean was born in January of 1846 in Jackson County Tennessee. He was married on May 14, 1865 to Margaret L. Chitwood, born in December of 1846. They lived in the Leonard Community of Clay County He was in the Civil War and served in Company D of the 9th Kentucky Infantry. Their children were Jeremiah S.; James M.; McDonald, born November 12, 1869; Ogley Rosetta, born 1871; Mahaley Armissie, born 1875; Elzona Belle, born 1878; Lusinda, born 1879; Mason, born January 1881; and Colonel, born in January 1886.

McDonald Bean was born on November 12, 1869. He died April 20, 1950. He married Bell Sweezy, born October 28, 1874. She died January 26, 1925. They had the following children: Carlie D., born May 24, 1892; Arnold P., born December 21, 1894; Ella Pearl, born in 1897; Brade; Ersie; Versie, born February 12, 1903; Drew; Tom Edd; and Otto, born July 18, 1914.

Carlie D. Bean was born May 24, 1892 and died on November 25, 1962. He was married on February 28, 1915 to Nellie Green.

Arnold P. Bean was born December 21, 1894. He died November 23, 1952. He married George Ann Bean, born March 22, 1889. She died March 7, 1956. Their children were Edris, Ray, Dan, and A.C.

James Bean was born September 16, 1854 in Jackson County, (now Clay County) Tennessee. He married Arcena Davis, born June 1, 1854 and died December 7, 1930. Their children were Sidney Stanton, born December 8, 1877; Lucy L., born 1879; Rena, born 1881; Haley, born 1882; Henderson, born 1883; Tennessee born August 31, 1886; Marion, born 1888; Ona, born 1891; Bedford, born 1894; Bettie, born 1895; and Fanna, born 1897.

Sidney Stanton Bean was born on December 8, 1877, and he died May 1, 1942. He married Martha Alice Browning, born March 3, 1882 and died January 23, 1963. They had the following children: Millard Bransford, born August 8, 1900; Ova Vesta, born November 17, 1901; James A., born December 11, 1903; Cena Jane, born January 8, 1906; Estelle Lillian, born September 8, 1908; Hazel Lee, born November 30, 1910; Elmore, born February 4, 1913; Allie, born February 4, 1913; Duel, born March 29, 1915; Dossie Odean, born May 14, 1917; Haley Gertrude, born February 1, 1919; Alma Ruth, born November 3, 1921; Ruby Molene, born February 14, 1924; and Alice Marie, born May 21, 1926.

CARLIE D. BEAN

Carlie D. Bean was born May 24, 1892, and he died November 25, 1962. He was the son of McDonald and Mattie Belle (Sweezy) Bean. He had six brothers and three sisters. He married Nellie Green February 28, 1915. He was a farmer, logger, agent for Raleigh Products, and he worked with law enforcement for approximately 30 years. He was a guard at Dale Hollow Dam. Nellie was a housewife. She loved flowers, gardening, children, and the Church. They attended the Church of Christ. Their children — Myrl, Lillian, Cleston, Hazel, Willodean, Ila Mae, Creola, Rosaleen, and Helen — were all born in Clay County

Carlie and Nellie (Green) Bean and Family

Myrl, born July 9, 1918, was married August 31, 1940 to Zelma Birdwell, born August 1, 1920, the daughter of Herod, Sr. and Lucy (Browning) Birdwell. They farmed until 1946 when they moved to Indianapolis, Indiana. They had one child at this time, Don Eugene. Myrl worked 10 years with the New York Central Railroad. He grew interested in politics. He was elected Ward Chairman and Precinct Committeeman for the Republican Party. They attended rallies to hear Richard Nixon, Gerald Ford, and Ronald Reagan speak. Zelma worked in politics, served as Parent Teacher Association President, and worked at a factory. She retired as cashier from the Marion County Clerk and Treasurer's Office. She belongs to the Order of the Eastern Star, and Myrl is a Mason. They believe in the Church of Christ. Their children are Don Eugene, Ronnie Wayne, and Novis Gayle.

Don Eugene was born January 15, 1945. He joined the United States Marines at age 18. He had schooling to be an insurance salesman. He left Indiana in 1985 and moved to Texas, where he worked in sales and in the office of Trucking Delivery. As he grew up, he was active in the Church, the Boy Scouts, the Explorers and Demolay.

Ronnie Wayne was born February 23, 1951. He received his certificate as an auto mechanic and now sells auto parts. He married Linda McCall February 18, 1972. Their children are Adam Wayne, born March 7, 1974; and Dustin Lee, born May 29, 1979. Adam and Dustin are the only Beans to carry on the Bean name for Carlie.

Novis Gayle was born December 16, 1952. She graduated from Harry Wood High School. Gayle took a course in Beauty Culture. She works at the City-County Building. She married David Frazier. They had one child, Talby Joe, born August 23, 1970. She next married Ted Cassidy, and they had two sons — Jason Andrew, born August 24, 1978, and Nicholas Eli, born on April 6, 1981.

LILLIAN BEAN PLUMLEE

Lillian Bean Plumlee was born June 9, 1920 in

Clay County Tennessee. She was the daughter of the late Carlie and Nellie (Green) Bean. Carlie and Nellie were the parents of nine children: Myrl, Lillian (Plumlee), Cleston, Hazel (Davis), Willodean (Thacker), Ila Mae (Kitchens), Creola (Eden), Rosaline (Hackett), and Helen (Carson). Their children attended the Milestown-Mt. Vernon School and were baptized in the Church of Christ. All the children now live in or around Indianapolis, Indiana, except for Cleston Bean who lives in Madison, Tennessee.

During World War II, Lillian moved to Louisville, Kentucky and worked until her marriage February 15, 1944 to Alva Plumlee, son of George and Glissie (Gulley) Plumlee of Clay County, Tennessee. They then moved to Camp Maxey, Texas until Alva was shipped overseas. He was discharged from the army in the fall of 1945.

They made various moves between Tennessee and Indiana until their last move to Indianapolis in 1952. They have lived in Lawrence, Indiana for the last thirty years, and their children graduated from Lawrence Central High School. Alva and Lillian were members of the Garfield Heights Church of Christ for thirty-three years and their children were baptized there. They have been involved for the last two years in helping to establish a new congregation, the New Palestine Church of Christ.

Lillian worked for twenty years at Western Electric and retired in 1975. Alva worked for twenty-six years at Chrysler and retired in 1980. They enjoy fishing.

Their son, Harold (Corky), was born on January 26, 1945 in Louisville, Kentucky and attended the early part of grade school at Oak Grove and Hermitage Springs in Clay County. Harold served in the army from 1965 until 1967 as a medic. He has worked for the last twenty-two years at Chrysler and lives in Indianapolis, Indiana.

Their second child, Bonita Carol was born on April 15, 1949 in Lebanon, Tennessee. Bonita worked as a keypunch operator at Fort Harrison, Indiana until her marriage March 20, 1971 to Dennis Dressler of Pigeon, Michigan. They have two daughters, Jennifer Robin, born March 20, 1973, and Casey Renee, born June 5, 1979. They live near Greenfield, Indiana and attend the New Palestine Church of Christ.

Their second daughter, Janet Faye, was born April 24, 1951 in Beech Grove, Indiana. Janet worked ten years at Western Electric. For the past five years, she has been employed as a Military Pay Clerk at Fort Harrison, Indiana and lives in Lawrence, Indiana.

HAZEL E. BEAN DAVIS

Hazel Elise (Bean) Davis was born June 22, 1926 in Clay County. She was the fourth child of Carlie and Nellie (Green) Bean. Hazel married Ether Davis, son of Bedford and Cora Bell (Davis) Davis. They were married in Tompkinsville, Kentucky December 15, 1943. At this time, Ether was serving in World War II. Ether was wounded in Bastogne, Belguim on January 2, 1945. Hazel and Ether have lived in Indianapolis, Indiana since December 28, 1952. Ether retired from Chrysler Corporation in 1981, with 28 years service. They have four children, Steve, Kaye, Sherri, and Candi.

Steve Alton Davis was born March 8, 1947. Steve attended David Lipscomb College in Nashville, Tennessee after graduating from Franklin Central High School in Indianapolis, Indiana. While in college he met and married Rebecca McPherson from Russellville, Kentucky. They have two children, Paul Russell, born June 4, 1969, and Shannon Heather, born June 15, 1970. Steve now works for Indy Lighting, and his children both attend Lawrence Central High School. They reside in Lawrence, Indiana.

Glenda Kaye (Davis) Bittorie was born November 2, 1948. Kaye graduated from Franklin Central High School, Indianapolis, Indiana in June of 1966. On July 2, 1966, she married John H. Bittorie from Columbus, Georgia. Kaye and John have two daughters, Lora Michelle, born June 10, 1967, and Tara Dawnelle, born February 18, 1969. John is an electronic engineer for T.R.W., and Kaye works for a law firm. Michelle attends Macon Junior College in Macon, Georgia, and Tara attends high school in Warner Robins, Georgia.

Sherri Leigh (Davis) Pruitt was born April 9, 1957. Sherri graduated from Franklin Central High School, Indianapolis, Indiana. She married Paul David Pruitt of Beech Grove, Indiana, January 10, 1976. Paul is making a career in the Air Force. He has eleven years service. Sherri and Paul have one daughter, Amber Rhiannon, born December 15, 1982. They are expecting a second child in August of 1986. Sherri is a housewife. They now live in Trotwood, Ohio.

Candace Renee Davis was born on September 27, 1966. Candi graduated from Franklin Central High School, Indianapolis, Indiana. She is in her second year at Indiana University School of Nursing. Candi is living in Bloomington, Indiana while attending school. She works at Hill's Department Store.

MATTIE W. BEAN THACKER

Mattie Willodean (Bean) Thacker was born May 29, 1929 in Clay County, Tennessee. Dean was the fifth child of the late Carlie and Nellie (Green) Bean. She moved to Indianapolis, Indiana on July 1, 1947. On May 14, 1948, she married Edward Leon Thacker, the son of Harry and Edith (Nickerson) Thacker of Bedford, Indiana. Leon is employed with Southeastern Supply Company, and Dean is employed at Fort Harrison, Indiana. They reside in Lawrence, Indiana. Leon and Dean have six children, Linda, Dale, Jerry, Dennis, Sheryl, and Carla.

Linda Sue was born July 15, 1949 in Indianapolis, Indiana. Linda works as a sales representative for Dellen Oldsmobile. She married Bill Allen, and they have three children, Brant, born May 27, 1969; Cory, born August 18, 1974; and Amber, born April 25, 1980. They reside in Castleton, Indiana.

Edward Dale was born June 26, 1950 in Indianapolis, Indiana. Dale served in the Vietnam War. He married Carol Below, and they have three children, Shelley Renee, born May 28, 1971; Denise Lynn, born July 11, 1973; and Thomas Shane, born December 3, 1976. Carol and the children now live in Arizona. Dale is now married to Rita Smith. Dale and Rita manage a motel in Lawrence, Indiana.

Jerry Neal was born November 16, 1951 in Indianapolis, Indiana. Jerry married Donna Cordell, and they have one daughter, Carla Dannaille, born August 10, 1982. They reside in Lawrence, Indiana.

Dennis Ray was born January 9, 1953 in Indianapolis, Indiana. Dennis graduated from Indiana University with a degree in Business and Real Estate. He married Michelle, and they have one daughter, Nicole, born December 10, 1981. Dennis now lives in Denver, Colorado.

Sheryl Ann was born January 11, 1955 in Indianapolis, Indiana. Sheryl married John Fortune, and they have two daughters, Tonya, born March 11, 1974, and Ericka, born on March 2, 1976. Sheryl works at Fort Harrison, Indiana and she and her daughters live in Lawrence, Indiana.

Carla Nell was born March 23, 1964 in Sarasota, Florida. She was named after her grandparents, Carlie and Nellie Bean. Carla married Phil Melick, and they have two daughters, Christina Dean, born, July 29, 1983, and Kristan Marie, born, September 12, 1985. She works at Fort Harrison, Indiana and they reside in Lawrence, Indiana.

ILA MAE BEAN KITCHENS

Ila Mae (Bean) Kitchens was the sixth child born to Carlie and Nellie (Green) Bean. She was born February 3, 1932 in Clay County, Tennessee. Ila moved to Indianapolis, Indiana in April of 1950. She was married to Boyce Kitchens, formerly of Morgantown, Kentucky, February 24, 1951. Ila began employment at Western Electric in 1955 and retired in 1985 with 28 years service. Boyce is employed at Eimlendgen Corporation in Indianapolis, Indiana. Ila and Boyce reside in Wanamaker, Indiana and have attended the Garfield Heights Church of Christ for 30 years. They are the parents of two children, Marsha Dianne and Gerald Taylor.

Marsha Dianne was born January 16, 1952 in Beech Grove, Indiana. She married Edward Lockhart of Paoli, Indiana and they had one child, Angela Dawn, born November 29, 1976, in Corydon, Indiana. Marsha graduated from Franklin Central High School and is now employed at Fort Benjamin Harrison as a payroll clerk. Marsha and her daughter reside in Lawrence, Indiana.

Gerald Taylor was born June 20, 1954 in Beech Grove, Indiana. Gerald attends Purdue University and will receive his degree in chemistry. He is employed at Curtis Industries. Gerald married Deborah Lynn Gidcumb of Morgantown, Kentucky and they had one son, Gerald Taylor, II, born December 22, 1972 at Fort Knox, Kentucky. Gerald is now married to Kimberly Bauman, who has one son, David Wayne Bowling. They reside in Indianapolis, Indiana.

CREOLA BEAN EDON

Creola Bean Edon was born June 1, 1934 in Clay County, Tennessee. She was the seventh of nine children born to Carlie and Nellie (Green) Bean. Creola moved to Indianapolis, Indiana in 1952 and began employment at Western Electric in 1953. She married Hall Edon, formerly of Cave City, Kentucky. Hall is employed at Standard Die Supply in Indianapolis. Creola retired from Western Electric in 1985 after thirty years service. They reside in Greenfield, Indiana. Hall and Creola are the parents of four children, Carol, Alan, Terry, and Barry.

Carol Ann, their only daughter, was born December 19, 1954 in Beech Grove, Indiana. Carol

attended Professional Careers Institute and is now a CMA in bone studies. Carol married George Combs, and they had one son, Chad Eric, born July 30, 1975. She is now married to Joe Nahmias, and they reside in Greenwood, Indiana.

Alan Lane was born July 19, 1956 in Beech Grove, Indiana. Alan attended Indiana University and graduated with a degree in Business Transportation. He is now employed with Churchill Truck Lines as a sales representative. Alan and his wife, Sherry, have two children, Derek, born August 1983, and Ashley, born August 1985. They reside in Beech Grove, Indiana.

Terry Edward was born August 17, 1960 in Beech Grove, Indiana. Terry graduated from Indiana Central with a degree in Business. He is employed with Fiber Materials as an industrial salesman. Terry married Cheryl Caughman, and they reside in Fairland, Indiana.

Barry Neal was born March 4, 1965 in Beech Grove, Indiana. Barry is attending Purdue University, studying Industrial Engineering Technology. He is employed at Standard Die Supply with his father. Barry married Renee McCorkle, and they have one son, Tyler, born in October 1984. They reside in Carthage, Indiana. — *Submitted by Creola Edon*

ANNA R. BEAN HACKETT

Anna Rosaleen Bean Hackett was born March 9, 1937 in Clay County, Tennessee. She was the sixth daughter and eighth child of Carlie and Nellie Green Bean. Rosaleen moved to Indianapolis, Indiana in 1954, and there she met and married James C. Hackett of Red Boiling Springs, Tennessee. James was born June 15, 1935, and he is the son of Clifton and Gladys Huffines Hackett of Red Boiling Springs, Tennessee. Anna and James are the parents of three children, Rita Elene, Lisa Gaye, and Jeffery Scott.

Rita Elene was born February 9, 1957 in Beech Grove, Indiana. She married Brian Nassif of Indianapolis, Indiana and they have two children, Barry Dean, born March 22, 1978, and La Christa Dawn, born November 22, 1979. Rita is currently attending Indiana University and is studying to be a registered nurse. Brian is employed by the Allison Motor Division. They reside in Greenwood, Indiana.

Lisa Gaye was born October 22, 1960 in Beech Grove, Indiana. She married Jimmy Coop of Indianapolis, Indiana. Jimmy's father, James Coop, was reared in Glasgow, Kentucky. They have two children, James Michael, born May 9, 1979, and Chad William, born May 30, 1983. Lisa is training to be a medical assistant, and Jimmy owns a sales and service business. They reside in Indianapolis, Indiana.

Jeffery Scott was born September 9, 1962 in Beech Grove, Indiana. Jeff resides in Beech Grove, Indiana and he works at a work center. He enjoys helping his father who preaches for the New Palestine Church of Christ. James is also employed with Nabisco Brands as a production supervisor. Anna was employed with the Western Electric Company for twenty-five years. — *Submitted by Anna Rosaleen Bean Hackett*

HELEN BEAN CARSON

Helen Bean Carson was born January 5, 1940 in Clay County, Tennessee. She was the youngest of nine children born to Carlie and Nellie Green

Bean. Carlie Bean was the son of McDonald (Mack) Bean and Mattie Belle Sweezy. Carlie was born May 24, 1892 in Clay County, Tennessee and he died November 25, 1962 in Clay County, Tennessee. Nellie Green Bean was the daughter of William Green and Anna Nelson. Nellie was born February 10, 1899 in Burkesville, Kentucky and she died August 31, 1974 in Indianapolis, Indiana. They are both buried at the Smith Chapel Cemetery in Red Boiling Springs, Tennessee.

Helen Bean attended Hermitage Springs School in Clay County. In 1956, she moved to Indianapolis, Indiana. Helen married Walter Eugene Carson, born January 1, 1934, in Franklin, Indiana. Helen is retired from Western Electric, and Eugene works at Kargo U-Haul. They reside in Lawrence, Indiana and have two children. Their oldest child, Richard Eugene Carson, was born August 24, 1957 in Beech Grove, Indiana. Richard graduated from Lawrence Central High School and is employed in home repairs and remodeling. He resides in Lawrence, Indiana.

Their youngest child, Heather Marie Green, was born 15 years later on the same day as her brother. She was born on August 24, 1972 in Indianapolis, Indiana. Heather attends Belzer Middle School in Lawrence, Indiana and is active in choir. Heather is the youngest grandchild of Carlie and Nellie Bean.

Helen Carson and her family return to Tennessee once a year, with the rest of the Bean family, to pay tribute to her parents, Carlie and Nellie, on Memorial Day weekend. — *Submitted by Helen Carson*

SIDNEY BEAN

Sidney Stanton Bean, born December 8, 1877 in Clay County, Tennessee, was the oldest of eight children born to James Andrew Bean and Arcena Harriet Davis. James A. was born September 16, 1854 and died January 4, 1934. His wife, Arcena, was born June 1, 1854 and died December 7, 1930. They are both buried in the Hill Cemetery in Clay County, Tennessee. Sidney S. (known as Sid) was a farmer and a lover of horses. He always owned a good riding horse. He was married September 8, 1899 at Miles Cross Roads in Clay County to Martha Alice Browning, born March 30, 1883. Martha A. was the daughter of Andrew Browning and Nancy Jane Lundy Browning. Sidney S. and Martha A. had 14 children, Bransford, Ova, James, Cena Jane, Estelle, Hazel, Allie and Elmore (twins), Duel, Dossie, Haley, Ruth, Ruby, and Marie. Sidney died May 1, 1942, and Martha A. died January 2, 1963. They are both buried in the Hill Cemetery in Clay County, Tennessee.

Alma Ruth Bean, the twelfth child of Sidney S. and Martha A. Bean, was born November 3,

Sidney and Martha Bean w/Bransford and Ova

1921 in Clay County, Tennessee. She was married September 22, 1940 in Celina, Tennessee to Dumas Earl Grace, who was born August 27, 1918 in Clay County, Tennessee. Dumas is the son of Wiley Wilson Grace and Vadie Ann Armer Grace. Dumas served in World War II in the 121st Mechanized Calvary in Europe. Dumas and Ruth live in the Mount Vernon Community of Clay County and attend church at the Mount Vernon Church of Christ. They have one son, Jimmy Neal Grace, born January 28, 1944 in Toledo, Ohio — Lucas County. The Graces moved back to Clay County from Ohio in 1948. Jimmy graduated from Tennessee Technological University, Cookeville, Tennessee with a major in Accounting. He spent two years in the National Guard, worked with the General Accounting Office for several years and is now associated with Powell, Booth & Grace Accounting Firm in Atlanta, Georgia. Jimmy was married to Elizabeth Bowman Baxter January 28, 1972 in Atlanta, Georgia. Elizabeth was born June 15, 1943 in Kinston, North Carolina. She is the daughter of Joe F. and Sara Bowman Baxter. Jimmy and Elizabeth are the parents of two children, Stewart Alexander Grace, born October 10, 1979, and John Mullen Grace, born August 10, 1981.

HAZEL LEE BEAN

Hazel Lee Bean was born on November 30, 1910 in Clay County, Tennessee. The sixth child of Sidney and Martha Alice Bean resided at home until she married Henry Cole in August 1929 in Decatur, Illinois, where her only child, Henry Dean Cole, was born September 18, 1930.

Lee divorced Henry and married Earl F. Bell in Las Vegas, Nevada in January 1952. Lee and Earl later moved to Mesa, Arizona, where they resided for 24 years. Earl and Lee were divorced in 1976. Lee married Al Hakonson in November 1977. Al suffered a heart attack and passed away in January 1985.

Lee now resides in Bakersfield, California with her son, Hank, and his wife, Audrey. Lee now has three grandchildren and two great grandchildren to keep her company in Bakersfield.

ALLIE BEAN REHEIS

Allie Bean Reheis was born February 4, 1913 in the Miles Crossroads Community of Clay County, Tennessee. The daughter of Stanton and Martha Alice Browning Bean, she was married February 2, 1931 to John Raymond Reheis, who was born May 27, 1905, in Illinois. They live in Mesa, Arizona. They have five children (1) Paul Clebern Reheis, born November 16, 1931, was married October 11, 1951 to Anita Joy Bradshaw, who was born August 26, 1931. They have

John and Allie Reheis

six children. (A) Daniel Paul was born November 14, 1952 and was married July 9, 1982 to Rena Hancock, who was born February 3, 1955. Their children are David, born January 22, 1985, and Smantha, born February 3, 1986. (B) Benjamin Ray was born March 27, 1954 and was married June 14, 1974 to Connie Jane Malherbe, born July 17, 1957. Their daughter is Trisha Lee Ann, born June 16, 1975. Benjamin married the second time, July 27, 1982, Sharell Denise Smith, born July 20, 1955. (C) Larry Alan was born September 7, 1955 and was married September 27, 1974 to Faye Lynn Rush, who was born June 1, 1956. Their daughter is Lisa Kay, born March 15, 1976. (D) Cari, born April 3, 1957, was married on March 31, 1977 to Gerald Lee, born October 22, 1953. Their children are Beckey, born June 17, 1978; Sally, born March 31, 1980; Brian Lee, born July 31, 1981; and Stacy, born October 1, 1984. (E) Tammi, born January 19, 1960, was married March 30, 1982 to Randell Val Nelson, born September 20, 1960. Their son is Joshua Randell, born December 24, 1985. (F) Judi, who was born October 23, 1964, was married June 24, 1983 to Stuart Reid Taylor, born August 29, 1962. Their child is Danielle, born August 1, 1984. (2) Mary Alice Reheis was born March 13, 1934 and was married October 15, 1955 to William Donald Dukate, born April 18, 1931. They adopted two children, Mary Claudi and John Lancaster. (3) Patsy Elaine Reheis was born November 10, 1936 and was married August 1, 1958 to Cecil Evert Martin, born January 24, 1935. Their children are: (A) Jeffery Everett, born August 18, 1959, was married June 16, 1978, to Christi Lee Ward, born March 17, 1962. Their children are Shawn Everett, born January 9, 1979, and Amanda Lynn, born July 9, 1981. (B) Michelle was born December 6, 1960 and was married July 10, 1982 to Clayton Ralph Black, born April 27, 1959. Their child is Michael Clayton, born June 15, 1983. (C) Allison was born August 27, 1964 and was married May 20, 1983 to Eugene Morgan Price, born August 22, 1962. Their child is Courtney Elaine, born February 6, 1985. (4) Jerry Ray Reheis was born August 17, 1942 and was married June 30, 1961 to Lonnie Tryon, born February 15, 1943. Their children are: (A) Robert Scott was born April 4, 1962 and was married March 12, 1983 to Sharlene Kay Flake, born February 11, 1960. Their child is Dayne Allen, born March 27, 1985. (B) Wanda was born March 31, 1963 and was married July 10, 1981 to Carl Emmett Nischan, born July 10, 1959. Their children are Jordan Carl, born November 4, 1982, and Carlee, born April 2, 1984. (C) Raymond Blake was born June 12, 1964 and was married April 12, 1986 to April Peterson, born April 2, 1966. (D) Heidi was born July 5, 1970. (E) Jeremy was born September 26, 1972. (5) Stephen Michael Reheis, born March 10, 1948, was married December 13, 1973 to Patricia Ann Standage, born September 12, 1948. Their child is Spencer, born April 5, 1975. They divorced in 1981 and then he was married October 1, 1982 to Donna Ann Rollins, born November 29, 1954.

MARIE BEAN RHOTON

Marie Bean Rhoton was born May 21, 1926 in Clay County. She was married to Cornell Rhoton September 11, 1945 at Tompkinsville, Ken-

Marie (Bean) Rhoton Family

tucky. Cornell was born January 2, 1921 in Monroe County, Kentucky. He is the son of Cay and Sylvia (Crawford) Rhoton. Cornell was in the Air Force during World War II. He served nineteen months in England out of the thirty-seven months spent in the Air Force.

Marie and Cornell have three children. Judy Sharon was born January 22, 1947; Terry Neal was born October 3, 1950; and Jeffrey Lynn was born March 15, 1964.

Judy married Larry Tim Ross at Celina, Tennessee. Larry is the son of Roy and Nell (Pitcock) Ross of Monroe County, Kentucky. They have four children, Larry Tim, Jr., born December 3, 1965; Mark Douglas, born June 12, 1967; Jonathan Blake, born March 23, 1972; and April Dawn, born August 18, 1973.

Terry married Jane Hale July 23, 1972. Jane is the daughter of James and Ina Faye (Cain) Hale of Monroe County, Kentucky. Terry and Jane have one son, Eric Lee, born December 30, 1977. — Submitted by Marie Bean Rhoton

JAMES W. "BILL" BEAN, SR.

James William "Bill" Bean was born July 7, 1885 in Clay County. He died November 14, 1942. He was married February 24, 1907 to Mildred Hall Pedigo, who was born November 23, 1884. She died September 2, 1960. James William "Bill" was a schoolteacher in Clay County for 20 years and a rural mail carrier for 17 years in the West End of Clay County and a farmer. He also served as President of the National Rural Carrier's Association. Mildred and Bill were members of the Leonard Church of

James W. Bean

Christ. They were the parents of nine children, Cleburn, James William "Will", Marie, Olin, Max, Iris, Morris, Harold and Horace.

James William "Will", Jr. was born March 16, 1910 in Clay County. He was married October 19, 1938 to Irene Davis who was born March 22, 1916. He is a retired farmer and schoolteacher. Will and Irene live in the Leonard Community of Clay County, and they are members of the Leonard Church of Christ. They are the parents of four children, Wendell, Linda, James William "Jimmy", III, and Brenda.

James William "Jimmy", III was born April 20, 1951. He is married to Nancy Hudson, born April 1, 1955. Jimmy is a 32nd Degree Mason and a member of the Red Boiling Springs Masonic Lodge No. 585. Jimmy and Nancy are the parents of three children, Crystal, Melanie and Kayla.

THE BEASON FAMILY

Zachary Taylor Beason, born in Pickett County in 1849 and died in 1915, was the son of Jacob Beason and Martha (Smith) Beason. Zachary married Nancy Kimber Heard, born in 1856 and died in 1924, and they set up housekeeping at the head of Ashburn's Creek in Pickett County, Tennessee.

Zachary and Kim had twelve children: Dillard; Marthan, an infant that died at birth; Leonard; Bernard; Louvernie; Haggard Taylor; Pernie Lee; Clinie Day; Grathard; Molard; and Millard. Tragically, five of these children died before the age of ten. Leonard died at age 33 as a result of an accident. He was cutting staves when the axe flew off the handle and struck his leg. They were unable to stop the bleeding and he died within a few days. His death was only 19 days after that of his father.

Molard Beason, born in 1898 and died in 1974, was the youngest child to survive to adulthood. He lived at home, helping farm, and cutting and rafting timber on the Obey River. Baseball was a favorite pastime during leisure hours.

Near the end of World War I, Molard was called to serve. Because their mother had suffered a stroke, Bernard decided it would be better if he served in Molard's place so that Molard could remain at home to care for her. The two brothers headed to Byrdstown to see if this would be possible, stopping on the way at the home of Porter Harrison, who had a telephone. There they learned that the war was already over so neither had to serve.

Corda, Keith, Norma, Molard and Wilma Beason

When Molard was in his twenties, he left Ashburn's Creek for a short time to work in timber in California. Upon his return, he married Corda Phillips, born in 1910 and died in 1977, the daughter of Samuel Silas Phillips, born in 1859 and died in 1919, and his second wife, Martha Ellen Morgan, born in 1873 and died in 1955. The Phillips family lived on the Obey River. Molard and Corda had four children, the first one dying only two months after birth. Their other children are Norma Jean (Beason) Brown, Wilma Dean (Beason) Nevans, and Molard Keith Beason.

In 1944, the Beasons moved from their home on Ashburn's Creek to a farm in Gamaliel, Kentucky because their land was bought for the building of Dale Hollow Dam and Lake. Here Molard and Corda spent the remainder of their days.

Two of their children, Norma and Keith, still live near Gamaliel. Wilma married Ezell Nevans of Celina, Tennessee and moved to Indianapolis. They moved back to Celina in 1956 where they have lived ever since. Wilma and Ezell own and operate Celina Lumber Company, a builders' supply and hardware store, which they bought from H.C. Swann and wife in 1962 in partnership with Ed and Jewell Qualls. They have been the sole owners since 1964, working alongside their two sons, Gary and Danny Nevans. They attend Celina Church of Christ. Wilma and Ezell have two grandchildren, Lorissa and Leigh Ann Nevans.

ADA CONDRA BILBREY

Ada Condra, born August 12, 1903, married Sidney Edward Bilbrey August 21, 1921. Sidney was born October 8, 1897 and died February 13, 1979. He was a barber in Celina, Tennessee. They had nine children.

Sidney and Ada Bilbrey

Dorothy, born December 19, 1923, married Lester Odle on June 29, 1941. Lester died March 1, 1956. They had two children: Carol, born June 8, 1942, and Danny, born February 5, 1944. Carol married Jim Lynn and they had two children: Craig, born December 26, 1964, and Sherrie, born August 23, 1966. Danny married Joan Ridge, and they have two children: Dwayne, born February 6, 1965, and Joey, born January 27, 1967. Dorothy later married Bill Sissiom.

Donald, born February 28, 1925, married Jean Brown May 6, 1949. They have no children.

Doris, born May 17, 1927, married Robert L. Jackson December 21, 1946. They have two children: Robert Lynn, born October 1, 1953, and Donnetta, born December 28, 1958. Donnetta married Randy Jones on April 22, 1977. They have two children: Misty Amber, born October 21, 1977, and Brian Franklin, born May 14, 1986.

Dorene was born November 10, 1929. She is unmarried. She works at OshKosh B'Gosh in Celina. She is a member of the Celina Church of Christ.

Lorene, born November 10, 1929, married William Long and they have two children: Deborah, born July 7, 1950, and Dale, born November 5, 1959. Deborah married Kenneth Biles in 1976. They have two children: Timothy, born June 26, 1977, and Andrea, born April 24, 1979.

Lexie, born June 26, 1935, married Jack Shupper February 18, 1955. They have two chil-

dren: Charles, born July 21, 1957, and Terry born February 14, 1961. Charles married Connie Willinger. They have two children: Cara, born April 11, 1981, and Carrissi, born September 28, 1984.

Evelyn, born September 19, 1936, married Paul Brown April 28, 1955. They have four children. Theresa, born February 11, 1956, married Roger Isenberg, and they have one child, Melanie, born August 11, 1975; Beverly, born January 26, 1957, married Bill Tresdale, and they have one child, Tabitha, born July 17, 1978; Linea, born August 16, 1961; and Gary, born May 5, 1964.

David, born February 3, 1939, married Janie Webb on June 4, 1966. They have one daughter, Lori, born July 12, 1968. David and Janie are divorced. He is a barber in Celina, Tennessee.

James, born June 17, 1942, married Linda Brown June 11, 1966. They have one daughter, Amy, born May 26, 1968.

JOHN BILES

Missionaries discovered the first Biles on the coast of England calling them Byes because of the multitudes of twins/triplets. Future generations moved to London becoming Bies, the name eventually developed into Biles.

William and Charles Biles, brothers, voyaged to America around 1590, settling in North Carolina, prospering in the Virginia House of Burgesses and the Second Continental Congress. An island was named Biles Island, and it was once the residence of William Biles.

Descendant John Biles, born in 1795, and Catherine Walton, born in 1798, were married on December 28, 1810 and moved west to settle in Clay County around 1813. John Condra Biles, born on March 8, 1830 and died on October 12, 1902, was the fifth of their six children. He and Martha "Patsy" Browning, born on January 10, 1832 and died in 1915, were married in 1852.

William Condra Biles, born on June 6, 1854 and died June 18, 1940, was the eldest of their nine children. He and Lavada Elizabeth York, born June 29, 1874 and died August 5, 1970, were married April 11, 1892 in Clay County. Bill and Vada had four children: Guy Frank, born November 10, 1895 and died March 22, 1979; Samuel Rowin, born May 8, 1903 and died June 4, 1982; Mabel Elise, born February 16, 1908; and William Poe, born August 19, 1910. Bill was a merchant, miller, and pharmacist, and Vada was a teacher.

Guy married Sally Rose in 1940 in California. They had one daughter, Carol Jean. Rowin married Pauline Clark June 1, 1935. They have one daughter, Lavada Carol. They lived in Indianapolis. Elise married Clofton Otis Prince, Jr. November 4, 1944 in Winchester, Tennessee. They have three sons, Thomas Clofton, Mark Dickson, and Harry Biles. Poe married Gladys Glee Brandon on October 9, 1938. Gladys, born July 3, 1918 in Gamaliel, Kentucky, is the daughter of Bransford Brandon and Alice Hale, the granddaughter of Martin Brandon and Clara Keith and Alexander Hale and Sarah Jane Crowe, and the great granddaughter of Logan Hale and Catherine Ford and James Nelson Crowe and Elizabeth Ford.

Poe and Gladys have three children, Mary Alice, born August 9, 1940; Charles William, born August 22, 1942; and Jane Ellen, born January

1, 1954. Poe and Gladys moved to Red Boiling Springs, Tennessee in 1950. Poe, a retired teacher of forty-three years in Clay and Macon Counties, presently serves as City Judge. Gladys is a retired City Clerk of seventeen years. Mary Alice, Vice-President of Macon Bank and Trust, is married to Eddie Dean Morgan. They have a son, Chad William Guffey, born April 6, 1971. Charles, Principal of Red Boiling Springs School, has three children, Charla Beth, born September 20, 1967; Gregory Halsell, born July 8, 1969; and Leslie Rae, born January 22, 1971. Jane is a teacher in Macon County

JOHN ALEXANDER BIRDWELL

John Alexander Birdwell was born in 1823 near Tompkinsville, Kentucky. He was the fifth in a family of two sons and three daughters born to Alexander and Elizabeth Copass Birdwell. Alexander was born in 1787 in Sullivan County, Tennessee. He died in 1866 in Monroe County, Kentucky. His wife, Elizabeth, was born in 1784 in Virginia, and she died in 1870 in Monroe County, Kentucky. Elizabeth was the daughter of William Copass, who was born in 1747 in Virginia. He was in the Revolutionary War and fought in the Battle of Yorktown. John Alexander was a gunsmith and a farmer. During the Civil War, he enlisted in the Union Army and served in the Fifth Kentucky Calvary as a bugler. He was married January 11, 1846 in Jackson (now Clay) County, Tennessee to Nancy Condra, who was born in 1816 and died in 1899. She was the daughter of William and Mary Gass Condra. John and Nancy were the parents of five children, Louisa (Gass), Alexander, William, Elizabeth (Likens), and Mary (Gulley).

Nancy (Condra) Birdwell and Chalista Birdwell

John Alexander Birdwell

ALEXANDER BIRDWELL

Alexander Birdwell was born June 27, 1849 in Jackson County, Tennessee. He was the son of John Alexander Birdwell (born in 1823 – died in 1870) and Nancy Condra Birdwell (born 1816 –

Alexander Birdwell

died 1899). He was the grandson of Alexander Birdwell (born 1787 – died 1866) and Elizabeth Copass Birdwell (born 1784 – died 1870). He married Nancy Bernettie Spear in 1874 in Clay County. Nancy was born in 1855, the daughter of Zachariah Spear and Susan Mary (Leaster) Spear. She was the granddaughter of Levi Spear (born 1794 – died 1863) and Elizabeth (Petitt) Spear, born in 1806.

Bernettie Birdwell

Alexander was a farmer and a carpenter. He built barges on the Cumberland River at Celina, Tennessee. He lived in the Miles Cross Roads Community of Clay County. He and Nancy had nine children, Zachariah, born 1875; Samuel, born 1878; Chalista, born 1880; Herod, born April 18, 1884; William, born 1887; Elishie, born 1890; Susan Mary, born 1893; Alexander, born 1895; and Dewey, born 1899.

Alexander, Sr. died February 2, 1929, and Bernettie died June 15, 1930. They are buried in the Mount Vernon Cemetery in Clay County.

HEROD BIRDWELL, SR.

Herod Birdwell, Sr. was born April 18, 1884 in the West End of Clay County, Tennessee. He was the son of Alexander Birdwell (born 1849 – died 1929) and Bernettie Spear Birdwell (born 1855 – died 1930). He was the grandson of John Alexander Birdwell (born 1823 – died 1870) and Nancy Condra Birdwell (born 1816 – died 1899) and Zachariah Spear (born 1826) and Susan Mary Leaster Spear (born 1827).

Herod, Sr. married Lucy B. Browning September 10, 1905. Lucy was born May 20, 1886, the daughter of Andrew Jackson Miles Browning

(born 1862 – died 1893) and Nancy Jane (Lundy) Browning (born 1859 – died 1920). She was the granddaughter of John Jackson Miles (born 1835 – died 1923) and Anna Jane Browning Miles (born 1839 – died 1908) and Elijah Lundy (born 1840) and Louisa Hull Lundy (born 1840 – died 1921).

Lucy B. Birdwell   Herod Birdwell, Sr.

Herod, Sr. attended Montvale College in Celina. He taught school in Clay County for many years. He was a member of the Clay County Board of Education and a member of the Clay County Court. He was a farmer and a merchant. Herod, Sr. and Lucy were members of the Church of Christ and attended services at the Mount Vernon Church of Christ.

Herod, Sr. and Lucy were the parents of twelve children, Ulysses, born June 14, 1906; Laura (Cherry), born September 24, 1907; Beulah (Grissom), born May 27, 1909; Clura, born January 26, 1911; Bee (Carnahan), born March 21, 1913; Dezzie, born 1914 and died 1924; Hulet Arnold, born July 31, 1916; Herod, Jr., born October 7, 1918; Zelma, born August 1, 1920; Earnest, born April 2, 1922; Andrew, born and died in 1923; and Carlos, born October 7, 1924.

Herod, Sr. died December 28, 1958. Lucy B. died August 19, 1972. They are buried in Mount Vernon Cemetery at Miles Cross Roads in Clay County.

ARNOLD BIRDWELL

Hulet Arnold Birdwell was born July 31, 1916 in Clay County, Tennessee. He was the son of Herod Birdwell, Sr. (born 1884 – died 1958) and Lucy B. (Browning) Birdwell (born 1886 – died 1972). He was the grandson of Alexander Birdwell (born 1849 – died 1929) and Bernettie (Spear) Birdwell (born 1855 – died 1930) and Andrew Jackson Miles Browning (born 1862 – died 1893) and Nancy Jane (Lundy) Browning (born 1859 – died 1920).

Arnold has lived most of his life in the Miles Cross Roads Community of Clay County except for a brief stay in Toledo, Ohio when his father went there to work around 1929. The family stayed there only a few months before returning to Clay County. Arnold attended Mount Vernon Elementary School.

On December 17, 1937, Arnold married Jelima Jewel Copas. The wedding took place at Tompkinsville, Kentucky. Jewel was born January 24, 1921 in Clay County. She was the daughter of Edward Austin Copass (born 1874 – died 1941) and Daisy Lena (Copas) Copass (born

1887 — died 1970) and the granddaughter of Nathan Richard Copass (born 1835 — died 1898) and Nancy B. Harlan Copas (born 1836 — died 1889) and Irea Greenberry Steven Copas (born 1860 — died 1933) and Sarah Matilda (Coulter) Copas (born 1861 — died 1921).

Arnold and Jewel grew up next door to each other. After their marriage, they purchased the farm that Arnold grew up on from his parents and then enlarged this farm by purchasing the farm adjoining theirs. Arnold is a farmer and he has worked as a carpenter. Jewel is a housewife. She helps with the various farming activities and she is an accomplished seamstress. Arnold and Jewel are members of the Mount Vernon Church of Christ.

Arnold and Jewel Birdwell

They have five children. Kenneth Myers was born November 27, 1938. In 1958, he married Creola Purcell. They have three children, Donnie Reed; Pamela Diane; and Kenny Wayne.

Their second son, Oliver Dayton, was born August 30, 1941. In 1966, he married Brenda Faye Carter. They have two children, Daytona Lynn and Jonathan Dayton Carter.

Coleda Faye was born September 22, 1943. She married Donald Stevens. They have four children, Don Curtis; Sharon Kay; Jackie Neal; and Sandra Lannett.

Audrey Denise Birdwell

Nelda Kay was born January 22, 1950. She married Lemuel Allen; and they have one daughter, Lisa Cheryl.

Audrey Denise, their youngest child, was born on September 6, 1966. She now resides in Nashville. She works in a lab at Rand McNally Publishers.

All of Arnold and Jewel's children were educated in the Clay County School System.

KENNETH MYERS BIRDWELL

Kenneth Myers Birdwell was born November 27, 1938 in Clay County, Tennessee. He is the son of Arnold and Jewel Copas Birdwell. On May

Creola and Kenneth Birdwell, Kenny, Pamela, Nannett and Donnie

22, 1958 in Macon County, Tennessee, he married Creola Aline Purcell, who was born January 17, 1941 in Clay County. She is the daughter of Mosey and Mamie Rush Purcell. They live in the Hermitage Springs Community of Clay County. Kenneth is a farmer and owns and operates a garage. He is a former member of the Clay County Court. They are both members of the Church of Christ. They have three children, Donnie Reed, born February 22, 1960; Pamela Diane, born January 22, 1963; and Kenny Wayne, born November 17, 1970. Donnie is married to the former Nannett Cherry.

DONNIE REED BIRDWELL

Donnie Reed Birdwell was born February 22, 1960 in Macon County, Tennessee, the son of Kenneth and Creola (Purcell) Birdwell and the grandson of Arnold and Jewel (Copas) Birdwell and Mosey and Mamie (Rush) Purcell. Donnie is a graduate of Hermitage Springs High School and Hartsville Vocational School in Hartsville, Tennessee. He works for Davis Electronics in Lafayette, Tennessee.

Arnold and Jewel Birdwell, Nannett and Donnie Birdwell, Mamie and Mosey Purcell

On September 30, 1983 he married Nannett Cherry, who was born February 1, 1962. She is the daughter of Jasper Cherry, Jr. and Nyoka (Smith) Cherry of Clay County, Tennessee. She is the granddaughter of Jasper Cherry, Sr. and Pearl (Bean) Cherry and Domer and Madge (Anderson) Smith. She is also a graduate of Hermitage Springs High School. She is a housewife. Donnie and Nannett are members of Mount Vernon Church of Christ. They live in the Hermitage Springs Community of Clay County, Tennessee.

DAYTON BIRDWELL

Dayton Birdwell was born August 30, 1941 in the Miles Cross Roads Community of Clay County, Tennessee. He is the son of Hulet Arnold Birdwell, born July 31, 1916, and Jelima Jewel Copas Birdwell, born January 24, 1921. Arnold

and Jewel have five children, Kenneth Myers, Dayton, Coleda Faye, Nelda Kay, and Audrey Denise. Dayton's grandparents were Herod Birdwell, Sr., born 1884 — died 1958, and Lucy B. Browning Birdwell, born 1886 — died 1972, and Edward Austin Copas, born 1874 — died 1941, and Daisy Lena (Copas) Copas, born 1887 — died 1970. The Birdwell and Copas families were originally from Sullivan and Washington Counties in East Tennessee.

Dayton and Brenda Birdwell

Dayton grew up on his father's farm in a small settlement called Happy Hollow in the Miles Cross Roads Community. He attended Mount Vernon Elementary School and graduated from Hermitage Springs High School. After graduation, he attended the Nashville University of Beauty in Nashville, Tennessee and became a hairstylist. After graduation, he worked for Ray Reed Hairstyling in Nashville. While still a teenager, he decided to return to Clay County and set up his own salon in the Miles Cross Roads Community. He has operated a salon in this community for over twenty five years. He is a licensed cosmetology instructor in the State of Tennessee.

Johnathan Dayton Birdwell   Daytona Lynn Birdwell

On June 6, 1966, Dayton married Brenda Faye Carter, born March 26, 1948, in Monroe County, Kentucky, the daughter of Elzie Elsworth Carter, born in 1913 and died in 1965, and Mamie Darlene (Botts) Carter, born in 1922. Brenda is the granddaughter of Samuel Bell Flippin and Bertha Huston (Walker) Carter and Fred and Milon Beatrice (Bushong) Botts. Brenda is also a hairstylist. Brenda and Dayton lived in the Miles Cross Roads Community for eleven years before moving to Tompkinsville, Kentucky, where they also own and operate a hairstyling salon. Dayton is an assistant librarian at the William B. Harlan Memorial Library in Tompkinsville. He is a member of the Mt. Gilead Church of Christ near Tompkinsville. He is a member of the Republican

Party. Dayton and Brenda have two children, Daytona Lynn, born November 18, 1969 in Celina, Tennessee, is a senior at Monroe County High School in Tompkinsville. Johnathan Dayton Carter, born January 19, 1973 in Nashville, Tennessee, is in the eighth grade at Gamaliel Middle School in Gamaliel, Kentucky.

COLEDA F. BIRDWELL STEVENS

Coleda Faye Birdwell was born September 22, 1943 in Clay County, Tennessee. She is the daughter of Arnold and Jewel (Copas) Birdwell. She married Donald Stevens September 14, 1963. The wedding took place in Macon County,

Donald and Coleda Stevens

Tennessee. Donald is the son of Paul and Pearl (White) Stevens. Coleda and Donald live in Macon County. She is employed at a greeting card company in Lafayette, Tennessee. He is a farmer and a truck driver. Coleda is a member of the Church of Christ.

Sharon, Sandra, Jackie and Don Curtis Stevens

Coleda and Donald have four children, Don Curtis, born September 11, 1965; Sharon Kay, born June 23, 1967; Jackie Neal, born July 8, 1968; and Sandra Lanett, born June 11, 1973.

NELDA KAY BIRDWELL ALLEN

Nelda Kay Birdwell was born January 22, 1950 in Clay County, Tennessee, the daughter of Hulet Arnold and Jelima Jewel Copas Birdwell. She is a graduate of Hermitage Springs High School. She attended Ray Reed School of Cosmetology in Nashville, Tennessee and is a licensed cosmetologist. She is presently employed at Rand McNally Publishers in Nashville, Tennessee. She was married December 20, 1970 to Lemuel Allen, born October 4, 1949 in Jackson County, Tennessee. He is the son of Leo and Mable Francis Martin Allen and the grandson of Berry and Rebecca Coffelt Allen and Oscar and Bornie Spivy Martin. He grew up in the Oak Grove Community of Clay County, Tennessee.

He has four brothers, Oscar, Orville, Dudney, and Arlis and four sisters, Dorothy, Marie, Georgia Ruth, and Martha. All five of the Allen brothers served in the Army; Oscar and Arlis served in Korea and Orville, Dudney, and Lemuel served in the Vietnam War.

Nelda, Lemuel and Lisa Allen

Lemuel is also a graduate of Hermitage Springs High School. He is employed at Rand McNally Publishers in Nashville, Tennessee where he is a supervisor. Nelda and Lemuel are members of the Church of Christ. They reside in Hermitage, Tennessee. They have a daughter, Lisa Cheryl, born May 8, 1975.

HEROD BIRDWELL, JR.

Herod Birdwell, Jr. was born October 7, 1918 in the Mount Vernon Community of Clay County. He is the fourth son of the late Herod Birdwell, Sr. and Lucy B. Browning Birdwell. Herod is the grandson of Alexander Birdwell and Bernettie Spear Birdwell, and Andrew Browning and Nancy Jane Lundy Browning.

Herod attended elementary school at Mount Vernon, graduated from Hermitage Springs High School, and attended Austin Peay State College until he was inducted into the military service in 1941. He served in Field Artillery in the United States, as well as in England, France, Luxemburg and Germany. While in Europe, he served in the Third Army commanded by General George S. Patton. He was discharged in 1945 with the rank of First Lieutenant. After leaving the service, he continued his education and received a Bachelor of Science Degree in Agriculture from the University of Tennessee in Knoxville, and later completed a Master of Arts Degree from Tennessee Technological University in Cookeville. Herod taught Vocational Agriculture for 23 years, seventeen years at Hermitage Springs High School and six years at Red Boiling Springs, where he served as principal for two years prior to resigning to become Director of the Tri-County Vocational School, where he served for 5½ years until his retirement in 1980.

Herod Birdwell, Jr.   Adele Birdwell

Herod married Adele Cherry on July 5, 1944. Adele was born in the Arcot Community of Clay County on January 23, 1927. She is the second daughter of Orville Newell Cherry and Ethel Reecer Cherry. She is the granddaughter of William Jackson Cherry and Mary Lou Dalton, and William Leander Reecer and Minnie Franklin Reecer.

Adele attended elementary school at Arcot and graduated from Celina High School in Celina in 1944. She received a Bachelor of Science Degree in Elementary Education from Middle Tennessee State University in Murfreesboro, and a Master of Arts Degree in Guidance and Counseling from Tennessee Technological University. Adele worked in the Clay County School System for 30 years teaching school at Union Hill, Mount Vernon, Hermitage Springs, and Celina K-8. She taught grades 1-9, worked as guidance counselor, and served as a career educational specialist with the Clay County Urban/Rural School Development Program. She retired in 1984.

Herod and Adele attend church at the Hermitage Springs Church of Christ. Herod serves on the Citizens Advisory Council in Clay County.

Herod and Adele are the parents of Phyllis Jean, born August 28, 1946, and Constance Dianne, born January 17, 1949.

Phyllis married Bobby Loyd Birdwell of Jackson County August 26, 1969. They are the parents of Michael Loyd, born August 21, 1971, and Amy Jean, born September 28, 1973. Michael is a student at Jackson County High School, and Amy is a student at Fox Elementary School in Gainesboro. Phyllis teaches third grade at Gainesboro Elementary and lives in Gainesboro.

Constance Dianne married Andrew Joel Lynn December 23, 1968. They are the parents of Scott Joseph, born July 7, 1973, and Todd Houston, born October 24, 1980. Scott is a student at Celina K-8. Connie teaches first grade at Celina K-8 and lives in Celina.

EARNEST BIRDWELL

Earnest Cancel Birdwell was born April 2, 1922 in Clay County, Tennessee. He is the son of Herod and Lucy Bee (Browning) Birdwell. He grew up in the Miles Cross Roads Community of Clay County, Tennessee and attended Mount Vernon Elementary School.

Earnest and Evelyn Birdwell

On April 5, 1947, he married Evelyn Cherry, born March 28, 1928, the daughter of Estes and Ercie (Condra) Cherry. Evelyn attended Arcot Elementary School and graduated from Celina High School.

Earnest is a veteran of World War II. He served in the Army Air Force from February 1943 to February 1946. He served in China, Burma and India.

Earnest and Evelyn live in the Hermitage Springs Community of Clay County where they have owned and operated Birdwell's Plumbing and Electric Store for the past 26 years. Evelyn attends the Hermitage Springs Church of Christ.

Earnest and Evelyn have one son, Jerry Neal, born January 28, 1948. He married Holly Graves, and they have two sons, Neil Earnest and Michael Robert.

JERRY NEIL BIRDWELL

Jerry Neil Birdwell was born January 28, 1948. He is the son of Ernest and Evelyn Cherry Birdwell. Jerry was married to Holly Renee Graves of Newark, Delaware June 22, 1977. Holly is the daughter of Robert Pyle Graves and Edna Greenplate Graves of Newark, Delaware. Jerry is a Technical Sergeant in the United States Air Force. Holly is a Staff Sergeant in the United States Air Force. Jerry is a veteran of the Vietnam War. He was stationed in Vietnam, Korea, Texas, Illinois, and Florida during his first four years in the service. As joint spouses, they have served in New Jersey, Alaska, Texas and Ilinois.

Holly, Michael, Neil and Jerry Birdwell

Jerry and Holly have two children. Neil Ernest was born August 21, 1980, and Michael Robert was born March 7, 1982. Neil and Michael were both born in Anchorage, Alaska.

WILLIAM "BILLY" BIRDWELL

Many of the barns and houses built by William "Billy" Birdwell (1887-1966) are still standing. They are a tribute to his carpentry skills and ability to get the most out of his helpers.

William and Beulah Birdwell

In 1913 William was married to Alice Beulah Hill (1895-1952). She was the oldest daughter of Daniel and Laura Netherton Hill. She was raised near the Clementsville church house. The accompanying picture was made by one of the oaks at Clementsville about 1912. That huge tree still stands by the new church house.

The Birdwell's house is still standing on the Mount Vernon road. The grandchildren still return to look at their youthful handprints in the concrete steps. The large white house with a pine tree framed driveway is a familiar landmark.

William was the fourth child of Alexander Birdwell (1849-1929) and Bernetta Spears Birdwell (1855-1930). He was raised near Union Hill. The old home is now owned by his niece, Maylene Roberts. William was very fond of raising berries and fruits. He was often seen walking on roads or taking short cuts across fields while eating fruits or shelling peanuts.

Beulah Birdwell was a woman of strong character. She bore six children and helped with various field work as well as maintained the household. She was a kind woman who kept everything going while her husband was away on carpentry jobs or working from sunup to sunset on jobs near home.

William "Billy" Birdwell was noted for his memory of historical and chronological facts. He prided himself in knowing the Presidents and most everyone's genealogy. He entertained his helpers at work with frequent jokes or witty sayings.

The children of the Birdwells are Ruby, who married Dalice Brady; Wade, who married Nina Fox; Oma, who married Elmo Henson; Ray, who married Wilma Waddell; Anna, who married Elbert Henson; and Ruth, who married Emmett Atwood. Ray lives in Humboldt, Anna at Adams, and Ruth in Nashville, Tennessee. The other three now live in Clay County.

William and Beulah are buried in the Pitcock Cemetery at Oak Grove.

WADE H. AND NINA BIRDWELL

Wade H. Birdwell was born October 23, 1916. He is the son of Beulah Hill and William (Billy) Birdwell. He was married to Nina Fox March 27, 1940 in Tompkinsville, Kentucky. Nina is the daughter of Daniel and Minnie Oliver Fox. Wade is a retired brick mason, carpenter and part-time farmer. They have three children, Carolyn, Stanley and Terry. Carolyn was born in Clay County, December 18, 1940. She married Oscar Allen, April 1, 1960. She is the librarian at Ezell Harding Christian School in Nashville, Tennessee. Stanley was born August 20, 1945, in Clay County. He graduated from Tennessee Technological University June 3, 1968. He married Nell Rich, October 12, 1970. He taught school in Clay County in 1968-69. He is employed as a sales representative in Nashville, Tennessee. Terry was born May 9, 1951 in Jackson County. He graduated from Tennessee Technological University in 1972. He married Wilma Tucker from Asheville, North Carolina August 24, 1973.

Nina and Wade Birdwell

Wade and Nina live in the Mount Vernon Community of Clay County. They attend the Church of Christ at Hermitage Springs.

AMOS J. BIRDWELL

Amos J. Birdwell was born April 14, 1930 in the Union Hill Community of Clay County, Tennessee, and is the son of Alexander and Myrtle Turner Birdwell. He moved to Columbus, Indiana in 1942. He served in the Korean War. He was married January 1955 to Thelma C. Wilson.

Amos J. and Thelma Birdwell

They have four daughters: Devita Lyne, who is unmarried and owns her own business; Myra D. married Mark David Foster and they have a son, Griffin David, born April 20, 1986; Trina K. married Kurt Duncan Buck and they have one son Mason Daniel, born May 21, 1982; and Nicohl who is a student in the 11th grade.

Amos and Thelma have been involved in their own real estate business since 1964.

DEWEY BIRDWELL

Dewey Birdwell was born in Western Clay County on March 30, 1899. He was the seventh son and the ninth child of Alexander and Nancy Bernette Birdwell. Dewey's father, Alexander, was born on June 27, 1849 in Jackson County (now Clay County) and died on February 20, 1929. Nancy Bernette, Dewey's mother, was also born in Jackson County on August 9, 1855. She died June 5, 1930. They were married in 1874 and lived at the Miles Crossroads Community. Like their father, all of Alexander's sons farmed at one time or another. Some took up other occupations such as carpentry, also learned from their father. Others were teachers and one was a business man. Dewey and his older brother, Alexander Jr., went into the wildcat whiskey business — making, selling, and drinking whiskey. His two sisters were housewives and mothers.

Dewey Birdwell

Dewey married his childhood sweetheart, Versa Etta Cherry, in 1918. They raised six children, Edna; Bernice; Clovis; Weltha J.; Allan C.;

and Veda J. Dewey saw the error of his ways in 1930, and with his wife, Versa, joined the Church of Christ. They were members for life. He had to find a better and legal way to supplement his meager farm income, so he ran for 2nd District Highway Commissioner and was defeated in the late 1930's or early 1940's. He ran a second time and was elected. This job paid $100.00 a month, and the term was for two years. Dewey also traded hogs on the side and did well in a limited sort of way.

World War II came and Dewey's two oldest sons entered service. Jobs were plentiful in the north, and after staying there three months alone, on June 14, 1944, Dewey moved his family to Indianapolis, Indiana, where he was employed by the United States Rubber Company until his retirement when he was sixty-two years old. On October 28, 1973, Dewey's wife, Versa, passed away. Twelve years later, he followed her. Dewey was a country poet and wrote about simple things: of people, friends, family, and politics. Many of his poems have been published by newspapers in Clay County. Both he and his wife of fifty-five years are buried in a family cemetery in Western Clay County, home again to stay.

SYLVIA ELISE BOLES

Sylvia Elise Boles was born February 11, 1932 in Jackson County, Tennessee. She was the daughter of Nora and John Cox of Jackson County, Tennessee. She was one of eleven children. Sylvia married Clifford Boles on May 10, 1956.

Sylvia Elise Boles

Clifford was born on March 9, 1937, the son of Ella and Cormer Boles. He attended Beech Springs School and Baptist Ridge School. Sylvia has worked at OshKosh B'Gosh in Celina for seven years. They have one daughter, Betty, born July 27, 1953. She married Donnie Hammock; and they have one daughter, Teresa, born August 30, 1973. They have two sons, David Boles and Doyle Cox. David was born August 21, 1966. He married Brenda Boles of the Dry Creek Community. Brenda was born September 10, 1966. David and Brenda have one son, Anthony, born February 27, 1984. Doyle is unmarried. He was born February 24, 1956. Sylvia now resides on Baptist Ridge. — *Submitted by Teresa Hammock*

ADOS A. BOONE

Ados A. Boone was born November 26, 1923, in Clay County, Tennessee. He is the son of Oscar Samuel Boone and Montana Lois Dyer Boone. Oscar and Montana were the parents of three children, Hazel (Halsell), Ados Boone and Avos (Halsell).

Ados is the grandson of Stephen Campbell Boone and Priscilla Anderson Boone and Samuel Dyer and Ermine Poore Dyer.

Ados attended schools in Clay County, Tennessee. He is a semi-retired merchant.

Ados married Lilliam Ruth Lockett of West Irvine, Kentucky on March 31, 1945. Lillian was born in Irvine, Kentucky on June 7, 1928, the daughter of John C. Lockett and Lucy Kirby Lockett. She is the granddaughter of John Lockett and Molly Crouch Lockett and Frank Kirby and Lula Hamilton Kirby. Lillian attended schools in Estil County, Kentucky. Ados and Lillian presently own and operate the Celina Dairy Chef.

Ados and Lillian are the parents of two children, Judy Boone Bailey, born May 22, 1946, and Donna Boone Dowell, born September 28, 1950. Judy married Ronald D. Bailey in October 1968; and they own a grocery store. Donna married Robert Michael Dowell June 19, 1970, and they own the Fentress County Flower Shop. Michael is also a druggist.

Judy and Ronald live in Tompkinsville, Kentucky, and they have one child, Ronald Shea, born July 6, 1970.

Donna and Mike live in Jamestown, Tennessee, and they have two children, Michelle Lea, born July 23, 1972, and Robert Michael, born September 25, 1977.

Ados and Lillian live in Celina, Tennessee and attend the Celina Church of Christ.

PAUL ALEXANDER BOYCE

Paul Alexander Boyce was born December 14, 1942, in Lexington, Kentucky. He is the son of William Alexander Boyce and Leola Frances Piper Boyce. After moves with church workers to Pine Ridge, Kentucky; Cedarville, Ohio; Knoxville, Tennessee; and Pleasant Hill, Tennessee, the family moved to Crossville where William was farm manager for the Evans Brothers. The Boyce family moved to Celina, Tennessee in 1967, where William Boyce was farm manager for Dr. Art Cardona.

Paul, Layne, Phyliss and Loren Boyce

Paul is the grandson of Sarah Eliza Waldron of New York and Alexander Boyce of Boston, who moved to Pleasant Hill, Tennessee, and Bessie Lewis and Zina Melvin Piper of Illinois.

Paul attended Cumberland County, Tennessee schools and graduated from Cumberland County High School in 1960. He attended Martin College in Pulaski, Tennessee in 1961-62, Tennessee Technological University from 1962-65, and Tennessee Technological University from 1969-70. He served in the Peace Corps in India from 1966-68. He is presently a farmer in Clay County. The family lives on the Jordan Holtam farm in the Knob Creek area. He is Scoutmaster for Boy Scout Troop 191 and enjoys photography.

Paul was married to Phyllis Ann Robinson, formerly of Mountain City, Tennessee, of Celina on December 20, 1969. Phyliss was born in Mountain City on February 21, 1945, the daughter of Samuel Everett and Theda Mae Winchell Robinson. She is the granddaughter of Ida Elizabeth Gentry and Moore Monroe Robinson of Mountain City and Ella Mae Greer and John Loren Winchell of Iowa.

Phyliss attended Johnson County, Tennessee schools, graduating from Johnson County High School in 1963. She graduated from Berea College, Berea, Kentucky, in 1968. She completed her Masters Degree from the University of Tennessee in Agricultural Extension Education in 1977. Phyliss came to Clay County as Home Demonstration Agent in March 1968. She was promoted to Associate Extension Agent in 1975; to Extension Agent in 1981; and to Extension Agent and Leader in 1985. She has received the Tennessee Home Economics Research Award; the Distinguished Service Award of the National Association of Extension Home Economists; the Distinguished Service Award of the National Association of Extension 4-H Agents; and in 1985, the E.J. Chapman Travel-Study Scholarship. In addition, she is co-sponsor of the Tennessee 4-H Food Preservation Project. Phyliss is involved in the American Cancer Society in Clay County; Dale Hollow Chamber of Commerce; and the Clay County Advisory Committee for Better Schools.

Paul and Phyliss are parents of Loren Alexander, born June 15, 1971, and Layne Ross, born July 27, 1973. Loren is a student at Celina High School, and Layne is a student at Celina K-8. Both are active in Scouts and 4-H.

Paul, Phyliss, Loren, and Layne attend the Celina United Methodist Church.

HOMER ALVIE BRADY

Homer Alvie Brady was born February 12, 1928 in Clay County. He is the son of Walter Benton Brady and Stella May McCormick Brady. He is the grandson of W.Y. and S.A. Brady and J.B. and Nan Dodson McCormick.

He was a farmer in Clay County until the past two years when he became disabled. He attended elementary school at Union Hill.

He was married to Bertha Likens on October 7, 1953. She died as the result of a tractor accident on May 17, 1954.

Homer, Charlene, Douglas, Anna and Linda Brady

He then married Charlene Nell Spivey Green February 21, 1970. Charlene is the daughter of Haskell and Cleo Ethridge Spivey. She was born January 3, 1939. She is the granddaughter of W.O. and Florette Cherry Spivey and Albert and

Lassie Avie Cowan Ethridge. Charlene attended elementary school at Moss and in Indianapolis, Indiana. She graduated from Celina High School in 1958. She attended Draughon's Business College in Nashville, Tennessee.

Homer and Charlene are the parents of Douglas Eugene Green, born December 2, 1961; Anna Mae Brady, born August 21, 1971; and Linda Faye Brady, born March 20, 1978. Douglas Eugene graduated from Hermitage Springs High School in 1980. He is presently employed as a draftsman at Honest Abe Log Homes. Anna and Linda are students at Hermitage Springs School.

Charlene is presently employed by the Clay County Board of Education, and she works at Hermitage Springs School.

Charlene, Anna, and Linda attend Union Hill Church of Christ.

JAMES MICHAEL BRIGGS

James Michael (Jim) Briggs was born December 22, 1938 in Tifton Georgia. He is the son of Agnes Vick Briggs and the late Harold Briggs, who died in 1947 in Thomasville, Georgia. After his death, the family moved to Tampa, Florida. Jim is the second child in a family of three children. One brother, Harold, lives in Tampa, Florida, as well as his mother, Agnes Briggs. One sister, Barbara Briggs Yancey, lives in Lakeland, Florida.

James, Betty, Michael and John Briggs

Jim's father, Harold Briggs, was born May 1, 1899 in Manchester, England. He was the son of Percy Briggs and Anne Bedford Briggs, both of Manchester, England. When he was 17 years old, the family moved to Cleveland, Ohio, where Mr. Briggs was a brick mason. Jim's mother, Agnes Vick Briggs, was born February 2, 1907, in Meigs, Georgia. She is the daughter of Ezekial Vick and Katharine Johnston Vick.

Jim attended school in Tampa, Florida through the eighth grade. He and his brother, Harold, attended high school at St. Andrews School in Sewanee, Tennessee, graduating in 1957. He served in the United States Navy from 1957 to 1961. He attended Georgia State University from 1973 to 1975. He worked as Office Manager for Dresser Industries in Atlanta, Georgia from 1969 to 1978. Jim attended Mid-America School of Mortuary Science in Jeffersonville, Indiana, graduating in 1981. He has been employed at the Upton Funeral Home since 1979. Jim enjoys reading, computers and sailing. He is a member of the Celina Lions Club and the Tennessee Funeral Directors Association.

Jim was married to Betty Sue Upton on December 11, 1971, in Atlanta, Georgia. Betty was born July 17, 1945 in Cookeville, Tennessee.

She is the daughter of Willie Butler Upton, born May 27, 1921 in Celina, Tennessee, and Edwina Smith Upton, born March 4, 1925 in Celina, Tennessee. She is the granddaughter of Mary Velma Goodpasture Smith and the late Thomas Cecil Smith and Belle Butler Upton and the late Willie Clayton Upton, all of Celina, Tennessee.

Betty attended Clay County Schools, graduating from Celina High School in 1963. She graduated from Tennessee Technological University in 1967. She worked at the Tennessee Department of Public Welfare, as a counselor from 1967 to 1970, before moving to Atlanta, Georgia. She was employed at Peachtree-Parkwood Psychiatric Hospital in Atlanta, from 1970 to 1973.

Jim and Betty moved from Atlanta to Celina in 1978. Jim was employed at the Clay County Ambulance Service before entering Mid-America School of Mortuary Science. Betty was employed at Tennessee Department of Human Services from 1981-1985 as a social counselor.

Jim and Betty are the parents of Michael Butler Briggs, born October 10, 1973, and John Harold Briggs, born January 22, 1975. Michael and John are both students at Celina K-8 School.

SAMUEL BROWN

Samuel Brown was born in 1826 in Jackson County, Tennessee. He married Adalaine (Adeline) Masters of Hilham, Tennessee. She was born in 1836, the daughter of James and Polly Masters. Adeline had two brothers, William, born in 1832, and Hillary, born in 1840, and two sisters, Sarah, born in 1841 who married Bill Daugherty, and Tennessee, born in 1844 who married (first name unknown) Christian.

Samuel was a farmer in what is now the Arcot Community of Clay County. In 1956, an elderly Arcot resident described him as "a fine figure of a man who rode a great black horse." Samuel served in the Confederate Army. On one occasion, the Yankee Army came to his home searching for him, but they failed to find him as his wife, Adalaine (Adeline), had hidden him in the garden by covering him with sweet potato vines.

James McHenry Brown and John Breckinridge Brown

Samuel and Adalaine had ten children. John Breckenridge, born in 1860, married Ida Chapman July 1, 1892. They had eight children. John Breckenridge died on October 8, 1947, and Ida died January 3, 1958. James McHenry "Jim" was born January 6, 1861. He married Martha Jane Harpe July 3, 1889. They had thirteen children. "Jim" died November 23, 1944, and Martha died September 3, 1956. Sib was born in 1857. He married Lou Edwards. They had four children: John B.; Mary, who first married B. Tom Morris and later remarried after moving to

East Tennessee; Mamie, who married Thomas Hayes; and Gypsy Ann, born December 18, 1884, who married Walter G. Masters, born June 3, 1877. Gypsy Ann and Walter were married October 18, 1905. Gypsy died February 23, 1968, and Walter Masters died February 4, 1960. Sib died at an early age and is buried in the McColgin Cemetery.

Mollie was born July 22, 1863. She married H.T. Harpe, who was born September 11, 1854. They had twelve children. Sarah was born in 1866. She married Jim Eldridge. they had two children, Robbie and Hugh. Mattie, born in 1868, married Rucker Dale. They had two children. Belle, born in 1870, married Walter Thompson. They had three children, Effie and twins, Daisy and Violet. Stone, age 11, and Bea, age 9, both died of yellow fever. Sarah, Mattie, Rhettie, and Belle all left Tennessee and moved to Texas. All of the sons remained in Tennessee.

Samuel died November 9, 1903; and Adalaine (Adeline) died February 5, 1922. Both are buried in the McColgin Cemetery in the Arcot Community.

JAMES McHENRY "JIM" AND MARTHA BROWN

James McHenry "Jim" Brown was the second son of Samuel and Adalaine (Adeline) Masters Brown. He was born January 6, 1861. He married Martha Jane "Sis" Harpe July 3, 1889. Martha Jane was born January 7, 1872, the daughter of H.T. and Mary (Sarah) Atchley Harpe. After Martha Jane's mother died, her father, H.T. Harpe, married Jim Brown's sister, Mollie Brown; thereby making H.T., Jim's father-in-law and his brother-in-law and making Mollie, Martha's stepmother and her sister-in-law.

James McHenry "Jim" and Martha Jane "Sis" Brown

Jim's first farm was just above the Arcot School. He sold this farm and bought a large tract on Dry Creek once owned by Samuel and then Denton Mack Plumlee. Jim and Martha Jane were almost totally self-sufficient during this era; and what they could not produce themselves, they purchased from riverboats, the store at Butler's Landing, and later from "rolling stores" which came through the neighborhood.

Jim and Martha had thirteen children. All thirteen lived to adulthood. Herman, born May 5, 1890, attended school at Montvale Academy. He married Versie Crowder, born October 15, 1895, the daughter of Smith and Armentia (Mintie) Brown Crowder, January 8, 1911. They had seven children. Herman died May 9, 1960. Versie died June 20, 1980. They are buried in the Macedonia Cemetery.

Jefferson Davis (J.D.), born December 10, 1891, married Bertha Pedigo, the daughter of James and Martha Pedigo, December 23, 1914.

They had two daughters. J.D. died May 11, 1944. Bertha died June 26, 1964. They are buried in the McColgin Cemetery.

Adam, born January 16, 1893, married Fannie Sallee, born April 6, 1899, the daughter of Abram T. and Mollie Martin Sallee, on October 14, 1917. They had one daughter, Ada Dean. Adam died of influenza during World War I on October 6, 1918. He is buried in the McColgin Cemetery.

Hunter "Bill" was born November 25, 1895. He served in the Army during World War I. He was a victim of rheumatoid arthritis and was paralized the last eight years of his life. He died November 7, 1974, and is buried in the McColgin Cemetery.

Bob "Brack", born June 13, 1898, married Elsie Eads, born April 9, 1899, the daughter of Barlow and Mattie White Eads, on December 23, 1923. They had five children. Bob and Elsie lived in the Pine Hill Community where Bob was a farmer. Elsie died April 12, 1976 and Bob died February 28, 1977. They are buried in the Kendall Cemetery in the Pine Hill Community.

Luke "Ben", born October 4, 1899, married Cora Craighead, born March 28, 1903, the daughter of Willie and Martha Gulley Craighead, on April 3, 1919. They had eleven children. Luke and Cora lived in the Pine Hill Community where Luke was a farmer. He served one term as district road supervisor. Luke died August 28, 1985 and is buried in the Moss Cemetery.

Jesse "Fay", born August 31, 1901, married Minnie Welch, born June 10, 1911, the daughter of Clint and Mandy Rich Welch, on October 2, 1927. They had eight children. Jesse and Minnie lived in the Pine Hill Community where Jesse was a farmer. Jesse died March 21, 1980 and is buried in the Moss Cemetery.

Sam T. "Slick", born November 16, 1903, married Gladys Gilpatrick, born August 24, 1905, the daughter of James and Mattie Masters Gilpatrick, on November 5, 1922. Sam worked until his retirement in Detroit, Michigan. He returned to Celina to farm after his retirement. He and Gladys have five children.

Ethel, born September 9, 1905, married Lonnie Crowder, born April 30, 1902, the son of Bishop Radford and Mary Plumlee Crowder, on September 23, 1923. They have one daughter. Lonnie died August 11, 1963 and is buried in the McColgin Cemetery.

Willette, born January 26, 1908, married Ivo Pedigo, born November 17, 1904, the son of James and Martha Pedigo, on August 24, 1924. They have four children. Ivo died September 28, 1952. He is buried at Hermitage Springs.

Malcolm, born April 1, 1910, married Iva Rich, born June 14, 1915, the daughter of Albert Grundy and Melissa Denton Rich, on March 23, 1930. They have three children. Malcolm died February 2, 1978, and Iva died May 14, 1978. They are buried at Union Hill.

Lillie, born July 15, 1913, married Vanus Eads, born April 4, 1912, the son of Barlow and Mattie White Eads, on November 26, 1933. They have two children.

Cordell "Pete", born April 22, 1916, married Ada Short, born April 3, 1914, the daughter of Sally and Frank Short, on June 3, 1933. They had four children. Cordell next married Maude Evitts of Michigan and they have three children.

Cordell lives in Michigan.

"Jim" Brown died November 23, 1944. Martha Jane Brown died September 3, 1956. They are buried in the McColgin Cemetery.

J.D. AND BERTHA BROWN

Jefferson Davis (J.D.) Brown was born December 10, 1891. He was the son of James McHenry and Martha Harpe Brown of the Arcot Community. He married Bertha Pearl Pedigo December 23, 1914. Bertha was born May 24, 1895, the daughter of James and Martha Pedigo of Oak Grove. J.D. attended Montvale Academy. Bertha taught school at New Hope and Highland before her marriage.

J.D., Jewell and Bertha Brown

J.D. was a farmer in the Dry Creek area of the Arcot Community. Bertha taught school in their home for a term so that the children in this area would not have to go so far to attend school. J.D. and Bertha were devout members of the Church of Christ. J.D. was a song leader for the Arcot Church of Christ and later for the Turkey Creek Church of Christ.

J.D. and Bertha had two daughters, Jewell Elizabeth, born on December 1, 1915, and Fannie Mae, born October 4, 1922. Fannie Mae married Carmon Mabry and they have four children, Brenda, Dale, Linda, and Mark.

J.D. died May 11, 1944, Bertha died June 26, 1964. They are buried in the McColgin Cemetery at Arcot.

Bob and Elsie Brown

BOB AND ELSIE BROWN

Bob Brown was born June 13, 1898, the son of James McHenry and Martha Jane Harpe Brown. He married Elsie Eads on December 23, 1923. Elsie was the daughter of Barlow and Mattie White Eads. She was born April 9, 1899. Bob was a farmer in the Pine Hill Community of Clay County. He and Elsie were members of the Arcot Church of Christ. They had five children, Gertrude, Barlow, Eulis, Daniel, and Melvin.

Gertrude married Jack Green June 1, 1946. They have two children, Richard and Patricia, and three grandchildren.

Barlow married Billie J. Johnson December 23, 1949. They have three children, Ronnie, Jimmy, and Judy. They have five grandchildren.

Eulis married Jean Crowder December 23, 1949. They have two children, Pam and Kelley. They have one grandchild.

Melvin married Linda Rose Cherry September 4, 1965. They have two children, Melissa and Jamie.

Elsie died April 12, 1976. Bob died February 28, 1977. They are buried in the Kendall Cemetery in the Pine Hill Community.

LUKE AND CORA BROWN

Luke Brown was born October 4, 1899, the son of James McHenry and Martha Jane Harpe Brown of the Arcot Community of Clay County On April 3, 1919, he married Cora Craighead, born March 28, 1903, the daughter of Willie and Martha Gulley Craighead. Luke and Cora lived most of their married lives in the Pine Hill Community where Luke was a farmer. He served one term as a district highway supervisor. He and Cora were members of the Pine Hill Church of Christ.

Luke and Cora Brown

Luke and Cora were the parents of eleven children — seven sons and four daughters. Three of the children died in infancy.

Willie Jim (Tom) was born December 18, 1921. He married Mona Moore, the daughter of Esco and Nora Eads Moore. They have six children: Buster, Eldon (deceased), Clyde, Dianna, Joy and Wendy. Clyde married Peggy Overstreet, and they have one daughter, Hannah. Dianna married Ronnie Webb and they have two sons, Mickie and Michael. Joy married Dennis Rhoton, and they have one daughter.

Willis Lee Rue (Biggon) was born May 10, 1924. He was killed in action in World War II on June 2, 1945 in the Philippine Islands (Luzon). He is buried in the Arlington National Cemetery in Virginia.

Iva Dean was born on February 13, 1926. She married Vancil Eads, the son of Ocrus and Melvina Plumlee Eads. They have four children: twins that died at birth, Randall and Vonda. Randall married Tony Pierce, and they have a son, David. Randall has a daughter, Melissa, by a previous marriage. Vonda married Johnny Gulley, and they have three children: Rachel, Jonathan and Joshua.

Robert Eugene was born August 21, 1929. He married Louise Moss, the daughter of Raymond and Maudie Moss. They have one son, Ronnie who has three children. Robert died May 31, 1950. He is buried in the Moss Cemetery.

Martha Bonnell (Pat) was born December 26, 1931. She married Clarence Turner, the son of

Sid and Katherine Smith Turner. They have four children, John David, Kathy (deceased), Timothy, and Tammy. John David married Margie Boles, and they have twins, Shana and Trever. John David has a son, J.J., by a previous marriage. Timothy married Vonda Birdwell. Tammy married Kenny Birdwell, and they have one son, T.J.

Elbert Aaron was born on April 19, 1934. He married Frances Plumlee, the daughter of Ed and Alice Pruitt Plumlee. They have five children, Danny, Deborah, Sherry, Stacey, and an infant that died at birth. Danny has one son, Jamie. Deborah married Larry Sagar, and they have one daughter, Amy. Deborah also has a daughter, Kristy, by a previous marriage. Sherry married Arnold Holman, and they have two children, Wesley and Lorie. Stacey married Karon Berrhop.

Clyde Thurman (Fiddler) was born September 28, 1936. He married Martha Scott, the daughter of Marvin and Edress Watson Scott. They have two sons, Martin and Michael.

Mary Louise was born November 7, 1939. She married Joe Melton, the son of Herman and Mary Sevier Melton. They have three children: Stephen, Beth, and Samuel. Stephen married Patsy Webb. Beth married Steve Forkum. Sam is a student at Celina High School.

Luke died August 28, 1985. He is buried in the Moss Cemetery.

JESSE AND MINNIE BROWN

Jesse Brown was born August 31, 1901, the son of James McHenry and Martha Harpe Brown. He grew up in the Dry Creek Section of the Arcot Community. He attended school at Arcot.

Minnie and Jesse Brown

On October 2, 1927, he married Minnie Welch, the daughter to Clint and Mandy Rich Welch. Minnie was born June 10, 1911.

Jesse and Minnie bought a farm in the Pine Hill Community early in their married life and moved there.

Jesse and Minnie had eight children. Elise lives in Nashville, where she is a seamstress and makes costumes for the country music entertainers. Wayne and Glen Carrol "Tiny" both work in Indiana. Billie Dorris died in infancy. Clint married Mable Brady and they live in Hendersonville. Juanita married David Cherry (deceased). She works at OshKosh B'Gosh at Hermitage Springs. Joanna married Herman Rhoton. She works at OshKosh B'Gosh at Hermitage Springs. Roy married Shirley Brady. He lives in the Pine Hill Community where he is a farmer.

Jesse attended the Pine Hill Church of Christ, where he was a member for several years. Jesse died March 21, 1980. Minnie still lives at Pine Hill and attends the Pine Hill Church of Christ, where she has been a member for several years.

SAM AND GLADYS BROWN

Sam Turner Brown was born November 16, 1903. He was the son of James McHenry and Martha Jane Harpe Brown of the Arcot Community. On November 5, 1922, he married Gladys Gilpatrick, the daughter of William and Mattie Masters Gilpatrick of Overton County. Gladys was born August 24, 1905 in Overton County.

The Sam T. Brown Family

Sam and Gladys worked in Detroit, Michigan for approximately twenty years before they retired and moved back to Celina, Tennessee. Sam is a farmer and operates a trailer court; and Gladys is a housewife. Sam is an avid fisherman and gardener. Sam and his son, Francis Selvin "Brownie", founded the Clay County Nursing Home in Celina. Sam and Gladys attend the Celina Church of Christ.

Sam and Gladys had five children. Francis Selvin "Brownie" married Norma Dean Key. "Brownie" was a farmer. He was a member of the Clay County Court, and a member of various civic organizations. Brownie died June 25, 1978. Norma works at OshKosh B'Gosh and lives in Celina. Brownie and Norma have two sons, Keith and Mike, who live in Lebanon. They both work in the trucking industry. Mike married Debbie Bailey; and they have two children, Johnny and Brandi. Keith married Beverly Sharp; and they have two children, Allison and Adam.

Eva Nell married Bill Redmond. Eva Nell received her Bachelor of Science Degree from David Lipscomb College and her Masters Degree from Tennessee State University. She attended the University of Tennessee in Knoxville where she worked on her doctorate. She taught at David Lipscomb College in the Department of Home Economics. She is presently employed at Opryland, U.S.A. in Nashville. Bill worked at Dale Hollow Dam, Old Hickory Dam, and retired while he was working for the Corps of Engineers at Percy Priest Dam. Bill and Eva Nell live in Donelson, Tennessee.

Dora Lee married Lewis Walker. She lives in Tipton, Indiana. She has worked at Delco in Kokomo, Indiana for approximately 30 years. She and Lewis have one daughter, Donna. Donna married Carl Wright of Doyle, Tennessee, and they have three boys, Timothy, Christopher, and Zachary. They live in Tipton, Indiana, where Carl is a Church of Christ preacher and Donna works part-time in a flower shop.

James Turner married Evelyn Strong. James is a construction worker; and Evelyn works at OshKosh in Celina. James and Evelyn have one daughter, Kandi. Kandi received her Bachelor of Science Degree from Tennessee Technological

University. She is currently working and attending school in New Mexico. James and Evelyn live near Moss, Tennessee.

Jean married Perry Richard "Dick" Royse. Jean is an L.P.N. and works part-time at the Clay County Hospital. Both Jean and "Dick" were previously employed as administrators of the Clay County Nursing Home. Dick is a retired Naval officer. Jean and Dick attend Celina Church of Christ. They have four children: Mike, Pat, Tammy, and Bill and one granddaughter, Shannon Renee. Jean and Dick enjoy outdoor recreational activities, particularly houseboating on Dale Hollow Lake. Dick also serves as part-time preacher for the Church of Christ.

CORDELL BROWN

Cordell "Pete" Brown was born April 22, 1916. He was the youngest child of James McHenry and Martha Jane Harpe Brown. He spent his early years in the Arcot Community. On June 3, 1933, he married Ada Short, the daughter of Sally and Frank Short of the Pine Hill Community of Clay County. Cordell farmed during the early years of their marriage. They had four children: Anna Jane, Lonnie Alvin, Nelda Ruth, and Daisy Lou. All four of these children now reside in Clay County.

Cordell Brown

In the mid 1940's Cordell moved to Michigan where he still resides. After he and Ada divorced, he married Maude Evitts of Michigan. They have three children: Mela Louise, William Russell, and David Lee. Cordell is retired and now enjoys hunting and fishing.

FRANCIS "BROWNIE" BROWN

"Brownie" Brown was born on July 29, 1924. He was the son of Sam T. and Gladys Gilpatrick Brown. He was the grandson of James McHenry and Martha Jane Harpe Brown and "Bill" and Mattie Gilpatrick of Overton County. "Brownie" grew up in the Arcot Community and attended school there.

On August 29, 1948, he married Norma Key. Norma was born on October 9, 1931, the daughter of Ester and Ina Short Key of the Kettle Creek Community. They left Clay County in 1948 and went to Detroit, Michigan. "Brownie" worked for Hudson Motor Car and then for Jones Transfer Company. In 1959, they returned to Clay County to a farm they had purchased on Knob Creek in the Arcot Community. They farmed there until 1977, when they sold the Knob Creek farm and moved to a farm they purchased on Pine Branch known as the Edens and Cordell Hull Farm.

"Brownie" served on the Clay County Court. He and his father, Sam T., were instrumental in the development and construction of the Clay

County Nursing Home, and "Brownie" served as the first president (chairman) of its Board of Directors. He was a member of the Celina Lions Club and took part in numerous community and civic activities. He was a member of the Arcot Church of Christ and was very active in all the activities of the church.

Norma worked on the farm; then at OshKosh B'Gosh; then at the Dairy Queen when it was owned by her son, Michael; then for the Upper Cumberland Human Resource Agency; and then back to OshKosh. Norma has always been active in civic affairs. She is a member of the Arcot Church of Christ where she is a Sunday School teacher.

Norma and "Brownie" have two sons, Michael and Keith. Michael was born September 18, 1950, and Keith was born August 31, 1957. Both sons graduated from Celina High School. Michael graduated from Middle Tennessee State University. Michael married Debbie Bailey, and they have two children, Johnny and Brandi. Keith married Beverly Sharp, and they have two children, Allison and Adam. Both families live in Lebanon, Tennessee.

"Brownie" died June 25, 1978. He is buried in the McColgin Cemetery in the Arcot Community. Norma now resides in Celina.

EZRA (SPUDDY) BROWN

Ezra Brown was born November 28, 1920 in the Arcot Community of Clay County. He was the second son of the late Jesse Herman and Versie Lee Crowder Brown. He was the grandson of the late James McHenry and Martha Jane Harpe Brown, and Smith (Son) and Armentia (Minty) Brown Crowder.

Ezra (Spuddy) Brown

Ezra attended school at Midway. He farmed, worked at sawmills, and he worked at a United States Warehouse in Michigan until he left to serve in the Army on July 17, 1941. He took his basic training at Fort Oglethorpe, Georgia. He served in England for one year where he was a cook at the First General Hospital. He was discharged December 10, 1946 with the rank of Corporal. He went back to farming, logging, and his speciality, cooking. He has cooked at several different places. He is presently cooking at James and Linda's Barbeque in Celina.

On January 19, 1946, he married Grace Marie Pitcock. The wedding took place in Tompkinsville, Kentucky. Grace is the oldest daughter of Otis Clyde Pitcock and the late Eula C. Mayberry Pitcock. She is the granddaughter of Bethel and Mary Elizabeth Philpot Pitcock and Amos Wesley and Mary Elizabeth Langford Mayberry. She attended school at New Liberty in Overton County and Dry Creek in Clay County. She is presently

employed at OshKosh B'Gosh in Celina, where she has worked for 30 years. She has served on the Board of Directors for the Cordell Hull Economic Opportunity Corporation from 1981-1986, representing the United Garment Workers of America Local 401.

Ezra and Grace attend the Arcot Church of Christ. Ezra was one of the organizers of the Brown Reunion held each year on the Sunday closest to the Fourth of July.

Ezra and Grace have four children: Eddy Clyde, born November 1, 1946; Mary Lee, born December 15, 1947; Jerry Dwayne, born December 9, 1949; and Priscilla Ann, born March 6, 1951.

EDDY CLYDE BROWN

Eddy Clyde Brown was born November 1, 1946 in Cookeville, Tennessee. Eddy is the first son of Ezra and Grace Marie Brown. He is the grandson of the late Herman and Versa Crowder Brown, and Otis Pitcock and the late Eula Pitcock.

Eddy Clyde Brown

Eddy attended Celina Elementary School and graduated from Celina High School in 1964. Eddy was inducted into the service in 1966. He served in field communications in the Vietnam Conflict; and he also served a tour in Germany. He was discharged in 1969 with the rank of sergeant. After leaving service he attended State Tech in Memphis and Volunteer State College in Gallatin, Tennessee. He presently owns and manages Salvage Paneling Center in Madison, Tennessee.

Eddy married Janice Kay Morrow March 27, 1970, the daughter of John Thomas Morrow and the late Margaret Jewell Morrow of Madison, Tennessee. Eddy and Janice have two children — John Steven and Natalie Rochelle. Eddy, Janice, John and Natalie now reside in Hendersonville, Tennessee.

JERRY DWAYNE BROWN

Jerry Dwayne Brown was born December 9, 1949 in Moss, Tennessee. He is the second son of Ezra "Spuddy" Brown and Grace Pitcock Brown. He lived in Moss, Tennessee. with his brother, Eddy Clyde, and sisters, Mary Lee and Priscilla. Jerry is the grandson of the late Jessie Herman Brown and Versie Lee Crowder Brown of Moss, Tennessee and Otis Clyde Pitcock and the late Eula C. Mayberry Pitcock of Celina, Tennessee.

Jerry attended Celina Elementary School and graduated from Celina High School in 1967. He served in the United States Army from 1969 to 1971. He served 17 months in Germany. He is presently employed at the Cordell Hull Power Plant at Carthage, Tennessee. He lives on the Old Bennett's Ferry Road on the M.D. Cherry

Jerry Dwayne Brown

place in Arcot. He enjoys hunting and woodworking.

Jerry married Ruth E. Meadows on December 20, 1969 at the Celina Church of Christ. Ruth was born March 31, 1950 in Toledo, Ohio. She is the daughter of Mike and Nellie Walker Meadows Schassberger and the late Luke Lee Meadows of Clay County. She is the granddaughter of Mackie Anderson Walker and the late Wade Walker and the late B.E. and Etta Jane Wheeler Meadows of Clay County. Ruth graduated from Lucas County High School in 1968. She attended Stautzenburger College of Business in Toledo, Ohio. Ruth has worked at Clay County Manor, Incorporated since May of 1975.

Jerry and Ruth are the parents of two children. Jeffery Dwayne was born December 7, 1972, and Misty Lou was born November 11, 1976. Jeff and Misty enjoy the sports programs. Jeff plays football and summer baseball. He also participates in 4-H Club activities. Misty plays little league softball. They are students at Celina K-8 School.

MARY LEE BROWN HAMPTON

Mary Lee Brown Hampton was born December 15, 1947 in the Arcot Community of Clay County. She is the oldest daughter of Ezra and Grace Marie Pitcock Brown. She is the granddaughter of the late Jessie Herman and Versie Lee Crowder Brown and Otis Pitcock and the late Eula C. Pitcock.

Mary Lee attended first grade at Arcot Elementary School. After the school closed in 1954, she attended Celina Elementary School and graduated from Celina High School in 1965. Mary Lee attended Tennessee Technological University in Cookeville, Tennessee.

On September 1, 1968, Mary Lee married L. Alan Hampton, of Nashville, Tennessee. The wedding was held at the Celina Methodist Church. Alan was born June 10, 1946 in Davenport, Iowa. He is the son of the late Richard Ray Hampton and Georgia Baker Hampton Smith. He graduated from Tennessee Technological University in 1968. Mary Lee and Alan lived in Fort Richardson, Alaska from 1968 to 1971, while Alan was serving in the United States Army. They next lived in Harlingen, Texas and San Antonio, Texas. In 1977, they returned to Tennessee residing in Goodlettsville. They presently live in Nashville at 3003 Hobbs Road.

Mary Lee and Alan have two daughters, Lynne Ann, born July 23, 1970 in Anchorage, Alaska, and Melissa Lee, born May 12, 1975 in San Antonio, Texas. They attend Harpeth Hall School in Nashville where they are active in drama, music, and dance programs. One of their favorite past-times is a trip to the country — Clay County!

After seventeen years in the communications industry, Alan and Mary Lee formed their own company, New Tech Communications in 1985. The company currently sells, installs, and services cellular mobile telephones and is planning to expand into other areas of communication.

PRISCILLA ANN BROWN TINNON

Priscilla Ann Brown Tinnon, the youngest child of Ezra and Grace Marie Pitcock Brown, was born March 6, 1952 in the Dry Creek Section of the Arcot Community of Clay County. She was born in the house where her paternal grandparents, Jessie Herman and Versie Lee Crowder Brown, raised their children. This house was restored in 1981 by Priscilla's brother, Jerry Dwayne Brown, and her great uncle, Vanus "Sandy" Eads. It is fondly known as "The Old House," and she and her brother, Eddy Clyde Brown, now own it.

Her maternal grandparents are Otis Clyde Pitcock and the late Eula C. Pitcock, who once lived in the old Hugh Roberts' log house in Celina.

Priscilla attended Celina Elementary School. She graduated from Celina High School in 1970 and attended Middle Tennessee State University where she met Frank "Bobby" Robertson Tinnon of Goodlettsville, Tennessee. They were married July 10, 1971 at the Celina Methodist Church of Celina, Tennessee.

Bobby was born September 30, 1949 in Davidson County. He is the son of the late Frank Robertson Tinnon and Sara Wallace Wade Tinnon. Bobby attended school at Goodlettsville Elementary School, Goodlettsville High School; and he graduated from Sewanee Military Academy in 1967 and from Middle Tennessee State University in 1974.

Priscilla and Bobby have one daughter, Amanda Brown Tinnon, born September 4, 1980. Amanda attends Davidson Christian Academy in Nashville, Tennessee.

Priscilla is presently employed part-time at Trickett Oldsmobile-Honda in Madison, Tennessee. Bobby is employed at Fiberglass Specialists, Incorporated in Goodlettsville, Tennessee.

Priscilla, Bobby and Amanda now reside in Goodlettsville, Tennessee.

REED BROWN

Reed Brown was born April 4, 1923 on Dry Creek near Moss, Tennessee. He is the sixth child of Herman Brown, born on May 5, 1890 and died May 9, 1960, and Versie (Crowder) Brown, born October 15, 1897 and died June 20, 1980. Reed had four sisters. They are Ila (deceased), Oline (deceased), Edith Odle Netherton of Moss, Tennessee and Louise (deceased). He had three brothers, Ray (Cap) (deceased), Ezra (Spuddie) of Moss, Tennessee and Raymond of Cookeville, Tennessee.

Hilda, Reed and Gary Brown

Reed was married to Louise Rich, born May 20, 1927, on December 28, 1948. She was the daughter of Sid and Kate (Stockton) Rich. Louise had two brothers, Clifton and Tim Rich, both of Celina, Tennessee. Louise died March 2, 1977.

Louise Brown

Reed and Louise had three children, Rita Ilene, Hilda Joy, and Gary Neal. Rita was born April 16, 1950. She is married to Thomas Ennis. They have one son, Thomas Christopher Ennis. Woodbury, Tennessee is their hometown. Hilda was born January 20, 1952, and Gary was born April 26, 1958. They both live in the Midway Community near Moss, Tennessee.

Rita, Chris and Thomas Ennis

Reed owns a 220 acre farm in the Midway Community on which he and Gary raise beef cattle and feeder pigs.

JOHN BRECKINRIDGE BROWN

John Breckinridge Brown was born in 1860, the son of Samuel and Adalaine Masters Brown. He was a farmer in the Arcot Community of Clay County. On July 1, 1892, he married Ida Chapman. They had eight children. Frank married Hester Rogers on September 5, 1913. They lived in the Butler's Landing Community of Clay County. Frank served as Clay County Highway Commissioner for a number of years. Frank died November 3, 1981; and Hester died October 21, 1974. They are buried in the Butler's Landing Cemetery.

Bertha married Wade Stone December 25, 1912. They lived in the Arcot Community where Wade was a farmer. They had four children: John T., Robert Lewis, Billy, and Marie. Bertha died November 10, 1971. Wade and Bertha are buried in the Stone Cemetery in the Beech Bethany Community of Clay County.

Lester married Lattie Cherry October 29, 1916. They lived in the Arcot Community of Clay County. Lester was a farmer, a district road supervisor, and a member of the Clay County Court. Lester died on January 13, 1981. He and Lattie are buried in the Brown Family Cemetery in the Arcot Community.

Ida Chapman Brown (center), Ethel Crowder, Mary Wood, Jewell Brown, Alvirta Brown Copas, and Fannie Mae Brown Mabry, and Pauline Pedigo Carver

Maude married James Robinson December 29, 1927. Maude resides in the Arcot Community of Clay County. She has two children. James Edward lives in Lebanon; and Norma Jean (Hawkins) lives at Arcot.

Charlie married Pearl Spears December 26, 1925. They live in the Arcot Community. They had six children. Charlie is a farmer. He, at one time, drove a grader for the Clay County Highway Department. Pearl is a retired schoolteacher.

Jack married Marie Farris November 10, 1926. Marie was the daughter of Hubert and Laura Crowder Farris. Jack and Marie lived on Brimstone for a number of years where Jack was a farmer and a logger. They later purchased a farm near Fountain Run, Kentucky and moved there. Jack died on July 22, 1965; and Marie died January 30, 1986. They are buried near Fountain Run.

Homer married Captola Pitcock October 29, 1942. They lived in the Arcot Community where Homer was a farmer. Captola taught school in the Clay County School System until her retirement. Homer died November 10, 1965. He is buried in the Pitcock Cemetery near Oak Grove. After Homer's death, Captola moved to Oak Grove.

Carmon, Ida Lou, Lavelle and Melvin Brown

Alvirtta married Eula Copas September 12, 1936. Eula was a farmer. He and Alvirtta owned a farm between Arcot and Moss. Alvirtta was a teacher with the Clay County School System, and she also served as Attendance Supervisor. At the time of her retirement, she was teaching at Celina High School. Eula died January 3, 1977. He is buried in the Pitcock Cemetery near Oak Grove. After Eula's death, Alvirtta moved to Celina, where she now resides.

John Breckinridge died October 8, 1947. Ida died January 3, 1958. They are buried in the Brown (Langford) Cemetery on the farm they owned in the Arcot Community.

ARMON LESTER BROWN

Lester Brown was born on December 9, 1896 in Clay County, Tennessee. He was one of eight children born to John B. Brown and Ida Chapman Brown. Farming was his main occupation. He served as District Road Supervisor and was a member of Clay County Court. Lester owned real estate in Celina, including the original law office of Cordell Hull who served as Secretary of State to President Franklin D. Roosevelt. He was instrumental in establishing the Clay County Hospital. In 1916 he married Lattie Cherry. Lattie was one of ten children, born February 7, 1900 to William J. Cherry and Mary Lou Dalton. The first years of their married life were spent in the Turkey Creek Community, but the most of their lives were spent in the Arcot Community. They lived in the Dr. Wilson McColgan home, a famous landmark in the County. The home was built of brick made on Dr. McColgan's farm by slaves in 1858. Lester and Lattie were the parents of four children, Carmon Cornell, Lavelle, Melvin Lester and Ida Lou. Lattie died April 15, 1958; Lester died January 13, 1981. Melvin inherited the old homeplace.

Carmon was born October 3, 1917. After graduating from Celina High School, he attended college at Tennessee Polytechnic Institute where he received his Bachelor of Science degree. In 1936, he married Frankie Mayfield. They lived in Celina. Carmon and Frankie were the parents of two children, Lester Mayfield and Carmon Mel. Carmon taught in the elementary schools of Clay County for years and served as principal of Celina High School. He served as Superintendent of Clay County Schools during the years of 1965 to 1967, dying before his term expired. Frankie continued his term of office.

Lavelle was born on October 21, 1919. After finishing high school, she went to Western Kentucky State Teachers College for two years, then transferred to The University of Tennessee where she received a Bachelor of Science degree. She taught elementary school in Clay County one year and taught home economics in high school in Benton, Tennessee one year. Then she served as University of Tennessee Extension Home Agent (4-H Club Work) in Winchester, Tennessee. In those years when one married she had to quit working in this position. In 1947, Lavelle married Leo Alvin Sharp. They live in Sevierville, Tennessee. They are the parents of one child, Leo Alvin, Jr.

Melvin was born October 7, 1921. After finishing high school, he entered college at Tennessee Polytechnic Institute before World War II; then he entered service school at Purdue University as a member of the Naval Air Corps. His training was in aviation, radio and gunnery. After the war, he went back to Tennessee Polytechnic Institute and got a Bachelor of Science degree. He was football coach at Benton, Tennessee. In 1949, he married Katherine Watson. They were the parents of three children, Lester Watson, William Mack, and Melvin Eddy. They lived in Celina while he served as Superintendent of Clay County Schools during the years of 1948 to 1958. Then they moved to Cookeville, where he owned a sporting goods store.

Ida Lou was born July 11, 1932. After finishing high school, she attended The University of Tennessee where she received the following degrees: Bachelor of Science, Master of Science, and a doctorate in education. In 1952 Ida Lou married William Alexander Stephens. They had four children, Melaney Lou, Billie Michelle, Armon Bates, and William Alexander, Jr. She served as Bledsoe County School Lunch Supervisor and University of Tennessee Extension Home Demonstration agent in Pikeville. After moving to Knoxville, she was an elementary school classroom teacher and is now principal of Linden Elementary School in Oak Ridge. In 1985, Ida Lou married Lee B. Vandewalker. — *Submitted by Lavelle Brown Sharp*

CHARLIE BROWN

Charlie Brown was born in 1903 near Celina at Arcot. He was the fifth son of eight sons and daughters of John B. and Ida Chapman Brown. All of his brothers and sisters are deceased, except Maude Robinson and Alvirtta Copas.

Charlie married Pearl Spear December 26, 1925, the daughter of V.B. and Frances Watson Spear. Pearl had two sisters, Winnie and one who died in infancy. She had two brothers, Dewey Clyde Spear who was killed in Toledo, Ohio in March of 1929, and Raymon Spear who now lives in Nashville.

Charlie and Pearl Brown

Charlie was a farmer and an operator of a county road grader. Pearl taught school for 23 years. She received her college education by commuting to and from Tennessee Tech in Cookeville on Saturdays, in the summers and by taking correspondence courses. Charlie and Pearl are both retired and are living on their farm at Arcot where oil wells were drilled and much oil was produced. They attend the Arcot Church of Christ.

Charlie and Pearl, who have been married for 61 years, have the following children: Joe Clyde who lives in Knoxville; John Edwin who died in 1977 after becoming choked on a piece of steak and is buried in the Brown Family Cemetery on the farm at Arcot; James Carrol, who many know as "Jimmy;" and Jerry Lynn.

WILLIAM LAFAYETTE BROWN

William Lafayette Brown was born November 24, 1858 in Celina, Tennessee. (Jackson County, now Clay County). He was the son of John Jasper Brown and Elizabeth Jane Walker. He married Lillie Maxey, the daughter of Dr. Elza and Nancy Jane Richardson Maxey of Monroe County, Kentucky. He and Lillie had two sons, Luke Walker and Walter Faye, and two daughters, Ethel and Nina. Faye married Minnie Hamilton. They had one daughter, Billie Fay. Luke married Willette Lowry. They had two sons, Lyon and Lyle. Ethel married Horace Anderson. They had two children, Ray Draper and Ruth Brown. Nina

married H.F. Srygley. The had one daughter, Joyce, and two sons, Donald Brown and Hubbard, Jr.

William Lafayette built a large Victorian home on a hill near the town square in Celina. His two sons built homes on each side of him. They operated a general store on the banks of the Cumberland River. The merchandise was brought in on steamboats from Nashville, The river often rose out of its banks during wet seasons and flooded the buildings near the river. Therefore, a new store was built on higher ground on the town square.

W.L. was a leader in the Church of Christ, where he taught Bible classes and preached. He owned a car but never learned to drive. On Sunday afternoons, he would look for someone to take him to other congregations to preach. He was President of the Celina Bank, and he helped to establish the schools in Clay County. He became a close personal friend of Cordell Hull, whom he had known since Cordell was a young man. When W.L. died, Cordell sent Lillie Brown a telegram saying, "I have lost the best friend I ever had." W.L. was a kind and generous man. When his sister, Ethel, and her husband, Horace, died, he took their two children, ages two and four, and gave them a home and sent them to college. When W.L. died, people brought money to his wife and said, "He never sent me a bill."

Billie Fay is the only member of this Brown family now living in Celina, where she was a teacher and librarian until her retirement from the Clay County School System.

ZACHARIAH BROWN

Zachariah Brown, son of John and Jerutha Brown, was born in Virginia (c) 1759. He married Susannah Rippetoe, daughter of Peter and Sary Rippetoe, on the 25th of July in 1798 in Amherst County, Virginia. They migrated to Overton County, (now Clay) Tennessee prior to 1830. Before 1840, they were living in Jackson County in District Five. Their children were: Pleasant W., Catherine, Susannah, Matilda, and probably others. Catherine married Henry Spotwood Painter. Tradition has it that at age 100, Zachariah walked to the river and was baptized. It is believed that he died at age 101, in 1860 and is the Z.B. Brown buried in the Pleas Brown Cemetery on the lower end of Brimstone Creek.

John P. and Sarah A. Brown

Pleasant W. Brown was born in Virginia (c) 1799. He married a lady named Sarah (surname unknown) in Tennessee (c) 1826. He owned many acres of land which were partially in Jackson and Clay Counties after Clay County was formed. Pleasant and Sarah were the parents of 14 children: Lucinda, born (c) 1827; Zachariah, born (c) 1838; James P., born July 17, 1829;

Morening, born (c) 1831; Susannah, born (c) 1839; Elizabeth, born (c) 1841; William C., born (c) 1843; Peter H., born February 1844; Sarah, born (c) 1846; Pleasant S., born January 20, 1848; and David Joel, born 1850. Two of these children, Elizabeth, who married Jim West, and David J., who married Cinderella Plumlee, moved to Arkansas in 1880.

Four sons, William C., John P., Peter H., and Leroy, served in the Confederate Army during the Civil War. Leroy and John both enlisted in the 8th Tennessee Calvary (later called the 13th). Leroy was captured near Perryville by Colonel P.B. Hawkins of the 11th Kentucky Volunteers and was taken to Camp Douglas, Illinois arriving there on January 27, 1862. He died March 12, 1863 and is buried in Oak Woods Cemetery in Chicago, Illinois. John P. served under George Dibrill and Mounce Gore. He was captured and was being taken to Louisville, Kentucky when he managed to escape near Green River. He was captured by the "Home Guards." He fought in the battles of Franklin, Nashville, and Murfreesboro.

John P. married Sarah Ann Plumlee, the daughter of Kendall and Mariar (Johnson) Plumlee, on September 9, 1858. They lived on Turkey Creek and were the parents of ten children: Martha Jane, born 1859; William Washington, born 1861; Zarriah Jackson, born 1866; Araminta Marvella, born 1868; Alonzo Lee, born 1869; Mary Ann, born 1873; Sarah Ellen, born (c) 1875; John Jasper, born March 23, 1878; George Thompson, born 1881; and Rettie Belle, born 1884. John P. sold his one-thirteenth share of his father's estate to P.M. Tinsley on October 9, 1879. Sarah's father willed her the home and land on Turkey Creek on August 30, 1888. John P. and Sarah A. were members of the Church of Christ. They had been married 70 years and 10 days when John P. died in 1928 at the age of 92. Sarah died in 1929 at the age of 88. Both are buried in the Macedonia Cemetery in Clay County

John Jasper Brown first married Lucinda C. Grace December 7, 1899. She was the daughter of Stewart F. and Sarah Mariar (Smith) Grace. John J. and Lucinda were the parents of Arson B. and Aria Glenn. Lucinda died August 21, 1903, and is buried in the Cherry-Denton Cemetery in Union Hill. John J.'s second wife was Nancy Strong, and his third wife was Zelma Denton. John J. died in 1957 in Texas. He was a member of the Church of Christ.

Many descendants of Zachariah and Susannah Brown still live in Clay County, Tennessee and as with any family, many are scattered throughout the United States. — *Submitted by a great, great, great granddaughter — Frankie Estell Brown Johnson.*

BROWNING

The Browning Family is one of the oldest and first families in America.

John Browning was born in 1370 or 1380. He married Elinor Fitz-Nicoll. Their son, William, was born in 1410. His son, John, was born in 1440 and was married in 1465 to Margaret Harding. Their son, Richard, born in 1468, was married in 1490 to Elizabeth Parsons. Their son, John, born in 1519, was married to Joan Tovey in 1541. Their son, John, born in 1554, was married in

1580 to Mary Codrinton. Their son, Captain John, born in 1588 in England, came to America in 1622 on the ship, Abbigail. He settled in Elizabeth City, Virginia and served three terms in the House of Burgesses. His son, William, born about 1615 in England, came to America with his father. He lived at Jamestown, Virginia. His son, John, was born in 1646. He had a son named John, born in either 1666 or 1676. This John had a son named William, born in 1710, in Culpepper County, Virginia. He settled in Maryland. William's son, Charles, was born in 1748 and died in 1821. He was married to Martha Hazlewood, born in 1768 and died December, 16, 1842. She was the daughter of Thomas and Mary (Lancaster) Hazlewood of South Carolina. Mary Lancaster's father was William Lancaster. His father was also William Lancaster. Thomas Hazlewood was the son of Randolph and Ann Hazlewood. Randolph's father was William Hazlewood.

Andrew J. Miles Browning   Nancy Jane (Lundy) Browning

Charles Browning fought in the Revolutionary War. He fought in the Battle of Kings Mountain. He was wounded in that battle. He moved from Union County, South Carolina to Monroe County, Kentucky about 1803. His children were: William, born 1787; Lavinia, born 1790; Nancy, born February 11, 1792; Rebecca, born 1796; Hawkins, born 1797, died 1882; Charles, born 1799; Elizabeth, born 1800; and Martha, born May 8, 1808, died April 15, 1885.

Hawkins Browning was born in 1797 in Union County, South Carolina, and he died in 1882 in Clay County, Tennessee. He married Elizabeth Kirby, who was born in 1804 in Barren County, Kentucky, the daughter of Robert and Kesiah (McCoy) Kirby. Hawkins and Elizabeth moved to Clay County, then a part of Jackson County, Tennessee, around 1830. They lived in the Miles Cross Roads Community. Their children were Hester; Kesiah; Martha, born in 1832; Mary, born in 1836; Robert S.; Anna Jane, born in 1839, died in 1908; Meredith; and James.

Martha Browning, born in 1832, married John C. Biles. Their children were: William, Scott, Elizabeth, Katherine, Margaret, James, Emeline, and Pleas T.

Anna Jane Browning was born in 1839 and died in 1908. She married John Jackson Miles, born in 1835 and died in 1923. Their eldest son, Andrew Jackson, was born in 1862 and died in 1893. He married Nancy Jane Lundy, born in 1859 and died in 1920. They had three children, Martha Alice, Lucy Bee, born May 20, 1886, and Maggie.

HENRY RICH BROWNING

Henry Rich Browning was born March 5, 186? He married Arie Russell November 25, 188? She was the daughter of Silas and Matilda (Cornwell) Russell. Rice and Ari had the following children: Mary Elizabeth, born 1885; William Seldon, born 1887; Silas Radford, born 1890; Matilda Susan, born 1892, died 1964; Nellie C., born June 13, 1885, died April 15, 1979; Loma Almeda, born 1898, died 1973; Robert Lee, born 1900, died 1972; Charlie Edward, born 1904, died 1979; Mattie Avo, born 1907, died 1936; Dire Estes, born 1910, died 1965.

Henry R. and Arie Browning

Nellie Browning married Lester Braden Davis, born April 24, 1892, died September 14, 1965. They had the following children: Bertha Olene, born 1914, died 1928; Loma Irene, born 1916; Bedford Leonard, born 1917; Brady Milford, born 1919; Thadius Hilman, born and died 1921; Hillus Guy, born 1923; Ulyes Hershell, born 1925, died 1972; Helen Annise, born 1928; Charles Elbert, born 1933; Carl Delbert, born and died 1933; and Clyde Carvel, born 1935.

Irene Davis married James William Bean. Children: Wendell Leonard, born 1941; Linda June, born 1945, died 1949; James William, III, born 1951; Brenda Jean, born 1954. Wendell Bean married Dorothy Duke, and they had one child, Tracy. Jimmy Bean married Nancy Hudson, and they had two children, Christal and Melanie. Brenda Bean married David Williams, and they have one child, Joseph Alexander, born in 1980.

Bedford Davis married Edna Ritter. Children: Rita, born 1951; Michael, born 1955; Karen, born 1957; Kay, born 1961; James Lester, born 1966. Rita Davis married Delwin Watson, and they have one child, Lovie, born in 1977. Michael Davis married Lana Swanader.

Milford Davis married Nell Sampson, and they have one child, Wanda Kay, born in 1947. Wanda Davis married Dr. Terry Shee, and they have one child, Laura, born in 1976.

Hillus Davis married Loucille McCarter. Children: Shirley Ann, born 1948; Cathy Diane, born 1950; Larry Neal, born 1953; Jackie Lynn, born 1956. Cathy Davis married Jeff Johnston, and they have two children, Jeffrey and Rebecca. Larry Davis married Vickie Utley, and they have four children, Robert, William, Jessica, and Carl. Jackie Davis married Pamela North, and they have two children, Andy and Amy.

Ulyes Davis married Jewel Pedigo. Children: Nannette Joan, born 1953, and Tony Marvin, born 1956. Joan Davis married Gene Holland, and they have two children, Eric and Kelly. Tony Davis married Diane Ridge.

Annise Davis married Vandal Clifton Crawford. Children are Phyllis Eloise, born June 15, 1948; David Lee, born December 25, 1951; Stephen, born March 30, 1956, died April 1, 1956; ...d Martha Denise, born October 25, 1957. Elo... Crawford married Roy Woodard. Children: Allan Roy, born 1970; Clifton David, born 1972; Michael Thomas, born 1975; Adam Paul, born 1977; and Cody Phillip, born 1979. David Crawford married Brenda Smith, and they have two children, Stephanie, born in 1970, and Latisha, born in 1972. Martha Crawford married Dwight Allen Smith, and they have one child, Joseph Dwight, born November 15, 1976.

Charles Davis married Louise Rhoten. Children: Linda Joyce, born 1955; Randy Martin, born 1957; Priscilla Lou, born 1959; and Jeffrey Lynn, born 1965. Linda Davis married Barry Plumlee. Children: Misty April, born in 1973; Rhonda Joy, born in 1975; and Barry Dale, Jr., born in 1978. Randy Davis married Carlene Leopard, and they have one child, Carrie. Priscilla Davis has one child, Jesse.

Clyde Davis married Vella Franklin, and they have two children, Jerry Dean, born 1956, and Pamela Jean, born 1958. Jerry Davis married Sheila Long, and they have one child, Melanie. Pamela Davis married Randy Keene, and they have one child, Patrick.

JACKIE AND KATHLEEN BROWNING

Jackie Layne Browning was born June 4, 1950. He is the fourth of six sons born to Press Browning Jr. and Adell West Browning. Jackie traces his ancestry to the old Browning family who came to America from England.

Kathleen Wilkerson was born April 26, 1950, the second of three children born to Earl R. Wilkerson and Anna J. Franklin of the Union Hill community. It is rumored that the Wilkerson family came to America from England and that they once served in the King's Court. The Franklin family is believed to be of Swedish and Dutch origin.

Jackie and Kathleen both graduated from Hermitage Springs School. After marriage, Jackie and Kathleen moved to Indianapolis, Indiana, living there for two years. After moving back to Tennessee, Jackie became a farmer holding other jobs along the way. Jackie is now employed full time as a truck driver for Buford Trucking Company in Celina, Tennessee. Kathleen is employed by OshKosh B'Gosh in Hermitage Springs.

Jackie and Kathleen have two sons, Jason Earl, born November 18, 1969, and Joseph Todd, born April 10, 1972. Both boys have red hair and bear the name "red wings".

The family belongs to the Pentecostal Church (Charity Tabernacle). Kathleen was ordained a minister on March 17, 1984 in Scottsville, Kentucky. under the Conference and Bishop Edward Shelton.

JAHUE SMITH BROWNING

Jahue Smith Browning was born July 3, 1870 in Clay County, Tennessee. He was married twice. He first married Minnie Evans, born June 20, 1872. She died May 17, 1902. They had five children, one of whom died at birth. The other four were James, Algenous, Jahue Smith, Jr., and Hova. After Minnie's death, Jahue Smith, or "Uncle Coon" as he was called by most people, married Eva Lena Armstrong in 1902. She was born July 8, 1886. They had ten children, Clara

Viola, Maudie, Lora, Rentford, Leona, Virgil, Estil, Clodean, Thomas, and Daisy. "Uncle Coon" was a farmer in the Milestown (Mount Vernon) community. He died December 22, 1951. Eva Lena died November 8, 1945.

Clara Viola Browning was born September 11, 1903 in Clay County. She died February 24, 1979. She was married June 11, 1928 to James William Hatcher, who was born June 18, 1905 and died August 3, 1973. He was the son of Rutherford B. Hatcher, born March 9, 1879 and died March 14, 1958, and Mary Etta Gulley, born May 13, 1885 and died March 14, 1958. Viola and Bill had a grocery store in the Milestown Community for twenty-five years. Viola and Bill had two children, Verda Pauline and Joyce Mae.

Verda Pauline Hatcher, born March 17, 1929 in Toledo, Ohio, married Cleston Harold Bean on October 16, 1946. He was born January 29, 1923. They have one daughter, Patricia Lynn. They live in Madison, Tennessee.

Joyce Mae Hatcher, born August 21, 1935 in Clay County, married Bobby Waymon Bean May 15, 1953. He was born May 31, 1935. They have two children, Gary Waymon and Karen Denise.

Patricia Lynn Bean, born July 13, 1955, married Jerry Dean White. They have three children, David, born November 3, 1975; Harold, born October 15, 1977; and Catherine, born February 2, 1984.

Gary Waymon Bean, born May 24, 1954, married twice. His first wife was Detra England. They had two children, Theresa Kay, born April 5, 1976, and James Harlin, born August 29, 1979. He later married Tammy Kay Brawner. They have one daughter, Tara Deshea, born September 18, 1985.

Karen Denise Bean, born March 6, 1956, married William Lawrence Sawyer. They have two children, Christopher William, born August 8, 1976, and Felicia Renee, born May 16, 1981.

JAMES DELBERT BROWNING

James Delbert Browning was born March 30, 1933 in the Leonard Community of Clay County. He was the son of Silas and Neva (Cherry) Browning. He was married March 8, 1952 to Bonnie Elise Copass, who was born June 27, 1933 in Clay County. She was the daughter of Millard Fillmore and Elsie Mae (McLerran) Copass. Delbert attended Hermitage Springs High School where he graduated in 1951. Bonnie attended Celina High School until the end of the eleventh grade in 1952. They lived in the Mount Vernon Community of Clay County for a year after they were married. They then moved to Indianapolis, Indiana, where Delbert worked for the American Can Company, Handschy Ink Company and I.P.I. Corporation. In 1972, Delbert was transferred to Rochester, New York by I.P.I. After one year, he moved back to Indianapolis, Indiana. In 1982, he

James Delbert and Bonnie Browning

was transferred to Glasgow, Kentucky where he died on August 17, 1984 of a massive heart attack.

Bonnie worked for the Perry Township School System in Indiana as a cook for 16 years. After the death of her husband, she moved back to Clay County and built a log home in the Moss Community. She is now employed by the Clay County School System as a cook at the Hermitage Springs School.

Delbert and Bonnie have two children, Roger and Connie Dianna. They also have three grandchildren, Chris Hughes, Corey Browning and Matthew Strong.

Bonnie is a member of the Church of Christ. She enjoys bowling.

JUANITA BROWNING

Juanita Browning was born January 11, 1937 in Clay County, Tennessee. She is the daughter of Earl D. Browning, born May 1, 1909, and Goldie (Cherry) Browning, born June 23, 1912.

Juanita Browning

She has a sister, Geneva, who married Wilmer Lee Delk. Juanita is the granddaughter of Benton Browning, born in 1885 and died in 1958, and Carrie (Long) Browning, born in 1889, and Grover and Bertha (Long) Cherry. She grew up in the Miles Cross Roads Community of Clay County. She attended Mount Vernon Elementary School. She is employed at the OshKosh Plant at Hermitage Springs. She is a member of the Church of Christ.

PLEAS BROWNING

Pleas Browning was born 1901 in Clay County, Tennessee, the son of Ead and Lee Ann (Vinson) Browning. He married Cena Smith, who was born April 1, 1904, the daughter of James Porter and Haley (Bean) Smith. Pleas was a well driller and a farmer. He was a member of the Church of Christ. Cena is also a member of the Church of Christ, and she attends the Milestown Church of Christ. She lives in the Miles Cross Roads Community of Clay County, Tennessee.

Pleas and Cena Browning

They had eighteen children, including four sets of twins. Their children are Glumus; Edna; Collean; Wilma; Harold; Charley Ray; Corrina Joyce, born March 2, 1936 and died March 2, 1962; Robbie Sue; James, born March 4, 1940; Judy; and twins, Douglas and Donald, born October 13, 1942 (Donald died the same day); and twins, Linda and Brenda, born December 31, 1944; (Linda died January 7, 1945, and Brenda died January 12, 1945); and twins, Annie and Dannie, born July 8, 1947, (Annie died July 17, 1947, and Dannie died July 9, 1947); and twins, Jimmy and Sandra.

ROGER BROWNING

Roger Browning, born May 20, 1953 in Wilson County, Tennessee, is a direct descendant of one of the oldest families in America — the Brownings. Captain John Browning was born about 1588 in England. He was the first of this Browning line to come to America. He came here in 1622 on the ship, Abigail, and settled in Elizabeth City, Virginia. He served in The House of Burgesses. His son, William, was born in 1615 in England. He came to America with his father and lived at Jamestown, Virginia. Will had a son, John, born about 1646 in Virginia. John had a son, John, Jr., born about 1666 in Virginia. John, Jr. had a son, William, born in 1710 in Culpepper County, Virginia. William settled in Maryland. He had a son, Charles, born around 1748 in Maryland. He died in 1821 in the southern part of Monroe County, Kentucky. He was in the Revolutionary War and fought in the Battle of Kings Mountain. He was wounded in that battle. He married Martha Hazlewood, who was born in 1768 in North Carolina and who died on December 12, 1842 in Jackson County (now Clay County), Tennessee. They lived in Union County, South Carolina before coming to Monroe County, Kentucky. Charles and Martha had a son, William, born in 1887 in Union County, South Carolina. He died on August 29, 1856 in Arkansas. He was married in 1820 in Monroe County, Kentucky to Nancy Kirby, born in 1800 in Barren County, Kentucky. She died in 1867 in Missouri. They moved to Arkansas in the 1840's. They had a son, Robert, born on January 2, 1825 in Monroe County, Kentucky. He died in 1871 in Clay County, Tennessee. He married Nellie Rogers, born on August 7, 1828. She died on May 1, 1868 in Jackson County (now Clay County), Tennessee.

Roger Browning Family

Robert and Nellie had a son, Henry Rice, born on February 5, 1862 in Arkansas. He married Arie Russell, born on November 25, 1884. They lived in the Leonard Community of Clay County. Their son, Silas, was born on February 27, 1890. He died in 1982. He married Neva Cherry, born

September 26, 1892. She died January 26, 1949. They lived in the Leonard Community. Their son, Delbert, was born on March 30, 1933, and he died August 17, 1984. He married Bonnie Copas, born June 27, 1933. She was the daughter of Millard and Elcie (McLerran) Copas. Delbert and Bonnie were the parents of two children — Roger, born May 20, 1953, and Connie, born January 18, 1956. Roger Brownning was born May 20, 1953. He married Darla Dalton. Their son, Corey was born November 10, 1977. They live in Indianapolis, Indiana.

WILLIAM THOMAS BUFORD

William Thomas Buford was born January 18, 1855 in Rock Springs Community of Overton (now Clay) County, Tennessee. He was the son of Edwin R. Buford (1825-1897) and Isabella Taylor Buford (1827-1909). His grandparents were John B. and Polly Edwards Buford and Warren and Polly Johnson Taylor.

William T. and Sarah Buford Family

On January 9, 1887, William Thomas was married to Sarah Alice Davis, who was born March 14, 1867 in the Rock Springs Community. She was the daughter of Samuel Tramel Davis (1835-1871) and Susan Mary Jennings Davis (1842-1903). They lived in Clay and Overton County, Tennessee. They had nine children: Charles T., Clarence R., Ada Neely, Cecil H., Haskell L., Luther M., Willie D., Elizabeth Chilton and Lou Bilbrey.

William Thomas died November 29, 1935. Sarah Alice died November 30, 1948.

CLARENCE R. BUFORD

Clarence R. Buford, son of William Thomas Buford and Sarah Alice Davis Buford, was born January 31, 1890 in the Pleasant Grove Community of Clay County. His grandparents were Edwin R. and Isobell Taylor Buford and Samuel Tramel and Susan Mary Jennings Davis.

On October 24, 1914 Clarence R. married Jennie Lee Overstreet, born October 4, 1892. She was the daughter of Calvin Wise and Belle Waddle Overstreet. To this union was born one daughter, Isobell. Jennie Lee died April 26, 1918.

On November 30, 1919, Clarence R. married Nancy C. (Nannie) Clark, who was born August 13, 1892 in Pickett County, Tennessee. She was the daughter of William Levi and Mary (Betty) Elizabeth Martin Clark. Their children are Lavelle, Wynell, W. Clark (Buster), John T., Edward, Launa, Billie, and Catherine (died infant).

Clarence R. lived his life in Clay County except for two years in California. He was a land owner and livestock dealer in the Fox Springs Communi-

ty until the building of Dale Hollow Dam. He then moved to Celina, Tennessee. He died May 1, 1975. Nannie Buford lives in Celina. She will soon be 94 years old.

Clarence and Nannie Buford

Isobell married Grady Paul Garrett. They had two children, Paul Martin and Jennie Ruth. Paul Martin married Eula Chloe Kendall. They have three daughters, Cynthia, Pauletta and Margie. Pauletta married Roger Brady. They have two children: Lora and Robert. Jennie Ruth married Robert Elton Crowther. They had two sons, Mark Andrew and Steven Earl. Jennie died January 10, 1982 in Bowie, Maryland.

Lavelle is semi-retired and lives in Okeechobee, Florida.

Wynell married Grayson Roylston. They have six children, Stephen, Nancy, Joseph, William (Bill) Clark, Johnny and David. Nancy married Larry Blalock. They have one son, Jeremy.

W. Clark (Buster) married Viola Ethridge. They have four children, Katherine, Patricia, Betty Sue and Micheal. Katherine married Harris Radford. Pat married Jens E. Valle. Suzi married Gregory Giannoni. They have one son, Ryan. Mike married Jennifer Perry.

John T. married Virginia Hunter. He has one daughter, Crystal.

Edward married Betty Poindexter. They have four sons, Ricky Edward, Ronnie Edwin, John Thomas and Jimmy Martin. Ronny married Unok Han. John Thomas married Patty Boatman.

Launa married Henry Boyd Stone. They live on a farm in the Arcot community.

Billie married Bobby Mitchel Stone. They have two daughters, Gaye Ann and Donna Gail. Donna married Andrew (Andy) Scott. Billie and Bobby live in the Arcot Community.

GEORGE T. BURNETTE, SR.

George Thomas Burnette, born July 26, 1908, married Elise Kendall, born May 4, 1910, in Clay County, Tennessee. They had thirteen children all born in Clay County. The children appear in order of birth as follows:

Elise Burnette

William Roy, born October 29, 1927, married Hazel Mae Scott. They have four children: William Roy "Butch", Gerald Lee "Jerry", Susan Starr, and Tiffany Dawn.

Juanita, born November 4, 1929, married Harry Thomas Dale, and they have one son, Harry Thomas, Jr.

David Rex, born October 5, 1931, married Arnell Odle. They have two daughters, Debra Lynn and Tracy Deann.

Virginia Wanda, born November 10, 1933, married Bobby Lynn Odle. They had two daughters, Beth Ann and Pamela Jo.

George Thomas, Jr., born August 8, 1936, married Rhea Rita Lynas. They have five children, George Thomas, III, Michelle, Kimberly Elaine, Sheila Dawn, and Mark Allen.

Addie Jo, born March 18, 1938, married Joseph Winton Williams. They have five children, Brenda Kaye, Beverly Faye, Cheryl Yvonne, Tammy Jo, and Joseph Winton, Jr.

The Burnettes as they participated in the Bicentennial: Susan, Butch, Jerry, Hazel, Roy and Tiffany

Jimmy Carroll, born June 29, 1940, married Barbara Dell Rouse. They have three sons, Barry Wayne, Michael Lynn, and Christopher Brian.

Ralph Harrold, born August 4, 1942, married Onieta Hanks Wilson. He has three stepchildren, Evette, Donnie, and Rose Anne.

Marcia Ann, born August 2, 1944, married Billy Hugh Bailey. They have two sons and one daughter, Billy Kevin, Kristi Jo, and Kenny Lee.

Janell, born November 3, 1946, married Robert Alan Baumgartner. They have three children, Anthony Robert, Craig Alan, and Jenni Anne.

Eddy Dale, born February 4, 1948, married Barbara Hayes. They have two sons, Ronald Bryan and Shawn Ryan. They divorced and he married Deborah Joan Wilson. They have one daughter, Cera Layn.

Charles Jones, born February 16, 1950, married Deloris Rouse Conkin. He has a stepdaughter, Kimberly.

Vickie Lynn, born August 23, 1954, married Benny McLerran. They have one daughter, Melanie Lynn.

In addition to the thirteen children and their spouses, George has 32 grandchildren, 14 great-grandchildren, 4 step-grandchildren, and 6 step-great-grandchildren. At the present time all are living, except grandmother Elise, who passed away at the age of 74 on April 29, 1985. This brief history is fondly dedicated to the memory of that lovely lady. — . Submitted by Susan Starr Burnette

WILLIAM ROY BURNETTE

The oldest of thirteen children, William Roy Burnette was born in Clay County on October 29, 1927. Roy lived his early years in Clay County near Boles, Kentucky before moving to Indiana where he stayed for ten years. Also during this time in the late 40's, he served in the Air Force. While living in Tipton, he met and later married Hazel Mae Scott, originally from Arkansas. After marrying, they decided to return to Roy's home and go into business in Boles.

It wasn't much easier in the late 40's to begin a business than it is today. Roy and Hazel actually started out by a single small investment leading to larger investments which eventually lead to ownership of Burnette's General Merchandise Store on the Tennessee/Kentucky line. Roy also served as Postmaster in Boles for eleven years at the general store, where locals gathered to swap tales and politics on a daily basis. The old store still stands and is operated today by Roy's father, George Burnette.

While running the store in Boles, Roy and Hazel had a son, William Roy "Butch," born December 25, 1949. One year and a day later, Gerald Lee "Jerry" was born. Susan Starr arrived on June 20, 1956. On these special occasions, Dr. Champ E. Clark enjoyed some good country cooking while waiting for the three to be born. Grandpa George and Grandma Elise lived up on the hill at the old Burnette homeplace where they all worked together on the farm and in the business. Roy and Hazel started the B & B Distributing Company in 1959, then moved to Celina in 1960.

On August 7, 1967, they added another to their lot, Tiffany Dawn. Dr. Clark was said to make a record run from Celina to Livingston with his passenger, Hazel, before Tiffany arrived at the Lady Ann Hospital.

Their firstborn, "Butch" is now Vice-President of sales at B & B Distributing Company in Celina. "Butch" lives in Celina with his wife, the former Joan Marie McLerran, and their two children, William Joseph and Amanda Joy.

Jerry is now Southern Region Sales Manager at Honest Abe Log Homes in Moss, Tennessee. Jerry is married to the former Donna Snow King. They live in Celina and have five children, Stephen, Ryan, Gretchen Lee, Tara Amber, and Caleb King.

Susan Starr is a Registered Nurse and also lives in Celina. She is employed as Director/Instructor of Practical Nursing at the Livingston State Area Vocational Technical School in Livingston.

Tiffany Dawn recently graduated from Celina High School and is attending David Lipscomb College in Nashville.

As a group, Roy's family has always been encouraged to be involved in their community. They have been active participants over the years in scouting, school activities, sports, civic clubs, and community projects. Roy and his family are all members of the Church of Christ. They have always been proud of their county and have never expressed a desire to leave it for very long. The boys actually stated, "It'd be worse than twisting a sore-tailed cat trying to get them out of Clay County again," after serving four years from home in the United States Coast Guard. Their sisters seem to be following the same general idea. It is pretty evident that Clay County is home to this family. — Submitted by Susan Starr Burnette

CHARLES W. BURRIS

John M. Burris and a brother, Rheuben, came to the "Colonies" from Manchester, England with the British Forces and settled in Virginia at the forks of the Allegheny and Monongahela Rivers. John M. married Hannah Oliver. A son, John M., was born February 14, 1781 near Pittsburgh and Morgantown, West Virginia. When this son was a young man, he ran away from home, taking with him a large, shelf-sized, cherry clock (now in the possession of Geneva Burris Spear). He hunted and fished along the Cumberland River and settled four miles northeast of Gainesboro in Jackson County. To keep his father from finding him, he changed the spelling of his last name, which was originally spelled Burroughs, to Burris. His later letter to relatives related his extreme loneliness and described his primitive housekeeping activiites.

In the latter part of 1855, John M. married a widow, Elizabeth Jarvis McClarrian. They had twins born December 10, 1856, Winfield Scott and Eliza Jane. John M. Burris died December 26, 1861. Seventeen years later, March 9, 1878, Elizabeth was approved for $8.00 a month widow's pension, since John M. was a private of Captain David Smith's Company Militia.

Winfield Scott Burris married Alice Kendall of Clay County, and they had three children. Martha married Albert Goolsby, and they had one son, Charles Albert. They lived in California. Belle married W. Prather and lived in Gallatin, Tennessee. Charles Wade Burris married Willia Alma Duke of Overton County May 24, 1925. They had four children, Geneva, Charles W., Wilma Jean and Duke.

Geneva Burris was born March 28, 1927. She married Walter V. Spear of Cumberland County, Kentucky. They have one daughter, Deborah Joan, who married Jimmy H. Nevins. Deborah and Jimmy have one son, Charles Neil, who is a student at David Lipscomb College. Deborah is a teacher with the Clay County School System.

Charles W. Burris, Jr. was born February 10, 1929. He married Geneva Warden of Overton County. They have one daughter, Sandra Renee, who teaches in the Monroe County, Kentucky. School System. Sandra has one daughter, Amanda. They live in Tompkinsville, Kentucky.

Wilma Jean Hayes was born February 2, 1931. She is employed by the Bank of Celina. She has three children. Her daughter, Sharon Suzanne "Sue," is married to Dr. John H. Stone, and they have one son, Samuel Adam, who attends Celina K-8 School. John and Sue live in Celina where John practices dentistry, and Sue is employed as a teacher by the Clay County School System. Wilma's sons, Michael Burris and Steve, both reside in Nashville. Michael is employed at Pillsbury in Murfreesboro as Maintenance Engineer. Steve is employed with the State of Tennessee as Director of Personnel with the Department of Finance and Administration.

Duke Burris was born January 25, 1933. He and his wife, Yvonne, live in Greenwood, Indiana. Duke has been employed by Bryant Heating and Air Conditioning Factory for the past 20 years. His two sons are Duke Burris, Jr. and Charles Thomas Burris. Duke is employed as manager for a grocery store chain, and Charles Thomas is a student.

Charles W. Burris died November 24, 1970. His widow, "Bill" continues to reside at the homesite in Celina. A portion of this homesite was the "Fairgrounds" for many years. (Pictures of the "Fairgrounds" are shown in other sections of the Clay County History.)

THOMAS BUTLER

Thomas Butler was born August 12, 1777 in South Carolina. He was married to Polly McClure February 3, 1801. To them were born nine children: James Bailey born November 30, 1801; Catherine born February 3, 1804; Clarenda, born June 19, 1806; Polly, born November 11, 1808, John Price, born February 3, 1811; Thomas Jefferson, born 1813; LeAnn born July 4, 1815; Leroy Bonapart, born August 22, 1823.

Leroy Bonapart "Tuck" Butler, married Elizabeth Dale, daughter of William and Martha Goodpasture Dale. They had seven children born to them: Martha (Bailey); Mary Louisia (Beck); Marcella "Cell" never married; Jane Ann (Kirkpatrick); Bennett S. died young November 18, 1862; Sarah Dulcenna (Overstreet); and John Dale Butler.

John Dale Butler married Martha Susan Hampton, daughter of John Reed Hampton and Sarah Jane Hawkins Hampton. To them were born five children: Belle (Upton); George; Lula Mae (Clark); Herman Reed; and Hugh.

Belle married Clayton Upton, September 28, 1919. He was a farmer on Mitchell Creek, near the Clay and Overton County line, now under waters of Dale Hollow Dam. They had one son, Willie Butler Upton, born May 27, 1921. He attended the public schools of Clay County, graduating from Celina High School in 1941. He married Edwina Smith June 28, 1941 at Byrdstown, Tennessee. He served in the United States Navy during World War II. After being discharged from service at the close of World War II, he entered Gupton-Jones College of Mortuary Science, graduating June 1949. He and his wife, Edwina, came back to Celina and bought the Rich Funeral Home and renamed it Upton Funeral Home. They have operated this business for thirty-seven and one-half years (1986). They have one daughter, Betty Sue Briggs. She and her husband, Jim Briggs, are also associated with the Upton Funeral Home. They have two sons: Michael Butler Briggs and John Harold Briggs.

COLONEL BAILEY BUTLER

Colonel Bailey Butler was born May 3, 1779 in King George County, Virginia. He died October 12, 1842 at Butler's Landing in what is now Clay County, Tennessee. He was a Master Mason and fought in the Indian Wars of his time. He was married three times. He first married Adeline Walker. They had two children: Adeline Butler, born in 1815, and Franklin Walker Butler, born in 1817. He next married Sallie Scantlant. They had two children: Thomas Harvey, born in 1819 and Lucetta born in 1828. Thomas Harvey Butler was a Captain in the Army of the Confederacy and served as Secretary of the State of Tennessee from 1870-1873. He was Secretary of State of Tennessee when Clay County was organized. Lucetta Butler married L.T. Armstrong, a merchant, a pilot, and an officer in the Army of the Confederacy.

Colonel Bailey Butler next married Mary "Polly" Stafford who was born June 11, 1807. To this union, the following children were born: Scantland, born 1835; Susan; Martha, born 1841; Sam G., born 1831; Mirian, born 1832; and Bailey, Jr. Mary "Polly" Butler died January 23, 1874.

Colonel Butler was a surveyor, a farmer, and a miner. He owned an operated a salt peter mine.

He is buried in a small cemetery at the mouth of Turkey Creek across the river from Butler's Landing.

JAMES CARNAHAN

James Carnahan, born around 1804 in South Carolina, married Elizabeth (surname unknown), born around 1810 in Tennessee. They lived in the Miles Cross Roads Community of Clay County They had the following children: James M.; William, born 1830; Larken; Franklin; Cyrene; Martha; Bransford; Clerenda; and John L., born October 27, 1845.

Earnest and Bee Carnahan and grandson Leon Carnahan

William, born in 1830, married Catherine McCarter, born March 3, 1850 — died August 13, 1924, in Clay County. William was in the Union Army during the Civil War and served in Company I, 59th Ohio Infantry. William and Catherine are buried in the Browning Cemetery in the West End of Clay County. They had the following children: Miram M., born 1868; James F., born July 17, 1870; George B., born 1873; and Eliza J., born 1875. James F. married Rebecca Vinson, born March 13, 1876 — died February 8, 1953. They lived in the Miles Cross Roads Community of Clay County. He was a farmer. They are buried in the Browning Cemetery in the Miles Cross Roads Community. Their son, Earnest Carnahan, married Della Bee Birdwell, born March 2, 1913 in Clay County and died December 4, 1976 in Dearborn, Michigan. Earnest worked for General Motors at Detroit, Michigan. They are buried in the Cadillac Memorial Gardens West at Garden City, Michigan. They had two sons: Glynn Edward, and Doyle Leon.

Glynn Edward was born March 7, 1940. In 1965, he married Diane Thomas in Garden City, Michigan. They have two children, Kyle Edward and Christie Noel.

Doyle Leon Carnahan married Phyliss Baker. Their children are Doyle Leon, Kimberly Ann, and Karen.

JEPTHA CAPSHAW

Jeptha Capshaw is a descendant of the following:

Essick Capshaw, a Scotchman, came from Wales. He settled in Baltimore in 1740. He married a Widow Johnson who owned a plantation. They had two sons, Essick, II and William. After the death of their parents, they migrated to North Carolina and settled as farmers on the Roanoke River. They were very unalike in temperament. Essick was passionate and often got himself into trouble, while William was quiet, peaceful and loved by his neighbors. During the Revolutionary War, Essick was a Whig and William, a Troy.

William Capshaw married a lady named Watkins in Virginia. They had eight children: Esther, James, Rebecca, Josiah, David, William, II, Daniel and Elinor.

William Capshaw, II came to Alabama in 1808 when the Country was a wilderness and began to raise cotton. He and his brother, Dave, invented a cotton gin and made a good profit. William married Widow Palmer and had nine children: William, III, James Wesley, David, Jonithan, Sallie, Esther, Dollie, Matilda, and Nancy.

Jonithan Capshaw married Celia Parsley, sister to James Wesley Capshaw's wife, Nancy Parsley. Jonithan and Celia moved from McMinnville to Long Hungry near Red Boiling Springs, Tennessee and built a log house and a water mill which he operated. Later they moved to Hermitage

Parrie, Jeptha, Elizabeth and Nellie Mattie, John, Eva, Dave, Emma, Sarah, William P. and Vada

Springs and built another water mill. They were the parents of five children: Jeptha, Dave, Abraham, Margaret and Hanna.

Jeptha Capshaw, born in 1851 and died in 1934, married Elizabeth Biles, born in 1859 and died in 1947. They built a large house on the Capshaw farm and reared ten children. Mattie married Roscoe Meador. John married Mary Biles. Sarah married Jess Copas and G.D. Osgathorpe. Dave never married. Emma married R.H. Wilson. Vada married Sam McCoin. Eva married Ben Williams. William Pleas married Bess Crawford and Lona Walker. Nell never married. Parrie Lee married Joe Hutson.

Jeptha Capshaw was a double cousin to Robert Bird Capshaw, son of James Wesley Capshaw. Robert was a lawyer in Cookeville and married Alice Whitson. They were the parents of Estill, Coran and Hulon. Now in 1986, the younger generation can see the following markers in Cookeville, Tennessee: The name — ROBERT BIRD CAPSHAW — over the front entrance of the school for which he gave the land; the UPPER CUMBERLAND REGIONAL LIBRARY standing where his old home stood; a MONUMENT in the CITY CEMETERY with six family names on it; Leigh Capshaw's NEW HOME — Estil's son and only family survivor; and CAPSHAW CONDOMINIUMS being built by Leigh Capshaw.

LONA WALKER CAPSHAW

Lona Walker Capshaw was born March 8, 1908 in Clay County, Tennessee. She is a descendant of Benton Thomas Walker, born September 18, 1886 and died August 14, 1954, and Dovie Reecer Walker, born April 2, 1892 and died January 3, 1974.

William P. and Lona Capshaw

Lona attended Liberty Hill Elementary School on Proctor Creek in Clay County. She graduated from Celina High School and attended Tennessee Polytechnic Institute and Middle Tennessee State Teachers College. Since they did not offer Vocational Home Economics, she transferred to Peabody College in Nashville, Tennessee during her senior year and received a Bachelor of Science degree in Vocational Home Economics in 1945. She later did her graduate work at the University of Tennessee in Knoxville.

Lona taught in elementary schools and at Celina High School. When she received her degree from Peabody, she accepted a position at Hermitage Springs High School teaching Vocational Home Economics where she remained until she retired in 1973. Now in 1986, Lona is living in the Hermitage Springs community with many of her students near by and enjoys them very much because they are so kind and thoughtful.

When Lona married W.P. Capshaw from Gamaliel, Kentucky, December 24, 1955, they built a home in Hermitage Springs, which they enjoyed together for 30 years. W.P. was born on March 4, 1898, the son of Jeptha Capshaw (1852-1934) and Elizabeth Biles Capshaw (1871-1947). W.P. died August 12, 1985 and is buried in the Gamaliel, Kentucky Cemetery.

W.P. attended Tennessee Polytechnic Institute and Western Kentucky College. He was a farmer. He served several years as an elder for the Hermitage Springs Church of Christ. The Church of Christ has been a beacon in W.P. and Lona's life — a life of devotion and work.

Lona has a stepson, Joe Capshaw, born on October 31, 1929. He is an engineer and also an elder for the Clear Lake Church of Christ in Houston, Texas. He married Rosemary Kent in 1956. She was born April 3, 1928. She was formerly a Chicago schoolteacher. They are parents of three children, Susan, born May 5, 1959, is an engineer; Patricia, born November 15, 1960, is a teacher in the Houston school system and is married to Corwin Snyder; and William Kent, born May 17, 1964, is a senior in college. W.P. and Lona enjoyed many visits with them as well as traveling with them to various places. — *Submitted by Lona W. Capshaw*

JOSEPH BROWN CARVER

The Carver family of Clay County are the descendants of John Carver, who came from Carver's Creek near Wilmington, North Carolina. Three young Carver men came from North Carolina to settle in middle Tennessee and Southern Kentucky. Neal settled in Kentucky; Thomas settled in Wilson County, Tennessee; and John settled in Jackson County, Tennessee. John married Polly Dycus. They were the parents of Joseph R. Carver, born 1813 — died 1877, who married Martha Crabtree. They were the parents of James Milton Carver, born 1844 — died 1920, who married Sallie Hoover. Their son, Bedford Stokley Carver, born 1871 — died 1953, married Beatrice Brewington. They were the parents of Jack, Comer, Joseph Brown (Joe), Willodean, and Don.

Joe and Blanche Carver

Joseph Brown (Joe) Carver was born May 7, 1915 in Jackson County at North Springs, Tennessee. He graduated from Middle Tennessee State Teachers College in Murfreesboro, Tennessee, with a Bachelor of Science Degree. He worked for three years in Cleveland, Ohio. He served for 38 years in the field of education, teaching in Jackson and Clay Counties. The last

14 years of his teaching career were spent as principal of Hermitage Springs School, grades kindergarten through 12. The family lives on a farm in the Hermitage Springs Community, where Joe enjoys being a cattle farmer.

Joe married Blanche McLerran of Clay County. Blanche was the daughter of Albert Harrison and Zona Caruthers McLerran. She is the granddaughter of Benjamin McLerran and Amanda Louisa Eads McLerran of Clay County and of Allen Wakefield Caruthers and Gracie Jane Whitaker Caruthers of Jackson County. Blanche attended school in Toledo, Ohio, Old Hickory, Tennessee and Clay County, graduating from Hermitage Springs High School. She attended Tennessee Polytechnic Institute completing one year of study. She is presently Registrar-at-Large of Clay County and a contributer to "Life Styles", a regular column in the **Citizen-Statesman,** a Clay County newspaper.

Joe and Blanche are the parents of two children, Bobby Joe, born June 2, 1941 in Jackson County, and June Carmen, born June 26, 1948 in Clay County.

Bobby Joe Carver

Bobby received his Bachelor of Science and Master of Arts Degrees from Tennessee Polytechnic Institute in Cookeville, Tennessee. He served five years as principal of Macon County schools before joining the Naval Air Force from which he received an honorable medical discharge. He is the owner of Tooley and Carver Insurance Agency of Lafayette, Tennessee. He is the owner of his grandparents (McLerran) farm in Hermitage Springs.

Carmen married Harry T. Matthews, Jr. of Uniontown, Pennsylvania. They have a home on the farm of Carmen's grandparents, Harrison and Zona Carathers McLerran, in Hermitage Springs. They are the parents of Julie and Phillip. (See Harry T. Matthews family.)

JUNIOR LESLIE CHAFFIN

Geraldine Gentry was born December 31, 1946, the daughter of George D. and Louvenia Rush Gentry. She is the granddaughter of Edmond Anthony and Polly Jane Chaffin Gentry, and Cyrus Haden Rush, Sr. and Mary Lou Loftis Rush. Geraldine attended elementary school at Mount Vernon, and she graduated from Hermitage Springs High School in 1964.

On December 30, 1964, Geraldine married Junior Leslie Chaffin. Junior is the son of Maggie and Wesley Heitt Chaffin. He attended schools at Draper's Cross Roads and Red Boiling Springs, Tennessee.

97

The Geraldine and Junior Chaffin Family

Geraldine and Junior have the following children: Marvin Leslie, Teresa Ann, and Donald Wesley.

Marvin Leslie Chaffin was born December 12, 1965. He attended Ray Waldron Elementary School in Lavergne and graduated from Smyrna High School in 1984. He married Jerrie Linbaugh in November of 1984.

Teresa Ann Chaffin was born April 1, 1968. She attended Ray Waldron Elementary School and graduated from Smyrna High School on May 24, 1986. Teresa married Danny Edward Pisani on April 1, 1986.

Donald Wesley Chaffin was born March 29, 1971. He attended John Coleman School for grades one through three; Smyrna Elementary School for grades four through six; and Thurman Frances School for grades seven through nine. He entered Smyrna High School in the fall of 1986.

Geraldine and Junior live in the Fellowship Community of Rutherford County. Geraldine works at Better Bilt Aluminum in Smyrna; and Junior works for Ideal Cabinet in Lavergne.

CARY CHERRY

Cary Cherry was born in Norfolk County, Virginia in 1790. When he was nine years old, he traveled to Tennessee from Edgecombe County, North Carolina. His parents were Lemuel and Sarah McPherson Cherry. He had three brothers: John, Wilson, and Wiley. His sisters were Martha, Sarah, Elizabeth, and Mary. Elizabeth, who later married Hiram Denton, was born in Jackson County, Tennessee in 1800. They possibly arrived in Tennessee in 1799 after the Wilderness Wagon Road was completed in 1797 through the Gap. This family settled on the headwaters of Trace Creek. Earlier, Lemuel had a "Sugar Camp" on Garrison's Fork (Browning Creek).

Henry Clay, Daniel Boone and Napolean Cherry

Cary Cherry married Isabelle McAdoo after the War of 1812. The three brothers, Cary, John, and Wilson, were in the Battle of New Orleans on January 7 and 8, 1815. Cary and Isabelle had nine children: William Carroll, 1818; John McAdoo, 1820; Lemuel Boyd, 1822; Sarah Tracy, 1823; Prudence Lucinda, 1826; Louisa Minerva, 1828; Mary Jane, 1831; Craten Isabelle, 1833; and Cary S. (Bud) Cherry, 1837.

Cary S. Cherry, II was married in 1860 to Marinda Hestand, the daughter of Abrahm and Elizabeth Pennington Hestand. They, too, had nine children all born in Jackson and/or Clay County, Tennessee. They were: Chalista Isabelle, born 1862, married Henry McCormack; Lemuel Jackson, born 1864, married Lucetta McGaughan; John C. Breckenridge, born 1866, married Maryntha Woods; Daniel Boone, born 1869, married Alice Billingsly; Hettie Missourie, born 1871, married John T. Copass; William Witt, born 1874, married Mettie Dalton; Napolean, born 1877, never married; Elzady Florettie, born 1880, married William Onzie Spivey; and Henry Clay Cherry, born 1882, married Virginia Hughes McLerran.

Henry Clay Cherry and Virginia Hughes McLerran were married on his birthday, November 13, in 1904. She was the daughter of Benajy A. McLerran and Amanda Eads McLerran of Clay County, Tennessee. Clay and Virginia moved to Grayson County, Texas, where Obie Roland was born on September 5, 1905. In 1908, they moved to Park County, Wyoming, and homesteaded there close to Powell. Mary Sadie was born in 1910, and Cary Benjamin was born in Clay County, Tennessee in 1912. Henry Clay Cherry, Jr. was born in 1918 in Park County, Wyoming. Daniel Boone Cherry was born in 1927. The family moved to Redding, (Shasta County) California.

WILLIAM WITT CHERRY

William Witt Cherry was born on September 7, 1874 and died February 16, 1947. He was the son of Cary Stewart and Marinda (Hestand) Cherry. On March 5, 1901, Witt married Mettie Avanna Dalton, born on February 21, 1882, the daughter of Phillip Henry and Purlina (Wiggins) Dalton. Mettie died September 25, 1960. They lived on a farm near Turkey Creek on the Cumberland River. Later, they moved to Tompkinsville, Kentucky, on a farm where the Houchens Store and Tompkinsville Elementary School are

Mettie and Witt Cherry, Ola, Phillip, Ora and Jack

now located. Still later, they moved to a farm located at Cherry's Cross Roads, about three miles east of Hermitage Springs. They built a large frame house about 1921, before the final determination of where Highway 52 would run. The house had a porch on the north side and on the south side, so that the house would face the highway whichever way the highway ran. Many travelers and passersby enjoyed Mrs. Mettie's good cooking and the family's hospitality.

Witt and Mettie were the parents of six children. They are: Audra Atrus Cherry, born November 30, 1903 and died October 18, 1907; Ora Jeanette Cherry Clements, born October 31, 1905 and died December 17, 1985; William Jackson Cherry, born August 2, 1907 and died February 13, 1941; Ola Emma Cherry Gillenwater, born April 1, 1911; Phillip Bailey Cherry, born December 13, 1913 and died October 4, 1959; and Opal Irene Cherry Grace, born July 15, 1919.

WILSON CARROLL CHERRY

Wilson Carroll Cherry was born in 1817 in Jackson County, Tennessee. He was the son of Carey, Sr. and Isabella (McAdfoo) Cherry. They had the following children: James Boyd was born May 31, 1839 in Jackson County. He married America Minor on October 18, 1869. America was born May 23, 1845. They had the following children: William Bennett, born October 19, 1870, married Alta McGlasson, the daughter of Oliver and Sarah (Pendergrass) McGlasson. William died in Rutherford County, Tennessee, on April 24, 1940. John Wilson, born February 11, 1872, married Allie B. Carver. Wheeler Morgan, born April 22, 1874, married Nancy Rose. Wheeler died in Rutherford County on April 22, 1874. Harrison Thomas, born May 15, 1876, married Vallie Cowan. He died in Glasgow, Kentucky. Sarah (Sallie) Mary Margaret, born December 4, 1877, married Bedford Forrest Rogers. Mattie Florence, born December 13, 1879, married Osco Moore. America (Minor) Cherry died February 8, 1881. James Boyd Cherry then married Millie Green, born May 28, 1853. They had no children. James Boyd Cherry died on December 1919. Millie died March 30, 1928.

Eliza A.J. Cherry was born (ca.) 1845.

William Taylor Cherry was born December 13, 1849 in Jackson County. He married Mary K. (surname unknown), born October 24, 1848. William T. died November 4, 1898. Mary K. died October 1, 1910. Both are buried in Compton Cemetery in Monroe County, Kentucky.

Harrison Wayne Cherry was born January 20, 1851 in Jackson County. He first married Julia America Craton Cherry, the daughter of Alex Jackson and Elizabeth (Moore) Cherry. Julia America Craton Cherry was born November 25, 1859 in Jackson County. She died December 20, 1887. In 1888, Harrison married his second wife, Martha Adeline Hestand, the daughter of Barton Greenup and Mary (Freiley) Hestand. After her death on May 15, 1900, Harrison married his third wife, Lucetta "Sis" McLerran. His third marriage had no issue, but the other two marriages gave him thirteen children. Harrison died April 2, 1940 at Hermitage Springs, Tennessee.

Carroll T. "Doc" Cherry was born January 14, 1855 in Jackson County. He married Abigail "Abbie" G. Mullinix. "Doc" died November 29, 1901.

Isabella L. "Cetta" Cherry was born (ca.) 858. She died (ca.) 1899.
Sarah Cherry was born (ca.) 1860.
Ellen Cherry was born (ca.) 1862.
Mary J. Cherry was born (ca.) 1843.

Wilson Carroll Cherry died June 6, 1880. His wife, Mary (Crawford) Cherry, died March 7, 1882. Her will is on record at Celina, Tennessee.

HARRISON WAYNE CHERRY

Harrison Wayne Cherry was born on January 20, 1851 in Jackson County, Tennessee to Wilson Carroll and Mary (Crawford) Cherry. He was married three times. The first marriage was to Julia America Craton Cherry, the daughter of Alex Jackson and Elizabeth (Moore) Cherry. Julia America Craton Cherry was born November 25, 1859 in Jackson County, Tennessee. They had seven children. Bedford Cicero Cherry was born on April 29, 1875. He married Mattie Jesse Moore, the sister of Preston Barlow Moore. Bedford died in 1954. Mary A. Joda Cherry was born May 18, 1877. She married Henry H. Ford. She died in 1954. Sarah Frona Cherry was born October 19, 1879. She married Preston Barlow Moore April 3, 1897. Sara died October 17, 1963. Dora Belle Cherry was born October 10, 1882. She was married about 1898 to Shadrach William "Shade" Murray, the son of George W. and Sarah A. (Copass) Murray. "Shade" Murray died March 26, 1956. Dora died February 27, 1966. William Turner Cherry was born September 20, 1883. Myra Crayton Cherry was born January 30, 1886, and she died April 24, 1886. Harrison Benton Cherry was born August 3, 1887. He must have died after April 2, 1940, because Harrison W. Cherry, his father, died at his home on that date. Julia America Craton (Cherry) Cherry died December 20, 1887.

Harrison Wayne Cherry

Harrison Wayne Cherry then married Martha Adeline Hestand. This marriage was recorded November 6, 1888 in Tompkinsville, Kentucky. Martha A. Hestand was born October 20, 1865 to Barton and Mary (Freiley) Hestand. Harrison and Martha had six children. Delina S. "Della" Cherry was born August 5, 1889. She married Charles Ritter. Della died February 2, 1974. She and her husband are buried in the Bailey Cemetery in Hestand, Kentucky. Smith Raymond G. Cherry was born July 10, 1891. He died December 7, 1891. Cassie A. Cherry was born May 23, 1893. She married a Ritter. She died October 27, 1955. Oliver S. Cherry was born October 16, 1895. He died September 7, 1924. Callie C.

Cherry was born December 5, 1897. She married Amos E. Craighead. She died October 15, 1969. Buford E. Cherry was born September 27, 1899. He died April 3, 1947. Martha Adeline (Hestand) Cherry died May 15, 1900.

Harrison Wayne Cherry then married his third wife, Lucetta "Sis" McLerran. No record is known of any issue to this marriage. "Sis" McLerran was born about September of 1868. It is believed that his third wife also preceded Harrison in death. Harrison W. Cherry died April 2, 1940 at Hermitage Springs, Tennessee at the home of his son, Benton Cherry. His funeral services were held by Elder H.C. Osgathorp with burial in the second Cherry Cemetery north of Oak Grove.

Harrison Wayne Cherry spent most of his life in the West End of Clay County. He was a prominent farmer and operated a general store that still stands today. He was a member of the Church of Christ for many years.

LAWRENCE HUSTON CHERRY

Lawrence Huston Cherry was born May 22, 1881, the son of Carroll T. Cherry, born January 14, 1855 — died November 29, 1901, and Abbie G. Mullinix Cherry, born January 13, 1856 — died July 25, 1934. He was the grandson of Wilson Carroll and Mary Crawford Cherry and Israel W. and Minerva Ford Mullinix.

Lawrence married Nora A. Spear, born April 5, 1889 — died November 11, 1963, the daughter of Zachariah L. and Sarah Dorcas McLerran Spear. Lawrence and Nora lived in the Oak Grove Community of Clay County. He was a farmer. Lawrence and Nora are buried in the Pitcock Cemetery at Oak Grove.

They had the following children: John, Elmer, Bonnie, Lex, Huston, Wanda, and Mitchell.

Lex Cherry married Edith Moss, the daughter of Anthony Calvin Moss, born December 22, 1842 — died in 1935, and Lucy Marshall Moss, born February 28, 1876. Lex and Edith were merchants in the Oak Grove Community for many years. He also served as the Postmaster at Memorial, now Oak Grove. They were members of the Church of Christ.

Calvin Cherry

Allyson Cherry

Lex and Edith have four children: Calvin, Duke, Jan, and Joy. Duke Cherry married Ella Mae Bilbery, and they have one son, Calvin, born in 1969. Ella Mae died in 1969. Duke then married Peggy Layne. They have a daughter, Allyson.

GRADY LUTHER CHERRY

Grady Luther Cherry was born October 11, 1901 in Clay County, Tennessee. He was the youngest of six children born to Carroll Turner "Doe" Cherry, who was born in 1855 and died in 1901, and Abbie Gail Mullinix Cherry, who was born in 1856 and died in 1934. Grady died February 11, 1982.

Grady was married in November 1920 to Para Lou Johnson, who was born April 4, 1905 and died March 12, 1955, the daughter of John W. Johnson, born in 1856 and died in 1945, and Rosetta McLerran Johnson, born in 1871 and died in 1942. Grady and Para Lou had seven children: Oleta, Kenneth, Carl, Emma Lou, Luther Keith, Sid and Joan. Grady went to Toledo, Ohio in 1928. He worked in a factory twelve hours a day for 30¢ an hour. Para took in boarders. They came back to Clay County in late 1929. When the Depression began, he farmed and worked by the day for 50¢ and $1.00. In the fall he would go to Indiana and husk corn for about two months and would make about $100.00.

Oleta Cherry was born December 4, 1923. She married Charles W. Hine July 23, 1949.

Kenneth Mack Cherry was born May 21, 1926. He married Betty Jean Pierson July 21, 1956. They have two sons, Randy and Wayne. Randy Alan Cherry was married May 21, 1981 to Carol Ann Cisketti; they have one son, Daniel Alan. Wayne Dale Cherry was married October 19, 1985 to Tina Taets. Betty Cherry died February 22, 1975; Kenneth died January 26, 1981.

Carl Jess Cherry was born October 26, 1927. He was married December 8, 1960 to Gladys Bean.

Emma Lou Cherry was born March 25, 1930. She married John F. Spear in November 1947. They have one son, Oliver Lee. Emma Lou was killed in an automobile accident November 6, 1965.

Luther Keith Cherry was born March 23, 1932; he died March 28, 1932.

Sid Allen Cherry was born August 17, 1933. He married Mamie Elaine King April 5, 1952. They have two children, Teresa and Jeffery. Teresa Ann Cherry was married September 10, 1982 to Gerald Jay Coone. Jeffery Allen Cherry was struck by a car and killed at the age of nine on December 23, 1974.

Edith Joan Cherry was born May 5, 1939. She married Lonnie Helton June 4, 1961. They have one daughter, Shelia Gail; she married Kirk Stierwalt July 14, 1984.

JOHN McADOO CHERRY

John McAdoo Cherry was born around 1820 in Jackson County Tennessee. He is the son of Cary Cherry, Sr. and Isabella McAdoo Cherry. John M. married Louisa, born around 1835. They lived in the Union Hill Community of Clay County. Their children were: Camel, born 1853, Tilford, born 1855, Andrew and Boyd.

Andrew Cherry, born November 26, 1858 — died April 6, 1899, married Louisa J. Newman, born October 24, 1848. Their children were: Mary, born February 1885; George A., born December 16, 1885; and John Mac, born September 27, 1887.

Boyd Cherry, born November 11, 1861 — died October 23, 1938, married Craton Short, born February 2, 1862. Their children were: Effie, born October 30, 1886; John F., born March 27, 1889; Elizabeth, born July 28, 1891; Ada, born November 11, 1893; Etta, born November 11, 1893; and John Mack, born July 1899.

BRANSFORD L. CHERRY

Bransford L. Cherry was born January 4, 1918, the son of Mack L. and Mandy Baley (Jones) Cherry. He was the grandson of Andrew and Louisa (Newman) Cherry. Mack L. and Mandy B. Cherry were the parents of eleven children: Lou Ann (Crawford), Maullene, Bransford, Celistia (Chandler), Elsie (Reecer), Rentford, John Mack, Berniece (Hatcher-Levie), Willard R. Genevie (Birdwell-Campbell), and Beulah.

Bransford L. married Brilla Jane Rush, born December 12, 1918, the daughter of Cyrus H. Rush, Sr. and Mary Lou (Liftis) Rush. Brilla and Bransford were married July 3, 1937. They had eight children: Lourenia, Royce L., Mack Vancel, Wanda Fay, Carlon Joyce, Lois Kay, Lennis Troy, and Garnette Mark.

Lou Renia Cherry married Donald Lee Davis June 1, 1957. They have the following children: Donna Gail, Denise, Stacy, and Rita.

Denise married Mark Reece, and they have one son, Derrick.

Royce L. Cherry married Sharon Beicherrye, and they have two children, Donna Gail and Dennis L.

Dennis L. Cherry has two children, Christopher, and Roy Looner.

Mack Vancel Cherry married Jackie Starks. Their children are Vancel Ray and Kenny Mack.

Wanda Fay Cherry married Bob Waterman. They have two children, Robbie and Melissia.

Carlon Joyce Cherry married Dennis Hix, and they had two daughters, Cindy and Alisia. Joyce later married Jesse Browner, and they have one child, Jessica.

Lois Kay Cherry married Ronnie Hudson, and they have on child, Shannon.

Lennis Troy Cherry married Jean Leonard, and they have two children, Troy and Tonya.

Garnette Mark Cherry married Ruth Copas, and they have two children, Nathan and Tommy.

WILSON CHERRY, SR.

Wilson Cherry, Sr. was born around 1797 in North Carolina, and died in 1862 in Jackson County, Tennessee. He was the son of Lemuel and Sarah (McPherson) Cherry. He was in the Battle of New Orleans during the War of 1812. He was married twice — the first time to Catherine Hodge, born 1792, and the second time to Adaline (surname unknown), born 1843. He lived in the West End of Clay County which was at that time Jackson County. Wilson and Catherine had

General Cherry

the following children: Fines E., born 1820; Wilson H., born 1828; Lemuel S., born 1825; Julian, born 1827; Alex Jackson, born 1830; and Sarah E., born 1834. Wilson and Adaline had one child, Beauregard, born 1862.

Fines E. Cherry married Mary Wood. Their children were: Wilson, born 1845; Sarah, born 1848; Samuel H., born 1850; and General, born November 4, 1855.

General Cherry was married the first time on November 9, 1873 to Mary E. Dodd, born 1856. He was married the second time to Almerry Whitaker, born March 29, 1863 and who died March 15, 1928. General and Mary had the following children: Fines J.; Rosco; Mary, born March 13, 1880; Ada; Vina B.; and Josephine. General and Almerry's children were: Beulah, born March 19, 1889; Grover, born September 26, 1893; Sylvia C., born March 18, 1897; Melvin, born in 1898; and Vira.

Beulah Cherry, born March 19, 1889, died October 31, 1943, married Press Browning, born April 20, 1877, died August 29, 1957. Their children were: Delano, Claude, Orville, Argo, Dumas, Kit, Press, Jr., and Onalee.

Grover Cherry married Bertha Long, born 1895, died 1958. They had the following children: Goldie, born 1912; Goldman; Bonnie, born December 28, 1917; and Jewel. Goldie Cherry married Earl Browning, and they had two children, Geneva and Juanita.

Wilson H. Cherry, Jr. married Margaret J. Miles, born February 12, 1834. Their children were: Lavina, born 1858; James H., born June 18, 1860; and Taylor (Tailer).

James (Jim) Cherry   Jessie (Morton) Cherry

James H. Cherry, born June 18, 1860 and died July 28, 1923, married Jessie W. Morton, born May 1, 1873. died April 12, 1911. He was one of the largest landowners in the West End of Clay County. James and Jessie had the following children: Estes, Neva, Nora, Leone, Birtie, Earnest, Ervin, Versa, and Vernie.

Alexander Jackson Cherry was married the first time April 10, 1853 to Elizabeth Moore, born January 13, 1835. He was married the second time to Permelia Hestand. Alexander and Elizabeth had one child, Julia America, born November 25, 1859. He and Permelia had the following children: Turner, born December 30, 1863, and William Jackson, born March 4, 1865.

William Jackson Cherry, born March 4, 1865, died September 23, 1923, married Mary Lou Dalton, born December 13, 1876, died May 7, 1936. They had the following children: Orville, Melic (M.D.), Lattie, Myrth, Ephraim, Willie T., Estes, Raymond, Ray, and Lina. Orville married

William Jackson and Lou Cherry

Ethel Reecer. Melic married Edna Birdwell. Lattie married Lester Brown. Myrth married Ida Mary Goodpasture. Ephraim married Nellie Rhea Arms. Willie T. married Dean Grimsley. Estes married Ersie Condra. Raymond married Mable Rose. Ray married Mary Elizabeth Kyle. Lina married Woodrow Lorance.

ORVILLE NEWELL CHERRY

Orville Newell Cherry was born in the Denton's Cross Roads Community of Clay County on November 14, 1894. He is the oldest in a family of eight sons and three daughters born to William Jackson Cherry and Mary Lou Dalton Cherry. Orville is the grandson of Alexander Jackson Cherry and Permelia Hestand Cherry, and Philip H. Dalton and Purlina Wiggins Dalton.

Orville attended school at Beech Bethany, Moss, Arcot, and Montvale Academy.

Orville started farming at a very early age and farmed until he was in his late eighties. He has been active in Farm Bureau, serving for 18 years as President of the Clay County Farm Bureau, and he is an honorary director at the present time.

He married Ethel Reecer December 16, 1916. Ethel was born in the Proctor's Creek Community of Clay County December 6, 1900. She is the daughter of William Leander Reecer and Minnie E. Franklin Reecer. She is the granddaughter of Bud Reecer and Mary Jane Savage Reecer, and Thomas Franklin and Adeline Hill Franklin. Ethel attended school in Clay County. She has been a homemaker for most of her life and has done this with a great deal of pride. She has been active in the home demonstration club and the Farm Bureau.

Orville and Ethel Cherry

Orville and Ethel attend the Arcot Church of Christ, which Orville's father was instrumental in establishing. Orville has been a leader in this congregation for more than 50 years, and is a strong supporter of the First Sunday Singings which are held at various congregations throughout the

...nty on the first Sunday of each month.

18 ...rville and Ethel are the parents of seven children—four sons and three daughters.

...alph Thomas was born January 28, 1918. He ...ed Dorothy Eads, the daughter of Rich and ...nie Cunningham Eads. They have two children—Judy and Douglas. Judy married John ...tta, and Douglas married Rayna Hestand. Ralph died July 10, 1980 and is buried in the Cherry Family Cemetery in the Arcot Community.

Ina Lee was born November 20, 1919. She married Cordell Masters, the son of Bedford and Dulcenia Masters. They have one daughter, Carolyn. She was married to Jerry Hindman. Carolyn has one daughter, Heather Hindman.

William Newell was born November 25, 1921. He married Olivette Brown. They have twins— William Newell, II and Tara. Newell was a professor at the University of Tennessee for a number of years. He died July 28, 1984, and he is buried in Knoxville, Tennessee.

Minnie Adele was born January 23, 1927. She married Herod Birdwell, Jr. Herod is the son of Herod and Lucy Browning Birdwell. Adele and Herod have two daughters — Phyllis and Connie. Phyllis married Bobby Birdwell, and Connie married Andrew Joel Lynn. Phyllis has two children, Michael Loyd and Amy Jean; and Connie has two children, Scott Joseph and Todd Houston.

James Kenneth was born January 22, 1931. He married Ramona Haile, the daughter of Haschal and Ravenel Hollaway Haile. Kenneth and Ramona have two daughters — Linda Diane, who married Abdesslam Swalhah of Jordan, and Sarah Elizabeth, who was born May 6, 1964 and died in September of 1972.

Eva Nell was born October 25, 1933. She married Louis Plumlee, the son of Eulas and Georgia Stone Plumlee. Eva Nell and Louis have three children. Gary married Betty McClain, and they have two children — Brian and Melanie. Jayne Ann married Kevin Donaldson, and they have one daughter, Deanna. James Louis married Jamie Smith.

Robert Arol was born September 19, 1924, and he died September 3, 1928. He is buried in the Cherry Family Cemetery at Arcot.

Orville and Ethel have lived in the same house they moved into nearly 67 years ago. They live in the house built by the McColgins who settled the Arcot Community. The hall of their home once served as the Arcot Post Office. Orville and Ethel will celebrate their 70th wedding anniversary in December of 1986.

JAMES KENNETH CHERRY

James Kenneth Cherry was born January 22, 1931 in the Arcot Community of Clay County. He is the son of Orville Newell Cherry and Ethel Reecer Cherry. Kenneth is the grandson of William Jackson Cherry and Mary Lou Dalton Cherry, and William Leander Reecer and Minnie Eva Franklin Reecer of Clay County.

Kenneth attended grades 1-8 at Arcot School, and graduated from Celina High School. He spent two years at Tennessee Polytechnic Institute and received a Bachelor of Science Degree in Agriculture from the University of Tennessee in Knoxville, Tennessee.

For thirty-three years, Kenneth has been Secretary-Treasurer and Manager of the Tennessee Rural Health Improvement Association in Columbia, Tennessee. He has served on the Tennessee Voluntary Health Cost Containment Committee, and has been appointed by two governors on the Select Health Committee to study health costs. Kenneth has served on various state and national health committees to study health costs. He served on the Advisory Board of Maury County Hospital, as President of Linco, Inc. and President of Voluntary Trust Company.

James Kenneth and Ramona Cherry

Kenneth was married August 29, 1959 to Shirley Ramona Haile from Tompkinsville, Kentucky. Ramona is the daughter of Hascal Haile and Rawenel Holloway Haile. Ramona is the granddaughter of John H. Haile and Anna Laura Richardson Haile, and Herod Holloway and Lillie Eaton Holloway of Monroe County, Kentucky.

Ramona attended school in Monroe County and graduated from Tompkinsville High School. She attended David Lipscomb College and Tennessee Polytechnic Institute. Ramona has taught piano in schools in Tompkinsville, Kentucky and Columbia, Tennessee.

Kenneth and Ramona are the parents of Linda Dianne, born December 26, 1961, and Sara Elizabeth, born May 6, 1964 and died September 1972.

Linda attended school in Columbia and graduated from Central High School in 1980. She went two years to Columbia State College and received a Bachelor of Science and Masters of Arts Degree from George Peabody College at Vanderbilt University in Nashville. Linda was married August 20, 1983 to Abdesslam Swalhah, born April 1, 1960 in the Country of Jordan. They live in Columbia.

Kenneth and Ramona attend church at Greymere Church of Christ in Columbia, Tennessee.

MELIC DALTON CHERRY

Melic Dalton Cherry was born December 5, 1897, the son of William Jackson and Mary Lou Dalton Cherry of the Arcot Community of Clay County. Melic was educated in the schools of Clay County. After his parents' deaths, he purchased the Cherry farm. Melic was a farmer and a trader. He always had at least one pair of beautifully matched mules on his farm and often had more as he greatly admired these magnificent animals. Melic was always for the progress of Clay County and of the Arcot Community. He worked hard in the establishment of the Twin Lakes Telephone Cooperative in order to bring telephone service to Clay County. He was a member of the Bank of Celina Board of Directors, and at one time, he served as president of the Bank of Celina.

Melic was a member of the Arcot Church of Christ and took an active role in the affairs of the Church.

In the mid 1940's, Melic married Edna Birdwell, born August 31, 1903. She was from Sumner County. Edna taught English at Celina High School for several years. Although Melic and Edna had no children, their home was often the scene of parties being held for the young people of the area. They enjoyed having young people in their home; and the young people greatly admired and respected them. Edna also attended the Arcot Church of Christ where she was a Sunday School teacher for several years. Melic and Edna were antique collectors. Melic acquired an extensive collection of mustache cups, while Edna collected a variety of dishes and furniture which were very appropriate for the home built by Melic's father.

Edna died December 26, 1968; and Melic died November 19, 1969. They are buried in the Cherry Family Cemetery in the Arcot Community.

WYATT ESTES CHERRY

Wyatt Estes Cherry was born April 12, 1909. He was the son of William Jackson and Lou Dalton Cherry. He was married to Ersie Condra August 1, 1926. Ersie was born October 15, 1909. She was the daughter of Frank and Ona Gass Condra of Moss.

Estes and Ersie Cherry

Wyatt Estes was a farmer in the Arcot Community. He was a guide on Dale Hollow Lake. He was a member of the Arcot Church of Christ, and Ersie is still a member and attends the Arcot Church of Christ.

Wyatt Estes and Ersie have three children. Evelyn married Ernest Birdwell and lives at Hermitage Springs. Noel and his wife, Vickie, live in Cookeville. Anita married Fred Roach and lives near Celina.

Wyatt Estes Cherry died on September 27, 1960. He is buried in the Cherry Family Cemetery.

NOEL CHERRY

Noel Cherry was born November 5, 1943 in the Arcot Community of Clay County. He is the son of Estis and Ersie Cherry. Noel is the grandson of William Jackson and Mary Lou Dalton Cherry and Frank and Ona Gass Condra, all deceased. Noel attended Celina High School and graduated in 1961. He is a graduate of Middle Tennessee State University. Noel coached football and girls basketball at Gordonsville High School and Cookeville High School. He also coached football at Lawrenceburg High School and Carthage High School. He is presently at

Cookeville Junior High, where he coaches football and is a physical education teacher. Noel is married to the former Vickie Brook of Fayetteville, North Carolina. They have two children, Eric, age 14, and Tracy, age 11. Vickie is the granddaughter of Robert and Beatrice Brombell, and Esteline and Junious Brook. Vickie graduated from Grey's Creek High School in Fayetteville, North Carolina, and is completing her degree in Elementary Education at Tennessee Technological University where she will graduate in the summer of 1987. She is a substitute teacher in the Putnam County School System.

Noel Cherry Family

Noel, Vickie, Eric, and Tracy are members of Collegeside Church of Christ in Cookeville, Tennessee.

DR. ZACHARIAH CHOWNING

Zachariah Robinson Chowning was born May 6, 1811 in Virginia. He was the son of Chattin Chowning and Elizabeth Robinson Philpot Chowning. He married Rebecca McMillin, the daughter of James and Catherine Halsell McMillin, on March 10, 1839. The Chowning and McMillin families migrated to what is now Clay County and Monroe County, Kentucky, prior to the 1820 Census. Dr. Chowning died in Clay County on December 23, 1883. Mrs. Chowning was born January 29, 1821 in Kentucky, and died November 5, 1885 in Clay County. They were the parents of nine children: James Chattin, Jane Ann, William Barton, Gertrude Leanna, Marcella Maria, Ida Rebecca, Dr. John Thomas, Elizabeth and Ernest (female).

Zachariah was the brother of Thomas Jefferson, William Barton, Narcissa Ann, Elizabeth Hannah, Cassandra Philpott, John Chattin, John Wesley, Chattin Horatio, Sarah J., Mariah Jane and Virginia Benson. Rebecca Chowning was the sister of Milton, Catherine, Mary and possibly others unknown.

Ida Rebecca Chowning, born June 11, 1848-died January 13, 1937, married John Holford Officer March 5, 1870. John Officer was born July 7, 1845 — died March 10, 1912. Ida and John Officer had ten children. Judge William Robinson Officer married Nannie Bell Windle. Dr. Margaret Cook Officer married George Davis. J.T. Officer and Sallie Officer died young. Dr. Henry Ray Officer married Mollie Singleton. Mary Officer married Charles Jones Cullom. Edda Officer married Henry Norton Thompson. Aline Ernestine Officer married Henry Roe Denton. W.A. Officer never married.

Aline Ernestine Officer married Henry Roe Denton October 20, 1906. Henry was from Smith County, Tennessee, being born there December 27, 1885. Aline and Henry moved to

Blount County, Alabama. They had three children: John Roe, Robert Officer and Barbara Anne. Aline and Henry Denton died in Alabama.

John Roe Denton, born in 1908 — died in 1972, married Margaret Irene Ellis. They were the parents of: Dr. John Roe Denton, Jr., an orthopedic surgeon in New York, who is married but has no children, and Anne Elizabeth Denton Heidelberg of Long Beach, Mississippi, who is the mother of Charles Hood Heidelberg, Jr.

Dr. Robert Officer Denton, born in 1918, married Frances Louise Sheffield, deceased. They had six children: Frances Diane Broders, Dona Anne Johnson, Jane Aline McDonald, Robert Officer, Jr., Julie Catherine Neal, and Scott Joseph Denton.

Barbara Anne Denton, born 1928, married Paul Corley, and they had one child, Robert Denton Corley, who married Cynthia Diane Williams, and they had two children: Nathan Russell and Matthew Denton. Barbara Ann next married Walter Richard Brassell, Jr., born in 1912. They had two sons: Walter Richard III, unmarried, and John Porter, who married Vickie Lynn Helton, and they have one son, Adam Lee.

NORMAN CLANCY

Norman Clancy was born October 4, 1906 at Moss, Tennessee. He is the son of George Dibrel Clancy, born in 1870, and Florette Plumlee Clancy. George Dibrel was a merchant in Moss, Tennessee, and Florette was a housewife. They are the parents of thirteen children — five sons: Herbert, Norman, Woodrow, Estes, and Haywood, and eight daughters: Bertha (Reecer), Zora (Atchley), Jose (Pennington), Ethel (White), Pearl (Rhoton), Minnie (Rich), Sophia (Baxter), and Winnie (Klug).

Norman Clancy   Lena Clancy

Norman married Lena Walker of Celina, Tennessee, May 30, 1929. She was the daughter of Benton and Dovie Reecer Walker. She was born on April 15, 1911. Norman and Lena are the parents of two daughters, Nelline and Eva Dean.

Nelline was born on July 12, 1930. She is married to Dr. K.E. Bobb of Seymour, Indiana. Nelline was formerly married to Orville Willman, deceased. They were the parents of two sons and one daughter: Rodney, Tim and Deborah.

Rodney, born July 17, 1945, graduated from Western Kentucky State University with a degree in engineering. He is a building contractor. He is married to Margie Curry. She is also a graduate of Western Kentucky. She is a registered nurse. Rodney has a daughter, Chris, a student at Charlestown College in South Carolina.

Tim, born March 3, 1947, is not married. He is a building contractor.

Deborah, born February 18, 1950, graduated from Western Kentucky State University. She is a registered nurse at Seymour Hospital. She is married to Richard Findley of Seymour, Indiana. They have one son, Matthew, age eight.

Eva Dean, daughter of Norman and Lena Clancy, was born January 9, 1932. She graduated from Norton's School of Nursing in Louisville, Kentucky. She is a registered nurse. She was married to Leland Steely, a Certified Public Accountant of Corbin, Kentucky. He is deceased. They have two sons and one daughter: David, Susan, and Daniel.

David, born February 1, 1955, attended Western Kentucky State University. He is employed in Florida. Susan, born July 24, 1957, graduated from Eastern Kentucky State University. She is a Certified Public Accountant in Lexington, Kentucky. She is married to Jim Combs, who is in computer programming in Lexington, Kentucky. They are the parents of Laura Elizabeth and Daniel. Daniel is a senior at Eastern Kentucky State University majoring in Public Relations. He was born on October 23, 1963. Laura Elizabeth is two months old.

DR. CHAMP EDWARD CLARK

Dr. Champ Edward Clark was born May 1, 1912 in the Willow Grove Community of Clay County. He was the oldest child born to Dr. William Edward Clark and Amelia Mary Jane Holman Clark. He has four brothers: Dr. Jack Clark of Cookeville, Dr. Malcom Clark of Livingston, Joe Clark of Celina, and William Haggard Clark of Celina. He has one sister, Geneva Clark Fowler of Celina.

Dr. Clark married Ora Dean Garrett of Byrdstown December 23, 1936. She was the daughter of Dr. I.L. Garrett. Dr. Clark and Ora Dean have one son, Champ Edward Clark, II, born June 19, 1952. He is a dentist practicting dentistry in Monterey and Livingston. Ora Dean died in May of 1972.

Dr. Clark taught school in Clay County for eight years, beginning in 1932 and ending in 1942. He taught at Fairview and Willow Grove Schools.

Dr. Clark attended school at Willow Grove, Montvale Academy, the University of Tennessee, Tennessee Tech, Memphis State University and graduated from the University of Tennessee Medical School in Memphis in 1946. He did his internship at General Hospital in Nashville.

Dr. Edward Clark, around 1910

He returned to Clay County to practice medicine, opening his office July 1, 1947. His first office was upstairs next to the County Extension Agent's office. He remained there for five years before moving to his present location on the public square. He has been practicing medicine in Clay County for 39 years. He was the only doctor in the County for 25 of those 39 years.

When he first started practice, there were no telephones in the county. When someone needed a doctor, they had to rely on word of mouth to find him. In addition, to being the only doctor, he served as his own chauffeur driving 50,000 miles a year.

When Dr. Clark came to this county, the dams had not been built and the water would get out of the creek and riverbanks causing roads to be closed in various parts of the county. It was on such occasions that some of the following happened: One night he walked through the woods for four miles to visit a patient, then helped to carry her out on an army cot to a vehicle to be transported to the hospital for emergency surgery. He delivered nine babies in one night while doing his internship at General Hospital. He delivered four babies in one night in Clay County in individual homes with only word of mouth to tell where he could be found. He had to cross the high water on his horse, standing in the stirrups and holding high his bag to keep it from getting wet, but going on to deliver a baby.

Besides being an old-fashioned country doctor to most of the people in Clay County and the surrounding counties, "Doc," as he is known to most, is much more. He has always been the type of person that you can confide your innermost thought and problems to without ever having to worry that they would be repeated. If you needed a shoulder to cry on, his was available.

In addition to all his work in Clay County, he has worked at the Lady Ann Hospital in Livingston, Jackson County Hospital in Gainesboro, Cookeville General Hospital in Cookeville, and Monroe County Hospital in Tompkinsville, Kentucky.

Dr. Clark was, and still is, so dedicated to his profession that if he were needed he went — regardless of conditions, regardless of the family's ability to pay, and in many instances neglecting his own family to care for others.

Dr. Clark has given a lifetime of devotion to all the people in Clay County.

WILLIAM HAGGARD CLARK

William Haggard Clark was born in 1925, the son of Dr. Edward Clark and Amelia Holman Clark. Dr. Clark was a doctor in Clay and Overton Counties from 1909 to 1944. He graduated from the University of Tennessee, Nashville, in 1909. He married Amelia Holman in 1911. They had six children: Dr. Champ Clark, Celina, Tennessee; Dr. Jack Clark, Cookeville, Tennessee; Dr. Malcolm E. Clark, Livingston, Tennessee; Geneva Clark Fowler, Celina, Tennessee; Joe Clark, Celina, Tennessee; and William Haggard Clark, Celina, Tennessee.

William Haggard was born at Willow Grove, was educated in the Clay County Schools and graduated from Livingston Academy in 1943. He attended Tennessee Polytechnic Institute, and he graduated from the University of Tennessee, College of Pharmacy in 1947.

In 1948, he and his brother, Joe, bought the Maxey Drug Store on the square in Celina. In 1957, he became the sole owner of Clark Drug Store.

In 1948, William Haggard married Geraldine

Walling, the daughter of Jay Everette Walling and Mattie Jane Mooneyham Walling (deceased). Jay Everette then married Tomy Sain Walling. They live in McMinnville, Tennessee. Jay Walling and Mattie Walling both graduated from Buritte College in Spencer, Tennessee and attended Middle Tennessee State College in Murfreesboro. They both taught school in Warren County until Mattie's death in 1945. Geraldine taught school in McMinnville City Schools and in the Clay County School System. She was also a reading specialist for the Urban/Rural School Development Program in Clay County. She was teaching at Celina K-8 School at the time of her retirement in 1982, having completed 28 years of teaching. She now works part-time at Clark Drugs.

William and Geraldine have two daughters: Doris Jane, born in 1951, and Geneva Ann, born in 1954.

Doris Jane Clark married Steven Robbins, the son of Edward and Ellen Robbins of Pascagoula, Mississippi. Jane attended school in Clay County, graduating from Celina High School in 1969. In 1973, she graduated from the University of Tennessee. She received her Masters Degree in Education in 1977. Jane taught in the Clay County School System for seven years. Jane and Steve have two sons, William and Daniel. They live in Cookeville, Tennessee, where Steve is a mechanical engineer with Fleetguard. Steve graduated from the University of Tennessee in 1977 and from Tennessee Technological University College of Engineering in 1981.

Geneva Ann Clark married Richard Roberts, Jr. in 1983. He is the son of Richard and Betty Roberts of Celina. Ann attended the Clay County Schools, graduating from Celina High School in 1972. In 1977, she graduated from the University of Tennessee College of Pharmacy. She is a pharmacist at Clark Drugs in Celina working with her father. Richard, Jr. "Dick" and his family own and operate the Cedar Hill Marina, near Celina, Tennessee on Dale Hollow Lake.

Since Ann came to work for William Haggard in 1977, he has spent most of his time farming. He and Geraldine live on a farm on the Obey River near Celina.

JOHN MORRIS CLARK

John Morris Clark was born about 1818. He and his wife, Katherine, had at least seven children: Leroy M., Sarah A., L.L., B.W., Siseroe, Emmagene, and Samuel.

John Morris Clark

Samuel Alexander Clark was born in either 1850 or 1854. He married Jerusha Ann, born 1857, the daughter of James and Willie Hawkins Ross Bean. They had seven children.

Sumner Jones Clark, born 1878, married Dora

Browning. They had nine children: Isabelle, Cordell, Willie, Oshie, Vivian, Thelma, Velma, Clifton and Ernest.

Dick Avert Clark, born 1880, married Mary P. Birdwell. They had no children.

Barney Durent Clark, born 1883, married Vira Cherry. They had four children: Effie, Herman, Avo, and a daughter who died in infancy. After Vira's death, Barney married Christine Meador, a sister of Albert Meador. They had four children: Vernita, Eunice, Webb, and Samuel Alexander.

Fitzhugh Weaver, born 1886, had one son.

Sidney Edgar Clark, born 1890, married Carnell Davis, the daughter of Parlie and Matilda Browning Davis. They had three children: Mary Edalene, Shelby Johnson, and Charles Randall who died in infancy. Mary Edalene, born June 2, 1942, married Willie Pryor, Jr. They have five children: Charles Anthony, Richard Andrew, Timothy Allen, Rachel Yvonne, and Edgar Alvin. They have two grandchildren: Jennifer and Richard A. Pryor, Jr. Shelby J. married Bobbie Proctor and had two daughters: Bridget and Marcella. This marriage ended in divorce. Shelby then married Linda Sue Smith of Kansas. They have one daughter, Amy Marie, born February 3, 1984. Shelby has one grandson, Toby Erick Abrahamson.

Altie Maye Clark, born 1893, married "Bruce" Jenkins, a widower with five children. She had no children.

Ora B. Clark, born 1898, married Albert Meador and had three children: C.J.; Leon; and Willa Dean (Mrs. Comer Huffines). Ora has five grandsons. — *Submitted by Mary Edalene Clark Pryor*

WILLIAM LEVI CLARK

William Levi Clark was born September 22, 1851 in Pickett County. He was the son of Abraham Henderson Clark and Martha Caroline Huddleston Clark. His grandparents were Robert

Bettie Clark Family: John, Bettie, Denver, Nannie, Esther, Ida, Hettie

Clark and Julia Garrett Clark, and Fielding Huddleston and Martha Zachary Huddleston. William Levi married Mary Pendergrass in Pickett County. They had two daughters: Cratus Clark Young and Mary Clark Story. Mary P. Clark died. William Levi married Margaret Smith in Pickett County. They had two sons: Radford and Charles Edward. Margaret S. Clark died, and on June 23, 1889, William Levi married Mary (Betty) Elizabeth Martin, who was born December 26, 1865 in the Independence Community of Overton County, Tennessee. She was the daughter of Ephriam O. Martin and Jane Garrett Martin. They moved to Clay County in the Willow Grove Community. Children born to this union were: Harris, Nancy

C. (Nannie) Buford, Ida, Esther, Hettie Buford, John and Denver. William Levi died April 5, 1911. Betty Clark died December 25, 1949. Issue for Nancy C. (Nannie), see Clarence R. Buford Family.

CHRISTOPHER CLEMENTS

Christopher Clements, born about 1791, probably in Virginia, and his wife, Anna Fraim (Framil), were the parents of: Leroy S., born in 1824; Henderson M., born in 1827; William Montgomery, born in 1830; Andrew Jackson, born in 1832 and died in 1913; Sarah (Sally), born in 1835; Christopher, born in 1838; and George W., born April 17, 1839 and died February 16, 1931.

George Washington Clements   Isabelle Hamilton Clements

Most of the sons practiced medicine. William Montgomery graduated from Jefferson Medical College in Philadelphia, Pennsylvania in 1859, and served as a surgeon in the Civil War. Andrew J. served as a Union Army surgeon during the Civil War, and was, at one time, a member of the Tennessee Congress. Henderson practiced medicine and also served as a member of Congress. Sally was a teacher. After serving as an officer of the Union Army, George practiced law in Clay County.

The story is told by many older Clay Countians about George being in court in Celina on a particular case. It developed that he needed a certain record, deposition, or a piece of evidence he could only get in Nashville. So, when court broke for the day, he left Celina, rode horseback to Nashville, undoubtedly exchanging a winded mount for a fresh horse several times along the route, and was back at court in Celina the following morning when the next session began.

George Clements married Isabelle Hamilton, the daughter of Colonel Oliver Perry Hamilton and Helen Kirkpatrick Hamilton. Isabelle was born December 28, 1850, and died April 9, 1891. She and George had three sons: Worth Clements, born June 12, 1872, and died April 8, 1951; Rue Clements, born on May 10, 1878, and died November 13, 1951; and Christopher "Kit" Clements, born August 12, 1887, and died September 16, 1967.

WORTH CLEMENTS

Worth Clements was born June 12, 1872 and died April 8, 1951. He was the son of George W. and Isabelle Hamilton Clements. He married Sarah Isabelle Ray, who was born October 13, 1875 and died December 16, 1950; she was the daughter of G.B. and Eliza Condra Ray. Worth and Sarah had four children: Clarence W., born July

Worth and Sarah Clements, Madge and Claude Clements

7, 1893, and died January 15, 1968,; Maude (Cothron), born December 23, 1896; Claude Ensor, born September 10, 1904, died June 17, 1965; and Ila Madge (Green), born April 21, 1906.

CLARENCE AND NOVA CLEMENTS

Clarence Worth Clements was born July 7, 1893, the son of Worth and Bell (Ray) Clements. On February 17, 1917, at Campground Church, he married Nova Ritter, born September 2, 1897, the daughter of Nathan and Jane Woods Ritter. Clarence and Nova lived at Clementsville where he was a farmer, a merchant, and a justice

Clarence and Nova Clements

of the peace. They had seven children: Mary Ruth, born June 10, 1923; C.W., Jr., born March 9, 1925; Carson McCarthy, who died as an infant; Calvin C., born December 21, 1929; Connie Mack, born on April 30, 1933; Clark G., born May 26, 1935; and Carrell Norris, born August 8, 1937. Clarence died January 15, 1968; Nova died March 14, 1963.

MARY RUTH TUDOR

Mary Ruth Clements was born June 10, 1923, the daughter of Clarence and Nova Ritter Clements. She graduated from business college and worked as a bookkeeper. She married Kansel Tudor, who was born September 21, 1918, the son of Rome Curtis and Lucy (Bacon) Tudor. Kansel was a welder, served as a mess sergeant in the 8th U.S. Air Force, and presently farms near Summershade, Kentucky. Mary Ruth is a homemaker. They have two children: Cynthia Ann, born November 11, 1957, and Kansel Roger, born September 14, 1959. Cynthia has a Bachelor of Science degree from Western Kentucky University and a Master of Arts degree from the Citadel. She married Keith Kremer, born December 23, 1956, the son of Myron Kremer of Mandan, North Dakota. Keith served six years in the Navy and has a Bachelor of Science degree from

Kansel and Mary Ruth Tudor, Roger and Cynthia

the College of Charleston. They live in Charleston, South Carolina. Cynthia teaches Home Economics and Keith teaches Math and Computer Science at Goose Creek, South Carolina. They have one child, Jonathan Ryan, born October 8, 1984. Roger married Karen Denese Pitcock, born November 15, 1965, the daughter of Rex and Gloria (Kerney) Pitcock of Lucas, Kentucky. Roger is a farmer, mechanic, and a welder, and Karen works in Glasgow, Kentucky. They live near Summershade, Kentucky.

CLARENCE W. CLEMENTS, JR.

C.W. Clements, Jr. was born March 9, 1925, the son of Clarence Worth, Sr. and Nova Ritter Clements. He attended the University of Tennessee, served five years in the Navy and Naval

C.W. Clements, Jr.

Reserve, and presently farms in the Clementsville Community and lives near the family home. He also serves with the Farm Bureau and Soil Conservation Service.

CALVIN C. CLEMENTS

Calvin C. Clements was born December 21, 1929, the son of Clarence and Nova Ritter Clements. He married Mary Doyle Hix, who was born February 2, 1936, the daughter of Henry and Irene (Gee) Hix of Monroe County, Kentucky. Calvin served over four years in the U.S. Air Force. They live on a farm near Clements-

Calvin C. and Mary Doyle Clements

ville. He is a farmer. Mary Doyle works at Osh-Kosh in Hermitage Springs. They have three children: Calvin Steven, Pamela Jill, and Galene Ryan. Steven married Sandra Wilson, the daughter of Bobby and Jeanetta Wilson of Monroe County, Kentucky. They have one son, Russ Wilson Clements, age two. Steve works at a printing company in Glasgow, Kentucky, Sandra is the dietician at the Monroe County Medical Center. They live near Tompkinsville, Kentucky. Jill married Donald Geralds, the son of John and Elizabeth Geralds of Monroe County, Kentucky. Donald is a carpenter, and they live in Tompkinsville, Kentucky. Galene is a farmer and lives near Clementsville.

CONNIE MACK CLEMENTS

Connie Mack Clements was born April 30, 1933, the son of Clarence and Nova Ritter Clements. He married Mary Pearl Harlan, who was born February 19, 1934, the daughter of Ray and Della Harlan of Monroe County, Kentucky. They

Mary Pearl, Connie Mack and Larry Neal Clements

live and farm in the Clementsville Community of Clay County, Tennessee. He owns and operates a farm and garden supply store in Gainesboro, Tennessee, and is a director of the Clay County Bank. They have a son, Larry Neal, born July 6, 1962. He attended Cumberland University and Martin College where he played basketball; he also attended Tennessee Technological University. He works with the Clay County Bank in Celina.

CLARK G. CLEMENTS

Clark G. Clements was born May 26, 1935, the son of Clarence and Nova Ritter Clements. He is

Clark G. Clements

unmarried, and works at OshKosh at Hermitage Springs. He lives in Red Boiling Springs.

CARRELL NORRIS CLEMENTS

Carrell Norris Clements was born August 8,

Carrell and Mary Lou Clements

1937, the son of Clarence and Nova Ritter Clements. He married Mary Lou Dixon, who was born September 10, 1940, the daughter of Whitney and Piccola Lee Dixon of Moss, Tennessee. They live and farm at Clementsville, and Mary Lou works at OshKosh at Hermitage Springs.

Dr. Barton M. Clements

They have a son, Dr. Barton Matthew Clements, who was born June 27, 1960. He completed medical school at the University of Tennessee Medical School in Memphis, Tennessee, in June 1986.

DONNIE S. AND MAUDE COTHRON

Donnie Sullivan Cothron was born September 13, 1896 and died on September 19. He was a World War I veteran and a farmer in Macon County, Tennessee. He married Maude Clements, born December 23, 1896, the daughter of Worth and Belle (Ray) Clements. Maude is a graduate of Middle Tennessee State University, and taught in Clay and Macon Counties for many years.

Maude Cothron

Donnie and Maude have one son, Kermit Clements Cothron, born June 29, 1924. He is a

graduate of Middle Tennessee State University with a Bachelor of Science degree and Master of Education degree, of Tennessee Polytechnic Institute with an Ed.S. degree, and of Mississippi State University with a Ph.D degree. Kermit served in the United States Army, taught and farmed in Macon County, where they presently live.

CLAUDE ENSOR CLEMENTS

Claude Ensor Clements was born September 10, 1902, the son of Worth and Belle (Ray) Clements. He married Ora Jeanette Cherry, born October 31, 1905, the daughter of William Witt and Mettie Avanna (Dalton) Cherry. Claude attended Montvale Academy and graduated from Clay County High School in 1928. He attended Tennessee Polytechnic Institute and was a teacher in Clay County from 1928-1965. He also farmed. Claude and Ora taught in several schools, including Hermitage Springs, Laurel Bluff, Leonard, Mount Vernon, Oak Grove, and Union Hill. Mr. Claude was known as a stern disciplinarian, but many of his students will remember his fondness for western or cowboy adventure stories. They recall being gathered in his room on Friday afternoons to hear him tell these stories. Mr. Claude also drove an early "school bus". He picked up students in a horse-drawn wagon with narrow wooden benches on it and drove them to Hermitage Springs.

Claude and Ora Clements

Ora was in the first graduating class of Hermitage Springs High School in 1930. She attended Tennessee Polytechnic Institute and was a teacher from 1930-1970. She taught the lower grades, stressing reading and penmanship. She attended and was very interested in any school or community endeavor, and delighted in seeing her "little folks" growing into responsible family and community citizens.

Ora and Claude had two sons: Ray Dalton Clements, born May 3, 1934, and Mickey Fay Clements, born March 31, 1937. Claude died June 17, 1965; Ora died December 17, 1985.

RAY DALTON CLEMENTS

Ray Dalton Clements married Corrynne Smith, born June 19, 1939, in Dayton, Tennessee, the daughter of Claude Mason and Hazel (Green) Smith of Cookeville, Tennessee. Ray graduated from Tennessee Tech in 1958 with a Bachelor of Science degree and in 1975 with a Master of Arts degree. He is a former principal of Hermitage Springs High School and presently teaches vocational agriculture there. He is an army veteran and served as an army aviator in the Tennessee National Guard, and is presently a member of the United States Army Reserves. Corrynne graduat-

Sarah, Jeffrey, Laura, Ray and Corrynne

ed from Cookeville Central High School in 1957, and from Tennessee Tech in 1976. She taught in Clay County and is presently employed by the State of Tennessee Department of Human Services. Ray and Corrynne live between the communities of Oak Grove and Hermitage Springs in Clay County. They have three children. Laura Cathryn, born March 5, 1961, is married to William Timothy McLerran, the son of William Buford and Annie (Kendall) McLerran. Both are graduates of Tennessee Tech and are employed by the Clay County Board of Education. Jeffrey Ray, born April 18, 1963, has an Bachelor of Arts degree from Martin College in Pulaski, Tennessee, attended Middle Tennessee State University, and is presently serving in the United States Army at Fort Carson, Colorado. He played basketball at Martin College. Sarah Claudette, born August 3, 1967, is presently attending Tennessee Tech.

MICKEY FAY CLEMENTS

Mickey Fay Clements, Sr. married Nelda Ruth Brown, born April 17, 1939, the daughter of Cordell and Ada Short Brown. Mickey is Plant Manager of OshKosh B'Gosh in Hermitage Springs. Nelda graduated from Tennessee Technological University in 1979 with a Bachelor of Science degree and teaches at Red Boiling

Deanna, Nelda, Mickey III, Mickey Sr., Kerri, Mickey Jr., Mary Clements, Cherry Ann, and Johnny Hanks

Springs School. Their two children are: Cherry Ann, born April 11, 1957, and Mickey Fay, Jr., born March 3, 1960. Cherry Ann has a Bachelor of Science degree from Tennessee Technological University, and teaches at Hermitage Springs School. On October 20, 1984, she married Johnny Radford Hanks of Monroe County, Kentucky, the son of Kenneth and Barbara Hanks. Mickey, Jr. received his Bachelor of Science degree in Chemical Engineering from Tennessee Technological University in 1982. He is currently a 1st

Lietuenant in the United States Air Force at Eglin Air Force Base in Florida. He is married to Mary Angela Brooks, and they have one son, Mickey Fay Clements, III, born July 7, 1984. Mary Angela also has two daughters, Angela DeAnna Hendrix, born September 14, 1978, and Kerri Elizabeth Hendrix, born July 13, 1980.

WILLIAM E. AND MADGE GREEN

William Ether Green was born September 5, 1900 in Clay County, Tennessee and died August 14, 1984 in Shelby County, Illinois. He married Ila Madge Clements, the daughter of Worth and Belle (Ray) Clements, on February 7, 1926 at Hermitage Springs, Tennessee. They lived in Hermitage Springs and later in Findlay, Illinois. Ether farmed and worked at a grain elevator and Madge has retired from a garment manufacturing plant. They had three daughters: Joyce C. Green, born March 26, 1927 in Clay County, Tennessee; Beverly Joanne Green, born on March 17, 1932 in Shelby County, Illinois; and Shirley Jean Green, born August 25, 1933 in Shelby County, Illinois.

William and Madge (Clements) Green

On August 23, 1945, Joyce married Donald Dean Wilson, born April 13, 1923. They have one son, Stuart Dean Wilson, born April 16, 1949.

On August 10, 1951, Beverly Joanne married William F. Fisher, born January 2, 1931. They have four children: Becky, born September 15, 1952; Shirley Diane, born January 31, 1954; Kelli Lea, born September 5, 1955; and Steven Jay, born April 24, 1957. Joanne is married to Max Moses, born March 13, 1930. They live in Mt. Zion, Macon County, Illinois.

On June 4, 1951, Shirley married James Russell Brewer, born November 5, 1927. Their two sons are: Jimmie Lee Brewer, born February 2, 1953, and Dannie Gene Brewer, born February 25, 1955. James and Shirley live in Fayette County, Illinois.

RUE AND SAVANNAH CLEMENTS

Rue Clements was born May 10, 1878 and died November 13, 1951, the son of George W. Clements and Isabelle Hamilton Clements. He married Savannah Eads, born March 14, 1885 and died December 17, 1926, the daughter of George and Florantha Eads. Rue and Savannah lived near Clementsville. Their children were: Cancel, born June 25, 1906 and died January 17, 1977; Carlos George "Red", born January 10, 1912 and died February 21, 1955; Creed, born January 4, 1915 and died February 4, 1970; Reed born March 4, 1920 and died May

28, 1976; and Rue, Jr., born August 22, 1924.

Cancel was married to Jewel Long, the daughter of George and Annie Long of Hermitage Springs. Cancel and Jewel's children are: Inez Clements Carnahan, deceased; Bliss Clements, who lives in the Scottsville, Kentucky area; and Dan Clements, who lives in Florida. Cancel farmed and lived the latter part of his life near Gamaliel, Kentucky.

Creed Clements was a veteran, serving with the army during World War II in the Pacific. He lived in Clay County most of his life.

CARLOS CLEMENTS

Carlos Clements married Essie Murray, born May 25, 1909, the daughter of Haskel Benton and Lily May Billingsley Murray. They lived in the Clementsville area. Carlos farmed and was especially known for his skills in handling the horse and mule teams in the logging industry. Carlos and Essie had four children: James, born December 13, 1937; Billy Douglas, born September 8, 1939 and died September 9, 1950; Virginia, born and died on July 13, 1946; and Glen G. "Tinker", born June 23, 1947.

James married Katherine Abney, the daughter of Fred and Pearl Abney of the Baptist Ridge community. James and Katherine have one daughter, Sharon, born February 11, 1967. Sharon is a student at Middle Tennessee State University. James has worked for many years for the Chevrolet Company in Indianapolis, Indiana and is farming part-time in Clay County where their home is on Highway 52, between Moss and Celina.

Glen Clements is married to Judy Sporey and they live north of Lafayette, Tennessee, where they farm and are preparing to open a business in Lafayette. Glen is an army veteran. They have a son, Nathan Glen Clements, born July 2, 1984.

REED CLEMENTS

Reed Clements served in General Patton's command in the European Theatre during World War II. His decorations included three Bronze Stars and the Purple Heart. He was a farmer, living between Laurel Bluff and Hermitage Springs. He also drove a school bus for many years. He was married to Ruth Carter, the daughter of Grover and Edna Carter. Reed and Ruth have four children: Wanda, Diana, Sandra, and Deborah.

Reed Clements

Wanda married Douglas Ray, the son of Bascom Ray, Sr. and Della Slate Ray. Their children are: Lonnie Douglas, born August 29, 1956; Larry Joe, born September 30, 1957, deceased; Gary Donald, born August 15, 1958; Nyoka Kay, born August 12, 1959; Donnie Lee, born March 24, 1961; Patrick Eugene, born May 18, 1962, and died in 1965; and Ronnie David, born September 15, 1963.

Diana is married to Mervyn Holland of Gamaliel, Kentucky. Their first son, Layne, was born January 27, 1969, and died at age eight. Their second son, Anthony Reed, was born June 29, 1970. Mervyn Holland sells office equipment and supplies, and he and Diana have been involved in the restaurant business. Diana operated the Dairy Burger at Hermitage Springs and, more recently, the new barbeque restaurant there.

Sandra is married to Bobby Grace, born May 29, 1945, the son of M.R. Grace and Opal Cherry Grace. Sandra works at OshKosh at Hermitage Springs. Bobby farms and drives a truck. Their children are: Shelley Leigh, born September 14, 1973; Lucas Brandon, born September 30, 1975; and Nicholas Landon, born September 24, 1979. They also had a son who died as an infant.

Deborah married Donnie Cornwell, and they live in Louisville, Kentucky, where Donnie works at the Ford assembly plant. They have twin daughters, Donneta Cheryl and Dondra Lynn, born September 19, 1984.

RUE CLEMENTS, JR.

Rue Clements, Jr. married Onille Browning, the daughter of Mr. and Mrs. Press Browning, Sr. He is now married to Laura Katrina Lyons, who was born October 8, 1912. Her parents were George Lyons of Kentucky and Katrina Lyons of Wyoming. Rue served in the army in Europe during World War II. He was awarded the Purple Heart and three Battle Stars. Later, he served four years in the Air Force. Junior is also a barber and currently has a part-time shop in the high-rise apartment complex where he and Laura live in Denver, Colorado.

Troy, Judy, Rue Jr. and Laura Clements

On July 20, 1958, Junior was working in cross-country custom wheat combining. A tornado struck, picked up the truck in which another man and he were riding, and killed the other man. A family saw the truck destroyed and carried Junior to shelter. Many days later he awakened in a hospital. He has undergone twenty-two surgeries since that injury.

On a recent visit to relatives here in Clay County, Junior and Laura discovered that she, too, has relatives in this vicinity. She found some of her Lyons relatives who live in Monroe County, Kentucky. One of her cousins is James Lyons of Tompkinsville.

CHRISTOPHER KIT CLEMENTS

Christopher Kit Clements was born August 12, 1886 in Clementsville, Tennessee. He was a farmer, a horse trader, and a merchant at Clementsville, where he lived his entire life. He was married to Ada Belle Murray March 6, 1905 at the Campground Methodist Church by Brother Taylor.

Ada Belle Murray was born November 13, 1889 and died September 16, 1967. She was the daughter of Dr. John R. Murray, who was born June 21, 1849 and died June 20, 1896, and Eliza Coffel Murray, who was born December 16, 1858 and died February 12, 1929.

Christopher Kit was the youngest of three sons born to George and Isabelle Hamilton Clements.

Kit and Ada, as they were known to all their friends and relatives, were the parents of seven children: Lillian, born December 9, 1907; Charlie, born December 10, 1910; Thelma, born February 22, 1912; Elvin, born October 2, 1915; Elzie Rue, born August 29, 1919; Alma, born March 19, 1923; and Chloe, born January 3, 1926.

Christopher Kit died June 21, 1971.

LILLIAN CLEMENTS SPEAR

Lillian Clements was born December 9, 1907, at Clementsville, Tennessee. Lillian was married to Roy Spear July 5, 1928, at Lafayette, Tennessee. They were on their way to Detroit where Roy was employed and where they lived most of their lives, except the depression years, 1930 to 1934. They lived at Oak Grove during these years, where Lillian carried the mail on a star mail route from Moss to Red Boiling Springs and Roy taught school at various places in the county.

They returned to Michigan in 1934, where Roy went back to his old job at Chrysler Corporation, and Lillian started there also in 1941. Roy was superintendent of the power steering division of the Chrysler Corporation, Trenton, Michigan Plant, until its move to Indiana. He continued with the Corporation on various assignments until his retirement, with 34 years accredited service. Roy and Lillian returned to Oak Grove in Clay County in 1976, where they now live. They have three children: Helen, born February 3, 1931; Betty, born on July 7, 1932; and Anna, born August 19, 1934.

Helen Spear was married to William (Bill) Putty September 2, 1950. He is a licensed master electrician with additional training from Lawrence Tech in electronics. He is employed at the Pontiac Division of General Motors. Both Helen and Bill are very active in church work at the Roseville Church of Christ in Roseville, Michigan. Helen attended McComb County Community College, where she received an executive secretarial associate degree. She is employed as a personnel interviewer at Sears.

Helen's work for most of her life has been on jobs where much responsibility was involved. Her first job was at Chrysler Corporation, the day after graduation from high school, a job of trust and responsibility. During her high school days, she won the American Legion Essay Contest, competing against all the high schools in the State of Michigan — the subject: "What America Has Done For Me." Helen and Bill have three children, Michael, Laura, and Karen. Michael was born on May 18, 1957, in East Detroit, Michigan. He received his Bachelor of Science degree in Electrical Engineering from the University of Michigan and is working on his master's degree.

He is employed in the Research Lab at General Motors, working in microelectronic research. Laura was born April 13, 1959, in East Detroit, Michigan. She was married August 31, 1980, to Tom Davison in the Greenfield Village at the Martha Mary Chappel in Dearborn, Michigan. To this marriage were born two children: Tommie Davison, born July 31, 1981, and Benjamin Davison, born November 26, 1984. Laura has a degree from McComb County Community College in associated accounting and associated computers. Tom has a business degree from Wayne State University. He is employed at J.C. Penney as a sales manager. Karen Putty was born on July 27, 1965 and is working on her degree at Wayne State University. She is very active in both the school and church programs. She has been a member of the girls choir, and has had various numbers as both a soloist and in a duet. She will continue her study in the School of Pharmacy at Wayne State University this fall. Both Karen and Laura are Sunday school teachers of different age groups at Roseville Church of Christ.

Betty Spear was married to George Shahly August 14, 1952 in Grosse Pointe Park, Michigan. Betty was a very popular girl in high school. She was president of her class at Southeastern High in Detroit, Michigan, a very large school. This election was a new experience to Betty's parents, who had attended high school in Clay County. Betty said, "This was a real political maneuver, like running for Governor in the State of Tennessee." There was a campaign manager, campaign meetings, printing literature, fund raisings, and banquets, but Betty's parents said it was all worth it when she won. They enjoyed most of all her campaign song, "The Tennessee Waltz." Betty's future husband was a great force in that election. He was from a fine and well-known business family and he had a great influence on the final outcome. Betty is now working as manager of a financial corporation and is licensed to sell various kinds of insurance. She received training for this line of work from McComb County Community College. George Shahly is a director of Elementary Education in Frazier Public School System. George received his training for this from Wayne State University and the University of Michigan, where he has a Ph.D. in Ed.D. Betty and George have two children: Mark, born November 21, 1954, and Vicki, born April 15, 1958. Mark married Cindi Corpi August 21, 1976. He has a master's degree from the University of Michigan in geophysics and holds a supervisory position with Amoco Oil in Denver, Colorado. Cindi has a bachelor's degree in education from the University of Michigan, and is a special education teacher. They have one child, Aloma, born March 21, 1986. Vicki married Ronald Kessler in April 1986. She has a B.S. degree in English from the University of Michigan and is working on her Ph.D. in clinical psychophysics from the University of California at Berkeley. Ronald teaches at the University of Michigan and does consulting work in the field of education.

Anna Spear was married to Earl (Bucky) Stuart September 5, 1952 in Grosse Pointe Park, Michigan. Bucky is a supervisor at Federal Mogul in Hamilton, Alabama. Anna taught as a substitute teacher in Hamilton and was secretary to the Superintendent of Schools and the Board of Education in Marion County, Alabama. Anna and

Bucky have two children: Jeffrey, born October 11, 1955, in Columbus, Ohio, and Cindy, born January 8, 1965, in St. Clair, Michigan.

Jeffrey graduated from high school in St. Clair Shores, Michigan, and was a member of the school band. He completed the auto mechanics course at Motex of Chrysler Engineering and passed the test for licensing in all phases of automobile mechanics. He married Jeri Hall March 26, 1983. Jeri was born April 30, 1958. They live in California where Jeff is stationed with the United States Marines, working for the United States Navy's Air Fleet as a mechanic. His duties include supervising inspection, maintenance, safety, and approving for flight the air fleet on the base. Jeff is now in his eighth year in the Marines. Jeri works in private enterprise, but has extensive training in the Air Force and is a member of the Air Force Reserve. Her job primarily involves office work with the United States Government. Jeri is from Knoxville, Tennessee, and both she and Jeff enjoy coming to Clay County, and Tennessee may be their home again some day.

Cindy was a cheerleader in high school, and was runner-up in the Miss Alabama Teenager Pageant in her senior year. She married Tommy Burleson August 10, 1985, at the Church of Christ in Hamilton, Alabama, where the family attends church. Bucky is a deacon and custodian of their new building, and Anna teaches Sunday School in various classes. Cindy and Tommy were in college at the University of Alabama at the time of their marriage. They both returned to college after the wedding. Cindy is working on her degree in Computer Science and Tommy is working on his master's degree in Civil Engineering.

CHARLIE CLEMENTS

Charlie Clements was born December 20, 1910 in Clay County, Tennessee. He married Nova Carter, who was born on March 11, 1921, and died December 18, 1953. There were four children born to this marriage: Edith Marie, born November 4, 1937; Geneva, born and died August 13, 1940; Melba Sue, born February 10, 1945, and died November 21, 1949; and Brenda, born December 17, 1953, and died May 23, 1956.

Charlie was a farmer and lived at Oak Grove, only a few miles from the old homeplace at Clementsville, where he was born. Charlie was a hardworking man. He loved horses and spent a lot of time breaking and training them. He entered various horse shows and won many trophies and prizes.

All of Charlie's children, except Marie, died at a very young age. When Marie's mother died in 1953, Charlie and Marie were left alone. However, Charlie manages to keep the home together, and takes good care of Marie. At the age of 48, she still lives at home with Charlie.

THELMA CLEMENTS EADS

Thelma Clements was born February 22, 1912. She married D.A. (Hood) Eads July 6, 1930. There were two sons born to this marriage: Kenneth, born February 7, 1934, and Jimmie Dale, born October 5, 1936 and died April 21, 1937.

Hood was a farmer and served as Road Commissioner of Clay County for three terms. Thelma and Hood had many friends in Clay County. They were both members of the Butler's Landing Church of Christ.

Kenneth Eads was married to Elizabeth Anderson November 30, 1967. They are part owners/operators of Eads and Spear Flower Shop in Celina. Kenneth also works with the State Highway Department, a civil service job he has held many years. He and Liz have one daughter, Kenna Kay, born September 7, 1969. She married Doug Spivey, Jr. June 14, 1986 in a beautiful wedding at the Church of Christ in Celina, Tennessee. Kenna Kay is now working at Osh-Kosh in Celina but plans to continue school in the fall. Doug graduated from Celina High School in 1985 and is employed by Nielsen's of Gainesboro, Tennessee. Doug and Kenna Kay live at the old homeplace, where Hood and Thelma lived so many years.

Neither Thelma nor Hood lived to see their only grandchild grow up to be such a beautiful and happily married young woman. Hood died February 10, 1980; Thelma died September 2, 1983.

ELVIN CLEMENTS

Elvin Clements was born October 2, 1915 in Clay County, Tennessee, and died March 25, 1970. Elvin was the fourth child of Christopher Kit and Ada Belle Murray Clements and the only one of the children that never married. However, he was very much a family man, giving much support to his father and mother, and any other member of the family who needed his help. He served in the United States Army during World War II, on active duty from November 8, 1942 until October 5, 1943. He arrived for duty at Pearl Harbor March 15, 1943 and received an honorable discharge October 5, 1943.

Elvin took a course in vocational agriculture at Hermitage Springs High School. He was a good farmer and livestock producer.

ELZIE RUE CLEMENTS

Elzie Rue Clements was born August 29, 1919. He married Mildred Armstrong October 23, 1943. Elzie Rue served in the United States Navy in World War II. After the war, he settled down in Nashville, where he owned and operated a barbershop for many years. He bought the old homeplace farm at Clementsville and his family still owns it. He was a great lover of horses and an excellent rider. He enjoyed breaking and training horses and was fond of fine bridles, saddles, and harnesses. Elzie Rue (Dooger) had been a mason for many years and he went far beyond the rank of a Master Mason.

Mildred Armstrong Clements was born on May 1, 1923 in Virginia. She lives in Nashville where she and Dooger lived for many years and where the three children, Garry, Steve, and Susan, were raised. Dooger died November 6, 1982.

Garry Clements, born February 13, 1950, was married to Rellis Rutledge on July 30, 1977. They have two children: Kelly, born February 11, 1978, and Kiera, born on April 30, 1985. Garry finished high school in Nashville and attended Tennessee Tech. He served in the United States Navy. He is now on the police force in Nashville, and he and his family live in Donelson, Tennessee

Steve Clements, born August 24, 1952, was married to Linda Meadows July 19, 1974. Steve and Linda both finished high school in Nashville. Steve is now employed by the Nashville Auto-

Diesel College, where he recruits students for the college. He has the entire state of Virginia as his territory. He is also a part-time farmer engaged in raising purebred cattle on the old homeplace at Clementsville. Linda has worked many years doing office work for various companies in Nashville.

Susan Clements, born November 10, 1956, was married to Stanley Browning October 11, 1974. They have one son, Jamie, born July 27, 1976. Susan is now married to Rickey Farley. Susan and Rickey have one daughter, Brittney Jo, born August 8, 1985. Susan lived in Nashville during her childhood days, but completed her junior and senior years at Hermitage Springs High School. She now lives at Gallatin, Tennessee, and is employed by Gallatin Auto Parts. Rickey works in a supermarket and as an auto mechanic.

ALMA CLEMENTS GILPATRICK

Alma Clements was born March 19, 1923. She graduated from Hermitage Springs High School in 1945. She was married to Granville Gilpatrick November 26, 1948. To this marriage was born one son, Dennis Wayne Gilpatrick, on September 23, 1957.

Wayne graduated from Celina High School May 26, 1975. He had a short stay in the United States Army, but had an honorable discharge, due to health reasons in the family. Wayne has a natural love for cars and great desire to do mechanic work. He has had much training in this line of work.

Alma did not live long enough to see Wayne grow up, but people who knew her best remember how hard she worked and how well she cared for Wayne. Alma died May 25, 1971. Granville and Wayne now live at the old homeplace. Granville is a leader in the Church of Christ in that community. He is in the real estate business and is an auctioneer in Kentucky and Tennessee. Wayne is employed in Algood, Tennessee.

CHLOE CLEMENTS PLUMLEE

Chloe Clements was born January 3, 1926. She finished high school at Hermitage Springs in 1945. She worked at the Clay County Hospital at one time and at various factory jobs in the county. She was married to Hunter Plumlee in 1945 and divorced in 1963. To this marriage, two children were born.

Linda Sue Plumlee was born January 10, 1951. She graduated from Tompkinsville High School in Kentucky with honors. She now works at OshKosh in Celina, Tennessee. She was married to Larry Rich. To this marriage, one son was born. James was born February 3, 1969. He is in his senior year at Hermitage Springs High School this year. James is of the athletic type. He made the varsity team in both baseball and basketball.

Alvie Dwight Plumlee was born October 12, 1955. Dwight attended Tompkinsville Elementary School and Hermitage Springs High School. He was active in sports at both places. He was also very active in the vocational agriculture program as a member of various judging teams and took an active part in other clubs and other activities. Dwight is now a long distance truck driver.

BILLIE E. MARCOM COLLINS

Billie Edwin Marcom was born May 21, 1932. She is the daughter of Luke Brown Marcom and

Siddie Parsons Marcom. Billie is the granddaughter of W.A. and Anne Lowery Marcom of Celina and Edward Herbert and Ara Vena Willis Parsons of the Pine Branch Community of Clay County.

Billie attended Celina Elementary and Celina High School. She received her Bachelor of Science Degree in Education from Tennessee Polytechnic Institute.

In 1951, Billie began teaching in the Clay County School System. She has worked for the Clay County School System for two years as Supervisor of Instruction and for 30 years as a teacher at the elementary level.

Billie married James Harold Collins October 15, 1951. Harold is the son of James Walter and Flora Mae Nelson Collins of Celina. Harold is the grandson of John William and Maude Brown Collins and James Reason and Rettie Brown Nelson of the Willow Grove Community of Clay County.

Harold attended Celina Elementary and Celina High School. He attended Tennessee Polytechnic Institute for two years. He works for the State of Tennessee Highway Department of Clay County.

Billie Marcom Collins

Billie and Harold are the parents of Patricia Ann, born July 9, 1952; James William, born October 3, 1959; Mark Edwin, born November 20, 1960; and Luke, born July 18, 1969. Patricia Ann married John C. South, Jr. of Eden, North Carolina December 15, 1972. They have one daughter, April Michelle, born December 1, 1975.

Mark Edwin married Tammy Sue Melton June 19, 1980. Tammy is the daughter of George Allan and Betty Sue Sims Melton of Moss, Tennessee. She is the granddaughter of Herman and Mary Sevier Melton, and of Estis and Vealer Crawford Sims of Moss, Tennessee.

Billie Edwin and Harold live in Celina on part of the W.A. Marcom farm. Their son, Luke, is a junior at Celina High School. He still lives at home. Patricia and Mark live in Celina, and William lives in Cookeville.

JAMES WALTER COLLINS

James Walter Collins, born May 15, 1911, was the son of John William and Maude Brown Collins. James Walter lived at Pleasant Hill in the eastern section of Clay County. He married Flora Mae Nelson March 27, 1932. She was the daughter of James Reason and Rettie Belle Brown Nelson. She was born May 8, 1912. James Walter owned and operated Collins Lumber Company near Celina on Shanky Branch. He and Flora had three children: James Harold, Doris Helen, and Margaret Lillian.

Harold married Billie Edwin Marcom. Helen married Billy Lee West, son of Harris and Agnes

James and Flora Collins

Dillion West of Rickman. Helen has two children: Jeffery Harris and John Howard. Jeffery is employed by the Kroger Company, and John Howard is a student at Glencliff High School in Nashville. Helen is employed at National Linen Service in Nashville. Billy Lee died November 4, 1979.

Margaret married Allen Reid Webb, son of Domer and Carmen Key Webb. Margaret and Reid have one daughter, Lillian Renee. Renee married Randy Thomas Davis. They have one son, Matthew Thomas. Margaret works for the Tri-County Vocational School and the Clay County Board of Education.

JOE BOB COLLINS

Joe Bob Collins was born during the Civil War May 16, 1863 to parents who were passing through Clay and Overton Counties on their way to Eastern Tennessee. The parents worked for John and Frances Brown near Hilham. The Brown's were childless and took Joe Bob to raise as their own son. The parents moved on to the Sequatchie Valley. Joe Bob married Ova Alred of Hilham in Overton County. Ova was born June 2, 1869. She died March 21, 1943. Joe Bob was a farmer, deputy sheriff, and often took rafts of logs from Celina down the Cumberland River to Nashville. The trip usually took three weeks. He served as deputy sheriff several times, and finally gave up his badge at the age of 81. Joe Bob died July 7, 1948. He lived most of his life in Overton, Jackson, and Clay Counties, except for six years spent in Nashville in the late 1920's. Joe Bob and Ova were the parents of five children: Charlie (married Mattie Strong); Arnold (married Iva Rogers); Virgie (married Fay Strong); Nellie (died at 15); and Willie (married Livie Lynn).

Joe Bob and Ora Collins

Arnold Collins was born November 10, 1898 and died June 21, 1972. He married Iva Rogers, the daughter of Brant and Amanda (Bailey) Rogers of Jackson County. Iva was born December 30, 1903 and died May 14, 1981. Arnold worked for the Nashville Bridge Company in the late 1920's before returning to Clay County to be a farmer in the Brimstone Community. Arnold had

the opportunity to play baseball for the Nashville Vols as a shortstop, but he turned it down to go back to Clay County to raise his family. Arnold and Iva were the parents of seven children: Thelma, Judy, Bonnie, Faye, Jimmy, Eddie, and Betty.

Judy Collins was born May 23, 1931 in Clay County. She attended Celina High School. She married Jim Carter of the Oak Grove Community. Jim was born December 17, 1922 to Aubrey and Ona (Moss) Carter. He is the grandson of Anthony and Roxie McLerran Carter. Anthony Carter was a Justice of the Peace and lived in Moss, Hermitage Springs, and Oak Grove. Jim and Judy moved to Indianapolis, Indiana. They are the parents of two children, Linda and James.

Linda married John Jerry Dillon. She graduated from Tennessee Technological University in 1973. She worked for the Cordell Hull Economic Opportunity Corporation in Celina as a supervising teacher of the Enrichment and Development Center for the mentally handicapped pre-school children, ages 4-18. In 1974, Linda taught first and second grades in the Jackson County School System. She was a social worker and program coordinator for Hilltoppers of Crossville, a non-profit facility for mentally handicapped adults, and she worked for the same type program in Lebanon, Tennessee. She and her husband presently reside in Cookeville, Tennessee.

ROYCE HAROLD COLLINS

Royce Harold Collins was born July 7, 1946 on McCormack's Ridge in Clay County, Tennessee. He is the son of Everett Greene (Bulldog) Collins, born in Hilham, Tennessee, and Delma Beatrice Anderson Collins, born in Moss, Tennessee. Everett, Delma, and their six children left Clay County in 1956 and moved to a farm near Sheridan, Indiana where Everett worked as a farmer. Everett later got a job with Stokely Van Camp where he worked until he retired. Everett and Delma now live in the Pine Hill Community near Moss, Tennessee.

Royce, Bernadine, Rita and Kimberly Collins

Royce is the grandson of the late Charles Collins who was born in Hilham, Tennessee and Mattie Strong Collins (after Charles died, Mattie married Will Siebert) and Garland Hall Anderson, born in Boles, Kentucky, and Mary Alice McCormack Anderson, born in Moss, Tennessee. Royce attended school at Pine Hill and Brimstone in Tennessee prior to his family moving to Indiana. Royce attended schools in northern Indiana and graduated from Tipton High School in 1963 and from Howard W. Sams Technical Institute in 1965. He then moved to Bloomington, Indiana to take a job with RCA. Royce served in the Marine

Corps from 1966 to 1968. Royce is now President of Local 1424 of the International Brotherhood of Electrical Workers representing RCA workers in Bloomington. Royce was married to Bernadine Regina Taylor Collins of Bloomington, Indiana on July 3, 1968. Bernadine was born in Bloomington on July 20, 1948, the daughter of Huston Randolfe Taylor, born in Jasonville, Indiana, and Wanda Marie Carter Taylor, born in Bloomington, Indiana. She is the granddaughter of the late Alfred Elmo Taylor, born in Ohio County, Kentucky, and Emma Harrington Wines Taylor, born in Greene County, Indiana and the late Paul William Carter, born in Myrtle, Mississippi, and Lora O'Leatha Martindale Carter, born in Bloomington, Indiana. Bernadine attended schools in Monroe County, Indiana, graduating from Bloomington High School in 1967. Bernadine works at Columbia House Records in Bloomington. Royce and Bernadine are the parents of Rita Dianne, born March 29, 1969, and Kimberly Ann, born April 1, 1972. Rita is a student at Bloomington High School North, and Kimberly is a student at Tri-North Middle School. Both are active in concert, pep, and marching band and Kimberly in track.

JAMES THOMAS COLSON

J.T. Colson, son of Robert Colson and Valeria Ellen (Dulworth) Colson, was born November 5, 1895.

Jimmy served his country during World War I and is one of the few veterans from Clay County still living. Jimmy married Myrtle Watson December 18, 1927. To this union were born eight children — four survive.

James Colson

Johnny E. Colson married Mary V. Mabry and they had two daughters, Vickie (deceased) and Debbie. They live in Russell Springs, Kentucky. Edna married Thomas C. Davis, and they have two sons, Larry and Gary. They all live in Franklin, Indiana. Larry and his wife, Linda have one daughter, Libby. Anna M. Colson married Bill Coe, and they have two children, Taryn and Joey. Taryn graduated from David Lipscomb College and is employed in Cookeville, Tennessee and is working on her Masters at Tennessee Technological University. Joey Coe is attending Samford University in Birmingham, Alabama, and is a member of the varsity basketball team. He plans to coach when he graduates. Bob Colson married Connie Callis, and they have two daughters and one son. Rhonda is married and is attending Indiana-Purdue University in Indianapolis. Tina is attending David Lipscomb College and Jon is in high school and also plays basketball. They now live in Indianapolis, but moved to San Antonio, Texas in June of 1986.

Jimmy Colson is ninety years old, but is still very active. He goes to the community center everyday and plays rook. He likes to fish and still works in his garden. Jimmy was born in Clay County, Tennessee and has lived here all his life. He is a member of the Rock Springs Church of Christ, one of the oldest congregations in the United States.

ROBERT A. AND VALERIA E. COLSON

Thomas Colson was born in Frederick County, Virginia. His wife's name is unknown. Their children were Elizabeth, Thomas, William and George M.

George M. Colson, born (ac) 1780, married Susanna Granger. Their first son, William Allen, was born in North Carolina in 1802. The family moved to Overton County, Tennessee in 1803. Their children were John, born in 1804; Bethel, born in 1806; Mary, born in 1809; and James Madison, born in 1812. Sometime later they moved to Clay County.

Tessie, Valeria Ellen, Thomas, Willie, Lucy, Ira, Paul, Mattie and Amelia Colson

William Allen Colson married Martha Clary, who was born in 1802 and died in 1862. Their children were Mary Jane, born in 1825; Susan, born in 1829; Nancy, born in 1832; Sarah, born in 1834; Hannah Ellen, born in 1836; John R., born in 1839; Martha Emaline, born in 1840; Permelia Catherine, born in 1842; and George Washington, born in 1827. After Martha died, William Allen married Amanda Thomas. Their children were: James Hardy, Martha Geraldine, and Richard M. William Allen was elected or appointed Justice of the Peace for Clay County in 1871. He died in 1873.

George Washington Colson married Patsy Arms, who was born in 1827. Their children were John Henry, Willie, Katherine, Melia, and Robert Allen.

Robert Allen Colson, who was born in 1865 and died in 1942, married Valeria Ellen Dulworth, born in 1874 and died in 1955. They were farmers. They had nine children: James Thomas, born in 1895; Tessie Ann, born in 1898 and died in 1973; Willie George, born in 1901; Johnny Robert, born in 1903 and died in 1926; Lucy Edith, born in 1904 and died in 1980; Amelia Avo, born in 1907 and died in 1983; Ira Hill, born in 1910 and died in 1968; Mattie Emma, born in 1912 and died in 1985; and Edward Paul, born in 1914 and died in 1973.

Edward Paul Colson married Mary Magdalene Scott, who was born in 1923. They had seven children: Shelby Jeane, born in 1938; Nell Ruth, born in 1940; Edward Carl, born in 1941 and

died in 1971; Robbie Edwina, born in 1942; Lynda Ellen, born in 1944; Mildred Sue, born in 1946; and Daryl Wayne, born in 1949.

Nell Ruth Colson married James Artee Dale, who was born in 1936 and died in 1983. They had two children. Ricky Lynn was born in Celina, Tennessee in 1958. They moved to Indianapolis in 1966. James Carl was born there in 1972. Nell now lives in Camby, Indiana.

Ricky Lynn Dale married Beth Ann Baldwin, who was born in 1958. They have one son, James Robert, who was born in 1977. Ricky is employed by Peterbilt. They live in Indianapolis, Indiana.

RICHARD CONDRA

Richard Condra, born 1751 in Virginia, married Dorcas Cox, born in 1755 in Barren County, Kentucky. They had four children: John Elder, George, Elizabeth and Rhoda.

George Condra, born June 2, 1792 in Barren, (now Monroe) County, Kentucky, married Rebecca Browning, born March 1796 in South Carolina. George died around 1850, and Rebecca died in 1886. Rebecca was the daughter of Charles and Martha (Hazelwood) Browning. George and Rebecca had eight children: Green, Mary, Sarah, John Wolford, Catherine, William, Nancy, and George.

John Wolford Condra, born October, 13, 1820 in Jackson (now Clay) County, Tennessee, married Sarah Teressa Cherry, born March 21, 1823. John died August 8, 1899, and Sarah died September 22, 1883. Sarah was the daughter of Cary and Isabella (McAdoo) Cherry. Sarah and John had nine children: Mary Jane, Isabelle, Cary Newton, Nancy, Sarah, Eliza Ann, Carrel Columbus, Elizabeth, and Martha Ellen.

Cary Newton Condra, born July 7, 1846, married Arthula P. Pipkin, born November 29, 1851. Cary Newton died March 24, 1923, and Arthula died July 27, 1903. They had seven children: Martha Savannah, William Taylor, John Payton, Fannie Bell, Cora Missour, Newton Franklin, and James Luther. Cary Newton married the second time, Grace Caruthers, born March 22, 1865. They had a daughter, Zelma Lola, born August 11, 1907. Grace died December 27, 1943.

William Taylor Condra, born May 3, 1872, married Carrie Johnson, born August 30, 1879, the daughter of John and Margaret (Bean) Johnson. William died March 3, 1968, and Carrie died June 10, 1904. They had three children: Oscar, Amon, and Ada, born August 12, 1903.

NEWTON FRANKLIN CONDRA

Newton Franklin Condra was born on January 26, 1884. He was the son of Cary Newton and

Newton and Ona Condra

Arthula P. Condra. He married Ona Gass December 10, 1908. Ona was born July 12, 1893. She was the daughter of P. Harvey and Rebecca Savage Gass. They had one daughter, Ersie, who married Wyatt Estes Cherry.

Newton Franklin and Ona lived in the Moss Community. They made their living by farming. Newton Franklin died September 29, 1965. Ona Condra died September 2, 1985. They are buried in the Moss Cemetery.

JOHN WESLEY COPASS

John Wesley Copass, born in Washington County, Tennessee, was married to Leah Conkins. Their son, Nathan Richard, was born April 18, 1835 in Washington County and died in 1898 in Monroe County, Kentucky. He was married November 21, 1865 in Monroe County, Kentucky, to Nancy B. Harlan, born December 30, 1836 and died April 26, 1889. They are buried in the Mt. Zion Cemetery near Tompkinsville, Kentucky. Their children were Elijah Wesley, born September 7, 1867 and died January 26, 1922; James H., born April 3, 1869; Nathan Alunzo, born April 27, 1871; Edward Austin, born March 17, 1874 and died September 20, 1941; and Margaret, born February 22, 1877.

Nathan Richard Copass   Nancy B. Copass

Elijah Wesley Copass was born September 7, 1867 and died February 26, 1922. On January 30, 1886 he married Margaret Ellen Sheffield, born February 17, 1869 and died October 25, 1912. Their children were Lena, born in 1889; Willie Ducan, born March 14, 1891 and died June 30, 1920; Betty, born in 1893; Nancy, born in 1895 and died in 1896; Hester, born in 1897 and died in 1928; Clearance, born in 1899 and died in 1947; and Ella Ree, born August 21, 1912.

Edward A. Copass   Lena Copass

Willie Duncan, born March 14, 1891 and died June 30, 1920, married Lavada Birdwell, born in 1891. Their children were Ruby; Edna; and Duel,

who was born in 1917 and died in 1942.

Edna Copass married Ray Cassetty. Their children were Pat, Kay, and Dickie Ray.

EDWARD AUSTIN COPASS

Edward Austin Copass was born March 17, 1874 and died September 20, 1941. He was married twice. He was married June 5, 1892 to Sarah Arnett, born March 22, 1869 and died April 22, 1904. Their children were M.A., born in 1894 and died in 1894; Nancy Melinda, born January 22, 1897; Millard Fillmore, born January 11, 1899; and Florence, born March 12, 1902. He married the second time August 20, 1904 to Daisy Lena Copass, born June 17, 1887 and died March 18, 1970. Their children were James A., born November 25, 1905 and died August 5, 1907; Carlos Edward, born May 5, 1908; Dessie Aline, born August 26, 1911 and died in 1961; Delvie Marie, born February 21, 1914; Clura Hubert, born September 27, 1917; Jelima Jewell, born January 24, 1921; Pleas Reed, born August 15, 1923; Ozina Pauline, born February 28, 1926; Nellie May, born June 5, 1928; and Otis Ray, born June 26, 1934.

HARDY EDWARD COPAS

Hardy Edward Copas was born April 20, 1927 in Clay County. He is the son of Millard Fillmore Copas, born January 11, 1899 and Elcie Mae (McLerran) Copas, born November 4, 1909, the daughter of Hardy and Eva (Ritter) McLerran. Millard F. was the son of Edward Austin and Sarah (Aronett) Copas. Edward was the son of Nathan Richard and Nancy B. (Harlan) Copas. Nathan was the son of John Wesley and Leah (Conkins) Copas. John Wesley was the son of Thomas and Hannah (Jobe) Copas. Thomas was the son of William Copas, born in 1747 in Virginia and died around 1851 in Sullivan County, Tennessee at the age of 104. William was in the Revolutionary War.

Ruth, Hardy, Tony, Parnell and Mary Copas

Hardy E. Copas married Elizabeth Ruth McCarter June 4, 1966. Elizabeth was born on November 29, 1948, the daughter of Fillmore and Mae (Evans) McCarter. They live in the Pine Hill Community of Clay County. Hardy is a veteran and is currently employed by the Clay County School System. Elizabeth Ruth is employed at OshKosh at Hermitage Springs. They have three children: Mary Ruth, born December 27, 1967; Hardy Parnell, born October 27, 1969; and Tony Edward, born November 29, 1971. The children attend Hermitage Springs School where Mary was valedictorian of her senior class in 1986. Mary Ruth Copas married Eddie Hatcher, the son of Harold and Patricia Hatcher.

JOHN JACKSON COPASS

John Jackson Copass was born October 10, 1813 in Washington County, Tennessee. He died May 12, 1899 in Monroe County, Kentucky and was buried in the Soldier's Cemetery in Tompkinsville, Kentucky. He served in the Union Army during the Civil War. He was married three times. He first married Nancy Birdwell August 19, 1840 in Washington County, Tennessee. Nancy Birdwell was born in 1821. Their children were Mary, born in 1842; William, born in 1846; and Teany Angeline, born April 24, 1847 and died December 15, 1923.

Sarah and Ira G.S. Copass

John Jackson Copass next married, in 1853 in Monroe County, Kentucky, Susanna Pitcock, who was born in 1817 in Monroe County. Their children were Cintha Winton, born October 3, 1854; Nancy J., born March 28, 1857; James J., born December 8, 1859 and died February 13, 1930; Irea Greenberry Steven, born May 13, 1865; and Roda Elizabeth, born in 1863.

John Jackson Copass next married Nancy Carter February 22, 1894. They had no children.

Mary Copass, born in 1842, married Joseph Gulley. Their children were James W., born December 18, 1863 and died October 15, 1910; Felix; Hester W., born in 1871; Nancy Jane, born in 1872; Elvina M., born in 1876; Mary, born in 1878; and Daniel, born in 1880.

James W. Gulley, born December 18, 1863 and died October 15, 1940, married Mary J.M. Birdwell, born November 29, 1857 and died April 16, 1945. Their children were Etta, Nancy, Robert, Eliza, and Roxie.

Teany Angeline Copass, born April 24, 1847 and died December 15, 1923, married John Alexander Murray, born December 23, 1841 and died October 8, 1909. Their children were Thomas, born in 1869; Tilda, born June 24, 1869 and died March 13, 1940; Sally, born in 1872; Elizabeth, born in 1874; and Johnnie G., born in 1877 and died in 1953.

Tilda Murray, born June 24, 1869 and died March 13, 1940, married Robert S. Miles, born October 3, 1865 and died October 20, 1921. Their children were Arah, born October 3, 1889; Carlie, born in 1891; Allie, born in 1894; Carlos, born in 1896; and Ava, born in 1898 and died in 1913.

Cintha Winton Copass, born October 3, 1854 and died February 11, 1942, married William P. Hatcher February 20, 1872. Their children were Cardely, born in 1874 and died 1955; Rutherford, born March 9, 1879 and died March 30, 1958; Walter; Sarah, born in 1880 and died in 1915; Angelo; and Benton.

Roda Elizabeth Copass, born in 1863, married Marion Blann. Their children were Sam; John; Alzie; Lady M., born April 29, 1896 and died April 4, 1979; Martha; and Ozie.

Irea Greenberry Steven Copass, born May 13, 1865 and died September 26, 1933, was married October 4, 1882 to Sarah Matilda Colter, born in 1861 and died in 1921. Their children were James Avery, born in 1885 and died in 1963; Daisy Lena, born June 17, 1887 and died March 18, 1970; Susanna, born in 1892 and died in 1970; Edgar Elzie, born in 1896 and died in 1965; and Lucy, born in 1898 and died in 1967.

ANNISE DAVIS CRAWFORD

Annise Davis Crawford was born July 20, 1928 in Clay County, Tennessee. She is the daughter of Lester Braden Davis, born April 24, 1892, and Nellie C. Browning Davis, born June 13, 1895. On November 28, 1945, Annise married Vandal Clifton Crawford, born February 14, 1926. Vandal is the son of Irvin Crawford and Florida Coons Crawford. Annise and Vandal are the parents of Phyllis Eloise, born June 15, 1948; David Lee, born December 25, 1951; Stephen, born March 30, 1956 and died April 1, 1956; and Martha Denise, born October 25, 1957.

David, Eloise, Martha, Annise and Vandal Crawford

Eloise Crawford married David Roy Woodard. They have five sons: Allan Roy, born April 6, 1970; Clifton David, born January 22, 1972; Michael Thomas, born January 2, 1975; and Adam Paul, born October 11, 1977; and Cody Phillip, born January 29, 1979. David Crawford married Brenda Sue Smith. They have two daughters: Stephanie Denise, born May 19, 1970, and LaTisha Annette, born August 22, 1972. Martha Crawford married Dwight Allen Smith. They have one son, Joseph Dwight, born November 15, 1976. The lineage continues another generation, as Stephanie Crawford married David Kernell, and they became the parents of Brittany Nicole, born March 18, 1986.

SHELTON CRAIGHEAD

Shelton Craighead was born in Jackson County, Tennessee, the son of Stephen Craighead (1776), the great grandson of Peter Craighead (1750-1786) of Virginia. Peter took the Oath of Allegiance in Henry County, Virginia at the beginning of the Revolutionary War. Peter and his brother, John, came to Smith County, Tennessee. Peter's father was also named Peter, and his father was Robert Craighead of England.

Shelton married Isabelle Wilkerson and they had five children: Marion, Nathan, Mary, Sidney and George. Marion and Nathan married sisters, Unice Footen and Jane Copass, daughters of Thomas Copass and granddaughters of William Copass. The families lived near Oak Grove, except George who moved to Nashville. Mary married John Gulley.

Footen, Marion and Estie Craighead

Nathan and Jane Craighead had three children. Herman married Maxine Eads. Travis married Edna Mae Watkins. Glennie married Estus Cherry. They lived near Oak Grove in Clay County.

Marion and Footen were married October 7, 1877 and had ten children. Avery married Minnie Ritter; they moved to Barren County, Kentucky and had nine children. Destie married Hardin; they had five children and moved to California about 1920. Nettie married Andrew Netherton and had five children; they lived in Clay County and Monroe County, Kentucky. Isabelle married Clarence Burke, and they lived in Illinois and Florida. They had no children. Shelton married Minnie Hall. They moved to Illinois and had three daughters. Starkie married Peyton Smith and moved to Illinois and had six children. James B. married Barzillia Emmert and had four children. After Barzillia's death, Jim married Polly Rich, and they had one son. They lived in Monroe County, Kentucky. Willie married Pearl Huffines. They had no children. Estelle married Carl Henson. They had one child and lived in the Pine Hill area of Clay County.

On January 26, 1921, Barlow Craighead, born July 26, 1883, married Leah Ritter, born January 15, 1888. They had one son, Marion Ralph, born January 2, 1922. Leah died May 2, 1926, and Barlow died November 26, 1970.

On September 15, 1951, Ralph married Jo Frances Gates, born July 23, 1930. They had four children: Robert, who married Deborah Davis; Leah, who married Charles Savage; Kathy, who married Christopher Ridge; and Donna, who married Keith Ferguson. Leah and Charles Savage have two daughters, Anna Frances and Lara Christin. Kathy and Chris Ridge have one daughter, Abigail Marie.

Ralph, a veteran of World War II, retired after working 32 years for the State of Tennessee in teaching and social work. Jo Frances is a director for the Cordell Hull Head Start Program. They reside in the Boles Community on the farm where Ralph was born.

JEFFERSON CROSS

Jefferson Cross was born in 1813 in Tennessee. He married Rutha Hix, born 1816 in Carter County, Tennessee. They were living in Clay County in 1880. Their children were born in Sullivan County. Their children were Nancy J.; Abraham; James; Isaac, born September 14, 1845; John, born 1849; David, born 1850; Mar-

garet E.; Emily, born December 17, 1854, and Equiler.

Isaac Cross, born September 14, 1845 in Sullivan County-died February 3, 1913 at Union Hill in Clay County, married Nancy Abbie Carlisle, born September 14, 1844-died September 8, 1915, the daughter of William and Emaline Carlisle. Nancy and Isaac had the following children: Martin H.; William Abraham, born February 4, 1873; Sarah Jane, born February 26, 1874; John; and Stoman.

William Abraham Cross, born February 1873-died November 18, 1952, married Sarah Strong, born in 1875. Their children were Omer, born January 11, 1895; William, born 1896; and Stoman, born 1899.

Sarah Jane Cross, born February 26, 1874-died December 6, 1948, married Harlan Smith, born August 30, 1874-died November 9, 1931. Their children were Abbie, William Charles, Olga, Major, Sheridan, Carmon, Laura, Mattie and Catherine.

Vergil and Earnest Cross

David Cross, born in 1850, married Nancy Elizabeth Newman, born July 14, 1854-died October 8, 1934. Their children were: George Jefferson and William H., born July 12, 1881.

George Jefferson Cross, born June 20, 1875-died December 25, 1945, married Cora Speakman, born December 20, 1883-died April 20, 1967. Their children were Estes, Nellie, and Stella, born in 1901.

Estes Cross, born January 1, 1900-died January 15, 1959, married Lucy B. Birdwell. Their children were Irene, Neva, Eva, Alvin, Virginia, Ruth, Garry, and Carlon.

Nellie Cross married Angelo Barnes, and they had one son, George.

William H. Cross, born July 12, 1881-died November 26, 1948, married Pary Likens, born June 14, 1875-died May 8, 1849. Their children were Bertha, born March 27, 1902, Vergil, Earnest, and Lovel.

Vergil Cross, born in 1905-died February 2, 1981, married Ina York. Their children were Jewell, Mary, Betty, Rosie, Cancle, Ancil, and Gervous.

HENRY CROWDER

The name "Crowder" goes back to the middle English word, "crowdere," which means one who entertains or one who plays the "crowthe," a crude musical instrument. These people traveled throughout England entertaining the "gentry" or noblemen. This name is certainly appropriate to this group of Crowders as they were accomplished musicians who played the fiddle, the banjo, the guitar, the organ, and the harmonica. They were always in demand to play at weddings, parties, etc.

Henry Crowder was born in 1798, and his wife, Polly (surname unknown), was born in 1796 in the State of Kentucky. They had the following children: Harry (Harvey), Matthew and Polly. A young man named Jesse Walker, who was born in 1836, came from Kentucky to live with Henry and Polly giving credence to the belief that Polly was a Walker. Harry Crowder was born in 1827, and his wife, Abbe (surname unknown), was born in 1829. Susanna Walker, born in 1828, lived with Harry and Abbe. Harry and Abbe had the following children: Laurinda, Marian, Smith, Bishop Radford, James W., Belle, and D.R.

Laurinda married Roark Rich. Smith married Almenta (Mintie) Brown, the daughter of John P. and Sarah Plumlee Brown. They had the following children: Versie, who married Herman Brown; Mary Belle, who married Walter Spears; Nannie; Clure, who married Ersie Sherrell; and Edd. Smith operated Bennett's Ferry at Arcot for a number of years. He was living in Kentucky when he died in 1952. His wife, Almenta, died in 1954. They are buried in the Macedonia Cemetery in Clay County

Bishop Radford, Smith, Marian, and D.R. "Doc"

Bishop Radford, born April 11, 1862, married Mary Jane Plumlee. Marian married Martha (surname unknown), and they had the following children: Oles, born in 1895 and died in 1898; Foster, who married Annie B. Allen; and a daughter who died in infancy.

Belle Crowder, born in 1866 and died December 11, 1958, never married. She and her brother, D.R. "Dock," born in 1874 and died in 1943, lived on the Crowder farm until "Dock's" death. They are both buried in the Crowder Family Cemetery in Jackson County.

BISHOP RADFORD CROWDER

Bishop Radford "B.R." Crowder was born April 11, 1862. He married Mary Jane Plumlee, born May 19, 1874. She was the daughter of Samuel and Adeline Eads Plumlee. B.R. and Mary lived on a farm in the Dry Creek section of the Arcot Community where B.R. was a farmer. He sometimes worked with rafting. He was a musician and often entertained his neighbors by playing the fiddle over the telephone party line in the evenings. B.R. and Mary were noted for their hospitality, and they were always entertaining guests in their home. B.R. and Mary attended the Arcot Church of Christ, and like others in the neighborhood they traveled to and from Church in a buggy. B.R. and Mary had eight children.

Laura was born January 4, 1891. She married Hubert Farris, the son of C.T. and Sarah Farris.

Bishop Radford and Mary Plumlee Crowder

They had the following children: Marie, Edith, Fred, Wilson, and Laura Eagle. Laura died June 11, 1926. She is buried in the McColgin Cemetery. Marie married Jack Brown, the son of John and Ida Chapman Brown. Fred died young. Edith, Wilson, and Laura Eagle left Clay County for Ohio and California.

Alberta was born June 22, 1894. She married Jesse Rich, the son of Mr. and Mrs. Alfred Rich. They had the following children: Willis, Lina, Vesta, Woodrow, Ralph, Reed, Lavelle, and Joe. Alberta and Jesse are buried in the Macedonia Cemetery.

Radford Jordan was born January 8, 1897 and died August 1, 1898. He was buried in the Plumlee Cemetery on Dry Creek.

Comer was born September 12, 1900. He married Lattie Hestand, the daughter of Esco and Ethel Hestand. They had the following children: Nell, Mary, and Joe Freeman. Comer and Lattie left Clay County in the 1930's. Comer worked for the DuPont Company until his retirement. Comer died November 12, 1965, and Lattie died October 24, 1967. They are buried in the Spring Hill Cemetery in Nashville, Tennessee.

Lonnie, Mac Donald, and Marlin are listed under their own biographies.

Willie was born November 23, 1904 and died August 21, 1906. He is buried in the Plumlee Cemetery on Dry Creek.

Bishop Radford died August 25, 1932, and Mary died September 9, 1938. They are buried in the McColgin Cemetery in the Arcot Community.

LONNIE CROWDER

Lonnie Crowder was born April 30, 1902 in Clay County, Tennessee. He was the son of Bishop Radford and Mary Plumlee Crowder. Lonnie grew up in the Arcot Community and attended school there. Lonnie married Ethel Brown, who was born September 9, 1905. She was the daughter of James McHenry "Jim" and Martha Jane Harpe Brown of the Arcot Community. She attended school at Arcot. They were married at Celina, Tennessee September 23, 1923. Lonnie and Ethel lived in the Dry Creek section of Arcot during the early years of their marriage, where Lonnie was a farmer and made a few trips down the Cumberland River to Nashville on rafts. Lonnie and Ethel moved to Old Hickory in the 1930's where he worked at the E.I. DuPont Company. They moved from Old Hickory to Madison where Lonnie and Ethel attended the just organized Madison Church of Christ, which met at that time in a "dwelling" house.

In the early 1940's, Lonnie and Ethel moved back to Clay County to the Crowder farm which

they had purchased after the death of Lonnie's parents. They attended the Arcot Church of Christ where Lonnie was the song leader. He also led the singing for other congregations during their annual meetings and also directed the singing at many funerals. Singings were held in Lonnie and Ethel's home and in other homes in the community. Lonnie and Ethel were members of the Farm Bureau. Lonnie was a very active member of the Democratic Party in Clay County. Ethel was a member of the Arcot Home Demonstration Club. She also worked a short time in the Celina Elementary School Cafeteria. They were both very active in community affairs.

Lonnie and Ethel Crowder

Lonnie and Ethel have one daughter, Laquanah. She attended elementary school at Stratton in Madison and Arcot in Clay County. She graduated from Celina High School. She received a Bachelor of Science Degree in Business; a Master's Degree in Guidance and Counseling; and a Master's plus 45 in Administration and Supervision from Tennessee Technological University. She has worked for Brown Engineering Company at Marshall Space Flight Center in Huntsville, Alabama and for the Clay County School System as a teacher, a counselor, and an attendance supervisor. She was a career education specialist with the Clay County Urban/Rural Program. She has been a member of Kappa Delta Phi and Phi Delta Kappa. She has been a member of the Clay County Election Commission, a member of the Clay County Library Board, and is now a member of the Clay County Foster Care Review Board. She teaches a Sunday School Class at the Arcot Church of Christ.

Lonnie Crowder died August 11, 1963 of a massive heart attack. He is buried in the McColgin Cemetery in the Arcot Community.

MAC DONALD CROWDER

Mac "Donald" Crowder was born on June 20, 1906, the son of Bishop Radford and Mary Plumlee Crowder. Donald grew up in the Arcot Community and attended school there. He married Vina Rich who was born on March 1, 1908 to John and Rhoda Kellow Rich.

Donald and Vina lived at Arcot where Donald was a farmer. He worked part-time as a school bus driver and as a truck driver for the County Highway Department. Donald and Vina moved to the Midway Community where he continued to farm and to work part-time as a carpenter. From there, they moved to Moss where Donald became one of the first electricians in the area. Vina worked as cafeteria manager at the Moss Elementary School. They attended the Moss Church of Christ, and took part in many community activities. Donald was a member of the Democratic

Little Terry Crowder and his grandfathers Mac Donald Crowder and "Guard" Kendall

Party. He was noted for telling "funny stories and tall tales." As all of the Crowders, he loved to sing and was an excellent bass singer.

Donald and Vina had two children, Clotiel and Johnny Radford. They both attended school in Clay County. Clotiel married Don Craighead, the son of Herman and Maxey Craighead of the Oak Grove Community. They moved to Indiana. They have five children: Darrell, Dianne, Ricky, Pat, and John Mark.

Johnny Radford was born May 2, 1935. He graduated from Celina High School in 1953. He married Wanda Kendall October 29, 1955. She is the daughter of "Guard" and Annie Burnette Kendall of Moss. She attended Moss Elementary School and Celina High School. Johnny and Wanda own J-C Motor Company and Crowder's, a ladies dress shop, in Celina. Johnny served as a member of the Clay County Board of Education in the early 1960's. Johnny and Wanda have two sons. Terry was born September 5, 1956. He graduated from Celina High School in 1975. Terry married Paula Burris, the daughter of Benton and Katherine McClain Burris. They have one son, Tray Neil, born April 8, 1986. Terry works for J-C Motor Company. Timmie was born August 7, 1962. He graduated from Celina High School in 1980. Timmy works for Clothing World Apparel of Opelika, Alabama.

Donald Crowder was the first of the four Crowder brothers to die of a heart attack. He died April 12, 1958 and is buried in the Moss Cemetery.

MARLIN CROWDER

Marlin Crowder was born March 6, 1911. He was the son of Bishop Radford and Mary Plumlee Crowder of the Arcot Community. He attended school at Arcot. Marlin was in the United States Army during World War II and was stationed in Mississippi. He married Anna Fox of the Hermitage Springs Community. She was born July 22, 1918. After Marlin's discharge from the Army, he and Anna lived in Clay County where Marlin was

Marlin and Anna Crowder

a farmer, a carpenter, a painter, and a bus driver on the route between Celina and Cookeville, which ran daily during the 1940's and 1950's. Marlin and Anna later moved to Plainfield, Indiana.

Marlin and Anna had five daughters. Marilyn Ann was born August 1, 1945. She married Walter Stantz, and they have three daughters, Donna, Linda, and Pamela. Donna is married and has one daughter, Carrie. Linda is married and has one daughter, Suzanne. Marcella Jean was born May 28, 1949. She is married to Bob Stantz. She has three children, Larry, Anna, and John. Lana Joy married Keith Fehrman. She has two children, Leah and Nathan. She now lives in Smyrna, Tennessee where her husband works for the Nissan Plant. Diana Hope was born November 3, 1956. She married Wesley Mills. She has one son, David. Connie Lynn was born December 4, 1957. She married Charles Beck. She has one son, John Glen.

Marlin died of a massive heart attack January 13, 1975. He is buried in Plainfield, Indiana. Anna now lives in Smyrna, Tennessee.

WILLIE H. CUNNINGHAM

Willie H. Cunningham was born February 13, 1898 in Clay County, near Celina, Tennessee, to Willie T. and Viola (Adkins) Cunnngham. In 1921, he married Emma Lee Morris, the daughter of J.P. and Avo Pearl (Goolsby) Morris. They lived in Clay County all their lives. Willie H. died September 22, 1962. Emma Lee Cunningham died June 17, 1984. To them ten children were born: Clara, Gladys, Pearl, Earl, Hope, Wilma, Annabelle, Willie H., Jr., Joyce, and Judy. Willie H. Cunningham was a farmer and also a trapper.

Willie H. and Emma Cunningham

He loved the Cumberland River and often talked about the times he went to Nashville on a barge. He was also a thrash healer. Many people would bring their children to him to be doctored. Emma Lee Cunningham was a midwife and helped many women in childbirth. Willie H. and Emma Lee Cunningham attended the Church of Christ near Moss, Tennessee. — *Submitted by Pearl (Cunningham) Scott*

ALBERT JACKSON DALE

Albert Jackson Dale, born August 20, 1886, was the son of Wilburn Hamilton Dale (December 10, 1835-November 19, 1908) and his third wife, Nancy E. Sims (October 28, 1852-July 22, 1920). He was one of seven children born to this union. Others were Ova, Sam Fowler, Florence, Iva, Ellis Mitchell, and Jimmy Dale.

Jack and Emma Dale

Albert Jackson Dale (Jack) grew up in Butler's Landing. His father was a blacksmith by trade. His father, Wilburn Hamilton, was a Confederate soldier and one of six brothers who served in the war. He was said to be one of the best legal advisors in the county, even though he was not a licensed attorney. He was a member of the County Court and knew every voter in the county at that time. Albert Jackson possessed many of his father's attributes and was said to be walking in his father's footsteps in many ways.

Jack Dale was married to Emma Retta Terry (1888-1982), a beautiful young girl from Roaring River in Jackson County, who had lost her natural mother at an early age. She was very unhappy at home after this because of a stepmother who did not love and care for the existing children in the household of the prominent miller whom she had married. When Emma, then 19 years of age, fell in love with the handsome young Jack Dale, whom she adored and loved so dearly, leaving home was a long-awaited pleasure. To this marriage was born Dorothy Frances, Ray Walter, Elizabeth, Albert Jackson, Jr., Ellis Terry and Joe Austin Dale.

On September 12, 1925, Jack Dale wrote the following about the "Drouth of 1925." "During this year, we have had the worst drouth since the year 1881. It is raining here tonight, September 12, 1925, the first rain we have had to amount to anything since May 9, 1925. All crops are short, but men say there are more made this year than in 1881. I was at Butler's Landing, Tennessee on August 22, 1925 and seen a dog trot across the Cumberland River. All well and springs are dry except a few. The well in the courthouse yard has saved the town." (Signed A.J. Jack Dale).

In 1929, when the new bridge across the Cumberland River was officially opened to traffic, the Governor of the state, Henry Horton, was in Celina for the festivities. Jack was forever inviting guests for lunch so on this day, the governor was no exception. He went to the Dale home and enjoyed the "spread" Mrs. Emma was in the habit of preparing everyday of her life. Jack served as Circuit Court Clerk for many years. Judges and lawyers from out of town were always welcome at Jack's dinner table. At times, Emma never knew where her kitchen would be next because Jack made many house and farm trades without his family's knowledge. He would come home and say, "Well, we've gotta pack up and move, I've traded for a place down the road." Jack was responsible for building the first brick house in Celina, which still stands and is the residence of Mode Denning. It was also the first house in Celina to have an indoor bathroom.

Jack served as postmaster in Celina during the

Roosevelt administration. He was also co-owner of a dry goods store, Dale Brothers, run by him and his brother E.M. Dale.

JOHN B. DALE (JACK EBIE)

John Bethel Dale was born June 16, 1902, at Willow Grove, Tennessee, near the farm where his great great grandparents, William, Sr. and Rachel Irons Dale, from Virginia, settled in early 1800. His great grandfather William Dale, Jr., who fought with Andrew Jackson, was given a land grant to all land drained by the Obey River.

Jenny, Virginia and "Jack Ebie" Dale

He and his wife, Martha Goodpasture, settled near the site of Dale Hollow Dam. They raised a family of eleven children; five of their sons fought in the Civil War. William Jackson Dale was killed at the Battle of Chickamauga. He was survived by his wife, Leanne Butler Dale, and four children, William Thomas, Martha, James, and Virginia. William Thomas was married first to Molly Qualls. They had four children, Robert, Walter, James and Martha. William Thomas was married second to Ida Eastep. They had two children, Fanny and John Bethel. John Bethel's parents moved to Celina when he was six. He attended Montvale College where he finished eighth grade. He got a job with Sullivan Brothers who taught him how to operate gasoline engines. They ran freight boats from Celina to Willow Grove. This experience enabled him to get a job with Cumberland Hickory Company operating between Burnside and Paducah, Kentucky. In 1926, he met Virginia Harwood from Beckley, West Virginia. They were married February 5, 1928. Virginia's parents were Harry and Florence Griffith Harwood, natives of Wayne County, Pennsylvania, who moved to West Virginia in 1898. John and Virginia have three children, Harry Thomas, Hugh David and Virginia Florence. They owned and operated Clay Theatre from 1943-1960. They sold the theatre and moved to West Virginia where John and sons owned and operated Dale Drilling Company. He reitred in 1968 and returned to Celina where he now resides. He has five grandchildren, Harry Dale, Jr., David Dale, Jr., Virginia Dale Kyer, Carl Scott, John Dale Scott, and three great grandchildren, Harry Dale, III, Alan Kyer, Jr., and Joshua Kyer.

MARTHA BELLE DALE

Martha Belle Dale was born October 3, 1875, at Butler's Landing near Celina. She was the daughter of Wilburn Hamilton Dale (born December 10, 1835, died November 20, 1909), and Evelyn Hawkins (Hampton, Lacy) (born 1842, died 1877). Wilburn was the son of William Dale, Jr. (born December 25, 1806, married July 28, 1827, died 1877) and Martha Goodpasture (born

The Philip Henry Dalton Family

1806, died 1876). William, Jr. was the son of William Dale, Sr. (born September 1, 1771, married October 6, 1800) and Rachel Irons (born June 19, 1779). William Dale, Sr. was the son of Thomas Dale and Elizabeth Evans. Thomas was the son of John Dale and Elizabeth McKnight. John was the son of James Dale. Martha Goodpasture (born 1806, died 1876) was the daughter of John Goodpasture and Margery Bryan. Evelyn Hawkins, from Overton County, was the daughter of William Hawkins (born 1806), a land surveyor, and Elizabeth Hamilton (born 1816). She was the second wife of Wilburn Dale, and it was her third marriage. Her first two marriages were to T.H. Hampton and Lafton Lacy.

Wilburn Dale was also married three times; to Marie Mabry, to Evelyn Hawkins and to Nancy Sims. Evelyn Hawkins Dale died when Martha Belle was 18 months old and she lived with her aunt, Mrs. Tuck Butler, until her father married Nancy Sims. She lived with them until she was 11 years old, and then with her half-sister Lizzie Lacy Poindexter. She married Clark Fowler Smith when she was 17. Her stepmother, Nancy Sims, had seven children, James, Sam, Ellis, Jackson, Florence D. Taylor, Ova D. Ray, and Iva D. Fitzgerald.

The Dale family is one of the oldest in the state, coming from Virginia and North Carolina. William Dale, Jr. fought with Andrew Jackson in the Battle of New Orleans (1812), as did Adam Clenden Hamilton from Celina, and was given a land grant of "all the land that Obey River drains in Clay County, Tennessee." He was the father of five sons and six daughters. All sons fought in the Civil War, one being calvary Captain A.C. Dale, who served under General Nathan Bedford Forest. He sold his farm in "Dale Hollow" to William Hull, father of Cordell Hull, and served in the Civil War. When Dale Hollow Dam was built in the 1940's, Cordell Hull, Secretary of State for President Franklin D. Rosevelt, declined having it named for him; he wanted it to carry the name "Dale Hollow" for the family that owned so much of the land it covered.

Martha B. Smith, known throughout the area as "Aunt Matt," was mother of 11 children, earlier named in the account of Clark ("Uncle Clark")

Fowler Smith, her husband. She was a Christian wife, mother and homemaker, who thoroughly enjoyed herself wherever she was. She trained her children to be hardworking, disciplined and self-sufficient. She was truly respected and admired by everyone and her memory is a cherished one, having given so much to so many. — Submitted by Mrs. Isabelle Nevins Ross.

WILLIAM HAMILTON DALE

William Hamilton Dale first married a Miss Lacy. Their two children were Hunter and Miriah. William Hamilton Dale next married Evelyn Hawkins. Their daughter was named Martha. Martha married Clark Fowler Smith. Eleven children were born to this union: Ezra Clifton Smith; Fannie Evelyn Smith (Stone); Lizzie Ermine Smith (Waddell); Martha Gladys Smith (Stone); Della Lea Smith (Stone, Clark); W. Wade Smith, who married Mary B. Bland; Thelma Laura Smith (Nevins); Paul T. Smith; Luke Lee Smith, who married Martha James Mabry; Fred Clark Smith, who married Ina Eads; and Mary Belle Smith, who married Arthur Nevins.

WILLIAM DALE

The Dale family traces its roots back to a William Dale who died in January of 1758, in Richmond County, Virginia. The births of the children of William Dale and his wife, Frances (daughter of Tobias Phillips), are recorded in the North Farnham Parish Register, videlicet: William, September 1, 1737; Peter, October 5, 1739; Reuben, January 24, 1741; Elizabeth, March 31, 1745; Isaac, September 8, 1747; Frances, March 11, 1753; James, December 29, 1754; and Richard, December 1, 1757. Around 1768, the widow, Frances Dale, moved to Bedford County, Virginia, where she wrote her will in 1777.

The sons, William and James, were attracted to North Carolina's western lands. William entered a claim for 100 acres at the headwaters of Boone's Creek in Washington County (now Tennessee) July 26, 1779. William's estate was inventoried in 1792 by his widow, Margaret. Identified children of William and Margaret Dale include William, born September 7, 1778; Peggy, married to Enoch Fox; Thomas, born about 1789; and Julia Ann, born about 1791 and married to Joseph Hamilton. After the death of William in 1792, the Dale family migrated to Knox County, but in 1800, James moved on toward the Upper Cumberland Region.

William Dale (born 1778) had found his way to Jackson County where he married Rachel Irons (daughter of Edward Irons) October 6, 1800. Their marriage begot Elizabeth, born December 8, 1801, married Matthew Davis; John, born June 15, 1803; Sarah, born 1805, married Josiah Allen; William, born December 25, 1806; James Alfred, born 1808; Thomas, born 1810; and Edward, born 1815. In 1808, William Dale purchased from Samuel A. Martin a 449 acre tract on the south bank of the Obey River. On May 8, 1836, William Dale drowned in the Obey River, 16 miles from its mouth, while attempting to cross the river with a four-horse wagon loaded with merchandise. His son-in-law, Matthew Davis, acquired the 449 acre tract from the other heirs. William Dale's grandson, Captain James K.P. Davis, willed that this tract "remain in the family and their descendants as long as a very wise law will permit." Dale Hollow Dam stands at the lower end of this tract and the remainder lies beneath the lake. — *Submitted by John L. German, Wanamaker, Indiana*

PHILIP HENRY DALTON

William Dalton was born in England about 1797. En route with his family to the United States, he contracted smallpox when he was five years old and was put off the ship on Long Island. The family went on to Savannah, Georgia. A doctor, Ephriam Sharps, reared William in New York City. William Dalton married Elizabeth Varc Ness from Pennsylvania. Their children were Ephriam Sharps Dalton from Long Island, New York; Philip Henry Dalton, born December 25, 1833, died in January of 1901 in Clay County and buried in the Dalton Cemetery on Knob Creek; Absolam Dalton from Brooklyn, New York; Hart Dalton of Pomeray, Ohio; William Dalton, Jr. of Marsfield, Ohio; Emma Dalton, born in 1840, who married France Fox and lived in Ohio in 1924; Hannah Dalton, who married a Mr. O'Brian; and Rachel Dalton, who married Jake Wills.

Philip Henry Dalton was born in 1833 and died in 1901. His second wife, Purlina Wiggins, was born on March 29, 1850 in Putnam County, Tennessee. She died October 27, 1883 in Clay County. She is buried in the Dalton Cemetery on Knob Creek. They were the parents of six children. Ephriam Sharps Dalton, II was born March 9, 1871 in Sparta, Tennessee. He died February 25, 1941. He was married May 18, 1902 to Fannie Lenara Davis. Annie Martina Dalton was born December 2, 1872, and she died in 1954. She married William M. Smith. Mary Lou Dalton was born February 13, 1875 in Sparta, Tennessee, and she died April 7, 1936. She married Willie (William) J. Cherry. They are buried in the Cherry Family cemetery in the Arcot Community of Clay County. Dorothea Dalton was born February 25, 1877 and died at age six. She is buried in the Dalton Cemetery on Knob Creek. Malinda Dalton was born June 2, 1880 and died at age five. Mettie Avanna Dalton was born February 21, 1882 and died September 25, 1960. She was married to William Witt Cherry.

Philip Dalton sold his farm in Putnam and White Counties October 20, 1876 and bought a farm on Knob Creek in Clay County. After his death, Ephriam S. Dalton kept the home farm until 1928 or 1929. Philip Henry Dalton's third wife was Clara Lee Buford.

Philip Henry Dalton was born in New York January 25, 1833. He died January 10, 1901 on Knob Creek. He is buried in the Dalton Cemetery. He married Lucy Biggs September 8, 1842 in Cleveland, Ohio. She died before 1870 and was buried in Putnam, County, Tennessee. They had four children. Genneeta Dalton was born December 29, 1861 in Cleveland, Ohio. She married Watson Scarlett. Emma Dalton was born March 6, 1864 in Cleveland, Ohio. She married Bailey Holman. Annie Dalton was born March 16, 1866 in Cleveland, Ohio and died on February 22, 1910. She was married October 21, 1876 to Henry Butler. Philip and Lucy had twin sons who died young. Philip Henry Dalton served in the Ohio State Militia in the Civil War.

Ephriam Sharps Dalton II was born Mar. 9, 1871 in Sparta, Tennessee and died February 25, 1941 in Murfreesboro, Tennessee. He is buried in the Evergreen Cemetery. He married Fannie Lenora Davis on October 1, 1881 in Livingston, Tennessee. She died in Wilmington, Delaware May 21, 1970 and is buried in Murfreesboro, Tennessee. They had four children. Philip Henry Dalton, II was born February 16, 1903 and died February 28, 1974 in Murfreesboro. He married Jessie Purette, and they had one daughter, Elnora Dalton. Willis Davis Dalton was born September 24, 1904 and died November 24, 1979. He married Edith Verona Cassetty. They had one daughter, Alberta Sandell Dalton, born April 12, 1924. She married Joseph B. McCrary born October 10, 1920. They have one son, J. Dalton McCrary, born July 9, 1951. He married Susan Elaine Hopkins, born March 8, 1956. Clara Lee Dalton was born January 22, 1909 and died December 26, 1973. She is buried in the Evergreen Cemetery in Murfreesboro. Verda Lula Dalton was born December 23, 1912. She married Nolan Cecil Davenport.

HERMAN DANIELS

Herman Daniels was born July 22, 1914 in Celina, Tennessee. His parents were Ben and Mary Pruitt Daniels. Herman attended the following schools: Knob Creek, Arcot, Butler's Landing, Baptist Ridge and Tennessee Industrial School in Nashville. He worked at many places: farms, sawmills, elevator operator, laundromats, and at Oak Ridge as a railroad flagman.

Katie and Herman Daniels

He married Katie Smith July 26, 1946. Katie had four children at the time of her marriage to Herman: Bill, Loren, Louise, and Marie. Herman and Katie have one child, Barbara, who was born in Celina. — *Submitted by Kathy Smith*

MADDEN AND MAI DAVIS

Madden Davis was born December 25, 1894 in the Free Hills Community of Clay County. He was the son of Jenkins Davis and Mary Langford. Both his parents lived to a ripe old age, 104 and 106 respectively.

Mai Davis   Madden Davis

Madden attended a one-room country school in the back of an old log church. School sessions were only three months out of each year.

Madden married Hester Mai Hickman June 22, 1922. Mai is the daughter of Benjamin Hickman and Laura Thomas of the Free Hills Community. Mai has one daughter by a previous marriage by the name of Pearlie. Pearlie married Pete Stone. They now reside in Indianapolis, Indiana. They have three children: Charles, Walter, and Callie.

Madden and Mai have been in the restaurant business for many years. Their knowledge of cooking was gained at an early age. They cooked for the workers on the Joe Horton Steamboat which ran from Burkesville to Nashville on the Cumberland River for many years.

Mai and Madden attend the Free Hills Church of Christ and are faithful, devoted members.

ROBERT DAVIS

Robert Davis, born in 1804, married Annie York, born in 1807. They lived in the West end of Clay County, Tennessee. Their children were Allen, born August 27, 1824; Elizabeth, born 1829; Richard, born 1831; Jane, born 1833; Mary, born 1835; Andrew J., born 1839; Meredith, born 1840; Nancy L., born 1846; and Martha A., born 1849.

Allen Rufus and Adaline Davis

Allen Davis, born August 27, 1824 in Jackson County, Tennessee, died May 4, 1905 in Clay County, Tennessee. He married Loucinda (surname unknown). They lived in the West end of Clay County, Tennessee. He was in the Civil War. He served in Company E, 1st Tennessee Mounted Infantry of the Union Army. They had the following children: Robert N., born 1843; Anna J., born 1847; John C., born 1848; Arcena, born June 1, 1854; Stanton, born 1856; Allan Rufus, born 1860, Alexander, born 1862; and Henderson, born September 27, 1863.

Richard Davis, born in 1831, married Tabitha Jane York, born in 1831. They had one son, William A., born September 22, 1862.

Andrew J. Davis, born in 1839, married Tempy H. Bean, born in 1846. Their children were James M., born June 15, 1865; Robert, born 1868; Luisa J., born 1872; William Franklin, born 1876; John, born 1877; Baty, born May 1879; Luther, born August of 1881; and Lola, born in April 1884.

Allan Rufus Davis, born 1860 and died 1944, married Margaret Adaline Armer, born February 1863. They lived in the Miles Cross Roads Community of Clay County. Their children were Cora Bell, born August 27, 1884; Leo, born 1886; Meredith, born March 1889; Sarah A., born 1890; Andrew, born November 5, 1892; and Charlie, born in 1897.

Cora Bell Davis, born August 27, 1884 and died April 18, 1971, married Bedford Davis, born March 14, 1881 and died November 19, 1967. They lived in the Miles Cross Roads Community. He was a farmer. They were members of the Church of Christ. He was a song leader and taught music. They are buried in the Mount Vernon Cemetery in Clay County, Tennessee. Their children were Jewel, Thelma, Charlie Leslie, Arthur Wesley, and Ether. Charlie Davis married Josephine Huffines. They have one daughter, Kathy. Arthur Wesley Davis married Joyce Copas.

CATHY LYNN DAVIS

Cathy Lynn Davis was born January 20, 1954 in Macon County, Tennessee. She is the daughter of Charlie Leslie and Alma Josephine (Huffines) Davis. She is the granddaughter of William Bedford and Cora Bell (Davis) Davis, and William Fowler and Edith Ann (Roberts) Huffines.

Omar and Nadie Malik, Cathy and Gulrez Malik, Leslie and Joe Davis

Cathy attended Mount Vernon Elementary School and graduated from Hermitage Springs High School. She went to David Lipscomb College for one year and to Middle Tennessee State University for two years where she majored in pre-law. She met her husband, Gulrez (Gulu) Malik, while a student at Middle Tennessee State University. He was born January 10, 1949 in Karachi, Pakistan. He was the son of Nazir Ahmed and Mahmooda (Begum) Malik. While a student at M.T.S.U., he majored in computer science and math. After he received his Bachelor of Science Degree, he joined the United States Army and was stationed in Yuma, Arizona. While in the Army, he became an American citizen. Cathy and Gulrez have two children: Omar, born February 16, 1977 in Arizona, and Nadia, born March 10, 1980 in Denver, Colorado. Cathy and Gulrez live in Denver, Colorado. They are in business with his five brothers. They own T.J.'s Pizza, Oneida Park Shopping Center, and two parking lots at the Stapleton Airport.

WELDON DAVIS

Weldon Davis was born August 9, 1925, the son of Andrew and Susan Birdwell Davis.

Weldon married Clodean Browning, born February 4, 1924, the daughter of J.S. and Eva Armstrong Browning.

Clodean and Weldon Davis

Weldon works at Tennessee Mills at Hermitage Springs. Clodean is a homemaker.

They live at Route 2, Red Boiling Springs, Tennessee.

MATTHEW DAVIS

The Davis family in America can trace their lineage back to Noah through Japeth, his son Gomar, and on down through five tribes in ancient Britton, to Dales, and to Colonial America.

The Davises of Clay County apparently all descended from two or three of the sons of Matthew Davis of Surrey County, North Carolina. The names of two of the sons and one daughter are known. Thomas, who owned the present-day Will Terry farm; Leonard, born in 1735, who also bought land on Obey's River; and their sister, Mary, who married Hillory Masters, born 1745, and who became the ancestress of most, if not all, the Masters' family in the region. These were two of the five brothers who fought in the Battle of Kings Mountain. Leonard was said to have been at Valley Forge. All of the above came here in 1809 (by way of Warren County, Tennessee) from Surrey County, North Carolina. Two of the five brothers are said to have settled in East Tennessee.

Thomas married Butler, sister of Bailey Butler and his brothers who settled Butler's Landing. One of their children was William Robert, born in 1805, who married Elizabeth Keen, born in 1806. One of their children was Samuel Tramel Davis, born in 1835, who married Margaret Robbins, born in 1859. One of their children was William Jefferson Davis, born in 1885, who married Emma Buck, born in 1890.

Leonard Davis married Susannah Burris. They had the following children: Issac, born in 1794, who owned land where the town of Celina now stands and who married Susannah R . . . , born 1797; Leonard, Jr., born in 1797; William, born in 1799; Jacob; Benjamin, Dr. Jonathan; Molly (or Mary), who married Jonathan Roberts; Nancy, who married John Stone; Sarah, born in 1780, who married Hugh Roberts; and Lemuel, who moved to Cooper County, Missouri. He had a son named William Marion Davis, born in 1822, who was in the Mexican War. He married Nancy Stevens. One of their children was Jim Lee Davis who married Nancy Elizabeth Scott. Among their children were Archie Burton Davis and Winnie McLerran.

Matthew Davis, born in 1788, married Elizabeth Dale, born in 1800. They had the following children: A.J., Jack, William, Leonard, Tom, Rachel Rich, Margaret, Julia, Thurmond, Sarah Daugherty, Susan Masters, and James K. Polk. James K. Polk, born in 1842, married Sadie Hestand. They had the following children: Daisy Terry, Winnie Johnson, and William Jennings Bryan Davis. — *Submitted by Jim Hunter*

ROBERT AND ANNIE DAVIS

Robert Davis married Annie York. Their children were Andy, born in 1839; Allan; Stanton; Merriad; and Robert.

Andy Davis married Temple Bean, who was born in 1846. They had the following children: Jimmy, born June 15, 1865 and died April 8, 1940; Robert born in 1868; Louisa, born in 1872; Franklin, born in 1876; John, born in 1877; Bate, born in 1879; Luther; and Lula.

Olene, Irene, Bedford and Milford, Lester and Nellie Davis

Jimmy Davis married Laura Johnson, who was born in 1865. She died November 16, 1945. Their children were Radford, born May 28, 1886; Luther Martin, born March 30, 1888; Parlie, born August 2, 1889 and died May 24, 1966; Otis Brince, born July 18, 1890 and died in 1966; Lester Braden, born April 24, 1892 and died September 14, 1965; Nola, born February 8, 1894; Allie, born August 20, 1896; Norma, born May 8, 1897 and died February 7, 1970; Carlie,

Parlie and Matilda Davis

born May 24, 1899; Roxie, born November 28, 1900 and died in 1965; and Pearl, born March 21, 1909.

Parlie Davis married Matilda Browning. They had the following children: Estelle, born in 1908; Mizelle, born in 1910; Odell, born in 1911 and died in 1968; Carnell, born in 1913; Lorene, born in 1916; Beatrice, born in 1917; Shelba, born in 1925; Leslie and Edna, born in 1929; and Elise, born in 1932.

Lester Davis married Nellie Browning. They had the following children: Olene, born in 1914 and died in 1928; Irene, born in 1916; Bedford, born in 1917; Milford, born in 1919; Thaddeus, born and died in 1921; Hillus, born in 1923; Ullyses, born in 1925 and died in 1973; Annise, born in 1928; Charles, born in 1933; Carl, born and died in 1935; and Clyde, born in 1935.

IRVIN AND ESTELLE RUSSELL

Orie Estelle Davis was born November 3, 1908 in Clay County, Tennessee. She is the daughter of Parlie Davis and Matilda Susan Browning Davis. Parlie Davis was the son of Jimmy Davis and Laura Johnson Davis. Matilda Davis was the daughter of Henry Rice Browning and Arie Russell Browning.

Estelle Davis married Irvin Russell, born September 17, 1900. He was the son of Henry Farmer Russell and Mary Arena Davis Russell. Mary Arena Davis Russell was the daughter of Robert Davis and Eliza Reeves.

Estelle and Irvin Russell are the parents of three children, Alma Guin, born February 20, 1931; Jesse Lee, born March 9, 1935; and James Harvey, born August 9, 1936.

Alma Russell married Edward Miller. They are the parents of, Brian Douglas, born March 27, 1954; Jeffery Lynn, born July 22, 1955; Linda Carol, born July 23, 1956; Anthony Wayne, born January 18, 1958; Richard Allen, born January 1, 1959; Roger Lee, born May 16, 1961; Michael Thomas, born January 8, 1963; and Keith Russell, born August 30, 1964.

Jesse Russell married Lillian Cook. They are the parents of Laura Lee, born April 21, 1961, and Lisa Lee, born June 19, 1965.

James Russell married Edwina Kerr. They are the parents of Anita Jean, born May 2, 1960; Diana Michelle, born December 5, 1966; Aundrea Lynn, born August 17, 1968.

Anthony Wayne Miller married Susie Gessner. Diana Russell married Joseph Sloan. They are the parents of Ashley Marie, born March 16, 1984 and James Robert, born September 2, 1985. Laura Russell married Steve Evans. They are the parents of Tiffany Leigh, born September 16, 1980; and Jeanna Leigh, Jennifer Leigh, and Jessica Leigh all born January 4, 1984.

Laura Russell Evans holds a special distinction in her family by having the first set of triplets ever recorded in the history of her family.

BRADY MILFORD DAVIS

Brady Milford Davis was born March 13, 1919 in Clay County, Tennessee. He was the grandson of James Davis and Laura Johnson Davis. James was a farmer in Clay County and owned a sorghum mill and a blacksmith shop. James and Laura were the parents of twelve children: Radford, Luther, Parley, Otis, Lester, Nola, Norma, Allie, Carlie, Huldie, Roxie and Pearlie.

Lester Davis was born April 24, 1892. He was married to Nellie Browning, who was born on June 13, 1895, Christmas Day, 1913. Lester was a farmer in Clay County and also did a little moonshining. They were members of the Leonard Church of Christ. They were the parents of eleven children: Olean, Irene, Bedford, Milford, Hillman, Hillus, Ulyes, Annise, Charles, Carl, and Clyde.

Milford and Nell Davis

On October 3, 1946, Milford married Mary Nell Sampson, who was born in Clay County November 10, 1921. He attended the Union Hill Elementary School and the Leonard Elementary School. He served over three years in the Army during World War II. He was stationed on the Island of Saipan in the Pacific. He returned home December 3, 1945, and went to work for the L.O. Braden Electric Company. He and Nell moved to Louisville, Kentucky in April of 1950. He worked at General Mills and at General Electric, where he retired in 1975 after twenty-three years of service. He was a member of the Southeast Christian Church in Louisville and was a Kentucky Colonel. Milford and Nell are the parents of one daughter, Wanda Kay, who was born December 11, 1947. She married Dr. George Terry Shee September 29, 1973, and they have two daughters, Laura Kay Shee, born January 4, 1976, and Rebecca Lynn Shee, born June 21, 1980.

Nell passed away December 18, 1980 and Milford passed away November 12, 1985.

HARAM H. DECKARD

Haram H. Deckard was born in 1831 in Jackson County, Tennessee. He married Jane Hammer, who was born in 1833. They lived in Jackson County, Tennessee. They later moved to Monroe County, Kentucky. He was a farmer. During the Civil War, he enlisted in the Union Army and served in the Fifth Kentucky Cavalry. Haram and Jane had eight children: Nancy, Mary, John, Samuel, Kilpatrick, Christopher, Hiram J., and Caswell. Jane died in 1915 and Haram H. in 1920.

Hiram J. Deckard was born in 1871 in Monroe County, Kentucky. He married Melvina Long. She was the daughter of G.B. and Matilda Long of the Milestown Community in Clay County. They were the parents of six children: Lester, Dewey, Herman, Mamie, Millard, and Ted.

Millard Deckard was born in 1904 near Gamaliel, Kentucky. He attended school at Gamaliel. At the age of eighteen, he went to work in Illinois. In 1930, he purchased a farm in the Hermitage Springs area. He married Locie Eakle December 20, 1930. She is the daughter of Clayton Eakle and Vadie Slate. She was born May 3, 1909 in

Mamie, Melvina and Millard, Ted, Hiram J. and Dewey Deckard

the Clementsville community of Clay County. Clayton and Vadie had ten children: Locie, Howard, Melvin, Henry, Odessa, Elmer, Essie, Glen, Ancil, and Iree.

Millard and Locie are the parents of three children: Bernice, Shelby Jean, and Willis. Bernice married Leon White of Tompkinsville, Kentucky. She has three children: Gail, Jennifer, and Jerry. Jerry and Jennifer both graduated from Hermitage Springs High School, Jennifer in 1983, Jerry in 1985. They are both presently attending David Lipscomb College. Gail married Danny Knight of Red Boiling Springs, Tennessee in 1972. They have three children: Melanie, Christie, and Dustin. Willis graduated from Hermitage Springs High School in 1966. He is presently a farmer in Clay County. Shelby Jean graduated from Hermitage Springs High School in 1961. Millard died in 1962; Shelby Jean died in 1968. Locie is presently retired and enjoys sewing.

GENEVA BROWNING DELK

Geneva Browning was born September 27, 1935 in Clay County, Tennessee, the daughter of Earl and Goldie Cherry Browning. She has a sister, Juanita Browning. Geneva grew up in the Miles Cross Roads Community of Clay County, Tennessee. She attended the Mt. Vernon Elementary School. She was married October 10, 1953 to Wilmer Lee Delk, who was born September 6, 1932 in Clay County, Tennessee, the son of Clure and Clio Whitaker Delk. He moved to

Wilmer and Geneva Delk

Franklin, Kentucky and returned to Clay County when he married. Geneva was employed at OshKosh in Celina for ten years, then worked for Genesco in Red Boiling Springs for fifteen years. She is presently employed at OshKosh in Hermitage Springs; she has been a supervisor there for five years. Wilmer Lee has been employed for OshKosh for thirty years, twenty five years at Celina and five years at Hermitage Springs. They are members of the Mt. Vernon Church of Christ.

Lillie and Larry Delk

They live in the Miles Cross Roads Community of Clay County. They have a son, Larry; he married Lillie Davis. Larry is employed at OshKosh, he is a corporate director of quality assurance. Larry and Lillie live in the Hermitage Springs Community of Clay County.

ALFRED BOWEN DENTON

Alfred Bowen Denton was born October 29, 1851, on Brimstone Creek in Jackson County, Tennessee. He was the youngest in a family of four sons, John, Willliam, Grundy, and Alfred, and three daughters, Mary, Susan, and Sallie, born to Erasmus and Susan Hawkins Denton, the daughter of William Hawkins.

Alfred Denton Family

Erasmus Denton and family moved in 1853 to a farm on the Cumberland River where he died in January of 1863. He was buried in the family cemetery near their old home which still stands on the highway between Celina and Gainesboro. His wife, Susan, died later and was buried by his side.

Some of Alfred Denton's early ancestors are: parents, Erasmus and Susan H. Denton; grandparents, Abraham and Polly Williams Denton; great grandparents, Abraham, Sr. and Mourning Hogg Denton; great, great, grandparent Abraham Denton, Jr.; Denton; great, great, great grandparent, Abraham Denton, Sr.; great, great, great, great grandparents, Samuel and Mary Smith Denton; and great, great, great, great, great grandparents, the Reverend Richard and Helen Wendlblank Denton.

Richard Denton was born in Yorkshire, England in 1586. He was married to Helen Windlblank. He came to America between 1630-1635 with his five sons, John, Daniel, Timothy, Nathaniel, Richard, Jr., and Samuel. They were among the first settlers of Wethersfield, Connecticut. Richard later moved to Long Island, New York, where he founded the first Presbyterian Church. He returned to England, where he died in 1662.

Alfred Bowen Denton married Amanda Eliza-

beth Loftis in 1881, the daughter of Henry and Ellen Johnson Loftis. To this union were born three sons and six daughters. William E. married Florence Rogers. Mary Ellen married Jesse Young. Margaret (Maggie) married Fowler Kirkpatrick. Ina married John Plumlee Dale. Walter H. married Minnie Hansom. Bert married Ruby Stone. Sallie, Una, and Anna Bill remained single. All of the children are deceased except Una and Anna Bill. They live at the old home place in Celina on McMillan Street.

CLYDE T. AND CORETTA DENTON

Clyde Thomas Denton was born January 16, 1945 in Clay County, Tennessee. He was the fifth of six children born to Theron Denton and Dora Dean Hestand Denton. Theron Denton was born August 8, 1914 in Clay County, Tennessee. His wife, Dora Dean Hestand Denton, was born November 29, 1917 in Clay County.

Corretta and Tommy, Johnathan, Latisha and Scarlett Denton

Tommy attended Pine Hill Elementary School and was a 1962 graduate of Celina High School. He was a 1971 graduate from Tennessee Technological University and completed his Master's Degree from Tennessee Technological University in 1976.

Tommy was married to Coretta Osgathorp August 13, 1966. Coretta was born in Paris, Texas on February 14, 1945, the oldest daughter of Johnie Dillard Osgathorp and Myrtle Newman Osgathorp.

Coretta attended elementary school in Toledo, Ohio and Nashville, Tennessee. She was a 1963 graduate of Hermitage Springs High School. Coretta attended Middle Tennessee State University and was a 1975 graduate from Tennessee Technological University.

Tommy and Coretta are Clay County teachers and are the parents of three children. Scarlett Kaylin Denton was born December 21, 1967 and is a 1986 Hermitage Springs graduate. Latisha Dean Denton was born July 1, 1969 and is a senior at Hermitage Springs High School. Clyde Johnathan Denton was born August 14, 1972 and is a freshman at Hermitage Springs High School.

All three children have been active in 4-H, basketball, baseball, and softball.

Tommy, Coretta, Scarlett, Latisha and John live in the Pine Hill Community and attend the Pine Hill Church of Christ.

WILLIAM DONALDSON

The Donaldson family of Clay County can be traced to the 1600's in Scotland. The name has

been spelled different ways, the most common other spelling being "Donelson". The name started as "Donald" in the Old Country. The first family member to migrate to the United States was Patrick (1600-1725), who settled in Somerset County, Maryland before 1690. Humphrey Donaldson (1737-1781), a great grandson of Patrick, was born in Pennsylvania but moved to Caswell County, North Carolina. It was his sons who began the family migration to Middle Tennessee. Humphrey's offspring began the move to Tennessee sometime before 1793, although an exact date cannot be determined. Robert (1775-1849), a son of Humphrey, moved from North Carolina to Wilson County, Tennessee sometime after 1819. William Richmond "Bucky" (1800-1884) came to what is now Clay County (then known as Fox Springs in Overton County) sometime around 1820, where he met and married Mary "Polly" Hord. William was a two-term member of the state legislature. Robert Daniel (1832-1908) was born to William and Mary. Robert married Hannah Ellen Colson in 1855, and to the couple were born John Thomas (1865-1914) and four other children. John Thomas, who served as Clay County Clerk for twenty years, married Molly Davis. The couple had four children — Gertrude (1888-1890), William Hubert (1890-1967), Ruby Green (1892-1929), and Robert Lester (1895-1958) — before Molly's death in 1895.

The Donaldson Family

Hubert and Lester married sisters. Hubert married Rose Elam (no children), while Lester married Willie Grace "Bill" Elam. Rose and Willie were daughters of Sarah Elizabeth Gilpatrick and Robert E. Lee Elam of Hilham. Robert Elam was descended from Wesley Elam and Lydia Maynard. Lester and Willie had four children: Robbie Fowler, born in 1922; William Harold, born in 1929; Jack, born in 1932; and James Donald, born in 1935.

Robbie Fowler married Clyde Dowell of Monroe County, Kentucky. They have four children: Polly Hanna, born in 1941; Elsie Diane, born in 1939; Clyde Dowell, Jr. (Johnny), born in 1943; and Robert Michael, born in 1948. Hanna is married to Carl Plumlee and has two sons, Christopher, born in 1965, and Samuel, born in 1969. Diane married W.C. Burnette and later Thomas Crawford. Diane has one son, W.C. Burnette Jr., born in 1961. Mike married Donna Boone and has two children, Michelle Lee, born in 1972, and Robert Michael, born in 1977.

William Harold married Cleo Henson and has twins, William Lester and Mary Annette, born in 1960. Mary Annette is married to William Winningham of Livingston.

Jack married Wanda Hestand and has one son, Kevin Jack, born in 1958. Kevin married Jayne Plumlee and has one daughter, Deanna, born in 1985.

James Donald married Lois Eads Short and has two children, Jed (Short) Donaldson, born in 1954, and Sheree (Short) Donaldson, born in 1959. Jed is married to Cynthia Rasch, and Sheree is married to Frank Dennis Strong. Sheree and Dennis have one son, Adam Mitchell Strong.

HUMPHREY DONALDSON

Humphrey Donaldson was born about 1736 in Pennsylvania. He moved to Caswell County, North Carolina prior to 1767. He is believed to be a son of Andrew Donaldson, brother of Colonel John Donelson, a co-founder of Nashville, Tennessee. His wife was Mary Riley, born in 1745 and died in 1825. Their son, Robert Donaldson, one of ten children, was born in Orange County, North Carolina prior to 1775. He married Elizabeth Richmond January 16, 1799, the daughter of John Richmond of Ayr, Scotland. They emigrated from North Carolina to Wilson County, Tennessee along with his brothers: Andrew, William, Ebenezer, and Humphrey, II. Their son, William Richmond Donaldson, born in 1802 and died in 1884, married Mary Dabney Hord, born in 1802 and died in 1872. He was nicknamed "Bucky" and was a member of the Tennessee State Legislature in 1848-49 and again in 1861-62 when Tennessee seceded from the Union. Their son, John Humphrey Donaldson, born 1837 and died in a Union prison camp near Louisville, Kentucky, married Martha Emeline Colson, born April 2, 1834 and died June 16, 1878. They had two children, Stanwix and William Allen Beauregard (nicknamed "Burea"). Burea married Minerva Brown, and their children were John Humphrey, James Walker, Permelia, Ethel, Carlyle, Thomas, Dolly and Albert Lee. Albert Lee, born August 29, 1894 and died April 15, 1944, married Lou Ellen Nelson on March 28, 1920. Lou Ellen was born October 20, 1899 and died November 5, 1949. Their children are Robert Andres, born May 13, 1921 and died May 13, 1949; Mildred Elizabeth, born July 24, 1922; Wilbur L. "Bill," born November 5, 1923, and Champ Clark, born July 15, 1925.

Mildred Elizabeth married Charles Oscar Hillman, born September 28, 1918 and died July 26, 1970. They were married February 21, 1942. One of their children is Sharon Ann, born October 25, 1947, who married William David Bavoso, born November 3, 1946. They were married on August 30, 1969. Their children are Amy Rebecca, born in 1973; Katherine Elizabeth, born in 1977; David William, born in 1980; and John Carles, born in 1985. Mildred Elizabeth and Charles' second child is Lauren Lee, born July 7, 1951. She is a Wildlife Biologist with the United States Forestry Service.

Champ Clark Donaldson married Evelyn Delores Lissy June 22, 1946. She was born July 26, 1925. Their children are Martha Lou, born June 28, 1947, and who married Jeff Schleifer and has one daughter, Karen Schleifer; and Champ Clark Donaldson, Jr., born March 7, 1954.

The William Richmond Donaldson home was located at Fox Springs. The house was "L" shaped and consisted of a living room, five bedrooms, a dining room, and a kitchen located to the back of the living room. All of the rooms were 20 feet square, and the four halls were 15 feet wide. The dining room and kitchen were torn down in the 1920's. — *Submitted by Mildred Donaldson Hillman*

JED SHORT DONALDSON

Jed Short was born September 25, 1954 in Sagus, California. He is the son of the late Carlene Short and Lois and J.D. Donaldson of Celina. Jed attended Celina Elementary School and graduated from Celina High School. He attended Tennessee Technological University.

Cindy Rasch and Jed Short Donaldson

On June 5, 1982, Jed married Cynthia Lu Rasch, the daughter of the late Alvin Rasch and "Penny" Rasch. Cynthia attended Celina Elementary School and Celina High School. She received the Bachelor of Science Degree in German with a minor in History from Tennessee Technological University. She also received her Master's Degree from Tennessee Tech.

Shortly after their marriage, both Jed and Cindy began active duty in the United States Navy. Jed became an Aviation Electronics Technician after attending Naval schools in Memphis, Tennessee and Pensacola, Florida. He served as an aircrewman with Patrol Squadron Five in Jacksonville, Florida. Cindy attended Officer Candidate School in Newport, Rhode Island and Supply Corps School in Athens, Georgia. She served aboard the USS Yosemite (AD-19) for 2½ years and then transferred to the Naval Supply Center at Jacksonville. Jed and Cindy have been deployed to various locations in Europe, the Mediterranean, Africa, and the Middle East. They are now stationed in Jacksonville, Florida.

JOHN C. AND R. FRANCES DONALDSON

John Clark Donaldson was born September 21, 1942 in Celina, Tennessee. He is the only son of Rebecca Waddell Donaldson, born December 26, 1912 in Celina, Tennessee, and the late Cordell Clark Donaldson, born January 24, 1902 in Celina, Tennessee and died March 24, 1956 in Celina, Tennessee. His grandparents were John Thomas Donaldson, married to Ermine Brown, and Henry Winfield Waddell, married to Martha Dale. They are all deceased.

On August 25, 1962, John Clark married Ray Frances Rich, the daughter of the late Forrest Elwood Rich, born October 15, 1906 and died August 14, 1951, and the late Dorothy Frances Dale, born July 25, 1908 and died January 14, 1985. Her grandparents were Albert Jackson Dale, Sr. of Celina, who married Emma Retta Terry of Jackson County, Tennessee, and Joseph Rich of Celina, who married Laura Watson December 31, 1897. Frances is the sixth of seven children. She has three brothers, Forrest Dale (deceased), Robert Elwood, and Jack Terry, and three sisters, Elizabeth Ann, Lauretta, and Mary Emma. All seven children were born in Celina.

John and Frances both attended elementary and high school in Celina. John attended Tennessee Technological University for three years. After two years of college John and Frances married and lived one year in Cookeville where she attended Middle Tennessee Beauty School. John and Frances then moved to Auburn, Alabama, where John attended Auburn University School of Veterinary Medicine. While living in Auburn, their first child, John Cordell, was born April 5, 1965 at Lee Hospital.

Lea, John Clark, Lenea, Libby, Frances and Johnny Donaldson

In June of 1967 John graduated from Auburn and received his degree in Veterinary Medicine. After leaving Auburn John did his internship with Dr. Lecil Donaldson in Carthage, Tennessee. In August, 1967 John fulfilled his lifetime dream by returning to Celina as their first veterinarian. After moving back to Celina, they moved into the old Donaldson home, which had survived three other generations of Donaldsons. John wanted to raise his family where he and his parents, grandparents and great grandparents once lived.

On December 3, 1967 a daughter, Lauretta Lea, was born at Clay County Hospital. On February 8, 1971 another daughter, Jerri Lenea, was born at Clay County Hospital. On December 12, 1978, another daughter, Libbi Nichole, was born in Crossville, Tennessee.

John and Frances have raised their children on the small fifty-acre farm which has been in the Donaldson family for over one hundred years. They have enjoyed raising cattle, horses, hogs and sheep. They have all been active in community clubs and activities. The children have been very active in school, clubs and church. They all attend the Celina Church of Christ, where John and Frances' parents and grandparents attended.

JOHN RICHMOND DONALDSON

John Richmond Donaldson was born February 15, 1836 in Wilson County, Tennessee. He was the second of five sons born to Daniel L. Donaldson and Jestinia Howard. Daniel was born in 1810 and died in 1842 in Wilson County. Justinia was born in Overton County, Tennessee. She was the daughter of Stanwix and Justinia (Burrus) Howard. John Richmond Donaldson was a captain in the Confederate Army. He was married in Clay County, Tennessee to Permelia Catherine Colson of the Pea Ridge Community of Clay County. She was the daughter of William Allena

Agnes (Donaldson) and Jewell Terry

and Martha Clary Colson of Clay County and was born June 25, 1842. She died on May 20, 1917. John Richmond and Permelia Catherine lived on the farm that had belonged to her father in the Pea Ridge Community. They had one son, Andrew Thomas Donaldson.

Andrew Thomas Donaldson was born July 25, 1969 in Clay County. He died September 30, 1941. He was a farmer, County Court Clerk, and a leader in the community. He was married in 1893 to Minnie Avo Watson who was born May 25, 1873 in Cumberland County, Kentucky. She died March 25, 1947. They lived on the farm that had belonged to John Richmond Donaldson. They had one daughter, Agnes.

Agnes Donaldson was born December 17, 1896 in Clay County, Tennessee. She was married on April 5, 1925 to Jewell Winchester Terry who was born August 17, 1896 in the Pleasant Grove Community of Clay County. He died on April 21, 1980. Agnes attended Montvale Academy in Celina. She taught school at Plainview in Clay County for many years. She and Jewell lived on the Donaldson Farm which was declared a Century Club Farm in 1976 because it had been in the same family for more than 100 years. Agnes and Jewell had two daughters — Katherine and Aenona.

Aenona Terry was born January 22, 1928. She was married June 2, 1950 to Ronald Ragland Harper who was born on Mar. 10, 1924 in Macon County, Tennessee, the son of Arthur Burr and Nettie Ragland Harper. Aenona attended Tennessee Technological University and is a teacher in the Macon County School System. Ronald retired in 1981 from teaching at the University of Georgia. They taught several years in Portland, Oregon. They have two children, Terry, born August 18, 1952 and Beth, born August 18, 1954.

LEONARD JIMMIE DONALDSON

Leonard Jimmie Donaldson, born December 25, 1936, is the son of Burah W. Donaldson and Liza Chilton Donaldson. Burah W. Donaldson was

Leonard and Virginia, Joan and Joseph Donaldson

born January 10, 1910, and he married Liza Chilton July 25, 1931. Leonard's brothers and sisters are Lyle, Louise, Linda, and Lonnie. Leonard was the grandson of James Walter Donaldson, born October 31, 1887, and Rebecca Rayburn Donaldson. Leonard's father, Burah, died July 14, 1980; and his grandfather, James Walter Donaldson, died November 25, 1952.

Leonard was educated in the Clay County School System, graduating from Celina High School where he participated in athletics — particularly football. Leonard is a farmer in the Arcot Community and is employed at the Dale Hollow National Fish Hatchery.

On December 22, 1961, Leonard married Virginia Isabelle Holman, the daughter of the late Buford Holman and Clara Rich Holman of the Pine Branch Community. Virginia has the following brothers and sisters: Dorothy, Bailey Hall, Florence, Alice, Marjorie, and James Hill. She was born November 20, 1943. Virginia attended schools in Clay County, graduating from Celina High School. Virginia is a motivational trainer at Tri-County Vocational School, employed by the Upper Cumberland Human Resource Agency.

Leonard and Virginia have two children — Joan and Joseph. Joan was born December 23, 1966. She is a 1985 graduate of Celina High School and is presently enrolled at Tennessee Technological University. where she is majoring in nursing. She is employed part-time at Cookeville General Hospital. Joseph Leonard Donaldson was born January 22, 1973. He is a student at Celina K-8 School. He is very active in 4-H Club work. Joseph was a winner in the District and Regional National History Day Contest making him eligible to participate in the finals in Washington, D.C., where he placed tenth in 1986.

The family resides in the Arcot Community and attends the Arcot Church of Christ.

ANDERSON EADS

Anderson Eads was born in Tennessee in 1824. He first married Sally Cherry. They had three daughters: Kead (Cinderella), born (ca)1845; Sarilda (Surelda) born (ca) 1842; and Mary Adeline, born (ca) 1848. Sarilda (Surelda) married David G. Hestand who was killed during the Civil War by Captain "Jack" Bennett at the Jones-Peterman Ford on Obey River. Sarilda was a midwife. Mary Adeline Eads married Denton Mack Plumlee.

After Sally's death, Anderson married Sarah E. (Sadie) Plumlee, the daughter of Archibald and Ruth Odle Plumlee. (Archibald Plumlee was born in North Carolina in 1794. He served in the War of 1812 and fought in the Battle of New Orleans.) Anderson and Sarah were living in Jackson County, Tennessee in 1850. He was a farmer and he received ten land grants, south of Walker's Line, from the State of Kentucky between 1847 and 1869 totaling 511 acres in the Pine Hill-Brimstone section of what is now Clay County. The 1850 Jackson County census lists Anderson and Sarah as having the following children: Amanda, born in 1849; John A., born in 1850; Rosetta, born in 1856; Lucettia (Lusette), born in 1855; George A., born in 1858; Nancy; William Clint, born in 1863; Florintha, born in 1866; Smith

Sarah (Plumlee) and Anderson Eads

Barlow, born November 11, 1869; and Parlette, who died young. (In Robert D. Plumlee's book, *The Plumlee Family,* there is a discrepancy as to the number of children and the dates of birth when compared to the U.S. censuses of 1850 and 1880.)

After Sarah's death, Anderson married Ruth Cherry. They had the following children: Ella, Frank, Wade, Palo, and Lonnie. Wade and Palo both died at an early age.

After Ruth's death, Anderson married her sister, Hannah Cherry. They had one son, Nathan (Malanthan), who died at an early age.

Anderson Eads had four wives and 19 children. He died in September of 1900. He and at least three (perhaps all four) of his wives are buried in the Eads-Denton Cemetery in the Pine Hill Community of Clay County.

SMITH BARLOW EADS

Smith Barlow Eads, the youngest son of Sarah (Plumlee) and Anderson Eads, was born November 11, 1869 in Jackson County (now Clay County). He married Mattie White who was born in 1874. They had nine children.

O.T. (Ocrus) was born September 25, 1890. He married Melvina Plumlee. Zora was born December 5, 1892. She died young. Nora was born October 31, 1895. She married Esco Moore. Mae was born November 21, 1897. She married Phillip Clancy. Elsie was born April 9, 1899. She married Bob Brown. Omas was born July 13, 1902. He married Ruby Spears. Myrtle was born November 19, 1904. She died young. Amos was born August 15, 1908. He first married Sally Rich. He then married Mildred Cherry. Vanus was born April 24, 1912. He married Lillie Brown.

Mattie died in 1914 when Vanus, the youngest child, was two years old. Barlow moved to Illinois taking with him Mae, Omas, Amos, and Vanus. He worked in the coal mines near Christopher, Illinois. Mae met and married Phillip Clancy during this period. Barlow moved his family back to Clay County, with the exception of Mae, who remained in Illinois. Mae and Phillip Clancy had the following children: Nina Mae, Rosco, and Ray. Barlow made his home with Vanus and his wife in the Arcot Community. Vanus married Lillie Brown and they had two children — Lois Oleeta and Joel Howard. Barlow died May 2, 1944.

Barlow and Mattie are buried in the Eads-Denton Cemetery in the Pine Hill Community.

Ocrus Eads married Melvina Plumlee. They had the following children: Ancil, married Ada Condra; Danvus; Nola, married Edd Kendall; and Lanvus, married Lena Green. Vancil married Iva Dean Brown and they had two children — Randall and Vonda.

Nora Eads married Walter Esco Moore. They had the following children: Girvus, married Allie Copas; Kathleen, married Gerald Tood; Kenneth, married Sharolett (surname unknown); Glyleen Moore; Cancil Moore, married Joyce Smith; Evelyn Moore, married Jasper Collins; Myrtle Moore, married Jess Human; Taft Moore, married Willodean Watson; Mona Moore, married Willie Jim "Tom" Brown; Dalpho Moore married James Brazil; and Ralph, married Barbara (surname unknown).

Amos Eads married Mildred Cherry on May 28, 1933. They had two children. Wilma Geane was born on June 28, 1934. Eldon Darrell was born March 24, 1937. The couple moved to California where the family still lives. Wilma Geane married Eugene Paige. They had three children, Steven, Paul and Stacy. Darrell married Viola Forrest (Cricket). They have two children, Craig and Christine Eads. Chris is married to Craig Garnett.

Elsie Eads, born March 20, 1899, married Bob Brown on December 23, 1923. They had five children, Gertrude, Barlow, Eulis, Daniel and Melvin.

VANUS "SANDY" EADS

Vanus Eads was born April 24, 1912. He is the youngest son of Smith Barlow and Mattie White Eads. He is the grandson of Anderson and Sarah (Plumlee) Eads. He grew up in the Pine Hill Community of Clay County. He married Lillie Brown November 26, 1933. Lillie was born June 15, 1913, the daughter of James McHenry and Martha Jane Harpe Brown of the Arcot Community of Clay County.

Lillie Brown and Vanus "Sandy" Eads

Vanus and Lillie have lived in the Arcot Community for most of their married life. Vanus is a farmer, a carpenter, a retired highway employee, and he spent some time working in California. Lillie is a retired cafeteria manager at Celina K-8 School and has worked in restaurants in Celina. At present, she works at Donaldson Child Care Center in Celina. Vanus and Lillie attend the Arcot Church of Christ, where Vanus has been the song leader for more than twenty years. He and Lillie (along with others in the community) used to hold singings in their home, as the people in the community enjoyed getting together on Friday or Saturday nights for singings. Vanus is an accomplished guitar player.

Vanus and Lillie have two children: Lois, born October 23, 1934, and Joel, born July 21, 1943. Lois married Carlene Short in 1952. They had three children, Jed, Jeffery (died as an infant), and Sherry. After Carlene's death, Lois married J.D. Donaldson. Lois is a therapist and operates

Donaldson Child Care Center in Celina. Jed Short Donaldson married Cindy Rasch; and they both serve in the Armed Forces stationed in Florida. Sherry Short Donaldson married Phil Stephens in 1977. They had one son, Cale Stephens, born December 21, 1977 and died December 26, 1977. Sherry later married Dennis Strong, and they have one son, Adam, born May 1, 1983. Sherry is in the United States Army and is stationed at Fort Knox, Kentucky. Joel Eads married Gale Poindexter, the daughter of Fred and Myrtle Poindexter of the Oak Grove Community of Clay County. Their wedding took place at his sister Lois's home on May 8, 1970. Joel is the Maintenance Supervisor at Clay County Manor in Celina. Gale works at OshKosh in Celina. Joel and Gale have two children, Joey Lynn, born June 23, 1971, and Shana, born October 1, 1977. Shana attends Celina K-8 School. Joey attends Celina High School. Joey plays summer league baseball; and he and his father, Joel, are avid fishermen.

JOE EMERTON

Joe Emerton was born and raised in Clay County, Tennessee. He was a farmer and worked at other jobs also. His father, George Emerton, came from Kentucky. His mother was Lucy Perrin. They are both buried at the McDonald Cemetery on Baptist Ridge in Clay County.

Joe married Linnie Goolsby October 18, 1925. Their children and grandchildren are as follows:

Rose Emerton married Jesse Copeland, who was sheriff of Clay County for three terms. He is also a farmer. Their children are: William, who married Josephine Tinsley; and they had two children, Barbara and Carolyn. William died several years ago. Barbara married a Meadows and has two children, Sara Jo, Jessica and one stepchild, Jody Meadows. Carolyn Short, the second daughter, has two children, Christina Short and Robert (Sonny) Short.

William (Bill) Copeland had no children. Bobby Copeland married Judy Hall. They had no children. Both are deceased and are buried in the Tinsley Cemetery.

Hazel Copeland married Frank Strong. Their sons are Dennis, who has a son, Adam; Douglas; David; and Danny, who has a daughter, Nichole.

Jessie Lee Copeland married Jewel Tinsley; and they have three children, Lee, Donny, and Susie.

The Joe Emerton Family

Anna Copeland McBride has two sons, Jimmy and William. Charlie Copeland has two sons, Randy and James Lewis.

George Emerton has no children. Elsa Emerton married Joe Thomas Hampton and they have

two sons, Ed L. and Charles J. Ed L. has twin daughters, Dixie and Kettie. Ed married Jill Stewart. Charles J. married Sue Poindexter.

Glin Emerton married June Coffman, and they have two children, Richard and Michelle. Richard has two children, Jennifer June and Richard, Jr.

Ray Emerton married Geneva Webb, and they had one son, Michael, who was killed in an auto accident.

Thelma Jo Emerton never married. Howard Emerton married Sue Copeland and they have three children, Barry Lee, Timothy, and Jeffery.

Lucy Ann Emerton married Homer Copeland and they have one daughter, Pamela Ann.

Charles Emerton married Beulah Williams (deceased), and they had three children, Anita, Beverly, and Charles Eddie Emerton, Jr.

Fred Emerton married Mary Terry.

Joe and Linnie Emerton are buried in the Turkeytown Cemetery. Joe Emerton was born November 4, 1901, and died July 5, 1971; and Linnie was born February 27, 1901 and died March 29, 1967.

W.D. (BILL) FISKE

W.D. (Bill) Fiske, grandson of pioneer educator and surveryor Moses Fiske, was born in Hilham, Tennessee in April 1884. His first wife, Miss Cora Denton of Macon County, gave birth to two children, Moses and Fannie (both deceased). Cora died about 1900, and Mr. Fiske married Miss Ermine Hooten in July 1902.

W.D. "Bill" Fiske

From this second marriage, nine children were born and the following survive:

Alva A. Fiske, retired from the "Washington D.C. Star" and now resides in Nashville, Tennessee. Idera Fiske Brumfield is a retired Texas school teacher and now lives in San Antonio, Texas. Genie Elkin Fiske is retired from Gannett Publishing Corporation and resides in Lee County, Florida.

Marie Fiske Speck lives in Livingston, Tennessee and Janie Lou Fiske Yates now lives in Alice, Texas. Hallie Ruth, Gertie, Will and Ray Fiske are deceased.

Mr. Bill Fiske purchased "The Celina Messenger", a weekly newspaper being published in Celina by Charles P. Gray. The Fiskes moved to Celina in October 1910 and soon thereafter changed the name of the newspaper to BILL FISKE'S BUGLE and published same until his death in December 1935.

His widow, Mrs. Ermine Fiske, published the BUGLE until the mid-forties when the paper was sold to local businessmen. Mrs. Fiske died in August of 1980 at the age of 93.

Mr. Fiske was an attorney and also Secretary-Treasurer for the Moss National Farm Loan Association, an organization that helped many Clay Countians from losing their farms during the readjustments after World War I.

The Fiske family were residents of Clay County from October 1910 until August of 1980. Some or all of the family spend time in Celina and Clay County each year, and Alva A. Fiske, who left Celina in 1925, has not missed spending time in Celina for the past 61 years.

The Fiske family members still call Celina their home and are proud to do so. — Submitted by Bill Fiske

ISAIAH FITZGERALD

Isaiah Fitzgerald of Kentucky and Margaret Ann Gearhart of Tennessee were married October 28, 1858 at Celina, Tennessee by J.Y. Amonett. The ceremony was witnessed by N.R. Gearhart. The relationship of Mr. Gearhart to Margaret Ann is not known. Valentine Gearhart was Margaret Ann's father. Valentine is buried in the Fitzgerald Cemetery. His grave is marked, but his wife, who is also buried there, has an unmarked grave. Margaret did not remember her parents as they died while she was very young. Isaiah was born January 16, 1831. Margaret was born February 10, 1843. They were the parents of ten children — five boys and five girls. Some of the children were born in Clay County and some were born in Kentucky.

Lee, Allie, Clyde, Isiah, Lou Rhett, Mattie, Frank Walker, Father — Isaiah Fitzgerald, Mother — Margaret Ann Fitzgerald

Isaiah was of German ancestry. His forefathers came to Virginia, then across the mountains to Kentucky. Of all his relatives, only one is known by name, Marion. He lived all his life in Kentucky and is buried there.

Isaiah Fitzgerald was an officer in the Courthouse in Celina, and today there is a large piece of beautiful furniture where he kept his books. "Miss Ann" as she was called by most who knew her, was kept busy rearing her large family and tending a farm known at one time as the Fitzgerald Place. It was related by her to others that when the War broke out in Kentucky, her husband put her in a carriage with her two oldest children and sent her to Celina for safety. She came to her grandparents' farm and lived there until she died March 5, 1921. Isaiah died March 20, 1897. One son, James Tolbert Fitzgerald died before his parents in 1894, and he is buried near them. — Submitted by: Anne Elizabeth Fitzgerald Butler.

Isaiah and "Miss Ann" had five sons and five daughters: Lee, Allie, Clyde, Isaiah, Lou, Rhett, Mattie, Frank Walker, Tolbert, and Maude. Allie married a Kirkpatrick. Lou married an O'Brian, and Mattie married a Moore.

BIRTY CLARANCE FRANKLIN

Birty Clarance Franklin was born January 7, 1884 in Franklin, Kentucky. He died November 21, 1971 in Glasgow, Kentucky. He was the first in a family of two sons and five daughters born to William Nelson and Parlee (Agee) Franklin. William Nelson Franklin's family moved to the Bakerton Community of Clay County in 1887. Birty Clarance purchased a farm in 1919 in the Union Hill Community of Clay County where he was a farmer. He also owned and operated a sawmill and gristmill for a number of years.

Clarence Franklin

On December 26, 1909, he married Lillie M. Newman, born May 6, 1894 — died June 8, 1922. They had one daughter, Vassie J. Franklin, born October 20, 1915.

Birty Clarance next married Abbie (Smith) Franklin May 5, 1925. Abbie was born March 25, 1903. They had eleven children, five sons and six daughters.

Anna Jean Franklin, born August 28, 1929, married Earl R. Wilkerson April 17, 1948 in Glasgow, Kentucky. They presently reside in the Union Hill Community of Clay County. They have three children, Donna, Kathleen, and David. Donna is unmarried and lives at home. Kathleen married Jackie Browning; and they have two sons, Jason and Todd. David married Linda Trobaugh and they have one daughter, Kellie Michelle.

THOMAS J. FRANKLIN

Thomas J. Franklin was born May 12, 1839. He died June 24, 1910. He married Emma Hill, the daughter of Robert Clemmons and Ann Eliza (Medlock) Hill. Thomas J. and Emma are buried

Johnny, Ray and Mealie Franklin

in the Macedonia Cemetery located between Moss and Midway in Clay County.

Thomas J. and Emma had six daughters and one son. Florence married George Walker. Idera married Benjamin Walker. Lee Ann married John Walker. Mary married Jimmy Reecer. Minnie married Leander Reecer. Vick never married. Johnny married Mealie Reecer, the daughter of Elisha and Nan Reecer.

Johnny and Mealie (Reecer) Franklin had one son, Ray. Both Johnny and Ray died young, thus ending one generation with the Franklin name. They are buried in the Moss Cemetery above Vick Franklin's grave — no markers.

JESSE GASS

Jesse Gass was born around 1805 in Barren County, Kentucky. He died around 1865 in Jackson County (now Clay County). He was married twice. In the 1850 Census of Jackson County, Tennessee, he was listed with his first wife, Sarah, who was born around 1805 in Tennessee. Her surname is unknown. They had the following children: Richard, born 1830; William C., born 1832; Rachel, born 1834; Andrew J., born 1836; Nathan J., born 1837; John H., born 1839; James B., born 1841; Jesse Newton, born 1843; and Josiah S., born 1846. Jesse was married the second time to Louvina White, born in 1821, the daughter of Peter and Ann (Morey) White. Jesse and Lavina had the following children: Peter Harvey, born January 9, 1858; Francis M., born 1860; Sarah A., born 1862; Melvina E., born 1863; and Rhoda M. born 1865.

Francis M. Gass, born in 1860, was the first postmaster at the post office in Moss, Tennessee. He was appointed to this position January 15, 1883 at the age of 23.

John Harvey, Shelva Chester, Randell Gass and Billy Davis, Velma, Erma Lee, Beulah Gass, Creola Davis, Herman, Pauline and Juanita Gass

Peter Harvey Gass was born January 9, 1858, died August 24, 1946. He was a farmer. He kept honey bees and sold honey. He married Rebecca Savage, the daughter of Preston Leslie and Nancy (Hestand) Savage. Her third great grandfather was Henry Heistand from Zurich, Switzerland. After about three generations, they changed the spelling from Heistand to Hestand. Peter Harvey and Rebecca had four children, Ona, Bethel, Vestas, and Herman, born October 3, 1900. Ona Gass married Frank Condra. Ona was bitten by a mad dog around 1912. Her uncle, Banyon Savage, took her in a buggy to Bowling Green, Kentucky to a mad stone. The stone drew the poison from her wound, and she lived to be 92 years old.

Bethel Gass married Dovie Reneau. Bethel served in World War I.

Vestas Gass married Edna Pennington.

In 1922, Herman Gass, who was born October 3, 1900, and died June 23, 1986, married Beulah Copas, who was born April 20, 1907 in Clay County. She was the daughter of John and Hettie (Cherry) Copass. Herman was a carpenter and a farmer. He was the owner of a sawmill, a grocery store, and a restaurant. He sold his sawmill and went into the logging business. Herman and Beulah were members of the Moss Church of Christ. They had five children, Chester, John Harvey, Creola, Randell, and Shelvie.

Chester Gass married Pauline Cherry. John Harvey Gass married Erma Lee McLerran. They have three children, Patricia Darlene, Deborah Kay, and Michael Kevin. Creola Gass married Billie Davis. They have one daughter, Pamela Ann, who married Greg Pedigo, and they have one daughter, Amy Lynn. Randell Gass married Juanita Rush. They have one son, Bryan Neal. Shelvie Gass married Wilma Collins, and they have two sons, Christopher Sean and Shannon Wesley.

JOHN HARVEY GASS

John Harvey (J.H.) Gass was born May 3, 1927 in Clay County, Tennessee. He was the son of Herman and Beulah (Copass) Gass and the grandson of Peter Harvey and Rebecca (Savage) Gass and John and Hettie (Cherry) Copass and the great grandson of Jesse and Louvina (White) Gass. Louvina was the daughter of Peter and Ann (Morey) White. He was also the great grandson of Cary and Marinda (Hestand) Cherry and Thomas and Nancy (Gulley) Copass and Preston and Nancy (Hestand) Savage. He helped his mother run a restaurant at the Three-Way Inn in Moss, Tennessee around 1939 and 1940. At the time, the dam was being built at Dale Hollow. They sold hamburgers for five cents, a bowl of chili for ten cents, and a roast beef sandwich for fifteen cents. His dad was a carpenter and made two dollars a day at that time. He bought a sawmill in 1943, and John started driving a truck taking cross ties to Glasgow, Kentucky when he was sixteen years old. He served in the U.S. Air Force in 1946 and 1947. He has worked as a carpenter two years in Toledo, Ohio; for the New York Central Railroad; and two years in Indianapolis, Indiana for Hy Grods Meat Packing Company. For the last twenty years, he has worked for J.B. Cassetty Lumber Company at Red Boiling Springs, Tennessee, where he has been yard foreman for the last five years.

John Harvey married Erma Lee McLerran, who was born September 3, 1926 in Clay County, Tennessee, the daughter of Albert Harrison and Zona Mae (Carruthers) McLerran, granddaughter of Benaggie and Amanda Louise (Whitaker) Caruthers, and granddaughter of Alfred and Amanda Whitaker. Erma Lee graduated from Hermitage Springs High School in 1945. She spent most of her working years in garment factories. She went to work in a shirt factory in New Albany, Indiana one summer when she was out of school at the age of sixteen. She also worked in a five and ten cents store, an electric company, and a dress factory in Toledo, Ohio. She also did custom sewing at home for about

Michael Gass, John Harvey, Erma Lee, Patricia and Deborah

five years. She is presently employed at Clay Sportswear at Moss, Tennessee.

John Harvey and Erma Lee are the parents of three children: Patricia Darlene, born in 1948; Deborah Kaye, born in 1956; and Michael Kevin, born in 1960. They all attended grammar school at Moss, and they all graduated from Celina High School. Patricia Darlene graduated from the University of Tennessee at Knoxville with a degree in accounting. She is presently employed with the Internal Revenue Service in Nashville, Tennessee. She is married to Roger Wood. They have two sons, Christopher Dale and Gregory Austin. They live at Goodlettsville, Tennessee.

Deborah Kaye graduated from Middle Tennessee State University in Murfreesboro, Tennessee with a degree in early childhood education. She is a second grade teacher at Celina K-8 School in Celina, Tennessee. Deborah is married to Alan West. They have two children, Johnathan Lee and Leslie Christeen. They live in Celina, Tennessee.

Michael Kevin graduated from Middle Tennessee State University in Murfreesboro, Tennessee with a degree in business administration. He is presently employed with Service Merchandise in Nashville, Tennessee as an inventory systems analyst. He is married to Tamie Johnson. They live in Goodlettsville, Tennessee.

RANDELL GASS

Randell Gass was born May 1, 1943, the son of Herman and Beulah Copas Gass. He married Juanita Rush, the daughter of Cyrus H. and Odell Davis Rush. Randell is self-employed as a logging contractor. Junaita is employed at Clay Sportswear at Moss, Tennessee.

Randell, Juanita and Brian Gass

They live in the Miles Cross Roads Community of Clay County, Tennessee. They have one son, Brian Neal, born May 28, 1971.

GREEN BERRY GATES

Green Berry Crossarmstrong Gates (December 25, 1865 to February 18, 1957) married Dora Green Peterman (February 17, 1891 to August 19, 1942). Dora Green's grandfather was Archibald P. Green, who served as Clay County's first Trustee, elected February 4, 1871. Green Berry Gates was the son of Jacob William Gates (February 25, 1824 to January 10, 1896) and Fannie Frances Stone who came from Virginia and settled on Proctor Creek. Jacob W. Gates served in the Civil War, having joined May 17, 1861. In the mid-1800's, he founded and operated Gates Ferry on the Obey River, which G.B. Gates later operated. Jacob and Fannie had 10 children. Burrenus (February 21, 1849 to June 21, 1927) married James Bilyue September 19, 1867. They lived in Russellville, Kentucky. Mary Margaret (July 22, 1851 to August 6, 1928) married Jacob Bilyue October 29, 1868. They lived in Russellville, Kentucky. Haden W. (September 10, 1856 to January 26, 1949) married Rosa Butler August 4, 1892. They were medical doctors in Waco, Texas. Florentha (May 17, 1861 to May 4, 1945) married Phillip Bilyue Jan. 18, 1881. They lived in Russellville, Kentucky. Other children were Green Berry, Louisianna (1862 to July 7, 1915), Sibbie, Shirley Alice Stone, William Gates, last known to be in Roseville, Arkansas, and Bell Arms, wife of J.W. Arms, grandmother of Nellie R. Cherry.

Dora Green Gates was the only child born to Martha Green and Richard "Tin" Peterman. Martha passed away when Dora was a small child. Martha's parents were Arch and Mary Colson Green. Richard "Tin" Peterman was a brother to Lizzie Dale (mother of Dora Anderson, grandmother of Lorene Marcom and Nellie Cherry), Ida Davis (mother of Wilma Hunter), Julie Holman, and Mary Goodpasture. His second marriage was to Betty Dale. They moved to Celina, Texas and she bore nine sons, Henry, Riley, Sherd, Hugh, Clem, George, Cheatam, Earl and Richard.

Green B.C. Gates Family

For several years, G.B. Gates served as a Justice of the Peace in Clay County. He and other citizens were interested in a good education system and bought the land where the present Celina High School is located. He and others donated $50.00 each and purchased the athletic field property from Wid Maynard's father.

In 1914-1915, the Gates carried their seven children by wagon and moved to Spencer, Tennessee, where the school age children attended Burrett College, a private school for all grades.

Mr. Gates, a large landowner, resided on the

farm located behind the Dairy Queen and owned the 150 acres now in subdivisions. He also owned the farm where the fish hatchery is located. G.B. Gates and his family were members of the Church of Christ.

Green Berry Gates and Dora Peterman reared seven children. Carl Bennett Gates (May 2, 1896 to December 24, 1983) married Orpha Moore of White County upon his return from World War I. They spent their life in Sparta, where C.B. operated a grocery store and later did construction work. Orpha died in 1936, and C.B. married Frances Williams and they lived in Putnam County. Orpha and C.B. had one son, Carl Brents who lived in Birmingham, and had two sons, Rodney and Donald, and one daughter.

Hayden R. Gates (November 13, 1898 to October 26, 1982) married Ruth Walker (June 15, 1901) on July 28, 1921. They reared two daughters. Nellie (August 21, to February 3, 1977) married Leslie Upton (September 23, 1922 to August 30, 1942) and they had three children, Richard (January 30, 1944), Robert (October 4, 1948 to November 25, 1963) and Suzanne Roberts (November 8, 1950). Mary Lou (July 11, 1929) was married July 9, 1955 to Bob Mitchell (September 21, 1929), a druggist in Crossville, Tennessee. They have two children, Jim (July 12, 1962) and Beth (January 19, 1964).

Willett Gates (November 2, 1900) married Willett Martin Poindexter (November 6, 1916 to January 13, 1946) who was assistant Lockmaster on the Cumberland River. They had four children, Mamie Bennett and Dora Elizabeth who reside near Chicago; Dora has two sons. Geneva married Odell Pryor and has two sons. Franklin Gates Poindexter married Freddie Smith and has two daughters and one son.

Millard Green Gates (August 1, 1902 to January 17, 1985) married Olyne Hogan (October 18, 1912) April 15, 1939. They had one child, Shirley (December 26, 1945), who married William A. Bartlett. She has one daughter and one son. Millard was a farmer, and Olyne had a long teaching career.

Homer Anderson Gates (March 7, 1905) married Hazel Jeanie Goodpasture (June 9, 1909). They had one daughter. Jo Frances married Ralph Craighead and resides near Moss, Tennessee. They had four children, Robert Stanley (Deborah Davis), Marion Leah Savage (Charles), Kathie Gene Ridge (Christopher), and Donna (Ferguson) Keith. Homer taught school many years throughout Clay County. He went into government service from which he retired. He has continued to operate the farm in Peterman Bend.

Velva Gates Nevins (December 10, 1910) married Oather Nevins (April 16, 1908) on April 18, 1926. He worked at various locks on the Cumberland River and returned to Celina after 40 years. They had three children. Willett Davis Nevins (January 27, 1927 to September 17, 1964) had two sons. Garah Nevins (April 19, 1929) has two daughters; and Doyle Gates Nevins (September 19, 1939), who resides in Florida, has a daughter and son.

Martha Thurman (April 21, 1913) married Frank Thurman (October 14, 1910 to May 31, 1977) on August 11, 1936. Martha taught school, worked at OshKosh, and assisted Frank in his large farm operation. Frank was one of the founders of the Clay County Bank and Martha continued the role after his death. Martha resides in Celina.

JOHN NORWOOD GATES

John Norwood Gates was born in Kentucky March 8, 1805. He married Martha H. (Holman?) Trice who was born in Virginia September 19, 1808. John and Martha had eleven children. John Norwood and Martha Trice and eight of their eleven children left the Celina area in about 1858 for the six-month trip by wagon train to California. John and his son, Roscoe, both homesteaded in Tehama County. The hand built rock fences still stand on their former ranch 14 miles east of Red Bluff. The girls all married and helped to develop the areas of northern California.

Permelia Gates, born in 1826, died in 1895 in Clay County. She married Erwin Francis Langford. Their children were Isabella Langford, born 1842; Florentha, born 1843; Martha (Mattie), born 1845; Palo Alto, born 1847; Randolf Franklin, born 1849; Buena Vista, born 1851; Smith Barlow, born 1855; and Jalapia (Dappie), born 1857.

William Gates, born between 1827-1830, married Clarinda Butler. Their children were James B. Gates, born 1851; Mattie H., born 1852; Milliard Fillmore Gates, born 1853; Tandy H. Gates, born 1856; John Bell Gates, born 1859; and Robert Hulin Gates, born August 17, 1861.

John Trice Gates, born between 1830-1832, married Mary Elizabeth Lamb, born February 17, 1832. They had seven children: Savana Cobb, born July 19, 1855; Eurasta Frazier, born July 13, 1858; Palo Alto Gates, born February 13, 1860; Barzilla Gates, born June 6, 1862; Stanton Battle, born November 28, 1864; Erley Sperry Gates, born November 28, 1867; and Amelia (Pamelia), born July 4, 1869. John Trice and his second wife, Eliza J. Hale, had one daughter, (name unknown). John Trice and his third wife, Alice Jane Marler, had seven children: Maude, Lillian, Florence, Johnnie Mosler, James, Alice, and Bernice.

Tandy Holman Gates was born May 8, 1833. He died in Red Bluff, California on March 17, 1891. He was a farmer, a rancher, and a druggist.

Barzella Laura Gates, born December 10, 1840, married William Brazelle in California. They had the following children: Anna Z., Lillian, Minnie, Lula, Garce, Cora, Leslie (died young), and Bruce.

Roscoe Franklin Gates, born in 1842, married Josephine Margaret Beck. Their children were Martha Belle, born October 17, 1873; William Franklin, born September 7, 1875; Leon DeCatuer, born July 24, 1877; John Norwood, born January 1, 1880; and Della Grace, born March 14, 1882.

Arabella Gates, born July 7, 1842, married J.P. Eldridge. She and her husband worked in a lumber mill in Lyonsville, California, and the men who worked there named the mill after her, "Belle Mill."

Mary Gates, born May 7, 1845, married George Cottleib Winter. They had the following children: George A., born May 28, 1867; Martha Bell, born October 11, 1865; Henry William, born July 12, 1868; John Franklin, born October 25, 1869; Louis, born January 5, 1864; and Eva, born February 2, 1873. Mary married John C. Tipton after George's death. No children are recorded.

Almara Gates, born in 1846, was also called Almary and/or Elmary. She married Nelson Cash.

Tennessee Frances Gates, born June 4, 1850, married A.A. Kaufmann. They had the following children: Forrest, born 1868; Henry, born 1870; Mary, born 1873; Burtt, born 1877; Effie Bell, born 1874, and Ida Maye, born 1871.

Amanda Fitzellen Gates, born about 1851, married R. Lane. She married S.E. Banks after the death of Mr. Lane. — *Submitted by Marilyn Kelly Ornbaun*

GEORGE DONALD GENTRY

George Donald Gentry was born December 22, 1916, the third son of Edmond Anthona Gentry and Polly Jane Chaffin Gentry of Jackson County, Tennessee. He served his country in the armed forces from 1941-1945 during World War II. After the war, he came back to Clay County and became a farmer until his death September 12, 1982.

Danny, Louvenia, Shelia and Ercil, Geraldine, Gayle, George, Donald, Veachel and Lesa Gentry

He was married December 22, 1945 to Louvenia Rush, born on December 23, 1920 to Cyrus Haden Rush, Sr. and Mary Lou Loftis Rush of Clay County.

George Donald and Louvenia were blessed with seven children: Geraldine (born December 31, 1946), Ercil D. (born September 8, 1948), Sharon Gayle (born August 6, 1950), George Danny (born November 26, 1952), Veachel Rose (born October 10, 1954), Sheila Diane (born August 3, 1958), and Lesia Inez (born June 7, 1961).

Geraldine married Junior Chaffin from Macon County, Tennessee. Their children: Marvin Leslie (born December 12, 1965), Teresa Ann (born April 1, 1968), and Donald Wesley (born March 29, 1971). The Chaffins live in Smyrna, Tennessee.

Ercil D. married Joann Young from Macon County and they built their home next to the home of George Donald and Louvenia Gentry.

Sharon Gayle married William Richard Mosley from Nashville, Tennessee. They have a daughter, Rachel Gayle, born January 14, 1984, and they live in Nashville, Tennessee.

George Danny still lives at home and farms the home place.

Veachel Rose married Charles Thomas King from Clay County. They have one son, Michael Ted, born September 6, 1980, and they live in the Hermitage Springs Community of Clay County.

Sheila Diane married Thomas Foster Strong of Clay County. Their children are Amy Marie, born

December 10, 1977, and Kristofer Thomas, born May 26, 1981. Sheila lives in the Hermitage Springs Community of Clay County.

Lesia Inez married David Reece of Macon County, Tennessee. They have one daughter, Pamela Suzanne, born April 6, 1985. They also live near the Gentry's home near Miles Cross Roads.

ERCIL D. GENTRY

Ercil D. Gentry was born September 8, 1948, the second child of George D. and Louvenia Rush Gentry and the grandson of Edmond Anthona Gentry and Polly Jane Chaffin Gentry and Cyrus Haden Rush, Sr. and Mary Lou Loftis Rush. Ercil attended the Mt. Vernon grade school for eight years, then attended and graduated from Hermitage Springs High School in 1967. After high school, Ercil attended the Hartsville Vocational School where he received a certificate in welding. After vocational school he took a job at a leather company until he was called to serve his country in the latter part of 1968. He was sent to Vietnam where he served from August 1969 to October 1970.

Jo Ann and Ercil Gentry

On November 16, 1973, Ercil married Jo Ann Young, the daughter of William Johnnie and Evelyn Brooks Young. Jo Ann is the granddaughter of James Burl Young and Margaret Ann Swindle Young and Joseph Willie Brooks and Lassie Lillian Day Brooks. Jo Ann attended school at Red Boiling Springs and graduated in 1972. Jo Ann has worked in the garment industry since then.

Ercil and Jo Ann bought land from George D. and Louvenia Gentry near the Hermitage Springs Community and built their home. This land has been in Ercil's family since it was homesteaded in 1849. At that time, this part of Clay County was still part of Kentucky.

Ercil worked at the Hartsville Nuclear Plant until it closed. While there, he became a member of Boilermakers Local 455.

Jo Ann now works for OshKosh in Hermitage Springs. She has been there since 1985.

SHARON G. GENTRY MOSLEY

Sharon Gayle Gentry Mosley was born August 6, 1950, the daughter of George Donald and

Rachel, Gayle and William Mosley

Louvenia Rush Gentry. She has four sisters, Geraldine, Veachel, Sheila, and Lesia, and two brothers, Ercil and George Danny. She attended grades one through seven at Mount Vernon School and grades eight through twelve at Hermitage Springs School, where she graduated in 1969. She moved to Nashville in 1969 where she attended Draughn's Business College.

In 1981, Sharon Gayle married William R. Mosley. They have one daughter, Rachel Gayle, born in 1984. Sharon Gayle works for South Central Bell; and William works for Coleman Sausage Company. They attend the Church of Christ and William is a Church of Christ Minister. They live in Brentwood, Tennessee.

THOMAS F. GOODPASTURE

The first record to be found of the Goodpastures in America is a land survey in the Clerks Office of the Circuit Court for Augusta County, Virginia, dated 1753 for Jacob Goodpasture for the land lying on the North Branch of Lewis Creek in Brocks Gap, Virginia. In 1766, Abraham, orphan son of Jacob, by order of the court was bound to Daniel Pierre to learn reading, writing, arithmetic, and the trade of carpentry. In 1767, according to the church records, this was changed and Thomas Smith took Daniel Pierre's place for Abraham's schooling.

In 1778, Abraham Goodpasture married Martha Hamilton, daughter of Arthur Hamilton and Barbara Campbell. All their children, except the youngest one, were born on their Royal Oaks Plantation near Abbington, Virginia. In 1796, they sold Royal Oaks and moved to Knox County, and later to Overton County, Tennessee. The children born to them were William, John, James, Martha, Arthur, Margaret, Abraham, Jr., and Jefferson.

T.F. and Ida Goodpasture

Arthur, one of Abraham and Martha Goodpasture's sons, married Jane Mical in Overton County, Tennessee. They had seven children: Robert M., William J., Abraham H., Malinda, Sarah, Esther, and Martha.

Robert M., son of Arthur and Jane Goodpasture, first married Dorothy Andrews; second marriage was to Frances Andrews; and the third time was to Minerva Jane Sims Grimsley. To the first marriage were born: Eliza Ann, Orsenus, Martha, Daniel Milton, Sarah, Orleana J., John Henry, Nancy K., and Thomas Dennis. To the third marriage were born Martin and Emma Jane, who married Moses Staggs.

Daniel Milton, son of Robert and Dorothy Andrews Goodpasture, married Martha Ann Jennings and had two sons, Robert Wylie and Thomas Francis Goodpasture. Thomas Francis was married to Ida Mae Richardson, daughter of Car-

ol and Rebecca Barksdale Richardson. Their children were Della, (Mrs. Arthur Terry), Auburn, Winnie (Mrs. Harris Clark), Velma (Mrs. Cecil Smith), and Hazel (Mrs. Homer Gates).

Robert Wylie Goodpasture married Nancy Caterine Martin August 10, 1892. She was the daughter of William Brice Martin and Eliza Garner Buford. They had eight children, Carlie, Dauphie (Mrs. Leland Arms), Willette (Mrs. E.L. Monroe), Ida Mary (Mrs. Myrth Cherry), Jessie Thomas, Ollie (Mrs. Clifton Waddell), Robert Lee, and Hugh.

ALLEN GOOLSBY

Allen Goolsby came to Clay County from Jackson County. He was a farmer and part-time blacksmith and did many other jobs. He was born September 2, 1873 — died September 18, 1947. He married Minnie Lee Lurkes. She was born June 4, 1882 — died February 1, 1966. They lived on the top of the hill above Dry Mill Creek. Allen's father was James Allen Goolsby. His grandfather was Bill Goolsby. His grandmother was Jane McCanely.

The Allen Goolsby Family

Allen and Minnie had the following children: Linnie married Joe Emerton; and they had the following children: George, Rose (Copeland), Elsa (Hampton), Glin, Arlo Ray, Thelma Jo, Lucy (Copeland), Howard, Charles, and Fred.

Mary Goolsby married Arlo Boles. They had two sons, Clyde and Carl.

Wint Goolsby married Amelia Hawkins. Their children were Bill, Walton (Buddy) (deceased), Minnie Lou (Anderson), Marvena (Watkins), Marvin Goolsby, Henerita (Hall), and James Goolsby.

Champ Goolsby married Pearly Boles (deceased). Their children are Clifton, Marlin, Kenneth, and Vickie (Apple).

Ova Goolsby married Herman Boles. Their children are Louie, Adean (Reecer), Loyd, Glendon, Harvey, and Junior.

Easter Goolsby married Girstle Ellis. Their children are Joe Allen, (deceased), Barbara (Sells), Curtis, Janice Faye (Rolles), Champ, Mary B., Diane (Boles) and Billy.

Ruth Goolsby married Leon Boles. Their children are Sue (Johnson), Toby and Joyce Ann (Emerton).

Wallace Goolsby married Jimmy West. They had the following children: Charlene (Allred) and Lany Goolsby.

Agnes Goolsby married Bill Roberson. Their children are Betty Jean (Brown), and James.

Lyda Goolsby married Frank Book. Their daughter is Barbara (Wilkes), and they had one daughter who died in infancy.

Allen and Minnie had one daughter to die in infancy. They are buried in the Turkeytown Cemetery.

BONNIE (CHERRY) GRACE

Bonnie (Cherry) Grace was born December 28, 1917 in Clay County, Tennessee. She is the daughter of Grover and Bertha (Long) Cherry. Grover was the son of General and Almerry (Whitaker) Cherry. General was the son of Fines E. and Mary Cherry. Fines E. was the son of Wilson and Catherine (Hodge) Cherry. Wilson was the son of Lemuel and Sarah (McPherson) Cherry. Lemuel Cherry was one of the earliest settlers in Clay County, Tennessee.

Gene, Haskel, Bonnie and Ronald Grace

Bonnie Cherry married Haskel Grace, the son of Wilson and Vadie (Armer) Grace. Haskel was born November 3, 1914. Bonnie and Haskel live in the Miles Cross Roads Community of Clay County. They are the parents of two sons, Ronald Dean and Wallace Gene. Bonnie was employed at the Genesco Manufacturing Company in Red Boiling Springs until she retired May 11, 1982. Haskel was in the lumber business for many years. They are also farmers, owning a large amount of land in the Miles Cross Roads Community. Bonnie attends the Milestown Church of Christ where she is a member.

ARCHIBALD P. GREEN

Archibald P. Green was born October 12, 1823 and died March 1, 1901. He was the first person to serve as Trustee of Clay County, having been elected February 4, 1871. He served one term but declined to run for a second term. He was a large landowner, having owned numerous tracts of land in Clay County. He was one of the first merchants to operate a business in New Town. The New Town, containing ten acres, was bought from A.P. Green. It was laid off in lots and sold at auction in the spring of 1870.

Archibald Green represented the counties of Clay, Fentress, Jackson, Macon, Overton and Pickett in the State Senate, 45th General Assembly, from 1887 to 1889. A Democrat, he practiced law in Celina. He was one of the builders of the steamship, "Benton McMillan". He owned controlling interest in the steamer "John Fowler" on which he served as captain for two seasons before selling his interest.

He married Mary Jane Colson, who was born October 11, 1825 and died November 18, 1905. Mary Jane was the daughter of William Allen Colson and Martha Patsy Clary Colson. Archibald

and Mary Jane had six children: Sarah married McCajah Stone; Nancy married James Richard Stone; Hannah Katherine married Joe Rich; Martha married Richard "Tin" Peterman; Amelia married Dr. Stone Plumlee; and Millard married Bell McMillan.

Archibald and Mary Jane are buried in the Green family cemetery near the Baptist Church in Celina.

JOHN GRIMSLEY

John Grimsley, born February 23, 1809-died March 21, 1896, married Eleanor C. Profitt May 27, 1829. Eleanor was born January 20, 1820, and she died in January of 1876. Children were James P., Joseph L., George Keen (Fannie Gains Farmer), William F., John M., Elizabeth Emela, and Nancy Ellen. (The sixth child, an unnamed son, lived only five days.)

George Keen Grimsley married Fannie Gains Farmer on August 9, 1860. Fannie Gains was born December 22, 1842 and she died May 27, 1932. They lived in Overton County near Oakley, Tennessee. Children were E. Alice, Laura N., E. Ella, William J., George Virgil (Martha Ellen Clark), Ira Everette, and James E.

George Virgil Grimsley married Martha Ellen Clark in Oakley, Tennessee August 26, 1900. George was born October 2, 1878 and he died January 13, 1950. Martha Ellen was born on July 8, 1878 and died May 13, 1959. They moved to Willow Grove in the East End of Clay County in 1920, where Mr. Grimsley served as apprentice druggist under Dr. Edward Clark and Dr. W.F. Sidwell until Dale Hollow Dam was built and flooded Willow Grove. He was postmaster of the village for several years. Children were Edna Alice, George M. Cleston, Clara Fannie Lee Ann, Ina Ruth, and Willie Dean (Willie Turner Cherry).

Willie Dean Grimsley, born November 10, 1916, married Willie Turner Cherry April 28, 1934. Willie Turner Cherry was born May 5, 1906, and he died on May 14, 1972. He was the son of William Jackson Cherry and Mary Lou Dalton Cherry of the Arcot Community near Celina. Willie T. Cherry was elected by the people of Clay County to serve as Superintendent of Schools for three consecutive four year terms. His father, William Jackson, had served in the same position during his lifetime. (Willie T. Cherry is buried in Davidson County) Their children are: Betty Ruth Cherry married Raymond Chancey November 28, 1957. He is the son of Raymond Ronald Chancey and Ruth Brooks Chancey of Davidson County. Betty Ruth Cherry Chancey was born September 27, 1935. Betty Ruth and Raymond Ronald have two children, Ronica Lynn, born January 27, 1959, and Blake Allen Chancey, born September 11, 1962. Martha Lou Cherry, the second daughter of Willie T. and Willie Dean, was born July 7, 1946. She married Billy Joe Gaines June 19, 1964. He was the son of Ray N. and Mary Louise Driver Gaines of Macon County. They have one child, Von Jason Gaines, who was born June 13, 1965. — *Submitted by Mrs. W.T. Cherry*

VERNON AND JUDY GROCE

Harold Vernon Grove was born February 20, 1940 in Cumberland County, Kentucky. He is the son of Virgil and Claudine Williams Groce of Cumberland County, Kentucky. Vernon attended high school in Burkesville, Kentucky. He went

into the army in 1962 and continued in the National Guard until 1968. Vernon owned and operated a service station at Kettle, Kentucky for approximately two years. He was employed at OshKosh in Celina for 20 years. He is now employed with Southern Belle Dairy Company.

Elaine, Randy, Judy, Vernon and Robin Grace

On May 22, 1965, Vernon married Judy Lane Webb of Route 1, Celina, Tennessee, the daughter of Willard and Maxine Watson Webb of the Pea Ridge Community of Clay County. Judy was born May 22, 1947. She graduated from Celina High School in 1965. She has been employed at the Bank of Celina for 17 years.

Judy and Vernon have three children, Carol Elaine, Randy Harold, and Robin Lee. Carol Elaine was born June 8, 1966. She graduated from Celina High School in 1984. She is a junior at Tennessee Technological University. Randy Harold was born May 22, 1969. He is a senior at Celina High School. Robin Lee was born June 3, 1974. He is in the seventh grade at Celina K-8 School.

Judy and Vernon attend the Rock Springs Church of Christ, where Vernon has served as a deacon for the past eight years. They are both active in church and community affairs.

BENJAMIN AND SARAH HALSELL

Benjamin Halsell was the son of George Halsell of South Carolina. His mother's name is unknown. George Halsell was a patriot of the American Revolution, as he served on the Jury during that time and was therefore classified as a patriot. Benjamin Hallsell, born (ca) 1760 in Virginia, died prior to August of 1830 near Vernon in Cumberland Co., Kentucky, which was the site of land granted to him upon his arrival as one of the early settlers of this area. About 1785, he married Sarah Turner, born (ca) 1765 in Virginia — died (ca) 1820 in Cumberland County. It is assumed their graves are in the church cemetery near the Halsell home place near Vernon where many of the graves are unmarked. They had eight children. Rebecca Halsell, born 1790 — died May 1869, married John C. Bedford in 1805. Sarah (Sally) Halsell, born (ca) 1798 — died 1861, married Cabby Embree. Susannah Halsell, born 1789/91 — died June 19, 1858, married Radford Maxey in 1813. Thomas Turner Halsell, born 1786/88 — died September 27, 1853, married Rebecca Scott. John Halsell, born 1790/1800, married, but his wife's name is unknown. Benjamin Halsell, Jr. was born between 1790 and 1800. James P. Halsell was born between 1799 and 1805. Mary Ann, born April 3, 1805 – died September 29, 1855, married George Washington Whiteside (ca) 1823.

Mary Ann Halsell and George Washington Whiteside had the following children: Catherine E., who married Francie Andrews; Eliza A. Whiteside, who never married; Chilton Whiteside, who married Elizabeth Fidella Simms; Benjamin Whiteside, who married Mary Ann (Armstrong) Hughes, as her second husband; Mary Whiteside, who married William Hudspeth; and James Whiteside, who married Sarah Isabelle Fowler.

FRANK B. HALSELL

Frank B. Halsell, was born November 13, 1921, in Clay County, Tennessee. He is the son of Benjamin F. Halsell Jr. and Effie Mae Wood Halsell. Benjamin and Effie were the parents of thirteen children: Nemo, Beulah (Jobe), Buford, Nadine (Cropper), Pauline (Warren), Frank, Rachel (Norris), Mary (Hullinger), James, Fletcher, Robert, Elwyn and Woodrow.

Frank and Avos Halsell

Frank is the grandson of Jim Wood and Elizabeth Ann Boles Wood and Robert S. Halsell, Sr. and Ruth Agnes Gray Halsell, who came to Monroe County, Kentucky from South Carolina and settled in Martinsburg, Kentucky on the Cumberland River in 1806.

Frank attended schools in Monroe County, Kentucky, and Clay County, Tennessee. He served in the US Army during World War II and was awarded the Purple Heart for wounds received in the Battle of the Bulge. Frank has been active in politics since his discharge from the military in May 1945. In 1946, he served as Highway Commissioner. From 1950 to 1966, he served as Clay County Trustee. In 1966, he was elected Clay County Judge and served in the position until 1982. He is a Mason and Shriner and serves on the Board of Directors for Twin Lakes Telephone Cooperative and the Bank of Celina.

Frank was married to Avos Boone Halsell of Moss, Tennessee September 19, 1942. Avos was born in Clay County, Tennessee, February 22, 1926, the daughter of Oscar Samuel Boone and Montana Lois Dyer. She is the granddaughter of Stephen Campbell Boone and Priscilla Anderson Boone and Samuel Dyer and Ermine Poore Dyer. Avos attended schools in Clay County, Tennessee. She serves as Postmaster at Moss, Tennessee.

Frank and Avos are parents of three children: Gale Halsell Thompson, born October 30, 1944; Frankie Halsell Scott, born April 7, 1947; and Suzanne Halsell, born January 10, 1960. Gale married Joe W. Thompson August 23, 1962, and works for the Corps of Engineers in Celina, Tennessee. Frankie married Fred Scott January 4, 1964, and they own a grocery store in Celina, Tennessee. Suzanne lives in Auburn, Alabama and manages a store there.

Gale and Joe live in the Moss Community of Clay County and they have two children, Joe Frank, born September 16, 1963, and Lori Anne, born October 9, 1970.

Frankie and Fred live in Celina and have one child, Jeffrey Lee Scott, born October 30, 1966.

Frank and Avos live in the Moss Community of Clay County and attend the Church of Christ.

JAMES MITCHELL HAMILTON

James Mitchell Hamilton was born November 24, 1898 in the Bennett's Ferry (now Butler's Landing) area of Clay County. His father was William Carroll Hamilton, and his mother was Madge Stone Hamilton. William Carroll fought in the Civil War.

James Mitchell and Maude Hamilton, Evelyn, Ruth, Charles, Billy and Kenneth

James Mitchell went to his first school at Butler's Landing. Later he went to Hamilton School near his home. His father, William Carroll, built this school. James Mitchell later attended Montvale College in Celina.

James Mitchell married Maude Sims of Vernon, Kentucky May 24, 1924. Maude was born July 18, 1899, the daughter of Savanah Woods and William Patterson Sims. They were married in Monroe County, Kentucky. They lived on a farm in the Butler's Landing Community for 44 years before moving to Celina where they still live. James Mitchell worked on the building of Dale Hollow Dam; and during World War II, he worked as a guard at Oak Ridge. He also ran the toll booth when a toll was charged to cross the Cumberland River Bridge.

James Mitchell and Maude had six children. Evelyn married Freeman Swann. Willie Buford (Bill) married Josephine Napier. Charles Mitchell married Mary Ann King. Nina Ruth married Ned Parsons. James Ray died at 18 of cancer. Kenneth Edward married Linda Donaldson. James Mitchell and Maude have seven grandchildren and five great grandchildren.

James Mitchell and Maude celebrated their 62nd Wedding Anniversary in May of 1986. — *Submitted by grandson, Jason Hamilton*

ED L. HAMPTON

Ed L. Hampton was born December 21, 1951 in Celina, Tennessee. He is the son of Joe Thomas Hampton (deceased) and Elsa Lee Emerton Hampton, both of Celina. Ed is the grandson of Joe and Linnie Emerton and Charles and Nannie

Jill, Dixie, Kittie and Ed Hampton

Elizabeth (Bessie) Maynard Hampton. Ed has one brother, Charles Joseph Hampton of Celina.

Ed attended Clay County, Tennessee schools and was graduated from Celina High School in 1969. He attended Tennessee Tech University from 1969-73, and received a Masters Degree in Wildlife and Fisheries Science from Virginia Tech in 1976. He worked as an environmental consultant in Nashville, Tennessee from 1976-79. Since 1979, Ed has been pursuing a Ph.D. in Forestry at Virginia Tech. Since 1973, he has owned and operated a karate school in Blacksburg, Virginia. He currently holds a 4th degree Black Belt in Okinawan kempo and teaches karate full-time.

Ed was married to Letitia Ann Smith, formerly of Baxter, Tennessee, September 9, 1973. The couple were divorced in July 1981.

Ed was remarried June 6, 1984 to Dr. M. Jill Stewart, formerly of Augusta, Georgia. Jill was born in Augusta, Georgia February 7, 1953, the daughter of Lucian Delbert Stewart and Margaret Fiske Stewart. She is the granddaughter of the late Julian Francis Fiske and Kate Edwards Fiske of Georgia and of the late Charles Lucian Stewart and Essie Pearl Stewart of Kentucky.

Jill attended Richmond County, Georgia schools, graduating from the Academy of Richmond County in 1971. She was graduated from Georgia Southern College in 1975 with a B.S. degree in math. At Georgia Southern College, Jill was voted into Who's Who Among Students at American Colleges and Universities. She completed a Masters Degree in 1976 and a Ph.D. degree in 1980 in statistics at Virginia Tech. After graduation, she worked as a statistician for the Office of Power of the Tennessee Valley Authority in Chattanooga, Tennessee. From 1981 until 1985, Jill worked as an instructor of statistics for the Department of Management Science at Virginia Tech and received the Certificate of Teaching Excellence. The last year at Virginia Tech was shared with an instructorship at Radford University, Radford, Virginia. From 1985 until present, Jill has been employed by Radford University as an assistant professor of statistics.

Ed and Jill are the parents of twin girls, Kittie Zhou and Dixie Lee, born April 14, 1985 in Roanoke, Virginia.

THOMAS HARVEY HAMPTON

Thomas Harvey (Babe) Hampton was born December 20, 1860. He died March 19, 1935. He married Louana Adeline Carson December 1, 1885. She died November 7, 1900. They are buried in the Hall Cemetery on Mill Creek. They had four children. Bill J. Hampton was born March 4, 1887 and died February 17, 1958. He married Cleora Lewreth June 4, 1917. They had no children and lived in Texas.

Edd and Rose Fowler

Rose Hampton, born June 25, 1889 — died April 25, 1971, married E.P. Fowler June 15, 1910. They had one child who died at birth. He was named Ray Fowler. E.P. Fowler was one of the first cashiers of the bank that started in Old Town March 18, 1895, and he was active in this Bank of Celina until a few months before his death in 1948. Rose and E.P. are buried in the Hamilton Cemetery.

Pearl Hampton, born January 6, 1893 — died July 5, 1962, married Matt L. Fowler April 30, 1916. Matt was an Assistant County Agent. Pearl taught school and was a clerk in a store for many years. They had no children. Both are buried in the Hamilton Cemetery.

Charles Lee Hampton, born December 16, 1895 — died March 27, 1940, married Bessie Maynard on May 28, 1919. Bessie died Mar. 9, 1947. They are both buried at the Hamilton Cemetery. Charles and Bessie had two children. Joe Thomas Hampton married Elsa Lee Emerton. They have two sons, Ed L. and Charles Joseph. Ed L. has twin daughters, Dixie and Kittie. Ed married Jill Stewart. Charles Joseph married Sue Poindexter.

Charles Hampton was a 2nd Lieutenant in the Army during World War I and was scheduled to go into the Battle of the Argonne Forrest when peace was declared. He was a member of the county court, a mason, and he taught school for many years. Charles and Bessie's daughter, Charley Nelle, married Robert Cooper, and they have one daughter, Lori Cooper.

Thomas Harvey's father was William Carroll Hampton; his mother was Margaret E. Hawkins. William Carroll died of wounds received in battle in Lee County, Virginia, the 23rd of April, 1865. G.W. Hampton was his grandfather. Polly Hampton was his grandmother. Polly is buried on a hill at the Barlow Rose place near Butler's Landing.

MILTON R. HARGROVE

Milton R. Hargrove lived in the Willow Grove area of Clay County. He was a farmer and busi-

nessman, the son of William Hargrove and Elizabeth Baker, who came across the mountains from Virginia.

Milton R. Hargrove

Although Milton had very little formal education, he, along with others, helped to establish the first school at Willow Grove.

Milton married Mary Margaret Nelson, and they had two sons, John A. Hargrove, born in 1872, and William Edward Hargrove, born fifteen years later in 1887.

John A. married Eunice Hunter and had one daughter, Agnes. Agnes married Eddison Reeves "Ted" Smith, and they had three children, Betty Reeves, John Hunter (d.) and Mary Ann Smith.

William Edward married Gladys Jouett September 13, 1908 in Pickett County, Tennessee. They had three children, Margaret Grimsley Langford, John Milton "Jack" Hargrove and Edwina Napier. Margaret married Cleston Grimsley (d.) and had one daughter, Jean Reed. After the death of Cleston, Margaret married Lewis Langford (d.).

Jack Hargrove married Gladys Wiggins (d.). They had two children, Jacqueline Beth Tankersley and Reginald Gaines Hargrove. Jack died in 1965.

Edwina married Billy J. Napier (d.) They had five children, Jack Douglas, Donald Edwin, Betty Jane Holtam, Mary Linda Strong, and William Nelson "Bill" Napier.

William Edward Hargrove died February 2,

1966, and his wife Gladys died October 12, 1973.

Milton R. Hargrove's first wife died at a young age, and he later married Sally McDonald. Milton died March 12, 1922, and Sally died on June 28, 1949 in Celina. Milton and his first wife are buried in Nelson Cemetery in Overton County. Sally is buried in St. John Cemetery in Clay County. — *Submitted by great-grandson Don Napier*

H.T. "TILLY" HARPE

Hillary Tilemon "Tilly" Harpe (Harp) was born September 11, 1854. He was the son of Daniel and Charlotte Harpe and the grandson of Alvarine and Nancy Harpe. His grandfather, Alvarine, was a sleigh maker who lived in Lincoln County, Tennessee in 1830.

"Tilly" Harpe was living on Knob Creek in 1880 where he was a farmer. He also worked as a raft pilot. He first married Mary (Sarah) Atchley. There is a discrepancy as to the names of their children. Census records lists Will (Billy); Martha, born Jan. 7, 1871, married J.M. Brown; Mary; and Dealy. According to descendants, there was also a daughter, Maddie, and at least one child who died in infancy. The exact date of the death of Mary (Sarah) is not known, but she died at an early age and is buried on Turkey Creek.

"Tilly" then married Mollie Brown, born July 22, 1863, the daughter of Samuel and Adalaine Masters Brown. "Tilly" and Mollie had ten children who lived to adulthood. Jim married (wife's name unknown) and moved to Texas. Sally married Guy Hammer and moved to Texas. Sib married Ollie Giddings, who died in 1947. Sib and Ollie had twin sons, Ed and Fred, who live in Lafayette, Tennessee. Sib was born November 24, 1882 and died in March of 1985 at the age of 102. Sib made 25 trips down the Cumberland River from Celina to Nashville on log rafts for which he was paid $25 a trip. He quit his last regular job at age 85. In his later years, he enjoyed fishing and trading knives.

Addie was born May 31, 1892. She married Andrew Odle and lived in the Moss Community. She died July 11, 1944. Lula married "Tink" Brown and moved to Texas. Ernest Love was born April 13, 1895 and lived her entire life on a section of the Harpe Farm on Knob Creek. She was a member of the Arcot Church of Christ. She

The Family of Martha Harpe Brown in the 1930's

died May 31, 1975 and is buried in the McColgin Cemetery.

Guy married Ida Moss. They moved to Indiana in the mid 1940's. Bea married Tom Perrin, and they moved to Indiana. Bea is buried in the Macedonia Cemetery.

Kate was born January 23, 1905. She married Raymond Strong, who was born January 11, 1906. Kate died June 10, 1959. She is buried in the Macedonia Cemetery.

Tinsley was born August 8, 1911. He worked at a service station in Celina. He died in a car accident November 4, 1956. He is buried in the McColgin Cemetery.

In a newspaper interview published in the Macon County Times November 20, 1976, Sib Harp (Harpe) stated that he came from a family of 17 children. His father, H.T. Harp, had five children by his first wife, and 12 by his second wife, Mollie Brown. He further stated that all but three lived to be "grown up."

"Tilly" died December 16, 1923. Mollie died July 23, 1941. They are buried in the McColgin Cemetery.

EDDIE HATCHER

Eddie Hatcher was born September 19, 1965, the son of Harold Dean and Patricia (Davis) Hatcher. Harold Dean is the son of Hubert and Gertrude (Coonse) Hatcher. Hubert is the son of Walter and Nancy (Gulley) Hatcher. Walter is the son of William P. Hatcher, who was born October 15, 1848, and Wint (Copas) Hatcher, who was born October 3, 1854. William P. was the son of John Hatcher, who was born in 1820, and Mary (Birdwell) Hatcher, who was born April 9, 1812 in Washington County, Tennessee. She died October 4, 1879. She is buried in the Clementsville Cemetery in Clay County, Tennessee. She was the daughter of Alexander Birdwell, who was born in 1787 in East Tennessee, and Elizabeth (Copass) Birdwell, who was born in 1784 in Virginia. She died in 1870 in Monroe County, Kentucky. Her father, William Copass, was born in 1747 in Virginia and died in 1851 in Washington County, Tennessee. He was a Revolutionary War soldier.

Eddie and Mary Hatcher

Eddie Hatcher was married in 1986 to Mary Copas, who was born on December 27, 1967, the daughter of Hardie Edward and Elizabeth Ruth (McCarter) Copas. Eddie is a farmer and a mechanic. Eddie graduated from Hermitage Springs High School. Mary graduated from Hermitage Springs High School in 1986. She was valedictorian of her class.

JOHN AND BEVERLY HEATH

John C. Heath was born on October 12, 1947, in Louisville, Georgia. He is the son of William E. Heath, Sr. and Cornellia Ledbetter Heath. His ancestors lived in Virginia until they migrated to Georgia in the 1700's. He grew up in Louisville, Georgia, and thereafter lived in Atlanta for approximately fifteen years before moving to Celina, Tennessee.

John is the grandson of Homer Heath and Lily Boykin Heath and the Reverend Samuel Ledbetter and Emma Sharpe Ledbetter. He graduated from Georgia State University in 1970, and from Emory University Law School in 1975. He is currently an attorney in Celina, Tennessee.

John was married to Beverly Wright, formerly of Jamestown, Tennessee, June 21, 1975. Beverly was born May 27, 1947, and is the daughter of Elmo Wright and Blanche Mullinix Wright. She is the granddaughter of Oakley Wright and Christina Wright and Helen Mullinix and Porter Mullnix.

Beverly grew up in Jamestown, Tennessee, and received a Bachelor of Science degree in music from Tennessee Technological University in 1969. She taught school for several years and received a Master of Music Education degree from Northeast Louisiana University in 1971. She is currently employed by the Clay County School System as a teacher.

John and Beverly Heath are the parents of Andrew John Heath, born July 21, 1978, and Ryan Scott Heath, born October 19, 1980, both born in Atlanta.

Beverly and John Heath are members of the Celina Baptist Church, where Beverly is the choir director. In addition, John is the Cubmaster for the Celina Cub Scouts and is Municipal Judge for the City of Celina. Beverly has been active in the musical programs presented by the Hermitage Springs High School, as well as other musical events involving the Clay County School System.

MARION AND BELLE HENSON

Richard Marion Henson and Victoria Belle Delk were married in March of 1882 in Simpson County, Kentucky. They owned a small farm and ran a store in Franklin. Their first four children were born in Franklin: Ella, Bessie, Weaver and Kizzie. Ella and Bessie both died as young children and were buried in Simpson County. Around 1898, the Hensons moved to Clay County and settled on Knob Creek. Marion was a farmer during his Tennessee years.

This couple had eight children. The last four were born in Clay County, Carl, Pearl, Clarence, and Earl. Weaver married Verda Pedigo in 1913. They had four sons, Elmo, Elbert, Delbert, and Leon. Kizzie married Edward Smith, and they had

Marion and Bell Henson

two sons, Ray and Edward. Carl married Estil Craighead. They had one daughter, Mildred, who married John Johnson. Pearl married Oscar Condra, and they have one son, Eldon. Clarence married Mertie Hestand, and they had two children, Carol and David. The youngest daughter, Earl, married Azzie Kendall.

Marion's sisters were Sis and Kizzie. Sis married a Hawkins and Kizzie married David Goodrun. Both remained in or near Simpson County, Kentucky. Two brothers, Mance and Bryant, never married. Marion was apparently the youngest child, born about 1862, but his roots are hard to trace.

Belle Delk was born in 1866 to David and Para Lee (Morris) Delk (daughter of Richard and Surena Morris) in Jackson County. David Delk was born in 1842 to Jourdan and Charlotte Delk. David Delk served with the Confederates in the Civil War. He was imprisoned by the Union Army in Ohio.

Marion Henson died of pneumonia in 1912 and was buried in the Macedonia Cemetery. Belle Henson moved with her children from Knob Creek at about that time to the Clements farm on Highway 52 and three years later moved to the Pine Hill area. Belle survived until 1944. She is buried in the Moss Cemetery.

WEAVER AND VERDA HENSON

In 1913, Mack Weaver Henson and Verda Mae Pedigo were married in Clay County, Tennessee. To this union were born four sons, Elmo, Elbert, Delbert, and Leon. Before Verda married, she was a school teacher at Oak Grove School. After living in several rent houses, the Hensons bought the Pedigo home where Verda was raised. They moved there in 1927 and renovated the L-shaped, two-story house.

Weaver and Verda Henson

For many years the Hensons ran a country grocery located near their home. Mr. Henson also ran a rolling store in his truck to serve isolated families. They ran a gristmill and hammer mill at the same location. Many a "turn" of shelled corn was delivered on horseback behind a rider. A toll (1/5 part) was taken out to pay for grinding the corn meal.

The Hensons' four sons all attended Hermitage Springs High School. Elmo was the first to graduate, in 1933. Elbert was on the basketball team in the mid-30's. Delbert and Leon both served in America's Armed Forces. Delbert was in the Pacific Navy in World War II. Leon served in Korea. He died in a car wreck during that war.

The Hensons were founding members of the Oak Grove Church of Christ. Weaver really loved to sing in his deep bass voice. They had previously attended the Pine Hill Church near where Weaver's mother lived.

The Hensons have the following descendants: Elmo married Oma Birdwell. They have two sons, Fred and Roy. Fred married Linda Meachem. They have four children, Mark, Daniel, Heather, and Chris. They now live in Virginia. Roy married Joy Tolle. They have four children, Philip, Johnathan, Lorrie, and Amy. They now occupy the Weaver Henson home, formerly the home of Verda's parents.

Elbert married Anna Birdwell. They have five children, Patricia, Barbara, Margaret, Timothy, and Jerry. Patricia married Charlie Allen and has one son, Jeff. They live in Cookeville. Barbara married Jack Smith. They have one daughter, Julie, and they live in Nashville. Margaret now lives in Denver, Colorado. Timothy married Carla Hagan. They have two children, April and Reed, and they live at Adams, Tennessee. Jerry lives with his parents at Adams.

Delbert married Estelene Anderson and had three children, Gwen, Ricky and Lajuana. Gwen married Mike Buffo. Ricky married Debbie Sutherland. They have a daughter, Erin. Lajuana married Mark Roch. They all live in Indianapolis, Indiana.

Verda Henson died in 1966. Weaver survived until 1970. They are buried in the Pitcock Cemetery at Oak Grove.

ELMO AND OMA HENSON

Fred Elmo Henson was born in Clay County on October 17, 1914. He was the oldest of four sons born to Mack Weaver and Verda (Pedigo) Henson. Elmo attended Oak Grove Elementary School. He graduated from Hermitage Springs High School in 1933 and took a few courses at Tennessee Polytechnic Institute.

On December 24, 1939, Elmo married Oma Birdwell. She was the third of six children born to William and Beulah Hill Birdwell. She vividly remembers walking three miles to Mount Vernon Elementary School. Sometimes a covered wagon was available for transportation to school in the winter. Oma also attended Hermitage Springs High School, where she again walked with her numerous friends.

The Hensons have two sons. Fred was born on his father's birthday, October 17, 1940. He attended Mount Vernon Elementary School, Hermitage Springs High School and received his Bachelor of Science Degree in Business Administration in 1963. He has worked with the U.S. Department of Agriculture in Washington, D.C. since his graduation. He attended the Arlington Church of Christ, and it was there that he met his wife, Linda Meacham. Linda is the daughter of

Elmo and Oma Henson

Buford and Connie Meacham, who now live in LaGrange, Georgia. Linda attended schools in Virginia and completed a year at David Lipscomb College in Nashville. Fred and Linda have four children, Mark, age 17; David, age 15; Heather, age 10; and Chris, age 7. They now live in Burke, Virginia, where their children attend school. The family now attends church at Fairfax, Virginia.

Their second son, Roy, was born February 2, 1943. He attended Mount Vernon Elementary School, Hermitage Springs High School, and he graduated from David Lipscomb in 1964. He received his Masters Degree from Memphis State University. While a student at Memphis State, Roy married Joy Tolle in 1967. She is the daughter of Albert and Evelyn Tolle of Baton Rouge, Louisiana. Joy attended school in Baton Rouge. She received her B.S. Degree from Louisiana State University. Roy and Joy have four children: Philip, Jonathan, Lorrie, and Amy. They all attend Hermitage Springs School, where both parents are teachers.

Elmo and Oma moved to Cleveland, Ohio in 1942, where Elmo worked in a defense plant until 1945. They returned to Clay County and bought the farm where they now live. They have lived 39 years in the frame house they built in 1946.

FRED AND LINDA HENSON

Fred Henson, the first son of Elmo and Oma Birdwell Henson, was born October 17, 1940 in Clay County. Fred attended Mount Vernon Elementary School and graduated from Hermitage Springs High School in 1957 at the age of 16.

Fred, Linda, Mark, David, Heather and Chris Henson

After completing an electronics course with United Electronics in Louisville, Fred enrolled in David Lipscomb College where he served as a dormitory supervisor to help defray his college expenses. He graduated in 1963 with a Bachelor of Science Degree in Business Administration.

In August of 1967, Fred married Linda Meacham of Springfield, Virginia. At that time, Linda's father worked for the United States Government in Washington, D.C. Fred and Linda now live in Burke, Virginia.

Fred and Linda have the following children: Mark, David, Heather, and Chris.

Fred works for the United States Department of Agriculture in Washington, D.C. He and Linda are very active members of the Church of Christ.

ROY AND JOY HENSON

The Hensons were married in Memphis, Tennessee on August 20, 1967. At that time, Roy was attending Harding Graduate School, while Joy was a landscape architect with Robert Green

and Associates. While completing his Masters Degree at Memphis State, Roy taught two years at Memphis Southside. Joy continued her work in landscaping.

Two children were born to the Hensons in Memphis — Philip in January of 1969 and Jonathan in July of 1970. When Roy was hired by the Clay County School System in the fall of 1970, the family moved to Clay County. Roy's grandfather had died in June, so his house was available. In November the family purchased the Weaver Henson house and 100 acres of the Henson farm. Renovation of the house and yard were soon begun. The family was completed by the births of two daughters, Lorrie in July of 1973 and Amy in June of 1975.

Amy, Philip, Roy, Joy, Jonathan and Lorrie Henson

Roy Henson was born to Elmo and Oma Birdwell Henson in 1943 in the house he now occupies. This house was built about 1904 by his great grandparents, James and Martha Grider Pedigo, and then purchased by his grandparents, Weaver and Verda Pedigo Henson. Roy's first two years were spent in Cleveland, Ohio. Then the family returned to Clay County to farm. His education includes Mount Vernon Elementary School, Hermitage Springs High School, a Bachelor of Arts Degree from David Lipscomb College, and a Masters Degree from Memphis State University. He spent a year as a Missionary in Scotland in 1964-65. He began teaching in 1968 and continues teaching at Hermitage Springs Elementary School today. He has preached part-time at the Pine Hill Church of Christ since 1970.

Joy Tolle was born to Albert and Evelyn (Fredrikson) Tolle in January of 1942 in Baton Rouge, Louisiana. Her father was born in Hammond, Louisiana to parents who had moved there from Ohio. Albert is now retired from the Exxon Refinery in Baton Rouge. Joy's mother was born to immigrant parents from near Tonsberg and Stavanger, Norway. Evelyn's father was a sailor for several years beginning at age 14. Joy now has his sea desk. Evelyn interrupted her education at Louisiana State University to get married. While pursuing her secretarial career, she resumed her course work and graduated at age 66. Joy was educated in Baton Rouge Public Schools and got her Bachelor of Science Degree from Louisiana State University.

When Joy moved to Clay County, she attended Tennessee Technological University in Cookeville and earned her teacher's certificate. She is now completing fourteen years of teaching in the lower elementary grades. Her hobbies include flowers, landscaping, piano, travel and raising registered cairn terrier dogs.

The children have varied hobbies and interests: fishing, swimming, canoeing, sketching and painting, golf, et cetera. Jonathan loves handling machinery, while Philip is deep into astronomy.

LYNDELL MYRL HENSON

Lyndell Myrl Henson was born February 6, 1955 in Clay County, Tennessee. at the home of his grandmother, Dessie Rich. He is the son of Myrl Smith Henson, born January 10, 1916 and Naoma Rich Henson, born October 24, 1930. His father, Myrl Smith Henson, is a veteran of World War II.

Lyndell and Dana Henson

Lyndell is the grandson of Allie Smith Henson (daughter of Dave Smith and Effie Morton Smith) and Hugh Henson (son of William Henson and Elvira Emmitt Henson) and Dessie Cherry Rich (daughter of Boyd Cherry and Craton Short Cherry) and Hobert Rich (son of William Rich and Challotie Coffelt Rich). His grandfather, Hobert Rich, is a veteran of World War I.

Lyndell attended school in Clay County and he graduated from Hermitage Springs High School in 1973. He attended Middle Tennessee State University where he received his B.S. Degree in 1977. He is presently a teacher and a coach at Hermitage Springs School. Lyndell started his teaching career in 1977.

Lyndell was married to Dana Jean Birdwell of Clay County, Tennessee June 24, 1978. Dana was born in Overton County, Tennessee March 13, 1953. She is the daughter of Ulysses Birdwell and Versa Cherry Birdwell. Dana is the granddaughter of Lucy Browning Birdwell (daughter of Andrew and Nancy Lundy Browning) and Herod Birdwell (son of Alexander and Bernetta Spears Birdwell) and Elizabeth Long and Matthias (Mack) Cherry. Dana attended school in Clay County where she graduated from Hermitage Springs High School in 1971.

Lyndell has one brother, Ronnie, born in Clay County, Tennessee August 15, 1952.

DANIEL HILL

The house where Daniel and Laura Netherton Hill lived is still standing near Clementsville in Clay County. One of the granddaughters still remembers sliding her hands over the porch lattice when visiting her grandparents when she was a young girl. The farm is now owned by Fred Mullinix.

Daniel and Laura Hill

The Hills made their living as farmers at a time when survival was hard. Their seven children were Alice Beulah, who married William Birdwell; Glenna, who married Herbert McLerran; Johnnie, who married Pearl Odle; Hubert, who died of pneumonia in his early twenties; George, who married Anna Owens; Bascal, who married Ernestine Mattington; and Hardy, who never married. The Hills and all their children, except Beulah, moved to Indianapolis, Indiana about 1926 and never returned except for visits.

Daniel Hill's (1872-1944) father was William Hill (1815-1875) from Alabama. William served with the U.S. Army in the Mexican War and v the South in the Civil War. Daniel's mother Rutha Burford (1835-1921) from Carthage, T nessee. Rutha's parents were John and Nan McCollester Burford who married in Sumn County in 1817.

John's father, Daniel Burford, was a promin Baptist minister at Dixon Springs and served Register of Deeds at Carthage about 18 John's brother, Daniel Burford, served in state legislature and was House Speaker in 18.

Laura Louise Netherton was born in 1875 Jasper (1843-1921) and Marey Dyer Netherᵗ (1844-1916) in Clay County. Her brothers and sisters were Martin, James, Andrew, Abraham, Sarah, Turner, and Alta. Many of their relatives live in Clay County.

The Hill family carried water from a spring, which soon became the boys' work. To make their work more fun, Daniel's sons made small pits beneath the spring branch to shape and polish their flint marbles. An unusual trait of Daniel's was his cooking ability. Occasionally he surprised the family with a Sunday dinner when they returned from church. One grandchild remembers the day the chicken's head got cooked too — with the eyes still in.

Daniel's brothers were John, Will, and George. Four of Will's children live in Vicksburg, where they moved about 1921. His sister, Annie Hill Draper, died young but has living descendants in Gainesboro and Nashville.

Bud and Azie Kendall

Carry S. Cherry home now owned by Haskell Spivey.

Logging and rafting at the mouth of the Obey River in 1906

Hermitage Springs Church of Christ

Reviewing stand at Clay County Fairgrounds.

Celina — 1940's

Weaver Henson Store

JOHN HILL, SR.

John Hill, Sr. of Randolph County, North Carolina, was the ancestor of the Hill families of Overton and Clay Counties in the areas of Celina, Willow Grove, Hilham, Alpine, and Ivyton at the West Fork of the Obey River. At the present (1986) all of his children are not known, but the descendants of one son, John Jr., are listed.

John Hill, Jr. (1786-1866) married Catherine Means (1792-1886) and lived at Ivyton, West Fork of Obey River, Overton County, Tennessee. John, R. was a minister in the Christian Church (now Church of Christ). They had fifteen children, Thomas, born 1810; Robert Clemons "Clem," born 1811-1891; George W., born 1813; Siddy, born 1814; Malvina, born 1817; Lizindia, born 1818; Charlotty, born 1822; Catherine, born 1823; Margaret "Peggy", born 1825; Nancy, born 1826; Elizabeth, born 1828; Matilda, born 1830; Mary, born 1832; John, born 1834; and Andrew, born 1836-1862, killed in the Battle of Mill Springs, Wayne County, Kentucky. during the Civil War. Of the above family, legends still exist of the land and money owned by Margaret "Peggy" (Hill) McDonald, 1925-1909, the wife of Sells McDonald, 1812-1853 and her nephew "Abe" Hill, 1855-1910 of Ivyton.

Robert Clemons "Clem" Hill, 1811-1891, married Annie Eliza Medlock, ca 1817-ca 1876, the daughter of Charley Medlock, a full Cherokee Indian of Overton County, Tennessee, and lived at Hilham, Tennessee. "Clem" was trustee of Overton County, Tennessee for several years. They had eleven children. Jane married Amos McBride. Emma married Thomas S. Franklin,

Robert Clemons and Ann Eliza (Medlock) Hill

1839-1910. Mary married Carol Burchitt, 1848-1907. George Washington, 1840-1900, married Martha Ann Beaty, 1840-1885. John never married, and was killed by bushwhackers during the Civil War. Siddie Clementine "Sid", ca 1846-ca 1915, never married. Susan Catherine married February 5, 1873 Casper Caruthers Christian 1852-1892. They went to the Indian Territory of Oklahoma. Laura, 1852-1892, married Harvey Rich, 1845-1912. Adelia Ann, 1857-1874, married Alex Hawkins, 1849-1928. Martha married George Dailey. Vestina, 1859-1886, married Jesse Calvin Thompson, 1856-1920.

George Washington Hill, 1840-1900, of Hilham, Tennessee, first married Martha Ann Beaty, 1840-1885, the daughter of Thomas Beaty, 1801-1881 and his wife, Jane Mullenax, 1804-1893. George W. Hill was an elder and lay preacher in the Church of Christ for many years at Hilham, Tennessee. They had ten children. The first two infant sons were never named. Andrew Jackson "Andy," 1861-1913, married Sarah Elizabeth Cook, 1866-1923; Mary Jane, 1865-1958, married Dr. Thomas Arkley Langford, 1855-1942; John Thomas, born 1867, went to the Indian Territory and married there; Matilda Ann Alice, 1870-1963, married Joseph Andrew Maloney, 1862-1935; Robert Clemons "Clem," (Jr.), 1871-1899, married Alice Masters and went to the Indian Territory, Oklahoma; Nancy died in 1877; George Benton, ca 1880-1884; and Martha Evelyn died in 1878.

George Washington Hill, 1840-1900, married for the second time, Amanda Jane Thomas, 1852-1898, the daughter of James Byrd Thomas, 1804-1854, and Deborah Masters, 1818-1904. They had four children. William Byrd, 1886-1960, went to Texas and married Mattie B. Crowell of Wichita Falls, Texas; James Alva 1889-1890; Albert Ross "A.R.," 1890-1983, was a Church of Christ minister and he married Ferrell Kirby of Alabama; and Charley David, 1894-1932/33, went to Texas and Arkansas. George Washington Hill married for the third time, Emma Coffman, 1854-1948, and they did not have any children.

Andrew Jackson "Andy" Hill, 1861-1913, married Sarah Elizabeth Cook, 1866-1923, the daughter of Wilson Cook, 1843-1911, and Louisa

Smith, 1847-1923. They lived on Obey River in Clay County, Tennessee. They had four children. George Wilson, 1882-1922, married Emma Nora Upton, 1886-1950; Martha Louisiana, 1884-1884; and Mary Ann, 1885-1929, married Grover Cleveland Rich, 1884-1950, the son of Tom and Judy Ann (Bow) Rich; and Matilda Jane, 1887-1927, married Willie Daniel "Will" Webb, 1889-1936, the son of William Caleb "Bee" Webb, 1855-1924, and Sophia Susan "Suffie" Bow, 1858-1913, of Obey River, Clay County. They had two sons, Edward Carmack, 1910, married Mary Emma Blythe, the daughter of William Thomas Blythe and Renia Florence Watson, and Walter Estes Webb, 1915, who never married. — *Prepared by Walter E. Webb*

JOSHUA POLK "JOSH" HILL

Joshua Polk Hill, better known as "Josh", was born January 5, 1880. Josh was the son of Rubin Hill and Sarah Weaver Hill of the Free Hills Community in Clay County.

Josh attended a one-room country school in the community. This one-room building was an old log church. The school year was for only three months each year. Josh went for approximately seven years and studied a trade. He studied carpentry and became a very good carpenter. He built many homes in this community. Many of the homes he built are still standing, even though they are very old. Josh also worked on the Cumberland River with the rafting industry as long as it was in existence.

Josh married Fannie Beadaline Philpotts in 1902. Fannie was a schoolteacher. She taught for

Fannie and Josh Hill, Millard and Annie Hill

134

almost five years. She was 21 years of age when she married Josh. Josh and Fannie had eight children: Charles Cecil, born October 28, 1906; Lovie and Lila born and died March 27, 1909; John Thomas, born April 7, 1913; Sarah Willett, born March 27, 1910; Jessie Lee, born March 18, 1915; Millard Kyle, born March 6, 1919, and Jean, born July 6, 1921.

Josh was added to the Church (Free Hills Church of Christ) at an early age, approximately 12. He enjoyed working with young people and reading the Bible. He studied the Bible daily hoping to become a leader someday. This blessing was bestowed upon him at an early age (approximately 25) when he was given the position as a deacon, a position he held until his death at the age of 87.

HIRAM T. HINSON

Hiram Tinsley Hinson (Tin for short and also called Calep) was born in Jackson County on December 6, 1856. He brought his young family from Jennings Creek in Jackson County to Clay County about 1885 and settled in a spot halfway between Oak Grove and Union Hill. There he lived out his life as a farmer. He married Belle Wood, and the children of this union who lived to maturity were Roxie, who married Henry Austin Smith; George Bedford; and Dora, who married Bruce Turner.

George Bedford (Doc) Hinson was born January 1, 1873 and lived his life in the Union Hill-Oak Grove community. He married Minnie Jane Barnes whose ancestors came from Maury County. This union produced five children: Bessie (Clark), H.B. "Bud", Hade, Lassie and Kermit. Lassie and Kermit lived past maturity, but neither ever married.

H.B. "Bud" Hinson was born January 4, 1899. He married Lela Jewell Yates, whose mother was of the prolific Rich family and whose father was Tom Yates. He came from Adair County, Kentucky, and was one of the Yates Brothers singers famed in South-Central Kentucky. Bud and Jewell settled in Moss and raised a family. Bud carried a rural mail route from Moss for forty-four years, save one day, and in the early days he traveled on horseback or by horse and buggy. His oldest son, Royce, later carried a rural mail route out of Celina, and Royce's oldest son, for a short time, carried mail by airplane for a contract mail carrier, thus making three generations of mail carriers, the first beginning by horse, the second by automobile, and the third by airplane. The second son of H.B. and Jewell Hinson, Kuell, became a geneticist and settled in Florida at their state university. Their third son, Russell, became a judge in Hamilton County. Their youngest son, Aaron (Rip), became a merchant in Tompkinsville, Kentucky. Their daughter, Alma, taught school at Moss for a short time and married Keith Clark.

Hade Hinson married Inis Spears of Moss. His son, Willis, carried on the family tradition of mail carrying with a rural route out of Moss. His daughters, Vassey and Corine, settled in Indianapolis, Indiana, where Corine developed a custom manufacturing business serving customers nationwide.

The next generation of Hinsons scattered to the four winds. The Hinson family name originated in England. — *Submitted by Russell Hinson*

MARY ADDIE HINSON

Mary Addie Burnette Hinson was born September 7, 1926 near the Clementsville Community of Clay County. She is the daughter of Blanche Ritter Burnette and the late C.E. Burnette. She is the granddaughter of Nathan Ritter and Mary Wood Ritter and of Joseph H. Burnette and Addie Downing Burnette.

Suzanne, Sarah, Jeffery, Robert and David Hinson

Mary Addie attended school at Eminence and Moss. She graduated from Celina High School in 1944. She received her Bachelor of Science Degree from Tennessee Tech in 1965. For the past 30 years, she has taught in the Clay County School System.

Mary Addie was married on February 10, 1943 to Nolan Royce Hinson. Royce is the son of H. Budd Hinson and the late Lela Jewell Yates Hinson. He is the grandson of the late Bedford and Jane Barnes Hinson and of Elzady Rich and Thomas Yates all of Clay County.

Royce graduated from Celina High School. He was a mail carrier for Rural Route one of Celina for 22 years.

Mary Addie and Royce are the parents of five children. Jeffery Nolan was born October 15, 1946. He attended Moss Elementary School and graduated from Celina High School in 1964. He graduated from Tennessee Technological University in 1969. He married Freada Bailey, and they have two children, Cynthia Janette and Eric Reginald, who live in Memphis. Jeffery joined the Navy in 1970 and became a navy pilot. He now works for the Saudian Airlines in Jedda, Saudia Arabia.

Roger Alan was born February 15, 1948. He attended school at Moss and he graduated from Celina High School in 1965. He graduated from the University of Tennessee in 1969. He spent two years in the army in Vietnam. After the service, he returned to the University of Tennessee where he received his doctorate in Agricultural Economics. He is now employed at Louisiana State University. He has one son, Russell Frazier.

Sarah Kay was born November 13, 1951. She attended school at Moss, and she graduated from Celina High School. She graduated from Tennessee Technological University with a degree in Education. Sarah married James Lancaster of Woodbury, Tennessee. They have two sons, James Anthony and Kurt Hinson. They are living in Cleveland, Tennessee.

Suzanne was born August 29, 1953. She attended Moss Elementary School, and graduated from Celina High School in 1970. She attended Tennessee Technological University. Suzanne married Michael Goolsby. They have three children: Jennifer Nicole, born September 26, 1975;

Phillip Michael, born in September 1981; and Alex Keith, born December 8, 1983. Suzanne and her family live in Tacoma, Washington.

David Berl was born August 4, 1957. He graduated from Celina High School in 1975. He is a graduate of Middle Tennessee State University. David married Karn Och of Wheeling, West Virginia. They live in Memphis.

Mary Addie and Royce attend church at the Moss Church of Christ.

ARMEL FELIX HIX

Armel Felix Hix, born July 13, 1858 — died September 30, 1943, married Sara Jane Gilpatrick, born February 8, 1869-died May 31, 1938. They had eight children.

Oliver, born December 6, 1888, married Annie McCalpin. They had five children, Ruby, Woodrow, Cordell, Gloria Dean, and Charles.

Winton (born, 1-28 ?) married Lennie Jenkins. They had ten children, Fred, James, Elise, Edna Mae, Willie Gray, Leland, Claude, Freeman, Beatrice, and Harris.

George, born July 24, 1896, was married three times. He first married Annie Lou Smith; then Emma Swann; and then Maggie Hollis. He had no children.

Clure, born March 29, 1899, married Pearlie Buck. They had three children, Elmer Lee, Imogene, and a baby daughter.

Mallie, born August 3, 1901, married Tolliver Kirkpatrick. She had no children.

Comer, born February 21, 1904, married Minnie T. Smith. They had three children, John Hugh, Wendell, and Myra.

Annie Beatrice, born July 1, 1908 — died Oct. 12, 1960, married Vollie Swann. They had four children, Kenneth, Doyne and Doyle, and Gene.

Robert Lee Hix, born May 30, 1911 — died March 30, 1975, married Mae Smith. They have one daughter, Helen Frances, who married Mitchell Overstreet.

FOWLER HUFFINES

William Fowler Huffines was born June 30, 1906 in Kentucky, the son of Claude Sanford and Berry (Cherry) Huffines. He was married on March 21, 1928 in Clay County, Tennessee to Edith Ann Roberts, born August 7, 1906 at Hilham, Tennessee, the daughter of Jefferson Franklin and Mary Ellen (Ryans) Roberts. Fowler and Edith lived in the Baptist Ridge Community of Clay County, then moved to Butlers Landing before moving to the Miles Cross Roads Community of Clay County. He was a farmer. He served as a deputy sheriff of Clay County for eight years. He was also a constable in Clay County. He was a

Edith and Fowler Huffines

Church of Christ minister and preached for many churches in Clay County and Monroe County, Kentucky. He is buried in the Mt. Vernon Cemetery in Clay County. Edith attends the Milestown Church of Christ. They have two daughters. Alma Josephine, born June 9, 1929, married Leslie Davis; they have one daughter, Katy Lynn. Dorothy Lucille, born February 17, 1932, married Thomas Gerald McDonald. They have six children, Janice, Alma, Martha, Keith, Douglas, and Lana.

CORDELL HULL

Cordell Hulll was born at Olympus, Overton (now Pickett) County on October 2, 1871. He was the son of William and Elizabeth Riley Hull. His mother, Elizabeth Riley, was descended from Revolutionary Virginia settlers. William Hull was linked with Commodore Isaac Hull, whose achievements on Old Ironsides in the War of 1812 made the old frigate an enduring naval symbol. Cordell's brothers were Orestes, who became a doctor; Senadius Selwin (Nade), who moved to Texas; Wyoming, called the General; and Roy. When William "Uncle Billy" Hull died, he left a fortune estimated at $200,000 which he had amassed through farming, trading, lumbering, and sending his rafts of logs down the Wolf, the Obey and the Cumberland Rivers to market in Nashville.

From one of these rafts, Cordell Hull had his first glimpse of Nashville. Cordell also helped with the farming. His educational opportunities were limited. Cordell and his brothers attended rural schools for three month terms. As William Hull's finances improved, a school was sometimes conducted in his own home. Cordell attended Willow Grove School where Cordell won a debate affirming that Columbus deserved more credit for discovering America than did George Washington for defending it. This was Cordell's first appearance at a rostrum. At Montvale Academy in Celina, Cordell was instructed by Joseph S. McMillin, younger brother of Governor Benton McMillin. It is said that Cordell and some of his brothers did their own housekeeping in a rented house just off the public square in Celina. He later attended Kentucky Normal at Bowling Green and National Normal University at Lebanon, Ohio. He studied law in the offices of Pitts and Meeks in Nashville and John H. McMillin in Celina and finally studied in the historic law school, Cumberland University at Lebanon, Tennessee, where he obtained his degree June 4, 1891.

After completing his legal education, Cordell Hull returned to Celina and opened his office where he was a thoughtful, painstaking lawyer, whose advice could be accepted in litigated controversy. In time members of the Clay County Bar elected him as special judge to sit in the stead of Circuit Judge William T. Smith, who chanced to be absent. On April 18, 1903, he succeeded Judge William Smith by appointment of Governor James R. Frazier; and at the ensuing August election, Judge Hull was elected to fill out the remainder of the Smith term. As judge, he enforced the law vigorously, but not harshly, and impartially. The story is told that he once fined his father for talking too loudly in court.

In 1892, Cordell made his first race for political office, for floterial representative from Clay, Fentress, Overton, and Pickett Counties. He was two

Cordell Hull

months short of his twenty-first birthday, when he was elected floterial representative.

Cordell was sworn into the United States Volunteer Service with Company H, Fourth Tennessee when he was approaching his 27th birthday. The company was ordered to mobilize June 27, 1898 to fight in the war with Spain. On this date Cordell marched 41 "Mountain District" lads away to war. Celina was the place of departure; and the women of Celina presented Commander Hull with a basket of flowers. The regiment's service ended May 6, 1899.

Cordell resumed his law practice at Celina. In 1901 Cordell moved to Gainesboro where he was appointed to the Circuit bench. He was next elected to Congress and served from 1907-1921. He was chairman of the Democratic National Committee from 1921 to 1923. He served in the U.S. Senate from 1931-1933. On March 4, 1933, he was appointed Secretary of State by Franklin D. Roosevelt. He served in this position until Dec. 1, 1944, longer than any other man. In 1945, he was awarded the Nobel Peace Prize. He was also awarded the Woodrow Wilson Memorial Plaque; the Robert Dollar Award; the Pan American League Medal; the Veterans of Foreign Wars Distinguished Citizenship Medal; the Humanitarian Award of Variety Clubs; Peru's Grand Cross; and Order of the Sun.

Cordell worked to bring peace to the world. His reciprocal trade agreements act was based on the sound theory that nations that do business together generally become friendly nations. He worked tirelessly for the United Nations believing that it was man's present hope for sanity in world affairs. Before the Charter of the United Nations was actually finalized at the San Francisco Securities Conference in 1945, Cordell's health broke, and he could not attend the meeting. He was forced to resign his position and to enter the hospital for a prolonged rest. Yet his influence was felt in the finalized plans.

Cordell Hull lived the remainder of his life in Washington, D.C. where he died July 23, 1955. He is interred in the Washington Cathedral. — *excerpts from the Nashville Banner, July 23, 1955.*

KEITH AND FREEDA HULL

Keith and Freeda Hull were married June 23, 1962. Both are natives of Clay County. Keith is the son of the late Will and Dona Tidwell Hull. Freeda's father was the late George William Emberton, and her mother is Mona Bilbrey Emberton. Freeda's maternal grandparents are Delton

and Sarah Robbins Bilbrey, who are enjoying active lives at age 86.

The Hulls moved from their first home on Mill Creek to Celina on River Drive, better known as the Swann Bottom, in 1964. They have three children.

Johnny is the oldest of the three children. He was born December 31, 1963. He graduated from Nashville State Technical Institute where he received his Associate of Science Degree in Business Data Processing Technology. However, immediately after graduation, he bought a tractor trailer rig and leased out to Valley Trucking Company of Brownsville, Texas. At the present time, Johnny is enjoying being a truck driver and traveling throughout the United States.

Jimmy "Crank" Hull, the second son, was born January 24, 1968. He entered Tennessee Technological University this fall on a football scholarship. During the past several years, "Crank" has earned a name for himself and his teammates by displaying outstanding athletic ability.

An exciting day came November 12, 1971, when Jodi, a beautiful baby girl was born. She is a sophomore at Celina High this year. She enjoys sports and is active in basketball, softball, and baseball.

The Hull family attends the First Church of God near Celina.

HENRY RAY HUNLEY

Henry Ray Hunley was born July 23, 1926 in Cumberland County, Kentucky. He is the son of Henry Carvin Hunley and Della Johnson Hunley. The Hunley family moved to Red Boiling Springs, Tennessee before moving to Celina, Tennessee in 1938.

After attending Celina's public schools, he moved to Nashville, Tennessee in 1949 where he attended Nashville Auto Diesel School and then to Memphis, Tennessee where he graduated from Hemphill Diesel College in 1950. He served in the U.S. Armed Services in Japan from 1944 to 1946. He is presently employed with Browning and Farris Industries. The family lives in Donelson, Tennessee.

Henry Ray was married to Dauphine Walker December 28, 1947. Dauphine was born January 19, 1928, the daughter of Benton Thomas and Mary Dovie Reecer Walker.

Dauphine attended Clay County, Tennessee schools, graduating from Celina High School in 1947. She has been employed by the State of Tennessee since 1967.

Henry Ray and Dauphine are the parents of three daughters. Rita Gail was born October 8, 1948 in Celina. She married John Dean Carr

Henry R. and Dauphine Hunley

April 9, 1971, who was born November 25, 1946 in Nashville. Rita graduated from David Lipscomb College in 1970 and is a school teacher. John Dean graduated from David Lipscomb College in 1972 and is employed by South Central Bell in Birmingham, Alabama. They are the parents of Jonathan, born February 4, 1974, and April, born May 16, 1976.

Denise Evon was born December 24, 1953, in Knoxville, Tennessee. She married Jeffery Lather Bell, September 2, 1973, who was born September 9, 1954 in Kenton, Tennessee. Denise graduated from Freed-Hardeman College in 1973 and University of Tennessee at Martin in 1975. She is a school teacher. Jeffery attended Freed-Hardeman College, UT-Martin and the University of Tennessee in Knoxville, Tennessee where he received his Master's degree in 1979. He is an engineer with Tennessee Valley Authority in Knoxville.

Eloise was born November 26, 1963 in Nashville, Tennessee. She was married July 17, 1982 to Charles Wayne Robinson, who was born May 19, 1959 in Nashville. Eloise graduated from McGavock High School in 1982 and Wayne in 1977. Wayne is employed by United Parcel Service. They are the parents of Daniel Wayne, born February 17, 1985.

DEWEY WOODWARD JACKSON

Dewey Woodward Jackson was born August 18, 1898. He died February 17, 1983. He was one of six children born to William H. and Roxie Sweezy Jackson. He married Loma Almedia Browning August 4, 1917. She was born January 11, 1899, the daughter of Rice and Ara Russell Browning. Loma died July 11, 1973. Dewey and Loma had seven children, Edward, Felix, Robert, Lucille, Elise, Maxine, and Lawrence.

Robert was born December 9, 1921. He married Doris Bilbrey December 21, 1946. She is the daughter of Sidney Edward and Ada Condra Bilbrey. Robert is a farmer and is employed by the Tennessee Department of Forestry. They have two children: Robert Lynn Jackson, born October 1, 1953, is a veteran and a police sergeant in Lafayette. Elisa Donnetta, born December 28, 1958, married Randy Franklin Jones April 22,

Robert and Doris, Robert Lynn and Donetta Jackson

1977. Elisa is the manager of McDonalds and he is the engineer at Murfreesboro Medical Center in Murfreesboro. Elisa and Randy have one daughter, Misty Amber Jones, born October 21, 1977.

GEORGE W. JENKINS

George W. Jenkins, born 1798 in Tennessee, married Melvina, born 1809. Their children were John Bryan, Seburt Ellis and Martha J.

John Bryan Jenkins, born 1829, married Melvina Elizabeth Runnolds. They had the following children: Elbert, William, and Melvina Elizabeth. John Bryan next married Mary Elizabeth McCrackin, born in 1846. Their children were George Winton, James, Matthias, Robert, Harland C., and America.

Melvina Elizabeth Jenkins, born 1861-died 1953, married William Birdwell, born 1851-died 1896. They had the following children, John, born 1883; Dora Bell, born 1886; and Lavada. Melvina then married Clay Clark.

Dora Bell Birdwell, born 1886, married Hovey Browning. Their children were Myrtle, May, Madge, Lula, Kenneth, Girvous, Buford, Audey, Andrew, Osbin, and Hubert.

Melvina E. Jenkins and Great Grandchildren, Marin Ruth, Charlene and Jean Smith

Sebert Ellis Jenkins, born 1833 and died October 9, 1875, married Mary Jane Cherry, born February 11, 1831-died November 10, 1910. Their children were Cary Brock, born 1857; George J., born 1855; Martha, born 1859; Virginia, born 1862; Sebert L., born 1865; Gilbert N., born 1868; and Samuel R., born 1871.

Cary Brock Jenkins, born 1857, married Elizabeth J. McCoin. Their children were Hubert Jackson, born August 19, 1879; James Harliey; Ellis Mack; Leo Birt; Stella B.; Lattie; George T.; Kit; Loyd C.; Kermit; Dillon; Ethel Isabell; and Catherine.

Martha Jenkins, born 1846, married George W. Barnes. Their children were Newton, John, Angelo, and Palo.

Hubert Jackson Jenkins, born August 19, 1879-died December 26, 1961, married Leona Stanton, born October 30, 1888. They are buried in the Mount Vernon Cemetery in Clay County. Their children were Sid, Charley, Della, Georgia, and Maxie.

Sid Jenkins married Della Stafford. They had the following children: Dorothy, Shirley, and Dimple.

Charley Jenkins married Elma Hatcher, and they had two children, Barbara and Tony.

Della Jenkins married Drew Browning; and they had two children, Fred Donald and Helen Berneice. Fred Donald Browning married Iva Rose Green, and they had four children, Ronnie,

Michael, Mitchell and Randy. Helen Berneice Browning married Ray Copas, and they had two children, Carol Ann and Dwight.

Maxie Jenkins married Virgil Browning, and they had four children, Rallon, Duane, Diana Dean, and Billy Joe.

ELMA JENKINS

Elma B. Jenkins was born October 3, 1925. She was the ninth child born to Rulford B. Hatcher and Etta Gulley Hatcher. Elma married Charlie D. Jenkins. He was the son of Hubert Jenkins and Lenona Stanton Jenkins. He was a private first class in the army during World War II.

Elma Jenkins

Elma and Charlie have two children. Barbara Ann was born August 24, 1947. She married Paul David Jacobs from Ivel, Kentucky. They make their home in Ivel. They have one daughter, Reneea born August 24, 1973. Tony G. Jenkins was born August 10, 1949. He was in the army and served in Vietnam. He married Jan Stearwell of Indianapolis, Iindiana. They have one daughter, Cosima Ann, born October 20, 1974.

Elma and Charlie lived in Indianapolis for a number of years. Charlie died June 9, 1971. He is buried in the Mount Vernon Cemetery.

Elma retired from Western Electric in 1974 and moved back to Clay County where she built and founded the first Pentecostal Church in the county. The land for the church was donated by Joe Roberts. Labor was donated by Orville Hatcher, Nemo Halsell, Kennith Lee, Rickey Hatcher, Chester Scott, Foshen Wilkerson and his two sons, Wendell and Danny. The electricity was donated by Clay and Eddie Trobaugh. Funds were supplied by Elma. The church is called Charity Tabernacle and is located in the Mount Vernon Community.

JOHN WESLEY JOHNSON

John Wesley Johnson, born 1818, married Susan Katherine Cloninger, born 1824. They moved to Jackson County between 1860 and 1870. They had ten children.

Elizabeth P. Ann Johnson, born 1842, never married.

Mary Johnson married Whale Bledsoe and had at least five children, Ellen, Gypsy, Charles, Gomer, and Adolphie.

Jane Johnson married Jackie Jones and had three sons, Edgar, Havon, Hewey.

James married (first name unknown) Copas.

George Clark is believed to have gone to Oklahoma.

John Washington Clark, born 1856, married

John and Katherine Johnson

Margaret Bean, the daughter of James and Willie Hawkins Ross Bean. They had five children, Carrie, Herschel, Harley, Victoria, and Etta. After Margaret's death, John married Rosette E. McClaran, and they had two children, Parry and Haskell.

Jacob Benjamine Lafayette Johnson, born 1859, married Letha Malinda Green. They had six children, Elnora, Madora, Elmore, Lola, William, and Leo. Jacob died in Oklahoma in September of 1936.

Laura L., born 1865, married James Monroe (Jimmy) Davis, the son of Andrew and Tempa Davis. They had twelve children. Radford married Hester Browning. Luther married Nettie Whitaker. Nola married Bob Capshaw. Parlie married Matilda Browning, the daughter of Henry Rice and Arie Russell Browning. Otis married Delphia York, the granddaughter of Thomas and Margaret Chitwood Bean. Lester married Nellie Browning. Norma had a daughter, Maudean. Allie married Gerther Mosley. Huldah Jane was born in 1900 and died in 1909. Carlie married Lona McCarter. Roxie married Roy Allen. Pearlie married Abraham Cross.

Abraham Lincoln Johnson, born about 1873, moved to Oklahoma. He married Sally Horton, and they had the following children: Jessie, Josie, Jeff, and Alton.

There are no records of Caldona Johnson.

Several of Jimmy and Laura Johnson Davis' grandchildren and several of John Washington Johnson's grandchildren live in Clay County. Some of them are, Ada Bilbrey, Beatrice Davis Ritter, Harris Johnson, Annise Davis Crawford, and Leslie C. Davis. — submitted by Mary Edalene Clark Pryor.

WALTER N. JONES

Thomas L. Jones was the son of Jacob and Elizabeth Hodges Jones. Jacob died during the Civil War of the fever. Elizabeth Hodges Jones then married William Miller, a captain in the Civil War. William and Elizabeth Miller decided to leave North Carolina and relocate in Missouri taking the children of Jacob Jones with them. As they were traveling through Clay County, Tennessee, a wheel came off their covered wagon. A snow came while they were waiting to have the wheel repaired, so they decided to stay put for the winter. They bought 300 acres of land in the Oak Grove Communmity for fifty cents an acre. There was a log shed on the farm, so they pulled their covered wagon up to the shed and spent their first winter in Tennessee. The Millers later built a house on the farm and remained there for 15 years before moving to Macon County, Tennessee, where they spent the remainder of their lives. Thomas L. married Sarah (Sally) Brown, the

daughter of Ed and Liza Quarles Brown of Jackson County, Tennessee. They had the following children: Daisy, Walter N., Nina, Taylor, Frank, Rose, Lazzie, Celeste, Morgan, and Edna. When Walter N. was 24 years old, the family moved to Clay County and settled in the Turkey Creek Community.

Walter N., born May 8, 1881, married Mattie Osgathorp, born March 29, 1885, on October 16, 1910. Mattie was the daughter of Erasmus Gore Osgathorp and Rachel Presconia Plumlee Osgathorp of the Brimstone Community of Clay County. She was a graduate of Montvale Academy and taught school in Clay County. They had seven children, Rex E., Blanche, Thomas G., Frank, Lucille, John Dillard and Joe Ray.

Thomas Gaw married Edith Spivey and later married Elta Elkins. They were living in Ohio, where they had retired, when Thomas suffered a heart attack and died. They had no children.

Frank (deceased) married Beatrice Johnson of Clay County. They moved to Tipton, Indiana. They had three children, Phillip, Marsha, and Johnny. There are three grandchildren.

Lucille married Amos Reecer of Clay County, Tennessee. They moved to Kokomo, Indiana where Amos worked for some thirty years before retiring and returning to Tennessee. They now live in Red Boiling Springs. Lucille and Amos have no children of their own but enjoy their host of nieces and nephews.

John Dillard Jones married Dean Moss of Clay County, Tennessee. They had one son, Stephen Kent, who married Linda Dubree of Tompkinsville, Kentucky. They have two children, Jeremy and Jennifer. Kent was killed in a truck accident while yet a young man. John Dillard and Dean live near Summer Shade, Kentucky. Their grandchildren live nearby and enjoy helping with the farm chores.

Joe Ray Jones married Zelma Jean McBride July 9, 1949. They have four daughters. Brenda married Jimmy Dale Boles July 19, 1969. They have three daughters, Tina Carol, Michele Lenah, and Melissa Ann. Deloris married Wayne Rich June 29, 1970. They have two sons, Wayne Martin (Marty) and Joe Marcom (Joey). Sherry married Robert Kendall December 31, 1970. They have four children, David Robert, Donna, Debbi, and Dustin. Sherry later married Windel Burton July 1, 1983. Danette married John Bonnor July 16, 1983. They have two daughters, Ashley Tygh and Candice Sierra.

REX E. JONES

Rex E. was born July 26, 1912. He married Jessie M. Roberts, born October 13, 1915, on August 13, 1936. They have three children, Shirley Ann, Betty Jo, and Jack Lynn.

Shirley Ann was born on November 14, 1939. On November 16, 1962, she married Fred Melton, born March 7, 1939. Fred is the son of H.T. and Mary Melton. Shirley and Fred were educated in the Clay County School System. They live at Moss, Tennessee where Fred is a farmer. Shirley works at the Bank of Celina in Celina, Tennessee. They have one daughter Kimberly Gaye, born August 9, 1966. Kimberly is a student at Volunteer State College in Gallatin, Tennessee.

Betty Jo was born January 8, 1942. She is married to W.C. White, born January 3, 1942. W.C. and Betty Jo live in Celina. They own and

Rex and Jessee Jones

operate the Tennessee Mills Pallet Mill at Hermitage Springs. They have two sons — Thomas M., born March 25, 1965 and David Allan born February 5, 1967. Tom works with his father at the pallet mill. David is a student at Tennessee Technological University in Cookeville, Tennessee.

Jack Lynn was born September 2, 1943. He married Jean Taylor Smith. Both Jack and Jean Taylor were educated in the Clay County School System. Jack owns a Quik Shop market near Celina. Jack and Jean Taylor have one daughter, Lisa Lynn Jones, born September 17, 1963. Lisa is a student at Samford University in Birmingham, Alabama.

BLANCHE JONES EADS

Geneva Blanche Jones married David Ell Eads February 23, 1931. They have two children, Rita Geraldine Eads, born June 29, 1932, and James Thomas Eads, born February 2, 1935. Geraldine married Billy Gene Britton July 1, 1955. They live in Clarksville, Tennessee. Bill is a laboratory technician and owns Clarksville Medical Laboratory. Geraldine and Bill have four children, David Mark, Laurie Ann, Leah Elisabeth, and Thomas Carter.

Walter N. "Dock" and Mattie Jones Children — John D., Joe Ray, Rex, Frank, Thomas, Lucille and Blanche Jones (Eads)

David Mark Britton married Sylvia Allender September 7, 1980. They live in Morgantown, West Virginia, where Mark is employed at the University of West Virginia as a graduate assistant. They have two children, David Blair, born April 15, 1982 and John Thomas, born February 10, 1985.

Laurie Ann Britton was born June 3, 1961. Laurie lives in Clarksville, where she is employed at Clarksville Medical Laboratory.

Leah Elisabeth Britton was born August 4, 1965. She died in May of 1986.

Thomas Carter Britton was born July 13, 1966. He is a student at Tennessee Technological University in Cookeville, Tennessee; where he is majoring in electrical engineering.

James Thomas Eads married Jo Helen Lawson December 1, 1962. They are both graduates of Celina High School. They live in Celina, Tennessee, where they own and operate the Celina IGA Supermarket in conjunction with Linda and Kenneth Hamilton. James and Jo Helen have two daughters, Tracie Janee, born April 7, 1968 and Kristi Jo, born July 22, 1969. Tracie is a student at Tennessee Technological University in Cookeville, where she is a pre-med major. Kristi is a student at Celina High School.

DR. JOHN W. JOUETT

Dr. John W. Jouett was the son of John and Amanda Chilton Jouett. Born on January 18, 1849, Dr. Jouett practiced medicine in Clay County after graduating from the University of Louisville in Kentucky. He married Mary Ellen Clark November 29, 1885, and they were blessed with a large family.

John W. Jouett, M.D.

Nannie was born in 1889, John A. was born in 1890, Gladys Lee was born in 1893, Martha was born in 1895 and Joe was born in 1898.

Dr. Jouett passed away during an epidemic in 1902. Mary Ellen was left a widow with small children to raise, a farm to look after and expecting her sixth child. The youngest son, William Chilton Joett, was born several weeks later on December 16, 1902. Mary Ellen was aided in raising the family by her parents, Albert and Sally Ann Harrison Clark, who lived on a nearby farm.

The oldest daughter, Nan, married Albert Keisling. Their children were Alfred (d.), Kermit, and Claude (d.). Nan died in 1978. John married Bessie Parrott. Their children are Philena Blankenship, John Louis and Mildred Arney. John died in 1984. Gladys married William Edward Hargrove. Their children are Margaret Grimsley Langford, Jack (d.), and Edwina Napier. Gladys died in 1973. Martha married Claude Keisling, and after his death married Thurman Myers; Martha died in 1975. Joe married Linnie Parrott. Joe died in 1957. William married Nora Taylor. Their children are Ray, Noel and Franklin. William died in 1980.

Dr. John Jouett and his wife, Mary Ellen, are buried in Hatcher Hall Cemetery in Overton County, Tennessee. — *Submitted by great-grandson Don Napier*

JIM JULIAN

A well-known part-time citizen of Clay County was Jim Julian. He was born January 1, 1875 in the Bloomington Springs area of Putnam County. Jim worked hard and stayed with many different families in the area. He was often with the George W. Clements family at Clementsville and each of the succeeding generations in that line . . . In his words, "I come to Clay County from Jackson County with Harrison Smith, then from Harrison Smith to Aunt Janie Howard, from there to Uncle Gerd Lights, from there to Clementsville. Come here because they were going to put me in an orphan's home." His mother was killed by a train as she was picking up coal along the railroad tracks.

Jim Julian

Jim could not read or write much, but was proud of his ability to make his "J.J." signature. He went to Campground Church with Mrs. Worth Clements and other friends. He attached great importance to the Bible, and would quote scripture he had heard. In his later years, his birthday was celebrated on January 1st, and he usually spent the Christmas holidays and his birthday with the Clements in Clay County.

Jim had his funeral arrangements made for many years, with a beautiful cherry coffin made by Turner Netherton of Moss and his monument up in the Clementsville Cemetery. He died in November, 1976, in Putnam County. He did not know his actual birthdate, but records place it close enough to be sure he was over 100 years old. He was laid to rest in his work clothes, just as he requested, as if he were going to work.

ROY KEMP

Roy Kemp was the son of Albert and Eddie (Russell) Kemp of Defeated Creek, Tennessee. He married Ina Wood, the daughter of Marian Clements and Ollie (Spears) Wood of Tompkinsville, Kentucky. Roy and Ina live in the Hermitage Springs Community where he is a farmer and the operator of a catfish lake. Roy and Ina have four daughters, Frances, Shelby, Dorothy, and Alma.

Roy and Ina Kemp Grandchildren

Frances Kemp married Ralph Ethridge. They have two children, Michele and Michael. Michele Ethridge married Bobby Comer, and they have two children, Tyler and Tashena. Frances and Ralph own and operate the Hermitage Hills Restaurant in Hermitage Springs. Ralph is employed by the Tennessee State Highway Department. Frances and Ralph's son, Michael, served in the Marines.

Roy and Ina Kemp Great Grandchildren — Tyler and Tashena Comer

Shelby Kemp married Roger Smith. They live in Memphis, Tennessee, where she owns an upholstery shop. Roger is a truck driver. They have two daughters, Christina and Dawn. Christina is in the Navy, and Dawn is in the Army.

Ina and Roy Kemp, Shelby, Frances, Alma and Dorothy

Dorothy Kemp married Dale Collier. They live at Hermitage Springs, where they own and operate the Hermitage Springs Grocery. They also have a garage at Hermitage Springs.

Alma Kemp married Lawrence Hollis. They live at Red Boiling Springs, Tennessee, where they own the Hillwood Florist and a Family Discount Store. They have three children, Sherry, Stacy, and Junior.

BENJAMIN HARRISON KENDALL

Benjamin Harrison Kendall, son of John and Matilda (Welch) Kendall, was born April 28, 1886. Harrison had three sisters. They were Rindy Kendall, Creasy Collins, and Bird Collins. Harrison lived in Moss, until he died August 8, 1968.

Harrison Kendall was married to Florence (McLerran) Kendall, the daughter of William Harvey and Nancy (Grace) McLerran. Florence was born November 23, 1890 and died November 26, 1975. She had one brother, Isaac McLerran, and two sisters, Melia Green and Lucy McLerran.

Harrison and Florence had ten children, nine of whom are still living. They are Alf (deceased), Abert, Edd, Louie, Amon, Elsie Ogden, Annie McLerran, Nannie Anderson, Elma Key, and Lura Plumlee.

Alf Kendall, born June 6, 1910, was married to Ethel Rogers, the daughter of Doc and Rose Rogers. They had twins, who died at birth, and one daughter, Kathy (Kendall) Price. She is married to James Price and has three sons, Jason, B.J., and Cory. Her family lives in Celina. Alf died November 26, 1972.

Abert Kendall, born November 13, 1911, married Dovie Lee Reecer, the daughter of Hardy and Clora Reecer. They were the parents of five children, Arthur, Jimmy, George, Truvena Finley, all of Indiana, and Louise Arnett of Ohio. After his first wife died, Abert then married Lucy Reecer, the daughter of Fed and Nancy Reecer. They were the parents of five children, Robert, Richard, Randall, Rondall, and Wanda Netherton, all of Nashville, Tennessee. After Lucy died, Abert then married Lola Yates Anderson, the daughter of Tom and Elzadie Yates.

Edd Kendall, born May 30, 1914, was married to Nola Eads, the daughter of Ocrus T. and Melvina Eads. They have three daughters, Virginia Thurman, Virlinda Coots, and Virrinda Walker.

Louie Kendall, born July 21, 1927, is married to Emma McLerran, the daughter of Herman and Ollie McLerran. They are the parents of two children, Wanda Strong and Freddie Kendall.

Florence and Harrison Kendall

Amon Kendall, born November 30, 1929, was married to Dorothy Meadows, the daughter of Ernest and Lillie Meadows. They had two daughters, Kay Trobaugh and Sue Smith, and one son, who died at birth. Amon is now married to Neldine York, the daughter of Cortez York and Ova York. Amon and Dean are the parents of four children, Billy Ray, Shawn, Shannon, and Amanda.

Elsie (Kendall) Ogden, born May 3, 1918, was married to Charlie Ogden, the son of Mr. and Mrs. Bill Ogden of Tipton, Indiana. They had eight children, Lester, Roscoe, Glen (deceased), James, Mark, Morlene, Janice, and Celeste (deceased).

Annie (Kendall) McLerran, born December 8, 1920, is married to Buford McLerran, the son of Herman and Ollie McLerran. They have two children, Sandra and Timothy.

Nannie (Kendall) Anderson, born on March 23, 1923, is married to Homer Anderson, the son of Johnny and Nova Anderson. They have one daughter, Linda Smith.

Elma (Kendall) Key, born May 19, 1925, is married to Willie Key, the son of Kernel and Lula Key. They are the parents of five children, Ronnie, Junior, Sheila (deceased), Connie Deckard, and Debbie Key.

Lura (Kendall) Plumlee, born May 17, 1933, is married to Clyde Plumlee, the son of Walter and Glissie Plumlee. They are the parents of three

children, Barry, Bruce, and Barbara.

Edd, Louie, Amon, Annie, Nannie, Elma, and Lura all reside in Moss, Tennessee. Elsie lives in Tipton, Indiana, and Abert lives near Tompkinsville, Kentucky. Edd, Louie, Amon, Annie, Elma, and Lura all attend and are members of the Moss Church of Christ, where Louie is presently the song leader.

EDD E. KENDALL

Edd E. Kendall was born May 30, 1914 near Moss, Tennessee. He is the son of the late Benjamin Harrison Kendall and Florence McLerran Kendall and is the grandson of John and Matilda Welch Kendall and William Harvey and Nancy Grace McLerran. Edd has four brothers, three of whom are still living. They are Alf (deceased), Louie, and Amon Kendall, all of Moss, Tennessee, and Abert Kendall of Tompkinsville, Kentucky. His five sisters are Elsie Ogden of Tipton, Indiana, Annie McLerran, Nannie Anderson, Elma Key, and Lura Plumlee of Moss, Tennessee.

The Edd E. Kendall Family

Edd worked at Stokley's Tomato Packing Plant and Oak's Manufacturing Company in Tipton, Indiana until December 1950, when he and Joe Burnette of Celina opened a general store in Moss known as Burnette and Kendall's General Merchandise. Edd was later joined by Buford McLerran as a partner in this same store, and Edd now runs the store, which is still in the same location.

Edd was married to Nola Eads December 23, 1952. Nola was born October 25, 1917, and passed away February 16, 1972. She was the daughter of Ocrus T. Eads and Melvina Plumlee Eads. She was the granddaughter of Barlow and Mattie White Eads and John and Serrie Ann Denton Plumlee.

Nola had four brothers, Danvasa (deceased), Vancil of Moss, Ancil of California, and Lanvas of Indianapolis, Indiana. Nola was a housewife in Moss until her death.

Edd and Nola were the parents of Virginia Ann, born April 3, 1955; Virlinda Van, born March 10, 1957; and Virrinda Nan, born May 16, 1961.

Virginia graduated from Hermitage Springs High School. She has worked at Hermitage Springs OshKosh B'Gosh, and is now employed by Clay Sportswear in Moss. She married Edward Thurman, son of Maxey and Magdeline Thurman, and they have one son, Chad Edward. They live in the Pine Hill Community, near Moss, Tennessee.

Virlinda attended Celina High School and is now employed by Key Manufacturing Company in Tompkinsville, Kentucky. Virlinda married Keith Turner, son of Rex and Margie Turner, and

they had two children, Melanie and Wesley. Virlinda is now married to Mark Coots, son of Mary Humes. Virlinda and Mark have one son, Scott Marcus, and they live in Tompkinsville, Kentucky.

Virrinda attends Hermitage Springs School and is studying toward her high school diploma. She is employed by the Village Shop in Tompkinsville, Kentucky. She married Keith Walker, son of the late Roy Walker and Estelene Garrett of Gamaliel, Kentucky. Virrinda and Keith have two children, Heather and Heath, and they live near Gamaliel, Kentucky.

Edd now lives in Moss, Tennessee and is a member of the Moss Church of Christ.

JOY AND JAMES KEY

Joy McLerran was born April 14, 1958, the daughter of Louis and Lovie Armer McLerran of the Moss Community of Clay County. Joy attended elementary school at Moss and graduated from Celina High School in 1976.

She married James Key, the son of Peggy (Spear) and Shirley Jones of the Neely's Creek Community of Clay County. James was born March 16, 1957. He graduated from Celina High School in 1974, where he played varsity football.

Derrick and Christopher Key

Joy and James have two sons, James Derrick, born August 26, 1981, and Christopher Louis Edward, born January 19, 1985.

Joy works for the Clay County Board of Education as a secretary-bookkeeper. James works for Tri-County Electric Membership Corporation. The family attends Cave Springs Church of Christ. They are active in the activities of the Church and the community. The family lives in the Neely's Creek Community of Clay County.

WILLIAM FRANKLIN KILLMAN

William Franklin Killman was born February 9, 1890 in Cumberland County, Kentucky. He was the son of Henry Washburn Killman and Emaline Cane Killman. On January 22, 1911, he married Mary Jane Key. She was the daughter of Anderson Key and Adeline Smith Key. Mary was born in Cumberland County, Kentucky June 5, 1890.

Franklin lived in Cumberland County until the age of twenty-one when he married Mary. He earned his living by clear-cutting for the government, rafting logs for William Hull, the father of Cordell Hull, and he also worked in the rock quarry for the county. He was also constable for several years. Franklin died of cancer at his home November 21, 1959.

Mary and her family moved from Kentucky to the Pea Ridge Community when she was four

William F. and Mary Killman

years old. After Mary and Franklin married, Mary bought the farm from her father. Mary was a housewife. She hardly ever left her home except when visiting neighbors or when going to church. She attended Rock Springs Church of Christ until illness bonded her to a bed that lasted eighteen years of her life. Mary died November 23, 1985 at Livingston Community Hospital.

Franklin and Mary had elven children, six sons and five daughters — Charlie Killman, deceased; Fred Killman, presently living in Hendersonville, Tennessee; Domer Killman, deceased; Mashie Gray, presently living in Celina, Tennessee; Doshie Watson, deceased; Hubert Killman, presently living in the Pea Ridge Community; Avo Killman, a twin to Hubert, died at birth; Anna Cherry, deceased; and Frank Killman, Jr.

GARLAND KING

Garland King was born July 11, 1918 in the Oak Grove Community of Clay County. He is the son of Otto King and Etta Hestand King. He attended school at Oak Grove. In 1939 he joined the Civilian Conservation Corps Camp in Norris, Tennessee. In 1941 he was drafted into the Army. He stayed in the states two years, then he was sent overseas to the European Theater. He was in the 3rd Armored Division for two years and twenty-three days. While there, he was awarded the Silver Star and the Purple Heart.

Vola and Garland, Sr., Janie, Paul, Charles and Garland King, Jr.

Garland came back to Tennessee where he farmed and drove a school bus. He then worked for Robco Materials in Springfield, Tennessee until his retirement in 1985.

Garland was married to Vola Mae Long August 23, 1945. Vola was born near Hermitage Springs, Tennessee February 22, 1917, the daughter of B.F. Long and Bertha Jane Browning Long.

Vola attended Hermitage Springs School and graduated from Hermitage Springs in 1935. She attended Tennessee Polytechnic Institute in Cookeville, Tennessee. She taught school in Clay

County and worked for the N.Y.A. from 1943 to 1945. She worked in Toledo, Ohio, then came back to Tennessee to live. She taught school in 1969. From 1969 to 1983, she worked for the E.N.P. program for the Extension Office in Celina, Tennessee.

Garland and Vola are the parents of four children, Garland, Jr., born August 18, 1948; Janie Etta Kind McCarter, born December 12, 1949; Paul David, born September 5, 1951; and Charles Thomas, born August 17, 1953.

Garland, Jr. attended school at Hermitage Springs and graduated in 1966. He attended Nashville Auto Diesel College in Madison, Tennessee from 1966 to 1967. He was drafted into the Army in 1968 and stayed in the states for six months. He was then sent to Vietnam for six months. He came back to the states for six months and was sent to Vietnam until the war was over. Garland, Jr. was married to Sandy Bartley December 25, 1968. They are the parents of Jeffery Junior, born July 23, 1970, and Jason Ben, born November 23, 1974. Garland, Jr. and his family live in Hendersonville, Tennessee. Garland, Jr. is a mechanic at Lawson Brothers. Sandy works at Security Federal.

Janie attended school at Hermitage Springs and graduated in 1967. She started work at a garment factory. Janie married Jerry David McCarter February 16, 1968. Janie and David have three children, Lee Ann, born November 16, 1972; Kelly David, born May 13, 1977; and Corey D., born September 15, 1978. Jerry was drafted into the Army in 1968. He was sent to Vietnam for one year, then served one year in the states. He was awarded the Army Commendation Medal for Heroism on February 20, 1970. After the Army, he opened a garage for three years. In 1978, he started teaching at Cookeville, Tennessee.

Paul David attended school at Hermitage Springs and graduated in 1969. He graduated from Tennessee Technological University in Cookeville in 1973. He has a degree in animal science. He now works for Tennessee Mills at Hermitage Springs, Tennessee.

Charles married Veachel Gentry August 25, 1973. Veachel works at Macon Bank and Trust in Red Boiling Springs, Tennessee. Charles graduated from Hermitage Springs School in 1971. He attended the Vocational School in Cookeville, Tennessee. He now works at Tennessee Mills in Hermitage Springs, Tennessee. Charles and Veachel have one son, Michael Ted, born September 6, 1980.

HIRAM BEDFORD KING

Hiram Bedford King was born May 28, 1877 in Clay County, Tennessee. He was one of the eight children born to George Washington King, born in October 1845 and died in July, 1910, and Lucinda Copas King, born in April, 1851 and death unknown. He was married to Floy Reneau, born December 5, 1880 and died October 5, 1925, the daughter of Mr. and Mrs. Scott Reneau. They had two sons. George S. King was born May 20, 1920. He was killed in World War II in July, 1945. Joe Harris King was born September 22, 1912. He died September 4, 1978.

After Floy's death, Bedford was married to Lillie Ritter on March 7, 1929. She was the daughter of Smith Ritter, born in May, 1873 and

died in June, 1933, and Louella Copas Ritter, who was born in October, 1870 and died in November, 1924. They had four children, Edyth, John, Elaine and Mary Ann. Bedford was a Clay County School Board member for several years. All his children attended the Oak Grove School and Hermitage Springs High School. In the early years of the 1930's through early 1950, Bedford would mend shoes by hand for just about everyone in the Oak Grove Community. Prices ranged from 5¢ to 25¢. Lillie quilted quilts for people for as low as $1.25 each. They were both dedicated members of the Campground Methodist Church in the Oak Grove Community. Bedford died January 22, 1966.

Lillie Ritter and Hiram Bedford King

Edith Lou King was born August 18, 1931; she was married to Gard Copass. They have one daughter, Connie, who is married to Robert Lee Strong. They have one son, Robert Lee Strong, Jr.

John S. King was born October 5, 1933; he was married to Madelle Moore. They have two sons, John Mark King and Joel Bedford King.

Mamie Elaine King was born April 22, 1935; she was married to Sid A. Cherry. They have two children, Teresa and Jeffery. Jeffery Allen Cherry, at the age of nine, was struck by a car and killed December 23, 1974. Teresa Ann Cherry was married to Gerald Jay Coon September 10, 1982. Teresa graduated from Tennessee Technological University in August 1984 with a Bachelor of Science degree in Business Administration.

Mary Ann King was born June 3, 1939; she was married to Charles Mitchell Hamilton. They have one son, Christopher Neal Hamilton. They live in Celina, Tennessee.

WAYNE ROY KING

Wayne Roy King was born August 24, 1893 in Fentress County, Tennessee. He was the oldest son born to Dave and Mary Ellen Conatser King. Dave was born March 9, 1871. He married Mary Ellen Conatser July 4, 1892. They had three other children, Raymond, born December 27, 1895; Altie, born November 17, 1898; and Manuel, born July 11, 1900. Mary Ellen died June 15, 1946. Dave died April 27, 1952.

Wayne married Clio Ford June 29, 1913. They had eight children, Fred Wilson, Edna Olyne, Raymond Loys, Mildred Ailene, Clyde Milton, John David, Martha Lee, and Mary Inell.

When the riverboats no longer carried freight up to the port in Celina, Wayne began the first independent trucking company that hauled freight between Celina and Nashville. He later established W.R. King and Son Produce Company in Celina. This store, for many years, bought produce such as strawberries, peppers, walnuts

Dave and Mary Ellen King Manvel, Wayne, Raymond and Altie

and herbs from local farmers to be hauled to other places. He ran this store until his retirement in the 1950's.

Clio and Wayne were both members of the Celina Church of Christ. Clio died on October 26, 1959. Wayne later married Pearl Greenwood Stover and they lived in Celina until his death September 22, 1982.

CLYDE MILTON KING

Clyde Milton King was born October 30, 1923 at Hestand, Kentucky. He is the son of Wayne Roy and Clio (Ford) King and the grandson of Dave and Mary Ellen King and John T. and Edna Ford. He graduated from Celina High School in 1943, where he was a member of the 15th District Championship basketball team. On October 30, 1943, he married Daisy Ruth Vanatta, daughter of Joseph and Daisy Snow Vanatta of Nashville. They have three children, Joseph Wayne, born December 2, 1946; Sandra Faye, born November 10, 1948; and Donna Snow, born September 1, 1950.

Clyde Milton King Family

During World War II he served for three years with the 61st Portable Surgical Hospital, operating in the South Pacific, as a surgical technician. From 1946 to 1948, Clyde was with the Corps of Engineers. He was on the Board of Aldermen for the City of Celina from 1955 to 1957. He served as Mayor of Celina from 1957 to 1961. He has been with the Bank of Celina since 1948, where he now serves as Chairman of the Board. Many honors have been bestowed on him, one of the most meaningful to him being the Silver Beaver Award for his work with the Boy Scouts. As a member of the Clay County Industrial Board, he has been active in recruiting industry for Clay County. He has been on the board of the Tri-County Electric Membership Corporation since 1968. He now serves as an elder of the Celina Church of Christ.

Joseph Wayne King is married to Melva Kay (Heck) of New Lebanon, Ohio. They have five daughters, Diana Lynn, Ginger Dawn, Kristie Rae, Nikki Noel, and Cherese Leigh.

Sandra is married to Kerry Lane Eads. They have three children, Cammille Starr, Tamara Kay and Michael Roy.

Donna is married to Gerald Burnette. They have five children, Robert Stephen, Phillip Ryan, Gretchen Lee, Tara Amber, and Caleb King.

JOHN C. KIRKPATRICK

John C. Kirkpatrick bought a farm at the mouth of Kettle Creek July 27, 1847 from Horton and Lucinda Kirkpatrick. He had two daughters, Fannie Kazira and Mary E.

Fannie Kazira Kirkpatrick Overstreet, "Cousin Fannie," was born October 11, 1852. She would tell stories about the soldiers coming to her home on Kettle Creek when she was a young girl. It is said that their home was not burned because a white flag was hung on the surrounding fence at all times during the Civil War. She was widely traveled for a woman in her time. She attended the Worlds Fair in St. Louis in 1904.

Steamboats would stop at the Overstreet Landing on the Cumberland River where a loading station was operated, complete with pens for livestock and warehouses.

"Cousin Fannie" had one son, Johnny Chism, who married Lucy Richardson. They had one son, John Harmon, who was born October 27, 1909. Lucy died in 1913. Johnny remarried Fannie Murly. They had one son, Robert Chism. Robert has one daughter, Nikki, and one grandson, Todd.

John Harmon married Alice Artimsia Arms in 1927. They had three children, John Thomas, Harmon Mitchell, and Dayse Lucille. Mitchell the only child to marry. He married Helen Frances Hix in 1952. They have four children and one grandchild. Peggy Lucille married Clyde Walter Brown in 1973. Hanna Michelle, their daughter, was born April 25, 1977. (This is 128 years after the birth of her great-great-grandmother.) Jane Helen married Larry Eugene Scott in 1983. Henry Mitchell married Cora Rosetta Roach in 1985. Lee Agnell married Jeffery Allen Poindexter in 1982.

John Harmon called himself "A jack of all trades and good at none." He was, however, a farmer, lumberman, oil man, and political leader. In his youth he would slip to the oil fields just over into Kentucky. He ran his first lumber mill when he was sixteen. He was well-known and traveled. He traveled often to Washington D.C. where he met with government leaders such as Cordell Hull, Albert Gore, and Joe L. Evins. These people and others were also his good friends and visited in his home.

Mitchell served as a page in the United States Senate in Washington D.C. at the age of twelve. He is one of the youngest persons ever to hold that post. Mitchell had his own airplane at the age of seventeen. He was often seen buzzing over the fields of Clay County in his J-3 Cub.

HUGH AND MARION KYLE

The Kyle surname originated from the name of a district called Kyle, which is located in Ayrshire in southwestern Scotland.

Daniel Kyle, the ancestor of the Kyles in Clay County, was born in Scotland. His wife was Elizabeth (surname unknown). He came to America before the Revolutionary War and settled in what is now Cumberland County, North Carolina. He died in Cumberland County.

Hugh Kyle, the son of Daniel, was born in North Carolina in 1777. He married Marion McLean April 7, 1803 in Cumberland County. She was born in Scotland.

In 1810 Hugh Kyle, his wife and family left North Carolina and settled in Overton (now Clay) County, Tennessee, where he bought several acres of land as shown by early Overton County deeds. He was a farmer and ordained Presbyterian minister. He was a soldier in the War of 1812. The date of his death is unknown.

Hugh and Marion Kyle had seven children, Hector McLean, Daniel, Robert, John, Sarah, Catherina and Jennette.

Hector McLean Kyle was born July 8, 1810 in North Carolina. He married Rebecca Sympson, the daughter of Henry Sympson of Monroe County, Kentucky, December 26, 1844. He was a farmer and lived on the Kyle farm which was located near Kyle Branch in Clay County. He and his wife reared eight children, William Robert, Catherine, Hugh Henry, Sarah Elizabeth, James, Mary, Oliver and Inez. Rebecca Kyle died September 28, 1976 and Hector Kyle died July 4, 1884. They are buried near the Kyle homeplace, but the graves were moved to the Donaldson Cemetery when Dale Hollow Dam was constructed. The old Kyle farm was flooded by waters of the lake.

Hugh Henry Kyle was born in Overton County November 19, 1851. He married Martha Dale, the daughter of William Jackson and Leanna (Butler) Dale February 22, 1874 in Clay County. They were the parents of six children, Millard Jackson, Floyd, Charles Lee, Frank, Elizabeth, and a daughter, who died in infancy.

Hugh Henry Kyle was one of the pioneers in the timber business of the Upper Cumberland. Between 1870 and 1880, he and other Clay County timbermen began to cut hardwood timber near the river and raft it to Nashville. His sons, Frank, Charles, and Millard Jackson, joined their father in the business. He was one of Celina's first mayors. He died January 12, 1920, and Martha Kyle died November 15, 1926. They are buried in the Kyle Cemetery near Celina.

Millard Jackson Kyle was born in Clay County December 9, 1874. He married Belle Mabry, the daughter of Thomas J. and Mary Ann (Savage) Mabry, January 7, 1899. They had seven children, Hugh Mabry, Charles, Cass, Ross, Thomas, John R., Mary Elizabeth and Martha Belle.

Millard Kyle, a lifelong resident of Clay County, was for many years engaged in the timber business. He was a raftsman and a river pilot. In later years he was a prominent Clay County farmer. He died in Celina December 18, 1944. Belle Kyle died August 16, 1954.

Hugh Mabry Kyle was born in Celina January 17, 1900. He was educated at Morgan School and Castle Heights Military Academy. He married Mattie Meadows, the daughter of Thomas L. and Ann (Dale) Meadows February 25, 1922 in Celina. For 30 years he was with the Farmers Home Administration. He retired in 1966. Hugh and Mattie Kyle have lived in Celina since their marriage and are the parents of Frances Kyle Brinton of Nashville, Tennessee and Doris Kyle Crowe of Lexington, Kentucky. — *Compiled by Frances Kyle Brinton*

JAMES HOUSTON KYLE

James Houston Kyle was born June 5, 1942, in Overton County to John Wilson Kyle and Sarah Ann (Jackson) Kyle. John was a coal miner at Brushy Mountain and farmed when he was at home in Overton County. Sarah was a housewife and lives today at Timothy on the property of her son. They were the parents of four children, R.E., Sally (Kyle) Davis, Jackson, and James Houston. They lived in Overton County until James Houston was about 8 years old. The family moved to the Arcot Community and lived on the Clark Smith farm where Sarah worked day work as housekeeper for the Clark Smith and "Camel" Roberts families. The Kyle family moved to Arcot at the time of John Wilson Kyle's death. James Houston attended school at Cedar Grove in Overton Co. for two years and then Celina Elementary School and Celina High School. James Houston attended high school to within 3 months of his high school graduation. He had turned 18 years old and had to go to work to help support the family. He worked at odd jobs until he started work with Clark Buford Bait Company. He continues his work with Buford's as a truck driver, traveling in many states supplying minnows to bait shops.

Jessica, Sheila, James and James, Jr. Kyle

Sheila Ann Chippoway was born August 2, 1955, at the Monroe County Hospital in Tompkinsville, Kentucky, to R.O. and Ella Mae (Jones) Chippoway. R.O. and Ella lived in Indiana following their marriage. Ella Mae returned to Clay County where she and Sheila lived with Ella's mother and father, Ben H. and Mona (Moss) Jones. They lived on the Orville Cherry farm, where Ben and Mona worked for the Cherry family. Sheila and her mother moved to Moss where she attended school until she had finished the 7th grade. She continued school at Celina High School through the 9th grade. Sheila Ann Chippoway and James Houston Kyle were married May 15, 1971. Sheila worked for Crotty Corporation from 1974-81, when the family moved to Cordele, Georgia, where Houston worked for Buford Bait Company. She started work for Celina Apparel in September 1984, where she still works,

Sheila and Houston are parents of James Houston Kyle, Jr, born September 30, 1983, and Jessica Ann Kyle, born November 4, 1985. The family resides in Riverside Subdivision in Celina, Tennessee.

ORA RANDOLPH LANGFORD

Ora Randolph Langford was born November 16, 1897 in Jackson County, Tennessee. She is the daughter of Frank and Mary Mayberry Ran-

Robert Langford and Great Granddaughter, Kathy

dolph. Frank Randolph was born in White County, Tennessee, the son of Gilbert and Susie Randolph. He died August 24, 1940, at the age of 72. Mary Mayberry Randolph was born in Jackson County, Tennessee. She was the daughter of Jessie and Elizabeth Mayberry. She passed away September 7, 1962, at the age of 89.

Ora Randolph married Robert Langford July 27, 1912. Robert Langford was born in Clay County on October 19, 1891. Robert and Ora lived on Mill Creek where Robert was a farmer. Robert passed away on November 3, 1969. He is buried in the McDonald Cemetery in Clay County. After Robert's death, Ora moved to a new home about three miles out of Celina on the Butler's Landing Road.

Ora was the manager of the Celina Elementary School Cafeteria for a number of years. She has also worked in a summer Head Start Program, and she has been a baby sitter. In 1978, Ora was selected as the Clay County Mother of the Year. Ora has been a member of the Church of Christ for many years, and she now attends the Celina Church of Christ.

Ora Langford and Great Grandson, Edmond Langford

Ora and Robert Langford have ten children. Pauline was born May 24, 1914. She married Huel Hawkins, and they have four children, Linda, Sandra, Douglas, and Lawrence. Minor was born August 29, 1916. He married Lizzie Holt, and they have two children, Gary and Joy. Grady was born September 28, 1918. He married Edith Dulworth, and they have one daughter, Alice. Martha was born February 18, 1921. She married Albert Rich, and their children are Shirley, Joyce, Linda, Dwayne, and Larry. Haskel was born March 31, 1923. He married Sarah Meadows, and they have two children, Carl and Katherine. Mary Agnes was born September 19, 1925. She married Joe Henry Spivey, and they have one son, Joe Robert. Cecil was born July 16, 1928. He married Frances Pennington, and they have three children, Champ, Cecil, Jr., and Kathy. Forrest was born December 7, 1930. He

married Elsie McBride, and their children are Peggy, Jewell, Vivian, Jackie and Timothy. Harold was born on Aug. 17, 1933, and he died on August 31, 1934. Reba was born July 23, 1935. She married Claude Boles, and they have two sons, Michael and Mark.

Ora and Robert have 25 grandchildren, 36 great grandchildren, and six great-great grandchildren.

THOMAS AND RACHEL LANGFORD

Thomas Langford and Rachel Riley were married April 4, 1926. Thomas was born May 30, 1907, the son of Rufus M. and Celina Martin Langford. His maternal grandparents were Jessie M. and Nancy Martin. His paternal grandparents were George and Elizabeth Langford.

Rachel was born September 2, 1908, the daughter of Robert Robinson (Bob) and Trudie Chilton Riley. Her maternal grandparents were A.P. (Bud) and Sarah Brown Chilton, and her paternal grandparents were Captain John Riley and Rachel Martin Riley.

Eddie and Mary Price, and Betty, Riley, Rachel and Thomas Langford

Thomas and Rachel have lived in Clay County all their lives. They graduated from Celina High School in 1927. They moved to Celina from Fox Springs when the area was flooded by Dale Hollow Dam. They were in the hardware business for many years. Thomas served on the Clay County Board of Education for eight years. He was on the Board at the time that Celina High School gymnasium, Celina High School and Hermitage Springs High School were built. Rachel has been a music teacher in the Clay County School System, and has given private piano lessons. After her retirement, she has been a substitute teacher; and she currently works at the Clay County Community Center. The Langford family attends the Celina Methodist Church, where Rachel has been the pianist and organist for over fifty years. The Langfords have always been active members of the Democratic Party. Rachel is a cousin of Cordell Hull.

Thomas and Rachel have four children, Thomas Riley, born February 6, 1928; Betty Ruth, born on May 28, 1930; Eddie Mae, born April 10, 1935; and Mary Price (Sue) born September 22, 1937.

Thomas Riley is married to Betty Dowell. They have four children, Dr. Michael D. Langford of Nashville; Ted Robinson Langford of Cookeville; Bob Langford of Memphis; and Bill Riley Langford in the United States Navy stationed in Florida. Riley and Betty live in Cookeville where Riley works with the American Bank and Trust, and Betty is a teacher and real estate agent.

143

Betty Ruth is married to Robert M. (John) Teeples. They live in Celina. They have one son, John Patrick, who became a freshman at the University of the South of Sewanee in the fall of '86. John and Betty taught in the Clay County School System until their retirement in 1983. They are presently in the insurance business in the log cabin on the Square in Celina. John is the agent for State Farm Insurance.

Eddie Mae married Reid V. Williams (deceased) and lives in Glasgow, Kentucky. They have one daughter, Mary Suzanne who is a student at Western Kentucky University and an employee of T.J. Sampson Hospital in Glasgow, Kentucky. Eddie is a teacher at the Barren County High School in Glasgow.

Mary Price is married to David Emory Stooksbury, and they live in Germantown, Tennessee. David is employed by Tennessee Eastman Company, and Mary is an interior decorator with Paul Neville Company of Germantown. Mary and David have two sons, David Riley, age 13, and Andrew Price, age 8. Both boys attend school in Germantown.

Rachel and Thomas taught their children to love one another and that getting an education was the top priority. All their children have college degrees.

Thomas Langford died January 5, 1982. He is buried in the Fitzgerald Cemetery in Celina.

THOMAS RILEY LANGFORD

Thomas Riley Langford was born February 6, 1928 in Celina, Tennessee. He is the son of Thomas and Rachel Riley Langford. Thomas married Betty Robinson Dowell August 3, 1951. Betty is the daughter of Dr. Cecil Dowell and the late Ruth Officer Dowell of Livingston.

Betty Dowell and Thomas Riley Langford

Thomas and Betty have five sons, Thomas Riley, Jr., born October 15, 1952 and died January 27, 1956; Michael Dowell, born April 4, 1955; Ted Robinson, born October 21, 1956; William Robert, born April 1, 1958; and William Riley, born December 27, 1963.

Michael is married to Jan Curtis. They have a daughter, Julie Ann. Mike graduated from Vanderbilt Medical School and is now an anesthesiologist in Nashville and Franklin, Tennessee.

Ted married Lisa Gaw. They live in Cookeville, Tennessee, where Ted is a carpenter and painter with Don Haile Decorators.

Bob married Lisa Cifaldi. They have two children, a son, John, and a daughter, Emily. Bob is employed by Howard Miller Clock Company. They live in Memphis.

Bill Riley married Beth Brooks. They have two daughters, Mary Elizabeth and Emily Ruth. Bill is

in the United States Navy and is stationed in Jacksonville, Florida.

Thomas Riley and Betty live in Cookeville, Tennessee. Thomas Riley graduated from the University of Kentucky and got his Master of Arts Degree in Agriculture from the University of Tennessee. He worked for the University of Tennessee for several years. They lived in India for six years, and Thomas worked as a consultant in agriculture to the University of Bangalore. After returning from India, Thomas joined the staff of the First National Bank in Cookeville. In 1980, he joined the staff of American Bank and Trust, where he is now Vice President of Marketing and Public Relations.

Betty is a graduate of Tennessee Technological University. She teaches in the Putnam County School System and sells real estate with the American Way Real Estate Company in Cookeville.

Thomas and Betty live in Cookeville. Both are very active in community activities, golf, and in being able to at last "do their own thing." They are active in the First Methodist Church in Cookeville.

EDDIE LANGFORD WILLIAMS

Eddie Mae Langford was born April 10, 1935. She is a graduate of Celina High School, class of 1953; and she received her Bachelor of Science Degree from Tennessee Polytechnic Institute in 1957. She is the daughter of Thomas and Rachel Riley Langford.

Eddie, Suzanne and Reid Williams

Eddie Mae began her teaching career at Hermitage Springs High School where she taught for one year. She taught at Celina High School for five years, and she is currently teaching English at Barren County High School in Glasgow, Kentucky.

She married Reid Victor Williams July 12, 1962. Reid was born August 15, 1924. He was a graduate of Western Kentucky University. For several years, he was a teacher and a coach at Tompkinsville High School in Tompkinsville, Kentucky. Later he became a district manager for Equitable Life Insurance Company. Reid served in the United States Navy during World War II.

Eddie and Reid have a daughter, Mary Suzanne, who was born October 18, 1963. She is a graduate of Glasgow High School, class of 1981. She is employed in the office of T.J. Samson Hospital in Glasgow, Kentucky. She is attending Western Kentucky University, where she is majoring in business administration.

Reid passed away January 12, 1984. He is buried in the Glasgow Municipal Cemetery, Glasgow, Kentucky. Eddie and Suzanne now live in Glasgow.

MARY LANGFORD STOOKSBURY

Mary Price (Sue) Langford is the daughter of Thomas and Rachel Riley Langford of Celina, Tennessee. She graduated from Celina High School in 1955 and from Tennessee Polytechnic Institute in 1959. After working for the Clay County ASC Office in the summer of 1959, she went to Kingsport, Tennessee to work as a secretary for Tennessee Eastman Company.

Andrew Price and David Riley, Mary Price Langford and David Stooksbury

On March 23, 1963, Sue married David Emory Stooksbury, who worked for Eastman Chemical Products, Incorporated (the sales division of Tennessee Eastman). David was born and reared in Andersonville, Tennessee. He graduated from the University of Tennessee in 1960.

In June 1972, Sue and David were transferred to Memphis, Tennessee where David is a sales representative for Eastman Chemicals.

On January 1, 1973, David Riley Stooksbury was born. He attended Mother's Day Out at Germantown United Methodist Church, nursery school at Emanuel Methodist Church, and Germantown Elementary School. At present, he is in the seventh grade at Germantown Middle School where he made the basketball and football teams. This is his third year to play competitive baseball for the Germantown Youth Athletic Association. He participates in track and is a member of the 4 x 100 relay team. He was a Cub Scout and a Boy Scout. He is an avid reader about the Civil War.

On January 10, 1978, Andrew Price Stooksbury was born. He attended Mother's Day Out at Germantown United Methodist Church and nursery school at Germantown High School. At present, he is in the second grade at Germantown Elementary School. He plays soccer, basketball, and baseball.

The Stooksburys are active members of the Germantown United Methodist Church and Sunday School. Sue works part-time at an interior decorating firm, Paul Neville Interiors. They belong to Windyke Country Club. The Stooksburys reside in Germantown.

MELVIN LEONARD

John Leonard was born in 1793 in South Carolina. His wife, Elizabeth, was born in 1794 in Tennessee. They entered a parcel of land south of Walker's line in Smith County on March 6, 1826. He received a land grant of fifty acres, surveyed March 26, 1826, on which they lived. They had four boys, Obediah, born in 1827; twins, William and Robert, born in 1830; and

The Leonard Family: Melvin, Lula, Dorothy, Mary, Elise, Grace and Rebecca Kendall, Ray, James, John and Charles Leonard

Lemuel, born in 1834. Obediah and Lemuel fought in the Civil War. Obediah was shot and killed January 2, 1863 at Murfreesboro, Tennessee during the war. Lemuel died October 19, 1862 of typhoid fever in a Nashville hospital. Between September 18, 1834 and April 15, 1850, John received 621 more acres in Smith and Jackson Counties, making a total of 671 acres which is mostly in Clay County now with a cave known as "The Leonard Cave".

They built the Leonard School, the Leonard Church of Christ and gave land for the Leonard Cemetery. A church directory dates back as early as May 1, 1852, about the time the present building was built. They met in the schoolhouse before that.

William married Harriet Armour. He farmed and hewed logs for people to build houses. They had three boys and seven girls, Loucinda, Ellen, Louisa, Pheba, Amanda, Sherman, Martha, Obe, James, and Rose. They moved to Illinois and stayed for a while. William and Obe died and were buried there. Harriet and the other children moved back to Clay County.

James, born June 20, 1875, married Charity Pedigo, who was born January 29, 1878. He was a farmer and cut logs for people. They had seven boys and two girls, Melvin, Elbert, Richard, twins Carl and Earl, Bertha, Cordell, Mable and Dye. They moved to Walter Hill in Rutherford County about 1922.

Melvin, born July 18, 1899, married Lula Bean, who was born January 1, 1897. They had five boys and six girls, Dorothy, Kendall, Ray, James, Mary, John, Charles, twins Elise and Louise, Grace, and Rebecca. Louise died at six weeks of age. Melvin farmed and cut and hauled logs. They moved on a wagon to Walter Hill and stayed two years. They came back and stayed until December 1934, then went back to Walter Hill and raised cotton and corn. They bought a farm and moved to Sky Harbor, stayed nine years, then moved to Murfreesboro in 1952. He is now retired from Avco Corporation, where he worked eleven years. His wife, Lula, died December 24, 1984.

Kendall has been a mechanic all his life, at present with Sears. Ray is a barber and cabinet maker. James has done maintenance for Coca-Cola for 36 years in Murfreesboro. John has worked at Aladdin for 34 years. Charles is a Church of Christ minister and owner of Leonard's Bi-Rite grocery in Loretto, Tennessee. Dorothy, Mary, Elise and Grace are homemakers. Rebecca never married and has been the owner and operator of a hair styling salon for 25 years in Murfreesboro.

HANANIAH LINCOLN

Hananiah Lincoln was a first cousin of President Abraham Lincoln's grandfather. Abraham, the grandfather of the President, was killed by Indians when Thomas, the father of the President, was six years old and this Thomas lived with Hananiah part of the time.

Hananiah moved around alot. At the first session of the Cumberland County Court held in said county Tuesday, July 2, 1799, Hananiah procured a commission from the Governor, James Garrard, and was appointed Sheriff of Cumberland County, Kentucky. Cumberland County Court Book "A" recorded this, and this is another indication of the civic and political prestige of the pioneer Lincoln family, as the job of Sheriff was a coveted one.

After becoming Sheriff in 1799, Hananiah attempted to take up land on Renox (Renicks) Creek, which was near Burkesville, the county seat, but this land had a prior claim, and the following year he took up more land on Meschack Creek in Monroe County. A number of records indicate Hananiah during his terms as the first sheriff survived the Burkesville Courthouse fire. After this term his descendants stated that he made a trip to Missouri with Daniel Boone. He did not like it there and returned to the Cumberland area to live in Jackson County, Tennessee in the Tinsley's Bottom area of that county, quite near his old home on the Meshack Creek.

Hananiah Lincoln's first wife evidently died soon after they moved to Cumberland County, as

records show that he married Lucy Wison February 14, 1801. Descendants of Hananiah state that he and Lucy are buried in Tinsley's Bottom in Tennessee on the farm. The exact sites of the graves were known as late as 1860, but now seem to have been obscured.

The known children of Hananiah and his first wife are Moses Jefferies Lincoln, Thomas Lincoln, Austin Lincoln, Sarah Lincoln Peterman, and Lucy Lincoln Hills.

CARRIE LONG

Carrie Long was born in 1889 in Clay County, Tennessee. She was the daughter of William T. Long, who was born June 4, 1855 in Jackson County, Tennessee. He died January 31, 1921.

William and Molly Long

He was a lawyer. He married Molley (Molly) J. Mosley who was born January 16, 1859 and died August 14, 1920. She was the daughter of Andy Mosley. William was the son of George W. Long, who was born January 22, 1831 and died May 25, 1907, and Elizabeth (Birdwell) Long, born October 9, 1829 and died March 6, 1912. She was the daughter of Joseph Birdwell, born in 1803, and Jane Birdwell. George W. was a farmer in the Hermitage Springs Community of Clay County. They are buried in the Turner Cemetery near Hermitage Springs.

Carrie (Long) Browning

Carrie Long married Benton Browning, who was born in 1885 and died in 1958. He was a farmer in the Miles Cross Roads Community of Clay County. Their children were Gertie (Bean); Earl D., born June 1, 1909; Huey, born April 11, 1912; Edna; and Edward. Earl D. Browning was born June 1, 1909, and married Goldie Cherry, born June 23, 1912 and died June 10, 1967. They had the following children: Geneva (Delk), Juanita, and Huey, born April 11, 1912. Huey was killed in World War II.

BENJAMIN FRANKLIN LONG

Benjamin Franklin Long, the son of William and Molly Long, was born September 13, 1887. He married Bertha Jane Browning, the daughter of Leeann and Ead Browning. She was born November 1, 1892. They had six children. Two of the children died very young. Vera Marie Long died at age three. Vergie Lee was born January 16, 1913. Vola Mae was born February 22, 1917. Charles Arbory died at the age of two months. Cohn Rudolph was born November 7, 1929. Earl Lewis was born December 9, 1935.

Benjamin, Bertha, Vergie and Vola Long

Vergie Lee Long married Bernard Larry O'Neal from Smyrna, Tennessee in 1935. She and Larry have two children. Robert Larry O'Neal, born March 2, 1938, married Sarah Elizabeth Baggett from Clarksville, Tennessee. They have three sons, Garry Michael O'Neal, born September 9, 1959; Larry Dewayne O'Neal, born April 16, 1961; and Donald Keith O'Neal, born October 22, 1968. Carolyn Dean O'Neal was born July 17, 1943.

Benjamin Long died October 21, 1977. Bertha Jane Long died April 21, 1969.

WILLIAM (BILL) LONG

William "Bill" Long was born June 4, 1855 in Jackson County, Tennessee. He died January 31, 1921. He married Molly Mosley in 1876. Molly was born January 16, 1859 and died August 14, 1920. They lived in Clay County, Tennessee. He was a lawyer and a farmer. They had ten children, five boys and five girls. They were Elizabeth, born August 19, 1877; Tennessee; Virginia; Rad; Bennie; Carrie; Fowler; Ethel; Rue; and Melvin.

Elizabeth Long was born August 19, 1877 and she died September 25, 1950. On February 26, 1898, she married Mack Cherry, who died October 16, 1955. They had eight children: Albert; Ora; Jasper; Raymond; Amos; born June 25, 1909; Versa; Ocia; and Ruby.

Amos Cherry, born June 25, 1909, married Laura Birdwell on April 13, 1929. The marriage took place in Toledo, Ohio. Laura was born September 24, 1907, and she died February 20, 1982. Amos was a farmer and worked for the State and the Agricultural Stabilization and Conservation Service for 32 years. He retired in 1968. Amos and Laura have one daughter, Doris, born September 13, 1935 in Clay County, Tennessee. She married Ronald Purcell May 20, 1955. Ronald was born June 16, 1936. They have two children, Vivian, born July 7, 1956 in Macon County, Tennessee, and Dennis, born December 6, 1960 in Macon County, Tennessee.

Vivian Purcell married Kenneth Goolsby July

28, 1974. Kenneth was born September 28, 1954 in Jackson County, Tennessee. They have two children, Michael, born February 9, 1975, and Brian, born December 10, 1978. Dennis Purcell married Melanie Meadows March 7, 1980. Melanie was born in Louisville, Kentucky. They have two children, Misty, born December 2, 1980, and Nathan, born August 13, 1984.

LOUIS REED LONG

Louis Reed Long was born June 16, 1947 in Clay County, Tennessee. He is the son of Lemuel Reed Long and Irene Cross Long. Louis is the grandson of Rue Henry Long and Belinda "Nannie" Long and Estes and Lucy Birdwell Cross of Union Hill. Louis has two sisters — Helen Long Pennington has three children: Linda Gail Bunter, Troy Curtis Swan, and Kimberly Pennington; and Karen Donna Long Franklin, who has one son, Daniel.

Louis attended Hermitage Springs Elementary and High Schools. He graduated in 1966. Louis is employed by Huffines Industries.

Louis and Dorothy Long

Louis married Dorothy Carlene Lee of Red Boiling Springs, Tennessee June 1, 1968. Dorothy was born in Lebanon, Tennessee August 10, 1950. She is the daughter of Homer Doyle Lee and Mary Alice Bartley Lee. She is the granddaughter of Becie Lee Hudson and Charles Clarence Lee and Lucy Irene Vinson and Charles Benton Bartley of Red Boiling Springs. Dorothy had two sisters — Linda Carver of Cookeville and Melissa Ann Lee of Red Boiling Springs. She has one brother, Larry K. Lee of Red Boiling Springs. She is employed by the Cigna Corporation.

Louis and Dorothy live in Goodlettsville, Tennessee. They attend church at Kemper Heights Church of Christ.

LUNDY

John Lundy was born in 1813 in South Carolina. He died in 1896 in Jackson County. He married Jane (last name unknown), born in 1803. Their children were Elijah, born in 1836; Acena, born in 1838; Thomas, born in 1842; Mary Ann, born in 1842; Celina, born in 1846; Susana, born in 1847; and William, born in 1848.

Elijah Lundy, born in 1836, married Louisa M. Hull, born in 1840 and died in 1921. They lived in the west end of Clay County, Tennessee. He was a farmer owning 740 acres on Pine Lick. He is buried in the Clementsville Cemetery in Clay County. Louisa was buried in the Mt. Vernon Cemetery at Miles Cross Roads. Their children were Nancy Jane, born Oct. 6, 1859; Malen Hulet, born December 29, 1864; Martha Elizabeth, born October 29, 1867; James Andrew, born

Louisa Lundy

June 30, 1872; Mary Emeline, born in 1877; and William Allen, born in 1879.

Nancy Jane Lundy was born October 6, 1859. She died January 20, 1920. She was married three times. She married Andrew Jackson Price December 16, 1875. Their children were Louisa Josiefine, born December 16, 1876 and died February 4, 1952; and Thomas Henderson, born December 31, 1878 and died in 1947. Nancy then married Andrew J. Browning June 18, 1882. He was born May 12, 1862 and died December 6, 1893. Their children were; Martha Alice, born March 30, 1883 and died January 2, 1963; Lucy Bee, born May 20, 1886 and died August 19, 1972; and Maggie, born January 8, 1890 and died March 11, 1962. Nancy next married Manuel T. Armer on September 30, 1895.

James Andrew Lundy, born June 30, 1872, married Betty Brown. Their children were Christean, Estell, Ruby, Earnest, and Odell.

Estell Lundy married Guy Deckard. Their children were Grace, Gene, Elane, Shirley, and Kathy.

Mary Ann Lundy, born in 1842, married John Crowder. Their children were Lucetta, born in 1866; Susie Jane, born in 1867; Lafayette, born in 1870; James Phillip, born in 1873; Thomas Sylvester, born in 1878; John Lee; and George.

Celina Lundy, born in 1846, married David Lynn. Their children were James A., born in 1866; Mary J., born in 1868; John, born in 1870; Clementine, born in 1872; Casanda, born in 1874; Joseph L., born in 1877; and Nettie, born May 28, 1880.

William Lundy, born in 1848, married Sarah J. (surname unknown), born in 1854. Their children were Dr. Elijah Galey, born in 1876, a physician in Nashville, and Mary J., born in 1879.

Dr. Elijah Galey Lundy's children were Jessie, George, Thomas, John, Mary, and Lorena. Mary Lundy married Larence Forrest. Lorena Lundy married Calvin Coe.

ASA LYNN

Asa Lynn, born 1777 — died 1868, lived in what is now the Roaring River area of Jackson County. He was married first to Elizabeth Loftis, who died October 3, 1844. In 1845, he married Mary Regan. They had twelve children. The third child — a son named Andrew Lynn was born in 1832. He married Susie Whitaker, born in 1836. She was the daughter of Lucy Hampton and Nathan Whitaker. Andrew and Susie lived in the Dry Creek area of Clay County. They had twelve children. The seventh son born to Andrew and Susie Lynn was George Hampton Lynn, born September 20, 1869 — died February 27, 1959.

As a young man, George Hampton "Hamp"

returned to the Roaring River area of Jackson County to work. There Hamp met and married Dakota "Dee T." Stone, born July 22, 1873 — died February 27, 1960. Dee Stone Lynn was the daughter of Louisana Johnson Stone, born December 28, 1851, and Dr. Samuel T. Stone, born December 23, 1846. Dee Stone Lynn was the granddaughter of Martha Whitaker and Dave Johnson. Martha Whitaker Johnson was a sister to Susie Whitaker Lynn, the mother of Hamp Lynn. Martha and Susie Whitaker were the granddaughters of Andrew Hampton, Jr.

When Hamp and Dee Stone Lynn were married, they moved, with a wagon containing their possessions — a cookstove and an iron bed — to the Tinsley's Bottom Community to work for the Tinsley family. (Sixty-six years later through hard work and perseverance, Hamp and Dee Lynn owned almost all of Tinsley's Bottom.)

Hamp and Dee Stone Lynn had three sons. Ruffin Johnson Lynn was born April 24, 1894 and died 1904. Sam Lee Lynn was born in 1896. He married Margaret Tinsley. They had three daughters, Alice Ruth Lynn Warden, Sammie Lynn Chaffin, and Elizabeth Dee Lynn Martin. Hamp and Dee's third son was Girstle Harley Lynn, born November 18, 1898. Hamp and Dee Stone Lynn lived all of their married life in Tinsley's Bottom. They are buried in the Rich Cemetery in Tinsley's Bottom.

Girstle Lynn married Georgia May Flynn, born January 22, 1900, the daughter of Major and Virginia Rich Flynn of the Sugar Creek Community of Jackson County.

Girstle and Georgia lived in Tinsley's Bottom where Girstle continued to add to the farm started by his father. Girstle and Georgia had ten children: Sam Harley, born September 8, 1922; Carl Hampton, born April 4, 1924; Girstle Houston (Junior), born February 5, 1926; Virginia Dee, born March 7, 1928; George T. (Jack), born January 23, 1930; Lucy Bryan, born February 11, 1932; Helen Frances, born October 25, 1934; Fred Russell, born December 20, 1937; Jim Randall, born November 18, 1937; and Andrew Joe, born September 4, 1945.

Georgia Flynn Lynn died in October of 1972. Girstle died in 1974. They are buried in the Rich Cemetery in Tinsley's Bottom.

CALVIN AND MYRTLE MABRY

Thomas Jefferson Mabry ws born August 18, 1841 in England. He immigrated to North Carolina, from North Carolina he moved to Smith County, Tennessee, and from Smith County to Clay County in the Bennett's Ferry Community, now known as Arcot. Thomas Jefferson Mabry married Mary Ann Savage, who was born July 16, 1843. Thomas Jefferson farmed and ran a ferry. Mary Ann was a housewife. Thomas Jefferson and Mary Ann had nine children, Will, Sally, Savage, Lovie, Belle, Jay, Beulah, Mildred, and Calvin. Thomas Jefferson died July 14, 1920, and Mary Ann died December 14, 1921.

Calvin Jackson (C.J.) Mabry was born May 26, 1889, the youngest of nine children. He moved to Clay County with his family when he was six years old. In 1917, he married Ollie Myrtle Flynn, who was born July 20, 1898. Myrtle was the

The Calvin and Myrtle Mabry Family

daughter of Major and Virginia (Jennie) Rich Flynn. Major and Virginia had eight children, Myrtle, Flora, Walter, Georgia, Carl, Mamie Love, Maude and Earl.

Calvin and Myrtle lived in the Bennett's Ferry Community, now known as Arcot. Calvin was a farmer and, after his father's death, ran the ferry that crossed the Cumberland River until 1934, when the ferry closed. Myrtle ran a general store for several years. Calvin served as a justice of the peace from the first district for more than 35 years. He served as County Judge of Clay County for eleven years, from August 18, 1955 to September of 1966. He is remembered by many as the man most responsible for getting school buses in the Clay County school system, working for several years on that project before seeing it become a reality. Calvin was affectionately referred to as "Judge Mabry". Calvin and Myrtle had five children, Flynn, Carmon, Major, Thomas Jefferson II, and Mary Virginia. Both Calvin and Myrtle were members of the Church of Christ. Myrtle died June 11, 1965, and Calvin died January 20, 1978.

Flynn Mabry was born November 2, 1919. She married George Hampton (Hamp) Galbreath of Gainesboro, Tennessee. Flynn and Hamp have five children, Kenneth, Kaye, Ann, Jane, and Robert. They live in Cookeville, Tennessee.

Carmon Mabry was born November 27, 1921. He married Fannie Mae Brown of the Arcot community. Carmon and Fannie Mae had four children, Brenda, Dale, Linda, and Mark. They live in the Arcot Community.

Major J. Mabry was born December 29, 1922. He married Jean Harwood of Celina. They have two sons, Randy and Richard (Rick). They live in the Arcot Community.

Thomas Jefferson Mabry, II was born on June 15, 1928. He married Jettie Mae Jones of Abilene, Texas. They had three children, Kathleen, Thomas Jefferson, III, and Carolyn Joyce. Tom lives in the Arcot Community. Jettie Mae died November 12, 1985.

Mary Virginia Mabry was born November 12, 1933. She married Johnny Elmo Colson of the Pea Ridge Community. They had two daughters, Vickie Sue and Debbie. Vickie was killed in an automobile accident in 1971. Elmo and Mary live in Russell Springs, Kentucky.

CARMON MABRY

Carmon Mabry was born November 27, 1921, the second son of Calvin Jackson and Myrtle Flynn Mabry. On December 24, 1945, Carmon married Fannie Mae Brown, the daughter of Jef-

ferson Davis (J.D.) Brown and Bertha Pearl (Pedigo) Brown. Fannie Mae was born October 4, 1922. Carmon is a farmer. Fannie Mae has worked at OshKosh B'Gosh in Celina for the past 34 years. Carmon and Fannie Mae are both members of the Arcot Church of Christ. They have four children, Brenda Faye, born November 2, 1946; Allen Dale, born October 8, 1947; Linda Kaye, born April 30, 1949; and Mark Davis, born January 9, 1955.

On November 25, 1970, Brenda married Kenneth Ray Kirby, born April 3, 1946. Kenneth is from the Antioch Community of Jackson County. Kenneth works at Hevi-Duty Electric Company in Celina. Brenda received her Bachelor of Science and Master of Arts degrees from Tennessee Technological University; she is a teacher in the Clay County school system. Kenneth and Brenda have one son, Phillip Lynn, born November 8, 1973. Kenneth and Brenda are members of the Arcot Church of Christ. They live in the Arcot Community.

Fannie and Carmon Mabry

On June 12, 1967, Dale married Elizabeth Diane Spicer, born September 24, 1947. Diane is from the Copeland's Cove Community of Overton County. Dale and Diane both received their Bachelor of Science degrees from Middle Tennessee State University. Dale is a park ranger at Standing Stone State Park in Overton County. Diane is a teacher in the Overton County school system. Dale and Diane have two daughters, Dana Sue, born February 6, 1975, and Rachel Diane, born December 3, 1980. Dale and Diane are members of the Livingston Church of Christ. They live in Livingston, Tennessee.

On June 27, 1970, Linda married Cecil Wayne Rhoton, born December 27, 1944. Wayne is from the Midway Community of Clay County. Wayne works at Hevi-Duty Electric Company in Celina, and Linda works at OshKosh B'Gosh in Celina. They have two children, Kevin Wayne, born June 24, 1971, and Mackenzie Lee, born March 2, 1986. Linda is a member of the Arcot Church of Christ. They live in the Midway Community of Clay County.

On November 18, 1983, Mark married Cynthia (Cindy) Biggs, born June 11, 1964. Cindy is from Hendersonville, Tennessee. Mark and Cindy work at OshKosh B'Gosh in Hermitage Springs. They have no children. They live in the Oak Grove Community of Clay County.

WILLIAM LUTHER MARTIN

William Butler "Luke" Martin was born April 18, 1916 in Lilydale in Pickett County, Tennessee. He is the son of Luther Osco and Ada Harrison Martin. He has ten brothers and sisters. His wife, Willie Ann Hay, was born October 3, 1918, the daughter of Willie Herbert and Bertha Ann Marcom Hay. She has one older brother, Ray Hay, and a younger sister, Evelyn Hay Bailey. Willie and Luke grew up in farming families.

They were married in Tompkinsville, Kentucky on April 10, 1937, and lived in the Willow Grove Community where they owned a small general store. Here their first child, Ann Hay Martin, was born October 26, 1942. She married Bennie Hestand March 10, 1962. They have two children — Boyd and Cindy Hestand.

In 1943, Luke and Willie moved because the government bought all of Willow Grove to build Dale Hollow Dam and Lake. They moved to a farm near Celina and had a flower shop in Celina. Luke later worked for the Corps of Engineers. Their second child, Joy Evelyn Martin, was born January 13, 1951. Joy married Robert M. Corley August 31, 1969. They have two children — Heather and Bobby.

Luke Martin is now retired from the Corps of Engineers. He works in politics and is a deacon in the First Baptist Church of Celina. Willie is a homemaker, active in church affairs, and helps to raise her four grandchildren. Today, most of the remaining Hay family lives in Clay County. — *Submitted by Heather Corley.*

REBA RUSH McCARTER

Reba Rush was born June 1, 1926, the daughter of Sam and Tennessee Bean Rush of Clay County. She is the granddaughter of Cyrus H. and Elizabeth Bean Rush and James and Arcena Davis Bean.

Darrell, Jerry, Linda and Gary, Reba and William McCarter

Reba married Willard McCarter. They live in the Hermitage Springs Community of Clay County, Tennessee. She is employed at OshKosh at Hermitage Springs. They have four children, Darrell, Jerry, Linda (Perdue) and Gary.

COLONEL JAMES McCOLGAN

Colonel James McColgan was born September 18, 1773, the son of the Edward McColgan, born in 1745. Colonel McColgan served in the Indian Wars under Wayne in Miami. He married Nancy Hughlette, born May 27, 1790.

The McColgans immigrated to Virginia from Ireland in the late 1700's. Colonel McColgan was one of two men who laid out the lots for "Old Town" Celina in the early 1840's on the land they had purchased from a gentleman in Wilson County, Tennessee.

The McColgans lived in what is now the Arcot

Dr. Wilson McColgan   Dr. Talleyrand McColgan

Community, a community they named.

James and Nancy had a son, Wilson T. McColgan, born August 1, 1825. He married Ann Eaton, born March 1, 1824. Wilson became a doctor. Little is known about the early years of the young doctor's life. In this remote section of Tennessee, the practice of medicine was not a full-time occupation. Dr. McColgan became interested in woodworking and furniture making. He and his friends made a printing press which was later used in the publication of the journal, *The Country Doctor*. His son, James Talleyrand "Tallow Ann", was born August 8, 1845. He married Loretta Hix, born in 1847. James Talleyrand also became a doctor, and he assisted his father in practice and in the publication of *The Country Doctor*. The Doctors McColgan selected the name *The Country Doctor* because "we have a very high appreciation and regard for the hard worked and poorly paid country and village practitioner." The McColgans next launched a campaign in July of 1890 to organize the Upper Cumberland Medical Society. The first meeting was held in Celina in November of 1890, but no one showed up but the Doctors McColgan. Dr. Wilson McColgan finally got the Society off to a sound start in 1894. He rode his horse to Cookeville in October of 1894 for a meeting where five doctors were present. Under his prodding, there were 50 doctors present at the two-day meeting in Cookeville in May of 1895. By 1897, the meetings had become one of the grand social events of the season, and members in Carthage, Cookeville, and Celina vied with each other to entertain the 150 to 200 doctors who came from as far away as Nashville.

"Old Doctor Wilson McColgan," who lived to be 85, was revered as "The Grand Old Roman, the pride and glory of his fellow practitioners of the Upper Cumberland Valley," the founder and long campaigner for the Society.

Dr. Wilson McColgan not only practiced medicine, but he was a slave owner on the Cumberland. By 1858, he had constructed an imposing 14 room brick house in the Arcot Community. He and his son, Dr. Talleyrand McColgan, were inseparable companions, riding the buggy together to make house calls. When Talleyrand was a young boy, he attended Bloomington Seminary.

James Talleyrand promptly enlisted in the Confederate Army when the Civil War erupted. He served with General Nathan B. Forrest in the 8th Tennessee Infantry in 1861. By 1862, he was involved in combat in Mill Springs and Shiloh with the 28th Tennessee Infantry. The decorated young soldier received a message that his father had been shot by the soldiers of the Union Army and that the home place had been shelled by gun-

boats on the Cumberland. He was released from active duty to go back to Arcot to attend his wounded father. After a few months, he had the opportunity to become a member of the famed General John Morgan's Raiders. Soon after joining the raiders, he and the troops rode north from Sparta toward Kentucky. For three more years, the back roads and paths of Kentucky and Ohio would be his home. During an expedition into Ohio, the Raiders were camped at Buffington Island. Union troops surrounded the group, but McColgan managed to escape. He was eventually captured and sent to the federal prison at Camp Douglas, Illinois.

Good fortune placed Sgt. McColgan in a cell with a German doctor who had gone to the south to assist in the Confederate cause. They devised a scheme for his release. He was to chew pokeberries, spit and cough up the red juice. The German physician convinced the prison authorities that his cell mate had tuberculosis. The federal officials notified Dr. Wilson McColgin back in Arcot that he must come at once and get his tubercular son. Dr. McColgan hitched his buggy up and drove the 400 miles to get his son.

After a period of recuperation, the young man headed to Nashville and enrolled in the University of Nashville Medical School. He later transferred and was graduated from the New Orleans Medical College. He then returned to Arcot to practice with his father.

Dr. Wilson T. McColgan died November 17, 1910. He is buried in the McColgan Cemetery at Arcot.

Dr. James McColgan continued to practice medicine until his death April 15, 1929. He was 83. He is buried in the Confederate Cemetery in Nashville. — *data taken from "The Sunday Magazine" of the Nashville Tennessean, June 13, 1971; and from personal notes of James Talleyrand McColgin, Jr. of Nashville. Tn.*

BENJAMIN McLERRAN

Benjamin (Benage) McLerran was born in Monroe County, Kentucky January 10, 1844. He was the son of John H. McLerran, born 1783 in Monroe County, Kentucky, and Dorcas Jarvis, the daughter of Bennett Jarvis and Sarah Cochran Jarvis.

Benjamin married Amanda Louisa Eads, born July 28, 1849 in Jackson County, Tennessee, the daughter of Anderson Eads, born in 1843 in North Carolina and Sarah E. Plumlee, born in 1828 in Jackson County, Tennessee.

Benjamin and Amanda had nine daughters and three sons. Lucette Bell married Harrison Cherry. Rosetta Elizabeth married John Johnson. Sarah Dorcas first married a Spear and then a Condra. Mary Adeline married David Kendall. None of the remaining daughters' husbands first names are known. Floretta and Virginia Hughes both married men with the surname of Cherry. Nancy married a Copass. Roxey married a Carter, and Amanda Blair married a King.

John Anderson (John Ann) McLerran, born March 4, 1870, married Orpha Moore. They had six children. Mamie married Elvin Cherry, and they had two children, Nan Ella and Bernella. Berah married Paul Stone, and they had four children, Henry Boyd, Orpha Coe, Bobby, and Shirley. Two sons, "Wart" and "Garl" never married. Caskar first married Ruby Plumlee. He then married Vada Biles Green. Ottie married Lassie Chitwood, and they had three sons. Dayton married Elizabeth White, and they have two sons, Jock and Scott. Harold married Christine Cochrin, and they have two children, Deborah and Douglas. John Howard married Corinne Reneau, and they have three sons, John Howard, Jr., Joe, and Al. Joe married Debbie Asberry, and they have two children, Joe Lee and Samantha. Al married Lisa Halsell, and they have one child, Ryan.

Barlow McLerran married Barca Clancy. Barlow was born January 26, 1876. They left Tennessee early in life to live in Texas, and their descendants live there today.

Albert Harrison, born February 9, 1888, married Zona May Caruthers. (See Albert Harrison McLerran.)

Benjamin McLerran served in the Union Army in the Civil War and was a prisoner at the Confederate Prison in Andersonville, Georgia for seven months prior to the end of the war. He was listed in the Special Census of 1890 of living soldiers of the Civil War. At the end of the War, he was so weak from having existed on a diet of a pint of corn meal per day, ground up with the cob, that he was carried out on the back of a fellow prisoner, Hughes Brown, hence, the name of one of his daughters, Virginia Hughes. Later in a deed dated June 16, 1886, he gave land and a building to be used as a school and "meeting-house." After such a sad war, it was appropriately named New Hope.

Benjamin's oldest brother, Bennett McLerran, served in the Confederate Army during the Civil War and was killed — another example of brother against brother.

Benjamin and Amanda made the journey by stagecoach and train to St. Louis, Missouri in 1904 to attend the World's Fair. They ate ice cream for the first time as it was introduced at this fair.

Benjamin and Amanda are buried on the family farm near Oak Grove. — *Submitted by Blanche McLerran Carver*

ALBERT HARRISON McLERRAN

Albert Harrison McLerran, born in Clay County, February 9, 1888, married Zona May Caruthers of Jackson County, who was born May 21, 1886. Zona was the daughter of Allen Wakefield and Gracie Jane Whitaker Caruthers. Allen was the son of Frank and Susan Moreland Caruthers. Gracie was the daughter of Alfred and Amanda Johnson Whitaker.

Albert Harrison McLerran   Zona McLerran

Harrison and Zona had six children. Edna married Richard Sandys, and they have four children,

Delores, Richard, Thomas, and David Harrison. Edna lives in Toledo, Ohio.

Ruby married Leonard Porter, and they have four children, Donald, Richard, Linda, and Noel. They live in Dickson, Tennessee.

Thelma died at age three during the flu epidemic of 1918.

Blanche married Joe Carver, and they have two children, Bobby Joe and June Carmen. Blanche and Joe live at Hermitage Springs.

Noel, the only son, born June 2, 1922, was killed December 16, 1944 in the South Pacific during World War II.

Erma Lee married John Harvey Gass, and they have three children, Darlene, Deborah, and Michael. Erma Lee and John Harvey live at Moss, Tennessee.

Harrison and Zona lived in Herrin, Illinois, Toledo, Ohio, Old Hickory, and Clay County. They are buried, along with their son, Noel, in the Pitcock Cemetery near Oak Grove.

Their grandchildren, Bobby Carver and Carmen Mathews, own the family farm at Hermitage Springs.

Deloris, Edna's daughter, lives in Grand Rapids, Michigan. She married Don Davey. They have the following children: Denice, Dianne, and Darrell. Denice married Jim Loufties, and they have two children, Michelle and Sara. Dianne is an electrical engineer and lives in New Orleans, Louisiana. Darrell, an engineer, lives in Ann Arbor Michigan. He is married to Sue (surname unknown) and they have one son, Charles Edward.

Richard, Edna's son, is a teacher and lives in Toledo, Ohio. He married Zana Fulkerson, and they have one son, Erik.

Thomas, Edna's son, owns "Sandys and Associates" in Toledo, Ohio. He married Kathy Schimmeur, and they are the parents of Timothy, Amy, and Laura.

David Harrison, Edna's son, is a teacher and lives in Toledo, Ohio. He married Janice (surname unknown), and they have the following children: Christopher Noel, Jonathan, and Nichlous.

Donald, Ruby's son, is retired from the United States Navy and lives in Italy. He married Joni (surname unknown), and they have two children Jenny and Jack. Jenny married Wayne Spear, and they have two sons, Jeremy and Joshua. They live in Clarksville, Tennessee.

Richard, Ruby's son, is a C.P.A. and lives in Dickson, Tennessee. He is married to Norma Baker and they have one daughter, Marcia.

Linda Faye, Ruby's daughter, married Michael Becard, and they have one daughter, Tina. They live in Dickson.

Noel, Ruby's son, lives in Chicago, Illinois.

Darlene, Erma Lee's daughter, works for the Internal Revenue Service. She is married to Roger Wood, and they have two sons, Christopher and Gregory. They live in Goodlettsville, Tennessee.

Deborah, Erma Lee's daughter, is a teacher. She is married to Alan West, and they have two children, Jonathan Lee and Leslie Cristeen.

Michael Kevin, Erma Lee's son, is an accountant. He is married to Tami Johnson. They live in Goodlettsville, Tennessee.

HERMAN McLERRAN

Herman McLerran, born December 7, 1890, was the son of George and Louella Spears

Herman and Ollie McLerran

McLerran. He had one sister, Martha Welch, who was married to Herman Welch.

Herman was married to Ollie Head, born June 11, 1896. She was the daughter of William Harvey and Marinda Reecer Head. Ollie had six brothers, Lonnie, Claude, Clyde, Lester, Eddie, and Chester Head, and five sisters, Bertha Dunning, Lula Walker, Ersie Meadows, Minnie Walker, and Lela Head.

Herman and Ollie were the parents of eight children, six of whom are still living. They are Raymond (deceased), Buford, Bedford, Lester, Fred, Emma, Flora, and Robert (died at 3 years of age).

Raymond McLerran, born November 30, 1917, was married to Nettie Hix, daughter of Edd and Verna Hix. Raymond and Nettie had four children, Coell, Dwayne, Arcella Alsup, and Shirley Woodrum, all of Indianapolis, Indiana. Raymond died August 8, 1979.

Buford McLerran, born March 21, 1920, is married to Annie Kendall, daughter of Harrison and Florence Kendall. They are the parents of Sandra and Tim McLerran, and they live at Moss, Tennessee.

Bedford McLerran, born September 9, 1925, is married to Annie Woods, daughter of Dee and Ella Woods, and they are the parents of five children, Dudley, Kenneth, Nolan, Junior, and Rita Bilbrey. They all live near Red Boiling Springs, Tennessee.

Lester McLerran, born January 14, 1933, is unmarried and lives in Moss, Tennessee.

Fred McLerran, born May 10, 1935, is married to Betty Tinsley, daughter of Hugh and Fannie Tinsley. Fred and Betty have one daughter, Ashlea, and they live in Hopkinsville, Kentucky.

Emma (McLerran) Kendall, born December 9, 1922, is married to Louie Kendall, son of Harrison and Florence Kendall. They have two children, Wanda Strong and Freddie Kendall.

Flora (McLerran) Kendall, born October 21, 1929, is married to Lecil Anderson, son of Rossie and Maggie Anderson. They are the parents of four children, Jean Pennington, Judy Rich, Connie Trobaugh, and Ray Anderson (deceased).

WILLIAM BUFORD McLERRAN

William Buford McLerran was born March 21, 1920, near Moss, Tennessee. He is the son of the late Herman and Ollie Head McLerran, and the grandson of George and Louella Spears McLerran, and William Harvey and Marinda Reecer Head. Buford had four brothers, three of whom are presently living. They are Raymond (deceased), Indianapolis, Indiana; Bedford, Red Boiling Springs, Tennessee; Lester, Moss, Tennessee; and Fred, Hopkinsville, Kentucky. Buford also had two sisters, Emma Kendall and Flora Ander-

Sandra and Annie, Tim, Laura and Burford McLerran

son, both of whom are living near Moss, Tennessee.

Buford worked with the Richardson Rubber Company in Indianapolis, Indiana in 1946 and 1947. He worked with Nebert Hestand's Lumber Company from 1948 to 1969, hauling firewood to people in Clay County and surrounding counties, and he also worked with Brian Crabtree's Lumber Company in Moss, Tennessee from 1947 to 1965. He and Edd Kendall were also partners in McLerran and Kendall's General Merchandise near Moss from 1952 to 1961. He is now retired.

Buford was married to the former Annie Mary Kendall November 27, 1952. Annie was born December 8, 1920, near Moss, Tennessee, to the late Benjamin Harrison and Florence McLerran Kendall. She is the granddaughter of John and Matilda Welch Kendall, and William Harvey and Nancy Grace McLerran. She worked at the Richardson Rubber Company in 1946 and 1947, and is a housewife now.

Annie had five brothers, four of whom are living now. They are Alf (deceased), Edd, Louie, and Amon Kendall, all of Moss, Tennessee, and Abert of Tompkinsville, Kentucky. She also had four sisters, Elsie Ogden of Tipton, Indiana, Elma Key, Nannie Anderson, and Lura Plumlee, all three of Moss, Tennessee.

Buford and Annie are the parents of Sandra Lee McLerran, born April 4, 1954, and William Timothy McLerran, born January 8, 1957.

Sandra graduated from Celina High School in 1971, and from Tennessee Technological University in August, 1976. She has been teaching at Hermitage Springs School since October, 1974, and is presently teaching seventh and eighth grade language arts.

Tim graduated from Celina High School in 1974 and from Tennessee Technological University in 1978. He studied Wildlife Management at Tennessee Technological University in 1983, and worked with the Kentucky Wildlife Resources Agency in Hopkinsville, Kentucky in conjunction with his course work. He has been teaching math at Hermitage Springs School for seven years. He married Laura Clements, daughter of Ray and Corrynne Clements, July 30, 1983. Laura is also employed by the Clay County Board of Education as Food Service Supervisor for the school system. Tim and Laura live near Hermitage Springs, Tennessee.

Buford, Annie, and Sandra live at Moss, Tennessee, and attend church at the Moss Church of Christ.

ISAAC McLERRAN

Isaac McLerran was born March 8, 1887. He died June 10, 1948. He was the son of Harvey and Nancy (Grace) McLerran and the grandson of

Isaac and Bonsie McLerran w/Belva

William (Billy) and Elizabeth (Betsy) Hestand McLerran.

Isaac married Bonsie Veachel Waddle May 13, 1917. She was the daughter of Napoleon Bonaparte and Amanda Melvina (Tranbarger) Waddle. Bonsie was born February 14, 1893. She died December 28, 1982. Isaac and Bonsie both had common school educations and were well-read for their time. They were members of the Republican Party. The majority of the McLerrans are members or believers in the Church of Christ. They are family people and landholders. Isaac and Bonsie were well-known for their honesty and integrity. He was a well-known farmer in the Moss Community.

Isaac and Bonsie had six children. Belva May was born February 17, 1918. On June 29, 1941, she married James Pennington. They had two daughters, Donna Rachel and Gloria Ann Pennington.

James Abe McLerran was born January 11, 1920. He married Sylvia Walker. They had one son, James Steven. James was a veteran of World War II serving from October of 1941 until October of 1945. He was on the German front. James died June 2, 1971.

Henry Louis McLerran was born October 18, 1920. He married Lovie Armer. They have three children, Louis Lynn, Joan Marie, and Joy Frances. Louis served in World War II from August of 1942 until December of 1945. He was on the Japanese front. Lewis is a farmer; and he works for the Tennessee Highway Department in Clay County. He served on the Clay County Board of Education for a number of years. He is an Ex-Chairman of the Clay County Republican Party.

Sylvia D. McLerran was born December 22, 1925. She died of measles on January 12, 1938.

Lovie Frances McLerran was born December 17, 1928. She married Elbert Likens. She lives in Indianapolis, Indiana.

Charles Eugene McLerran was born January 24, 1932. He married Wanda Hollinsworth. They have two children, Bonnie and Barry. Charles was called into duty during the Korean War and served from December 1952 until December of 1954. He is Chairman of the Clay County Republican Party.

HARRY T. MATTHEWS

Harry T. Matthews, Jr. was born July 1, 1946 in Uniontown, Pennsylvania. He is the son of Harry T. and Margaret Bierer Matthews. He graduated from Fairchance Georges High School in Uniontown. He worked for the Federal Bureau of Investigation in Washington, D.C. and spent four years in the Air Force. He graduated from Middle Tennessee State University with a Bache-

lor of Science Degree. He received his Masters Degree from Tennessee Technological University. He taught school in Clay and Macon Counties for 12 years. He is currently in management.

Harry T. Matthews   Carmen Matthews

Phillip Allen and Julie Michelle Matthews

Harry T. married June Carmen Carver, the daughter of Joe and Blanche McLerran Carver of Hermitage Springs. Carmen graduated from Middle Tennessee State University with a Bachelor of Science Degree. She teaches at Fairlane Elementary School in Lafayette. Harry T. and Carmen have two children, Julie Michelle, born September 12, 1974, and Phillip Allen, born August 21, 1978.

JOE MEADOWS

Joe Meadows was born November 12, 1911 in the Flynn's Lick Community of Jackson County, Tennessee. At the age of six, he moved to Clay County. He is the son of Bryon Elijah and Etta Wheeler Meadows. He married Belva Anderson, born March 23, 1916, the daughter of John Alfred and Josephine Daniels Anderson.

Joe and Belva have nine children. Joe Clifton

The Joe and Belva Meadows Family

was born January 1, 1936 and died July 23, 1936. Marie was born June 20, 1937. Jean was born September 8, 1938. Russell was born March 4, 1940. Travis (Duck) was born February 3,

1943. Justina was born September 27, 1944 and died April 22, 1945. Willie (Dude) was born February 27, 1945. Bobby D. was born October 4, 1947. Kathy was born August 29, 1954.

Joe and Belva live in the New Hope Community of Clay County.

MARIE MEADOWS STEPHENS

Marie Meadows was born June 20, 1937 in Clay County, Tennessee. She is the daughter of Joe and Belva Anderson Meadows. She married Wayne Stephens. They live in Cheatham County, Tennessee. They have three children, Danny, Keith, and Joseph Ward.

Wayne and Marie Meadows Stephens

Danny married Aletha Andrews, and they have three children, Danny, Jr., Juanita Marie, and Sharon.

Keith married Lisa Bowe, and they have two children, Jessica and Michelle.

JEAN MEADOWS FINCH

Jean Meadows was born September 8, 1938, the daughter of Joe and Belva Anderson Mead-

Ronnie Parsons, Mary E. Taylor, Jean and Inzer Finch

ows of the New Hope Community. She first married Avery Hull Parsons, and they had two children, Ronnie and Mary Ellen. After Mr. Parsons death, Jean married Inzer Finch, born July 18, 1933. He works at the Ford Glass Plant.

Ronnie Parsons is a minister and lives at Willow Grove in Clay County.

Mary Ellen Parsons married Mark Taylor and they have two children, Phillip and Susan.

JAMES McMILLIN

James McMillin, born (ca) 1786 in Virginia — died in 1876 in Cumberland County, Kentucky, married Catherine Halsell, born (ca) 1792 in South Carolina — died (ca) 1870 in Clay County, Tennessee. James McMillin was one of the early settlers in the area of Turkey Neck Bend, which is situated on the line of Cumberland County, Kentucky and Clay County, Tennessee. James

McMillin was the son of Daniel McMillin, an immigrant to Maryland shortly before the Revolutionary War and who served as a Sergeant in this war until being injured by a horse kicking him which left him disabled for the rest of his life. Daniel McMillin was living in Augusta County, West Virginia after the war. Daniel McMillin and Eleanor Keenan McMillin had the following children: Elizabeth, born (ca) 1790; Archibald, born October 12, 1801; James, born (ca) 1783; John W., born (ca) 1785; and Patrick Keenan, born 1788. Elizabeth married Richard Cross. Archibald married Pattie Dickens. James married Catherine Halsell (ca) 1805. John W. married Nancy (surname unknown). Patrick Keenan married Mary Long. They were the grandparents of Benton McMillin, a governor of Tennessee.

Daniel McMillin next married Jane Scounce. They had four children. Julie Ann, born 1814, married Edmund Johns and then John Greene. Franklin, born 1816, died young. Stephen, born 1818, married Eliza Wade. Margaret, born 1819, died young.

James and Catherine Halsell McMillin had four children. Milton, born (ca) 1815, married Angeline (surname unknown). Rebecca, born January 29, 1821, married Dr. Zachariah Robinson Chowning. Katherine, born (ca) 1824, never married. Mary married E.L. Gardenhire.

RUSSELL MEADOWS

Russell Meadows was born March 4, 1940 in Clay County, Tennessee. He is the son of Joe and Belva Anderson Meadows of New Hope.

Sarah, Terry, Russell and Shirley Meadows

Joe and his wife, Shirley, live at Moss, Tennessee. He owns and operates a garage. Shirley works at OshKosh B'Gosh at Hermitage Springs. They have one son, Terry. He is married to Sarah Keisling, the daughter of Mary Jo and Andrew Keisling.

TRAVIS (DUCK) MEADOWS

Travis (Duck) Meadows was born February 3, 1943 in Clay County, Tennessee. He is the son of Joe and Belva Anderson Meadows. He married Shirley Smith. They have three children, Gregg, Jeanetta, and Travis Lee. Travis died August 5, 1979.

WILLIE (DUDE) MEADOWS

Willie Elvin (Dude) Meadows was born February 27, 1945, the son of Joe and Belva Anderson Meadows. He married Elwanda Rush, born December 25, 1945 and died January 1, 1979, the daughter of Cyrus Hayden and Odell (Davis) Rush. She was a teacher in Clay, Macon, and Sumner Counties. They had one son, Joseph Hayden.

"Dude", Barbara, Jesse, Sarah and Joseph Meadows

Willie next married Barbara Copeland, the daughter of the late William Copeland and Josephine Copeland. Willie is a logger and farmer. Barbara is a student of nursing. They have two children, Sarah and Jesse Elvin.

BOBBY D. MEADOWS

Bobby D. Meadows was born October 4, 1947 in Clay County, Tennessee, the son of Joe and Belva Anderson Meadows. He married Sue Rush, born July 31, 1948, the daughter of the late Cyrus Hayden Rush and Odell Davis Rush. Bobby is presently Circuit Court Clerk of Clay County.

Bobby, Sue, Robin and Robert Meadows

He is also a farmer. Sue is a substitute teacher and a housewife. They live in the Mount Vernon Community of Clay County. They have two sons, Robin Dale, born February 25, 1973, and Robert Heath, born February 21, 1977. The boys are students at Hermitage Springs School.

KATHY MEADOWS REAGAN

Kathy Meadows wsa born August 29, 1954, the daughter of Joe and Belva Anderson Mead-

Beverly, Crystal, Kathy, James Carl and James Reagan

ows. She married James Reagan, who was born November 17, 1952. They live in the Willow

Grove Community of Clay County. James works at Clay Sportswear at Moss, Tennessee. Kathy is a homemaker. They have three children, Beverly, Crystal, and James Carl.

DALE AND PANDORA REAGAN

Dale is the son of J.C. and Jewel Reagan of the Willow Grove Community. Pandora Hendley Reagan is the foster daughter of Joe and Belva Meadows of the New Hope Community of Clay County.

Scotty, Pandora, Tina and Dale Reagan

Dale and Pandora live at Route 2, Celina, Tennessee. They have twins named Scotty and Tina.

Dale and Pandora both work at Clay Sportswear in Moss, Tennessee.

THOMAS L. MEADOWS

Thomas Laton Meadows, the son of Milton and Sarah Barksdale (Davis) Meadows, was born in Overton County, Tennessee May 27, 1865.

He was the grandson of Jason and Harriet (Walker) Meadows. Jason Meadows came from Virginia to Jackson County, Tennessee shortly after 1800.

In 1856, Milton Meadows came to Horse Creek in Overton (now Clay) County. Thomas Meadows and his brothers and sisters grew up there. He was educated in the Clay County schools. He was married January 26, 1895 in Clay County to Ann Dale, the daughter of Priscilla (Chism) and Cleon E. Dale. They had three children. Inez was born October 8, 1895 and died April 18, 1973. She married Selvin Sallee. Ward Dale was born November 16, 1897 and died December 6, 1905. Mattie was born April 28, 1900. She married Hugh Kyle. Ann Dale died in Celina April 12, 1943.

In the years following his marriage, Thomas Meadows was engaged in farming and lived near Vernon, Kentucky. In 1909 he moved to Celina and was, until after World War I, the proprietor of the Riverside Hotel. He served as Sheriff of Clay Co. and held the office of County Registrar.

He was a fun-loving man with a ready wit and sense of humor. He was known affectionately as "Pa" by his grandchildren. He was a devoted family man and liked simple things, his garden, the circus, the County Fair, and his favorite radio show, "Lum 'n Abner".

Thomas Meadows died September 8, 1944 in Celina. He did not leave great wealth or material possessions, but left a legacy of love and affection to all who knew and remembered him. — *Submitted by Frances Kyle Brinton*

CECIL CHARLIE MELTON

Cecil Charlie Melton was born April 6, 1900 on a farm in the Willow Grove Community of Clay County. He was the second of fifteen children born to William Thomas Melton and Sarah Perlina Davis Melton. He attended school at Willow Grove, St. John, and Ashburns Creek. At about the age of eighteen he enlisted in the Army and served for three years at Fort Oglethorpe, Georgia and Camp McClelland, Arkansas.

Mae and Charlie Melton

On January 15, 1924 Charlie Melton married Della Mae Thrasher at Willow Grove. Mae was born February 16, 1908 and was reared by her grandfather, Otis Thrasher; his first wife, Mary Sherrell Thrasher; and his second wife, Margaret Watson Thrasher. She attended St. John School.

From 1925 to 1927, Charlie and Mae lived in Arkansas while he worked for the Midland Valley Railroad. Their second child was born in Arkansas. All other children were born in Clay County. The Melton family returned to the family farm in the Willow Grove Community and lived there until 1946 when they moved to a farm in Moss. The following year they returned to Willow Grove, where they lived until 1973 when they moved to their current home near Livingston.

Charlie Melton served as a member of the Clay County Court, representing the Fourth Civil District, in the late 60's and early 70's.

The Melton's have ten children: Bonnie Lee Shipley (1924); Ruby Alyne Hurley (1926); Margaret Christine Brown (1928); Tommie Arlene Adams (1931); Mary Elizabeth Richardson (1933); Charles Fay (Billy) Melton (1935); Regina Ruth Melton (1938-1970); Helen Louise Ledbetter (1942); James Doyle Melton (1945); and Wanda Sue Cravens (1949).

HERMAN T. MELTON

Herman T. Melton was one of fifteen children born to W.T. (Tom) Melton, the son of Jonathan Daunt Melton and Betty Raburn Melton, and Perlina Davis Melton, the daughter of J.K.P. Davis and Melina Ray Davis. Herman's brothers and sisters were Ben, Auda, Pauline, Charlie, Jewell (deceased at an early age), Clara, Joe, Sula, Nannie, J.D., Anna Laura, Edna, Saraphine, and Warren.

The family was born and raised in the Willow Grove Community of Clay County. The children grew up and scattered to various areas of the country. When Dale Hollow Lake was formed, most of the families in this area were forced to relocate. Mr. Tom and his family moved to the Turkey Creek Community of Clay County.

Herman T. (1899-1985) married Mary Dean Sevier (1900-1970), the daughter of George Washington Sevier, Jr. and Dulcie Stone Sevier. George Washington Sevier, Sr. was a fourth gen-

eration descendant of John Sevier, the first governor of Tennessee.

Herman T. and Mary had ten children, Alene (Mrs. James Ames of Brazil, Indiana); Kathleen (Mrs. Charlie Brady of Moss, Tennessee); Aaron Paul (deceased); Bobbie (married Freda Aaxum and lives in Columbus, Indiana); Frances Moore Fox (husband deceased) of Newhaul, California; Walter T. "Billy" (married Mildred Polston and resides in Moss, Tennessee); Joe (married Louise Brown and resides in Moss, Tennessee); Betty (Mrs. Clifton "Bud" Smith of Celina, Tennessee); Fred (married Shirley Jones and resides in Moss, Tennessee); and George (married Betty Sims and resides at Oak Grove). There are 29 grandchildren and 18 great grandchildren.

Herman and Mary moved to Moss, Tennessee in the early 1940's. Herman was a dedicated farmer and a lover of the soil. He was known well for his famous, humorous yarns. He enjoyed talking to anyone who would listen. He especially loved to recall the days when his children were young and he and his wife, Mary, would go far and near to watch one of the children play ball.

Mary was a talented woman who loved to knit and crochet. She also loved sports. While knitting, she would keep scores of any ball games being played. This enabled her to tell her boys the scores when they came in from working in the fields.

Herman was a very generous man. He would give anyone anything if they ask it of him. On many occasions, he would give his children (all nine) monetary gifts, but he never expected anything in return. Herman never wanted to inconvenience anyone. Herman and Mary loved their family and were very proud of each and every one of them.

Herman and Mary are buried in the Fellowship Cemetery in Overton County.

RICKEY T. MELTON

Rickey Terrell Melton was born August 1, 1957. He is the son of Warren G. and Norene (Stover) Melton of Celina. Rickey grew up in the Arcot Community of Clay County. He attended Celina Elementary School and graduated from Celina High School, where he was a member of the varsity football squad.

On February 17, 1979, Rickey married Tammy Reecer. Tammy was born in Beech Grove, Indiana August 17, 1961. She is the daughter of Carl and Nina McLerran Reecer. Tammy grew up near Moss. She attended Moss Elementary School and graduated from Celina High School.

Rickey and Tammy live in the Pea Ridge Community, where Rickey is a farmer. Rickey and

Rickey T., Tammy, Erica and Nicholas Melton

Tammy enjoy all types of athletic activities, both as participants and as spectators. Tammy works at the Clay County Hospital in the medical records office.

Rickey and Tammy have two children, Erica, born January 12, 1981; and Nicholas, born May 13, 1983. The children are enrolled at Donaldson Child Care Center in Celina. The family attends the Arcot Church of Christ, where Tammy is a member.

GEORGE MILES

George Miles was born May 1, 1802 in Virginia. He died October 12, 1894 in Edmonson County, Kentucky. He married Sarah Prewitt, born March 1, 1816 in Tennessee. She died March 14, 1897 in Edmonson County, Kentucky. Her parents were born in Virginia. George's father was born in England, and his mother was born in Virginia. George received nine land grants from the State of Kentucky. They were all in Jackson County, (now Clay County) Tennessee. The first grant was made in 1835 and the last one in 1852. He had a total of 842 acres in land grants. Sarah and George had eleven children. Elender, born November 4, 1832, married Robert Davis. Margaret J. was born February 12, 1834. John Jackson was born October 18, 1835. William Calvin, born March 17, 1837, married Jerusha Kendell. Elizabeth Catherine, born December 2, 1838, married Elijah Sanders. Martha Jane, born January 18, 1842, married George Edward Blair. She died in 1919. George Marion was born December 2, 1843. Elijah was born August 1, 1847. Jasper Newton was born in 1848 and married Mary J. Merdith. Sarah Ann was born August 5, 1849, and she married W.S. Davis. Robert Tilford was born in 1851 and married Louisa Jane Demuburn.

Sarah and George Miles

In 1857, George bought 265 acres of land in Edmonson County, Kentucky on the north side of the Green River at the mouth of Buffalo Creek. It is believed that this is the year that George and Sarah moved from Jackson County to Edmonson County, Kentucky.

Margaret J. Miles, born February 12, 1834, was married twice. She first married Wilson H. Cherry, and they had three children, Lavinia; James H., born June 18, 1869; and Tailer, born in 1863. Margaret next married William H. Grider, and they had three children, twins, Sarah E. and Martha E., born June 30, 1871, and Mirandy, born April 5, 1874.

JOHN JACKSON MILES

John Jackson Miles was born October 18, 1835. He died October 9, 1923. He was a member of the first county court of Clay County, Tennessee. He was a farmer and owned over 2,000 acres in the West End of Clay County. During the Civil War, he joined the Union Army on May 20, 1864 and served in Company A, First Regiment Capitol Guards at Frankfort, Kentucky. After the war, he was a merchant, ran a lumber mill, and served as the postmaster at Miles Cross Roads.

John Jackson Miles

His son, Andrew Jackson, was born May 15, 1862 and died on December 6, 1893. This son was by his second wife, Anna Jane Browning, who was born February 10, 1839 and died October 15, 1908. Andrew Jackson was married June 18, 1882 to Nancy Jane Lundy, born October 6, 1859, and died December 30, 1920. Their children were Martha Alice, born March 30, 1883; Lucy Bee, born May 20, 1886; and Maggie, born August 1, 1890.

Martha Alice married Sidney Stanton Bean. Their children are Bransford, James, Ovie, Estell, Hazel, Allie, Elmore, Duel, Dossey, Haley, Ruth, Ruby, and Marie. Martha Alice died January 2, 1963.

Lucy Bee was married September 10, 1905 to Herod Birdwell, born April 18, 1884, and died December 28, 1958. Their children are Ulysses, Laura, Beulah, Clura, Bee, Dezzie, Hulet Arnold, Herod, Jr., Zelma, Earnest, and Carlos. Lucy Bee died August 19, 1972.

Maggie married Merdith Davis. Their children are Phocian, Willie, Ruffis, Charlie, Christeen, Clearence, Roy, Moline, Pauline, Buford, and Tom Frank. Maggie died November 11, 1962.

Hulet Arnold Birdwell was born July 31, 1916. He was married December 17, 1937 to Jelima Jewel Copass, born January 24, 1921. Their children are Kenneth, Dayton, Coleda, Nelda, and Denise.

ALFRED G. MOORE

During the early years of the 1800's, there were a number of families with the surname Moore living in the Clay County area. It is known that Alfred was the oldest of his family being born in what is now Clay County around 1813 and dying in 1907. His known brothers and sisters were Elzie, Witt, and Polly. They are believed to have been the children of Garrett Moore, but this has not yet been proven. Alfred was said to have had either 12 or 13 children, one of which was John Whitson Moore, born in 1843. In 1869, he married Malinda M. Hestand, who was born in 1842. He was by trade a herder. His main livelihood was to herd sheep to market, earning him the nickname of "Sheep John." Some of his known brothers and sisters were Lige, Josep William, Ellen, and Jane. John W. Moore died 1934 in Monroe County, Kentucky. His wife, Malinda, died in 1925 in Monroe County, Kentucky. Their children were Susan, Preston, Jasper, Mattie, and Winfield.

Susan F. Moore was born August 7, 1871 and died October 25, 1936. She married Jerry S. Bean. Their children were Norman, Thurman, Ada, Hobert, Delbert, and Jesse. Norman Bean was born in 1894 and died in 1952. His children were Glendale, Wilma, Mary, and Clara. Thurman Bean was born in 1896 and died in 1969. His children were Jesse, Louise, Anita and Elmer. Ada Bean was born in 1901 and died in 1976. Her children were Douglas and Carsie Crabtree. Hobert Bean, 1907-1920, died young. Delbert Bean was born in 1909, and his children were Thomas, Iva, Billie, Betty, Bobby, Jimmy and Jerry. Jesse Bean was born in 1911 and died in 1985. His children were Corrine and Jerry.

Preston B. Moore was born October 31, 1873 and died December 17, 1958. He married Sarah F. Cherry. Their children were Dewey, Charles, Dona, and Ona. Dewey Moore was born in 1893 and died in 1976. His children were Mildred, Calvin, and Jackson. Charles W. Moore was born in 1901 and died in 1974. His children were Opal, Otis, Mabel, Charles Jr., Clyde, Ruth, Hettie, and Don. Dona Moore was born in 1904. Her children were Creed, Carl, Thelma, Sara, Mildred, David, and Carol Kendall. Ona Moore was born in 1911. Her children were Raymond, David, Mary and Joyce Wilkes.

Jasper L. Moore was born February 19, 1877 and died April 4, 1921. He married Louisa Butler. Their children were Emily, Barlow, and Simmie. Emily Moore was born in 1904; and her children were Allie, William, Anna and Mabel Odle. Barlow Moore was born in 1906 and died in 1983. His children were Delvie and Golda. Simmie Moore was born in 1909; and her children were Jack, Bedford, Jr., Delores, James, Elmer, Rosie, Lester, Harlie, Carlie, Anna, and Linda Johnson.

Susan F. Bean, Melinda and John W. Moore

Mattie Moore was born September 31, 1879, and she died March 19, 1974. She married Bedford Cherry. Their children were Roxie, Rosie, Amos, Lillian, Amy, Lattie, and Clifton. Roxie Cherry was born in 1901 and had the following children: Oma, Alma, Amy, Oscar, and Lloyd Rhoton. Rosie Cherry was born in 1903 and died in 1925. Amos Cherry was born in 1906, and his children were Edith and James. Lillian Cherry was born in 1907 and died in 1907. Amy Cherry was born in 1909. Her children were Mabel, Opal, Hettie, Bethal, Radford, Bobby, Mattie,

David, Billie, and Aubrey Dodson. Lattie Cherry was born in 1919, and she had one child, Clifton Osborne. Clifton Cherry was born in 1922 and died in 1978. His children were Broderick, Michael, and Gregory.

Winfield S. Moore was born April 3, 1882 and died October 11, 1971. He married Margie Marsh. Their children were Etter, Effy, Oscar, Frank, Charles, and Hilda. Etter Moore was born in 1909; her children were Annamai and Claridy. Effy Moore was born in 1913. Oscar Moore was born in 1911 and died in 1912. Mary Moore was born in 1916; her children were Donald, Eugene, Virginia, Cecil, Linda, and Louise Jenkins. Frank Moore was born in 1920 and died in 1980; his children were Jerry, Rebecca, Jacqueline, Frances, and Carolyn. Charles Moore was born in 1924; his children were Peggy, Barbara, and Deborah. Hilda Moore was born in 1933. Her children were: Gary, Terry, and Darrel Jones, and Donny Hagen.

ANTHONY CALVIN MOSS

Anthony Calvin Moss was born December 22, 1842 in Jackson County, Tennessee, in what is now Clay County. He died December 17, 1935. His parents were James and Mary Moss, and he was the third child in a family of four boys and three girls. He was first married to Jane Moore, who died about 1897. He was married a second time to Lucy Marshall December 8, 1899. She was the daughter of William H. and Mary Savage. She died February 8, 1970.

Anthony Calvin Moss

They were the parents of ten children. Seven were raised to be grown and married. Five are still living today. They are Eunice Cherry of Woodburn, Kentucky, Kate England of Louisville, Kentucky, Clifton Moss of Tompkinsville, Kentucky, Edith Cherry of Red Boiling Springs, Tennessee, and Dona Turner of Moss, Tennessee.

Anthony Calvin and Lucy lived on the same farm they bought just after they married until they died. They were members of the Church of Christ. Both were buried at the Pitcock Cemetery between Moss and Oak Grove in Clay County.

He was in the Civil War and was a Pvt. in Company D, 9 Regiment, Kentucky Volunteer Infantry. His brother Lindsay Moss was also in Company B, 9th Kentucky Infantry. He lost his life on August 31, 1862 and was buried in Memorial Cemetery, Nashville, Tennessee. Another brother, Dr. Barton H. Moss, married Mary Pedigo. They moved to Willow, Oklahoma, and never made but one visit back to Tennessee in 1928. He died in 1933 and was buried in Willow, Oklahoma.

Dona Moss and John Turner were married December 24, 1929. They own her father's farm that he lived on all his married life. It is located at Denton's Cross Roads near Moss. They are members of the Pine Hill Church of Christ. They have two sons, Gene and Billy Bruce, who is a veteran of the Vietnam War.

ANDREW JAY MOSS

Andrew Jay Moss served in the Civil War as a private in the Union Army from 1861 to December 1864. Though he lived on Brimstone, he served with the Volunteer Calvary in Kentucky. His father-in-law, Samuel A. Moore, who married Sally Denton Moore, also served in the Union Army and was in the Battle of Shiloh.

Andrew J. Moss

Andrew Jay Moss's parents were John Moss and Betsy VanHouser Moss.

Andrew Jay Moss married Roxana Moore and they had nine children: 1) James (Uncle Jim) Moss (b. May 4, 1867) (d. November 2, 1938); 2) Bell Moss (never married) (b. September 10, 1868) (d. May 30, 1939); 3) John Denton Moss (b February 20, 1871) (d. December 14, 1946); 4) Rogeta Moss (Aunt Roe) McLerran (b. October 7, 1873) (d. December 15, 1954); 5) Nora Moss Moore (b. June 23, 1877) (d. June 13, 1948); 6) Edward Moss (b. September 15, 1878) (d. September 31, 1905); 7) Mandy Lanaetta Moss (Aunt Settie) Russell (b. May 31, 1882) (d. 1964); 8) Sara Malica Moss Moore (b. September 22, 1888) (d. ___); and 9) Ida Moss Smith (b. September 18, 1885) (d. March 31, 1916).

Ida married Henry Luther Smith and they had two children: 1) Eula Mae Smith Hix Swann (b. January 16, 1912) and 2) Guy Smith (b. November 15, 1915) (d. June 1916).

Eula Mae Smith and Robert Lee Hix had one daughter, Helen Frances Hix. She married Harmon Mitchell Overstreet, and they have four children, and one grandchild.

JOHN ALEXANDER MURRAY

James Murray was born in 1821. He married

Tennie A. (Copas) Murray

Sarah Birdwell August 20, 1840 in Washington County, Tennessee. Sarah was born in 1817, the daughter of Alexander and Elizabeth (Copas) Birdwell. James and Sarah had the following children: John Alexander, born December 23, 1841; William P.; Jarrot; Samuel; Barbara J.; Elizabeth E.; George W., born August 25, 1850; Thomas and Amanda J.

John Alexander Murray was born December 23, 1841 and died October 8, 1909. He married Tennie Angeline Copas, born in 1845. She was the daughter of John Jackson and Nancy (Birdwell) Copas. John J. and Tennie had the following children: William, Thomas, Matilda, Sarah, and John.

Matilda Murray married Robert Miles. They had three children: Arah, Carlie, and Carlos.

GEORGE W. MURRAY

George W. Murray was born August 25, 1850 in Knoxville, Tennessee to James and Sarah (Birdwell) Murray. Sarah Birdwell was born in 1817 to Alexander and Elizabeth Copass Birdwell.

George W. Murray married Sarah A. Copass, the daughter of Thomas and Nancy (Gulley) Copas, March 29, 1873 in Jackson County, Tennessee. Sarah A. Copass was born in Red Boiling Springs, Tennessee September 18, 1849. They had six children born to them. All were born in Clay County, Tennessee.

Hova Turner Murray, born April 4, 1874 in Clay County, Tennessee, married Gid Colter. They had two children, Charles and Nellie. Hova Murray lost all three of them in a flu epidemic around the turn of the century. They are buried at Milestown, Tennessee in Clay County. Hova then married Ora Isabell Coffelt. Their children were Hattie Cleo; Vella Mae; Sidney Ether; Raymon Wilson; Guy Richard; Ruby Estelle; and Dimple Odell.

Milton Murray was born February 16, 1876 in Clay County, Tennessee. Milton married Hassie Belle Eakle in Clay County October 8, 1905. Milton and Hassie's children are Ted, Molean, Marie, Lillian, Edna, Ruth, Ralph, Nola, Eugene, and Howard. Milton died November 14, 1935 and is buried in Valier, Illinois; he died in Weaver, Illinois.

Franklin Murray was born in 1879 in Clay County, Tennessee. His wife was Verdie Allen. Their children were Fred, Rue, Lester and Metsi. The boys are all dead. Metsi married a man named McClain and lives in Detroit, Michigan. Franklin is said to have died in the 1930's.

Benton Murray was born February 18, 1882 in Clay County. Benton married Lola Newman December 18, 1910. Lola was born March 13, 1889. Benton E. Murray died May 25, 1958. Lola died January 30, 1929. They are both buried at Union Hill in Clay County. Their children were: Lansford Murray, born February 16, 1913, was married to Mary Lena Lawson on December 7, 1936. She was born February 14, 1919. Another child was Hazel Murray, born April 7, 1919. She married Dumas Anderson in August 1938. Another son of Benton's was Rassie, who married Betty Billingsley.

Rendie Murray was born August 28, 1884 in Clay County. She married Jay Cherry. One son was Lawrence Cherry of Herrin, Illinois. Lawrence was born August 22, 1904 in Tennessee.

Rendie died May 3, 1967 in Herrin, Illinois.

Shadrach W. "Shade Murray" Murray was born August 19, 1875 in Moss, Tennessee. About 1898 he married Dora Belle Cherry, a daughter of Harrison Wayne and Julia America Craton (Cherry) Cherry. Dora Bell was born October 10, 1882 in Red Boiling Springs, Tennessee. Shade Murray died March 26, 1956 in Moss, Tennessee. Dora Belle died February 27, 1966 in Red Boiling Springs, Tennessee. Both are buried in the Union Hill Cemetery in Clay County.

George W. and Sarah A. (Copass) Murray moved their family to the Herrin area of Williamson County in Illinois about 1909. George W. Murray died October 28, 1928 at his son Milton's home in Weaver, Illinois. Sarah A. (Copass) Murray died March 28, 1931 at the home of Lawrence Cherry in Herrin, Illinois. Both George and Sarah are buried in the City Cemetery in Herrin.

WILLIAM "SHADE" MURRAY

Shadrach William Murray was born August 19, 1875 in Clay County, Tennessee to George W. and Sarah A. (Copass) Murray. About 1898, he married Dora Belle Cherry, the daughter of Harrison Wayne and Julia America Craton (Cherry) Cherry. Dora was born October 10, 1882 in Red Boiling Springs. They had seven children.

William "Shade" and Dora Belle Murray

Clurie Elvin Murray was born April 10, 1899 in Clay County. He married Vella Proffitt, the daughter of Perry Thomas and Martha Etta (Thomas) Proffitt August 5, 1922 at Union Hill. Vella Proffitt was born May 5, 1904 at Tompkinsville, Kentucky. They had eleven children.

Gaynell Murray was born May 14, 1902 in Clay County. She married Ernest Bartlett September 4, 1921. They had two children.

Van Murray was born July 2, 1904 in Moss, Tennessee. He was married January 1, 1928 at Mount Vernon, Kentucky to Stella Ann Short. Stella was born August 4, 1904. They had nine children. Stella died September 11, 1978 at Tompkinsville. Van followed her in death January 17, 1982.

Porter D. Murray was born February 21, 1907. He died December 12, 1907, while still an infant.

Bransford Murray was born August 20, 1909 in Clay County. He married Craton Smith. Craton Smith was born September 30, 1913 in Clay County. They had four children.

America Murray was born August 25, 1911 in Oak Grove, Tennessee. She married Bethel B. Dodson August 26, 1928 in Oak Grove. They had two children. After Bethel's death on July 20, 1935, America married Herbert Smith. America and Herbert had one son, Randall H., born September 20, 1945 at Union Hill. Herbert Smith passed away September 25, 1946.

Carlos Wayne Murray was born September 14, 1913 in Clay County, Tennessee. He married Vassie Franklin November 18, 1933 in Tompkinsville, Kentucky. They had five children. Carlos died April 16, 1969 in Clay County.

Shade W. Murray died March 26, 1956 at Moss, Tennessee. His wife, Dora Belle, died February 27, 1966. They are both buried at Union Hill in Clay County, Tennessee.

EARL WILLIAM NAPIER

After having completed a tour of duty as an electrician in the United States Navy aboard the USS Yorktown, an aircraft carrier, Earl worked in the Norfolk Naval Shipyard in Portsmouth, Virginia. It was while living in Virginia that he met Nellie Marie Neal. On August 20, 1942, they were married and after World War II they chose to make Celina their new home. Earl, the son of William Watterson Napier and Jewell McClanahan Napier, was born in Trousdale County, Tennessee, and already had numerous relatives in Clay County, including his sister Beatrice Napier Waddell, his uncle Hubert H. "Blooney" Napier, and Aunt Annie "Red" Napier, who encouraged this upstart businessman and his new wife to open a restaurant. Earl was to become one of the most widely known "grassroots" politicians and restauranteurs in the history of the Upper Cumberland. Everywhere Earl went people quickly recognized him as Clay County's unofficial ambassador of goodwill, inviting everyone to attend the Annual Chittlin' Dinner which he and Marie started at Napier's Restaurant in the early 1950's. In the early 1970's, as President of the Dale Hollow Recreation Association, Earl helped organize and promote the annual free fish fry which has attracted thousands of visitors each summer to Donaldson Park in Celina and provided an occasion for Clay Countians to "come home". Each of these events attracted politicians who came to shake hands and other folks who came to enjoy the music which entertained them until late at night. Marie, the daughter of James Walter Neal and Ethel Jane Dunn Neal, was born in Alvarado, Virginia, on August 28, 1919. She knew that Earl loved Clay County, politics, and "the Big Orange". Earl and Marie rarely missed a University of Tennessee football game. Earl probably caught more fish by "word of mouth" than any other sportsman. He also regularly tested the character and thickness of his friends and acquaintances skins.

Earl was a 32nd degree Mason, a Shriner, and a Charter Member of the Celina Lions Club.

Cynthia Lacy, Allison Lacy, Raymond Lacy, Wanda Napier Lacy, Janet Napier Richardson, Doug Richardson, Marie Napier and Earl Napier

Earl and Marie have two daughters, Wanda Jane Napier, who was born March 30, 1949, and married Raymond E. Lacy August 29, 1970, and Janet Kathryn Napier, who was born August 5, 1951, and married Douglas Richardson September 14, 1985. Wanda and Raymond have two children, Cynthia Marie Lacy, born February 26, 1975, and Christy Allison Lacy, born February 2, 1977. Wanda teaches at Farragut High in Knoxville; Ray is an attorney with the Knoxville law firm of Lacy & Winchester, P.C. Janet teaches first grade at Dupont Elementary in Nashville. Doug is an industrial engineer with Heil Quaker in Nashville.

One of Earl's most well-known quotes was: "If you want to go to heaven you have to do four things – love and serve the Lord; be good to women and children; be a good Democrat; and think 'Big Orange.' " He did all these things.

WILLIAM GEORGE NAPIER

William George Napier was one of five children born to George and Nancy Short Napier. Born in Cave City, Kentucky in 1868, William raised a large family in Celina, instilling in them a pioneer spirit of independence, self-sufficiency and pride that has been handed down through the generations.

William George Napier, father to 18 children

William had two brothers (Ike and Jim) and two sisters (Minerva and Delilah).

A man of many occupations, William operated a boardinghouse and restaurant on the Cumberland for river travelers. He was a good cook and a skilled butcher. His sons helped him run a slaughterhouse, delivering fresh meat to neighbors who lived within walking distance of their homeplace in "Old Town". Among many other things, he preserved ice from ponds and in the summer, made, for many, their first taste of ice cream.

A good father, William married Marietta Hall of Jackson County and from this union came six children, Pearl, Ada, Watt, Tom, Hall and Hubert (Blooney). At the time of this writing in 1986, only Uncle Blooney is living. Pearl married Tommy Hogan, children – Hugh and Orville; Ada married Clay Hawkins, children – Malcolm, Vadius (d.), Vanus, Zelma, Gladys, and Champ; Watt married Jewel McClanahan, children – Earl (d.) and Beatrice; Watt then married Agnes Presley, children – Watt Jr. and Aubrey (d.); Tom married Willie Poteet, children – Billy, Louie, Joe, Dick, Margaret and Melba; he then married Grace Bratcher and had daughter Mary Lee; Hall married Thelma ?, children – Hall Jr. (d.) and Naomi; and Hubert married Annie West.

After an untimely death of his first wife, William married Lovie Reecer of Clay County. William's second family started with the birth of Annie, then came Bayless, Rosa, Amelia, Maxey (d.), Evoline, Fanny Pauline (d.), Karl (d.), Cass (d.), Joe Frank, Billy (d.) and Earl Thomas.

Annie married Edward Lee Ford, children — James (d.), Nancy and Clyde; Bayless married Nellie Wylie, children — Bayless Jr. and Josephine; Rosa married Andrew Scott, children — Dorothy, Cecil, Doris, Glenn, Burnice (d.), Maxey, Mary Evelyn, Connie and Martha; Amelia married George Martin, children — Florence, Billy, Virginia, Thomas, Kenneth, Jodie and Marilyn; Maxey married Bessie Marney; Evoline married Lawrence D. Pace, children — William Hardy (d.), Arnold (d.), Eva, Douglas and Billy Joe; Karl married Reba Averitt, children — Jackie, Karl Reece, Denny and Dianne; Cass married Louise White, children — Tommy; Joe Frank married Mary Smalling, children — Barbara and Brenda; and Earl Thomas married Gloria Olsen, children — Vickie, Valerie, Joey, Tommy, Victor and Doreen.

There are numerous great, and great-great grandchildren.

William died in March of 1929, and his widow met a construction worker from Alabama named Homer Calhoun, whom she married in 1932. Pa Calhoun became stepfather and step-grandfather to a loving family during the depression years and worked hard to help support his newly acquired dependents.

My father, Billy, was born in 1923. He married Edwina Hargrove in 1947. I have two brothers (Jack and Bill) and two sisters (Betsy Holtam and Linda Strong). Daddy died in 1967. — *Submitted by Don Napier*

HUBERT H. NAPIER

Hubert H. "Blooney" Napier was born June 11, 1900, the son of W.G. and Mary Etta Hall Napier. On April 1, 1923, Blooney married Annie "Red" West, the daughter of R.L. and Rebecca Evans West.

Annie "Red" and Hubert H. "Blooney" Napier

In 1925, "Blooney" and Red rented the old Stevens Building on the north side of the square, where the DX Service Station is now located. This was the first restaurant to have electric lights and an ice cream freezer to keep ice cream. In 1931, they moved their cafe to the Cordell Hull Building on the east side of the square where Roach's Service Station is now located. They were the first to serve "3-2 Beer." It was so popular that they would keep it in the cooler during the day and take it home at night to prevent someone from stealing it. In 1938, they moved the cafe to the building that is now Dr.

Clark's office. In 1941, they bought the grocery owned by "Greenie" Arms. They stayed there until the Dale Hollow Dam was built.

In 1950, "Red" and "Blooney" built Napier's Grocery on East Lake Avenue in Celina. This grocery was very popular with tourists and local residents as well. Even though they retired in 1962, their many friends who pass through Celina still ask about or stop by to see "Red" and "Blooney" who live in Celina.

ALBERT BURRIS NEELY

In the spring of 1885, Hugh Adolphus Neely and Martha Jane Hargis sold their farm in Overton County and made their way down a rough wagon trail to an area in Clay County, which later became known as Neelys Cross Roads. Their children were Virgil, Albert, Burdine, Ida, John, Emma, Mattie, Mary Etta, and Shird.

Lucy and Mary Etta and and Albert Neely

H.A. (Dolly) Neely was a member of the Clay County School Board for several years. He was also a recruiter for the Nashville School for the Blind. Many of the early teachers for the Neely's Cross Road School boarded in his home, including Dr. Cullom Sidwell.

His son Albert, commonly referred to as A.B. or Squire Neely, graduated from the Montvale Academy in Clay County. He worked as a clerk in the Will Murphy General Store in Hilham, Tennessee for a short time. It was here that he met and married Lucy May Murphy. Following their wedding they established their home in Neely's Cross Roads. Here Albert served as teacher in the local school, merchant in the Howard-Neely General Store, was a cabinet maker, carpenter, and farmer. He served several terms as a member of the County Court. When the need arose to refurbish the Courthouse, Mr. Neely was selected to repair the trim work around the building.

He was a member of the Celina Methodist Church where he served for many years as Sunday School Superintendent and song leader. He served as the secretary of the Cookeville Conference. He conducted, for many years, an afternoon Sunday School in the Neely's Cross Roads school house.

To Albert and Lucy were born seven children — Percy Carlyle (engineer), married Cecil Dunham and their children were Carlyle, Gary, and Jon; Milton Haskell (farmer) married Mabel Williams and their children were Sammy, Milton, Betty, Anna, Buddy, Judy and Tommy; Samuel Buford (engineer) married Elise Hoover and their children were Joann, Venetia, and Bobby; Stella (died as a child); Eula Mae (teacher) married Howard Story, and their children were Sara, Brenda and Bobby; Johnny Raymond (machinist) married

Patricia Davis, and their children were James, Jere, Jamie, Tony, Sherry, Judith, and Eddie; and Ruby Lee (teacher) married Rev. S.M. Shaw, and their children were Lucy, David and Rebecca.

Though the family was scattered over the nation to fill their calling in life, their rootage in Clay County was a very dominant factor in their lives. The hills, hollows, winding roads, and friendly people produce many memories of home. — *Submitted by Ruby Lee (Neely) Shaw*

ARTHUR NEVINS

Arthur Nevins was born August 24, 1903 at Neely's Creek near Celina, the son of William Joseph Nevins (b. Webb City, Missouri, July 11, 1857, died 1933) who, in 1894, moved to Celina by ox-cart, a 30-day journey. His mother was Belle Florence Hoover, born in Overton County, June 17, 1867, married November 25, 1902, died September 22, 1936). An uncle, John Wright owned the farm later bought by Alvin C. York. His grandfather, John Gee (b. August 28, 1825, d. October 4, 1867), of Irish descent, served in the Civil War; he and his wife, Mary Cole, did copper mining in Missouri.

Arthur Nevins' mother, Belle, was the daughter of Alexander Hoover and Nancy Reed; Alexander's parents were Henry and Rebecca. Alexander served in the Civil War with General Nathan Bedford Forest.

William Joseph Nevins first married Martha Black, and their children were Robert, John, Sherd, Martha, Charlie and Ruby. After Martha's death, he married Belle and to that union were born Arthur, Arlie (born March 9, 1906, died December 27, 1984) and Haskell (born 1909, died 1915).

Arthur married Thelma L. Smith (March 28, 1928) and they had one daughter, Isabelle (b. November 9, 1930). Thelma died June 11, 1937 and he married Mary Belle Smith (b. January 11, 1916 m. December 10, 1938, d. December 10, 1982). They had two children, Barbara Carol (b. May 12, 1940) and Joseph Clark (b. January 3, 1948).

Isabelle married Dr. Joseph C. Ross (married 1952) from Tompkinsville, Kentucky, and they had five children, Laura Ann Porter, Sharon Lynn Shaub, Jennifer Jo Goodman, Mary Martha Hearn, and Jefferson Arthur Ross. Their grandchildren are Nicole, Jonathan and Megan Shaub and Ian Embree and Mary Kendall Porter. Isabelle teaches at David Lipscomb College and Dr. Ross is Associate Vice-Chancellor for Health Affairs at Vanderbilt University.

Barbara married Merle Watson (1958) from Celina. They had three sons, Jackie Merle, Jerry Robert, and Joel Houston and a granddaughter, Jade. They purchased the John Arms farm, where they raised their sons. In 1983, they moved to Arthur Nevins farm where they have continued to live and work. Barbara works at the Gainesboro Nursing Home.

Joseph Clark and Jane Grider, from Tompkinsville, Kentucky, were married September 12, 1970. They had two children, Jennifer Erin and Andrew Clark. Joseph is a Vice-President of Third National Bank in Nashville, Tennessee.

Arthur Nevins attended school at Cave Springs, where Jim Reneau was his first teacher, then boarding school at Pleasant Grove and

Montvale Academy. He boarded with the Bill Dale and Bob Goodpasture families. He left school to help his father and started farming, logging, et cetera. Celina had no transportation except steamboats. He worked at various things including a spoke mill and raising tobacco. With the money he saved, he first bought 20 acres of land on Neely's Creek near Free Hills Road, and then bought land in Celina from Hubert Donaldson.

He started drilling for oil and leasing land in 1922. He made raft trips to Nashville to take logs. In 1930, he bought the John Stone farm and worked very hard to make it a productive farm; the 30's were hard times, and farmhands were paid 50¢ a day. He raised broomcorn, tobacco, soybeans, sugar cane, wheat, oats, corn, hay, cattle, hogs, truck crops of all kinds, and managed to pay his farm debts by oil leasing and cutting timber. He set the first acre of strawberries in Clay County in 1940's. He continued farming until 1983, when he moved to Lakeshore Home in Nashville, Tennessee.

He has been a hardworking, successful, honest, fun-loving, friendly man who can tell many interesting stories about happenings in Clay County. — *Submitted by Mrs. Isabelle Nevins Ross*

THOMAS W. NEVINS

Thomas W. Nevins (1859-1951) and Sarah Lee Fancher (1867-1949) were born in Celina, Tennessee. They were married March 30, 1882. In 1884, they, and two wagon loads of relatives, decided to move to Celina, Texas, a newly founded settlement out west. It was a long, hard journey to Texas, and the life was much different than these settlers had anticipated. Dust storms, tornadoes, and scorpions had T.W. and Sarah returning to Clay County after only five years. They returned with two children, Dora (Hall) and Samuel Robert. After their return, T.W. tended the ferry in Celina and Sarah kept schoolteachers as boarders. They had four more children: Hugh, Herman, Lucille (Smith), and Ann (Brown).

Samuel Robert Nevins (1889-1939) attended Montvale College in Celina and started farming at an early age. He also did odd jobs to support himself and to help his family. On December 1, 1913, he married Lena Mae Watson (1891-1982)

Lena Watson Nevins was the daughter of Joseph Newton Watson and Edna Scott. During the 1890's, her family lived in Martinsburg, Kentucky on the Cumberland River near what is now known as Burkesville. Joseph and Edna had six children: Reuben, John Hansford, Lena Mae (Nevins), Laura (Stone), Elizabeth (Parsons), and Alice (McClard). In 1902 the family moved to a farm in Vernon, Kentucky where they grew crops for their own needs and raised cattle and hogs to sell at market. In 1908, they moved near Celina. This is where the Watson family was living when Lena met and married Samuel Robert Nevins.

After their marriage, Samuel and Lena moved to the Pine Branch Community where Samuel owned a sawmill and farmed. They had seven children: Sam Phelmon, who died at age six; Lily Brownie (Young), of Heiskell, Tennessee; Ann Lee (Dalton), of Celina, Tennessee; Paul Erlic, who died at age eighteen; Estus Ezell, of Celina, Tennessee; Foy Joe, who died in 1984; and Joy Elizabeth (Burnette), of Celina, Tennessee.

Samuel and Lena's grandchildren include Brownie Young's five children (all of Heiskell, Tennessee), Samy (Cooper), Jimmy, Andrea (Hendron), Robert Clay, and Janet (Wampler). Other grandchildren are Ann Dalton's two daughters, Barbara, who died at age fourteen, and Margaret (Birdwell), of Celina, Tennessee, and Ezell Nevins' two sons, Gary and Danny, both of Celina Tennessee. Foy Joe Nevins has two children living near Detroit, Michigan. They are Sharon (Schwartz) and Steve. Joy Norman Burnette has two children, Sheila Norman, of Knoxville, Tennessee, and Billy Burnette, who is living in Celina, Tennessee.

DANNY AND TERESA NEVANS

Danny and Teresa Nevans have lived in Clay County since their marriage December 1, 1979. They live on the corner of Mitchell Street and Marcom Lane in Celina with their two daughters, Lorissa Renee, born May 13, 1983, and Leigh Ann, born February 26, 1986.

Danny was born September 11, 1957 and has lived in Celina all his life. He graduated from Celina High School in 1975, and then attended Tennessee Technological University where he received a Bachelor of Science degree in business management in 1979. He has been employed at Celina Lumber Company, the family business, since his graduation.

Danny is the son of Ezell Nevans (born in Clay County) and Wilma Beason Nevans (born in Pickett County, Tennessee). He is the grandson of Samuel Nevins (born in Celina, Texas 1889-1939) and Lena Watson Nevins (born in Martinsburg, Kentucky 1891-1982) and Molard Beason (born in Pickett County, Tennessee 1898-1974) and Corda Phillips Beason (born in Pickett County, Tennessee 1910-1977). Danny has one brother, Gary, who also lives in Celina.

Teresa was born in born in Indianapolis, Indiana May 31, 1959. Her family moved to Martinsville, Indiana in 1967 and to Scottdale, Pennsylvania in 1974. Her family moved back to Tennessee, the home state of both her parents, in 1975, to Lafayette, where Teresa graduated from Macon County High School in 1977. She then attended Tennessee Technological University where she received a Bachelor of Science degree in accounting in 1981. She has been employed as comptroller at the Bank of Celina since 1982.

Teresa is the daughter of Kenneth Gentry and Iva Lauderdale Gentry, both of whom were born in Macon County. She is the granddaughter of (William) Harvey Gentry (born in Macon County 1897-1960) and Lena Coons Gentry (born in Clay County 1910-1984) and Robert Lauderdale (born in Macon County 1896-1940) and Martha Gregory Lauderdale (born in Smith County 1907-1942). Teresa has one sister, Penny, who lives in Cookeville, Tennessee with her husband, Jack Hauskins, of Lafayette, Tennessee and their three children, Joshua, Holly, and Ryan.

GEORGE NEWMAN

George Newman was born in 1814 in Tennessee. He married Jerutha Pitcock, born in 1814 in Washington County, Tennessee. She was the daughter of John and Mary (Fisher) Pitcock. George's mother's name was Rhoda. George and Jerutha had the following children: Rhoda, born April 18, 1835; John F., born July 1839; Han-nah, born October 15, 1844; Louisa J., born October 24, 1848; and Nancy Elizabeth, born July 14, 1854.

Rhoda Newman married Thomas W. Vaughn, born April 26, 1845 — died April 15, 1923. Rhoda died February 19, 1919. They had the following children: John Washington, born January 13, 1866; Louisa Katherine, born September 6, 1867; and Lucy A., born 1870.

John F. Newman, born July 1839, first married Sarah Hunt June 5, 1858. Sarah was born in 1842. She was the daughter of John P. and Martha (Johnson) Hunt. They had one child, George W., born August 7, 1862. John F. next married Pelina E. Brown, born in 1848. They had the following children: Lovella, James H., John F., Jerusha, Butler W., Mary C., Clemma, and Martin.

George W. Newman, born August 7, 1862 — died March 12, 1948, married Mittie N. Morton, born March 1, 1871 — died April 28, 1952. Their children were Harley F., born March 15, 1887; Lola, born March 13, 1889; Lillie, born May 6, 1894; and Haskell, born August 18, 1906.

Harley F. Newman, born March 15, 1887 — died February 1, 1966, married Etta Cherry, born November 11, 1893. Their children were Lillie, Florence, Pam, Myrtle, Lawrence, Ridley.

Louisa J. Newman, born October 24, 1848, married Andrew Cherry, born November 26, 1858 — died April 6, 1899. Their children were Mary C., George A., born December 16, 1885; John Mack, born September 27, 1887; and Jerusha, born December 1, 1890.

George A. Cherry, born December 16, 1885 — died January 23, 1962, married Louisa Cross, born May 31, 1885 — died April 10, 1925. Their children were Oma, Ona, Andrew, Dona, Zona, Nadine, and Gertrude.

John Mack Cherry, born September 27, 1887 — died April 4, 1941, married Mandy Jones, born October 23, 1895. Their children were Luan, Rendford, John Mack, Bernice, Bransford, Willard, Celistia, and Genevive.

RICHARD OSGATHARP

The first Osgatharp in America was Richard. Family tradition, handed down through the generations, states that Richard was born in London, England about the year 1752. His father made and sold hats. When Richard was twelve years of age, he was sent out by his father to sell hats. The young boy went down to the docks, and there he was kidnapped by sailors (a common occurrence in those days). He was brought to America and sold as a bond servant.

The first written record of Richard is found in Surry County, North Carolina in 1771, where he is listed as a taxpayer. Records also show Richard to have served in the Revolution. He was a Primitive Baptist preacher, serving at one time in the Catawba Church of Burke County, North Carolina.

By 1778, Richard owned 300 acres of land in Burke County, was married and had several children, among them, two sons, Richard, Jr. and John, born in 1801. Richard, Jr. and his family migrated to Arkansas where they all died at an early age.

John moved to Jackson County, Tennessee after the death of his parents, probably around the year 1818. In 1825, he married Susannah Carlisle. They were the parents of eight children: Harrison, Tilman Jasper, Benton, Addison Perry, Harriett, Helen, Almira Edna, and Erasmus Gaw.

John was a farmer and a school teacher, and he held several civil offices. Susannah died in 1845, and John in 1887.

Erasmus Gaw Osgatharp was born January 1, 1843 in Jackson County (now Clay). He attended school at Concord. During the Civil War, Erasmus and three of his brothers served in the 13th Tennessee Cavalry Regiment (Dibrell's). In October of 1872, Erasmus married Rachel Prescovia Plumlee, daughter of George H. and Mary (Polly) Kirk Plumlee. They lived and farmed in the Brimstone Community of Clay County. Rachel died in 1922 and Erasmus in 1928. They are buried in the McGlasson Cemetery on Brimstone. Rachel and Erasmus were the parents of eleven children. G.D. first married Sally Etheridge, and then he married Sarah Capshaw. W.D. married Bea Painter. Hettie never married and died at an early age. Ida married Frank Jones. A.V. married Maryland Huffines. John Jasper married Nannie Meadows. Hanes Mitchell first married Arkie Huffines and then Mattie York. Mattie married Walter Jones. Virgil married Vallie Jenkins. — *Submitted by Betty F. Foor*

THE OSGATHARP BROTHERS

The Osgatharp brothers, Harrison, Tilman, Benton, Addison and Erasmus were born and raised on Brimstone Creek in Jackson (now Clay) County. Four of them served in the Civil War with the CSA. Harrison, the eldest remained on the farm. Addison joined the 28th Mounted Volunteer CSA and fought at Fort Donelson, Shiloh, Murfreesboro and Vicksburg. After reaching the rank of Captain, he changed sides and joined the Federal Forces as a private. He stayed around Nashville for the remainder of the war as a railroad guard. Erasmus Gaw joined the 8th Tennessee Calvary, Company G, known in the field as Dibrell's. On a raid into west Tennessee, he rode with General Forrest on a railroad destroying mission. They attacked the railroad and fortification at Jackson, Tennessee, and for a hundred miles north they destroyed bridges, tressels and stations. At Trenton the 8th exchanged their flintlocks and squirrel guns for modern Enfield Rifles. After raiding and burning for ten days, they met the Federals in a general battle at a place called Parker's Crossroads, 30 miles east of Jackson. Three hundred men were captured, including Erasmus. He was interned at Camp Douglas in Chicago for three months and then exchanged, where he rejoined his regiment at Columbia, Tennessee, in time for the big battle at Chickamuga. After this battle, he went to east Tennessee with General Wheeler where he was captured again on January 5, 1864. He was held in various places including the old Knoxville jail, the Nashville penitentiary sheds, the military prison at Louisville and finally at Rock Island, Illinois where he stayed until he became sick and weak. In March 1865, he was exchanged and released at Richmond, Virginia. He walked back home by way of Atlanta, Chattanooga and Nashville.

Brothers Benton G. and Tilman J. also joined the 8th Tennessee Calvary, Company G. and

fought at the battles of Atlanta, Calhoun, Cartersville, New Hope Church, Dallas, Kennesaw Mountain, Marietta and Peach Tree Creek, Georgia, Saltville, Virginia, and Averyboro, North Carolina. At Beulah, North Carolina, the regiment had its last fight. At Greensboro they were detailed to escort President Jefferson Davis and a million dollars in gold as he tried to escape to Mexico to carry on the fight, but the command decided to accept the surrender terms of General Grant. They surrendered at Washington, Georgia on May 11, 1865. They were allowed to keep their horses, but on the way home, they were taken into custody at Cleveland, Tennessee and their horses confiscated. So they had to walk home over the Cumberland Mountains. All four brothers returned to Brimstone after the war. My great grandfather, Erasmus Gaw, died in 1928, at the age of 85.

JOHN PAINTER, SR.

John Painter, Sr. was born around 1700. He married Hannah (surname unknown). They lived in the Shenandoah Valley of Virginia. His will was probated on March 5, 1771 in Frederick County, Virginia. John and Hannah had seven children: John, Jr., Robert, Thomas, Isaac, Hannah, Sarah, and Jane.

John Painter, Jr. had a son, Henry Spotwood, born April 2, 1814. He married Catherine E. Brown on September 14, 1846. Catherine was born January 18, 1816 and died July 20, 1887. Henry Spotwood bought a thirty-five acre farm in the Pricetown section of the Union Hill Community of Clay County. During the Civil War, he served in the Union Army with Company K, 37th Regiment of the Kentucky Infantry Volunteers from October 1, 1863 until February 1, 1865. While in the service, he contracted smallpox and was discharged. He died March 4, 1865. He is buried in a small family cemetery on his farm. While Henry Spotwood was sick, the neighbors were afraid to help his wife with him and her small children because of the smallpox. They would go and call to see if they needed anything to eat. They would get what she needed and leave it in the yard. The children would go out and get the supplies. When Henry Spotwood died, the neighbors made his coffin and took it to the yard. Catherine and the children placed him in the coffin and buried him on their farm. Catherine moved to Turkey Creek in order to be closer to her family so they could assist her with the children. While there, her daughter, Mary, died and she is buried on a hillside above their home on what is now the Philip Strong farm. After her daughter died, she moved to Pine Lick in Jackson County. She died and was buried there. She was later moved to the cemetery where her husband was buried in Pricetown and buried next to him.

Henry Spotwood and Catherine had seven children: John, born 1847; Zachariah, born October 25, 1849; Newton, born March 25, 1851; William, born January 20, 1853; Susana, born September 8, 1854; Mary, born December 20, 1856; and Patrick Henry, born August 14, 1860.

PATRICK HENRY PAINTER

Patrick Henry Painter was born August 14,

1860 in Jackson County, Tennessee, and he died December 28, 1959. On January 7, 1886 in Jackson County, Tennessee, he married Susan Genetta McCawley, born August 17, 1866 — died April 4, 1940. They are buried in the Keeling Cemetery in Jackson County.

Patrick Henry, Susan, Lee, John, Dee, Catherine, Ella, Ada, Gillock, May, Loren, Rosa and Gilbert Painter

Patrick and Susan had twelve children: Harley Lee, born April 3, 1887; John George, born September 20, 1888; Maggie Dee, born March 21, 1890; Sarah Catherine, born October 11, 1891; Infant, born and died 1892; Mary Ella, born October 1, 1893; Ada V., born April 6, 1895; Lindsey Gillock, born May 19, 1898, Stella May, born September 18, 1899; Loren Zachariah, born January 5, 1902; Rosa Bell, born November 24, 1903; and Gilbert Newton, born July 4, 1905. Ten of the children are still living in 1986. Two of the children, Harley Lee and John George, served in World War I. They enlisted November 13, 1917 in Gainesboro, Tennessee. They were in Battery D, 115 F.A., and served in England, France, and Germany. Lee was a blacksmith, and John hauled ammunition to the front line. They stayed together during the war and came home together.

Harley Lee was the first of the Painter children to die. He died May 5, 1984. He first married Mary Liz Keeling. His second wife was Ethel Savage.

John George Painter, born September 20, 1888, married Gillie May Watson on January 20,

Ten of the Painter Family and living as of July, 1986 — Sarah — 94, Dee — 96, John — 97, Lee died in 1984 at 97, Mary — 92, Ada — 91, Stella — 85, Loren — 84, Rosa — 82, Lindsey — 88 and Gilbert — 81.

1920. They live in the Hermitage Springs Community of Clay County. They have two children, Dorris (Potts) and Florene (Maxey).

Maggie Dee Painter, born March 21, 1890, married William Carter November 27, 1910. Sarah Catherine Painter, born October 11, 1891, married Dillard Spivey January 14, 1912. Mary Ella Painter, born October 1, 1893, married Mathew Crowder December 22, 1911. Ada V.

Painter, born April 6, 1895, married Johnny B. Mercer July 7, 1920. Lindsey Gillock Painter, born May 19, 1898, married Mamie Watson August 12, 1921. Stella May Painter, born September 18, 1899, married Sam Batts October 2, 1921. Loren Zachariah Painter, born January 5, 1902, married Edna Allen December 30, 1931. Rosa Bell Painter, born November 24, 1903, married Elbert Watson February 1, 1920. Gilbert Newton Painter, born July 4, 1905, married Nannie C. Allen April 20, 1924.

LURA DEAN ARMS PARSONS

Lura Dean Arms Parsons was born December 26, 1948 in Celina, Tennessee. She is the daughter of Walter B. Arms and the late Claudine White Arms. Lura was reared partially by her paternal grandparents, the late Tommie and Dayse Arms, and partially by Dewey and Helen Wells. Her maternal grandparents are Beulah Cunningham White of Celina and the late Ress White.

Amanda, Lura, Bill, Robert and James Parsons

Lura attended school in Celina, graduating in 1966. She is a 1980 graduate of Tennessee Technological University, graduating cum laude with a Bachelor of Science in Early Childhood Education, and a 1983 graduate of Tennessee Technological University, graduating with a Master of Arts degree maintaining a 4.0 average. She was a member of honorary societies which included Alpha Lambda Delta, Phi Kappa Phi, Kappa Delta Pi, and Pi Lambda Theta.

Lura's first teaching assignment was at Maple Grove Elementary, teaching a kindergarten-fourth grade regular classroom. Lura comes from a long line of teachers. Each of her paternal aunts and uncle, including her father, have taught for a period of time. Kindergarten at Celina K-8 is her present assignment. Lura has served in the local education association and is active with Tennessee Technological University Council of International Reading Association where she is recording secretary.

Lura was married to William (Bill) Hull Parsons, Jr. of Celina June 26, 1965. Bill is the son of William H. Parsons, Sr. and Ora Burnette Parsons. He is the grandson of the late Edly H. Parsons and Ara Willis Parsons of Celina, and Blanche Ritter Burnette of Celina and the late Carroll Estell Burnette.

After Bill's graduation from Celina High School in 1963, he served in the United States Army. Bill is employed by the United States Army Corps of Engineers and farms for a hobby, while Lura's hobby is raising registered collies.

Bill and Lura are the parents of James Wilson, born June 1, 1968; Robert Hull, born April 8, 1969; and Amanda Claudyne, born October 1, 1970.

James attended school in Celina graduating from Celina High School in 1986. Robert and Amanda attend school at Celina High School where Robert will be a senior and Amanda will be a junior.

Bill, Lura, James, Robert and Amanda attend church at the Church of Christ at the Pine Branch Community in Clay County. Bill is a part-time minister and a full-time teacher with the congregation.

JAMES AND MARTHA PEDIGO

James Pedigo was born November 21, 1869 to William Newton Pedigo and Nancy Woods Pedigo. Newton Pedigo was born in 1849 to Robert Pedigo (1822-1909) and Elizabeth Reeves (1825-1900). Nancy Woods was born in 1843 to William Henry Woods, born in 1806, and Cynthia K. Reeves, born in 1816.

James Pedigo married Martha Grider, who was born June 30, 1871. She had a twin Sarah; she also had another sister Mirandy, who was born April 5, 1874. They were the daughters of William H. Grider born 1836, and Margaret J. Miles Grider, born February 12, 1834. She was the daughter of George and Sarah (Prewitt) Miles. William H. Grider was son of John and Plelisha Grider.

Margaret J., Martha, Sarah and Mirandy Grider

James and Martha were married in Clay County November 1, 1891. Six children were born to this union: Verda Mae, born December 13, 1892; Bertha Pearl, born May 24, 1895; William Basil, born October 14, 1897; baby girl, born October 27, 1901 and died November 6, 1901; Johnny Ivo, born November 17, 1903; and Earl, born February 15, 1908. Verda married Mack Weaver Henson December 23, 1913. They had four sons: Elmo, Elbert, Delbert, and Leon. Bertha married J.D. Brown December 23, 1914. They had two daughters: Jewell Elizabeth and Fannie Mae. Basil married Mattie Grindstaff August 22, 1923. They had two children: Harold and Inez. Ivo married Willette Brown August 14, 1924. They had four children: Cecil, Ray, Pauline, and Shirley Jo. Earl was never married.

James and Martha Pedigo first lived in a log house near Oak Grove. About 1904, they built a large wood frame house near the same site which still stands. This house was next occupied by the Weaver Henson family (1927) and is currently inhabited by the Roy Henson family (great grandson of James Pedigo).

James Pedigo was a farmer and also ran a

Martha and James Pedigo

gristmill for the public. The Pedigos spent their last years in Hermitage Springs on Highway 52. James passed away September 12, 1942, and Martha passed away June 22, 1946. They are buried in the Hermitage Springs Cemetery.

The descendants of the Pedigos now are scattered. Basil was the last surviving child. He died in 1985. His children, Harold and Inez (Hinson), live in Tompkinsville, Kentucky. Three of Verda and Weaver Henson's sons survive today: Elmo in Clay County, Elbert in Robertson County (Adams, Tennessee), and Delbert in Indianapolis, Indiana. Bertha's daughters, Jewell and Fannie Mae, live on Dry Creek in the Arcot community of Clay County. Ivo's daughter, Pauline (Carver), lives in Macon County, Tennessee; and his son, Ray, lives in Clay County.

KIMBERLY PENNINGTON

Kimberly Pennington was born April 23, 1969. She is a descendant to Hannah (Boone) Pennington, a sister to the frontiersman, Daniel Boone. The Boone family originated in England. George Boone, who married Sarah Uppey, had a son, George, who was born about 1666 in England. He married Mary Maugridge. In 1717, George and Mary came to America and settled in Philadelphia, Pa. He died on July 27, 1744 in Berks County, Pennsylvania. Mary died February 2, 1740. Among their children was Squire Boone, born November 25, 1696 in England — died January 2, 1765 in Rowan Co., North Carolina. Squire married Sarah Morgan September 23, 1720 in Philadelphia. Sarah was born in 1700 and died in 1770 in Rowan County, North Carolina. They had eleven children, among whom was one Daniel Boone, the famous frontiersman. Another was a daughter, Hannah who was born August 24, 1746 in Philadelphia. She was married twice — first to John Stewart and then to Richard Pennington, who was born in 1752 in Pennsylvania. He served in the Revolutionary War. In 1798, Hannah and Richard moved to Barren, now Monroe County, Kentucky. Hannah

Kimberly Pennington

was a member of the Old Mulkey Church near Tompkinsville, Kentucky.

Around 1811, Hannah and Richard moved to White County, Tennessee. Richard died there December 21, 1813. Hannah returned to Monroe County to live with her son, Daniel Pennington. She died April 9, 1928 and is buried at the Old Mulkey Church Cemetery.

Hannah and Richard's children were Joshua, born February 23, 1778; Daniel, born December 3, 1781; Stewart, born June 10, 1784; and Abigail, born January 24, 1787.

Daniel Pennington, born Dec. 3, 1781 — died February 1, 1865, married Esther Fraley August 20, 1805 in Barren County, Kentucky. Esther was the daughter of Christian and Elizabeth (Harding) Fraley. Esther died April 30, 1854. Daniel and Esther had eleven children. One was Isaiah Crouch Pennington, born April 3, 1825 — died February 5, 1892, married Louisa Minerva Cherry March 25, 1846. Louisa was the daughter of Carey Cherry, born 1790 in Virginia and Isabella (McAdoo) Cherry. She was the granddaughter of Lemuel and Sarah (McPherson) Cherry. Isaiah and Louisa had eight children. One was Daniel, Rufus, born March 23, 1862 — died January 28, 1954. He married Leah Wood. They are buried in the Gamaliel Cemetery.

Their son, Jack, married Ovie Ritter. They have the following children: Dr. Vanis Pennington, Willard, David, and Lex Pennington. Lex Pennington married Helen Long, and their daughter, Kimberly, attends Hermitage Springs School.

JOSEPH PHILLIPS

Joseph Phillips was born in Wales in 1716. His wife, Mary, was a Welch maiden.

John Phillips, Sr., the son of Joseph and Mary, was born in Pembrokeshire Wales in 1745. He married Mary Stockton of Stockton Valley, Kentucky after coming to Kentucky.

Samuel Phillips, son of John Phillips, Sr., married Elizabeth Tompkins and moved to Pickett County. Samuel was born in 1797.

Anslum Phillips, the son of Samuel Phillips, married Jane Ellen McCraw from Fox Springs in Clay County. Anslum was born in 1839, and he was a farmer.

William Porter Phillips was the son of Anslum Phillips. He was born in 1870 in Pickett County. He married Ermon Rayborn.

Gratton D. Phillips, born in 1896, was a rural letter carrier and farmer in Clay County. He married Lorene Pickens. He was the son of William P. Phillips.

Geraldine Phillips was the daughter of Gratton D. Phillips. She was born in 1922 and married Eugene Winston Smalling. She was a rural mail carrier in Clay County. She now lives in Red Boiling Springs.

Phillips Meredith Smalling, born 1960, is the son of Geraldine and Winston Smalling. He married Jane Thompson of Tompkinsville, Kentucky. He is an attorney in Pickett County. They have one daughter, Danielle Meredith, born 1985.

Gwendolyn Phillips, born in 1924, is the daughter of Gratton D. and Lorene Phillips. She married Paul K. Sadler and lives in Red Boiling Springs, Tennessee.

Paulette Clark Pippin, born in 1950, the daughter of Gwendolyn and Paul Sadler, has three children: Nicole Clark, Benjamin Clark, and

Giner Clark. She is employed by the City of Red Boiling Springs.

Regina Sadler Cassetty, born 1951, the daughter of Gwendolyn and Paul Sadler, has two children, Kristy and Ashley Cassetty. Regina lives in Red Boiling Springs, Tennessee. She is the speech teacher in Macon, County.

OTIS PITCOCK

Otis Pitcock was born September 8, 1903 in the Turkeytown Community of Clay County. He is the son of the late George Bethel Pitcock and Mary Elizabeth Philpot Pitcock. He attended the New Liberty Elementary School in Overton County. He worked at farming, sawmilling, logging and carpentry. He helped to clear the land for Dale Hollow Lake. He has helped in building many homes and businesses in Clay County including OshKosh B'Gosh. He was employed at OshKosh B'Gosh as a carpenter and maintenance person for many years.

Mary and Bethel Pitcock, Otis Pitcock's parents

On October 7, 1923, Otis married the late Eula C. Maybery in Jackson, County, Tennessee. Eula was born September 11, 1905 in Louisiana. She was the daughter of the late Amos Wesley Maybery and Mary Elizabeth Langford and the granddaughter of the late Corey Maybery and Betsy Gentry Maybery and Milt Langford and Elizabeth Allen Langford. Eula was a housewife and helped with the farming.

In 1945 Otis and Eula moved to Celina. They had previously lived in the Beech Flat Community of Clay County. They attended the Celina Church of Christ where Eula was very active until her death January 26, 1981. Otis is still active in the church.

Otis and Eula had ten children. They are Thurman Harold, born December 7, 1924; Grace Marie Pitcock Brown, born November 3, 1926; the late George Wesley, born December 25, 1928 and died April 21, 1964; Lola Christine Pitcock Rains, born September 25, 1931; Nola Katherine Pitcock Smith, born October 29, 1933; Mary Creola Pitcock Halsell, born January 31, 1936; Herman Byrdle, born May 10, 1938; infant daughter, born and died in 1944; Darvis Lee, born April 9, 1946; and Janice Dean Pitcock Arms, born November 2, 1947.

ALVA CREED PLUMLEE

John Garner Plumlee was born in 1856 in Clay County, Tennessee. He was the only child of Job and Jennie (Pennington) Plumlee. John married Margaret Isabell Denton on August 31, 1877. He traveled cutting timber for the Jess Wyman Steve Company and died in Illinois around 1920. John and Margaret had ten children.

Glissie Plumlee Family

George Washington Plumlee was their sixth child. He was born in 1896 in Clay County, Tennessee. In 1915, he married Glissie Gulley, the daughter of John and Mary (Craighead) Gulley. Glissie was born October 20, 1900 and died in December of 1980 in Clay County, Tennessee. George and Glissie had four children: Alva Creed, Donnie Duel, Bertha Olyne, and Walter Clyde. Later, George Plumlee moved to California and married Mary Minerva Gallimore. They had nine children. George died in November of 1974 in California.

Duel Plumlee was born March 24, 1919 in Clay County, Tennessee. She married Herman Netherton. Duel died March 5, 1969 in Tipton, Indiana and her husband still resides there.

Olyne Plumlee was born in Arkansas on August 3, 1921 and died in 1940 in Clay County, Tennessee.

Clyde Plumlee was born January 24, 1924 in Clay County, Tennessee. He married Lura Kendall. They have three children and live in Moss, Tennessee.

Alva Creed Plumlee was born in Shirley, Arkansas on July 3, 1916. He was raised in Clay County and attended Oak Grove School. From 1934-1939, Alva worked in the Civil Conservation Corps. In 1942, he entered the Army and took basic training at Camp Van Doran. On February 15, 1944, he married Lillian Pauline Bean, the daughter of Carlie and Nellie (Green) Bean. Lillian was born June 9, 1920 in Clay County. Alva was sent overseas in 1944. He was in the 99th Infantry Division and was in England, France, Germany, and Belgium. He was in the Battle of the Bulge and was discharged in the fall of 1945.

DR. DAVE PLUMLEE

Dr. Dave Plumlee obtained his M.D. Degree; and rather than seek the plaudits of an alien world in a steam heated office in some city, he returned to his people in the hills of Tennessee to practice. He soon found that these people often needed legal council as well as medical help. He studied law and was admitted to the bar. He was an able barrister and a learned doctor, as he practiced both medicine and surgery. Many cases, had they been reported to medical journals, would have been marked along the path of progress in medical science.

Early in life, Dr. Dave married and he and his wife had several children. Illness came to his wife, and though brother doctors came and administered, she was taken away. After a few years, the doctor married again, a young woman much his junior, and in due course, they had a daughter.

During all these years, Doctor Dave served the

people of the hills, his people. Where sickness or suffering, there he was always to be found, never asking, "Can they pay?", always rendering the same kind of service whether in the single room cabin in the hills or in the big house on the farm in the valley.

Much sickness, colds, pneumonia, et cetera among his people grew more numerous and severe as that February 29th came along. On this February 29th was born that daughter who would make young again the heart of a dad of three score years. March came with howling winds, blowing rain and snow, filling and overflowing streams, freezing the ground, and making white the whole countryside. The calls came from the hills — pneumonia and other serious illnesses. Thankful that the creator had given him a new daughter and that both child and mother were showing every sign of proper progress, the doctor went to those who were suffering, though he had a severe cold. Far into the hills, over bridle paths that were frozen and slick, he traveled to that home in the hills where a mother was nearing to the brink of death with pneumonia. As the sun came forth, he stepped from that cabin, tired and worn but knowing that he had saved this mother to care for her brood. His cough was heavier, tighter, and now he thought of himself — that he best get home and do battle with pneumonia himself.

The doctors came to him as he had gone to his people, but it was too late. Pneumonia in its most severe form! Soon his life was burned out.

Upon an early March Sunday afternoon, gathered from hill and dale for miles around, simple, honest, country folks, the purest of the purest of the Anglo-Saxon in America, came to pay a last tribute of respect to one who had truly given his life for them. Over there stood a man whose broken limb Doctor Dave had set, a woman who survived a caesarean, a man with an arm shattered from the accidental discharge of a shotgun which had been amputated by Doctor Dave with a common carpenter's saw. They came to quietly say, "We'll miss you Doctor Dave."

And now the last journey — the trip to the graveyard on the cedar point in the bend of the Cumberland River. There was no hearse. There were no roads. He was borne on the shoulders of those for whom he had lived and for whom he had died, murmuring with the hundreds gathered on that snow clad hill, "We'll miss you, Doctor Dave."

Dr. Dave Plumlee died March 9, 1912. This tribute was written several years later by Hampton Maxey for publication in a medical journal.

CAPTAIN LUE W. PLUMLEE

Captain Plumlee was born in Celina in 1887, the son of Weaver Plumlee, the grandson of Lorenza and Annie Mary Plumlee, and the great-grandson of Denton Mack and Adeline Plumlee, all of the Dry Creek Section of the Arcot Community.

Captain Plumlee was born to the river as his father, Captain L.T. Plumlee, was a raftsman and riverboatman of long experience. He made over 400 trips, rafting and operating his own sternwheelers on the Upper Cumberland. Young Lue was just a boy when he began his river learning. He made his first trip downriver as a raftsman in the early 1900's. Sometime around 1913, he

Captain Lue W. Plumlee

went to steamboating. He steered on the Jo Horton Falls, handled all kinds of workboats and towboats. He piloted his father's sternwheelers, the Quick Step, the J.J. Gore, and the L.T. Plumlee, hauling freight and livestock regularly up the river from Carthage to Burkesville, Kentucky and up to the Obey from Celina. Since the 1950's, Captain Lue has piloted such steamboats as the Avalon and the Belle of Louisville, excursion boats, and he brought the famous Delta Queen up the Cumberland on her last trip to Nasvhille. — Excerpts from The Nashville Banner Monday, August 18, 1969.

SAMUEL PLUMLEE

Samuel Plumlee was born in 1825. He was the son of Denton Plumlee, born in 1803, and Nancy Johnson Plumlee, born in 1806. He was the grandson of John Plumlee, born in 1766, and the great-grandson of William Plumlee, who married Phebe Denton, of Shenandoah County, Virginia, a direct descendant of Richard Denton, a minister who came to New England between 1630-1635 from Wethersfield, England to form a settlement called Rippowams, later called Stamford, Connecticut. Samuel was given the nickname, "Black Sam," to distinguish him from his first cousin, Samuel (Red Sam), who was the son of John Plumlee.

Samuel and Nancy Arterberry Plumlee

Samuel Plumlee married Nancy Arterberry, who was born September 2, 1828. Samuel and Nancy had the following children: Mary A., born in 1847; Denton Mack, born in 1848; and Martha J., born in 1853.

The Plumlees farmed, operated a riverboat landing at the mouth of Dry Creek, owned riverboats, constructed rafts to take down the river to Nashville, and built a school for their children and the children whose parents worked for the Plumlees. They were a fun-loving family and enjoyed fishing, hunting, trapping, singing, and playing musical instruments. They had a racetrack where

horse races were held. Their home was the scene of frequent parties and any type of activity — corn huskings, hog killings, barn raisings, quilting bees, et cetera — was always accompanied with good food, music, singing, and games.

The exact date of Samuel's death is not known. Nancy died May 22, 1887. They were buried in the Plumlee Family Cemetery on Dry Creek in the Arcot Community.

DENTON MACK PLUMLEE

Denton Mack Plumlee, born in 1848, was the son of Samuel and Nancy Arterberry Plumlee. He married Adeline Eads, born in 1848, the daughter of Anderson and Sally Cherry Eads. They lived in the Dry Creek section of the Arcot Community where Denton Mack was a farmer. Denton Mack and his father, Samuel, owned a large acreage of land and were awarded several acres of land under the Federal Land Grants, south of Walker's line, between 1847 and 1867.

Denton Mack and Adeline had eight children, Lorenza, Sam Anderson, Amanda, Mary Jane, Nan, Alva, Lonnie, and Everette. Lorenza (Captain L.T. Plumlee), born in 1868, was a raftsman and a riverboatman who operated three sternwheelers, the "Quick Step," the "J.J. Gore," and the "L.T. Plumlee," hauling freight and livestock regularly from Carthage to Burkesville, Kentucky and up the Obey River from Celina. Lorenza married Anna Mary (surname unknown).

Sam Anderson, born in 1871, was married twice — first to Lizzie (surname unkown) and then to Ollie McBride. Sam moved from Clay County to Smith County, Tennessee, where he was a commercial fisherman along the Cumberland River.

Mary Jane, born in 1874, married Bishop Radford Crowder. She was the only child to remain in Clay County. Amanda married Ambrose Speakman and moved to White County, Tennessee. There is no record of Nan, born in 1872 or Everette ever being married. Lonnie, born in 1870, died young. Alva, born in 1876, was married twice — first to a Hall (first name unknown) and then to Alice Reecer. They moved to Barren County, Kentucky where he was a farmer.

Denton Mack and Adeline were buried in the Plumlee Family Cemetery on Dry Creek in the Arcot Community. (This cemetery has been virtually destroyed through neglect and only a monument or two remain.)

EDWARD PURCELL

Edward Purcell, born in Ireland, married a Miss Ethridge. Their children were Jeremiah, James, and Hardy.

Hardy Purcell, born in 1777 or 1778 in North Carolina, married Elizabeth Manning, born in 1778. He was in the War of 1812 and served under General Andrew Jackson in the Battle of New Orleans. Their children were Edward, born September 13, 1810; Alfred, born in 1812; Tabitha, born in 1813; William Manning, born October 8, 1818; Lewis; Isaac; Temperance; and Topsy.

William Manning Purcell, born October 8, 1818 — died November 22, 1869, married Priscilla Welch, born November 18, 1823, on April 6, 1843. William was a teacher and later became a physician practicing medicine at Moss in Clay County. William and Priscilla had the following children: Hovey Allen; John P.; Samuel; Mary J.; Martha; and Miles N. Priscilla died August 11, 1859. William then married Elizabeth Hestand, born May 14, 1834 — died September 1, 1907. William and Elizabeth had the following children: Priscilla, William, Jahue McPherson, Elizabeth, and Camilia.

Catherine Purcell, Mosey and Mamie Purcell

Jahue McPherson Purcell, born August 13, 1865 — died December 25, 1919, married Roxie Catherine Gulley, born December 2, 1866 — died December 29, 1965. Their children were Pearlie, born October 11, 1887; Mattie, born July 20, 1889; Rue, born December 2, 1890; Carlos, born December 12, 1892; Sanford, born August 30, 1895; Willard, born February 13, 1899; Jay, born October 21, 1902; Mai, born June 5, 1905; and Mosey born November 2, 1910. Jahue and Roxie Catherine are buried in the Biles Cemetery in Clay County.

Mosey Purcell, born November 2, 1910, married Mami Rush. Their children were Eugene, Ronald, and Creola Aline.

Eugene Purcell married Virginia Cross. Ronald Purcell, born June 16, 1936 in Clay County, married Doris Cherry. Their children are Vivina, born July 7, 1956; and Dennis, born December 6, 1960. Dennis married Melanie Meadows, and they have two children, Misty, born December 2, 1980, and Nathan, born August 13, 1984.

Creola Aline Purcell married Kenneth Birdwell, born November 27, 1938. Their children are Donnie Reed, born February 22, 1960; Pamela Dianne, born January 22, 1963; and Kenny Wayne, born November 27, 1960.

JESSIE REECER

Jessie Reecer, born in Jackson County, Tennessee January 20, 1861, married Rebecca Nevins, born in 1862. To this union four children

Perry and Allie, Roy and Amos Reecer

were born: Jimmy, Perry, Lilly and Tommie Reecer. Jessie died in January of 1894.

Perry Reecer married Allie Odle December 24, 1904. They lived in Moss, Tennessee. They had two sons, Roy and Amos.

Amos Reecer married Lucille Jones, the daughter of Walter N. (Dock) and Mattie Osgathorp Jones of Clay County. Amos and Lucille have no children. They lived in Kokomo, Indiana for thirty years before retiring and returning to their present home in Red Boiling Springs, Tennessee in 1972.

Roy Reecer married Esther Spires from Kentucky. They have four children. Wilma June Reecer, born May 6, 1931 in Indianapolis, Indiana, married Junior Alonzo Garner. They have two children. Danny Carl, born in Kokomo, Indiana, married Arna Katherine Sheller, and they have four children — Matthew Wade, Julia Dawn, Melissa Noelle, and Jesse Alonzo. Alonia Luann, the daughter of Wilma June and Alonzo Garner, was born in Kokomo, Indiana, where she married Joseph Allen Huskins. They have three children: Joseph Nickolas Ryan, Jeremiah Christian Zane, and Zachariah David.

Rebecca Evins Reecer (Perry Reecer's mother)

Gloria Mooneen Reecer was born in Indianapolis, Indiana October 11, 1933. She married David Lee Creviston. They have three sons. Thomas David married Constance Mae Yerden, and they have three children, Richard Thomas, Treva Laurinda, and Sarah Rachelle. Larry Dean married Susan Diane (Dusek) Gentry, and they have two sons, Scott Allen Gentry and Brian Lee Gentry. Rondle Dale married Cindy Sue Levine, and they have two children, Susan Marie and Adam James.

William Perry Reecer, born in Moss, Tennessee June 23, 1941, married Janet Arlean Boyd, and they have four children. Gloria Jean married Rod Thomas, and they have three children, Destiny Renee, Kyle Emerson Brian, and Tara Velma Rae. Tammy Dee married Kent Muisick and they had one child, William Garrett. (The other two children of William Perry and Janet Boyd Reecer were not listed.)

Roy Dale Reecer was born September 11, 1946. He married Alberta Cerbus. They have two sons, Adam Douglas and Richard Kane.

TIM TOLLIE REECER

Tim Tollie Reecer was born March 16, 1919. He grew up at Liberty Hill on Big Proctor Creek, four miles west of Celina, Tennessee. He was the sixth child of five boys and two girls born to Tollie Thomas and Gertrude Walker Reecer. Gertrude died at the age of 83 and Tollie died at the age of 90.

Tim attended Liberty Hill Grade School which

Tim Tollie Reecer Family

was a one-teacher school. He graduated from Celina High School. He attended Middle Tennessee State Teachers College in Murfreesboro, and received his Bachelor of Science Degree from Tennessee Polytechnic Institute in Cookeville, Tennessee. He taught school in Clay County for many years. He retired in March of 1981 at the age of 62. He is now self-employed in industrial arts.

Tim is married to Armella Plumlee Reecer. They have four sons, Melvin, Thomas, Tim Edward, and Truman. They have eight grandchildren and one great-grandchild. Tim and Armella are members of and attend the Celina Church of Christ. — *Submitted by Tiffany Reecer*

JAMES H. RENEAU

James H. Reneau was born November 7, 1887 in Celina, Tennessee. His family was from the Wolf River area. He married Della Elam, who was born in Hilham, Tennessee, and later moved to the Indian Territory in Oklahoma. Her family moved back to Willow Grove, then to Hilham, and finally settled in Celina. They were married September 11, 1910 in "Old Town" Celina. "Mr. Jim" and Mrs. Della both taught school at Montvale Academy and then in the public schools of Clay County. They taught at Pine Branch and Neely's Creek. After being married, they moved to Fox Springs at the mouth of Mitchell's Creek which is now Dale Hollow Lake. At Fox Springs, "Mr. Jim" farmed and Mrs. Della taught school. When "Mr. Jim" was elected tax assessor, they moved back to Celina. Later, "Mr. Jim" was elected County Court Clerk and held that office for 16 years. He went to law school at Cumberland Law School and started law practice in 1928. His law partners were M.C. Sidwell, Don White, and Charlie Haile. Mrs. Della was Relief Director for Clay County in the 1930's. She wrote a book about her job and workers in the 1940's entitled *Grapefruit Gussie*.

Della, James Houston, Sr. "Baby" & J.H. Reneau, Jr.

"Mr. Jim" and Mrs. Della had seven children: "Baby," J.H. Reneau, Jr., Ruby Dean, Elizabeth "Tooby," William Herman "Dickey," Mary Ruth "Oopie," and Eddie Sue. "Baby" was born December 22, 1911. She married Roy B. Smith in 1936, and they live in Clarksville, Tennessee. "Baby" served as County Court Clerk in Clay County from 1934-1938. She was the first woman to serve in this position in the State of Tennessee, and she was also the youngest person to hold this position. Roy was the agriculture teacher at Celina. Roy later worked for the Soil Conservation Service. "Baby" and Roy have one son, Dr. James Smith of Clarksville. He is married to Elaine Schmit, and they have three children, Jimmy, Christy, and David.

James Houston Reneau, Jr. was born June 6, 1915. He married Mary Emma Scobey of Nashville November 28, 1935. "Daddy Jim" served in the Navy in World War II. He is the only State Senator from Clay County; and he served two terms starting in 1946. He graduated from Cumberland Law School in 1937 and practiced law in Celina for 44 years. He served as Clerk and Master and as County Court Clerk. Mary Emma "Mama Mae" ran Holly Creek Boat Dock for 27 years. They have three children, Jimmy, III, Corinne, and Mary Loyd. Jimmy, III is a lawyer in Celina, and he is serving his first term as General Sessions Judge. He is married to Margaret Bearden of Nashville. Margaret has two daughters, Gina and Dawn. Gina is married to Rusty Getter of Dallas, Texas. They have three daughters, Brooke, Courtney, and Brittany. Dawn is a paralegal and works and lives in Louisville, Kentucky. Corinne is married to John Howard McLerran. They have three sons, Johnny, Joe, and Al. Joe is married to Debbie Asberry, and they have two children, "Little" Joe and Samantha. Alex "Al" is married to Lisa Halsell, and they have one child, Ryan Wade. Mary Loyd is a retired high school band director and is presently attending law school in Nashville.

The third child of "Mr. Jim" and Mrs. Della was Ruby Dean Reneau, born October 16, 1919 and died December 21, 1919.

Elizabeth "Tooby" Reneau was born December 14, 1921. She married Tommy Talley of Nashville. "Tooby" worked for the Tennessee Department of Education. She attended Tennessee Polytechnic Institute and taught school in Clay County at Butlers Landing. She died December 18, 1953 at the age of 32.

Will Herman "Dickey" Reneau was born April 5, 1923. He is married to Geneva Reding of Courtland, Alabama. "Dickey" served in the United States Army during World Ward II. He worked for the United States Corps of Engineers for 33 years as an inspector of dams and bridges. "Dickey" is serving his first term as Mayor of Celina. Geneva is secretary at Celina High School, a position she has held for 21 years. They have one daughter, Sarah Elizabeth. She is married to Greg Burch, and they have one daughter, Virginia. Elizabeth teaches at Celina High School; and Greg works for Twin Lakes Telephone Company.

Mary Ruth "Oopie" Reneau was born December 10, 1924. "Oopie" attended David Lipscomb College. She served as County Court Clerk of Clay County. She also served as Executive Secretary for the Cordell Hull Development Corpora-

tion for many years. She was Clerk and Master for three years. "Oopie" died April 26, 1984.

Eddie Sue Reneau was born July 23, 1927. She was married to Carley B. Hurd of Tompkinsville, Kentucky. She worked in Louisville as a computer programmer. They had one daughter, Neil. Eddie Sue died July 1, 1965.

ELISHA RICH

Elisha (Lish) Rich was a first strictly Clay County progenitor of the prolific Rich family which blossomed and flourished in the Moss to Midway area. He was born in Jackson County in January of 1829, but it is not clear whether that was an area of present Jackson County or a part of Jackson that contributed to the formation of Clay County. His father was James Rich, married to Virginia Peake. Tradition has it that these Riches were a part of the party that came up the Cumberland River by boat and separated, a portion going toward Overton County and a portion coming toward the community where so many were born and lived.

Lish Rich was a farmer and also operated a water-powered gristmill. He married Mary Strong, and they made their home in a four-room, log house on the Mill Road between Moss and Midway, that was built by John Leek Maxey before the Civil War and was still standing in 1986. He was living in that house when he left his family to enlist in the Union Army July 1, 1860. The children would hide in the cellar of the house which was entered by a trap door in the middle of the big room to avoid the Celina Guerillas, better known as Hamilton's Raiders. He came back and got his oldest son, William, who at age 14 or 15, became one of the youngest enlisted soldiers in the Civil War.

The other sons of Lish Rich were Jim (father of John, Robert, Elisha, and Bedie); John (father of twenty-two children among whom were Sid, Aus, Herman, Lester, Vina, Buford, and Dorothy); and Roark (father of Harrison, Rad, Buford, and Nina). Jim was born on September 10, 1848; and John was born January 20, 1850.

Elisha's son, Will, born March 20, 1847, had eleven children among whom were Bone, Hobert, Ed, Clyde, and Arizona. Will was a Church of Christ preacher and Elisha's second son, Jim, was a Baptist preacher. The Rich Brothers' public formal debate over the plan of salvation was talked about in the area for decades. Lish also had daughters; namely Tennessee (Ten), Arizona, Missouri (Zood), Louisiana (Zan), and America.

Many descendants of Lish Rich became active in Clay County affairs. Among them are the children of Will's daughter, Arizona, namely Nelson Grace, a long-time businessman in Celina; Rasmus Grace, a farmer in the west end of the county; and the descendants of Missouri (Zood) through her daughter, Elzada Yates, and Elzada's daughter, Jewell (Hinson), mother of Royce Hinson, a long-time mail carrier in Celina, and through Elzada's daughter, Lola (Anderson) whose daughter, Chloe Nell (Moore), a long-time businesswoman in Celina. — *Submitted by Russell Hinson*

WILLIAM RICH

William Rich was born March 20, 1847 in Jackson County, (now Clay County) Tennessee. He was the son of Elisha Rich, born November 2, 1828 and died June 4, 1907, and Mary (Strong)

Rich, born June 15, 1829 and died May 19, 1912. Elisha owned a water-powered gristmill near Moss. He was in the Civil War and served in Company B of the 37th Kentucky Volunteer Infantry. Elisha was the son of James and Virginia (Peake) Rich. Elisha and Mary were the parents of nine children: William, born March 20, 1847; James, born September 10, 1848; John, born January 20, 1850; America, born in 1854; Missouri, born February 15, 1855; Virginia, born May 17, 1860; Jonathan Roark, born 1863; Tennessee, born February 6, 1869; and Louisiana, born 1873. William Rich was also in the Civil War. He served in Company B of 37th Kentucky Volunteer Infantry. He was married three times. He was first married January 25, 1865 to Sarah J. Foster, who was born July 22, 1848 and died January 25, 1871. He was then married August 2, 1871 to Amanda Isabelle Head, who was born December 14, 1848 and died August 25, 1895. He then married Charlotte Bell Coffelt January 19, 1896. Charlotte B. Coffelt was born September 6, 1862.

William Rich — 1847-1924

William and Sarah had the following children: James Frank, born March 19, 1867, and Marty J., born January 15, 1869. William and Amanda Isabell had the following children: Benton F., born July 27, 1873; Martha J., born April 27, 1875; Florintha F., born April 18, 1877; Grundy, born November 18, 1881; Arizona, born July 30, 1886; Omer, born in 1893; Louisiana, born in 1883; and Amanda, born in 1874. William and Charlotte Bell had the following children: Herbert Wilson, born January 16, 1897; Edmond H., born May 23, 1899; and Clyde, born March 1, 1902.

Hobert Wilson Rich was born January 16, 1897 and died June 29, 1965. He married Dessie M. Cherry, born October 14, 1896. They had the following children: Naoma, Creola, Doyle, Noel, Alvie, and Janetta.

Edmond H. Rich, born May 23, 1899, was married twice. He first married Maxie Smith, born April 24, 1900 and died September 3, 1943. They were the parents of Geneva, William Lee, and Buford. Edmond H. then married Marie Copas. They had no children.

Clyde Rich, born March 1, 1902, married Laura Smith. They had the following children: Ruth, Laura, Irene, Corrine, Hack, and Dow.

EDMOND H. RICH

Edmond H. Rich was born May 23, 1899 in Clay County, Tennessee. He was the son of William and Charlotte (Coffelt) Rich. Charlotte was the daughter of Jacob and Elizabeth (Thompson) Coffelt. Edmond was married twice. He first mar-

Edmond H. and Marie Rich

ried Maxie Smith, born April 24, 1900 — died September 3, 1943, the daughter of Henry Austin and Roxie (Hinson) Smith. Maxie is buried in the Hinson Cemetery in Union Hill. Edmond and Maxie had the following children: Buford, Geneva, William Lee, and Edward, born in 1929 and died 1931. William Lee married Genil Cherry, and they have one daughter, Marilyn.

Edmond next married Marie (Copas) Cherry, born February 21, 1914. They had no children.

Marie was previously married to Omas Cherry, born December 2, 1908 — died July 9, 1965, the son of Breckenridge and Maryntha (Wood) Cherry. Marie and Omas had five children. Robbie Genil, born April 23, 1934, married William Lee Rich, and they have one daughter, Marilyn. Inez, born March 15, 1936, married Donald Copass, and they have two children, Shela and Danny. Lena, born August 2, 1938, married Lex Smith, and they have three children: Reta, Allen, and Troy. Runell, born March 31, 1940, married Douglas Kemp, and they have one daughter, Kim. Carlon Sue, born August 12, 1944 — died September 2, 1944.

Edmond drove a road grader for 43 years, retiring at the age of 79. Edmond and Marie live in the Union Hill Community of Clay County. They are members of the Union Hill Church of Christ.

JOHN RICH

John Rich was born January 20, 1850 in Jackson County, (now Clay County) Tennessee. He was the son Elisha and Mary (Strong) Rich. Elisha was the son of James and Virginia (Peake) Rich. John had four sisters. They were Zane, Jennie, Zude, and Tin. He had three brothers. They were Will, Jim, and Roark. John was a farmer in the Midway and Macedonia Communities of Clay County. He was married three times. He first married L.A. (Missona) Welch, who was born February 2, 1852 and died April 15, 1894. They had the following children: Elisha, born August 26, 1872; Nancy (Nanny), born in 1874; Rosetta, born in 1876; Loudia, born in 1878; Leo (Doc); Albert; Dappie, born December 18, 1888; and Phillip, born May 30, 1892 and died March 17, 1976.

John was married the second time to Lenora Barbara Watson from the Turkeyneck Bend Area, who was born in July of 1864 and died February 17, 1905. They had the following children: Lovie, born in 1896; Sid, born May 4, 1898; Aus, born June 6, 1900 and died February 18, 1982; and Herman, born August 20 1902 and died March 31, 1975.

John was married the third time to Rhoda Kellow, who was born August 20, 1882 and died

May 26, 1961, the daughter of Arch and Mary Ann Kellow. They had the following children: Vina, born March 1, 1908; James Lester, born April 17, 1909 and died October 8, 1976; Stella; John Buford; and Dorothy. John and Rhoda were members of the Midway Church of Christ. John died September 6, 1932. He and his wives are buried in the Macedonia Cemetery.

Elisha Rich married Mollie Brown. They had the following children: Haskel, Wade, Luther, Zelma, Bill, and Zurie. Rosetta Rich married Tim Stevens. They had one son, Fowler. Phillip first married Jeddie Johnson. They had three children, Alma, Eva Dee, and James Phillip (Sonny Boy). Phillip married Rosie White the second time. Lovie Rich married Alto White. They had four children, Clema, Delno, Clarsie, and Wilburn. Sidney Rich married Kate Stockton and they had the following children: Clifton, Louise, and Tim. Herman Rich married Robbie Kidwell the first time. They had one son, James Earl.

Dorothy, John and Elva Rich

Herman married Ila Adams the second time. James Lester Rich married Jewel Huffines and they had the following children: Sybil, Iva Mae, Joanna, Quell, Geniel, and Durrell. Stella Rich married Hubert Atchley. Vina Rich first married Donald Crowder, and they had two children, Clotiel and Johnny Radford. She then married Lemuel Smith. Dorothy Rich married Willis "Bill" Arms, and they have one daughter, Dorothy Martin. John Buford "Boose" Rich first married Edith Lee, and they had two sons, Bobby and Johnnie. He then married Ada Short. Johnnie Rich married Betty Carter, and they have the following children: Teresa Ann, Dana Gail, Jennifer Lynn, and John Barry.

JOE RICH

Joe Rich, born April 12, 1839, the son of Alfred and Nancy Bowman Rich, spent his childhood on a 200 acre farm in Clay County (then Jackson County). It was worth about $3,000 when the war began. A log house, with two rooms and an upstairs with a kitchen separate but near the house, was home to Joe until he entered the War in 1861 as a Confederate soldier. On the farm, he had helped his father, who was a blacksmith and a farmer, make plows, wagons, and carts while his mother spent her time cooking, spinning yarn and weaving cloth. No servants or slaves were employed in this household. However, others in the community owned slaves during this time. Joe attended common public schools, but he never attended a "subscription school" for over six weeks. His entire schooling totaled only four months. Schools were in session only two or three months a year, and attendance was very irregular.

Forrest Ellwood, Joe, Laura and Hester Rich

Joe Rich enlisted in the Army of Confederacy in Clarksville, Tennessee in June or July of 1861 and was sent first to Bowling Green, Kentucky. He engaged in battle first at Shiloh. He went from there to Carence, Mississippi, then on to the Upper Fort at Vicksburg to fire upon warships as they traveled up and down the river. From there, his troops journeyed to territory near the capitol of Louisiana where they fought all one Sunday. Soon they returned to Murfreesboro, Tennessee. He also served under General Bragg at Missionary Ridge and Chickamauga. During these years, Joe spent only three days in a hospital. He was awarded his discharge at Columbus, Mississippi in May of 1865.

Joe Rich first married Catherine Green and to this union was born eight children. When this wife died, Joe was approximately fifty years of age. While attending a community picnic one Sunday afternoon, Joe saw a beautiful brunette with long curls blowing in the wind as she ran across an open field. Joe turned to his friend and said. "I want to marry that girl." A courtship followed, and Laura Belle Watson, 25 years old, was married to Joe Rich, 58 years old, December 31, 1897. To this union was born Hester in 1902 and Forrest Ellwood in 1906. Hester died at the age of 16 of pneumonia. She was engaged to marry Joe Pole Overstreet at the time. She was buried with a gold watch he had given her.

Joe and Laura traveled to New Mexico when the children were young. They made the trip in covered wagons. There Joe worked on a dairy farm and was closely associated with the Indians. He learned many things from them. His homeland was Tennessee; so he returned and spent his remaining years in Clay County. He died in 1933. To the Clay Countians who knew Joe Rich, he was remembered as a dedicated Confederate hero who always walked in a noticeable, straight, upright manner as though he were still marching in General Bragg's Army. He was an upstanding citizen who stood for honesty, integrity, and all the values Americans cherish; but most of all he was remembered as a loving and proud husband, father and grandfather.

Forrest Ellwood Rich, the son of Joe Rich, married Dorothy Frances Dale February 3, 1929 in Clay County. They traveled to Nashville by steamboat on the Cumberland River for a one-night honeymoon.

Forrest was known for his skills as a carpenter; and Dorothy was an accomplished pianist. Forrest and Dorothy had seven children: Forrest Dale, 1929; Robert Ellwood, 1936; Elizabeth Ann, 1938; Lauretta, 1940; Jack Terry, 1943; Ray Frances, 1944; and Mary Emma, 1947.

Laura Belle Watson Rich died in July of 1958.

Forrest Ellwood Rich died August 14, 1951. Dorothy Frances Dale Rich died January 14, 1984. Forrest Dale Rich died November 17, 1978.

JOHN H. RICHARDSON

John H. Richardson, born about 1787 in Virginia, was the son of Williamson Richardson, of Virginia, who was born in England. He was among the first settlers of what is now Fentress County, Tennessee, a portion of Kentucky before the revision of the state line between the State of Kentucky and Tennessee. John H. was appointed Clerk of the County Court when the county was created and held the office by appointment until it became law that the clerk be elected by the people. He was successively elected every term until his death, about 40 years later.

John H. Richardson married Abigail Hildreth in 1805. Abigail was the daughter of Geoffrey and Lillie Bowen Hildreth. To this union was born twelve children, the seventh being William H. Richardson. He was married to Julia Ann Kirkpatrick September 3, 1841. She was the daughter of William and Tabitha Wallace Kirkpatrick of Monroe County, Kentucky. To them was born Carol H., Tabitha (Shives), Ellen (Coe), William K., Geoffry H., Almarine, Albert, Lucy (Smith), Robert, Belle (Smith), and Thomas.

Carol H. Richardson (1842-1923) was married to Rebecca Barksdale (1848-1892). Rebecca was the daughter of John Barksdale and Elizabeth Nevins Barksdale. They had ten children: Ida Mae (Goodpasture), Lucettie died young, Mattie Belle (Dowell), Annie Laura (Haile), Mary Elizabeth (Rich), John, Russ, who died at the age of 31, George died young, Irene (Tinsley), and Barlow.

Carol and Rebecca lived on a farm that was part of the land deeded to William Barksdale in 1804 by Sampson Williams. William Barksdale was the grandfather of Rebecca Barksdale. This land remained in the Barksdale family until it was inundated by the Dale Hollow Dam in 1943, 139 years later. This land was located just above Dale Hollow Dam. Pleasant Grove Park and Recreation Area are part of this farm.

Ida Mae Richardson (1870-1952) was married to Thomas Frances Goodpasture (1871-1957) August 27, 1889. To them was born five children: Della (1890-1979) married Arthur Terry; Auburn (1893-1967) married Ethel Keisling, and his second marriage was to Mattie Terry; Winnie (1897-1972) married Harris Clark; Velma (1903-) married Cecil Smith; and Hazel (1909-) married Homer Gates.

MICHAEL RICHARDSON

Michael Gordon Richardson was born September 10, 1949 in Oak Ridge, Tennessee. He is the son of Everett Gordon Richardson and Jane Elizabeth (Garland) Richardson. He graduated from Oak Ridge High School in 1967 and enlisted in the United States Navy that same year. Upon leaving the service in 1971, Mike continued in the Navy Reserve and entered Tennessee Technological University at Cookeville, Tennessee. He graduated in June, 1975 with a Bachelor of Science degree in Agriculture. He managed a feed and garden store in Oak Ridge until February of 1977 when he accepted a position with the United States Department of Agriculture Soil Conservation Service. Mike worked for the Soil Conser-

vation Service in Williamson County and Overton County prior to coming to Clay County in January of 1979. He is presently the district conservationist for Clay County and is active in many civic organizations, including Cub Scouts, Chamber of Commerce, Sportsmans Club, Rural Area Development Committee, and Homecoming '86. Mike enjoys hunting, fishing, golf, bowling, and is a student of karate.

Mike was married to Linda Louise Smith of Janesville, Wisconsin on June 9, 1973. Linda was born in Janesville, January 5, 1950. She is the daughter of Robert Wayne Smith and Dorothy Joyce (Pope) Smith.

Linda attended Rock County, Wisconsin schools, graduating in 1967. She attended the University of Wisconsin at Madison until June of 1971, graduating Magna Cum Laude with a Bachelor of Science in physical medicine and a certificate in physical therapy. She moved to Oak Ridge, Tennessee in 1971 where she met Mike. Linda has worked as staff and/or chief physical therapist at hospitals, rehabilitation centers, nursing homes, and for private and state home health agencies in Oak Ridge, Knoxville, Nashville, and several east and middle Tennessee counties. She is currently Chief of Physical Therapy at the Clay County Hospital and serves the nursing home and home health care agency here.

Linda helped start a parent support group to buy playground equipment for the Celina K-8 School, then helped initiate a Parent-Teacher Organization for Celina schools in 1985, and was elected the Parent-Teacher Organization's first president. She is also active in the local chapter of the American Cancer Society.

Mike and Linda are the parents of John Michael, born May 6, 1978, and Laurel Diana, born September 21, 1982. John is a student at Celina K-8 and is active in Cub Scouts and karate. Laurel attends Carrie and Herman Brown's day care home.

ROBERT R. RILEY

"Uncle Bob," Robert Robinson Riley was born at Fox Springs in 1855, the son of John and Rachel (Martin) Riley. He was the grandson of Isaac Riley, a veteran of George Washington's army, who later emigrated from the Shenandoah Valley in Virginia, to what is now Pickett County, Tennessee, settling on a large tract of land on the Wolf River. His mother, Rachel (Martin) Riley, was a daughter of Joseph Martin, who was with John Sevier and others when Ferguson was driven from King's Mountain. He moved from North Carolina in 1804, settling on a large tract of land on Obed's (Obey) River in what is now Clay County, Tennessee.

"Uncle Bob" Riley

Rachel Martin first married William B. Chowning. By him she had three children: Joe Chat Chowning, Larissa (who married Joshua L. Chilton), and Seraphine (who married Dudley Hunter, and after his death, Thaddeus Kyle). Mr. Chowning was a casualty of a yellow fever epidemic in New Orleans where he had gone by flatboat to market his grain, tobacco and livestock.

John and Rachel had the following children: Robert Robinson "Uncle Bob"; William Albert, who died in young manhood; Ruth Frances, who married Dr. W.N. Gray; and Sterling Price, who married James W. Henson.

"Uncle Bob's" formal education was limited, but his knowledge was extensive and covered a wide range of subjects. He once said, "I was educated in the University of Hard Knocks and did post graduate study in the School of Experience." He was a natural mathematician and an omnivorous reader. He was conversant with current events. He was a champion of schools and did much to promote educational progress within his sphere of action.

At an early age, "Uncle Bob" showed signs of being mischievous, a prankster, and a perpetrator of harmless, but amusing, practical jokes.

"When 'Uncle Bob' reached the age of 21, he was 'set free' by his father. This was an old custom that prevailed for almost a century in this section of the country. He was presented with a horse, a bridle, a saddle, and a saddle blanket and was then 'free' to choose his own course in life or to follow his own inclinations. If the young man chose to live in his parents' home, he was welcome to do so. John Riley allowed his son to cultivate a crop on his land; and no rent was charged. He made a good crop of corn the first year of his 'freedom' but so did everyone else; so 'Uncle Bob' distilled his crop into corn liquor. (There was no law against this practice.) He found this to be unremunerative and otherwise distasteful as it was only worth about 25 cents a gallon.

"He had dreamed of becoming a 'woodsman', later called 'lumberman.' " His uncle, William Hull, had already engaged in this business. "Uncle Bob's" mother loaned him $800 to go with his $200 to get the $1000 needed to go into business with "Uncle Billy" Hull, who had devised the plan of shipping logs to Nashville by making rafts and floating them down creeks to the Obey and Cumberland Rivers and thence to Nashville. The firm of Hull and Riley would buy a tract of timber, each paying half the price and operating expenses. Profits and/or losses were shared equally. When the land was stripped of timber, it was sold for a small price to someone who could not pay more. Hull wanted to deed the property outright, but "Uncle Bob" reserved all oil and mineral rights. This was one of the differences which led to the dissolution of the firm. Their joint venture was a great success financially, and each man was now in a position to go it alone.

"Uncle Bob" later moved his operation to Fentress County where he stood with the miners in their opposition to mine operators. "Uncle Bob" did not believe in the methods of dealing with men who were forced to submit to injustice and indignities in order to support themselves and the mine operators became furious at his "meddling" as they called it. "Uncle Bob" was ambushed in August of 1903. Dr. M.B. Capps thought that "Uncle Bob" was mortally wounded. He called for Dr. Duncan Eve, Dean of Vanderbilt Medical College, to come. The railroad track was cleared and in six hours, Dr. Eve and his staff were in Wilder by the bedside having come straight through by train. Dr. Eve said that he could just be kept comfortable until the end. "Uncle Bob" heard this and told him that if the doctor wished he would serve as pallbearer at the doctor's funeral. "Uncle Bob" survived and did serve as pallbearer at the doctor's funeral.

In 1907, "Uncle Bob" settled on his father's farm. He was a prosperous and highly respected citizen. Not long afterward, he married Mrs. Trudie Brown, the widow of John Brown and the daughter of A.P. Chilton. They had three children, Rachel, who married Thomas Langford, John Albert, and Marshall, who died in infancy.

He lived in Celina for a few years while his son and daughter were in school, commuting back and forth to the farm, He was a favorite of all "teenage" and under boys and girls because of his pranks, jokes and escapades which he often related to them. One of the most often told and enjoyed stories goes as follows: On one occasion "Uncle Bob" rode from his father's farm to Willow Grove, about six miles away. The route crossed a ridge community known as Sourwood. As he was passing the small country store, one of the more than half a dozen or more loafers on the store porch greeted him and said: "Stop a bit and tell us one of your big lies, Bob." Without slackening the pace of his horse, he answered, "No, I ain't got no time. Old Aunt Jane Chowning died suddenly this morning and I am on my way to Mt. Pisgah to help dig her grave." (In those days, when someone died, the neighbors would gather at the cemetery to dig the grave.) The storekeeper closed his place of business, and he and the loafers gathered their picks and shovels and started to Mt. Pisgah to help dig Aunt Jane's grave. Enroute, they passed her home, and as they came in sight, they saw the good old lady seated on her front porch churning and singing "Oh, they tell me of a home far beyond the skies, Oh, they tell me of an unclouded day." Late in the afternoon, as "Uncle Bob" was returning, one of the men said: "Bob, why did you tell us that big lie about Aunt Jane?" Bob said "You fellows wanted me to stop and tell you one of my big lies and I did not have time."

He loved sports of all kinds, boxing, wrestling, horse racing, hunting and fishing. He loved life; he loved his family and his friends. He loved fun; he loved to do good deeds, but, overall and above all, he loved honor, which to him was the most sublime word in any language. — Taken from an article by Charles P. Gray.

WILLIAM JAMES RITTER
William James Ritter was born June 9, 1818 in Tennessee. He married Leah Jobe, who was born November 28, 1820. They had four children, Abigail, who married Henry Fowler; Katie Ritter; Nathan, who married Mary Word; and James Taylor, who married Kittie Brandon. The Ritter family lived in the Centerville area of Clay County and nearby Monroe County, Kentucky.

Nathan and Mary were large landowners near Centerville and reared five daughters. Elizabeth Hill moved to Mississippi. Clarence and Nova Clements operated a general store in Centerville and were farmers. Estil and Blanche Burnette operated general stores at Boles and Moss and a dry goods store in Celina. Archie and Ruth Mullinix lived near Centerville. Archie was a school bus driver and farmer. Buford and Ruby Watkins moved to Ohio.

James Taylor Ritter, who was born February 25, 1861, married Kittie Brandon, who was born February 29, 1862. They had six children, Minnie, William, Charlie, Leah, Nathan, and Eva. Minnie married Avery Craighead and had nine children. They lived in or near Barren County, Kentucky. William married Callie Gulley; they had one son, Hilburn. Charlie married Della Cherry and moved to Monroe County, Kentucky. They had three children. Nathan married Texie Capshaw. They had three children and lived in Tompkinsville, Kentucky. Eva married Hardy McLerran and lived in Illinois and Clay County.

Hilburn Ritter was born January 11, 1906 in Clay County. On December 23, 1929, he married Willie Nelson, who was born June 30, 1906. They had two daughters, Eloise and Neva.

Neva married Eugene King. They lived in Iowa and had three children.

Eloise married Louis Taylor and lived in Murfreesboro, Tennessee where Louis was Brigadier General in the Tennessee National Guard. They had one child, Deborah, who earned a law degree from the University of Tennessee, and was on Governor Lamar Alexander's staff in the State Capitol. Deborah married William Howard Tate. They have two children, Will and Taylor. They reside in Nashville, Tennessee.

FRED WAYNE ROACH
Fred Wayne Roach was born March 17, 1950. He is the son of Waymon Lee and Elise Hull Roach. He was married May 28, 1972 to Anita Cherry, who was born October 18, 1950. She is the daughter of Wyatt Estes and Ersie Condra Cherry.

Fred, Lance and Anita Roach

Fred is a truck driver and is employed by the Celina Oil Company. Anita is employed by the Bank of Celina.

Fred and Anita have one son, Lance Wyatt, who was born March 29, 1979. Lance attends Celina K-8 School. Anita is a member of the Arcot Church of Christ.

SMITH ROBERTS
Smith Roberts was born February 14, 1881 and died February 18, 1957. He was the son of Carol, born in 1848, and Martha Whitaker Roberts, born in 1852. They had nine children, Meda Alice, Edd, Lula, Mandy, Smith, Granville, Bob, Carlie, and Donie.

Smith married Mary Cherry in May 1903.

Smith and Mary Roberts

Mary was born March 13, 1880 and died July 13, 1974. She was the daughter of General, born November 4, 1854, and Mary Ellen Dodd Cherry. They had six children, Vina Cherry Richardson, Jeff Cherry, Rosco Cherry, Mary Cherry Roberts, Josie Cherry, and Ada Cherry Davenport. General Cherry then married Almary Whitaker and they had five children, Vira Cherry Clark, Beulah Cherry Browning, Grover Cherry, Sylvia Cherry Browning, and Melvin Cherry.

Mary was the granddaughter of Finis and Polly Wood Cherry. They had four children, Wilson Cherry; Sarah Cherry; Sam Cherry, who got killed in the army; and General Cherry. Finis was killed in the Civil War. Polly then married Ernie Brown. Mary was the great granddaughter of Wilson Cherry, Sr. and Catherine Hodge Cherry.

Wilson Cherry and Elizabeth Whitaker Cherry had six children, Radford, Roscoe, Finis, Palo, Smith, and Draper.

Smith and Mary Roberts had eight children.

1. Avo was born June 26, 1906 and died July 22, 1907.

2. Irvin was born December 7, 1907. He married Maylene Birdwell, born September 25, 1908. They had three sons.

Irvin was born October 30, 1934. He married Priscilla Copas, born October 14, 1943, April 26, 1961. They have three children, Angela Yvonne, born December 14, 1964; Pamela Diane, born October 30, 1969; and Gina Renee, born March 9, 1974.

Michael was born March 15, 1938. He married Brenda Wilson, born July 27, 1941, December 25, 1958. They have one daughter, Michelle, born August 2, 1961. She married Randall Edward Hedges, born May 29, 1957, August 15, 1981. They have two children, Michael Nelson, born March 4, 1983, and Daniel Howard, born May 17, 1986.

Joe was born July 7, 1943. He married Carol Murray, born December 17, 1947, December 19, 1964. They have two sons, Robert, born June 5, 1966, and Shane, born July 8, 1970.

Irvin was killed working on the construction of the Dale Hollow Dam July 22, 1943.

3. Cancel was born May 12, 1913.

4. Sylvia was born October 9, 1918 and died August 22, 1919.

5. Herman was born September 13, 1920 and died March 18, 1984.

GUY AND JEWEL ROBERTS
Guy was one of the eight children born to Smith and Mary Roberts. He was born in the Mt. Vernon Community of Clay County November 26, 1909. He is a retired school teacher and farmer and has lived in Mt. Vernon all his life. On

Jewell, Guy, Sue, Dean, and Joann Roberts

November 27, 1934, he married Jewel Reeves who was born June 11, 1915. She died March 21, 1983. They had three children, Sue, Joann, and Ronald Dean.

Sue was born September 23, 1935. She has been a factory worker and is presently employed at the Hermitage Springs Bank. She married A.C. Bean who was born October 26, 1931. He died Sept. 25, 1974. They had one daughter, Gail, born April 7, 1954. She married Dale Beaty and they have one son, Michael, born August 14, 1973. Sue then married Bobby Wilburn, born September 3, 1934. They live in the Mt. Vernon Community.

Joann was born June 13, 1937. She married Veachel Williams, who was born March 10, 1934. They have two children, Sharon, born January 12, 1959, and Ronald, born November 23, 1967. Joann and Veachel moved to Georgia where they now reside.

Ronald Dean was born November 11, 1940. He attended Tennessee Polytechnic Institute and has been a schoolteacher and principal in the Clay County Schools for several years. He married Deborah Armer, who was born September 3, 1952. They have two children, Chris, born October 16, 1974, and Nicole, born December 1, 1978.

CLURE AND NELLIE BIRDWELL

Nellie was one of the eight children born to Smith and Mary Roberts. She was born in the Mt. Vernon Community May 10, 1916. On December 25, 1934, she married Clure Birdwell who was born January 26, 1911. He was the son of Mr. and Mrs. Herod Birdwell, Sr. Nellie has been a housewife all her life and Clure has been a farmer, factory worker, grocer, and carpenter. He is now retired. They had two sons. Dillard Eugene was born November 19, 1943 and died November 3, 1944.

Donald Ray, Clure and Nellie (Roberts) Birdwell

Donald Ray was born December 14, 1935. He married Louise Clark of Celina, Tennessee. She was born November 2, 1939. They moved to Red Boiling Springs, Tennessee, where Donald Ray started working for Macon Bank and Trust Company. He is now the president of this bank. They have three sons, Don, Doug, and Robert.

Don was born October 21, 1958. He married Jill Dycus, born in February 1954. They have one daughter, Laveda Donyelle, born April 2, 1986.

Doug was born May 15, 1960. He married Linda Mesker, who was born in January 1967.

Robert was born June 10, 1965. He married Cathy Smith, who was born in June 1966. They have one son, Derik, born December 26, 1985.

WILLIAM ROBERTS, SR.

William (Billy) Kirkpatrick Roberts, Sr. was born March 29, 1851 and died May 18, 1880. Billy, Sr. married Nancy Tinsley. She was from Tinsley's Bottom. Helen Arms Wells was her namesake and granddaughter. Billy was a descendant of Hugh Roberts, who originally built the old log "Roberts House" in Pennsylvania in 1780. Hugh tore it down and made it into a large raft, floated it down the Ohio and Cumberland Rivers to Celina, Tennessee and rebuilt it on the "Old Roberts Hill" in Clay County.

William Roberts, Jr., Campbelle and Laura

Billy was a farmer, and ran a tanning farm tanning leather. Billy and Nancy lived on the "Roberts Hill", which is near the present location of Clay County Hospital. Their children were Campbelle, Horace, Roxie, and Billy, Jr.

Campbelle married Lizzie Whaley. Their children were Nannie Belle, Hugh, Horace, Bruce, Elizabeth, Dorothy, Esther, and Campbelle Jewell. Horace died at about two years of age. Roxie married Elbert Clark. Their children were Anna (who married Willie Hugh Stone. Their children were Lillian, Jean and Mary Jo.); Willie; Nora Alice; John; Malcolm; Joe; and Steve. Billy, Jr. married Laura Belle Arms. Their children were Campbelle, Lester, and Willie George. Campbelle married Wealthia Nevins. They had no children. Lester married Ruthie Cook. They had one daughter, Louise. Willie George married Katherine Sims. They had one daughter, Sue. Her children are Jeffrey Arms, Jerry Arms, Jan Laura Arms, Willie George Allred, and Julianne Allred.

Billy, Sr. died May 18, 1880 and is buried on his property behind the "Roberts Hill". Nancy's second husband was John Henry Stone. They had eight children. My mother, Dayse Lucretia, was one of those children. — *Submitted by Helen Arms Wells*

ISAAC C. RUSH

Isaac C. Rush was born February 13, 1832 in Monroe County, Kentucky and died March 15, 1899 in Clay County, Tennessee. He was the son of Benjamin Rush, who was born in North Carolina July 16, 1782 and who died October 9, 1843 in Monroe Co., Kentucky, and Rachel (Springer) Rush, who was born April 26, 1786 in Union County, South Carolina and who died March 17, 1884 in Monroe Co., Kentucky. Rachel was married the second time December 24, 1853 to William Chism. Rachel was the daughter of Ezekiel Springer, who was born in 1754, and Rebecca (Collins) Springer. Ezekiel was the son of Charles Springer, who was born in 1735, the son of James Springer, born in 1703. James Springer was the son of Charles Springer, who was born in 1658, the son of Christopher Springer, born in 1592. Benjamin and Rachel (Springer) Rush were married July 1, 1803 in Barren County, Kentucky by the Reverend John Mulkey. They were members of the Old Mulkey Church near Tompkinsville, Kentucky.

Isaac C. Rush married in 1849 Brilla Moore, who was born December 25, 1830 and died March 5, 1900. She was the daughter of John W. Moore, born 1804. Isaac C. was in the Union Army during the Civil War. He served in The Fifth Kentucky Calvary. He moved to Clay County (then Jackson County) around 1866 and settled between Miles Cross Roads and Hermitage Springs. He built a log house on his farm. This house is still standing today.

Isaac and Brilla were the parents of nine children: Elswick; Lemuel; Lucettie, born May 11, 1857; Newton; Levi S.; Cyrus Haden, Sr., born September 31, 1861; John E.; Martha, born December 15, 1873; and George Anderson. Lucettie Rush, born May 11, 1857 and died July 27, 1934, married John Carnahan, born 1845 and died 1920. Their children were Isaac, Minnie, Rutha, and Brillie.

Isaac C. Rush Home

Cyrus Haden Rush, Sr. lived in the log house after his father. He was first married to Elizabeth Bean, the daughter of James C. and Sarah Bean. Cyrus H. and Elizabeth were married December 1, 1881. Their children were Sarah (born December 8, 1886 and died December 11, 1965); Sam (born September 13, 1888 and died September 18, 1974); Ada B. (born January 11, 1892 and died July 17, 1958). Elizabeth Bean Rush died April 22, 1914. Cyrus Haden, Sr. then married Mary Lou Loftis from Jackson County, Tennessee.

Cyrus H. and Mary Lou had three children, Cyrus Haden, Jr. (born April 16, 1917); Brilla Jane (born December 12, 1918); and Louvenia (born December 23, 1920).

Louvenia Rush married George Donald Gentry in 1945. They moved to the Rush home place in

1955, to the house that Louvenia's grandfather built.

The Rush log home is over one hundred years old. Louvenia Rush Gentry still lives in the "House," which has had several additions since it was built, but which still has the original big logs and huge beams.

George Donald died in September of 1982. Donald and Louvenia made a living farming and raised their seven children from farm income. George Danny Gentry, their fourth child, still farms "the place."

CYRUS HADEN RUSH, SR.

Cyrus Haden Rush, Sr. was born March 31, 1861. He married Mary Lou Loftis of Jackson County, Tennessee March 12, 1916. Mary was born on February 5, 1888. They had three children, Cyrus Haden, Jr., Brilla, and Louvenia.

Brilla married Bransford Cherry. They have eight children, Lourenia, Royce, Vancel, Wanda, Joyce, Lois, Lennis, and Garnett.

Louvenia married Donald Gentry. They have seven children, Geraldine, Ercil, Gail, Danny, Vachel, Sheila and Lesia.

Andrew Davis, born November 5, 1892, married Susan Mary Birdwell August 29, 1914. Susan Mary was born November 29, 1893. They lived on a farm in the Mount Vernon Community. They had two children, Odell and Weldon. Weldon married Clodean Browning.

Cyrus and Odell Rush, Jr.

Cyrus Haden Rush, Jr. was born April 16, 1917. He married Odell Davis December 31, 1939. Odell was born February 13, 1918. They lived in Clay County, in the Mount Vernon Community, for five years before moving to Indianapolis, Indiana in 1944. They lived there for about seven years. They had four children during this time. However, all four were born in Tennessee. Cyrus worked at the United States Rubber Plant, and Odell worked at Cramer's Furniture Plant. Around 1952, Cyrus and Odell moved back to Clay Co. and bought the "Coon" Browning farm. Their fifth child was born in 1954. Cyrus worked as a farmer until he retired in 1979. Cyrus passed away September 21, 1983. Odell taught school at Mount Vernon, Union Hill, Hermitage Springs and Oak Grove, a one-teacher school. She also taught at Enon and Red Boiling Springs in Macon County. She is now retired.

Cyrus and Odell had the following children: Juanita, Dean, Elwanda, Sue and Peggy. Juanita married Randall Gass, a logger, and they have one son, Brian. Juanita works at Clay Sportswear.

Dean married Gayla Hewitt, a housewife, and they have two sons, Kevin and Waylon. Dean teaches at Central Elementary in Lafayette.

Elwanda married Willie (Dude) Meadows, and they had one son, Jody. Elwanda taught at Headstart in Celina and at Enon Elementary in Macon County. She also taught in Sumner County. Due to illness, she was forced into an early retirement. She passed away January 11, 1979.

Sue married Bobby Meadows, presently Clay County Circuit Court Clerk. They have two sons, Robin and Robert. Sue is a beautician and substitutes at Hermitage Springs School.

Peggy married Jerry Kirby who works for the State Department of Transportation. Peggy teaches special education classes at Hermitage Springs School.

SAM RUSH

Sam Rush was born September 13, 1888 in the west end of Clay County, Tennessee. He was the son of Cyrus Haden Rush, Sr. and Elizabeth Bean Rush. He married Celina Alise Tennessee Bean, who was born August 31, 1886 and died March 19, 1965. She was the daughter of James and Arcena Davis Bean. They lived near the Hermitage Springs Community of Clay County. Sam was a well driller in Clay and surrounding counties. He died September 19, 1978. Sam and Celina Alise are buried in the Mount Vernon Cemetery in the west end of Clay County.

Tennessee and Sam Rush

They were the parents of six children: Mamie (Purcell), born February 3, 1912; Amie (Pedigo), born January 15, 1914; Flevel, born September 22, 1916; Beford Herman, born February 14, 1919; Elise (Green), born August 5, 1920; and Reba (McCarter), born June 1, 1926.

LEVIN J. SAVAGE, JR.

Levin J. Savage, Jr. was born in Surry County, North Carolina in 1789. Rachel Odle Savage was born June 20, 1846 and died February 4, 1928. They were the parents of three children, Andrew, Julia, and Mary Belle.

Aunt Rach (Big Mammy to her grandchildren) was best known as a midwife. She lived near the New Hope Church of Christ, and really believed that it was her duty to see that people were at church each Sunday. She would travel through the crowd on the church grounds, inviting people to dinner at her house. This was evidence that she cared about people, as she was a member of the Baptist Church.

CHARLES BARTON SAVAGE

Charles Barton Savage, born December 24, 1951, the only son of Willie Virgil Savage, born

Leah and Charles B. Savage and daughters, Anna and Lara

December 6, 1924, and Edith Christine Bailey, born April 25, 1932, was reared in the Vernon Community of Clay County. His three sisters are Virginia Carolyn, born December 7, 1949; Vickie Lou, born September 23, 1956; and Rita Ann, born October 19, 1959. Carolyn married Keith Plumlee, born November 15, 1950, and they have a daughter, Casey Ann, born February 15, 1977. Vickie married David Harrell, born April 6, 1952, and they have two sons, David Christopher, born September 5, 1973, and William Bradley, born December 9, 1975. Rita married Robert Thompson Deal, born March 4, 1957, and they have two sons, Robert Ryan, born October 29, 1980, and Ross Matthew, born March 12, 1984.

Charles is the grandson of Hugh Barton Bailey, born June 27, 1906, and Mary Daffo Weaver, born March 22, 1911, and Charlie Edgar Savage, who died June 7, 1926, and Carmack Edward Dunning, born August 20, 1901.

Charles married Marion Leah Craighead, born October 24, 1956, August 15, 1981. She is the second of four children born to Marion Ralph Craighead, born January 2, 1922, and Jo Frances Gates, born July 23, 1930. Other siblings of Ralph and Jo Frances Craighead are: Robert Stanley, born May 3, 1955, is married to Deborah Davis, born April 5, 1959; Kathie Gene, born May 10, 1955, is married to Christopher Ridge, born April 12, 1958, and they have one daughter, Abigail Marie, born December 19, 1981; and Donna Frances, born August 19, 1960, is married to Keith Knox Ferguson, born November 16, 1956.

Charles and Leah have two daughters, Anna Frances, born November 23, 1983, and Lara Christen, born January 23, 1985, and they reside in Moss. Charles is a farmer, and Leah teaches vocational food management at the Tri-County Vocational School.

JAMES BUCHANAN SCOTT

James Buchanan (Buck) Scott, the son of Alfred Scott and Nancy (Scott) Scott, was born March 8, 1857 near the Cumberland County, Kentucky/Clay County, Tennessee line. His siblings were Andrew Jackson, born January 5, 1854; Ollie Jane, born March 11, 1855; Mary Eunice, born April 1, 1860; Winfield, born October 13, 1861; John, born August 12, 1864; Milt, born May 10, 1867; and Joe, born July 12, 1869.

Ollie Frances Willis, the daughter of Charlie Willis and Euna (Williams) Willis, was born December 25, 1861 in Cumberland County, Kentucky. Her siblings were Miles and Lina. Her half-brothers were Albert, Curtis, and Ambrose

James Buchanan and Ollie Frances Scott

Watson, and a half-sister, Alice Watson. Charlie Willis was with the 5th Kentucky Calvary during the Civil War and fought for the Union. He died of measles during the Battle of Lookout Mountain and is buried at Chattanooga.

Buck Scott married Ollie Frances Willis April 19, 1879. They lived in the Willis Bottom section of Clay County, an area now covered by the Dale Hollow Reservior. To this union were born 14 children. They were Miles Winfield, born July 19, 1880 and died January 12, 1882; Perry Brance, born January 5, 1882; Erasie Virgil, born November 27, 1883; Walter Howard, born November 13, 1885; Dora Alice, born December 22, 1888 and died August 24, 1908; William Carlie, born February 8, 1890; Ambrose Rite, born February 20, 1892; George Curtis, born March 28, 1894; Charlie Finis, born March 16, 1896; Alta Mae, born May 21, 1899 and died December 16, 1899; Mary Eunice, born October 1, 1902; Cordie Homer, born August 28, 1908 and two children who died at birth.

Brance married Ora Scott, and they had nine children, Lester, Nellie, Pearl, Paul, Warren, Christine, Gracie, Elbert, and Bessie. They moved to the Vernon Community in Monroe County, Kentucky.

Virgil married Flossie Spears and they had ten children, Denver, Gordon, Grady, Nova, Josephine, Lucille, Mary Elizabeth, Haskell, Maxwell, and Willie Mae. They moved to Indianapolis, Indiana, when they were forced to move from the Willis Bottom area because of the Dale Hollow Dam.

Howard married Delia Spears, and they had eight children, with seven living to adulthood. They were Raymond, Lela, Frances, James, Russell, Joe, and Quinton. They moved to Granite, Oklahoma and then to Bells, California.

Carlie married Ada Spears, and they had seven children, James, Ivy, Cecil, Vecheal, Louise, John Hubert, and Paul. They moved to Hendersonville, Tennessee.

Ambrose married Melia Thompson, and they had two children, Winona and Cero. They moved to Nashville, Tennessee.

George Curtis married Avo Ledbetter, and they had seven children, George, Jr., Jack, Ruth, Betty, Ollie, Joyce, and Mary Etta. They remained in the Clay County area.

Charlie married Belle Davis, and they had five children, Hoye, Troy, Quanita, Opal, and Frances. They moved to Danville, Indiana when they were forced to move because of the Dale Hollow Dam.

Mary Eunice never married and lived in Clay County until her death.

Homer married Dollie Thompson, and they

had two children, Gemilla and Bruce. They moved to Nashville, Tennessee.

James Buchanan and Ollie Frances Scott and their children, Dora, Eunice, Brance, Charlie, Ambrose and Homer, are buried in the Scott Cemetery (land given by Alfred Scott) in Cumberland County, Kentucky. George Curtis is buried in Celina; Howard is buried in Bells, California; Virgil is buried in Indianapolis; and Carlie is buried in Hendersonville.

The only descendants from this family that continue to live in the Clay County area are two daughters of George Curtis, Joyce (Scott) Witham and Mary Etta (Scott) Sherrell, and one son of Brance, Elbert Scott.

ELBERT T. SCOTT

Elbert T. Scott was born February 27, 1922 in Vernon, Kentucky. He is the son of Perry Brance Scott and Ora Catherine Scott. Elbert attended Monroe County, Kentucky schools and graduated from Tompkinsville High School in 1940. He is presently a farmer and used auto dealer in the Beech Bethany Community.

Elbert and Ruby Scott

He entered the military service, United States Army, in December, 1942. Elbert served for three and a half years and then was released to the reserves as a First Lieutenant.

Elbert worked at the Dale Hollow Powerhouse and Dam until he was again called to active duty during the Korean conflict. During this time he was Battery Commander of Battery 'A', 623rd Field Artillery, Kentucky National Guard, Tompkinsville, Kentucky. Elbert was promoted to Captain while in Korea. Upon returning home, he again went to work at the Dale Hollow Powerhouse with the United States Corps of Engineers, holding a number of titles until his retirement February 27, 1979. During the last 15 years of service, prior to his retirement, Elbert was the Powerhouse Superintendent.

Elbert was married to Ruby Fowler Stone of Celina May 10, 1942. Ruby is the daughter of Amos Tinsley Stone and Martha Gladys Smith. She is the granddaughter of Clark Fowler Smith and Mattie Belle Dale and John H. Stone and Nannie H. Tinsley.

Ruby attended Beech Bethany Grade School and graduated from Celina High School in 1937. She was employed by the Bank of Celina, where she worked until October 1942.

Elbert and Ruby have two children, Emma Jean, born February 2, 1945, and Perry Stone Scott, born July 2, 1955.

Elbert and Ruby are members of the Church of Christ.

EMMA JEAN SCOTT

Emma Jean Scott was born February 2, 1945.

Rachel, Rawlin, Perry and Joyce Scott and Edmond Langford

She is the daughter of Elbert and Ruby Stone Scott. She attended Celina Elementary School and graduated from Celina High School. She married Kirk Baxter, the son of Bazz and Della Harlan Baxter of Monroe County, Kentucky. Kirk attended and graduated from Monroe County, Kentucky Schools. They live near Tompkinsville, Kentucky.

Kirk is employed by the Kentucky Department of Transportation as a highway foreman. Emma Jean is employed by the United States Postal Service. Emma Jean is a member of the Church of Christ and attends the Germany Church of Christ at Hestand, Kentucky.

Emma Jean and Kirk have one child, Amy. Amy is married to Stevie Hale, the son of Archie and Dimple Bowe Hale. Amy has two sons, Jordan Baxter and Jacob Scott Hale. Amy and Stevie live near Old Mulkey in Kentucky. Both Amy and Stevie graduated from Monroe County Schools. Stevie is employed at Belden, and Amy is employed at the Deposit Bank of Monroe County. Amy is a member of the Germany Church of Christ.

PERRY STONE SCOTT

Perry Stone Scott was born in the Monroe County Hospital, Tompkinsville, Kentucky July 2, 1955. He is the son of Elbert T. Scott and Ruby Fowler Stone. Perry is the grandson of Amos Tinsley Stone and Martha Gladys Smith and Perry Brance Scott and Ora Catherine Scott. Perry has one older sister, Emma Jean Scott.

Perry attended the Clay County schools; he graduated from Celina High School in 1973.

Perry started working for HONDA of Cookeville, Tennessee as a mechanic after he graduated from high school. He was employed at this place for two years. During the next year, he was a business partner and half owner of the Ossa Motorcycle Shop in Celina, Tennessee. The shop closed, and Perry worked on a ship in the Gulf of Mexico. During the next eight years, Perry worked offshore as a shipmate and eventually was promoted to Captain. He worked in Guayaquil, Ecuador; Bombay, India; and during the time between 1983-1986 in Saudi Arabia, and Dubayy, United Arab Emirates on the Persian Gulf. Perry is presently employed at OshKosh B'Gosh as quality assurance auditor.

During the year 1983, Perry, with the help of his father and family, built the log house that he and his family now live in on Proctor Creek, Beech Bethany Community.

Perry married Joyce Elaine Boles Langford

November 24, 1976. Joyce's grandfather, Barton Bailey, was the Justice of the Peace who performed the marriage ceremony. Joyce is the daughter of Wilma Jean Bailey and Clint Boles. She is the granddaughter of Hugh Barton Bailey and Mary Daffo Weaver. Joyce attended the Clay County schools; she graduated from Celina High School in 1968. Joyce attended Tennessee Technological University and graduated with the following degrees: Bachelor of Science in Vocational Home Economics in 1973; Master of Arts in Secondary Education in 1980; completed 45 quarter hours beyond a master's level in 1982; and Bachelor of Science in Nursing in 1985. Joyce taught vocational Home Economics at Celina High School during 1973-83. Joyce also works part-time for the Clay County Hospital as a registered nurse and works full-time for the Clay County Board of Education.

Perry and Joyce are the parents of three children, two sons and a daughter. Robert Edmond Lee Langford was born February 15, 1969. He is the son of Champ Edmond Langford and Joyce. He is the grandson of Cecil Frank Langford and Frances Lee Pennington and Wilma Jean Bailey and Clint Boles. He is a senior at Celina High School. He is employed at Austin's Bi-Rite. Rachel Lorraine Scott was born December 28, 1977. She attends Celina K-8 and is in the second grade. Rawlin Preston Scott was born March 5, 1980. He was born on his mother's birthday. Rawlin attends Celina K-8 and is in kindergarten. The family attends the Church of Christ.

GEORGE CURTIS SCOTT

George Curtis Scott was born March 28, 1894 in the Willis Bottom section of Clay County, an area now covered by the Dale Hollow Reservoir. Willis Bottom was located in the northeast part of Clay County adjacent to Cumberland County, Kentucky. He was the son of James Buchanan (Buck) Scott and Ollie Frances (Willis) Scott. He was the tenth of fourteen children.

George Curtis and Avo Scott, and sister, Eunice Scott

George Curtis attended school at Willis Bottom and Willow Grove. At the age of 20, he decided to enlist in the Army, a decision his father was violently opposed to. On April 15, 1915, he walked from Willis Bottom to Willow Grove to do some shopping for the family and to take some ducks to sell that belonged to his sister, Eunice. When he arrived at Willow Grove, he sold the ducks and used the money to hire a horse to take him to Cookeville and enlist in the Army. He lied about his age, and told the Army officer he was 21 years old, the age he had to be without parental consent. He left that day for the training, and did not return to Clay County for more than four years. However, he did repay his sister for the

"duck money" he had used. He was later sent to France, where he served under General Pershing during World War I.

Avo Ledbetter was born June 10, 1907 to James Porter and Mary Etta (Hammon) Ledbetter in the Highland Community of Overton County, Tennessee. She was one of eleven children.

George Curtis and Avo Ledbetter were married September 22, 1927. They began their married life in Fort Sheridan, Illinois, but later returned to Clay County to live. To this union were born seven children. They are George Curtis, Jr., born October 7, 1928; Jack, born December 24, 1929; Anna Ruth, born August 3, 1931; Betty Jean, born December 31, 1932; Ollie Frances, born April 5, 1934; Mabel Joyce, born September 16, 1935; and Mary Etta, born October 2, 1948.

George, Jr. married Lois Kuhuien, and they presently live in Lexington, Kentucky. They have two children, Stephen and Lisa.

Jack married Eva Nelle Goolsby, and they have two daughters, Terrie and Tammie. Jack and Eva Nelle live in Nashville.

Ruth married John Crawford, and they live in Buhl, Idaho. They have six children, Jim, Connie (Crawford) Christofferson, Nick, Brian, Mary, and Stacie.

Betty married Earl Lyons, and they have three children, Gregg, Rebecca, and Teresa. Betty lives in Burley, Idaho.

Ollie married Harold Hutcherson and they have three children, David, Thomas (died 1968), and Scott. Ollie presently lives in Hollywood, Florida.

Joyce married Edward Witham, and they have two sons, Curtis and Thomas. They live on Kettle Creek in Clay County on the farm where Joyce was born.

Mary Etta married Donald Sherrell, and they live in Celina.

George Curtis served a total of 22 years in the Army on active or reserve duty. He also worked as a raftsman who navigated logs on the Cumberland River to Nashville and then walked home to Clay County. He died in January, 1974 at the age of 79. Avo Scott continues to live in Celina.

JAMES CHARLIE SCOTT

James Charlie Scott, the son of Clement Kelly Scott and Mary L. (Cleary) Scott, was born April 26, 1883 in the Kettle Creek Community of Cumberland County, Kentucky. He was the second of 12 children. His siblings were Ruthie Ann, born November 19, 1881; Mary Ellen, born July 21, 1885; Myrtie, born August 15, 1890; Fanny, born March 15, 1892; Tom T., born June 29, 1896; Elmer D., born May 12, 1897; Velura, born January 12, 1899; Ova, born March 24, 1901; Clema, born December 24, 1902; George Arvel, born March 2, 1904; and Lura Macel, born October 21, 1907.

Artha Ladora Riley, born May 19, 1879, was the daughter of Jim Riley and Martha E. (Vinson) Riley. Her family lived in the Willis Bottom section of Clay County, an area now covered by the Dale Hollow Reservoir. She was one of eight children. Her siblings were John Lewis, Joe, Gilbert Alma, Sarah, and Velura. Artha married Richard Wells the first time, and two children were born to this union. They were Sam and Lela Wells. After Richard Wells death, Artha married

Mattie, Lucy, Charlie, Lura, Artie, Woodrow, Carmon Scott, Sam Wells, Lela Kerr, Wilma and Brance Scott

Charlie Scott.

Charlie Scott and Artha (Riley) Wells were married March 18, 1903. To this union were born eight children. They were Eddy Brance, born December 30, 1903; Wilma Pauline, born May 3, 1905; Charlie Carmon, born February 24, 1907; Mattie Ann, born March 4, 1909; Lucy Ira, born March 23, 1911; Lura Allene, born October 1, 1912; Ray Woodrow, born February 14, 1916; and James Paul, born February 5, 1921.

Eddy Brance married Amelia Avo Colson. They had two children, Eldon Bransford and Eddie Randall. Brance and Amelia are buried in the Rock Springs Cemetery.

Wilma married Prentice Watson. They had six children, Flord Norman, Mayford James, Georgie Newton, Edith Yvonne, Paul Leonard, and Prentice Eugene. Wilma and Prentice are buried in the Scott Cemetery in Cumberland County, Kentucky.

Carmon married Ocie Groce, and they had four children. They are Ray, Richard, Roger, and Ronnie. Carmon is buried in the Ashlock Cemetery, and Ocie Scott lives in Burkesville, Kentucky.

Mattie married R.B. Capps, and they had one son, James Edward, that died shortly after birth. Mattie and Brance live in the Ashlock Community of Cumberland County, Ky near the Clay County line.

Lucy married Cordell Sherrell, and they have five sons. They are Edward, Elbert, Eddy, Harlon, and Donald. Lucy and Cordell live on Pea Ridge in Clay County.

Lura married Frank Stephens, and they have four children. They are Joe, James, Jerry, and Jean. Lura and Frank live on Pea Ridge in Clay County.

Woodrow married Dorothy Roach, and they had one daughter, Minnie Pearl. Woodrow is buried in the Roach Cemetery in the Ashlock Community of Cumberland County, Kentucky. Dorothy Scott lives in Indianapolis, Indiana.

Paul married Elsie Scott, and they have five children. They are Floyd Cornell, Jackie Woodrow (died at birth), Timmy, Patricia, and Terry.

Charlie Scott died December 24, 1969 and Artha Scott died December 15, 1958. They are buried in the Ashlock Cemetery.

JOHN DOUGLAS MARY SCOTT

John Scott, who was born in 1761 and died in 1843, married Sophia Murray in Pittsylvania County, Virginia. He served in the Revolutionary Army in the Fifth Regiment of the Virginia Continental Line in Captain Williams' Company. He enlisted in 1777 and received his discharge in 1783 when General Washington resigned his command of the army. They had six children, William, Nathaniel, Shadrach, Dallas, John and Betsy. They settled in Cumberland County, Kentucky.

William Scott, who was born in 1783, married Sallie Scott. They had five children, William, Jr., Nimrod, John, Robert and George W.

William Scott, Jr., who was born in 1807 and died in 1880, married Harriet Pruitt. They had six children, George Allen, William, Susan, Jefferson D., Edwin and Isabella.

John Douglas and Mary Ellen Scott

George Allen Scott was born in 1853 and died in 1910. His wife was Harriette Watson. They had seven children, Kirk, John, Douglas, Walter, Emory, Mary, Evie, and Minnie.

John Douglas Scott, who was born in 1883 and died in 1956, married Mary Ellen Scott, who was born in 1886 and died in 1962. They had seven children, Vella 1905-1984; Stella 1908; Homer 1910-1978; Domer 1916-1968; Leonard 1917-1976; Ola 1919; and Mary Magdalene 1923.

Mary Magdalene Scott married Edward Paul Colson, born in 1914 and died in 1973. They had seven children: Shelby Jean, 1938; Nell Ruth, 1940; Edward Carl, 1941-1971; Robbie Edwina, 1942; Lynda Ellen, 1944; Mildred Sue, 1946; and Daryl Wayne, 1949. Mary Magdalene later married Ben Nolan, born in 1919 and died in 1960. They had one daughter, Patricia Ann. Mary now lives in Cookeville, Tennessee.

Lynda Ellen Colson married Edward Estill Larimore, who was born in Greensburg, Kentucky in 1932. They have one daughter, Kathy Jo, born in 1973. They now live in Indianapolis, Indiana.

SEWELL

The name Sewell is inseparably connected with the history and development of this section of Tennessee. The Sewells came from the Clear River Settlement of North Carolina to what was then Carter (now Johnson) County, Tennessee, near the close of the eighteenth century. Not many years later, three brothers (there were seven brothers and one sister in this family), William D., J.A., and Stephen Sewell, moved across the Cumberland Mountains and settled among the rugged hills on the waters of the Wolf River, only a few miles northeast of Willow Grove. They were of English descent and were Baptists. William D. was a Baptist preacher and served as minister of the old Mount Zion Baptist Church for more than forty years. Little is known of his brother, J.A., except that he voted for the exclusion of his nephew, William B. Sewell, from the Baptist Church because he had "communed with the Campbellites". Before crossing the moun-

tains, Stephen married Annie Brown, of German descent, in Carter County. There were fourteen children born to Stephen and Annie Sewell; twelve of these, seven sons and five daughters, lived to be grown. The other two, a son and a daughter, died in infancy and childhood.

Few families in the last century have contributed as much to the cause of the Church of Christ as that of Stephen and Annie Sewell. Originally Baptists, the parents were brought to the Church of Christ through the influence and teachings of their eldest son, William B., who had been taught by his wife, who was a member of the Church of Christ. Before marriage she was a Miss Turner, a relative of Dr. Turner who established the church at Willow Grove.

Isaac C. Sewell rendered great service to the Church of Christ, being a good song leader, an efficient schoolteacher, and an acceptable preacher. He did not travel and preach so extensively as his brothers. He was never married. There is an old moss-covered slab in the Sewell graveyard, near the old homestead, which bears this inscription: "Isaac C. Sewell, born June 6, 1822, died March 29, 1900. There is no death that seemeth transition."

Caleb W. Sewell studied grammar under Isaac T. Reneau at Salt Lick Bend in Kentucky and later entered Bethany College. It seems that he was, while there, a favorite of the Campbells, especially Mrs. A. Campbell, who gave him a silk cap for his mother, Mrs. Stephen Sewell. The gift was cherished so highly that it was never worn, and when "Mother Sewell" died, she was buried in this cap. Caleb worked for a number of years in Louisville, Kentucky, but after the death of his wife, July 11, 1894, and because of failing health, he returned to the old Sewell home, where he died September 8, 1911. He was buried beside his brothers, William and Isaac, in the family graveyard.

The youngest of "the four preaching boys", as they were affectionately called by their old friends, the lamented Elisha G. Sewell, was one of the editors of the Gospel Advocate for more than a half century.

BENJAMIN BEUGREGARD SHERRELL

Benjamin Beugregard Sherrell, born January 3, 1861 near the Willow Grove area, was the son of Jessie and Elizabeth (Ashlock) Sherrell. His father was first married to Thersy Dalton, and they had six children. They were George Washington, born 1844; Salley; Elizabeth; Rebecca; Nancy; and John, born 1856. Thersy Dalton died and Jessie married his first wife's niece, Elizabeth Ashlock. To this union were born ten children, with nine living to adulthood. They were Benjamin; Robert Lee, born 1863; Mary Etta, born 1866; Sidney, born 1869; Jane Ann, born 1871; James Andrew, born 1874; Margaret Ellen, born 1877; Millard, born 1879, and George Walter, born 1882. Elizabeth (Ashlock) Sherrell raised her nine children, as well as the children from Jessie's marriage to her aunt.

Jessie and his oldest son, George Washington (about 16 at the time), fought for the Confederacy during the Civil War. Jessie and George Washington were together at the Battle of Chickamauga. Jessie was wounded during the battle (lost an ear) and George Washington was believed

to be killed. Jessie was returned to a hospital in Nashville to recuperate. At that time the Union soldiers occupied Nashville and after swearing allegiance to the Union, he was allowed to return to his home in Clay County.

Benjamin and Belle (Watson) Sherrell

Ben could remember the Civil War and would relate stories of how his mother hid their meat in the haystacks to protect it from the guerrillas that frequented this area. He was a young boy of about five years old when his father returned from the war, and this was the first time he remembered seeing his father.

Missouri Belle Watson was born September 20, 1867 on Pea Ridge, the daughter of William (Bill) Watson and Elizabeth (Williams) Watson. She was one of eight children. Her siblings were John, Joe, Tom, George, Etta, Margaret, and Martha.

Ben Sherrell married Belle Watson February 29, 1886. They bought a farm on Pea Ridge called "Old Jerusalem". To this union were born nine children, with six living to adulthood. Their children were Charlie, born January 13, 1890; Edda, born February 8, 1892; Eula, born September 16, 1894; Lela, born February 21, 1898; Minnie, born June 28, 1902; and Cordell, born August 5, 1908.

Charlie married Pearlie Key, and they had no children. Charlie drowned in the Obey River below the present Dale Hollow Dam at the age of 25 in 1916.

Edda married Clarence Bowe, and they had one daughter, Robbie. After Clarence Bowe's death, she married L.D. Huffer. Edda Huffer is 94 years old and lives in Clinton, Arkansas.

Eula married Dan Webb, and they had four sons. They are: Grady, Savage, Marshall and J.B. Webb. Marshall Webb was killed April 7, 1945 during World War II and is buried in Germany. Eula Webb died in 1980 and is buried in the Thompson/Webb Cemetery on Pea Ridge.

Lela married O.C. (Tee) Waddell, and they had no children. Lela Waddell is 88 years old and lives in Celina.

Minnie married Elzie Conner, and they have six children. They are Herman, Lorene, Shirley, Fred, Joyce and Jackie. Minnie Conner is 83 years old, and she and Elzie live in Livingston, Tennessee.

Cordell married Lucy Scott, and they have five children. They are Edward, Elbert, Eddy Ray, Harlon, and Donald. Cordell and Lucy live on the farm that Benjamin bought over a 100 years ago on Pea Ridge.

Benjamin and Belle Sherrell were married 69 years before Belle's death August 1, 1955. Ben lived to be almost 102. He died August 16, 1962.

They are buried in the Williams Cemetery on Pea Ridge.

CLIFFORD AND LUCY SHERRELL

Clifford Cordell Sherrell, the son of Benjamin Beugregard and Missouri Belle (Watson) Sherrell, was born August 5, 1908 on Pea Ridge in Clay County. He was the youngest child of nine children with six living to adulthood. His sisters are Edda, Eula, Lela, and Minnie. His only brother, Charlie, drowned in the Obey River in January 1916 at the age of 25.

Lucy Scott and Cordell Sherrell

Lucy Ira Scott was born March 23, 1911, in the Kettle Creek Community of Cumberland County, Kentucky. Her parents were Charlie Scott and Arthie (Riley) Scott. Her siblings were Brance, Wilma, Carmen, Mattie, Laura, Woodrow, Paul, and a half brother, Sam Wells, and a half sister, Lela Wells.

Cordell and Lucy were married November 24, 1928 by George Henry Watson near the Kentucky state line while sitting on their mules. After paying the expenses for their marriage, they had $1.00 left to begin their married life. Five children were born to this union. They are Jessie Edward, born November 13, 1929; Elbert Lee, born September 9, 1931; Eddie Ray, born November 20, 1934; Harlon D., born July 5, 1938; and Clifford Donald, born November 23, 1940.

Edward married Wilma Thompson, the daughter of Domer and Flossie Thompson, and they have four children. They are Eddie Dean, Harold, Belinda (Sherrell) McCoy, and Nathan. Edward and Wilma presently live at Kettle, Kentucky.

Elbert married Annie Thompson, the daughter of Dennis and Dollie Thompson and they have two daughters, Vicki (Sherrell) Sewell and JoAnn (Sherrell) Hestand. Elbert and Annie live in Franklin, Indiana.

Eddie Ray married Betty Sue Key, the daughter of Cordell and Rosie Key, and they live in Marysville, Indiana. They have three children, Clifford Ray, Kathy, and Anthony.

Harlon married Marcella Thompson, the daughter of Marshall and Ona Thompson, and they have three children. They are Elaine (Sherrell) Smith, Tammy, and Jeffery. Harlon and Marcella live in the Pea Ridge Community.

Donald married Mary Etta Scott, the daughter of George Curtis and Avo Scott, and they live in Celina. Donald has two children, Kimberly (Sherrell) Moore and David.

Cordell and Lucy continue to live in the Pea Ridge section on the farm where Cordell was born, the farm bought by Benjamin Sherrell over a 100 years ago. They have been lifelong farmers.

OTHA AND BONNIE SHIPLEY

Bonnie Lee Melton was born October 28, 1924 at Willow Grove in Clay County, Tennessee. She is the oldest of ten children born to Cecil Charlie Melton and Della Mae Thrasher Melton. She grew up on the Melton farm in the Willow Grove Community and attended the St. John School.

Otha and Bonnie Shipley

Otha Chasten (Babe) Shipley was born October 23, 1910 at Lillydale in Clinton County, Kentucky. He was the seventh of ten children born to Nathan Thomas Shipley and Clementine (Tine) Boles Shipley. He grew up on a farm on the banks of the Wolf River and Van's Branch in Clinton County. The farm was on the Tennessee-Kentucky border. The Shipley family later moved to Miller's Mill, also in Clinton County, before returning to their farm on the Wolf River, where they remained until the farm was flooded by Dale Hollow Lake in 1942. Otha attended school at Leonard Oak, Lee's Chapel, and Sulpher Springs.

David, Damon and Janet (Shipley) Yates

Bonnie Melton and Otha Shipley were married in Jamestown, Kentucky January 15, 1945. They moved to Anderson, Indiana where they were employed by Delco Remy, a division of General Motors, for twenty-five years each. In 1950 they purchased a farm near New Castle, Indiana.

One daughter, Janet Faye Shipley, was born January 26, 1954 at the Henry County Memorial Hospital in New Castle, Indiana. She attended school at Blountville Elementary School and Union School in Modoc, Indiana.

In 1968 the Shipley family moved back to Clay County. They purchased a farm on Highway 53, approximately two miles south of Celina.

Janet graduated from Celina High School in 1972. She received her Bachelor of Science degree from Tennessee Technological University in 1976 and her Master of Arts degree from Austin Peay in 1980. She married David Anthony Yates at the Celina Church of Christ September 4, 1976. They now reside in Lyles in Hickman County, Tennessee where Janet teaches school. David is a civil engineer and Vice-President of Robbins, Yates and Associates, Inc., Consulting Engineers. They have one son, Damon Anthony Yates, born March 31, 1982.

DAVID FRANKLIN SHORT

David Franklin "Frank" Short was born in Clay County, Tennessee September 8, 1874. He was the son of Adeline Willmore and Caleb W. Short. On June 4, 1894, he married Sarah Susanne (Sally) Moore. She was the daughter of Denton and Melinda Ann Rogers Moore. "Frank" and "Sally" lived in the Pine Hill Community of Clay County where he was a farmer. "Frank" loved music and enjoyed buck dancing. "Sally" enjoyed crocheting and entertaining company, as visitors were always welcome. She enjoyed participating in the activiites of the Pine Hill Church of Christ where she was a member. "Frank" Short died March 30, 1956; and "Sally" Short died August 13, 1965.

David Franklin (Frank) and Sarah (Sally) Short

"Frank" and "Sally" had seven children, Ezra Dumas, Dovie May, Bonnie Lee, Mary Dimple, Ada Crayton, Edwin Leon, and Fred.

Ezra Dumas Short was born January 1, 1901. On December 12, 1924, he married Rosa Vaughn, the daughter of Joe and Allie Cherry Vaughn. They have seven children, Lorene, Carlene, Dumas Eugene, Barbara Esteline, Charles Lee, Sarah Alice, and David Richard. In 1958, he married Dimple Willadean Copas, and they had four children, Fred Leon, Kenneth Ray, Linda Kay, and Brenda Faye. Dumas died December 2, 1966.

Dovie Mae Short was born September 9, 1905. On December 28, 1923, she married Lester Thomas Watson, the son of Luther and Lille Reecer Watson. They had four children, Chester Lyle, Frank Martin, Mary Edith, and James Thomas. Lester worked for the Corps of Engineers. Lester and Dovie have made their home in Ashland City, Tennessee since the 1950's. Lester passed away January 11, 1986.

Bonnie Lee Short was born July 27, 1908. On April 5, 1930, she married Harry Lee, the son of Peyton Monroe and Freelove Brown Lee. Bonnie Lee and Harry Lee had seven children, Clyde Alvin, Doris Jean, Fred Cedric, Joyce Ann, Johnny Denton, William Peyton, and Janice Fay. Harry and Bonnie moved to Toledo, Ohio in the 1930's. They returned to Clay County. Harry returned to Detroit, Michigan to work. All their children were educated in Clay County. After an early retirement, Harry returned to Clay County where he and Bonnie lived in the Mount Vernon Community. Harry Lee died in April of 1986.

Mary Dimple Short was born March 20, 1911. On January 15, 1929, she married Willie Copass, the son of George and Nancy McLerran Copass. They had one child, Betty Sue. Dimple died on November 23, 1947. After her mother's death, Betty Sue lived with her aunt, Laura McLerran.

Ada Crayton Short was born April 3 1914. On June 3, 1933, she married Cordell Brown, the son of James McHenry and Martha Jane Harpe Brown. They have four children, Anna Jane, Lonnie Alvin, Nelda Ruth, and Daisy Lou. Ada next married Joe William Smith, who was killed in 1956 in a hunting accident. On August 1, 1960, she married John Buford Rich. Ada and John Buford now reside in Moss, Tennessee.

Edwin Leon Short was born November 3, 1917. He was killed in action in World War II in the European Theater.

Fred Short was born January 20, 1924. He was killed in action in World War II in the Pacific Theater.

ADA CRAYTON SHORT RICH

Ada Crayton Short was born in Clay County, Tennessee April 3, 1914. She was the daughter of David Franklin (Frank) and Sarah Susanne (Sally) Moore Short. She grew up in the Pine Hill Community and attended school there. On June 3, 1933, she married Cordell Brown, the son of James McHenry and Martha Jane Harpe Brown. They had four children. Anna Jane was born April 11, 1934. She married Phillip Strong September 19, 1952. He was the son of Mose and Doshie Reecer Strong. Anna and Phillip have three children, James Martin, Susan Beth, and Julie Rose Strong. Susan Beth has two children, Jada and Luke Bland. Anna and Phillip live in the Turkey Creek Community of Clay County.

Daisy, Nelda, Anna and Lonnie, Alvin and Ada Crayton Short Rich

Lonnie Alvin was born April 5, 1936. In 1964, he married Charlotte Smith, the daughter of Leon Hays Smith of Dennison, Texas. They had one son, Lonnie Edward. In 1973, Lonnie Alvin married Beyhan Beser, the daughter of Mehmet and Seher Beser of Ankara, Turkey, and they have one son, James Devrin. Lonnie Alvin is a retired gunnery mechanic for Northrop Corporation in Saudi Arabia. Lonnie Alvin also spent 22 years in the United States Air Force. Lonnie Alvin now resides in Celina.

Nelda Ruth was born April 17, 1939. On June 8, 1956, she married Mickey Fay Clements, the son of Claude and Ora Cherry Clements. They

have two children, Cherry Ann and Mickey Fay Clements, Jr. Nelda and Mickey live near Hermitage Springs, Tennessee. Nelda is a teacher in the Macon County School System; and Mickey is the Manager of OshKosh of Hermitage Springs. Cherry Ann married Johnny Hanks, and she teaches at Hermitage Springs. Mickey, Jr. is married and has one son. He is in the United States Armed Forces and is stationed in Florida.

Daisy Lou was born December 12, 1942. On July 1, 1961, she married Eugene Renodin, the son of Glen Ryle and Lucy Marie Fisher Renodin, of Romulus, Michigan. Daisy and Eugene moved from Michigan to the Midway Community of Clay County. Daisy has worked for the Cordell Hull Community Service Agency for a number of years as a field coordinator. Eugene works with the maintenance division of OshKosh at Hermitage Springs. Daisy and Eugene have two daughters, Susan Lee and Debra Ann. Susan Lee is a senior at Tennessee Technological University in Cookeville, Tennessee, and Debra Ann works for OshKosh at Hermitage Springs.

Ada next married Joe William Smith November 23, 1951. He was killed in a hunting accident in 1956. After Joe William's death, Ada married John Buford Rich August 1, 1960. Ada and John Buford live in Moss, Tennessee.

MADISON SIDWELL

Madison Sidwell married Elizabeth Maxfield. They had three sons and one daughter.

John Ephison Sidwell, born July 9, 1863, married Mattie Bennett May 6, 1891. They had three children, Watterson Grady, Paul Bennett, and Paula Elizabeth. John Ephison was a physician and practiced medicine at Fox Springs.

Milton C. was born at Speck, Tennessee. He was an attorney and practiced law with Cordell Hull at Celina, Tennessee. He first married Celia Stewart, and they had one son, Walter F., who became a physician. He practiced medicine at Willow Grove and Celina. Walter F. married Ada Arms; and they had four children, Frank, Tissie, Kenneth Boyd "Bub," and Ben. Frank was a teacher at Willow Grove and Celina before becoming a doctor. Tissie married John Bryant, a judge in Cookeville, and they had one son, John Milton, who became a doctor. Kenneth Boyd was a schoolteacher in Kentucky, where he still resides at Cave City. Ben resided in Livingston but is now deceased. Milton C. next married Alva A. Mitchell of Celina. They had a daughter, Ada, who married Hugh Williamson, a doctor. They had a son, Herman Edgar, who first married Kate Shanks of Cookeville. He then married Hettie Windle of Butler's Landing. They had four children, Frances, Ada Lee, Milton, and another son.

Cullom Sidwell first married Ada (surname unknown), and they had three children who died in infancy. Cullom then married Eunice Martin. They had two children. Ruth married Winfried Kirby of Cookeville, and Paul married Patsy Kennedy of Soddy Daisy, Tennessee. Paul and Patsy now live in Alabama.

Fannie Sidwell married Abraham M. Kimes. She died November 8, 1937. She is buried at Mt. Pisgah in eastern Clay County.

Among the descendants of Madison Sidwell have been eight doctors, one dentist, and two attorneys.

DR. J.E. SIDWELL

John Ephison Sidwell was born July 9, 1863. He married Mattie Bennett of Lillydale May 6, 1891. She was born June 28, 1867, the daughter of Captain Jake Bennett. She was born in Conyers, Georgia.

John Ephison was the son of Madison and Elizabeth Maxfield Sidwell. He received his medical training in Nashville. He practiced medicine at Fox Springs about nine miles up the Obey River from Celina. (This area is now covered by Dale Hollow Lake.)

Dr. John Ephison and Mattie Sidwell

John Ephison and Mattie had three children. Watterson Grady Sidwell was born May 13, 1893 at Speck, Tennessee. He attended Burritt College at Spencer, Tennessee and received his law degree from Vanderbilt University in Nashville. He married Mary Sue Maxwell August 23, 1929 at Devereau, Georgia. Mary Sue was born October 30, 1901. Grady and Sue made their home in Celina. Grady practiced law here for approximately forty years. He served as General Sessions Judge for a number of years. He served in the Tennessee State Legislature. He was a Mason and a member of the Eastern Star. Sue taught school in Celina for a number of years. When she retired, she was teaching English and biology at Celina High School. Sue was a member of the Eastern Star. Grady and Sue attended the Celina United Methodist Church. Grady died in April of 1967, and Sue died in January of 1985. They are buried in the Fitzgerald Cemetery.

Paul Bennett Sidwell was born March 11, 1896 at Fox Springs. He died in November of 1900 of scarlet fever. He is buried at Mt. Pisgah in eastern Clay County.

Paula Elizabeth was born October 8, 1900 at Fox Springs. She attended elementary school at Fox Springs. She had four years of high school and two years of college at Tennessee Polytechnic Institute in Cookeville. She received her Bachelor of Science Degree in Home Economics from Peabody College in Nashville. She taught home economics for two years at Celina High School and then at Charlotte, Tennessee for four years. Paula is a member of the Eastern Star and has served in different capacities — secretary, et cetera. She is a member of the Celina United Methodist Church. Paula lives in Celina.

John Ephison and Mattie Sidwell are buried in Mt. Pisgah Cemetery in eastern Clay County.

GERALDINE SMALLING

Geraldine Phillips Smalling, one of the handful of pioneer women rural mail carriers in the United States, served the people of Clay County for forty years in this capacity.

The daughter of Gratton D. and Lorene Pickens Phillips of Clay County, she grew up at Lillydale and attended the Lillydale School through the eighth grade. At the age of eighteen, after high school graduation and one year of college, she was appointed Rural Letter Carrier out of the Lillydale Post Office in 1941.

Geraldine (Phillips) Smalling

In those days roads in the area were mostly dirt, and carrying the mail was considered a man's job. Women simply did not do this type of rugged work. However, "Gerry's" uncle, Louis Elder, urged her to take the examination for the route which was left vacant after the untimely death of her father, Gratton Phillips. Most people bluntly told her that she could not handle the job. One lady, Mary Wells, of Byrdstown told her that it all depended on how much determination she had. That was all the encouragement she needed to embark on her new career.

The people soon learned that she was determined enough when she walked three miles during the winter months on part of the route where the roads were impassable in an automobile. Soon the people on the route were always out ready to lend a helping hand in times of car trouble or snow and ice.

Dale Hollow Dam was started shortly after Geraldine's appointment, and in February of 1943 the Lillydale Post Office was discontinued. The Lillydale area would be flooded by the waters of Dale Hollow Lake. She was transferred to Route 4 out of the Red Boiling Springs Post Office in Macon County. It was with joy that she learned that most of Route 4 was located in Clay County and that she would still be serving her own people. Hermitage Springs School was served by Route 4 as was Mt. Vernon and Leonard schools, all part of the Clay County school system. Again there was surprise and unbelief. The people on Route 4 had always had a man who was their rural carrier. Proving that she could do the job started all over again. Although there was no part of the route that had to be served on foot, there were plenty of dirt roads and unbridged streams. During the winter months snow and ice on the narrow roads added to the hazards. Creek flooding was sometimes very difficult to contend with. However, she stayed on and became part of the lives of the people on that route. *The Nashville Tennessean* did a feature story about her and the Route 4 patrons in their Sunday Magazine section.

Her daily rounds continued until 1981 when she retired. The years had brought many changes in roads and the type of vehicles needed for carrying the mail. Geraldine likes to feel that she helped pave the way for the hundreds of women who now serve as rural letter carriers throughout the country.

CLARK FOWLER SMITH

Clark F. Smith was born February 13, 1890 in Celina, Tennessee, the son of Matthew Mordecai Smith and Frances Fowler. Matthew M. was the son of Mordecai Miller Smith, who served in the Civil War, and Nancy Roberts. Mordecai M. was the son of Charles Smith and Sarah Hord. Frances F. was the daughter of Christopher Clark Fowler and Elizabeth Elliott Hamilton. Nancy Roberts, born in Mt. Airy, North Carolina, was a daughter of Jonathan Roberts and Mary Davis. Sarah Hord was a daughter of Stanwix Hord and Justinia Burrus. Stanwix was the son of Sarah Carr, who was the daughter of William Carr and Elizabeth Winston, who was the daughter of John Winston from Virginia. William Carr was the son of Thomas Carr, Jr. and Mary Dabney. Justinia Burrus was the daughter of Thomas Burrus and Susanna Martin. Susanna was the daughter of General Joseph Martin (born in 1700, in England) and Susanna Chiles. Her father, John Chiles (born 1669-70) lived in the first brick house in Jamestown, Virginia as the second owner; he was the son of Walter Chiles, II (born in 1636, in England) and married Mary Page (born 1647), daughter of Lt. Col. John Page (born 1627). Mary Page helped select the site for William and Mary College; her portrait hangs in the library there. Lt. Col. Chiles, father of Walter Chiles, II (born 1600), married Elizabeth (1634), then later Alice Lukin, who after his death married Lt. Col. John Page (1656). His statue is located at the entrance to Jamestown, Virginia.

Amos T. and Martha Gladys Stone

C.F. Smith attended school at Fox Springs and Montvale Academy with Cordell Hull. He had three brothers, Wade, William and Nard; two sisters, Lockie Beck and Mallie Lowery; two half-brothers; and one half-sister. He married Martha Belle Dale, (born February 12, 1893), daughter of Wilburn Hamilton Dale and Evelyn Hawkins, at the home of Tuck Butler. Wilburn Dale, who served in the Civil War, was the son of William Dale, Jr. and Martha Goodpasture. The C.F. Smiths lived on different farms near Celina until 1930, when they settled in Arcot Community and remained there until their deaths, his January 11, 1963 and hers February 3, 1967. Both are buried in Edens Cemetery.

They had 11 children, Ezra Clifton; Fannie Evelyn, who married H.W. Stone, and had three sons, Ray Fowler, Thomas Lovell, and an infant son; Lizzie Ermine, who married W.F. Waddell, and had one daughter, Mattie Lucille Bowe; Martha Gladys, who married Amos T. Stone, and had five children, Nardie Copas, Ruby Scott, Mattie Clark, Evelyn, and Harold; Della Lea, who married Lee Stone, and had three children, Elizabeth Pendleton, John Fowler, Wade Tinsley, and her

second marriage was to Radford Clark; W. Wade, who married Mary Bland, and had two daughters, Mary Ann Barnes and Virginia Norris; Thelma Laura, who married Arthur Nevins, and had one daughter, Isabelle Ross; Paul T.; Luke Lea, who married James Mabry, and had four children, Gene, Cherrie Nell, Lois Evans and Jay Jeffery; Fred Clark, who married Ina Eads, and had three children, Freddie Poindexter, Clark Fowler and infant son; and Mary Belle, who married Arthur Nevins, and had two children, Barbara C. Watson and Joseph Clark.

There are many relatives of this family. A book "The Smiths and Dales of Middle Tennessee" by W.W. Smith was written after 30 years of research and published in 1979. This account is dedicated to W.W. Smith in memory of his family he loved so deeply. This country was made better by families like this. — *Submitted by Mrs. Isabelle Nevins Ross*

DENNIS WILLIAM SMITH

Dennis William Smith was born January 8, 1948 in Celina, Tennessee. He is the son of William George (Bill) Smith and Una Hilda Donavon Smith. He is the grandson of Dayton and Annie Smith. Dennis's mother was a World War II bride from England.

Monica, Nina, Dennis, William and Duane Smith

Dennis attended school at Celina Elementary School and Celina High School. He graduated from Celina High School in 1966. He spent two years at Cumberland College in Lebanon, Tennessee and received a Bachelor of Science Degree from Middle Tennessee State University in 1970. He received a Master's Degree from Tennessee Technological University in 1974.

Dennis has taught school for 16 years in the Clay County School System. He has taught science, physical education, and has coached football at both the high school and junior high levels. Dennis has served as a member of the Clay County Court representing the Fifth District of Clay County.

Dennis was married on Sept. 10, 1966 to Nina Pearl McLerran from the Moss Community of Clay County. Nina is the daughter of Willie George McLerran and Emma Dee Strong McLerran. Nina is the granddaughter of Harlan and Nina McLerran of the Moss Community and of Frank and Pearl Strong of the Midway Community.

Nina attended school in Clay County and graduated from Celina High School in 1966. Nina attended Cumberland College. Nina has worked as a food service supervisor at both the Clay

County Hospital and the Clay County Nursing Home.

Dennis and Nina are the parents of Dennis Duane Smith, born June 24, 1968; William Patrick Smith, born February 13, 1971; and Monica Leann Smith, born October 10, 1978. Dennis Duane is a 1986 graduate of Celina High School and is attending Elizabethtown Community College in Elizabethtown, Kentucky. William Patrick and Monica are students in the Clay County School System.

Dennis and Nina have lived in the New Hope Community of Clay County for the past 12 years. They are members of the New Hope Church of Christ.

JOSEPH DWIGHT SMITH

Joseph Dwight Smith, born November 15, 1976, is a descendant of one of the oldest families in Clay County.

Joseph Smith is the son of Martha Crawford Smith and Dwight Allen Smith. Martha Smith is the daughter of Annise Davis and Vandal Crawford. Annise Davis Crawford is the daughter of Lester Braden Davis and Nellie Browning. She had eight brothers and sisters: Olene; Irene, who married James William Bean II; Bedford, who married Edna Ritter; Milford, who married Nell Sampson; Hillus, who married Loucille McCarter; Ullyses, who married Jewell Pedigo; Charles, who married Louise Rhoton; and Clyde, who married Vella Franklin. Vandal Crawford is the son of Irvin Crawford and Florida Coons. He is one of three children. His brothers were Noble, who was killed in the Korean War, and Darris, who married Elizabeth Bilbrey.

Joseph Dwight Smith

Lester Davis was the son of Jimmy Davis and Laura Johnson. His brothers and sisters were Radford, Parlie, Otis, Nola, Allie, Norma, Carlie, Roxie, Luther and Pearl. Nellie C. Browning was the daughter of Henry Rice Browning and Arie Russell. Her brothers and sisters were Elizabeth, Seldon, Silas, Matilda, Loma, Robert, Charlie, Avo and Estes.

Irvin Crawford was the son of Sam Crawford and Martha Rush. He had one sister, Ruth. Florida Coons was the daughter of Larry Coons and Lucy Kirby. Her brothers and sisters were Ethel, Jim, Charlie, Pluma, Will, Pete, Henry and Odell.

Jimmy Davis was the son of Andy Davis and Temple Bean. Laura Johnson was the daughter of John Johnson and Catherine Clunner. Rice Browning was the son of Robert Browning and Nellie Rodgers. Arie Russell was the daughter of Silas Russell and Matilda Cornwell. Sam Crawford was the son of Johnathan Crawford and Nancy Copas. Martha Rush was the daughter of

Isaac Rush and Brilla Moore. Larry Coons was the son of Parasetta Coons. Lucy Kirby was the daughter of Claiborne Kirby and Fannie Bean.

Dwight Smith is the son of Donald Smith and Rita Jo Watson. Rita Jo Watson was the daughter of Van Watson and Ethel Capps. She has one brother, Gene. Van Watson was the son of Richard Watson and Lani Boone.

PAUL TRUMAN AND LEXIE SMITH

Paul Truman Smith was born August 14, 1903; and he died November 7, 1976. He was the only child of Steve and Martha Boles Smith. He married Lexie Myra Hix, the daughter of Ben and Belle Crowder Hix. Lexie had the following brothers and sisters: Minnie Spivey, Grace Loftis, Mamie Forkum, Mary Loftis, Martha Hawkins, Fred Hix, and Dewey Hix.

Paul and Lexie Smith

Paul and Lexie had four children. Lois Christine, born August 12, 1929, married Wheeler Turner Marshall, and they had one daughter, Emily Ann Coffelt. Clifton Ray (Bud) Smith, born February 7, 1931, married Betty Ruth Melton, and they have three children, David Ray, Jeffrey Robin, and Marty. Velma Louise, born October 13, 1931, married Howard Reever "Posey" Young, and they have two children, Winton Edward and Myra Flo. Ralph Edward Smith was born May 17, 1937 and died July 3, 1941.

Paul and Lexie lived in the Butler's Landing Community of Clay County. Paul was a farmer and sawmill operator. He loved music and was song leader for the Butler's Landing Church of Christ for 40 years. Paul also served as a Justice of the Peace for 16 years. Lexie enjoyed raising her children on the farm and was a faithful member of the Church of Christ. She enjoyed making fancy quilts and pillows.

RANDALL H. SMITH

Randall H. Smith was born September 20, 1945 in the Union Hill Community of Clay County. He is the son of Hubert and America C. Smith. Randall is the grandson of Shade W. and Dora B. Murray and Henry Austin and Roxie Smith, all of Clay County.

Randall attended elementary school at Union Hill and Hermitage Springs. He graduated from Hermitage Springs High School in 1965. He received his Bachelor of Science Degree in Business Administration from Middle Tennessee State University in 1970. He received his Masters of Education Degree in 1976 from Middle Tennessee State University; and in 1981, he received the Education Specialist Degree from Tennessee Technological University.

Hubert and America Smith

Randall has taught in the Clay County School System since 1970. He has taught at both the high school and elementary levels at Hermitage Springs School and at Celina K-8 School. Since 1984, he has served as a part-time coordinator for the Better Schools Program in Clay County. Randall also works as a tax consultant and has an office at Hermitage Springs.

Randell H. Smith

Randall attends church at the Oak Grove Church of Christ, where he is a member. He has served as President of the Clay County Teachers Association and is a member of the Tennessee Education Association and the National Education Association. He was a charter member of the Hermitage Springs Jaycees and the Ruritan service organizations. He is a member of the West End Community Club.

THOMAS PAYNE SMITH

Thomas Payne Smith was born January 26, 1843 and died January 12, 1925, in Overton County, Tennessee. He was the son of William Smith and Sally Barksdale. He married Polly Ann Upton. Polly was born August 17, 1844 and died February 27, 1916. She was the daughter of Riley Upton and Martha Ann Peterman Upton. They were the parents of ten children, Stephen I.K.; Jim Riley; Sarah B. (Dale) and William Lee, who were twins; John; Zeda Ann (Cook); Tom Bedford; Palo; Aria (Davis); and Alexis.

Stephen I.K. Smith was born January 7, 1867 and died February 1, 1931. He was married January 30, 1891 to Rebecca Lou Maynord. She was born December 7, 1873 and died June 9, 1945. She was the daughter of Lewis Maynord and Elizabeth Garrett Maynord. They owned a farm near Timothy, Tennessee, where all their children were born. They moved to Clay County and bought a farm in the Pleasant Grove Community. They were the parents of seven children: Ether (1893-1958) married Oliver George; Arthur (1896-1968) married Mary Poindexter; Ermine

(1898-1967) married Shirley Sullivan; Thomas Cecil (1901-1957) married Velma Goodpasture; Verda (1904-1928) married W.D. Buford; Willie Haston (1907-1976) married Martha Rule Nevins; and Zelpha (1912-) married first Jim Bailey and then C.T. Martin.

Thomas Cecil was born November 2, 1901 and died April 24, 1957. He was married to Velma Goodpasture on February 9, 1921. She was born April 1, 1903. Cecil and Velma grew up on adjoining farms. They were parents of two children, Carl Hildreth Smith and Edwina Smith Upton. Carl was born November 30, 1922. He was married to Dorothy Camplin May 10, 1947. She was born November 18, 1922, the daughter of Finley Camplin and Myrtle Dillingham Camplin of Beech Creek, Kentucky. They live in Jacksonville, Florida. They have two daughters, Donna Kay and Tamera Beth.

Donna Kay was born August 5, 1948. She attended David Lipscomb College. She is married to Rudy Staggs of Hohenwald, Tennessee. They have three children, Todd, Ryan, and Ashley. They live in Columbia, Tennessee.

Tamera Beth was born August 20, 1957. She graduated from David Lipscomb College. She is married to Joe Spivey of South Bend, Indiana. Joe also graduated from David Lipscomb College. Joe is an accountant and Tamera works for the telephone company. They live in Nashville.

VANCIL SMITH

Vancil Smith was born January 22, 1916, the son of Luther and Eliza (Cherry) Smith. On March 8, 1935, he married Mae York, who was born December 2, 1918 in Clay County, the daughter of Clinton and Dona (Bean) York. They live in the Union Hill Community of Clay County where Vancil is a farmer. Mae worked at OshKosh in Celina until her retirement. Vancil and Mae have a large collection of antiques, and they sometimes hold antique auctions at their home. Mae and Vancil have nine children.

Kathleen, Neal, Linda, Sherry, Coell, Vancil, Brenda, Mae, R.J., Donnie and Genevieve Smith

Coell Smith, born December 22, 1935, married Anna Bell Cunningham. They have two daughters, Sheila and Diane.

R.J. (Jack) Smith, born December 15, 1937, married Laura Bell Maden. They have two sons, Bryan and Troy.

Genevieve Smith, born May 1, 1940, first married Bobby Craighead. They had two children, Liz and Curtis. Genevieve then married Noah Pharris, and they have a son, Keith.

Kathleen "Kat" Smith was born June 20, 1942. She married Lincoln Wilkerson, and they have two sons: Kerry and Terry.

Linda Smith, born September 22, 1944, married John Anderson. They have three children,

Annette, Barry, and Glen.

Donnie Smith, born September 16, 1946, has four daughters, Linda, Kathleen, Lydia, and Elizabeth.

Brenda Smith was born December 10, 1949. She married Douglas Browning, and they have four children, Stacy, Tracie, Stephanie, and Valerie.

Neal Smith, born February 16, 1953, married Debbie Perrian. They have three sons, Neal, Jeremy, and Bart.

Sherry Smith, born January 11, 1955, married Eddie Hatcher, and they have two children, Shawn, and Shannon.

DILLARD FRANKLIN SPARKS

Dillard Franklin Sparks (born October 29, 1899 — died July 10, 1973) was born in Estil County, Kentucky. He was the son of John G. and Melina Ella Moore Sparks. His grandfather was Daniel C. Sparks. His great grandfather was Isaac Sparks, Jr., and his great great grandfather was Isaac Sparks, Sr.

Dillard left home at the age of 17 to work in the oil fields. This became his lifelong avocation. While working in Bowling Green, Kentucky, he met Zetta Mae (Spinks) Smith, the daughter of James Ellis and Margaret Melvina Spinks of Anna, Kentucky. They were married in 1924. Zetta Mae was divorced from Sam Smith and had two sons, Royce and James, ages eight and four at this time. Dillard and Zetta had two children, Jane Marie, born in 1928, and Joe Neal, born in 1932, while they were living in Glasgow, Kentucky. Dillard first came to Clay County, Tennessee in 1928. He boarded at the homes of Fred Smith of Kettle, Kentucky and Mark Hayes in Celina returning home to Glasgow on weekends. The family moved to Clay County on a permanent basis in 1939, and Dillard formed a drilling partnership with Harmon Overstreet. This partnership was disolved in 1952, and Dillard was joined in the drilling business by his son, Joe Neil, who had graduated from Celina High School in 1950. These men drilled oil, gas, and water wells for 29 years, drilling approximately 700 water wells, and over 200 wells for gas and oil. Dillard retired from full-time drilling in 1963. His son, Joe Neil, continued to work at the occupation until 1980 when he started to work at Hevi-Duty Electric in Celina. Their daughter, Jane Marie, married Edward C. (Holy) Swan in 1949, and they made their home in Celina where Edward was head mechanic at OshKosh. Edward died of cancer in 1972. Edward and Jane Marie have three children living, Lisa, Leann, and Travis. They have one grandchild, Caitlin Collins. Joe Neil married Dorothy Mae Keisling in 1958, and they have two daughters, Linda and Betty. Zetta's son, Royce, has made his home in Belleville, Missouri, where he served as Mayor for 12 years before resigning to become County Commissioner. He is now retired. Royce married Arlene Pitcher, and they have four children, Paul, Charles, Elvis, and Ruthann, and Royce has a son, Richard, by a previous marriage. They have three grandchildren, Sarah, Jim, and Phillip. James Smith was killed in 1985. He was married to Myra Hix of Clay County who was killed in a car accident in 1980. They had five children, Joe, James R., John, Jeff, and Melanie. The four sons continue to operate the family business, and Me-

lanie lives in Houston, Texas. There are two grandchildren, Leslie and Melissa.

ZACHARIAH SPEAR

Zachariah Spear was born in 1826 in Monroe County, Kentucky. He was the son of Levi Spear, Jr., who was born in 1797 in Surry County, North Carolina. He died in 1856 in Monroe County, Kentucky. He was the great grandson of Levi Spear, Sr. of North Carolina. Levi settled in Monroe County, Kentucky about 1800, and he died there about 1825. Levi Spear, Jr. was married March 8, 1819 in Surry County, North Carolina to Elizabeth Pettitt, daughter of Benjamin and Charity (Skidmore) Pettitt of North Carolina. Levi and Elizabeth had the following children: Bennett, born February 1, 1820; Samuel, born in 1822; John Crouch, born in 1824; Zachariah, born in 1826; Levi, born in 1832; George W. born in 1835; Mary (Tade), born in 1836; Burnette (Casteel), born August 2, 1840; Austin, born in 1842; and Lucettie Catherine (Smith), born April 5, 1845.

Zachariah Spear   Susan Mary Spear

John Crouch Spear was married twice. He first married Nancy Hestand. Their children were Amanda (Stockton), born in 1847; Mary (Smith), born in 1849; Zachariah, born March 2, 1851; Laura (Smith), born in 1853; Bernetta, born January 6, 1857 (married Hamilton S. Reecer in 1876); Lucetta (Wilson), born in 1862; and David Austin, born October 8, 1864. John Crouch then married Louisa A. Potter. Their children were Miney G. (Smires), born in 1868; Archibald Bennett, born in 1872; Lillie W. (Moss), born in 1874; Donna (Moss), born in 1876; and Faye W. (Odle), born in 1884.

Zachariah Spear (born in 1826) married Susan Mary Leaster. They moved to Missouri in the late 1840's, but returned to Jackson (now Clay) County before 1855. Zachariah was a farmer and a blacksmith. They lived in the Moss Community. They are buried on McFarland Creek near the Tennessee-Kentucky line. They had the following children: Samuel J., born September 8, 1849; Nancy Bernetta, born August 9, 1855 (married in 1874, Alexander Birdwell, born 1849 and died 1929); Susan Mary (Carter), born September 10, 1858; Amanda C. (Stephens), born in 1867; and Zachariah L., born in 1869. Zachariah L. married Sarah Dorcas McLerran. They had the following children: Nora, born April 5, 1889; Ellis; and Amos.

Lucettie Catherine Spear, born April 5, 1845, married Thomas Jefferson Smith, born in 1834. Their children were Payton, born in 1868; Henry Austin, born in 1872; Eli Harlan, born August 30, 1874; Levi Denton, born August 30, 1874; and

Mack. Lucettie Catherine died April 4, 1904.

SAMUEL J. SPEAR

Samuel J. Spear was born September 8, 1849 in Missouri. He was the son of Zachariah and Susan Mary Leaster Spear. While a young boy, Samuel and his parents returned to Clay County (then Jackson County). Samuel was a blacksmith, a farmer, and a minister. On September 15, 1870, Samuel married Permelia L. Burnette, the daughter of Moses and Ester Potter Burnette.

Vanus B. and Frances Spear

Permelia was born April 3, 1849 in Jackson County, Tennessee. They had the following children: Tolle Alto Spear, born June 8, 1871 and died September 20, 1872; Louella Florence Spear, born May 12, 1873 and died July 13, 1962; Vanus Beauregarde Spear, born June 24, 1874 and died September 27, 1924; Nancy Bernetta Spear, born July 15, 1876; Denton Alexander Spear, born March 12, 1878 and died September 23, 1933; Amanda Austrila Spear, born February 15, 1880 and died September 3, 1880; Loretta Beck Spear, born September 3, 1881 and died October 3, 1928; and Mary Myrtle Spear, born May 28, 1886 and died December 17, 1972. Louella Florence Spear married George McLerran August 31, 1887. They had two children, Martha and Herman. Nancy Bernetta Spear married Varney Greenwood, and they had the following children: Vora, Edward, and Elma. Loretta Beck Spear married Luther J. Savage March 3, 1901, and they had the following children: Fred, Ferry, Edward, Charlie, Nova, Luke, and Ollie Belle. Mary Myrtle Spear married William Martin Savage, and they had the following children: Vernon, Wade, Malcom, Mary Belle, and Cecil. Samuel Spear died January 22, 1930. Permelia died July 25, 1923. Vanus Beauregarde Spear, born June 24, 1874, was a blacksmith, a carpenter, and a law enforcement officer. He married Lenora Frances Adeline Watson December 24, 1897. She was the daughter of Robert S. and Jane Baxter Watson. They had the following children: Dewey Clyde, Lula E., Raymond C., Pearl, and Winnie. Dewey Clyde married Katheryn Rich April 14, 1928. Dewey died March 13, 1929 in Toledo, Ohio. Lula E. was born March 24, 1901 and died July 3, 1901. Raymond C. Spear was born February 23, 1905. He married Bonnie Waddell January 19, 1940. After Bonnie's death, Raymond married Lennie Reed November 4, 1969. Pearl married Charlie Brown on December 26, 1925. They had the following children: Charlie Frances (died young), Lula Belle (died in infancy), Joe Clyde, John Edwin (deceased), James Carol (Jimmy), and Jerry Lynn. Winnie married Robert Brown February 26,

1928, and they had the following children: Evelyn and Robert Hugh. Pearl and Winnie were both teachers in the Clay County School System. Vanus B. Spear was shot and killed in the Butlers Landing schoolhouse on the night of September 27, 1924 while performing his duties as coroner and acting sheriff of Clay County. Lenora Frances died March 15, 1944. They are buried in the New Hope-Spear Cemetery in the New Hope Community near Moss.

ALEX SPEAR

Denton Alexander Spear, born March 11, 1878 – died September 23, 1933, married Mary Belle Savage, born July 24, 1882 – died February 13, 1972, on July 15, 1900. Alex was born in the Moss Community of Clay County, and Mary Belle was born in the Proctor Creek Community of Clay County. The early years of their marriage were spent in the New Hope Community. They later lived in Midway, Pine Hill, and Celina. Alex was a farmer and a blacksmith. For many years, he served as a law enforcement officer. He served as deputy sheriff and was the Sheriff of Clay County from 1928-1932. Mary Belle was a housewife and mother. She devoted much of her life to the work of the Baptist Church at Celina. She was one of the five charter members of the church. During the great depression, she solicited funds from businesses and individuals to purchase the lot where the church now stands and to erect a rough church building thereon. On a front pew in the new church building is a bronze plaque placed there in her memory. She was a loving mother who impressed on her children the value of honesty and integrity and the importance of a good education.

Alex and Mary Belle had ten children: Frank Allen, born February 25, 1901; Leslie Levi, born September 29, 1902; Ruby Mae, born September 6, 1904; Roy Edward; Orland Eston, born May 10, 1909; Charlie Ray, born November 15, 1911; Mattie Mason, born October 2, 1914; Cordell Denton, born January 30, 1918; Willis Earl, born March 5, 1920; and Anna Marie, born November 26, 1921.

FRANK ALLEN SPEAR

Frank Allen Spear was born in 1901 at Moss in Clay County, Tennessee. He was the first child of Denton Alexander Spear and Mary Belle Savage Spear. He had six brothers and three sisters.

He graduated from Celina High School and received a Bachelor of Arts Degree from Berea College, Berea, Kentucky, in 1928. In 1933, he received a Masters of Art Degree from Peabody College in Nashville, Tennessee.

Mr. Spear had a career in education serving as a classroom teacher in several locations in and

Mr. and Mrs. Frank Allen Spear and Children — 1951

outside Clay County. He served as principal of the high schools in Willow Grove, Hermitage Springs, and Big Sandy in Tennessee, and Buchanan High School in Georgia.

Mr. Spear had a military career in the United States Army Reserve as a chaplain and attained the rank of Lieutenant Colonel. During World War II, he served in Hawaii, the Philippines, New Guinea, and other Pacific Islands under the command of General Douglas McArthur. Among the citations he received were battle stars for the Central Pacific and Leyte Island conflicts.

In 1934 Colonel Spear entered the United States Postal Service from which he retired in 1956. He died in 1982 in Nashville, Tennessee.

Nova Grey Dulworth Spear was the youngest child of nine children born to John Robert Dulworth and Tennessee Emma Kerr Dulworth. She was born in 1910 in Willis Bottom, grew up in Willow Grove, and graduated from Celina High School, all located in Clay County. In later years, she was an interior decorator with Sears and Cain-Sloan department stores in Nashville. She currently resides in Madison, a suburb of Nashville, at the Madison Church of Christ's Golden Age Village Retirement Home.

These two native Clay Countians married in 1931. In subsequent years they made their home in eight states and reared five children. Their children are Mary Emma Spear Stamps, a teacher at Goodpasture Christian School in Madison, Tennessee; Rebe Lee Spear Hagewood, a retired Metropolitan Nashville teacher; Frank Allen Spear, Jr., a United States Patent Examiner in Washington, D.C.; Clara Nell Spear Cundiff, a nurse in the Nashville area; and Danny Joe Spear, a Nashville businessman. They have ten grandchildren and one great grandchild. — *Submitted by Mary Spear Stamps*

LESLIE LEVI SPEAR

Leslie Levi Spear was born September 29, 1902 at Moss, Tennessee. He married Elfry Thompson, who was born October 4, 1921.

After attending Clay County High School, Leslie attended Draughons Business College in Nashville, and the Ford Trade School at the Ford Rouge Plant in Dearborn, Michigan, where he completed a course in toolmaking and served his apprenticeship. He worked for many years at this same plant as a toolmaker, and later at Oak Ridge, Tennessee on United States Defense projects, until his retirement.

Leslie was also very active in church work. He worked with various congregations in Michigan and has held gospel meetings in many locations here in Tennessee. He also wrote and published a book, *The True Religion and Religion of Others*.

Leslie and Elfry now live in Nashville, Tennessee. They have two sons, Dean Thompson and Billy Duke. Dean works with the United States Postal Service in Nashville, and Billy works for Boeing Corporation in Seattle, Washington.

RUBY MAE SPEAR

Ruby Mae Spear was born September 6, 1904 at New Hope near Moss, Tennessee. She married Omas Eads October 4, 1921. They had one son, James Opal Eads, who now lives in Ohio. After Ruby and Omas were divorced, Ruby married Don Rittgers.

Ruby was the oldest girl in a family of seven

boys and three girls. While the family was living at Pine Hill, Ruby entered high school at Moss; and her younger brother, Roy, was chosen to drive the horse and buggy from Pine Hill daily. After her high school days at Moss and Celina, she entered Berea College at Berea, Kentucky. She taught school at Midway and Pine Hill for a short time. Ruby was a talented organist; and she played at Saturday night "Singings" in the Spear home. Ruby was living in Ohio at the time of her death on April 7, 1980.

ROY EDWARD SPEAR

Roy Edward Spear was born October 9, 1906. On July 5, 1928, he married Lillian Clements. They have three daughters, Helen, Betty, and Anna. They have seven grandchildren and three great grandchildren.

Roy graduated from Clay County High School in 1926. The senior class picnic was held on the grounds of the Allons Church only seven miles away; and other activities included a trip to Livingston twenty miles away. Roy's life with a family of ten and his work with some of the great names of trade and industry brought him much joy, but his days as a teacher in Clay County were the most rewarding of all.

ORLAND ESTON SPEAR

Orland Eston Spear was born May 10, 1909 at New Hope in Clay County. He died April 4, 1984 in Clawson, Michigan. On May 25, 1935, he married Ila Tidwell.

Eston lived in Celina during his school years. He was very active in sports making varsity in all three major sports at Clay County High School. He worked for the State Highway Department in the early and mid 1930's. Eston was the only one of the seven sons in the family to learn the trade of his father, blacksmithing. When he started working in the auto industry in Michigan, he started as a millwright, without the usual factory training period for this trade; and within a very short time, he passed an examination and was certified by the State of Michigan as a machine builder. He said to his older brother, Roy, "What I learned from papa in that little, dirty blacksmith shop done the trick." This blacksmith shop was located near the present day Fire Department in Celina. His wife, Ila, also finished high school at Celina and worked for sometime in the factories of Michigan. After her death, Eston lived alone at the homeplace in Michigan. Eston and Ila had two children, Betty June, who died in infancy, and James Douglas (Jim), who lives in Troy, Michigan.

CHARLES RAY SPEAR

Charles Ray Spear was born November 15, 1911 in Celina, Tennessee. He died October 16, 1975. He married Vallie Pitcock February 12, 1937 and was later divorced.

Charles Ray possessed a talent for learning. He was seen on numerous occasions in the study hall at Clay County High School with a western novel concealed in a history book, and yet, he graduated as salutatorian of his class. After high school, he received a Bachelor of Science Degree from Berea College and a Masters Degree from the University of Tennessee. He served in the United States Navy during World War II. After the war, he worked for a short period of time with the State Agriculture Department. He later worked

in Michigan at various factory jobs.

Charles was an outstanding professional checker player, and he won many important matches in Ohio and Michigan, after learning to play in Clay County.

Charles Ray worked in Michigan until his retirement. From his first marriage, he has one son, Alex Neil, who lives in Dearborn Heights, Michigan. Charles Ray's second wife was Louise Brown. They had no children. His third marriage was to Dorothy Settles, and they have two children, Michael, who is in the United States Army, and Brenda, who lives in Michigan.

MATTIE MASON SPEAR

Mattie Mason Spear was born October 2, 1914 in Celina, Tennessee. She graduated from Celina High School at age 16. After the death of her father, she lived in Toledo, Ohio, where she met and married Lester Leroy Snyder February 6, 1937. They had two children, Patsy Ann and Denton Leroy. Mattie Mason later moved to Detroit, Mi. and worked in a defense plant during World War II. She later married Johnnie Howell, a native of Jackson County, November 21, 1958. Upon retirement, Mattie Mason and Johnnie moved to Daytona, Florida.

CORDELL DENTON SPEAR

Cordell Denton Spear was born January 30, 1918 in the Midway Community of Clay County. On June 23, 1928, Cordell died as a result of a drowning accident. He was ten years old. His teachers commented on his school reports that he was a sweet, bright child. He is remembered by his younger sister as having diplomatic and leadership traits — planning and organizing tasks and chores in such a way that they became fun and games. He could always be relied upon to do whatever he attempted well.

WILLIS EARL SPEAR

Willis Earl Spear was born March 5, 1920 in the Pine Hill Community of Clay County. He died April 13, 1980 in Celina, Tennessee. Willis was stricken with a serious illness at age one and a half, which was lengthy and left him physically handicapped. He graduated from Celina High School in 1939. He was extremely interested in school sports and seldom missed a game. Although he could not participate, he served as manager for the teams. He was very popular with his peers and was elected president of his high school classes. He graduated from Cumberland Law School in 1944 and passed the state bar examination that same year. He worked for a short time for the legal department of the Atomic Energy Commission in Oak Ridge, Tennessee. He returned to Celina and entered private practice of law; and for the last several years of his life, he served as General Sessions Judge of Clay County. He was active in the Masonic Order and became a Shriner. He served as Worthy Patron of the Eastern Star. He was active in the Baptist Church in Celina and was a Sunday School teacher there. He enjoyed golfing and had the distinction of making two holes-in-one during his lifetime. He liked to fish and in the 1950's, he caught what was then a world record largemouth bass. Because of his many inter-related physical problems, he was forced to retire in 1978. However, he remained mentally active and devoted much

of his time to the research of the genealogy of his family and the history of Clay County.

ANNA MARIE SPEAR

Anna Marie Spear was born November 26, 1921 in the Pine Hill Community of Clay County. She moved to Celina when she was two years old. She graduated from Celina High School in 1939. She was active in the sports program, playing on the basketball team for four years. She received a Bachelor of Science Degree from Carson-Newman College in 1944. While in college she met and married DuPont D. Smith from Spring City, Tennessee. They moved to Oak Ridge, Tennessee in 1944 and lived there until 1979. Marie and DuPont had three sons, David, Daniel, and Donald (died in 1981). Marie returned to school at the University of Tennessee and earned a Masters Degree in Education. She taught in the Oak Ridge School System from 1958 until 1983. She and her family moved to Kingston, Tennessee in 1979.

"AUNT ADD" STAFFORD

Arminey Adeline Williams was born December 1, 1863 in the Dry Mill Creek section of Clay County. Her father was one of the "fighting Williams," a family of men who wore long hair, widebrimmed hats, and carried loaded guns, after the style of Buffalo Bill. They kept fine livestock, and old-timers remember that they used to come riding up to the courthouses in Livingston and Celina brandishing their guns as they rode. They were feuding, as well as fighting, men but they were strict with their children. "Aunt Add" and her six sisters and five brothers were never allowed to do anything that smacked of pleasure. They could not go to night church meetings, much less to dances; and "Aunt Add" always told her mother that she was going to have dances if she ever had a home of her own.

Add Stafford

"Aunt Add" was married to five different men, but she was always addressed by the name of her third husband, Sam Stafford, the only one of her husbands separated from her by death. Her full name was Arminey Adeline Williams Boles Carmack Stafford Brown White. True to her word to her mother that she was going to have dances, she held a dance on "Old Christmas," January 5, for anybody who cared to come; and the walls of her six-room, two-story farmhouse bulged with merrymakers until long after January 5 became January 6. They danced in the living room, dining room, the kitchen, and the upstairs bedroom; and "Aunt Add" always had the lightest foot of them all. Although she stopped dancing at 65, she was considered "the dancingest thing you ever saw." She taught her "children and neighbors' children" to dance, and she held dancing parties at her house every time she had an excuse — such as a logrolling, a cornhusking, and a corn-shelling. She also took her "children and neighbors' children" to the town square of Celina on the fourth of July to square dance, an event that was "enjoyed by all." "Aunt Add" reared seventeen children, none of them her own, but always referred to as her "children."

When "Aunt Add" and Arg Boles married, they bought a farm and worked hard paying for it, but when she left him after nine years of marriage, she put her money into the next farm. She put up a house and started farming on her own.

Sometime around the turn of the century, she started logging. For 25 years, she stayed in the woods, working like a man, riding herd on her logging crews. Wearing overalls, she handled three span of mules at a time, snaking logs out of the Clay County hills. She was a familiar sight in the streets of Livingston and Celina, cracking a whip as she drove a four-mule team to a logging wagon. She sent four or five rafts of logs a year to Nashville. She kept two or three logging teams in the woods and ten teams of mules in the barn, and for 18 months at one stretch she cleared $80 a day.

With her profits, she bought more land, and that meant more woods to clear. Before she finished paying for one farm, she bought the adjoining one. She followed her mules with a plow, cultivating her land. She hauled staves. She once took a contract to handle timber for a Kentucky firm which made whiskey barrels, bought ten new wagons, hired a crew, and finally sold out the contract and equipment.

Perhaps the largest taxpayer in Clay County, and a heavy contributor to the coffers of Overton, Jackson, and Putnam counties as well, she owned approximately 2000 acres of land, and she also owned houses and lots in Livingston and in Cookeville. Twenty tenant families sharecropped her farm land for one-half of the proceeds. She had a healthy respect for a dollar and a reputation in the Upper Cumberland as an exacting employer. Therefore, she could well afford the luxury of mass hospitality.

In the Upper Cumberland, people who speak of the "good old days" are likely to be remembering the parties at "Aunt Add" Stafford's on Easter Sunday, when she "set" dinner for as many as 2000 hearty appetites whetted by dancing which started at sunup and continued after the midday meal until the darkness fell on Dry Mill Creek. One person recalled that "Aunt Add" killed 7 beef and 60 fat hens in preparation for one of her last Easter dinners, adding to this 26 hams which came from her smokehouse and 400 cakes and 600 pies which served as dessert. Five cooks kept three wood stoves going at full tilt in her yard for a solid week before the party, and ten more stoves blazed in the homes of her tenants to whom she furnished the food to be cooked for the feast. At this particular feast, "Aunt Add" had a man at the gate to register the guests before they passed into her one-acre garden, where the food was set out on wire fencing, stretched the full length of the garden on both sides and covered with bolts of brown domestic. When he had totaled up his register, the final count was 2,100. The Stafford hospitality was free to all comers, and attendance seldom fell

below 1500. "Aunt Add" was fond of saying, "Anybody is welcomed at my house."

Arminey Adeline Williams Boles Carmack Stafford Brown White is still a legendary figure in the Upper Cumberland. She was an experienced lumberjack, a crack shot, a famed hostess, a political heavyweight, and a woman who had reared seventeen children, none of them her own. *Submitted by Mrs. Malcom Young*

JOHN MIKE STOCKTON

John Mike Stockton, born April 11, 1871 — died April 17, 1955, was the son of Alvin and Amandy Spears Stockton. He had six sisters. They were Maretta Eads, Lounette Brown, Sally Hestand, Fannie Reecer, Pearl Netherton, and Florentia (Poode) Reecer. He had three brothers. They were Walter, Benton, and Randolph Stockton.

John, Kate, Delmar, Homer and Vinnie Stockton

John Mike married Vinnie Boyles, born September 10, 1884 — died January 1, 1943. Vinnie was the daughter of Newton Boyles and Nancy Lee Grissham Boyles. She was orphaned in the Ozark Mountains. Newton and Nancy decided to go west taking their four children, Othela A., Elles D., Luther, and Vinnie. Upon reaching the Ozarks, Nancy and the two older children died. Around 1889, after working three years in the Ozarks, Newton started walking to Carlisle, Arkansas with the two younger children. While on the road, Newton died leaving Luther, age seven, and Vinnie, age five. Newton had told the children they were going to catch a train back to Glasgow, Kentucky and then go to Moss, Tennessee. A black family took the children and cared for them until the officials came and Luther told them they were on their way to Moss, Tennessee. The postmaster in Carlisle wrote to Moss to verify Luther's statement. After receiving verification, the children were tagged and placed on the train for Glasgow and eventually to Moss.

John Mike and Vinnie has six children. They are Delmar Earl (deceased), Della Blanche (Kate) (deceased), Homer (Cracker), Emma, Mandy Lee, and Kathleen.

Delmar Earl Stockton, born March 31, 1904 — died December 3, 1965, married Rettie Strong, the daughter of Bart and Alta (McAlpin) Strong. They had three children, Bonnie Boone, Sandal Francis, and John Bart (deceased). The family lived in Indiana.

Della Blanche "Kate" (Stockton) Rich was born October 22, 1905. She married Sidney Perrin Rich, the son of John and Barbara (Watson) Rich. They had three children, Clifton, Louise

Brown (deceased), and Tim. Kate died January 5, 1980.

Homer (Cracker) Stockton, born October 27, 1907, married Zelma Rich, the daughter of Elisha and Molly (Brown) Rich. They had two sons, Tommy and Jimmy of Louisville, Kentucky.

Emma Stockton was born June 28, 1910. She married Willis "Bill" Rich, the son of Jesse and Laberta Crowder Rich. They have two children, Willis and LaRue Turner of Kentucky.

Mandy Lee Stockton was born November 19, 1912. She married Clark Cunningham, the son of Willie and Viola (Atkins) Cunningham. They have two sons, Clark Mitchell and Bart Jackson, of Moss, Tennessee. Mandy Lee has always been called "Dan" by her family and friends.

Kathleen Stockton, born July 17, 1915, married Andrew Davis, the son of Columbus and Della Cook Davis. They have three children, Chuck of Illinois, Eddie of Virginia, and Sharlene Allen of Indiana.

JOHN HENRY STONE

Ancestors of the Stone Family were some of the first settlers in what is now Clay County, Tennessee. They came to America as early as 1628 and settled in Virginia, and eventually they came from Virginia to Tennessee and Kentucky.

Uriah Stone came from Virginia to Kentucky and down the Cumberland in 1766. Stones River, near Nashville, was named for him. Again, in 1769, he and a party of hunters, all from Virginia and North Carolina, explored the Caney Fork and the Roaring Rivers. They camped at the present site of Celina, Tennessee.

John Henry and Nannie (Tinsley, Roberts) Stone

Uriah Stone later settled in what was Jackson County (now perhaps Kentucky), just south of the George Stephens Place, the state line having been changed. While we are not certain, it does appear that he is our ancestor.

George Washington Stone married a widow, Mrs. Martha Hunter, about 1784. They had nine children, John, Frank, Ecibius, Michajah, Billie, Richard, Archibald, James and George. James was my great grandfather.

James Stone married Nancy Peterman about 1820, and they had the following children: George, Martha, Sinah, Margaret, Lewis, John, and Rebecca. John was my grandfather.

James Stone operated a flatboat and often went down to New Orleans with freight. He was a farmer and merchant, and he died from cholera which he contacted at New Orleans in 1838.

John Henry Stone (1830-1921) first married Sarah Anne Gearhart, about 1856. Their children were Hugh (1857-1947), William Riley (1858-1922), James (1860-1924), Susan Mary (1863-?), Thomas (1865-1942), Robert (1867-1868), Sallie

(1869-1959), Ben (1871-1912), John (1873-1944), and Addiville (1877-1878). John Henry's second marriage was to the widow of Billie Roberts, Nannie Tinsley Roberts, who already had three children, Campbell, Billie, and Roxie Roberts. Then John Sr. and Nannie were the parents of eight children, George, Amos, Daisy, Alice, Columbus, Claude, Charlie, and Lee.

John Stone was a fine athlete when he was young. He was a Confederate soldier about 3½ years in the cavalry of General Nathan Bedford Forest, much of the time, a scout. He was sent to Texas to secure horses. He had 75 grandchildren and 16 stepgrandchildren.

After the Civil War, many young people looked westward, for there were increased opportunities there with much land to be homesteaded. Many found good land at very low prices. Three of John Stone's sons settled in Texas and reared families there. Two daughters and their husbands moved there and eventually reared large families. Three sons, Thomas, John, and Ben, remained in Tennessee. Of John Stone's children by his second wife, George went to Texas and spent the rest of his life there. Campbell and Roxie Roberts both married and moved to Arkansas. *History Given By Mr. Hubert E. Stone*

JOHN HENRY STONE, SR.

(Red) John Henry Stone, Sr., was born July 31, 1830 and died November 6, 1921. He was the son of James Stone and Nancy Peterman Stone.

Red John first married Sarah Gearheart who was the daughter of William and Sarah Roberts Gearheart. They had several children. Benjaman Franklin Stone was one of them. He served as a Chaplain in the United States Army during World War I. Ben's first wife was Lovie Arms, a sister to Tommy Arms and Laura (Arms) Roberts. Ben and Lovie's children were Robert, Lura and Laura. Ben's second wife was Docia Plumlee. They had one child, Bennie.

John H. and Nancy Tinsley Stone

Red John's second wife was Nancy (Tinsley) Roberts. Nancy was born November 10, 1851 and died December 29, 1929. She was the daughter of Amos Kirkpatrick Tinsley by his first wife, Arminta Kirkpatrick. Their children were George Pembroke; Amos Tinsley; Dayse Lucretia (married Tommy Arms; their six children are Alice, Nancy Helen, Edith, Billy Amos, Laura Lee and Walter); Alice Stone; Claude; Christopher Columbus Stone; Lee; and Charles Stone.

Many of the Stone family lived in England as far back as 1212 A.D., when Robert Stone was recorded as having lived in Oxford, England. The original Stones (Danish origin) in America were George Stone, Captain William Stone, Matthew Stone, and John Stone, who all settled in Virginia, migrating to Kentucky and to Tennessee. James and John settled in Clay County, Tennessee.

(Red) John Henry Stone, Sr. was a farmer, liking to hunt the fox. Living to be ninety-one years of age, Red John was a consistant member of the Christian Church, now called the Church of Christ. He donated the land for the old Beech Bethany Church of Christ. He died on a Sunday night, November 6, 1921, at his home on Proctor Creek near Beech Bethany. *Submitted by Helen Arms Wells*

JOHN AND SUZANNE STONE

John Howard Stone was born June 14, 1948 in Overton County, Livingston, Tennessee. He is the son of John Tom Stone and Nelle Lynch Stone. John T. Stone was raised in the Arcot Community with brothers, Billy and Louis, and sister, Marie. John Howard is the grandson of Wade Stone and Bertha Brown Stone of Celina, Tennessee and Ben Lynch and Roxie Mitchell Lynch of the Butler's Landing Community of Clay County.

Sam, Sue and John H. Stone

John Howard attended Clay County schools between 1954 and 1966. He then attended Tennessee Technological University from 1969-1972, getting a dental degree from the University of Tennessee Dental School in 1971. He opened a dental office in Celina in January, 1973.

John Howard was married to Sharon Suzanne Hayes Stone June 9, 1973. Suzanne was born in Detroit, Michigan December 10, 1949, the daughter of Hugh Ellis Hayes and Wilma Burris Hayes. She is the granddaughter of Charles W. Burris, Sr. and Willie Duke Burris, formerly of Overton County, and Willie Hugh Hayes and Willette Masters Hayes of Celina, Tennessee. Suzanne had two brothers, Michael and Steve.

Suzanne attended Wayne County schools in Detroit, Michigan from 1954-1956. She then moved with her family to Celina, Tennessee and completed her schooling in the Clay County schools graduating in 1967. She attended Tennessee Technological University and received a Bachelor of Science degree in Home Economics in 1971. She later returned to the university and earned a teacher's certificate and became a teacher in the Clay County schools.

On Feb. 19, 1979, John Howard and Suzanne became the parents of a son named Samuel Adam Stone. He was born at Cookeville General Hospital in Putnam County, Tennessee.

John Howard and family attend the Celina Church of Christ.

John Howard's hobbies and interests include hunting and archery. John Howard has made several trips to Colorado, Wyoming, and other western states to hunt deer, antelope and elk. He also has won many trophies for his archery skills.

Other ancestors of John Howard include Thomas Stone and Mary Coe Stone; John Brown and Ida Chapman Brown; Sarah Ann Gearheart Stone and John Henry Stone; and James Stone and Nancy Jefferson Peterman Stone.

PAUL STONE

Paul Stone was born in the Arcot Community of Clay County May 19, 1904. He was the seventh of eight children born to Tom and Mary Coe Stone. Paul attended the lower grades of school in a one-room, one-teacher school located at Knob Creek. He attended high school in Celina.

Paul and Mandy Berah McLerran were married September 10, 1925. Berah, the daughter of John Anderson and Orpha Moore McLerran, was the youngest of six children. She was born August 23, 1906 in Moss. She attended school through two years of high school in Moss. She then attended school in Celina and Murfreesboro.

Shirley, Henry, Paul, Berah, Bobby and Orpha Stone

After their marriage, Paul and Berah made their home in the Arcot Community where he was engaged in farming. She has been an active homemaker for sixty years. The Stones have attended the Arcot Church of Christ from their early years of marriage to the present. They are both members of the Church of Christ.

Paul served as Clay County Tax Assessor for twenty-eight years. He has held the position of Grand Jury Foreman since 1982.

Paul and Berah have four children, two sons, Henry Boyd and Bobby Mitchell, and two daughters, Orpha Coe and Shirley Ann.

Henry Boyd married Launa Gay Buford, the daughter of C.R. and Nannie Clark Buford. The Bufords lived in the Willow Grove Community before impoundment of Dale Hollow Lake. Bobby Mitchell married Billie June Buford, a sister to Henry's wife, Launa. Bobby and Billie have two daughters, Gaye Ann and Donna Gail. Donna Gail is married to Andy Scott.

Orpha Coe married Charles J. Masters, the son of Walter G. and Gypsy Brown Masters. Orpha Coe and Charles have seven children—three daughters and four sons. Their daughters are Sharon Kaye, Mary Katherine and Joyce Stone. Sharon married Bill Harward, and they have two sons, William and Benjamin. Mary Katherine married Bobby Hyatt, and they have three children, Rachel, Matthew and Mandy. Joyce Stone married Bill Johnson, and they have one child, a daughter, Sydney. The four sons of Orpha Coe and Charles are Charles Stephen, Paul Gray, John Thomas, and Joseph Michael. Charles Stephen married Sloan Easton; they have two sons, Jayson and Eric. Paul Gray married Deborah Macon. John Thomas married Lindy Leath. Michael is a high school student.

Shirley married David Sharp, the son of Vina Watson and Leslie Sharp. David and Shirley have one son, David Alan, who is a college student.

ROY LEE STRONG

Roy Lee Strong was born January 27, 1924 in Clay County, Tennessee. He is the son of Fay and Virgie Frances (Collins) Strong. He married Geraldine Johnson May 29, 1947. Geraldine was born April 4, 1930, the daughter of Garrett and Bertha Alice Johnson.

Roy and Geraldine have lived in the Brimstone and Turkey Creek Communities of Clay County except for a short time that they lived in Indianapolis, Indiana. Roy was a farmer. He died of cancer February 25, 1977. Geraldine is a housewife and is employed by OshKosh. She is a member of the Church of Christ.

Roy and Geraldine have nine children, Robert, Sharon Kay, Paul, Clark, Randall, Eva, Ina, Shelba, and Lisa.

RANDELL NEIL STRONG

Randell Neil Strong was born August 8, 1957 in Clay County, Tennessee. He is the son of Roy and Geraldine (Johnson) Strong. He grew up in the Brimstone Community. He graduated from Hermitage Springs High School in 1975. He was married July 9, 1981 to Connie Diana Browning.

Randell, Matthew and Connie Strong

Connie was born January 18, 1956 in Indianapolis, Indiana. She is the daughter of Delbert and Bonnie (Copass) Browning. She graduated from Southport High School in Indianapolis, Indiana in 1974. She was employed by Burger Chef, Dunham Rubber and Belting, Eli Lilly and Company, and RCA Corporation before moving to Clay County in 1981. Randell is employed at Green Forest Wood Products, and Connie works for OshKosh at Hermitage Springs. They live in the Pine Hill Community of Clay County. Connie is a member of the Church of Christ. They have one son, James Matthew.

WILLIAM FRANK SWAN

William Frank Swan was born April 6, 1867. He was the son of John Alexander Swan and Matilda E. (Farris) Swan. His sister was Sarah (Swan) Flynn. He was the grandson of George Lane Swan. John was born in 1836 and died in 1922 in Jackson County. His wife was born March 6, 1842 and died April 21, 1919 in Jackson County.

W.L. (Windy), Delilah, holding Lisa and Edward Swan

William Frank married Delilah Edmonds, the daughter of Tom Edmonds, February 1, 1885. William Frank was a preacher. He and Delilah had 13 children, John Thomas, Mary Jane, Martha A., Tilda, Cora, Lena, William Luther, Henry Clay, Avo Hulty, Millard Wesley, Sallie Lou, Harrison Cecil, and Delilah Mae. William Luther was born January 25, 1896 and died October 6, 1966. He was an oil field worker, farmer, carpenter, and sawmill operator. On November 28, 1920, he married Mona Della Freeman, the daughter of John M. Freeman and Margaret C. (Halliburton) Freeman. Mona Della was born April 13, 1893 in Macon County; and she died July 27, 1975. William and Della had five children, Jesse Freeman, Edward Carrington, Thomas Edmond, Luther Dell, and Delilah Katherine.

Jesse Freeman was born January 30, 1922 in Coalinga, California. He was married November 6, 1948 to Evelyn Hamilton, the daughter of Jim Mitchell and Maude Hamilton. Evelyn was born March 8, 1925. Jesse Freeman and Evelyn have one daughter, Jessie Ann, who married James Beason on April 14, 1972. They have one daughter, Mellisa.

Edward was born June 26, 1924 in Coalinga, California. He died April 18, 1972 in Clay County. On September 17, 1949, he married Jane Marie Sparks, the daughter of Dillard and Zetta Sparks. Jane Marie was born November 19, 1928. Jane and Edward had five children: Barbara Elaine, born and died February 28, 1952; Lisa Ellen, born February 28, 1952; Leann Marie, born January 24, 1955; Julie Katherine, born and died January 16, 1961; Edward Alan, born and died July 2, 1962; and one adopted son, Travis Mark, who was born March 22, 1962. Lisa was married August 31, 1974 to Greg Teeples of Nashville, Tennessee. Leann was married April 14, 1973 to Domer Collins. They have one daughter, Caitlin.

Thomas was born September 4, 1926. Luther was born July 15, 1928. Katherine was born March 6, 1930. On August 30, 1953, she married Robert Dillon, the son of Joe and Ada Dillon of Livingston, Tn. Robert was born August 21, 1924. Katherine and Robert have two daughters, Roberta Jean and Lila Deann. Roberta was married to Mark Cobbe of Dayton, Ohio September 16, 1978. They have one daughter, Sara.

HENRY CLAY SWANN

Henry Clay Swann was born January 16, 1899, on Hamilton Branch in Jackson County. He was one of thirteen children born to William Frank and Deliah Edmunds Swann. All thirteen children survived except Sally Lou who died at two from whooping cough. His paternal grandfather was a miller, but very little is known of his maternal grandparents.

He grew up on Sugar Creek in Jackson County, as the son of a father who farmed, cut timber, practiced as a lay veterinarian and preached in the Church of Christ.

During his teen years he became known for his adventurous spirit, as well as his mechanical abilities. One adventure was to raft logs down the Cumberland River in 1915, at age 16. The salary was $25 for eight days, six days to Nashville and two days return on the steamboat "Joe Horton Falls".

Inez, Nora, James and Henry Swann

In January, 1918, at eighteen, he left Tennessee for California to make his fortune. He departed Sugar Creek on the steamboat "Dudney" and left Nashville by rail three days later. He remained in California for eight months, but was corresponding with a young lady from Overton County, Nora Fleming. Affairs of the heart prevailed and he returned to Tennessee where he and Nora were married December 15, 1918.

He and his bride remained in Tennessee until September 1919, when California called again, and he, Nora, and 9 months old daughter, Inez, headed west by train. The young family stayed in California until 1924, with Henry working in the oil fields. A son, James Henry, was born in 1921. In 1924 they visited Tennessee, crossing the desert on plank roads in a Model T, returning to California where they remained until 1926.

The family moved to Clay County in 1927, where a son, Wayne Fleming, was born. In 1928, Henry opened a general store in Butler's Landing, but the depression hit, so in 1929 he moved to Grey John Hill to cut timber as his father had done. He continued this until 1939, operating a portable sawmill in Clay County, Jackson County, and Monroe County, Kentucky. In 1940, he moved to Celina on six acres of land purchased for $600 and opened Celina Lumber Company, which he operated until 1962. His last child, Linda, was born in 1940.

Henry and Nora Swann were married sixty years. She died September 5, 1978. "Daddy Swann," as he is affectionately known to his six grandchildren and seven great grandchildren, has been a source of strength and inspiration to his family, and at 87 his sense of adventure lives on.

GEORGE CLEMONS TAYLOR

George Clemons Taylor and his wife, Clora Cole, bought the S.B. Moulder farm in northwestern Clay County in 1924. The farm is located between Laurel Bluff and Hermitage Springs. The Poplar Bluff School was located on this farm.

George and Clora had five children, Agnes, Clarence, Louis, and twins, Alene and Alice. The children attended school at Laurel Bluff and Hermitage Springs. Three of the children graduated from college — Middle Tennessee State University, the University of Tennessee, and Tennessee Technological University. George Clemons died in 1955, and Clora died in 1969.

The George Clemons Taylor Family

Their farm is still in the family now belonging to Alene and her husband, Mitchell Turner. They have three children. Jerry and his wife, Barbara, and their two children, Brian and Jamie, live on an adjoining farm. Janet and her husband, Robert Hawkins, have three children, Robert and twins, Jonathon and Jessica, and also live on an adjoining farm. Michael lives in Nashville, Tennessee.

George Clemons and Clora's oldest daughter, Agnes, and her husband, Clifton Ray, are retired teachers and live in Jacksonville, Florida. They had four children. David, at the age of 21, was killed in a car accident. James and his wife, Janice, and their two children, Andrew and Amanda, live in Newbern, North Carolina. Charles is in the Navy. Sandra Reed and her daughter, Eilene, live in Jacksonville, Florida.

Clarence and his wife, Billie Ruth, and daughter, Sylvia, live in Indianapolis, Indiana. He is employed with Mail Transportation.

Louis had a long military career with many honors. His rank was Brigadier General when he retired. He and his wife, Eloise Ritter, had one daughter, Debi. Debi married William Tate, and they are both attorneys. Eloise was a teacher. Both Louis and Eloise are deceased. Debi and William Tate and their two sons, Will and Taylor, live in Nashville, Tennessee.

Alice Taylor married Bascom Ray, a photographer. They had three children, Kenny, Barbara, and Sylvia. Alice is a registered dietitian and is listed in Who's Who in the South and Southwest. Bascom Ray is deceased, and Alice lives in Springfield, Tennessee. Her son, Kenny, also lives in Springfield. Her daughter, Barbara Head, and her children, Trase and Alicia, live in Springfield. Sylvia and her husband, Mark Stiles, live in Athens, Georgia.

ROBERT MATTHEW TEEPLES

Robert Matthew Teeples was born March 23, 1926. He is the son of William Hunter and Tommie Masters Teeples. John attended Celina High

School, graduating in 1944. From high school, John entered the United States Navy, serving in the South Pacific during World War II. After leaving the Navy, John entered Tennessee Polytechnic Institute and graduated in 1950. He received his Master of Arts Degree from Tennessee Technological University in 1975. He was a coach in the Clay County Schools for many years, coaching girls' basketball, boys' basketball, and football. He was principal of Celina K-8 School, when he retired to be a full-time agent for State Farm Insurance. His office is in the Log Cabin on the Square.

John Teeples   Betty Teeples

John is married to Betty Ruth Langford, the daughter of Thomas and Rachel Langford of Celina. Betty attended Clay County Schools, graduating from Celina High School in 1947. Betty received her Bachelor of Science Degree from Tennessee Polytechnic Institute in 1956 and her Master of Arts Degree from Tennessee Technological University in 1973. Betty was a teacher with the Clay County School System, worked with Title I, and was Team Manager for the Urban/Rural School Development Program — a $750,000 grant awarded to Clay County for teacher training. She retired from teaching in 1983, and is now working with her husband in the insurance business.

John Patrick Teeples

Betty and John have one son, John Patrick, born December 12, 1967. Pat graduated from Celina High School in 1986, where he participated in football and baseball. He was active in various clubs, as well as 4-H Club activities. Pat enrolled in Sewanee, the University of the South, in 1986.

The family attends church at the Celina Methodist Church. John is a member of the Clay County Quarterly Court, having served for the past 14 years. He is a charter member of the Celina Lions Club. He has been a member of the Tri County Vocational School since its inception. He is Chair-

man of the Clay County Foster Care Review Board. Betty is a member of the Eastern Star, and she is chairman of the Clay County Citizens' Advisory Council for the betterment of the Clay County School System. John and Betty are members of the Celina Chamber of Commerce, and they are active in the Democratic Party.

JAMES BURTON TERRY

James Burton Terry was born March 15, 1847 in Putnam County, Tennessee. He was the oldest of fifteen children born to Vincent M. Terry and Sarah Katherine (Dowell) Terry. Vincent was born in 1824 and died in 1869 in Putnam County, Tennessee. His wife was born in 1829 in Putnam County and died in 1906 in Royce City, Texas. James Burton was a lover and breeder of fine horses. He was in the military service during the Civil War. He was married March 25, 1869 to Martha Ann Buford. Martha was born December 10, 1850 and died October 11, 1886 in Clay County, Tennessee. She was the daughter of Edwin R. Buford and Isabelle (Taylor) Buford. They had six children, Johnny, Edwin, Curtis, Robert, Lou (Peterman), and Lon. After her death, James Burton married Nancy Emma Holman August 20, 1892. She was the daughter of Robert N. Holman and Susan Millimersalis Stephens. She was born January 17, 1868 and died November 4, 1942 in the Pleasant Grove community of Clay County. They had four children, Arthur, Jewell, Willie, and Raymond.

Alfred and Katherine Clark, Sandra Shepherd, Pat Davis and Jim and Eddie Clark

Jewell Winchester Terry was born August 17, 1896 and died April 21, 1980 in Clay County. He attended Dixie College and served in the military during World War I. He was a farmer, a member of the school board, a Justice of the Peace, and an elder of the Rock Springs Church of Christ. He was married April 5, 1925 to Agnes Donaldson, who was born December 17, 1896 in Clay County. She was the daughter of Andrew Thomas Donaldson and Minnie Avo (Watson) Donaldson. She taught school at Plainview in Clay County for many years. Jewell and Agnes were the parents of two daughters, Katherine and Aenona.

Katherine Terry Clark was born January 13, 1926 in Clay County, Tennessee. She was married March 18, 1948 in Cookeville, Tennessee to Alfred Cornell Clark. Cornell was born on June 15, 1923 in the Willow Grove Community of Clay County. Cornell was the son of Charles Edward Clark and Mary Pearl (Upchurch) Clark. Katherine is a retired teacher, and Cornell is retired from the Agriculture Extension Service. They live in Cookeville, Tennessee. They have four children. Sandra Shepherd was born June 25, 1949. She works with Human Services in Putnam County and has two sons, Kent and Garrett. Pat Davis was born March 30, 1951. She is a lawyer in Nashville, Tennessee. Jim was born on October 31, 1954. He is a college English teacher. Eddie was born November 20, 1961. He recently graduated from Tennessee Technological University.

ARTHUR VIRGIL TERRY

Arthur Terry was born September 10, 1893 in Clay County, Tennessee. He was the son of James Burton (Burt) Terry and Nancy Emma (Holman) Terry. Arthur had two brothers, Raymond and Jewel, and one sister, Willie. He also had several half brothers and half sisters due to a previous marriage of his father.

Arthur and Della Terry

Arthur grew up in Tennessee and met his future bride, Della Mae (Goodpasture). She was the daughter of Tom Goodpasture and Ida (Richardson) Goodpasture. After they married and had one child, Cornell Savage Terry, they decided to move out west to Texas. Arthur had a half brother, Bob, who lived close to Dallas, Texas. Once they arrived in Texas, they found a small community in east Texas and settled down to make a home. They farmed and raised cattle. One more son was born, Ray Vincent Terry. Arthur eventually bought a general store in the country. His son, Cornell, carried on the tradition by starting a general store in the town of Emory, Texas. Ray Terry served in World War II and went on to be a hospital administrator. Cornell married Veda Rhea Lennon, and they had two sons, Lawrence Arthur and Tommy Frank. Ray married Audrey June Harrison, and they had one son, Dale Ray Terry. Lawrence carried on the tradition of general stores, but being a "college kid" tried to refine the operation and specialized in furniture. He married Linda Kay Shaffner, and they have two daughters, Anna Marie and Laura Anne. Tommy Frank died as a young child in 1956. Dale Terry married Joan Marie Fritz and they live in Dallas. Dale is executive vice-president of a large Dallas bank. They have one daughter, Erin Marie.

Arthur Terry died March 24, 1972. Della died October 12, 1979. They both loved Clay County and cherished the memories and the people of the area.

DAVID THOMAS THREET

David Thomas Threet was born February 4, 1947, in Celina, Tennessee. He is the son of Claston Thomas Threet and Velma Dona (Thompson) Threet. David is the grandson of Cosberry Threet and Ollie George Threet and John Thompson and Seretha (Webb) Thompson of Clay County.

Nathan, Rachel, Willie and David Threet

David attended school in Clay County and graduated from Celina High School in 1967. He spent three years at Middle Tennessee State University where he received the Bachelor of Science Degree in 1973. He did his postgraduate work at Tennessee Technological University and received the Masters of Arts Degree in Education and Administration in 1979.

For the past twelve years, David has been a teacher and a coach in the Clay County School System. He has served as assistant junior high football coach and as coach of the sixth grade football and basketball teams. He teaches social studies in the sixth grade. David is a member of the Clay County Education Association, the Tennessee Education Association, and the National Education Association. David is a member of the Celina Fire Department, the Clay County Rescue Squad, and the Democratic Party.

David is married to Winnie Lee Adams. Winnie is the daughter of Cordell Thomas Adams and Delia Mae (Scott) Adams of Clay County. She is the granddaughter of Miles Adams and Plina Perrin Adams of Clay County. Winnie attended school in Clay County and received her GED from Celina High School. She was employed for two years with the Upper Cumberland Human Resource Agency and is presently employed at the Crotty plant in Celina.

David and Winnie are the parents of Rachel Nicole Lee, born December 23, 1976, and David Nathan Thomas, born May 17, 1978. Rachel and Nathan are students at Celina K-8 School.

JOHN TINSLEY

The name Tinsley is English in origin and means "one who came from Tynee's Hill in Yorkshire." The name Tinsley appears in Virginia records as early as 1630. This is a date close to the founding of the first permanent English settlement in America at Jamestown, Virginia in 1607.

John Tinsley, born February 29, 1976 — died April 15, 1853, was an early settler in Tinsley's Bottom in Jackson County, Tennessee. John was married June 2, 1816 to Alice Mulkey, born April 19, 1797 — died January 16, 1874, the daughter of Reverend Philip Mulkey, a Disciples of Christ minister and founder of "Old Mulkey Meeting House," now a memorial state park in Monroe County, Kentucky. John and Alice were the parents of 15 children, including Thaddeus Sobieski Tinsley, born March 31, 1832 — died July 2, 1905. Thaddeus married Julia Ann Fowler July 13, 1854. Julia Ann was born September 24, 1837; and she died July 3, 1913. Thad and Julia migrated to Missouri from Tinsley's Bottom in February 1873, where they settled in Dallas County approximately four miles northwest of Buffalo.

Thad and Julia had ten children, including John Henry Tinsley, born March 24, 1858 — died January 26, 1932, who was born in Tinsley's Bottom and migrated to Missouri with his parents. John Henry married Mary Elizabeth Hendrickson Feb. 1, 1883. Mary Elizabeth was born August 18, 1862, and she died June 1, 1946. John Henry and Mary Elizabeth had ten children. As of 1963, there were seven generations in direct descent from John Tinsley.

THADDEUS SOBIESKI TINSLEY

Thaddeus Sobieski Tinsley was born March 31, 1832 in Tinsley's Bottom, Jackson County, Tennessee. He died July 2, 1905 in Dallas County, Missouri. He was the son of John Tinsley, born 1796 — died 1853, and Alice Mulkey Tinsley, born 1797 — died 1874.

Thaddeus Sobieski is a strange name for an Anglo-Saxon family such as Tinsley. His mother, the daughter of a minister, sister of a minister, granddaughter of a minister, and an avid reader, as well as a very religious person, selected this name from her many readings.

Thaddeus was married July 13, 1854 to Julia Ann Fowler, born September 24, 1837 — died July 3, 1913. She was born and grew up on a farm adjacent to Thad's in Tinsley's Bottom. Thaddeus became the President of Philomath Academy and was a teacher there. Thaddeus was also a preacher for the church which was located in the middle of a fine beech and poplar grove on a high bank of the Cumberland River. At about the time of the Civil War, Thaddeus and Julia and their four children moved across from Turkey Creek to take care of his widowed mother at the old family homestead in Tinsley's Bottom.

Thaddeus was not only a preacher and teacher but a successful farmer as well. Thaddeus and Julia were the parents of ten children. Thad and Julia celebrated their Golden Wedding Anniversary July 13, 1904. He lived one more year to age 73. Julia lived to be 76. When Thad died, Julia moved from the big house on the farm into a little house in Buffalo, Missouri. In 1913, she decided to visit her son, Clay, in Colorado, and the trip wore her out. She died a few hours after her arrival. She was buried in the Lindley Church Cemetery.

RILEY UPTON

Riley Upton was born April 25, 1823 on Mill Creek, Overton County, Tennessee. He married Martha Peterman September 22, 1843. She was the daughter of George Washington Peterman and Sarah Lincoln Peterman. To them were born ten children, Polly Ann "Smith"; Turner Michael; Riley; Sarah; Zeda Ann "Gentry"; Parillia "Holman"; Martha "Howard"; Belle "Hawkins"; James, and Joseph Jones Upton.

Turner Michael Upton was born January 3, 1846 on Mill Creek, Overton County Tennessee. He was married to Martha Dougherty December 18, 1864. To them were born eleven children, Minnie "Peterman"; Montie "Robbins"; Dennie Ann "Garrett", Bailey Peyton; Willie Clayton; Hattie "Stinson"; Joe Bob; Laura "Ward"; Emma "Hill" "Fisk" "Terry"; and Edda "Gibbons".

Willie Clayton Upton married first, Belle Garrett. They had a son named Larue who died in infancy. Belle died June 15, 1915. They are both buried at the Garrett Cemetery near Allons, Tennessee. Clayton married second Belle Butler, They had a son, Willie Butler Upton, born May 27, 1921. Clayton died January 25, 1944 and is buried in the Fitzgerald Cemetery, Celina, Tennessee.

Willie Butler Upton married Edwina Smith June 28, 1941. She is the daughter of Velma Goodpasture Smith and the late Cecil Smith. He died April 24, 1957, buried in Fitzgerald Cemetery, Celina, Tennessee. Butler and Edwina had one daughter, Betty Sue Upton, born July 17, 1945. She married James Michael Briggs December 11, 1971. They have two sons, Michael Butler Briggs and John Harold Briggs.

Butler and Edwina Upton have operated the Upton Funeral Home in Celina, Tennessee since 1949. Their son-in-law and daughter, Jim and Betty Briggs have joined them in this business.

Riley and Martha Upton lived from the time they married until their death almost 60 years later, on the same farm that Riley was born on. At their death the farm was purchased by a grandson, Clayton Upton, and a grandson-in-law, Spencer Garrett. Clayton later sold his part to the Garretts who lived there until they died, he in 1962, her in 1956. This farm remained in the Upton family for 119 years.

TURNER MIKE UPTON

Turner Mike Upton and Martha Dougherty Upton began housekeeping near Timothy, Tennessee. They lived in a log cabin on a farm they called the "Brushey Ridge Farm". The log cabin still stands on the old farm, but has been moved from its original site. All their children were born in this cabin. After the children were all grown, "Mike" and Martha moved to Hilham, Tennessee in the late 1890's and built a new house on a farm they had bought. This house still stands but is in a bad state of repair. This farm is now owned by Mr. and Mrs. Lenard Ward. Lenard is a grandson of Mike and Martha's.

Turner Mike Upton Family

The descendants of "Mike" and Martha Upton live in almost all the western states and many of the eastern states. The descendants of Riley and Martha "Peterman" Upton have a reunion every year at Cumberland Mountain State Park near Crossville, Tennessee.

CHARLIE VAUGHN

Charlie Vaughn was born and raised in the Alpine Community of Overton County. He attended Alpine Presbyterian High School. Mr.

Vaughn received a Bachelor of Science Degree from Tennessee Polytechnic Institute and a Masters Degree from Peabody College. Both degrees were in agriculture. In 1934, he became County Agent for Clay County. He held this position until his retirement in 1969. He was instrumental in the organization of the Farm Bureau, the Clay County Co-op, the Farmers Home Administration, the Agricultural Stabilization & Conservation Service, the Production Credit Association, Tri-County Electric, and Twin Lakes Telephone Cooperative.

Elsie Jo Vaughn and Children

Mr. Vaughn married Elsie Jo Pettit of White County, Tennessee. Mrs. Vaughn attended White County Schools and received a Bachelor of Science Degree in mathematics from Tennessee Polytechnic Institute. Both Mr. and Mrs. Vaughn were interested in athletics. Mr. Vaughn played for the Tennessee State Champs at Alpine Presbyterian High School and went to the National Finals in Chicago. He played collegiate basketball at Tennessee Polytechnic Institute. Mrs. Vaughn played for the Tennessee State Champions in basketball while at White County High School. She played collegiate basketball at Tennessee Polytechnic Institute. Mrs. Vaughn coached girls' basketball at Celina High early in her teaching career.

Charlie Vaughn

Mrs. Vaughn began her teaching career in Clay County in 1935. She taught mathematics at Celina High School for a number of years. She served as Junior Class sponsor for several years, and the beautiful banquets that she and her classes did for the Senior Classes are still remembered by Celina High School graduates. She was very innovative in the teaching of her mathematics classes, for example, correlating geometry and art. Mrs. Vaughn was the first woman to be elected Superintendent of Schools, and she was the first woman to serve as Principal of Celina Elementary School. She implemented one of the first breakfast programs for students in the State of Tennessee.

Both Mr. and Mrs. Vaughn were always working to improve Clay County — both educationally and economically. Neither ever really "retired."

Mr. and Mrs. Vaughn had three children, Charles Joseph who now lives in Alpine and has five children; Donna who lives in San Antonio and has two children; and Tammy who lives in Celina and has two children. All three of the Vaughn children were excellent athletes. They all three played basketball, and Charles Joseph was an outstanding quarterback for the Celina High School football team.

WILLIAM CAMPBELL WADDLE

William Waddle, born December 8, 1852 to Jimmy and Katie Waddle, was married to Lucretia Alice Stone (born October 2, 1859 to John and Martha Tinsley Stone) on Oct. 7, 1885. Bill was a farmer and logger on Mill Creek where his father homesteaded. He was Sheriff of Clay County, 1904 till 1906, living in the house adjoining the jail during this term, then moving back to Mill Creek, where he died. Four sons were born to this family, who attended Baptist Ridge School, also used as a church, with a dirt floor and benches made of split chestnut logs with no backs. Bedford and Butler attended Burrett College, Spencer, Tennessee. Willie attended Montvale Academy for two years, either walking or riding a horse.

Bedford, born September 6, 1886, married Rhea Graves, daughter of the Headmaster at Burrett College. They lived in Crystal Springs, Mississippi, where he was Mayor for several years and State Representative. After Rhea's death, he remarried, and his widow lives in Hattiesburg.

Butler (February 14, 1889-November 9, 1977) was a teacher and married his student, Minnie Moore. They operated a store on Baptist Ridge. He was an avid fisherman, nicknamed "Zibe."

James (September 18, 1890-September 1925) married Fannie Langford, daughter of Barlow and Martha Langford, and had four daughters:

Ruby married Clifton Loftis, a farmer at Butlers Landing, and she has two children, Jean Keys of Nashville, and James Riley of Livingston, who has three children.

Ruth lived in Nashville and worked for GENESCO and the State of Tennessee, until death in 1979.

Edith married Edgar Phillips and now lives on the farm homesteaded by her great grandfather.

James Wilma married Ray Birdwell, Clay Countian, and veteran of World War II. They have one son, Richard, and live in Humboldt.

Willie (August 14, 1894) married Lizzie Smith, daughter of Clark and Martha Dale Smith, September 16, 1915, and lived on the Arcot Road until her death in 1972, when he moved to Nashville. Willie, nicknamed "ATT" was a farmer, Circuit Court Clerk for 16 years, State Auditor under Governor McCord, an avid fisherman, and enjoyed guiding fishermen on Dale Hollow. Lucille, their only child, married Cornell Bowe, who entered the Army in 1942, and retired in 1969, with the rank of Lieutenant Colonel, serving through three wars. They had three children, Jeanna Boulware, Nashville, a teacher at David

Lipscomb College, who has two children, Jesse, Jr. of Nashville, District Sales Manager for Biggers Brothers Foods, who has two daughters; and Jennifer, a student at Abilene Christian University.

JAMES A. WALKER

James A. Walker is a descendant of Van Walker, born in 1824 in Tennessee. His father was born in North Carolina and his mother in Tennessee. Van married Marey Hill, born in 1830. Van was a farmer and Marey a keeper of the home. They were the parents of six children, John, George, Melvina, Jesse, Sarah, and Benjamin.

George Walker was born in 1860 in Clay County, Tennessee. He married Florence Franklin, the daughter of Tom Franklin. George and Florence were the parents of nine children, Gertrude, Benton, Elzie, Lesly, Clure, Bethel, Allie, Nina, and Myrtle.

Mary Mullins, James A., James Allen and Robert Benton Walker

Benton Walker was born September 18, 1886 in Clay County, Tennessee. He died August 14, 1954. He married Dovie Reecer, born April 2, 1892 in Clay County, Tennessee. She died January 3, 1974. They are buried in the Moss Cemetery. Dovie is the daughter of Hamilton Reecer, born in 1857, and Burnetta Spear Reecer, born in 1855. Benton and Dovie are the parents of Lona, Lena, Livie, Cecil, Dumas, Eulas, Pettious, Minnie, Edward, Clifford, Dauphine, James, Cristeen, and Durell.

Dovie Walker

James A. Walker was born November 14, 1929 in Clay County, Tennessee. After high school, he served three years in the Korean War. He later received his Bachelor of Science and Masters degrees from Middle Tennessee State University and his Rank 1 from Western Kentucky University. He accepted a position teaching at Pleasure Ridge Park High School in Louisville, Kentucky.

On August 16, 1969, James married Mary Mullins of Lebanon, Kentucky. She was born January 2, 1944, the daughter of Robert Shirrell

Mullins and Elizabeth Mouser Mullins. She was the granddaughter of Less Mullins and Mary Helm Mullins and Will Mouser and Ruth Yankee Mouser, all of Lebanon, Kentucky.

Mary received her Bachelor of Science degree from Eastern Kentucky State University, her Masters from Western Kentucky University and 30 hours above her Masters (Rank 1) from the University of Louisville. She now teaches math at Southern High School in Louisville, Kentucky.

James and Mary are the parents of two boys, James Allen, born February 10, 1974, and Robert Benton, born August 10, 1976. James Allen is a student at Jefferson County Traditional Middle School, and Robert Benton is at Audubon Traditional School. Both are on the Okolona Soccer Team in Louisville.

This family has a vacation home in Celina, Tennessee and they enjoy coming to Clay County. The family now attends the Highview Baptist Church in Louisville, Kentucky.

BENTON THOMAS WALKER

Benton Thomas Walker is a descendant of the following:

Van Walker was born in 1824 in Tennessee. His father was born in North Carolina, and his mother in Tennessee. Van married Marey, who was born in 1830. Van was a farmer and Marey a keeper of the home. The birthplace of Van Walker's descendants was in Clay County, Tennessee near Celina. Following is a list of Van and Marey's children and who they married: John married Lee Ann Franklin; George married Florence Franklin; Melvina married Joe Driver; Jesse married Ellie Benson; Sarah married Andrew Reecer; and Benjamin married Ida Franklin.

Benton Walker and his sister Gertrude

George Walker was born in 1860; he died in 1927. He married Florence Franklin, who died in 1923. She was the daughter of Tom and Emma Franklin. George and Florence were leaders in the Liberty Hill Church of Christ on Proctor Creek, four miles from Celina. Florence can be remembered sitting up front and singing so beautifully, and at night after services George would carry the old oil lamp high above his head for the people to see how to get out of the church house. Following is a list of their children and who they married: Gertrude married Tolley Reecer; Benton married Dovie Reecer; Elzie married Pearly Anderson; Lesley married Minnie Head; Allie married Jack McLerran; Clure married Mollie Reecer; Bethel married Lula Head; Nina married Harlin McLerran; and Myrtle died at age seven. George and Florence are buried in the Walker-Reecer Cemetery on Proctor Creek in Clay County, Tennessee.

Benton Walker was born September 18, 1886. He died August 14, 1954. He married Dovie Reecer in 1906. Dovie was born April 2, 1892 and died January 3, 1974. They are buried in the Moss Cemetery in Clay County. Dovie was the daughter of Hamilton Reecer, born in 1857, and Bernetta Spear Reecer, born in 1859. Bernetta was the daughter of John Crouch Spear, born in 1826, and Eliza Spear, born in 1834. Following is a list of Benton and Dovie's children and who they married: Lona married W.P. Capshaw; Lena married Norman Clancy; Livie married Carson Chitwood; Cecil married Olivia Marshall; Dumas married Hazel Smith; Eulas never married; Pettious married James Sullivan; Minnie Lee married Thomas Redford; Edward was killed in World War II; Clifford married Louise Waller and then Ann Nesbett; Dauphine married Ray Hunley; James married Mary Mullins; Christeen married Lesley West, Jr.; and Durell married Sue Weaver. *Submitted by Lona W. Capshaw*

DURELL WALKER

Durell Walker was born September 26, 1933 near Celina, Tennessee. He is the youngest son of Benton Thomas and Dovie (Reecer) Walker. He married Sue Weaver, who was born February 18, 1936, the daughter of the late Mozella Weaver. Durell and Sue have two children,: Steven Edward and Sharon Gaye.

Sue, Durell, Sharon and Steve Walker

Steven Edward was born June 26, 1956 in Jackson County, Tennessee. He is a graduate of Smith County High School and Tennessee Technological University in Cookeville, Tennessee. He has done graduate work at the University of Tennessee in Knoxville. He is currently employed by the University of Tennessee Extension Service in Macon County. On March 13, 1977, he married Beverly Ann Waller who was born July 12, 1957 in Smith County, Tennessee. Beverly is the daughter of Hiram and Maud (Dixon) Waller. Her grandparents are Luther and Hettie (McCormick) Waller and Alfred and Annie Lee (Graham) Dixon. Beverly is a graduate of Smith County High School, and she attended Volunteer State College in Gallatin, Tennessee. She is presently employed at the Regency Health Care Center in Red Boiling Springs, Tennessee. She is also a certified real estate broker. Steven and Beverly are the parents of two daughters, Christina, born July 3, 1979 in McMinn County, Tennessee, and Stephanie, born June 7, 1986 in Wilson County, Tennessee. Christina is a second grade student at Fairlane Elementary School in Lafayette, Tennessee.

Sharon Gaye Walker, born December 11, 1961 in Jackson County, Tennessee, is a graduate of Smith County High School and Tennessee Technological University. On May 24, 1986, she married Randall Kimes, the son of Mr. and Mrs. Henry Kimes, Jr. of Cookeville, Tennessee. His grandparents are Mr. and Mrs. Richard Bilbery and Daisy Kimes and the late Henry Kimes, Sr. Randall is a 1979 graduate of Tennessee Technological University. He is currently employed by the Univ. of Tennessee Extension Service in Clay County, Tennessee.

CRISTEEN AND LESLIE WEST

Cristeen Walker West was born September 9, 1931 near Celina, Tennessee. She was the daughter of Benton Walker and Dovie Reecer Walker. She was the granddaughter of George Walker and Florence Franklin Walker and Hamilton Reecer and Burnetta Spear Reecer all of Route 2, Celina, Tennessee.

Cristeen (Walker), Alan and Leslie West

Cristeen married Leslie West, Jr., who was born September 9, 1928. He was the son of Leslie West and Effie Davis West of Hermitage Springs. After he graduated from Hermitage Springs High School, he became an auto mechanic and car dealer.

Cristeen was employed in the Clay County school system for a period of 22 years, which ended with her death in 1974. Her obituary read:

"Cristeen West, age 42, of Celina died Monday morning, July 8, at the Clay County Hospital. She belonged to the Church of Christ and was a teacher.

The funeral was held Wednesday, July 10, at 1:00 p.m. at the Celina Church of Christ. Brother John Hollaway officiated. Burial was in the Moss Cemetery.

Survivors include her husband, Leslie West, Jr.; one son, Alan West of Celina; six brothers: Cecil Walker of Castalian Springs, Tennessee, Dumas Walker of Route 2, Celina, Eulas Walker of Tompkinsville, Kentucky, Clifford Walker of Indianapolis, Indiana, James Walker of Louisville, Kentucky, and Durell Walker of Carthage, Tennessee, and five sisters: Mrs. Lona W. Capshaw of Hermitage Springs, Tennessee, Mrs. Lena Clancy of Seymour, Indiana, Mrs. Pettious Sullivan of Ogden, Utah, Mrs. Minnie Lee Redford of Celina, Tennessee, and Mrs. Dauphine Hunley of Nashville, Tennessee.

She attended elementary school at Moss and high school at Celina. She also received her Bachelor of Arts and her Master of Arts at Tennessee

Technological University at Cookeville, Tennessee. She was employed by the Clay County Board of Education as an elementary guidance supervisor."

Leslie West, Jr. died August 24, 1980 and is buried in the Moss Cemetery. Leslie, Jr. and Cristeen are the parents of Alan Ward West, born December 7, 1953, in Celina, Tennessee. Alan is a graduate of Celina High School, and received his Bachelor of Science and Master's degrees from Tennessee Technological University in Cookeville, Tennessee. He is now employed by the Clay County Board of Education as Vice-Principal of Celina High School.

Alan married Deborah Gass of Moss, Tennessee August 27, 1976. She was born August 5, 1956, the daughter of J.H. Gass and Erma Lee McLerran Gass. She is the granddaughter of Herman Gass and Beulah Copas Gass and Harrison McLerran and Zona Cruthers McLerran, all of Clay County, Tennessee.

Deborah is a graduate of Celina High School and received her Bachelor of Science degree from Middle Tennessee State University in Murfreesboro, Tennessee. She is employed at Celina K-8 as a second grade teacher.

Alan and Deborah are the parents of Jonathan Lee, born December 21, 1980, and Leslie Cristeen, born October 23, 1983. Both are in Donaldson Day Care Center in Celina. *Submitted By Alan West*

CURTIS RANDALL WALKER

Curtis Randall Walker was born September 3, 1952 in the New Hope Community of Clay County. He is the son of Curtis Earl Walker and Daisy Morris Walker. Randall is the grandson of Elzie Walker and Pearly Anderson Walker and B. Tom Morris and Dona Morris of Clay County.

Kaylan, Courtney, Mallory, Randall and Carol Walker

Randall attended first grade at New Hope and finished elementary school at Celina Elementary. Randall graduated from Celina High School. He received a Bachelor of Science Degree from Tennessee Technological University in Health and Physical Education and later received his Masters Degree from Tennessee Technological University in Administration and Supervision.

He has taught school in Clay County for the past twelve years. He has taught at Maple Grove for five years and at Celina K-8 for the last seven years.

Randall was married December 22, 1977 to Teresa Carol Poindexter from the Pea Ridge Community of Clay County. Carol is the daughter of Cecil Poindexter and Maxie Watson Poin-

dexter. She is the granddaughter of William Poindexter and Mertie Poindexter and Vanus Watson and Ova Scott Watson.

Carol attended school in Clay County and graduated from Celina High School. She studied one year at Middle Tennessee State University. She has been employed by OshKosh B'Gosh in Celina for the past six years.

Randall and Carol are the parents of Kaylan Nacoe, born July 15, 1979; Courtney Brooke, born May 15, 1981; and Mallory Ellen, born February 23, 1985.

ELISE DONALDSON WATERS

Elise Donaldson Waters is a great granddaughter of William Richmond Donaldson of Wilson County and Clay County, Tennessee and Mary Dabney Hord of Virginia and Tennessee. She is a member of the Rachel Stockley Donelson Chapter of Daughters of the American Revolution, Old Hickory Chapter of the United States Daughters of 1812, Colonial Dames of the XVII Century, Huguenot Society, National Society of Magna Carta Dames, and the Ladies Hermitage Association.

Elise Donaldson Waters

The Donaldsons came from Scotland to Delaware Bay in 1716. The name was Donald, then Donaldson. Colonel John Donelson, one of the first settlers of Nashville, married Rachael Stockley of Virginia; and a daughter, Rachael, married Andrew Jackson. Colonel John spelled the surname Donelson, but his father and grandfather, John and Patrick, and his brothers, William and Andrew, spelled it Donaldson.

Robert Donaldson married Elizabeth Richmond. Andrew came from Maryland, Pennsylvania and Caswell County, North Carolina, to Wilson County, Tennessee in 1804.

William Richmond Donaldson, a son, went from Wilson County to visit relatives in Overton County in 1820. He married Mary Dabney Hord, the daughter of Justinia Burrus and Stanwix Hord. A son, Robert Daniel Donaldson, married Hannah Ellen Colson. Their home at Fox Springs is now under Dale Hollow Lake.

John Thomas Donaldson of Celina, Tennessee married Molly Davis. Their children were Gertie, Hubert, Ruby and Lester. Lester had the following children: Robbie, William Harold, Jack, and Donald. Hubert had no children.

John Thomas Donaldson's second wife was Ermine Brown, the daughter of James Lafayette Brown and Ava Glorianna Fowler Brown. Their children were Elise, Ben Allen, Cordell, Ava Belle, and Flo.

Cordell Donaldson married Rebecca Waddell.

They had one son, John Clark Donaldson. John Clark married Frances Rich, and they have four children, John Cordell, Lea, Lenea, and Libby. They are the fourth generation to live in the Donaldson home.

Flo Donaldson married Herman Taylor, and they had the following children: Herman Donald, Carolyn, Cordell, Barbara, and Anita. Carolyn married Larry Wilson, and they had two children, Jennifer and Elissa. Cordell married Glenda Van Dyke, and they had two children, Vonda and Valerie. Barbara married Otis Smith. Anita married Carlton Martin, and they have one son, Robert.

Elise Donaldson married W.D. Waters.

GENEVA GLADYS WATSON

Geneva Gladys Watson was born February 3, 1917 in Clay County. She is the daughter of Andrew Thomas and Lizzie Jane Watson. She is the granddaughter of Riley and Sarry Kerr from Cumberland County, Kentucky. Gladys attended school at the Plainview School on Pea Ridge. Gladys married Willie Herman Watson June 9, 1932. Herman was born in Cumberland County, Kentucky October 19, 1912, the son of Johnny Lee Kerr and Alice Sue Watson. Herman attended school at Kettle Creek. Herman and Gladys are the parents of ten children, Reneth, James, Randall, Ricky, Cornelia, Comell, Mary, Barbara, and Zelma. They have 25 grandchildren and 47 great grandchildren.

The Watson Family attends Ashlock Church of Christ in the Pea Ridge Community.

THOMAS AND CAROLYN WATSON

Thomas Watson was born April 19, 1944, the second son of Arthur Cleo and Melissa Florence (McLerran) Watson. He attended Clay County schools beginning at New Hope, a small one-room school, at the age of four. He transferred to Celina Elementary after the second grade where he continued his education through high school. While at Celina High School, he was a member of the basketball team that won the Fifteenth District Tournament in 1961. He was also a member of various clubs, including the Beta Club. He was third academically in his class in 1962. Thomas attended Tennessee Technological University at various times from 1962 to 1967. He transferred to Middle Tennessee State University in 1967, where he remained until he graduated after the fall semester of 1969 with a Bachelor of Science in Social Science. In 1970, he returned to Celina High School as a teacher and assistant basketball coach. In 1970, he served as junior high boys' basketball coach. Thomas was junior high boys' coach and senior high girls' coach in 1971-72. In 1972, he was hired as high school boys' basketball coach—a position he has held since that date. Through this period of time, Celina High School has enjoyed unprecedented success in boys' basketball, winning over 300 games, while losing less than 100. During Coach Watson's tenure, Celina High School has won nine district championships, five regional titles, and made three trips to the Tennessee Secondary Schools Athletic Association State Tournament. During the last three years Celina has won 108 games, while losing only six. During this period of time, many Celina players have won numerous individ-ual honors. Ten players have been selected to All-State teams and one, Joey Coe, was named All-American. Coach Watson has been selected District Coach of the Year seven times. In 1984 and 1985, he was selected to coach the East All-Stars by the Tennessee Athletic Coaches Association.

Thomas and Faye Watson

Carolyn Faye (Strong) Watson is the oldest child of nine born to Carlos Caye and Wealtha (Armer) Strong. She was born February 15, 1947. Faye attended elementary school at Moss, where she was a member of the basketball team. She attended school at Celina, where she was a member of the best basketball team in the history of the school, a team that won three straight district tournaments. Faye graduated from Celina High School in 1964. She and Thomas were married January 1, 1966. They moved to Murfreesboro in 1967, where he attended college while she worked to pay for his education. In 1970 they moved back to Celina. She continued to work as a garment factory employee eventually attaining the position of supervisor. She entered Tennessee Technological University on a full-time basis in 1970. While at Tennessee Technological University she was consistently on the honor roll. Faye graduated with honors with a degree in secondary education. She has taught junior high social studies at Celina K-8 since her graduation. Six of Faye's history students have won National History Day state titles and have finished as high as third in the national contests in Washington, D.C. Faye was selected to coach Celina High School's first girls' softball team for the 1986 season. This team finished second in the district, losing only to the eventual state runner-up. Faye is an excellent amateur tennis player. She has won over one hundred tennis titles throughout Middle Tennessee during the past ten years.

SAMUEL WEAVER

Samuel Weaver married Louise Butler. Their children were Tom, who had several children; James Bailey Weaver, born November 11, 1849; a daughter (first name unknown) who had several children; Anne Mary; Dodie; and Butler Kirkpatrick, who changed his name to Brown.

Samuel Weaver's second wife was Louise Langford. Their children were: Irving; Morgan; Mac; Fitzhugh; and Floretta. Floretta married Stone Plumlee. They had three children.

Samuel Weaver's third wife was Mary McMillan. Their children were Milton and Bedford.

James Bailey Weaver, born November 11, 1849, was married to Martha Elizabeth Arterberry March 7, 1878. Martha Elizabeth Arterberry was born September 18, 1859 and died January 14, 1929. She married a Mr. Kirk the second time. The children of James Bailey and Martha Arterberry Weaver were William Radford Weaver, born March 16, 1879 and died in the spring of 1961; Annie Lou Weaver (called Anne), born February 26, 1882 and died September 22, 1951; Mary Katherine (called Kate), born March 31, 1885; Sam Bedford Weaver, born August 6, 1891; and Ester Bryan Weaver, born July 15, 1896. William Radford Weaver married Rosa Jones March 9, 1909. Annie Lou Weaver married Jay A. Mabry May 5, 1901. Mary Katherine (Kate) married Rice Leek Maxey May 20, 1906.

The children of Rice Leek Maxey and Mary Katherine (Kate) Weaver were Robert Cullom, born May 30, 1907; John Oliver (called Jack), born November 29, 1909; Jay P. (called Peck), born November 28, 1911; Anne Rice, born November 4, 1913; James Weaver, born May 4, 1916; Sam Bedford, born July 12, 1918; Mary Haynie, born January 3, 1922; and Henry Philip, born July 12, 1925. Robert Cullom Maxey married Mary Willodean Roberts October 18, 1941. They were divorced. Robert Cullom Maxey then married Dorothy Dean Booth August 27, 1954. Their children were William Larry, born and died in infancy in 1955; Robert Cullom, Jr., born September 18, 1956; Mary Haynie, born November 6, 1957; Shirley Fay, born May 19, 1959; Cathy Dean, born January 3, 1961; Margaret Ann, born November 14, 1961; Hattie Laverne, born March 12, 1963; and Debra Wayne, date of birth not certain — possibly the fall of 1963 or spring of 1964.

Rose Weaver

John Oliver (Jack), the son of Rice Leek and Kate Weaver Maxey, married Mary Elizabeth Hayes August 6, 1949. John Oliver (Jack) and Mary Elizabeth Hayes Maxey had the following children: Edna Ruth, born July 24, 1951, and Robert Allen, born September 16, 1953. Robert Allen Maxey, the son of Jack and Mary Elizabeth Hayes Maxey, married Mary Elizabeth Sammons May 18, 1974.

Jay P. Maxey, the son of Kate Weaver and Rice Maxey, was a bachelor.

Anne Rice Maxey, the daughter of Rice Leek and Kate Weaver Maxey, married George Ray Burnett March 3, 1933. They had the following children: George Ray, Jr., born April 21, 1934; Jo Ann, born April 21, 1934; Beverly Gail, born August 21, 1937; Donald Maxey, born May 19, 1940; Frances Gabie, born December 23, 1941; Richard Lowrey, born March 31, 1944; Ralph Daniel, born May 13, 1947; William Marvin, born June 28, 1950; and Patricia Carol, born October 15, 1952.

James Weaver Maxey, the son of Kate Weaver

and Rice Leek Maxey, was married July 30, 1949 to Vivian Marie Hunter. Their children were Jimmie Neal Carol (stepson); William Radford, born February 10, 1951; Connie Jean, born June 9, 1953; Susan Dianne, born June 23, 1956; and Brenda Kay, born August 19, 1959.

Sam Bedford Maxey, the son of Kate Weaver and Rice Leek Maxey, married Dorothy Dodds Hudson April 8, 1945. Their children were Larry Bedford, born December 27, 1945; twins Dorothy Grace and Doris Faye, born November 10, 1947; Virginia Anne, born September 28, 1949; and Sibil Illeta, born September 3, 1951.

Mary Haynie Maxey, the daughter of Rice Leek and Kate Weaver Maxey, married Leeman Conn June 27, 1942. Their children were Maxey Conn, born February 22, 1943, and Patrick Ray Conn, born January 16, 1946.

Henry Philip Maxey, son of Rice Leek and Kate Weaver Maxey, married Delores Jo Thompson March 12, 1961. Their daughter, Debra Lyn, was born February 9, 1962 and died at birth.

JAMES BAILEY WEAVER

James Bailey Weaver was born in Jackson, now Clay, County, Tennessee November 11, 1849. He was the second child of Samuel Weaver and his wife, Marie Louisa Butler. Louisa was born in Butler's Landing September 2, 1819, and was the tenth child of Thomas Jefferson and Polly McClure Butler of Butler's Landing. According to the census records, Samuel was born March 22, 1822. Samuel and Louisa were married January 30, 1845 at Butler's Landing. William Thomas, their first child, was born in 1848, while Louisa was born in 1850. It is not clear whether they had another daughter, Elizabeth, born in 1852; but this was the year that Louisa died September 22. Samuel and Louisa owned land in the Seventh Civil District, as listed in the 1850 census. The land was located in what is known as Weaver's Bottom outside of Celina in the Butler's Landing area. The main crops were corn and tobacco, and cattle, and hogs were raised in this very fertile valley.

On March 7, 1878, J.B. Weaver and Martha Elizabeth Arterberry were married in Celina. Martha Weaver was the daughter of William Tyre and Catherine Black Arterberry. Both Catherine Black and William Tyre were born in Jackson County with Thompson and Elizabeth Jones Arterberry being his parents. Their land was later listed in Monroe County, Kentucky on McFarland's Creek.

James Bailey and Martha Weaver bought farmland and built a home which stands today in Weaver's Bottom and is still owned by a branch of the Weaver family. Five children were born of this marriage. William Radford was born March 16, 1879; and lived on the farm during his lifetime. He married Rosa Jones, and their children are Mary Daffo, Jim Tom, Willadean, Frank Bedford, Mocell, and Sam Jones. Frank Bedford Weaver and Mary Daffo, the wife of Bailey, live in the Butler's Landing area.

Annie Lou Weaver was born February 26, 1882 and married Jay Mabry. Their children are three daughters, Earl, Mary Jeff, and Martha James, and also four sons, Ed, Tom, Fred, and Charlie. Their farm is in the Moss area of Clay County, and is owned by one of the daughters.

Another daughter, Mary Katherine, married

Rice Leek Maxey in Celina May 20, 1906 and shortly thereafter moved to Crawford, Mississippi. Their children were Robert Cullom, John Oliver, Jay Peck, Anne Rice, James Weaver, Sam Bedford, Mary Haynie, and Henry Philip Maxey.

The youngest daughter, Ester Bryan, married Frank Edwin Campbell July 17, 1916 in Celina. They owned farmland in Kentucky in the Creelsboro area, but Frank Campbell was also a steamboat pilot on the Cumberland, making runs from Burnside to Nashville. The Campbell children are Joe Frank of Jamestown, Stella Elizabeth, Vivian Gould, Katherine Weaver, Nellie Hill, and Sam Edwin. Mrs. Bryan Campbell lives in Ashland City, Tennessee with a daughter, Mrs. Stella Powell.

By 1914, Samuel Bedford Weaver was in Casper, Wyoming, where he worked at an oil refinery. He enlisted at Fort Russell in 1916 and fought in France for eighteen months in the 99th Aero Squadron until November 11, 1918. Sam returned to his job in Casper, where he brought his wife, Alyce Chism Kerley of Barren County, Kentucky. Their children, Wanda Maye, Wayne Kerley, and Warren Bedford, live in Casper with their families, while Anna Patricia lives in Colorado.

After Louisa's death in 1852, Samuel was married to Adeline Langford Gates, and they had six children. E. Fitchie, Floretta, William Morgan, Ervin, Mac, and Fitzhugh grew up in Tennessee, with some of the boys moving to Hamilton County, Texas.

Samuel Weaver married for the third time when Adeline died, this time to Mary Elizabeth McMillan in 1873 in Celina. They had two children, Milton and Joseph Bedford. After this marriage Samuel bought land in Cumberland County, Kentucky, where he was buried after his death November 23, 1907.

James Bailey Weaver and his son, William Radford, are buried in a little cemetery on a hill above the family farmhouse in Weaver's Bottom. James died June 19, 1898 in a farming accident, when his youngest son was only seven years old.

According to records, J.B.'s older brother, William Thomas, was married to Elizabeth and farmed in the area, too. *Submitted by Wanda Weaver Walters*

JAMES C. WEBB

James C. Webb met Melissa White in Princeton, Indiana where they were married. They later moved back to Clay County. Melissa's ancestors were originally from Holland. They had twelve

James C. Webb Family

children, Walford Tilman, Winfield, Dan, Andrew, Ella, Mandy, Maggie, Lizzie, Seretha, Dulsina, Henry, and Hancock. The exact dates of James and Melissa's deaths are not known. The are buried on Pea Ridge.

WALFORD TILMAN WEBB

Walford Tilman "W.T." Webb was born October 26, 1900. He was the eleventh child in a family of six sons and six daughters born to James C. and Melissa White Webb.

"W.T." married Ida Roach. Ida was the daughter of Gabe and Manerva Roach. To this union was born five children, Cecil, Geneva, Otis, Willard, and Ollie Lena.

The Walford Tillman Webb Family

Cecil married Opal Key. They have two children, Billy and Donnie. Donnie has one daughter, Karen, and Billy has one son, Bryan. Geneva married Ray Emerton. They had one son, Michael, who was killed in a car accident. Otis married Willodean Thompson. Ollie Lena died in her early years. Willard is married to Maxine Watson of Cumberland County, Kentucky. Maxine is the daughter of Curb and Ora Watson. Willard and Maxine have three children, Judy, Harvey, and Ronnie. Judy is married to Vernon Groce of Cumberland County, Kentucky, the son of Virgil and Claudyne Groce. Vernon and Judy have three children, Elaine, Randy, and Robin. Harvey is married to Rosanna Bishop. Rosanna is the daughter of LeRoy and Clementine Bishop of Greensburg, Kentucky. Harvey has one son, Shannon, and one stepson, Kevin. Ronnie is married to Diana Brown, the daughter of Willie Jim "Tom" and Mona Moore Brown of Moss. Ronnie and Diana have two children, Mickey and Michael.

Ida Roach Webb died February 29, 1951.

W.T. later married Beatrice Stephens. Beatrice was the daughter of Poke and Myrtie Stephens of Clay County.

W.T. and Beatrice both died in February of 1979. They are buried on Pea Ridge.

OTIS AND WILLODEAN WEBB

Otis Webb was born October 24, 1922, the son of W.T. and Ida Roach Webb of the Pea Ridge Community. Otis attended school in Clay County. He served in the Civilian Conservation Corps. He worked in the construction of the Oak Ridge Atomic Energy Plant. He worked in the construction of Berry Field Airport near Nashville. He returned to Clay County where he drove a school bus and farmed. He built a grocery store which has served the community for 38 years. He has served as Co-Chairman of the Clay County Republican Party. He was a member of the Clay

Otis Webb   Willodean Webb

County Civitan Club.

Otis married Willodean Thompson December 24, 1946. Willodean was born December 2, 1930, the daughter of Willie Elmore Thompson and Mattie Velma Key Thompson. After her mother's death when she was only eight month's old, Willodean lived with her grandparents, J.S. and Emery Jane Watson Thompson. Willodean attended schools in Clay County graduating from Celina High School in 1948. She started teaching in the fall of 1948 at Plainview all the while continuing her college work at Tennessee Polytechnic Institute, where she received a Bachelor of Science Degree in 1954. In the fall of 1954, she started teaching social studies and English at Celina High School, where she was a teacher for 12 years. In 1965, she went to work for the Clay County Department of Human Services. She became Director of the Clay County Department of Human Services in 1978. Willodean has served as Chairman of the Clay County Heart Fund. In 1973, she received special recognition for raising the most money ever raised during one campaign for the Heart Fund in Clay County. She was active in the Civitan Club and was Chairman of the Miss Clay County Beauty Pageant for a number of years.

Otis and Willodean are members of the Rock Springs Church of Christ, where Otis has served as treasurer for more than 20 years and where Willodean is a Sunday School teacher.

Otis and Willodean live in the Pea Ridge Community and are active in community and county affairs.

JOHN WEBB

John Webb, ca 1695-1760, died in Dover, Kent County, Delaware. He had four children. By his first wife (name unknown) he had Caleb, ca 1750-1804, and Daniel, ca 1753-1827, who married Jean Young August 17, 1783 in Rowan County, North Carolina. By his second wife, Ann, he had Elizabeth, ca. 1756, who married Samuel Luckey, Sr., the blacksmith, and Sarah, ca. 1759, who married William James Davis, Sr., who died in 1788.

Caleb Webb, ca 1750-1804, furnished a substitute, aid and supplies to General Pickens' troops in the Revolutionary War for which he received on Nov. 4, 1784, a North Carolina State Grant No. 756, of 500 acres of land on the north bank of the South Yadkin River, then Rowan County, North Carolina. He died in Iredell County, North Carolina. He had six children by his first wife (name unknown). John, ca. 1783; Caleb, ca 1785; Andrew, Sr., 1788-1819, who married Mary Ann Coe of Surry County, North Carolina;

Elizabeth, ca 1791, who married Samuel Luckey, Jr.; Ann, ca 1793, who married Allen Morrow; and Sarah, ca 1795-1822, who never married, were the six children.

Caleb Webb married the second time December 11, 1797 in Surry County, North Carolina, Mary Ann Hudspeth, ca 1770-1842. They had three children. Hudspeth, 1799-1856, married Jestina Vitula Holman, 1824-1902. Giles W., 1801-1883, married Emily Holman, 1815-1881, and they moved about 1853 to Barnett, Missouri. Daniel, 1803-1864, married Mary Jane Gammon, 1832-1873. The above three brothers, along with their mother, Mary Ann (Hudspeth) Webb, moved in 1830 from Rowan and Iredell Counties, North Carolina to Overton (now Clay) County Tennessee on the Obey River.

Daniel Webb, 1803-1864, married Mary Jane Gammon, 1836-1873, the daughter of John and Rebecca Whitworth, and lived on the Obey River, now Clay County. They had two sons. William Caleb "Bee," 1855-1924, married Sophia Susan "Suffie," Bow, 1858-1913. Albert Kitchell, 1863-1921/22, married Minnie Grace Harp, 1883-1975, the daughter of Foster Montville Harp and Ellen Matheny Harp. Kitchell and Minnie moved in the spring of 1919 to Whiteright and Sherman, Texas. After the death of Daniel, his widow, Mary Jane, married Robert Frank Thurman, 1837-1922, the son of Allen Thurman.

Sophia Susan Bow Webb   William Caleb Webb

William Caleb "Bee" Webb, 1855-1924, of Obey River, married Sophia Susan "Suffie" Bow, 1858-1913, the daughter of Jesse and Judith (Arms) Bow. They had nine children, Stone P., 1876-1876; Dillard Bransford, 1878-1954, who married Lizzie Rich, 1882-1951, the daughter of Tom Rich; Alice Alma, 1880-1915, who married William Talton Terry, 1880-1958; Baylus Ross, 1882-1914, who never married; Edith Enner, 1884-1887; John Walter, 1886-1968, who married Edna Earl Monroe, 1898, the daughter of Willard Monroe; Willie Daniel "Will," 1889-1936, who married Matilda Jane Hill, 1887-1927; George Lester, 1891-1918, who never married; and Culver Vinson, 1895-1910, who never married.

Willie Daniel "Will" Webb, 1889-1936, married Matilda Jane Hill, 1887-1927, the daughter of Andrew Jackson "Andy", 1861-1913 and Sarah Elizabeth (Cook) Hill, 1966-1923. They had two sons. Edward Carmack was born in 1910 and married Mary Emma Blythe, the daughter of William Thomas Blythe. Walter Estes, born 1915, has never married. *Submitted by Walter E. Webb.*

DEWEY COLONEL WELLS

Dewey Colonel Wells was born April 11, 1909.

He is the son of William Hiram Wells, (1849-1933) and Martha Watson Wells.

Dewey married Nancy Helen Arms April 11, 1936. Helen was born December 6, 1910. She is the daughter of Archie Thomas (Tommy) Arms and Dayse (Stone) Arms. Dewey and Helen have no children of their own. Helen's niece, Lura (Arms) Parsons, and nephew, Walter Lee Arms, whose mother died young, lived with them. Lura Arms married William Parsons, Jr. Their children are James, Robert and Amanda. Walter Lee Arms married Judy Drewery. Their children are Bethany Jo and Walter Dewey Arms. Dewey and Helen are members of the Church of Christ.

Dewey attended school in Cumberland County, Kentucky and attended automobile college in Nashville, Tennessee in 1929. He was a farmer, oil driller, school bus driver, and United States mail carrier between Celina, Tennessee and Burkesville, Kentucky. Helen was a school teacher, attended Tennessee Polytechic Institute during the great depression era in 1932-1934, and received her Bachelor of Science Degree in 1956.

Helen and Dewey Wells

The first Wells name was in Normandy, France in the year 794 A.D. About 1125 A.D., Harold deVaux (Wells) and his three sons, Hubert, Rudolph and Robert, moved from Normandy to Norfold, Essex and Lincolnshire Counties, England. Hubert married and had Robert and William. This William became the progenitor of the noted Essex branch who came to America. Robert, his brother, of the Lincolnshire branch of Wells intermarried with royalty, and reared sons, William, Oliver and Henry. Descendants of William and Robert are the Wells who settled in Virginia, Kentucky and Tennessee.

Silas Wells (1810-1851), a son of William Wells, married Mary Smith in January 1830. They were the grandparents of Dewey Wells. Silas and Mary had 13 children. William Hiram Wells (1849-1933), the son of Silas and Mary, was Dewey C. Wells' father. William Hiram was a farmer and a financier. He ran a merchandise store, United States Post Office, meal and flour mills. He dealt in timber in Cumberland County, Kentucky and in staves for barrels in Louisville, Kentucky. He is buried in Donaldson Cemetery in Clay County, Tennessee, brought there by the United States Government prior to the building of Dale Hollow Dam. This William Hiram from Cumberland County Kentucky, married Martha Alice Watson, December 19, 1906, reared the six following children: Alpha, Dewey Colonel, Carmon, Anna, Dovie and Maxine.

ALAN WARD WEST

Alan Ward West was born in Tompkinsville,

Kentucky December 7, 1953. He is the only child of Leslie Owen West, Jr. (born September 7, 1928, died August 24, 1980) and Cristeen Walker West (born September 7, 1931, died July 8, 1974), who were lifelong residents of Clay County.

Leslie Cristeen, Jonathan Lee, Deborah and Alan West

Leslie West, Jr. was the son of Leslie Owen West, Sr. and Effie Mae Davis West of the Hermitage Springs Community. Cristeen Walker was one of fourteen children of Benton T. Walker (born September 18, 1886, died August 14, 1954) and Mary Dovie Reecer (born April 2, 1892, died January 3, 1974).

Alan has lived his entire life in Clay County. He was educated at Celina Elementary School, and he graduated from Celina High School in 1971. He received his Bachelor of Science Degree in Secondary Education — English from Tennessee Technological University in 1977 and his Masters Degree in Administration and Supervision in June 1985.

Alan was employed at Tri-County Vocational School for one year before joining the Tennessee Department of Employment Security in 1977. He became the Cooperative Education Instructor at Celina High School in 1979 and remains in that position at present. He also serves as Assistant Principal of Celina High School. Alan is Chairman of the Clay County Election Commission; and he is Captain of the Celina Volunteer Fire Department.

Alan married Deborah Kaye Gass August 27, 1976 at the Moss Church of Christ. Deborah, born August 5, 1956 in Tompkinsville, Kentucky, is the daughter of John Harvey (May 3, 1927) and Erma Lee McLerran (September 3, 1926) Gass. John is the son of Herman Gass (October 3, 1900) and Beulah Copas (April 20, 1906, died September 14, 1983) of Moss, Tennessee. Erma Lee is the daughter of Albert Harrison McLerran (February 9, 1888, died November 20, 1957) and Zona May Darruthers (May 20, 1887, died February 13, 1964) of Hermitage Springs, Tennessee. Deborah has one older sister, Patricia Darlene Gass Wood, and one younger brother, Michael Kevin Gass. Deborah attended Moss Elementary School and graduated from Celina High School. She received a Bachelor of Science Degree in Early Childhood Education from Middle Tennessee State University in 1978. Following graduation, Deborah was employed by the Clay County Department of Human Services for three years. She taught school at Red Boiling Springs during the 1982-83 school year. She taught kindergarten at Hermitage Springs School during 1983-84, and she has taught second grade at Celina K-8 since 1984.

Alan and Deborah have two children. Jonathan Lee was born December 21, 1980 in Jackson County, Tennessee. He is named for his maternal grandparents, John and Erma Lee Gass. Leslie Cristeen was born Oct. 23, 1983 in Jackson County, Tennessee. She is named for her paternal grandparents, Leslie and Cristeen West. The West family lives in Celina.

BOBBY EUGENE WESTMORELAND

Bobby Eugene Westmoreland was born in Celina, Tennessee July 6, 1939. He is the son of Lester and Irene Poindexter Westmoreland. Bobby attended schools in Celina and graduated from Celina High School in 1957. Bobby is the grandson of Tessie Colson and Bill Poindexter, and Nan Westmoreland is his grandmother on his father's side of the family. Nan's mother was Minerva Jane Napier, all of whom lived, grew up, and died in Clay County.

Bobby attended Western Kentucky University on a football and track scholarship, graduating in 1965 with a Bachelor of Science and Master of Arts degrees in biology and physical education.

Bobby married Mari Lynne Kinnebrew in 1962. Mari Lynne was born in Henderson, Texas July 17, 1942. Mari is the daughter of Marion Leonard and Edna Clark Kinnebrew, formerly of East Texas. They now reside in Pennsylvania. Mari is the granddaughter of Harvey and Nannie Neely Clark and Tom and Ethyl McClain Kinnebrew from East Texas. Mari is the great granddaughter of Mary Clark, an active member of the Daughters of the American Revolution (DAR).

Bobby worked as a coach and a teacher at Celina High School for six years and as a state employee for 15 years. Mari worked at the Celina Post Office for 10 years and is presently working as a property manager in Celina. Bobby is President of the Dale Hollow Shrine Club. He is a 32nd Degree Mason and a past member of Canton Lodge #481 in Celina. Mari is active in the Celina Bridge Club and the Order of the Eastern Star. Mari graduated from Glasgow, Kentucky High School in 1960 and from Tyler, Texas Junior College in 1962.

Bobby and Mari have four children, Lester Kenny, John Kevin, Jeana Ann, and Robert Kyle. All four are attending or have attended public schools in Celina. All of the family attend the Church of Christ in Celina. Bobby's father, Lester Westmoreland, built the first houseboats on Dale Hollow Lake in 1954. Before he died in 1973, he had built 125 of the same style houseboats.

Bobby's brother, Billy Westmoreland, is a very well-known television star in the fishing business. Billy travels all over the world in his position and holds 15-20 major fishing seminars each year throughout the United States. Each year in Oakland, California, a Billy Westmoreland Invitational Bass Tournament is held in his honor. Billy has been a fishing pro since 1965.

Shirley Nelson, the sister of Billy and Bobby, is President and Chief Executive Officer of Summitt Bank, Oakland California, with two branch banks in the Bay Area that she oversees. She is one of the few women in the United States with such a position. Shirley received her formal education in the schools in Celina. She has one son, Steve Nelson, age 21, who attends college in the Bay Area.

Irene Westmoreland, the mother of Bobby, Billy and Shirley, has always been a housewife and has worked hard at rearing her family.

JOHN BENJAMIN WHITE

John Benjamin (Ben) White was born in September 1842 in Cumberland County, Kentucky. He was probably the eldest of a family of three sons and two daughters born to Samuel and Catherine G. White. Samuel was born in (c) 1821 in Kentucky. Samuel was a farmer, and Catherine was a tailoress. Ben was also a farmer, and he was in the Civil War — probably the Confederate Army. In 1874, Ben married Juda Catherine Hopper, who was born in Tennessee December 23, 1856. She died July 28, 1934. Ben and Juda lived alternately in Cumberland County, Kentucky and in Clay County, Tennessee. Ben died sometime after 1910 in a veterans' home in Nashville, Tennessee. Ben and Juda were the parents of seven children, Zachariah W., James E., William, Nancy E. (Long), Robert Allen, Tramell, and John T.

Robert Allen White was born March 16, 1892 in Burkesville, Kentucky. He died October 19, 1940. He married Rosa May Warden December 25, 1921 in Clay County. Rosa was born February 23, 1904 in Overton County, Tennessee, the eldest of a family of two sons and two daughters born to Joseph K. and Lavina Adeline (Gaw) Warden. Allen was a farmer. He served in the United States Army in World War I, but was not sent overseas. In the 1930's, Allen worked for the Works Progress Administration. Allen and Rosa lived alternately in Overton County and Clay County. Rosa presently resides in Clay County. Allen and Rosa were the parents of five children, Raymond Edward, Paul Houston, Mary Pauline (Melton), Floyd Thomas, and Reba Dean (Moore).

Paul Houston White was born February 1, 1925 in Overton County. He married Versie Lola (Bill) Cunningham April 19, 1942 in Celina, where they now reside. "Bill" was born September 2, 1919 in Clay County, the fifth in a family of two sons and five daughters born to Sam and Julie Halie Ann (Bowman) Cunningham. Paul served in the 42nd Rainbow Combat Engineers Division and the 1901st Aviation Engineers Battalion during World War II. He served in the Pacific Ocean on Okinawa and in Korea. Paul has been a farmer, the manager of the Clay Farmers' Co-op, an employee of the Corps of Engineers, and is presently employed by the United States Postal Service as a rural mail carrier. He served as Clay County Trustee from 1966 until 1974. Paul and "Bill" are the parents of three children, Harlen Paul, Anna Rose (Warden), and Thomas Eddie.

Harlan Paul White was born October 28, 1944 in Cookeville, Tennessee. Harlan married Patricia Ann Ledbetter December 24, 1964 in Livingston, Tennessee. Patricia was born November 12, 1946 in Livingston, Tennessee, the sixth child in a family of two sons and seven daughters born to Roy Lee and Jewell Amelia (Flatt) Ledbetter. Harlan and Patricia are both employed by OshKosh B'Gosh, and they presently live in Celina. They are the parents of Melissa Deneen, born October 27, 1965; Leslie Michelle, born June 18, 1969; and Casey Harlan, born June 3, 1974.
Submitted by Melissa D. White

EARL HANCE WILKERSON

Stella was one of the eight children born to Smith and Mary Roberts. She was born March 31, 1905 in the Mt. Vernon Community of Clay County, Tennessee. She was married November 17, 1935, to Earl Hance Wilkerson, who was born May 22, 1896 in the Pine Hill community. He died April 8, 1977. Hance and Stella were both schoolteachers in the Clay County Schools. Hance taught for many years at Pine Hill, Brimstone, Eminence, and Celina High School, and served as Supervisor of Instruction before his retirement. He also served on the Clay County Quarterly Court for many years and was a leader in the Republican party all his life. Stella taught for many years at Pine Hill, Brimstone, Union Hill, Moss, and Hermitage Springs. They lived in Pine Hill all their married life. They had two children, Lincoln Smith and Peggy Ann.

Earl Hance and Stella Wilkerson

Lincoln was born in the Pine Hill community on April 23, 1938. He attended Tennessee Polytechnic Institute and the University of Georgia, where he received his doctor's degree. He has taught in the Clay County Schools and is now teaching at Vanderbilt University in Nashville. On January 28, 1961, he married Kathleeen Smith, who was born June 20, 1942. They have two sons, Kerry and Terry. Kerry was born February 8, 1962. On May 24, 1980, he married Regina Anderson who was born May 28, 1962. They moved to Cookeville, Tennessee to attend Tennessee Technological University and still reside there. They have one daughter, Teri Rae, born July 23, 1980. Terry was born August 2, 1964 and is working in Clay County.

Peggy was also born in the Pine Hill Community December 17, 1939. She attended Tennessee Technological University and Middle Tennessee State University where she received Bachelor of Science, Master of Education, and Ed.S. degrees in education. She has been a teacher and principal in the Clay County Schools for 27 years. On December 20, 1963, she married Howard Davis of the Hermitage Springs Community. He was born July 2, 1941. They have two children, Scottie Lee and Lesa Ann. Scottie was born November 8, 1964, and Lesa was born January 6, 1966.

LINCOLN WILKERSON

Lincoln Wilkerson was born November 20, 1861 and died January 9, 1926. Lincoln had one sister, Allie Wilkerson, born November 2, 1860.

Lincoln married Albina Gully. She was born November 20, 1860 and died July 29, 1943. She was the daughter of Thomas W. Gully, born December 21, 1835 and died August 23, 1916, and Eunice Gully, born November 22, 1824 and died

Lincoln and Albina Wilkerson

November 6, 1917. Albina had four brothers and sisters, Anna, born December 15, 1862; James Thomas, born February 3, 1865 and died April 6, 1881; Sarah B., born January 27, 1868 and died June 23, 1888; and Jacob L., born November 10, 1869 and died January 26, 1877.

Lincoln and Albina had four children.

1. Thomas was born November 25, 1887 and died February 13, 1976. He married Tennie Lee July 4, 1915. They had seven children, Blanche, Fred, T.S., Katheleene, Billy, Elizabeth, and Martha Sue.

2. Argailous was born October 20, 1890 and died March 5, 1982. He married Ada Ethel Cherry May 5, 1912. They had six children, Exie, Elba, Earl, Foch, Mary Etta, and Beverly.

3. Mary was born November 11, 1893 and died June 18, 1982. She married Carlos Plumlee, born February 15, 1895 and died June 8, 1968. They moved to Illinois and had four children.

Daffo was born March 4, 1922 and died March 6, 1922.

Lincoln (Billy), born March 25, 1928, married LaVern Gill, and they had one daughter, LaDonna, born October 7, 1951.

Kenneth, born March 27, 1930 and died November 14, 1959, married Ruth Loller. They had two children, Barbara, born December 10, 1955, and Steve, born June 20, 1958.

Bina was born September 17, 1933.

4. Earl Hance was born May 22, 1896 and died April 8, 1977. He married Stella Roberts, born March 31, 1905, November 17, 1935. They had two children, Lincoln Smith and Peggy Ann.

Lincoln was born April 23, 1938. He married Kathellen Smith, born June 20, 1942, January 28, 1961. They have two sons. Kerry was born February 8, 1962. He married Regina Anderson, born May 28, 1962, May 24, 1980. They have one daughter, Teri Rae, born July 23, 1980. Terry was born August 2, 1964.

Peggy was born December 17, 1939. She married Howard Davis, born July 2, 1941, December 20, 1963. They have two children, Scottie Lee, born November 8, 1964 and Lesa Ann, born January 6, 1966.

JOHN WILLIAMS

John Williams was born in Tennessee on January 15, 1822. His father William (Bill) was born in Virginia. William married Lucretia Stacy in 1816. Margaret (Peggy) Boles was born on October 27, 1831 in Tennessee. She and her husband, John Williams, are buried in the Turkeytown Cemetery. They had twelve children, all born on Dry Mill Creek. Five died young. They were farmers and stockmen on a small scale. During the winter, they trapped animals for the fur, which was sold

or bartered for items at the general store. Remember, Daniel Boone hunted and trapped in the Butlers Landing area before our ancestors arrived. A typical ledger at the store in 1841 read as follows:

"Stone, Samuel E.,
  1½ yds. blu domestic, .25; 1 lb. sugar 9¢;
  3 darning needles 6¢, cash loand .50"

William (Bill) Williams was born May 23, 1856, and he died March 11, 1930 near Cookeville. He and his wife are buried in the Turkeytown Cemetery. Bill operated a small store in Butlers Landing before moving to Putnam County. He married Elizabeth Jane Lynn February 27, 1872. They had one son, Palo, who married Bessie Christian. They had two sons, Billy Lewis and Fred Lynn.

Mary Pamela (Polly) Williams was born July 5, 1860, and she married W. David Lynn October 8, 1876 in Celina. They moved to Hollister, California before 1900, where they had an irrigated farm and grew cucumbers and tomatoes. They had a 50-cow dairy herd and a cream separator.

Tim Williams

Tim Williams was born April 1, 1863, and he married Laura Evelyn Fitzpatrick October 28, 1879. She died May 28, 1888 and is buried in the McDonald Cemetery, Clay County, Tennessee. They had four children, Sallie, John Boles, Susie, and Milton Coleman. Tim married Sarah Elizabeth Kirk at Livingston, Tennessee July 14, 1889. They moved to Vernon, Texas in 1891. They then settled at Hess, Oklahoma. They had nine children. Five died young. Their son, Joe Kirk, was born in Butlers Landing.

Sarah Alvina Williams married James Robert Kirkpatrick December 23, 1883 in Celina. They had six children. They were at Altus, Oklahoma in 1892. They later settled in Hedley, Texas, where both are buried.

Melia Williams married John W. Stone, and they had three children, John H.; Margaret, who married Arthur L. Young; and Bessie, who married Elmer Hammock. They lived in Jackson and Overton Counties.

Ida Sue Williams married Joseph Lemons November 11, 1900, at Celina. They are buried at Broken Arrow, Oklahoma. They had six children. *Submitted by V. Rex Williams*

JOHN WILSON

John Wilson came to this area in the early 1880's from North Carolina via South Carolina and Georgia. He married Deliah Kemp, and they settled on Jennings Creek in Jackson County. The 1850 census lists Deliah as a widow with the following children: Jesse, born in 1837; Haywood, born in 1839; Allen, born in 1842; Polly, born in 1843; and Savanah, born in 1849.

Haywood Ross Wilson was born December 7, 1839 in Jackson County, and he died May 21, 1926 at Hermitage Springs, Tennessee. He married Celina Wilson, who was born June 3, 1840. She was the daughter of Thomas H. Wilson, who was born in 1801 in South Carolina. Her mother was born in Georgia. They were the parents of seven children. James A. was unmarried. Asa T. married Sada Cowan of Georgia and had two children, Haywood and Ruby. Bell first married Sherman Leonard and had one daughter, Dora. Bell then married Milton Draper. Otis Frank married Lucy Reeves and had six daughters, Myrtle, Mattie, Edna, Iva, Willie and Ola. Bernetta married Bud Reeves and had seven children, Loren, Lois, Edith, Oral, Joe, Roy, and Lloyd. John married Betty Monroe and had two children, Paul and Odell. Radford Haywood married Emma Capshaw.

Radford Haywood was born July 31, 1883, and he died September 28, 1946. He was buried in the Gamaliel Cemetery in Gamaliel, Kentucky. He was married to Emma Capshaw, born February 4, 1889, the daughter of Jeptha and Elizabeth Capshaw. He was a bookkeeper in Jersey, Georgia, for several years before returning to farming. They purchased the farm from his father. Emma is a retired schoolteacher and continues to operate the farm which has been in continuous operation since 1872. On September 24, 1976, the Wilson farm was awarded the "Century Farm Family Land Heritage Ceritificate of Honor" from the Department of Agriculture.

The following are children born to the union of Radford and Emma: Myrleen and Ethleen (twins) and Oneta. Myrleen married Leo Clifford Davis of Mississippi (no children). Cliff is a retired accountant and merchant. Myrleen is a retired employee of Oak Ridge National Laboratory, Oak Ridge, Tennessee. They presently live in Knoxville. Ethleen married Maurice M. Anderson. They are the parents of Maurice M. Anderson, Jr.; Haywood Shields; and Donald Bayless. Maurice and Ethleen live in Columbia, Tennessee. Oneta married Billie D. Varnado of Mississippi. He died December 8, 1970. He was Safety Engineer for the Southeastern Region of the Navy Facilities Engineering Command. The children of this union are Douglas Wilson and Carol Elizabeth. Douglas Wilson Varnado married Linda Gray, the daughter of Dr. Joe and Harriette Gray of Nashville. Douglas graduated from Middle Tennessee State University, Tennessee State University, David Lipscomb College, and is a graduate student in the School of Divinity, Vanderbilt University. He is minister of the South Harpeth Church of Christ, the oldest Church of Christ in Davidson County, and teaches Bible at David Lipscomb College. Doug and Linda are the parents of Nicholas Gray and Katelin Emma. Carol Elizabeth Varnado graduated from David Lipscomb College, Peabody College of Vanderbilt University, and will graduate in June, 1986 from St. George's University School of Medicine, Grenada, West Indies. Oneta is Administrative Officer for the Nashville District of the United States Food and Drug Administration, Nashville, Tennessee.

ARCHIE NEVILLE WINDLE

Archie Neville Windle is the son of the late William Porter and Frances Ellen Coffee Windle.

He is the youngest of ten children. He was born July 19, 1908. He graduated from Celina High School in 1929, where he with his other brothers, played football. Neville has worked for the State of Tennessee, the Federal Government, and the Corps of Engineers during the building of Dale Hollow Dam in 1942. He was stationed in the South Pacific during World War II, attaining the rank of Staff Sergeant. His service with the 81st Division won him a letter of commendation from Major General Paul J. Mueller of the 81st "Wildcat" Infantry Division. After returning home from the Army, he opened a bait shop and in later years a service station. Neville retired from his business in 1971.

On October 14, 1954, Neville married Doye Green Knight, the daughter of Harve William and Grace Marie Green Knight of Hermitage Springs. Doye was born October 13, 1922, one of seven children. She graduated from Hermitage Springs High School in 1941, where she received all tournament awards in basketball. After graduation, she moved to Old Hickory, Tennessee where she was employed by the E.I. DuPont Company for 14 years. She also worked for Hudsons in Detroit, Michigan where she worked as a riveter making airplane wings. Doye has been working as a substitute teacher for the Clay County School System for the past 16 years.

Neville and Doye have one daughter, Amelia Beth Windle, born August 6, 1961 at the Jackson County Hospital. She is a 1979 graduate of Celina High School. After graduation, she worked for OshKosh at Hermitage Springs for two years. She is presently employed by the Clay County Board of Education as the Federal Projects Bookkeeper.

HAROLD E. WITHAM

Harold E. (Edd) Witham was born March 22, 1936 in Shelby County, Memphis, Tennessee. He is the second of seven children born to Roy F. and Catherine Witham, who now live in Nashville, Tennessee. He grew up and attended school in Davidson County, Tennessee. He left school at the age of seventeen to join the United States Marine Corps. On July 29, 1955, he married Joyce Scott, the daughter of the late George Curtis Scott, Sr. and Avo Ledbetter Scott. Joyce was born in the Kettle Creek-Pine Branch Community of Clay County September 16, 1935. She attended the Pine Branch School and graduated from high school in 1953. She attended business school in Nashville, Tennessee, where she met Edd.

Joyce, Edd, Roy Curtis and Thomas Edward Witham

They have two sons, Roy Curtis, born February 7, 1966 at Camp LeJeune, North Carolina

and Thomas Edward, born May 19, 1967 at Baton Rouge, Louisiana. Edd retired from the United States Marine Corps in March 1973, after serving twenty years. He served in Vietnam, the Far East, and Europe. While in service they lived in Virginia, Florida, North Carolina, Louisiana and New York.

They returned to Clay County to make their home. Edd returned to school and graduated from Tennessee Technological University in August 1979 with a degree in Health and Biology Education. In December 1978 they bought the farm that belonged to Joyce's family, where she was born and raised in the Kettle Creek-Pine Branch Community and where they now live.

Edd teaches at the Tri-County Vocational School; Joyce is Supervising Teacher at Celina Head Start. Curtis is a student at University of Tennessee at Knoxville. Tom is a student at David Lipscomb College, Nashville.

HOWARD AND LOUISE YOUNG

Howard Reever "Posey" Young was born on August 13, 1930 to Winton Herbert (Hub) and Flora Florene Lynch Young of the Butlers Landing Community of Clay County. "Posey" is the grandson of Marlin and Mary Smith Young of the Roaring River Community in Jackson County and Ben and Roxie Mitchell Lynch of the Butlers Landing Community. His sister, Mary Katherine, born July 7, 1928, is the wife of William F. Murley and lives in Dayton, Ohio.

Howard "Posey" and Louise Young

"Posey" was married May 25, 1951 to Velma Louise Smith of the Weavers Bottom Community in Clay County. Louise is the daughter of Paul Truman and Lexie Myra Hix Smith and the granddaughter of Steve and Martha Smith of Butlers Landing and Ben and Bell Hix of the Big Bottom Community of Jackson County. Her sister, Lois Christene, born August 12, 1929, married Wheeler Turner Marshall, and they have one daughter, Ann. Louise's brothers are Clifton Ray (Bud) Smith, who married Betty Ruth Melton, and Ralph Edward Smith, born May 17, 1937 — died July 3, 1941.

"Posey" served as a member of the United States Marine Corps from 1951-1953. He was stationed in Korea. He was a car dealer in Celina for 25 years. "Posey" works for the Upper Cumberland Development District, and Louise is secretary-bookkeeper for Dr. John H. Stone in Celina.

Posey and Louise have two children, Winton Edward, born September 26, 1953, and Myra

Flo, born January 5, 1961. They are the proud grandparents of Dylan Freeman and Harrison Reever Young, Winton's sons.

WINTON AND CASEY YOUNG

Winton Edward Young was born September 26, 1953 to (Posey) Howard Reever and Velma Louise Smith Young of the Butlers Landing Community of Clay County. Winton is the grandson of Winton Herbert (Hub) and Flora Florence Lynch Young and Paul Truman and Lexie Myra Hix Smith of Clay County. His younger sister is Myra Flo, born January 5, 1961, and named for her grandmothers.

Harrison, Casey, Winton and Dylan Young

Winton graduated from Celina High School in 1971. He earned a Bachelor of Science Degree in Physical Education from Middle Tennessee State University in 1976 and an Associates Degree from Cumberland Junior College in Lebanon, Tennessee.

Winton was married November 6, 1976 to Laurie Casey Freeman of Bells, Tennessee. They met at Cumberland College, which is the same University where Casey's parents met. Casey is the youngest daughter of Richard Edward, Jr. and (Scottie) Mary Scott Hassell Freeman of Bells, Tennessee. She is the granddaughter of Richard Edward and Mary Lellis Odell Casey Freeman of Bells and Alvin D. and Mary Nell Scott Hallsell of Humboldt, Tennessee. She has two sisters, Mary Lynn, born April 24, 1943, the wife of David Lynn Martindale of Jackson, Tennessee, and Sherry Scott, born February 26, 1941, the wife of Jesse Mack Kail of Bells, Tennessee.

Casey attended schools, grades one through ten, at Bells in Crockett County and graduated from high school at Old Hickory Academy in Jackson, Tennessee. She earned a Master of Science Degree in Speech Language Pathology from the University of Tennessee in Knoxville in 1982. She earned a Bachelor of Science Degree from Middle Tennessee State University in 1976 and an Associate Degree from Cumberland Junior College. She holds the Certificate of Clinical Competence with the American Speech Language and Hearing Association and has liscensure to practice in Tennessee and Kentucky.

Winton has worked with the State of Tennessee Department of Employment Security and on grants working with employers to help local people obtain jobs by training them with an employable skill and getting them job placements. He also is a substitute mail carrier. In addition to aiding many Clay, Macon, Overton, Pickett, and Putnam County people to find employment, Winton has played an active role in community activi-

ties and has held leadership roles in several civic organizations. Winton is an avid sports fan and is presently involved in helping Clay County obtain a golf course and swimming pool.

Casey works with the public schools as a Speech-Language Pathologist in Clay County and surrounding areas. She has a small private practice which focuses on speech and language problems of the adult population. She has been chosen as an Eminent Tennessean of the '80's and Who's Who Among Human Services Professionals. Her newspaper column in the Knoxville Journal won a national award for Articles in the Interest of Youth. Casey has also been active in community activities and has held leadership roles in several civic organizations.

The living room in Winton and Casey's home is the place where the first Clay County Court met for the purpose of selecting the site of the county seat.

Winton and Casey are the proud parents of two sons, Dylan Freeman, born August 6, 1983, and Harrison Reever, born on his Papa Freeman's birthday, July 18, 1985.

The family lives in the Butlers Landing Community of Clay County.

MYRA FLO YOUNG

Myra Flo Young was born January 5, 1961 to "Posey" Howard Reever and Velma Louise Smith Young of the Butlers Landing Community of Clay County. Myra is the granddaughter of Winton Herbert (Hub) and Flora Florence Lynch Young and Paul Truman and Lexie Myra Hix Smith of Clay County. Myra has an older brother, Winton Edward, born September 26, 1953. Myra Flo's name came from each of her grandmothers.

Myra attended Celina Elementary and graduated from Celina High School in 1979. She was active on the school newspaper and yearbook staffs. She was interested in photography; and she received the journalism award her senior year. Myra graduated from Middle Tennessee State University with a major in Advertising/Public Relations. Her activities in undergraduate school were the Campus Grounds Committee, Middle Tennessee State University Advertising Club, and Midlander (yearbook) Copy Editor for two years. Myra had the honor of being selected for outstanding senior project and was chosen to present her paper, "Three Generations of Women," about her mother, grandmother and great aunt, during Women's History Week at Roanoke College in Virginia in 1983. She has recently begun graduate school at Tennessee State University.

Myra is presently employed by Mid-Cumberland Human Resource Agency as the Coordinator of the Teenage Parent Program. She serves as a member of Planned Parenthood's Public Relations Board, the Council of Community Services, and the Young Leaders Council.

Celina Methodist Church (Masonic Lodge)

East Side of the Town Square — Destroyed by fire in the 1940's.

BUSINESS & TRIBUTE

B & B DISTRIBUTING COMPANY, INC.

B & B Distributing Company was founded by W. Roy Burnette and Lonus Bruton in 1959. B & B originally occupied three buildings near the old dry cleaners building on East Lake Avenue. In 1962, B & B moved to its present location on the Southwest corner of the public square on East Lake Avenue. In 1972, Roy and Hazel Burnette purchased the entire stock of B & B and have since been the sole owners.

B & B has been in business here for 27 years making it the oldest hardware, furniture, appliance, and merchandising store in Clay County.

CELINA OIL COMPANY

Celina Oil Company, operated by Keith and Freeda Hull, was purchased from Sun Oil Company and Charlie Bilbrey in 1978. It is located on River and Kyle Streets in "Old Town."

The Oil Company originated as C.C. Brown Oil Company and was later purchased by Wagoner Oil Company; and it later became Lynn Oil Company. It was then sold to Sun Oil Company and Charlie Bilbrey. The exact dates of these transactions are not known.

Celina Oil Company is a distributor of Sunoco gas and oil products. They also sell batteries, kerosene for home heating, and several brands of tires. The Company offers delivery service to farmers, resellers, and comsumers throughout Clay County and the surrounding areas.

BANK OF CELINA

The Bank of Celina is the oldest continuous business in Clay County. On March 2, 1895, the following people signed the application for the Bank Charter: J.T. Anderson, L.B. Anderson, A.G. Maxwell, H.H. Kyle, M.F. Green, George W. Stephens, and A.P. Green. W.L. Brown built the first building to house the Bank of Celina of lumber from an old store building which he had purchased from A.P. Green. This Bank was located in "Old Town". It has since been located at three other sites. The following committee was appointed to select a lot in "New Town" for the second bank on June 29, 1927: Frank Kyle, W.A. Marcom, and E.P. Fowler. The Bank was moved to the square in 1928. It has been at its present location since the new building was constructed on East Lake Avenue in 1970.

Since 1917, some of the members of the Board of Directors have been: W.L. Brown, H.H. Kyle, W.C. Williams, M.F. Hayes, F.B. Mayfield, Frank Kyle, Millard Kyle, J.B. Walker, W.A. Marcom, E.L. Young, J.A. Howard, W. Grady Sidwell, E.P. Fowler, W.F. Brown, C.C. Donaldson, R. L. Donaldson, J.H. Overstreet, C.W. Burris, Sr., M.D. Cherry, Edward Mayfield, C.M. King, M.R. Marcom, P.M. Cherry, and Frank Thurman.

The current officers and employees of the Bank of Celina are: Kerry L. Eads, President; J.D. Donaldson, Senior Vice President; William R. Marcom, Vice President; Joe W. King, Assistant Vice President; Ruth E. Dale, Cashier; Anita Roach, Assistant Cashier; Wilma J. Hayes, Teller;

Suzanne Roberts, Teller; Peggy Brown, Teller; Shirley Melton, Teller; Judy Groce, Bookkeeper; Laura Craighead, Bookkeeper; Teresa Nevans, Comptroller; Michael Bailey, Farm Agent; and Tammy Russell, Compliance Officer. Ronnie Brown is Vice President and Manager of the Hermitage Springs Branch of the Bank of Celina. Sue B. Wilburn is the Teller, and Jane Tandy is the Bookkeeper at the Hermitage Springs Branch Bank.

In 1986, the following serve as Directors of the Bank of Celina: L. Mayfield Brown, C.W. Burris, Jr., J.D. Donaldson, John Clark Donaldson, W.H. Donaldson, Kerry L. Eads, Frank B. Halsell, William R. Marcom, and W.B. Upton. Clyde King is Chairman of the Board of Directors.

CELINA LIONS CLUB

The Celina Lions Club was chartered in 1953 and has been in existence since that time. The Celina Lions Club functions as a service organization for Clay County with special emphasis placed upon sight conservation with eye exams and glasses provided for those in financial need. The Club offers assistance and support to other community activities such as the schools and other service organizations. The annual Easter Egg Hunt is sponsored by the Lions Club with many cash prizes being awarded at the Hunt each year. Yearly a "Clay County Citizen" is recognized by the Lions Club for outstanding accomplishment or service to the County. A Drug Awareness Essay Contest is sponsored in cooperation with the Clay County School System with the top winners being recognized with a plaque and cash award. Funds from the local Lions Club help support the Middle Tennessee Eye Bank and the Seeing Eye Dog Program.

The Annual Celina Lions Club Horse Show is held each year on the third Saturday night in June. The event attracts visitors from all over the State and from adjoining states. In October, the White Cane Road Block is conducted by the Lions Club.

The Lions Club meets the second and fourth Monday nights of each month.

Don Sherrell, President

CLAY COUNTY BANK

Clay County Bank became Celina's second banking institution in August of 1976 when seven area businessmen organized the bank with assets of $750,000. The original members of the Board of Directors were: Dr. C.E. Clark, Ralph W. Hamilton, T.H. Holland, R.L. Johnson, Joe Law, Kenneth Masters, Edward Mayfield and Frank Thurman.

The bank purchased property from Edward Mayfield which was located on the northeast corner of the public square. The property was completely remodeled to become the home of the Clay County Bank.

The bank was readily accepted by local citizens and a growth pattern developed early that continues today. The assets of the bank grew from the original $750,000 to over 2.4 million dollars in just six months. Three new members were added to the original Board of Directors — Billy Westmoreland, C.H. Buford, Jr., and Dr. Nora Tiongson.

By December 31, 1981, the assets had grown to over 8.8 million dollars; and the bank enlarged their original offices through the acquisition of adjacent property which underwent a complete facelift. The bank currently occupies a spacious, modern banking facility. The bank had grown at an average rate of over a million dollars a year.

The assets at this time totaled $11,263,008.05.

The present officers of the Clay County Bank are: Edward Mayfield, Chairman of the Board; David Browning, President; Carol Brown, Cashier; and Elaine Cherry, Assistant Cashier. Other employees are: Bookkeeper, Patsy Collins; Tammy Collins and Joy Corley, Tellers. The current members of the Board of Directors are: C.E. Clark, Kenneth Masters, Edward Mayfield, Nora B. Tiongson, Martha Thurman, C. Mack Clements, Carol Brown, Ralph Hamilton, David Browning, and R.V. Tiongson

THE CLAY COUNTY CHAMBER OF COMMERCE

The Dale Hollow-Clay County Chamber of Commerce was chartered with the State of Tennessee in 1977 by a group of Clay Countians who envisioned "people working together to make the Community a better place to live and to work."

The members hoped that the spirit in which the Chamber of Commerce was born would spread throughout the Community. It was believed then, as it is by many today, that the Chamber of Commerce could be the vehicle by which the entire community would begin an organized pattern of improvement.

The members worked aggressively in its early years to lay the groundwork for many projects — revitalizing the business community, developing utilities, working for the Appalachian Highway,

etc. After years of frustration, the benefits of much of the members' work is now being realized. The Chamber of Commerce is now setting accomplishable short-term goals in addition to the long-term goals in order that progress can be measured and interest kept alive.

Due to the generosity of the Twin Lakes Telephone Company, the Chamber of Commerce is now located in the building which once housed part of their operations. This office also serves as an information center for tourists.

For a period of time from 1981 until 1984, the Chamber of Commerce was virtually nonexistent. In 1984, interest again was revitalized due primarily to a stagnant economy.

The Chamber of Commerce has been instrumental in several recent projects: Water District

development, Hevi-Duty Access Road project, road improvements at the Fowler Curve; Welcome to Clay County signs, clean-up programs, the annual Christmas parade, etc.

It is currently cosponsoring with the Homecoming '86 Committee the construction and establishment of the "Clay County Museum of History." This building will contain information and articles of historical significance to Clay County and its people. It will also serve as a welcome center and tourist information center.

The officers of the Chamber of Commerce are: Wallace Walker, President; Jerry Burnette, Vice President; Melba Burch, Secretary; and John Heath, Treasurer.

CELINA LUMBER COMPANY

In 1962, Ezell and Je.... ....and Wilma Nevans and Edward ....ewell Qualls purchased the Celina Lumber Company from H.C. and Nora Swann. In 1964 Ezell and Wilma became the sole owners. The business was located on Cemetery Street until 1977 when a new building was constructed on Mitchell Street and the business moved to this location where the business is operated by Ezell and Wilma and their two sons — Gary and Danny.

OWNERS — Wilma and Ezell Nevans

CITIZEN-STATESMAN

'We make history...52 times a year'

The Citizen-Statesman is Clay County's only newspaper. It was created by the merger of two other weeklies, The Clay Citizen and The Clay Statesman. In business since 1968, the Citizen-Statesman offers advertisers a variety of readers in an area that includes all of Clay County and portions of Monroe County, Kentucky and other rural areas that surround Celina.

The Citizen-Statesman and its forerunners

have received many state press awards from the University of Tennessee and the Tennessee Press Association. Having won awards in everything from public service to editorials and best sports page, the newspaper is most proud of its title as best weekly newspaper in 1984.

Editorial offices are located on East Lake Avenue in Celina.

Donald E. Napier, Executive Editor of the Citizen-Statesman (right) and Kevin J. Donaldson, Managing Editor (left) are shown with two first-place awards from a recent Tennessee Press Association awards ceremony. In the center is Dr. Joseph Johnson, executive vice-president of the University of Tennessee.

CLAY COUNTY HOSPITAL

Prior to 1965, the citizens of Clay County had to rely on one doctor and no hospital for their healthcare needs. In 1961, the County Court started the process of establishing a hospital for Clay County. After completion of the hospital, the county had a problem locating doctors to come here and work in Celina. In 1965, physicians Aristides (Art) Cardona and Billy C. Nesbett started practice in the new 20 bed facility. The first administrator was Lloyd Black and Eva Craig was the Director of Nurses. On April 22, 1967, the County sold the hospital to Clay County Health Association. In 1974, the Clay County Health Association sold the hospital to the Clay County Health and Education Facility board which constructed additional bed capacity and an attached doctor's clinic. In August of 1980, Dr. Nora Bolanos Tiongson pruchased the lease-purchase agreement and leased to the Clay County Management Company, Inc. In February of 1982, Health Group, Incorporated of Nashville purchased Clay County Hospital; and in October of 1985, Paracelsus Healthcare Corporation of Pasadena, California purchased the facility. The Corporation also manages many other facilities in the southern United States, the western United States and in Europe. Paracelsus is privately owned by Dr. Kreukemeyer of West Germany.

Some of the many doctors who have practiced at Clay County Hospital are: Dr. Art Cardona, Dr. Billy C. Nesbett, Dr. R.G. Kloss, Dr. Renoaldo Olechea, Dr. Manual Crespo, Dr. Terry Raunsvall, Dr. Venice, Dr. Karty, Dr. Arun and Dr. Renu Bajaj. Those currently practicing here are: Dr. Robert Mauricio, Dr. Rod Tiongson, Dr. Arturo Runato, Dr. Nora Bolanos, Dr. Art Cardona and Dr. Michael D. Littell. The current management consists of: Carl Davis, Administrator; Robert Stockton, Controller; and Demetra Finley, Director of Nurses.

Carl Davis — Administrator, Margie Boone — Medical Records, Dr. Arturo Ruanto, Dr. R.V. Tiongson, Dr. Nora Bolonas (Tiongson) and Dr. Roberto Mauricio

Employees regularly receive awards for outstanding Service

CLARK DRUG STORE

Clark Drug Store, located on the square in Celina, has been in business since 1948 with the motto of being "The Friendly Store," as pharmacists W.H. Clark and Ann Roberts are ready to assist their customers 24 hours a day. Telephone numbers for the store are: 615-243-2673 during the day and 615-243-3317 at night.

Clark's in about 1950

Clark's Today

THE CLAY COUNTY SOIL CONSERVATION DISTRICT

The Clay County Soil Conservation District was organized under the provisions of the Tennessee SCD Enabling Act of 1939 to protect and promote the wise use of Clay County's natural resources. Those helping to organize the soil conservation district for Clay County were: County Agent Charles Vaughn, Frank Thurman, W.H. Langford, Grady Sidwell, W.D. Terry, Bill Fiske, and a Mr. Arnis. The following have served as SCD Supervisors: Amos Stone, W.D. Terry, J.H. Overstreet, Frank Thurman, Amo Osgathorpe, Elmo Henson, A.E. Craighead, Phillip Cherry, C.W. Clements, Jr., W.L. Russell, Harold Stone, Wayne Head, Bruce Turner, David Browning, Henry Boyd Stone, Joe Melton, Robert H. Jackson, Corinne McLerran, Rickey Melton, and John M. Hayes. SCD service personnel who have served in Clay County are: Frank Pharris, Wayne Thomas, Jack Enoch, Alfred Smith, Marion Simpson and Michael Richardson.

THE FIRST CLAY COUNTY SCD BOARD OF SUPERVISORS IN 1945

(L To R) Amos Stone, W.D. Terry, J.H. Overstreet, Frank Thurman, and Amo Osgathorpe.

CLARK BUFORD FISHERIES

Clark Buford Fisheries are located in three states and five cities. The home office is in Cordele, Georgia. Other fisheries are located in Eatonton, Georgia; Lake Okeechobee, Florida; Phenix City, Alabama; and Celina, Tennessee.

This flourishing industry was established in the 1950's by Clark Buford in Celina, Tennessee; and at that time, it was a one-man operation. The Celina operation is now managed by Mr. Buford's daughter, Kathy Radford. Other employees in the Celina organization are Houston Kyle, Donald Grace, Donnie Grace, Jim Boles, and Becky Rich.

CROTTY-TENNESSEE, INCORPORATED

Crotty-Tennessee, Incorporated is located on Joe L. Evins Drive in Celina, Tennessee. Crotty manufactures automotive parts — sun visors. The manager of Crotty is Bill White, a native Clay Countian. Crotty now employs 130 people.

"DIGGERS" RESTAURANT

"Diggers" was established in Clay County on July 8, 1986. The restaurant is located on the Bypass in Celina just below the Clay County Hospital. "Diggers" is home owned and operated by Teresa and Mayfield Brown. The name "Diggers" originated with the Brown's seven-year old daughter, Amora. The character, "Digger," depicts a friendly, country hound dog. The personality of "Digger" is carried over into the restaurant atmosphere which provides warm, friendly, and courteous service to everyone. "Diggers" offers five different styles of burgers, "Digger" dogs, super dogs, a wide variety of sandwiches, side orders of fries, tater tots, onion rings and fried mushrooms. There are also "Digger Delights," sundaes, strawberry short cake, hot fudge cake, and ice cream cones. Chicken, fish, and steak baskets along with pizza are featured items.

New ideas are tried every day to please the customers who frequent the spacious dining area; and those who use the drive through facilities available only at "Diggers."

A new feature offered at "Diggers" is the birthday party program for children which is developed around a menu selected by the birthday child with an option to have the party video filmed by Donnie Pealer. A wide variety of birthday cakes baked by Frances Donaldson and Betty Jo White is available from which the celebrant may make a selection to suit the individual taste.

Organizations and other groups are urged to make reservations to dine at "Diggers."

DIXIE LIMESTONE COMPANY

Dixie Limestone Company is owned and operated by Bobby Solomon. The Company provides agricultural limestone, crushed stone, and roadway materials to businesses, farmers, and other private individuals.

The Company is located by the Obey River on Highway 53 in Celina.

EADS AND SPEAR FLOWER & GIFT SHOP

Eads and Spear Flower and Gift Shop was established by Elizabeth Eads and Geneva Spear in 1976. The Shop is located on East Lake Avenue in Celina, and it offers a complete line of flowers and gifts suitable for all occasions with FTD and CARIK services.

Eads and Spear Flower and Gift Shop offers that personal touch that makes their work distinctive. They specialize in flowers for the home, for weddings, for funerals, and for Memorial Day. Elizabeth is in the Shop six days a week, and she is assisted in her work by Sue Willis.

HAMILTON'S DEPARTMENT STORE

HAMILTON'S DEPARTMENT STORE is a complete Family Clothing Store owned and operated by Charles and Mary Ann Hamilton since 1965.

The store was purchased from P.M. Cherry Dry Goods on January 11, 1965; and it was operated by the Hamiltons at this location in the Cherry Building on the Square in Celina for eleven years before moving to its present location on East Lake Avenue in 1976.

HEAD EQUIPMENT COMPANY

Head Equipment Company was established in the mid 1970's by Larry and Lucy Head. The Company is located between Moss and Oak Grove. The Company disassembles large construction and mining equipment for parts and components. These parts are then sold all over the United States and in some foreign countries. Parts have been shipped as far away as Australia and Singapore. They also rebuild and sell complete machines. The Company now employs 15 people.

OSHKOSH B'GOSH, INC.

OshKosh was founded by Frank E. Grove in 1895 and was called the Grove Manufacturing Company. In 1896, Mr. Grove sold his interests to Messrs. Jenkins and Clark who changed the name to OshKosh Clothing Manufacturing Co. and adopted the brand name "J & C" for their overalls. During the first year of operation, a Union was organized and a charter was granted to Local 126 of the United Garment Workers of America. Since that date the Union Label has been attached to all garments.

In 1910, the business changed hands when it went under the control of Will E. Pollock; and the name was changed to "OshKosh Overall Company" and the product name to OshKosh B'Gosh."

In 1934, Earl W. Wyman and his associates acquired the controlling interests from William E. Pollock who retired. Under the new management, the line was expanded to embrace garments of a utility nature and casual wear in addition to overalls. Again the name was changed. This time it was called "OshKosh B'Gosh, Incorporated" thus incorporating the trademark into the company name so that it might cover not only the famous OshKosh B'Gosh overall, but the many new garments added to the line.

In 1953, OshKosh B'Gosh, Inc. constructed a new plant at Celina, Tennessee in Clay County. The original building was a 24,000 square foot structure with a beginning work force of 95. This plant has been expanded until today. The manufacturing facility consists of 75,000 square feet of floor space and employs 393. There is a Corporate Finishing facility which consists of 18,000 square feet of floor space and employs 220 who process the pre-wash and pressing of garments for all ten OshKosh plants.

In 1979, OshKosh B'Gosh again expanded their capacity by constructing a 20,000 square foot building in Hermitage Springs, Tennessee which is also located in Clay County. This Division started with a work force of 49 employees manufacturing bib overalls. In December of 1981, the plant was expanded by adding 14,000 square feet to meet the demands of the Infants Snap Crotch bib overall. By the end of 1981, the Hermitage Springs plant employed 131 and as of July 1, 1986, the plant has 373 employees.

Today OshKosh B'Gosh Inc. has ten manufacturing plants — the original in Wisconsin, five in Tennessee and four in Kentucky. Corporate Headquarters is still located in the original building at 112 Otter Street, OshKosh, Wisconsin.

STATE CHAMPS — Members of the OshKosh B'Gosh softball team that won the Industrial State Championship pose with their trophy. Kneeling, L-R: Larry Watson, Alan Melton, Gary Watson, Ray Likens, Randy Hopper and Michael Cross. Standing, L-R: Celina Mfg. plant manager Eddie White, Ricky Watson, Tim Boles, James Trobaugh, Bo Bo Likens, Jeff Watson, Donald Ashlock and Hermitage Springs division plant manager Mickey Clements.

The advertising poster bearing the image of Uncle Sam with a protective hand on the head of a small boy has been with OshKosh for as long as anyone can remember. It is a symbol of strength and integrity.

JOHN C. HEATH, ATTORNEY

John C. Heath was born on October 12, 1947, in Louisville, Georgia. He is the son of William E. Heath, Sr., and Cornellia Ledbetter Heath. His ancestors lived in Virginia until they migrated to Georgia in the 1700's. John is the grandson of Homer Heath and Lily Boykin Heath and Reverend Samuel Ledbetter and Emma Sharpe Ledbetter. He graduated from Georgia State University in 1970 and from Emory University Law School in 1975. He is currently an attorney in Celina with his office located on the square.

John was married to Beverly Wright, who was born on May 27, 1947, on June 21, 1975. She is the daughter of Elmo Wright and Blanche Mullin Wright and the granddaughter of Oakley and Christina Wright and Helen and Porter Mullinix. Beverly grew up in Jamestown, Tennessee. She received a B.S. Degree in music from Tennessee Tech in 1969. She received a Master's Degree in Music Education from Northeast Louisiana University in 1971. She is currently employed by the Clay County Board of Education as a teacher at Celina High School.

John and Beverly are the parents of Andrew John Heath, born July 21, 1978, and Ryan Scott Heath, born October 19, 1980. Both are students at Celina K-8 School.

John and Beverly are members of the Celina Baptist Church, where Beverly is the choir director. John is Cubmaster for the Celina Cub Scouts and is Municipal Judge for Celina.

GS HEVI-DUTY ELECTRIC
P.O. BOX 334 • CELINA, TENNESSEE 38551

In July of 1974, with 27 employees, Hevi Duty started to manufacture transformers at the Celina plant. The first transformers the plant started to manufacture were 15 KVA transformers which weigh 180 pounds.

In September of 1975 a night shift was added.

At the present time the plant employees 80 people in a two shift operation. The company presently manufactures a line of dry type transformers from 15 KVA which weigh as much as 2000 pounds.

RENEAU & RENEAU — ATTORNEYS AT LAW

James H. Reneau, Sr. was licensed to practice law on August 14, 1928. In 1937, James H. Reneau, Jr. graduated from Cumberland University Law School at Lebanon, Tennessee and was licensed to practice law on August 26. Messrs. Reneau, Sr. and Jr. practiced law together until 1961, at which time James H. Reneau, III graduated from Cumberland University Law School and was admitted to the bar to practice law on August 12, 1961. After serving a brief period of time in the United States Army in Germany, Mr. Reneau, III joined his father and his grandfather in their law practice in Celina until Mr. Reneau, Sr.'s death in 1965. In 1963, Jimmy, III built the law office which presently houses the business. James H. Reneau, Jr. was awarded a Doctor of Jurisprudence Degree from the Cumberland School of Law of Samford University on April 17, 1979. In January 1981, James D. White, Jr. joined the firm as a law clerk while working toward his law degree at the University of Louisville, which he was awarded in May of 1982. Mr. Reneau, Jr., and Mr. Reneau, III practiced law together until Mr. Reneau, Jr.'s death in May of 1981. On May 2, 1983, Mr. White was admitted to the practice of law and continues to practice with this firm.

SCOTT'S BESTWAY

Frankie and Fred Scott purchased the Bestway Food Store from Ados and Lillian "Peachy" Boone in December of 1977. Scott's Bestway is located on East Lake Avenue in Celina. In addition to its complete line of food and household items, Scott's Bestway sells hunting and fishing licenses. They give quality stamps double the amount of the purchase.

The staff of Scott's Bestway is compromised of: Gary Stephens, Bobby Poindexter, Barry McLerran, Delilah Scott, Betty Webb, Peggy Riley, Alice Eads, Retha Pennington, Regina Rich, Paul Atchley, Lori Thompson, Luke Collins, Marty Rich, and Anna Coe.

SCOTT'S D-X SERVICE STATION

The D-X Service Station is located on the square of Celina. It was purchased by Boyd Scott in 1986. The Station is open six days a week with complete car service available. Members of Boyd's staff are: Waymon Estep, Lea McLerran, and "Butch" McLerran. Telephone 243-2563.

Swallows - Donaldson
Insurance Agency, Inc.

The Donaldson Insurance Agency was founded in 1929 by Mr. Fay Brown and Mr. W.H. (Hubert) Donaldson. It remained under the name Brown & Donaldson till Mr. Brown's death in the mid 40's. Mr. Hubert Donaldson maintained the agency until 1958 at which time W.H. (Corky) Donaldson took it over.

Corky operated the agency from 1958 till 1986. On July 1, 1986, the Donaldson Agency merged with the Swallows Agency of Livingston. The Agency is now known as the Swallows-Donaldson Insurance Agency, Inc. It represents approximately ten (10) major companies and offers a full line of insurance for all your needs.

WILMA'S RESTAURANT

Wilma's Restaurant is located on East Lake Avenue in Celina, Tennessee. It was originally established by Earl Napier over 30 years ago; and it was the site of the famous "chitlin suppers." Wilma Scott purchased the restaurant in November of 1982, and it was renamed Scott's Restaurant. In 1986, the name was changed to Wilma's.

Wilma and her capable staff — Debbie Clayburn, Bessie Key, Pauline Rich, Selma Young, Daryl Clayburn, Ricky Barlow, Michelle Grace, Marlene Pryor, David McClintock, and Michel Fox — prepare and serve outstanding meals and short orders throughout the day and evening. A delicious buffet and salad bar are available at lunch and dinner. Steaks, country ham, catfish, and homemade desserts are also restaurant specialties.

UPTON FUNERAL HOME

One of the oldest continous operating businesses in Clay County is the Upton Funeral Home. It was first organized about 1922 by the late H. Turner Netherton at Moss, Tennessee. At that time, he used a horse-drawn hearse and made most of his coffins, as they were called then. He also had a cabinet shop. He bought a motor hearse, a 1935 Ford, and he used it until he sold the business to Charlie Rich in 1943. Mr. Rich moved the business to Celina. He purchased a new 1957 Cadillac hearse — the first new machine of this type ever purchased in the County. Mr. Rich operated the business until August 5, 1949 when Mr. and Mrs. Butler Upton and Mr. and Mrs. Estil Burnette purchased the business which was located on Highway 52 in South Celina. In October of 1949, a new location was bought for the business. The old Montvale College building located just off the Courthouse square was bought and converted into a Funeral Home. The old Montvale College building was historic in that several famous people attended this school during the 1880's and early 1900's, including the late Cordell Hull, Secretary of State, under President Franklin D. Roosevelt.

Willie Butler and Edwina Upton purchased the Burnettes' share of the business in 1953. The old Montvale building has been enlarged; and the staff has been increased. Jimmy R. Hay has been with the firm for 21 years; and the Upton's daughter and son-in-law, Betty and Jim Briggs, are now associated with the business.

Upton Funeral Home

Horse Drawn Hearse

Coffin Shop

TRIBUTE

Mary Emma and J.H. "Jimmy" Reneau, Jr.

THE RENEAU'S OF HOLLY CREEK
1950-1986

J.H. "Little Jimmy" Reneau, III

Corinne Reneau McLerran

Mary Loyd Reneau

EPILOGUE

The "Homecoming '86" Committee and the staff of "History of Clay County Tennessee" wish to express their appreciation to all of those who have contributed to the publication of this book. If any name has been omitted from a list, if any significant historical fact, date, or event has not been included, or if the name of a contributor has been omitted, it was not intentional.

This is the first published history of Clay County since the one published by Isiah Fitzgerald many years ago. It is hoped that this book will be a treasured reference for future generations, and that someday another group will accept the task of expanding the "History of Clay County Tennessee" in order that Clay Countians may always have an up-to-date history of their county.

A birds eye view of the Court House and the downtown area of Celina.

Minnie, Fred and Ned Maxey,
Walter Fay and Minnie Brown

West Side of Public Square — 1940's.

Celina's last car dealership owned by Edward Mayfield and Ray Speck.

Napier's Cafe

"Blooney" and "Red" Napier

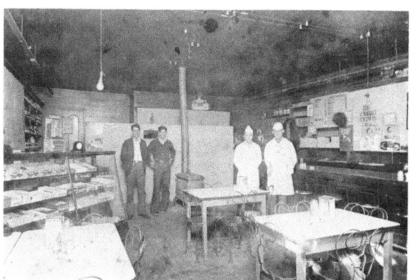

"Blooney" and "Red" Napier's Cafe.

Napier's Grocery on East Lake Avenue

W.L. Brown's Store on the square in Celina.

Law Office — Drug Store — Post Office

The Hayes Bros. — Cornell and John Mark show their corn crop to county agent Charlie Vaughn.

May and Madden Garrett observing their sows — about 1950.

Herman Burris resetting tobacco in the 1950's.

Moss Post Office

"Rolley Hole" Marble Champions — Ralph Roberts and Wayne Rhoton

As seen on national TV —
Billy Westmorland's "Fishing Diary"

E.H. Wilkerson and Esco Moore's Saw Mill

Young people of Arcot: Carmon Mabry, Mary Lee Harpe, Fannie Mae Brown, Oliver Stone, and Eva Nell Brown, Brownie Brown, Maudie Strong, Ila Cunningham, Dorthy Eads, Major "Cat" Mabry, Adele Cherry, Luara Farris, Jewel Brown and Lena Butler.

Martha Leonard Bean, John Bean, Elizabeth (Bets) Leonard, Dyer Leonard and Geneva (Navy) Leonard Davis.

Henry Stone's collection of antique tools.

Clay County 4-H Club

Celina graduates — 1930

Clementsville School: *First Row:* Clay Anderson, Genie Anderson, Buford Cherry, Claude Clements *Second Row:* Garland Anderson, Frank Gulley, Tabitha Fowler, Bessie Fowler, Callie Craighead, Maxie Craghead, Maude Clements, Sis Fowler, *Third Row:* Clarence Clements, Porter Billingsley, Dide Golden, Bee Gulley, Nettie Gulley, Leah Ritter, Alice Eakle, and Teacher Maria Birdwell

(On The Left) Eminence School — *First Row:* Roy Burnette, Corkey Burnette, Ray Moore, Chester White, Corinna Hatcher, Cleo Spear, Florence Plumlee, Mary Katherine Kendall, Doris C. Bilbrey, Irene Smith, Dean Pennington, Hazel Green and Ermis Sweezy. *Second Row:* Donald Bilbrey, Dallas Smith, Ados Boone, Eula Sweezy, Jack Billingsley, Eulas Sweezy, Darris Spear, George Lex Kendall, Harold Moore and Wayne Moore. *Third Row:* Pauline McLerran, Avos Boone, Louise Kendall, Anna Chitwood, Noel Head, Reed White, Vassie Smith, Wheeler Turner Marshall, Trilba Davis, Leon Cherry, Durward Green, Ray Head and Glenn Head. *Fourth Row:* Dorothy Bilbrey, Olivia Marshall, Nova Pennington, Evelyn Chitwood, Clara Pennington, Chloe Marshall, Willodale Short, Ora Burnette, Mary Addie Burnette, Ruby Plumlee, Zelma Moore and Chester Plumlee. *Fifth Row:* Earl Head, Ralph Craighead, John Halmoore, Ralph Plumlee, Dellie Netherton, Neville Chitwood, Cova Hatcher, Mae Pennington, Roy Spear — Teacher and Idera Fisk — Teacher.

Hermitage Springs School — 1925

Dramatics Club, 1938, Hermitage Springs High School
Front row: Belva McLerran, Louis Taylor, Blanche McLerran, Herod Birdwell, Jr., Herman Taylor. Second row: Zelma Birdwell, Oneta Wilson, Clifton Ray, Russell Hall. Third row: Nina Fox, Elizabeth Whitley, Mable Deckard. Back: Anna Fox

Ag. Class, 1942, at Hermitage Springs High School.
Front Row: C.W. Clements, Harold Williams, Fred Short, Noel McLerran, R.J. Bean, Teacher, E.C. Gunther. Second row: Bill Green, Weldon Meador, Jr., Harold Carlisle, Lawrence Newman, Ray Hall, Thomas Craighead, Rue Clements, Jr. Third row: Hillous Long, Dan Bean, Hollis Bean, Ray Bean, John Ray, Mitchell Turner. Fourth row: Bill Long, Ray Head, Edward Browning, Austin Taylor, Glyn Grace, Weldon Davis

Hermitage Springs — 1945 and 1946. *Front Row:* Fred Lee, James Long, Ann Justic, Nell Pedigo, Ina Ruth Pedigo, Gloria Lancaster, Myrna Bean, Edward Pedigo, Shelby Kemp, Jesse Cherry and Betty Armour. *Second Row:* Doris Purcell, Garth Right, Gerald Jenkins, Eurene Anderson, Joyce Deckard, Bobby Dean, Louie Long, Bobby Green — Teacher Miss Vera York. *Third Row:* Garndell King, Willis Davis, Dean Purcell, Judy Lancaster, James King, Dorris Cherry, Rosalene Newman. *Fourth Row:* Carl Hood, Billy Choate, Shirley Davis, Annie Davis, Ada Appleby, Unknown, Evelyn Pedigo, Unknown.

Leonard School

Midway School — 1938 — Hance Wilkerson — Teacher.

Mt. Vernon School — 1941: Sonnie Holmes, Charles Bean, Delbert Cherry, and Leslie Copass. *Second Row:* Guy Roberts — Teacher, Morrell Carlisle, Willodean Bean, Unknown, Pauline Pedigo, Evolyn Birdwell, Mildred Carlisle, Donald Head and Audey Browning. *Third Row:* Weltha Birdwell, Pauline Copas, Geneva Allen, Gladys Johnson, Lillian Birdwell, Flossie Rush, Glemus Crawford, Eldon Long and Claude Pedigo.

New Hope School — 1913 — Teacher — Bertha Pedigo

Katherine Roberts' class at Pine Branch School

Oak Grove School — 1916

Students at Pine Branch.

Pine Hill School — 1918

Plainview School

Pout Hill School group.

Turkey Creek School — Ben F. Brown — Teacher.

Union Hill School — 1917

Union Hill School — 1940

Arcot Church of Christ renovated 1970's.

Brimstone Church of Christ

Congregation — Celina Church of Christ — "Old Town" in the late 1800's or early 1900's.

Liberty Missionary Baptist Church

Macedonia Baptist Church

Moss Church of Christ

New Hope Church of Christ

Oak Grove Church of Christ

Pea Ridge — *First Row:* Myrtle Watson Colson, Ada Williams Johnson, Eula Sherrell Webb, Clyo Bowe Johnson and Agnes Donaldson Terry. *Second Row:* Coolie Johnson, Edgar Stephens, Andrew Johnson, Dan Webb, Jimmy Colson, Curb Watson, Jewell Terry and Leslie Spear — Minister.

Young men attending church at Pine Hill — Jesse Brown, Lonnie Crowder, Bob Brown, Luke Brown and Comer Crowder.

Pout Hill Church gathering.

Union Hill Church of Christ

Wesleyan Church at McCormick Ridge.

Fay Brown home — Celina

William J. Cherry's home.

Clarence Worth Clements home.

John Donaldson's home

The Parsons' house — home of Joe and Judy Fox

Almary Cherry standing on her front porch. House is now owned by granddaughter Bonnie Grace.

The Hayse Home

Jay Mabry's home.

Columbus Stone Farm — The site of Concord Academy and Church.

Gratton D. Phillips home at Lilly Dale.

Benton Thomas Walker home

Calvin Moss home, now owned by his daughter, Dona Turner.

Mount Vernon School building

Printed in the USA
CPSIA information can be obtained
at www.ICGtesting.com
JSHW060052150824
68134JS00032B/2713